CARNAL CRIMES

Sexual Assault Law in Canada, 1900–1975

The Osgoode Society is supported by a grant from
The Law Foundation of Ontario.

THE LAW
FOUNDATION
OF ONTARIO

The Society also thanks The Law Society of Upper Canada
for its continuing support.

CARNAL CRIMES

Sexual Assault Law in Canada, 1900–1975

CONSTANCE BACKHOUSE

Published for The Osgoode Society for Canadian Legal History
by Irwin Law

Toronto

Printed and bound in Canada by Irwin Law Inc.

ISBN 978-1-55221-178-6

Library and Archives Canada Cataloguing in Publication for the Hardcover

Backhouse, Constance, 1952–
Carnal crimes : sexual assault law in Canada, 1900–1975 / Constance Backhouse.

Includes bibliographical references and index.
ISBN 978-1-55221-151-9 (bound)
ISBN 978-1-55221-178-6 (pbk.)

1. Rape—Canada—History—20th century. 2. Sex crimes—Canada—History—20th
century. 3. Rape—Canada—Case studies. 4. Sex crimes—Canada—Case studies.
5. Sex discrimination against women—Canada—History—20th century.
6. Women—Legal status, laws, etc.—Canada—History—20th century.
I. Osgoode Society for Canadian Legal History II. Title.

KE8928.B32 2008	345.71'02532	C2008-904529-7
KF9325.B32 2008		

The publisher acknowledges the financial support of the Government of Canada
through the Book Publishing Industry Development Program (BPIDP) for its
publishing activities.

We acknowledge the assistance of the OMDC Book Fund, an initiative of
Ontario Media Development Corporation.

1 2 3 4 5   13 12 11 10 09

CONTENTS

FOREWORD

THIS IS AN ENGAGING and powerful book about sexual assault crimes in Canadian history, by Professor Constance Backhouse, whose previous books for the Osgoode Society have won major awards. Using a case-study approach, Professor Backhouse explores nine sexual assault trials from across the country throughout the twentieth century. We move from small towns to large cities, from the Maritimes to the Northwest Territories, from the suffrage era to the period of the women's liberation movement. Each chapter offers insight into the failure of the criminal justice system to protect women from sexual assault, and each is highly readable and provocative. The most moving chapters document the law's refusal to accommodate a woman who could only give evidence in sign language, and the heartbreak of a child rape trial. This book is the best kind of legal history — a vivid exploration of the past which also gives us the tools to assess the efficacy (or, in this case, lack of efficacy) of the legal system.

The purpose of the Osgoode Society for Canadian Legal History is to encourage research and writing on the history of Canadian law. The Society, which was incorporated in 1979 and is registered as a charity, was founded at the initiative of the Honourable R. Roy McMurtry, formerly attorney general for Ontario and chief justice of the province, and officials of the Law Society of Upper Canada. The Society seeks to stimulate the study of legal history in Canada by supporting researchers, collecting oral histories, and publishing volumes that contribute to legal-historical scholarship in Canada. It has published seventy books on the courts, the judiciary, and the legal profession, as well as on the history of crime and punishment, women and law, law and economy, the legal treatment of ethnic minorities, and famous cases and significant trials in all areas of the law.

Current directors of the Osgoode Society for Canadian Legal History are Robert Armstrong, Attorney General Chris Bentley, Kenneth Binks, Patrick Brode, Brian Bucknall, David Chernos, Kirby Chown, J. Douglas Ewart, Martin Friedland, John Honsberger, Horace Krever, Ian Kyer, Gavin MacKenzie, Virginia MacLean, Roy McMurtry, Jim Phillips, Paul Reinhardt, Joel Richler, William Ross, Paul Schabas, Robert Sharpe, James Spence, Mary Stokes, Richard Tinsley, and Michael Tulloch.

The annual report and information about membership may be obtained by writing to the Osgoode Society for Canadian Legal History, Osgoode Hall, 130 Queen Street West, Toronto, Ontario, M5H 2N6. Telephone: 416-947-3321. E-mail: mmacfarl@lsuc.on.ca. Website: Osgoodesociety.ca .

R. Roy McMurtry
President

Jim Phillips
Editor-in-Chief

ACKNOWLEDGMENTS

I SUSPECT ALL WRITERS have their own idiosyncratic preferences for setting. I prefer to write while looking through a window. I roll my computer right up to the best window I can find, and root there surrounded by boxes and books. This book has been written in front of many wonderful windows. It began in Perth, Western Australia, in 1999, from a library window in an artist's cottage that looked out on flowering hedges surrounded by raucous birds. It moved in 2000 to a window in Ottawa, which looked onto an upper wooden balcony with squirrels, crows, and pine cones, facing south over the beautiful Rideau River. It took a five-month sojourn in Montréal in 2004, where it looked out from a garret above a three-storied metal stair railing. For the first few months, layers of frost and ice impeded all view. With spring, the window magically opened to the bustle of St. Urbain Street in the ethnic mosaic of the Plateau below. In 2006, the writing project moved for six months to the medieval town of Lunel in the south of France. There I looked down from the centuries-old stone balcony of a former *écurie*, onto a private courtyard with towering laurel and bamboo trees. My gaze would wander to the fountain with a gargoyle frequented by white doves. Each window has added its distinctive cachet to the migrating mixture that became this book.

Many people have also contributed enormously to this book. First and foremost, the creative and brilliant research assistants whose work has helped to unearth much of the detail surrounding these cases: Monda Halpern, Kristen Clark, Pascal-Hugo Plourde, Marie-Josée Blais, Isabelle LeBreux, Alka Tanden, Belinda Peres, Rosemary Morrissette Rozyk, Raquel Chisholm,

Ella Forbes-Chilibeck, Michelle McLean, Peter Scrutton, Marie-Eve Ouellette, Megan Reid, Sabina Mok, and Carly Stringer. Some have gone on to write superb history themselves. Others have gone on to finish law school, to graduate school, and to legal practice. I wish them all the opportunity to write books from wonderful windows in their futures.

Colleagues in the academy, the legal profession, the medical profession, the judiciary, and many individuals connected with the cases profiled have also offered marvellous ideas, and shared their own remarkable research and knowledge: Sandra Archie, Donica Belisle, Ronda Bessner, Susan Binnie, Susan Boyd, Christine Boyle, Susan Burch, Clifton F. Carbin, Dianne Crosina, Elise Chenier, Dorothy Chunn, Tina Dion, Maureen Donald, Karen Dubinsky, Serge Durflinger, the Hon. Chief Justice Catherine Fraser, Donald Fyson, Chad Gaffield, Philip Girard, the Hon. Chief Justice Constance Glube, Michael Grossberg, Hendrik Hartog, Ian Kerr, Diane Kirkby, Andrée Lajoie, André Lapierre, Andrée Lévesque, Greg Marquis, Howard McConnell, John McLaren, Wendy Mitchinson, Renate Mohr, Delia Opekokew, Astrid Paidra, Joy Parr, Carol Patrie, Amos Peres, W. Wesley Pue, Joan Sangster, Christabelle Sethna, Elizabeth Sheehy, Susan Sterett, Carolyn Strange, Angela Stratiy, Jon Swainger, Walter Temelini, Mariana Valverde, Lynn Varty, Henry Vlug, and Brian Young.

As all historians are, I am indebted for the support of many talented archivists: Susan Lewthwaite of the Law Society of Upper Canada Archives, John Choles and Brian Miller of the Archives of Ontario, Barry Cahill, John Macleod, and Garry Shutlak of the Public Archives of Nova Scotia, Anne Watling of the Nova Scotia Barristers' Society, Kelly Casey of Dalhousie University Archives, Lydia Duncan of the Midale Library, Chris Gebhard of the Saskatchewan Archives Board, Luc Brazeau of the Archives nationales du Québec–Outaouais, Monique Voyer of the Division des archives de l'Université de Montréal, Jonathan H. Davidson of the Provincial Archives of Alberta, Tonya Barber of the Legal Archives Society of Alberta, Barry Haugrud of Vital Statistics Alberta, Robin Weber, Northwest Territories Archives, Andrew Martin of the Special Collections Division, Vancouver Public Library, Sheila Barnett of the World YWCA Archives, Marie Chidley of the Edmonton Public School Archives and Museum, Ann ten Cate of the B.C. Archives and Records Service.

Susan Lecorre and Véronique Larose of the University of Ottawa were extremely generous in providing administrative support. The anonymous readers who reviewed the manuscript provided excellent advice and suggestions. This book would not have come to final fruition without the invaluable assistance of Jim Phillips and Marilyn Macfarlane of the Osgoode Society, and Bill Kaplan, Jeffrey Miller, Pamela Erlichman, and Heather Raven of Irwin Law, Inc.

I am particularly honoured that Velma Demerson, one of the only women still living whose story appears here, wrote to me in 2000 in connection with her public legal campaign to seek redress for the injustices she experienced historically. She agreed to have her story included in this book, and allowed me to interview her at length, and to review the many boxes of research she had compiled on her own case. She has subsequently published her memoirs, and I hope that my additional analysis regarding the sexual assault aspects of her case may contribute in some small way to the growing recognition of the historical significance of her life.[1]

Windows are not conjured up by sorcery. I reflect often upon my great fortune to have obtained a full-time academic appointment as a law professor, which allows me not only the privilege of exposure to an invigorating influx of new generations of law students, but also the freedom to write books that fascinate me. I am much in debt to the University of Ottawa, which has offered extraordinary support for my research in honouring me with a University Research Chair, a University of Ottawa Award for Excellence in Research, and a Distinguished University Professorship. I am equally indebted for financial assistance from the Law Foundation of Ontario, the Social Sciences and Humanities Research Council of Canada, the Bora Laskin Human Rights Fellowship, the Jules and Gabrielle Léger Fellowship, and the Trudeau Fellowship. This book has also been published with the help of a grant from the Canadian Federation for the Humanities and Social Sciences, through the Aid to Scholarly Publications Program, using funds provided by the Social Sciences and Humanities Research Council of Canada.

I also wish to thank the people who have shared the homes and apartments attached to these wonderful windows, and offered daily feedback, advice, and inspiration: Diana Backhouse, Mark Feldthusen, Diana Majury, and Bruce Feldthusen, to all of whom this book is dedicated.

October 2007
Ottawa, Canada

CARNAL CRIMES

Sexual Assault Law in Canada, 1900–1975

Chapter 1

INTRODUCTION

SEXUAL ASSAULT HAS BEEN astonishingly widespread throughout Canadian history. It emerges out of disparities in power between men and women, adults and children, and those with and without the privileges of class, race, ethnicity, heterosexuality, physical/mental ability, and other variables that create hierarchies among individuals. To pursue the study of when and how people with power perpetrate sexual assault upon the less powerful is to begin to unmask inequalities that manifest themselves through sexual coercion and violence. To review how our legal system characterizes the wrong of sexual assault puts the phenomena into sharper focus. It brings us face to face with the raw power of law, along with the enormous potential and appalling failures at the root of the Canadian justice system.

This book takes nine cases of sexual assault, and profiles in detail the people, the places, and the legal proceedings involved, using a method that some have described as micro-history. It begins with the trial of Joseph Gray, a London, Ontario, teamster charged with raping a middle-aged boarding housekeeper, Mary Ann Burton, in 1907. It moves to Québec City in 1917, where fourteen-year-old Yvonne Collin testified she was gang-raped by eight young working-class men out for a spree in a dashing motor vehicle. It explores allegations of date rape in the Roaring Twenties, in Halifax in 1925, between a fashionable Simpson's salesclerk and a Dalhousie medical student. It retells the story of Velma Demerson, who told no one that she was raped in 1936 when she went out for a drive with an admirer in an automobile in Saint John, New Brunswick. It explains how the same woman, more than sixty years later, waged a public campaign for an apology and compensation for the wrongful confinement she suffered in the Toronto Mercer Reformatory in 1939 and 1940. Part of her complaint related to the "state sexual assault" she suffered while incarcerated. This entailed involuntary internal examinations and experimental medical treatment at the hands of Dr. Edna Guest.

The book continues by examining how disability affected the trial of Joe Probe, charged with the exploitative rape of a deaf woman, Beatrice Tisdale, in Weyburn, Saskatchewan, in 1942. It reviews the multiple ways in which children were disadvantaged through sexual victimization, in the 1951 prosecution of Ovila Soulière for indecent assault upon a five-year-old girl in Hull, Québec. It analyzes what appears to be the first trial of a female, Willimae Moore, charged with indecently assaulting another woman in the sexually charged environment of Yellowknife, Northwest Territories, in 1955. The book also considers the tragic case of Rose Marie Roper, a seventeen-year-old Esketemc Aboriginal from Alkali Lake, who was sexually assaulted by a group of young white men and left to die in 1967, on a deserted logging road near Williams Lake in the central interior of British Columbia. It finishes with a narrative of sexual harassment, where the proprietor of a hairdressing salon, Franco Angione, pleaded guilty to the indecent assault of his female employee in Windsor, Ontario, in 1974.

Historians of sexual assault often seek to preserve the anonymity of the victims and the accused by using pseudonyms or initials instead of real names. However, the research here is predicated upon lengthy explorations into the detailed backgrounds of the actual people involved, in an effort to magnify our understanding of how these events came to pass and their impact on the lives of individuals. To maintain the anonymity of the people involved contradicts the nature of this work. Most of the victims and accused are long dead. Where I have been unable to confirm that individuals accused of these sexual assaults are deceased, I have still chosen to use their real names, because their trials were matters of public record, and their names were published in the newspapers. I have treated the victims differently, although their names also appear in public court records and occasionally in newspapers. In later decades, the press chose not to identify them out of respect for the privacy of those whose only connection to the criminal justice system was their sexual victimization. This change met with the support of the feminist movement in the 1970s and subsequently resulted in legislative amendment to ensure that there would be no public disclosure in the media of the names of sexual assault victims. In the three instances where I was unable to confirm that the victims in the cases profiled here were deceased, or to secure their personal permission to use their names, I have indicated in the chapter that the name used is a pseudonym.[1]

The nine cases permit an analysis of many legal issues that affected sexual assault trials historically: the assessment of credibility of those who claimed victimization and those who denied responsibility, theories and practices of cross-examination, the role of physicians, the role of the press, the dynamics of gang rape as opposed to individually perpetrated rape, police investigation practices, the focus on women's prior sexual history and "previous chaste character," the concept of consent, the search for demonstrations of force and resistance, the doctrines of corroboration and recent complaint, the rules surrounding children's testimony, the nature of plea bargaining, conviction rates, sentencing, civil remedies, evolving theories about sexuality, and the complicating influences of class, race, ethnicity, antisemitism, disability, age, and homophobia.

The Sample from Which the Cases Were Selected

THE NINE CASES WERE selected from a compilation of sexual assault records from the whole of Canada for the years between 1900 and 1975. An earlier book, *Petticoats and Prejudice: Women and Law in Nineteenth-Century Canada*, considered the law of sexual assault prior to 1900.[1] The year 1975 was a natural cut-off point for this research because it was the first year that saw legislative changes to sexual assault law based upon the reform campaigns of the second wave of the Canadian women's movement. Parliament dramatically restructured the law of sexual assault with waves of legislative reform in 1975, 1982, 1987, 1992, and 1997.[2] For those who seek to evaluate the effectiveness of the post-1975 legislative reforms, it is critical to understand what the landscape looked like before these changes came to pass.

The starting point for a study of sexual assault law is the statutory framework within which all complaints are prosecuted. The pre-reform landscape includes all the federal legislation pertaining to sexual assault from the enactment of the first Criminal Code in 1892 through the addition of every statutory revision to 2000. The phrase "sexual assault" did not become a legal term until 1983, when it replaced a number of other offences, such as "rape" and "indecent assault." However, I have found it useful to use the term generally throughout the book, employing it in the broadest sense possible to encompass the wide range of sexual offences included in this review:

rape, carnal knowledge of girls under the age of consent, indecent assault on females, seduction, incest, corrupting children, indecent acts, gross indecency, buggery, unlawfully defiling women, abduction of women, procuring, communicating venereal disease, carnal knowledge of women with disabilities, exposure in public, bestiality, indecent assault on males, and sex-related murder. To assist future researchers, I have uploaded the details of the relevant legislation onto a website: www.constancebackhouse.ca. The website is organized in such a way that it should be useful to non-lawyers as well as lawyers. It permits readers to view all the sexual assault law that was in force in any specific year between 1892 and 2000. It also permits readers to follow a specific offence from its inception through its various amendments over time.

The pre-reform landscape also includes the *application* of this legislation, in the form of individual charges, preliminary inquiries, trials, and appeals. Some are documented through official law reports published by legal publishers for the use of lawyers and judges. I have collected and reviewed every such reported case on sexual assault law across Canada between 1900 and 1975. However, reported cases comprise only a portion of the cases tried, because they were selected for publication by the editors of the law reports only when the case was deemed to be significant on a point of law. The vast bulk of cases were never reported, and remain documented only in the records of Crown prosecutors, court files, judges' notebooks, jail registers, and occasional press accounts. Many of these records have been lost or destroyed, making it impossible ever to claim to have reviewed all the cases that were heard. Provincial archives hold portions of these records, although the case files are not consistent in the type of documentation that survives. Some files contain the official information, arrest warrants, bail documents, transcripts of magistrates' court proceedings, jurors' lists, indictments, trial transcripts, verdicts, judicial decisions, correspondence from counsel and judges, and occasionally appellate documents. Most files are only partially complete and often lack critical pieces, such as transcripts or any indication of the outcome. Some provinces withhold large portions of these surviving records, claiming privacy obligations.

Despite their inadequacy, without resort to archival records, any attempt to analyze sexual assault law would be woefully inadequate. I initially attempted to cull representative samples from selected archives, but discovered that it was futile to claim accuracy on this score. Archivists would advise me years after the sample was collected that they had discovered vast new series of boxes with additional records, or that they had only just learned that there were quantities of missing (lost or destroyed) records in samples they had previously produced as complete. When one reflects that even the surviving archival files disclose only the sexual assault complaints that were officially reported and prosecuted, the prospect of compiling a comprehensive or fully representative set of documents seems elusive indeed. That said, I have reviewed portions of archival records in selected counties and judicial districts in Nova Scotia, Québec, Ontario, Manitoba, Saskatchewan, Alberta, the Northwest Territories, and British Columbia between 1900 and 1975.

The large number of records collected from this research reinforces the conclusion that historically sexual assault was a commonplace occurrence. This review retrieved a total of 1202 cases, of which a number involved multiple accused individuals. The published law reports included 713 cases. These were supplemented by 494 non-reported archival cases. There is a discrepancy in the total because in 5 cases both archival records and reported cases were available. The provincial breakdown was as follows: British Columbia 179, Alberta 58, Northwest Territories 3, Yukon Territory 2, Saskatchewan 65, Manitoba 44, Ontario 356, Québec 143, New Brunswick 30, Nova Scotia 314, P.E.I. 6, Newfoundland 2. The disparity in numbers reflects more extensive research into the unreported archival records of some provinces.[3] Here is the chronological breakdown:

Pre-1900:	5	1935–1939:	47
1900–1904:	44	1940–1944:	61
1905–1909:	68	1945–1949:	87
1910–1914:	95	1950–1954:	59
1915–1919:	143	1955–1959:	64
1920–1924:	102	1960–1964:	53
1925–1929:	103	1965–1969:	85
1930–1934:	63	1970–1975:	123

A listing of the cases can also be found on the website www.constancebackhouse.ca.

I have chosen not to attempt any overall quantitative evaluation of this data, in part because the many decades, multiple locations, and partiality of the records make consistent comparisons impossible within a collection of this scope. Furthermore, while I do not criticize other scholars for drawing generalizations from large groups of cases, I do not believe that such historical research is substantially more reliable than microhistory. Findings based upon overviews can conceal critical aspects of the legal process as it operates in particular cases. I have come to believe that studying history through illustrative narratives is no less elucidating and far more interesting to researcher and readers alike. The larger scope of this research can be found in the lengthy research endnotes that indicate how aspects of the selected cases fit within the wider research findings.

This is by no means to suggest that the nine cases chosen for in-depth research could ever represent the fullness of the large pool of data collected. I have selected most of them for their potential to offer "illustrative examples" of the central themes that appeared in the sample. The selection was then further refined to ensure representation from the geographic diversity of Canada and the chronological sweep of the study. I have confined the cases primarily to heterosexual sexual assault prosecutions, with the exception of one chapter that examines the only female-to-female criminal prosecution in the pool. Although this is an exceptional rather than a "representative" case, I selected it because of its historical importance and comparative usefulness. Future researchers will want to examine how the treatment of same-sex male prosecutions compares to my findings here.

One of the most intriguing discoveries of the detailed research into the cases selected was how many of the other cases chosen for their "representativeness" began to reveal unusual features as further investigation into the people and events progressed. Midway through the study, I became concerned that I had simply made errors in selecting aberrational or exceptional cases, and jettisoned some, replacing them with others that appeared more "ordinary."[4] Yet with further probing, the replacement cases often revealed similar layers of complexity. It caused me to wonder whether all sexual assault cases that entered the realm of the courtroom were unusual in some respects. In fact, the most truly "representative" sexual assaults in this sample may have been Velma Demerson's rape in New Brunswick in 1936, which she chose to disclose to no one, and the multiple sexual assaults experienced by Rose Roper and her sisters as children in Alkali Lake, British Columbia, in the 1950s and 1960s, which went unreported and unprosecuted. Another interpretation is that most people's lives are complicated, and legal research that relies upon the written texts of reported decisions or even archival records misses much of significance. Probing below the surface of these documents into the times, places, events, and lives of the individuals who spawned the legal proceedings discloses a richness almost unimaginable to those who restrict their research to "black letter" legal doctrine.

Theoretical Frameworks

THE CAUSES, MEANINGS, AND significance of sexual assault are issues that have been hotly contested for decades. Early researchers tended to depict sexual assault as anomalous individual acts, perpetrated by mentally ill men who had not adjusted to proper masculine norms, against women and children who more than occasionally invited such overtures or failed to protect themselves properly. Psychiatrist Benjamin Karpman defined rapists as victims of an "uncontrollable urge" that was "infantile" in nature, and attributed their acts to a thwarted "natural" impulse to have intercourse with their mothers.[5] Psychologist David Abrahamsen blamed the wives of rapists for their spouses' criminal tendencies, asserting that the former "latently denied their femininity and showed an aggressive masculine orientation," thereby "stimulat[ing] their husbands into attempts to prove themselves."[6] Criminologist Menachem Amir described rape as a "deviation," a function of the "criminal subculture," and identified "victim-precipitation" as one of its causes.[7]

One of the first feminist theorists to take issue with such perspectives was Susan Brownmiller. She claimed that rape was a socially pervasive phenomenon, ubiquitous throughout history, and that it functioned as a "process of conscious intimidation by which *all men* keep *all women* in a state of fear."[8] The first feminist sociological surveys, commenced in the 1970s, provided concrete evidence of pervasiveness, demonstrating a shockingly high rate of sexual assaults upon women and girls, some by strangers but disproportionately by men known to the victims.[9] Robin Morgan argued that rape was not the product of a few sick individuals, but an act of "political terrorism," the inevitable consequence of a patriarchal culture.[10] Andrea Dworkin defined rape as a "colonizing act," a "function of male imperialism over and against women," and a violation of women's "right to self-determination."[11] Lorenne Clark and Debra Lewis expanded upon a "property analysis" of rape, arguing that "rape laws were never meant to protect all women" but were designed "to preserve valuable female sexual property for the exclusive ownership of those men who could afford to acquire and maintain it." Clark and Lewis claimed that the "violence" of sexual assault vastly outstripped the "sexual" components.[12]

Catharine MacKinnon took issue with the pure "violence" approach. She described sexual assault as "dominance eroticized," adding that sexual assault seemed "less an ordinary act of sexual desire directed toward the

wrong person than an expression of dominance laced with impersonal contempt, the habit of getting what one wants, and the perception (usually accurate) that the situation can be safely exploited in this way — all expressed
sexually . . . . The fact that [men] can do this seems itself to be sexually arous-
ing [for them]."[13] Other feminists, sometimes characterized as "sex radicals,"
critiqued what they described as "dominance feminism," claiming that sex
was potentially empowering for women. While their analysis stemmed primarily from debates about prostitution, pornography, and sado-masochism,
their arguments occasionally spilled over into sexual assault theory, as they
suggested that attempts to regulate sex and stifle sex-related expression were
potentially regressive and would subordinate women.[14]

Feminist theorists expanded upon these diverse premises within the
realm of law. Lorenne Clark and Debra Lewis documented the sexist enforcement of Canadian rape law, and called for a substantial legal redefini-
tion of rape.[15] Catharine MacKinnon critiqued traditional legal doctrines as
"conceptually inadequate" to deal with the "social reality of men's sexual
treatment of women," and challenged concepts of "objectivity" and "neutrality" as masking the inherent maleness of law.[16] Christine Boyle traced
many legal rules to the fears of male law-makers, "haunted by the spectre of
the innocent accused, the victim of a false charge," and argued that "given
the position of inequality of Canadian (and other) women, one should start
with the assumption that intercourse is non-consensual and look for evidence of consent, rather than the reverse."[17] Elizabeth Sheehy refined this
with feminist argument as to why evidence of prior sexual history should
not be admissible in court, and a critique of how the *Charter* had been used
to diminish gender equality in sexual assault law.[18]

Other theorists questioned feminist demands to reform the legal system to
recognize women's realities. Their concern was that the criminal justice system was a tool of the patriarchal state, ill situated to provide useful outcomes
for women, or communities disadvantaged by race, ethnicity, poverty, sexual
identity, or disability. Carol Smart queried the efficacy of all law: "We should
not make the mistake that law can provide the solution to the oppression
that it celebrates and sustains."[19] Katherine Franke argued that legal feminists had focused largely on the dangers of sexual violence without affirm-
ing the pleasures of sex and the desirability of sexual subcultures.[20] Dianne
Martin complained that feminist ideas and credibility were appropriated to
strengthen right-wing agendas that scapegoated the most vulnerable and
gave greater power to a retributive criminal justice system.[21] Laureen Snider

claimed that the criminal law lacked "transformative potential because of its particular role vis-à-vis the welfare state, dominant ideologies, and the struggle for change."[22] Their analyses built upon the work of Elizabeth Spelman, Angela Davis, bell hooks, Patricia Monture, Sherene Razack, Himani Bannerji, Philomena Essed, and Richard Delgado, who critiqued the universality of the concept of "gender." Critical race scholars insisted that not all women experienced sexual assault the same way and that female experiences varied greatly depending on class, race, and other identifying variables.[23]

The historical cases compiled for this book appear to bear out many parts of this rich feminist analysis, particularly with respect to the pervasiveness and sheer ordinariness of sexual assault. In the decades researched here, large numbers of women and children experienced sexual assault on urban streets, rural fields, in automobiles, in the home, and in the workplace. Where the trials illuminated the perspectives of the accused men, there is little evidence of psychiatric or other mental disturbance and in contrast, a sense that their actions were more accurately characterized by common understandings of masculine entitlement. While some of the victims might be criticized for risk-taking behaviour, most were simply going about their business at home or at work. Some were accosted by relative strangers, but most were assaulted by individuals they knew well.

The claim of feminist theorists that sexual assault is an inevitable outgrowth of patriarchy is bolstered by the gendered dynamics of the large majority of cases in this historical study, where male power and the subordination of women are clearly evident. However, the presence of two female perpetrators in the nine cases profiled complicates the patriarchal analysis. The lesbian prosecution reminds us that sexual coercion can be present in same-sex female relations. But the lesbian case discussed here differs significantly from the heterosexual prosecutions, both in terms of the act perpetrated and the legal response to it. Indeed, it can be understood as the response of a legal system intent upon enforcing compulsory heterosexuality, which Adrienne Rich has characterized itself as a central tenet of patriarchal supremacy.[24] The state-perpetrated abuse visited upon a reformatory inmate by a female physician is not so easily distinguished, and it reveals that women could become equally implicated in certain forms of serious sexual abuse. While some may argue that this poses a central challenge to the feminist perspective on sexual assault, in my view, it suggests instead that individual women occasionally aligned themselves with male-dominant ideologies and practices.

The cases profiled here provide strong support for the critiques raised by feminist legal theorists that rape law reflected male perspectives and dismissed women's realities. Both in formulation and enforcement, the legal system betrayed a deep distrust of female complainants, and an underlying misogyny that infused legal doctrines such as consent, corroboration, prior sexual history, and resistance, as well as legal practices such as charge-laying and cross-examination. The doubts expressed by some feminist theorists about the efficacy of law also appear to be legitimized by the historical data, where the results of engagement with law typically worked to the disadvantage of the women concerned. The cases in this study also amply bear out the premise that intersectional factors played a definitive role in women's historical experiences of sexual assault.

This book builds upon the path-breaking research of other Canadian historians who have explored sexual assault. Many began with regional studies. Terry Chapman, Lesley Erickson, and Dorothy Chunn examined sexual assault in Western Canada, while Jim Phillips explored some cases in eighteenth-century Halifax, and Marie-Aimée Cliche researched Québec.[25] Ruth Olsen and Patrick Connor studied Ontario rapes in the late eighteenth century and the Victorian era.[26] Carolyn Strange examined the sexual perils facing young, single, working-class women in Toronto at the turn of the century.[27] Karen Dubinsky's study of sexual crime in northern and rural Ontario supported a feminist analysis of the power dynamics of sexual violence, and it emphasized that women were not silent victims, but active in negotiating their own sexual encounters.[28] Joan Sangster examined aspects of incest and sexual abuse in her study of how the law attempted to regulate female sexuality in Ontario in the first half of the twentieth century.[29] Becki Ross, Mary Louise Adams, and Elise Chenier explored historical aspects of enforced heterosexuality and the resistance posed by lesbian practices.[30] This study expands upon the work of these earlier researchers with a specifically legal focus. In addition to a wider geographic, pan-Canadian range, it examines a lengthier and more contemporary time period, moving forward to when the first round of pro-feminist legislative reform commenced. It contains a multi-dimensional examination of the forces of intersectionality. And its detailed narrative, case-specific approach that delves into the intricacies of individual trials also distinguishes it from the earlier studies.

My objective is to demonstrate that the legal history of sexual assault offers an extraordinary window into the past. It appears to provide one of the best tools with which to gauge the status of women in comparison to men, while viewing the gender imbalance through the intersecting features of class, race, ethnicity, sexual identity, age, and disability. As courts probed into the nuances of sexual adventuring and sexual coercion, they exposed to public view the intricate intimate relations forged between men and women. Witnesses, lawyers, jurors, judges, and reporters described, explored, justified, and critiqued the dynamic, and often dangerous, practices that led to criminal sexual charges. The final verdicts were based upon credibility assessments that lay bare the prevailing notions of masculinity, femininity, sexuality, and respectability that were so often unarticulated in other forums. Sexual assault cases cut to the core of gender in all of its variations. The history of sexual assault unveils much of the foundation of sexual inequality in our time.

"DON'T YOU BULLY ME ... JUSTICE I WANT IF THERE IS JUSTICE TO BE HAD": The Rape of Mary Ann Burton, London, Ontario, 1907

"DON'T YOU BULLY ME," was the defiant retort of Mary Ann Burton, her bold command issued from the witness box in the London Police Court on 15 July 1907. "I want to speak justice, and justice I want if there is justice to be had." The stirring remark was kindled by a "searching and ruthless cross-examination," as it was described by the *London Free Press,* at the hands of criminal lawyer Edmund Allen Meredith, KC. Mary Ann Burton, who had launched a complaint of rape against Joseph Gray on 8 July 1907, had withstood Meredith's merciless grilling with courage and dignity. As her words indicated, she was incensed at both the substance and the tone of the interrogation.[1]

Women who made allegations of rape in early twentieth-century Canada rarely spoke with such temerity and force.[2] Those who suggested otherwise were responsible for perpetrating one of the greatest mythologies embedded in law. Seventeenth-century English jurist Sir Matthew Hale had been the first to pronounce that rape was "an accusation easily to be made" in his *Historia Placitorum Coronae* published posthumously in 1734.[3] This unsubstantiated dictum had come to be enshrined in the texts and judicial decisions of criminal justice systems throughout the Anglo-American legal world.[4] Despite the endless obeisance conferred upon Hale's homily, it was common knowledge that most rape victims made no public outcry at all. Women weighed the shame and embarrassment of public disclosure against the trauma of dealing with coercive sexual assault in private, and voted over-whelmingly for perennial silence.[5] The few women who did resort to the law for protection found themselves crushed in the process, typically tormented and abused on the witness stand by defence lawyers who stopped at nothing to besmirch the credibility of the "prosecutrix" as the rape complainant was anachronistically characterized.[6] What such women thought of their treat-ment is generally not recorded.

Mary Ann Burton is the exception, although few saw fit to recognize her for this in her own time. The wife of a tanner, Mrs. Burton was a poorly educated, working-class, heavy-set, woman of uncertain age. She lived in a dilapidated rental house in a rundown neighbourhood at the fork of the Thames River in London, Ontario. Working-class areas stuck out like a sore thumb in turn-of-the-century London, the "Forest City" that prided itself on the wealth of its inhabitants, the elaborate brick-and-stone structures that housed many of the province's key financial businesses, and the ornate resi-dential mansions that graced the parklike boulevards. The self-satisfaction of city burghers was pricked by pockets of unreclaimed poverty, such as the ramshackle row house that was home to Mrs. Burton. Like many of her class, Mary Ann Burton cooked and cleaned for a few boarders who paid to live in the upstairs of her modest dwelling. Her two-storey row house at 12 Dundas Street West backed onto the dump. Alongside it stood Lancaster Boat Builders, several other shambling residences, and assorted industrial factories, including the Dennis Wire & Iron Works and the Electric Construc-tion Company. The forbidding City Jail loomed over everything, just down the block and across the street.[7]

Mary Ann Burton's rape trial would not become a landmark legal prec-edent, so far as lawyers and judges were concerned. The records suggest that her efforts to "speak justice" were betrayed by her husband, the physician who examined her, the friends and neighbours who testified at her trial, the lawyers, the judge, and the press. There was little here that was noteworthy to those who parsed cases for legal rulings and precedent. The decision was not published in the law reports. It was an ordinary, run-of-the-mill rape trial. The jury was never asked to deliberate on the evidence. The outcome was an acquittal on a directed verdict. The Crown offered no appeal. The spirited resistance of Mary Ann Burton, thrown up in the face of all odds, has been buried in the archives for over a century. Her impassioned words deserve our attention this many years later, because she gave voice to what so many others must have thought, but dared not express.

London Room, London Public Library, PGO 66

Dundas Street West, c. 1940s, showing Dundas Street bridge and
Dennisteel Ltd., formerly Dennis Iron Works

The Events of 8 July 1907: Mrs. Burton's Narrative

WHAT TRANSPIRED ON MONDAY, 8 July 1907, will never be completely recoverable from the surviving documentation. Mary Ann Burton's description of the events was filtered through police investigators, prosecuting Crown attorneys, and the tightly structured criminal trial process. Yet hers was the most detailed version to survive in the records, because it was she who was the main focus of the judicial proceeding. Her story, pieced together as fully as possible from the remaining records, follows.

It was a hot and sultry afternoon in southwestern Ontario, with an ominous threat of thundershowers. Mrs. Burton had been out window-shopping with a friend, and arrived home at the height of the hazy midday heat. The row house was quiet and empty, her husband and boarders long since departed for work. Mrs. Burton began the tiresome task of putting the house to order. She scrubbed the two upstairs rooms, made the boarders' beds, swept out the stairs and passageway, and had a bite of cold dinner left over from Sunday. Then a friend and former male boarder of Mrs. Burton's, who now rented just down the street, dropped over.[8] Mrs. Burton interrupted the

Teamster and rig in muddy roads, c. 1908–1910.

visit because she had seen some workers over by the dump unloading scrap wood. She shouted to one of them, a man she did not know but would later learn was Joseph Gray, inquiring whether he would sell her a few loads of wooden blocks for fifty cents. Some of Mrs. Burton's neighbours had made previous arrangements with Gray to deliver scrap kindling that day.

Joseph Gray seemed affable enough. He was a young, reasonably well-to-do teamster, who owned his own team and rig, and worked under contract with the city, hauling discarded paving blocks to the dump.[9] Gray called out to one of his hired hands for help, and the two men deposited the wood outside Mrs. Burton's door. When she offered to pay Gray, he declined. Instead, he jumped down off his cart, peered into her kitchen, and hailed Mrs. Burton's former boarder like a long-lost buddy. "Hello Harry, how are you, old man?" he called out. Hauling wood was a dusty, thirst-inducing business, and Gray suggested that they should "give the boys a drink." He flipped Mrs. Burton's former boarder a quarter and told him to run over to the Grand Central Hotel on King and Ridout Streets to get some ale.

Mrs. Burton claimed that although they asked her to drink with them, she did not touch a drop, and that the men downed the ale in her back woodshed because she refused to let them drink in the house. Joseph Gray turned rude and familiar, announcing that "before he left that night," he would "have" her. "Get out of the house," retorted Mrs. Burton. "If you don't get out of the house, I will have you arrested." The party broke up right away, and everyone took off, leaving Mrs. Burton alone in her house. Shortly after 5 p.m., Joseph Gray reappeared. He strode swiftly through the woodshed, past the summer kitchen, and into the house.

Gray seized Mrs. Burton by the shoulder, and she struck her assailant "just by the scar at the back of his ear." Screaming, "Let me go, you dirty beast," she fought as fiercely as she could, struggling to reach the front door. Gray knocked her down and they both fell onto the floor of the front hall. Gray took hold of her breast with one hand, clasped her waist with the other, and lifted her bodily into the front bedroom adjacent to the hall. He threw her sideways across the bed, undid his trousers, and forced himself upon her sexually. She remembered begging, "For God's sake, let me out." Gray removed a large, filthy handkerchief from his pocket, stuffed it down her mouth, and gagged her with a stout rope tied securely around her neck. Mrs. Burton fainted, and Joseph Gray must have fled.

When she came to, the gagged woman could barely breathe. Unable to crawl to the door at first, she smashed the window in the hall in a desperate effort to call for help. Sometime later, she dragged herself through the passageway to the door, which she managed to open partially. Some passersby came to the rescue, ungagged her, and poured some water over the groaning woman to help her regain consciousness. Mrs. Burton was gasping for air and could scarcely speak. A crowd gathered to gawk at the badly bruised woman, and someone called the police. The police had more than a passing acquaintance with the residents of 12 Dundas Street, for the Burtons were frequently entangled in violent marital disputes. This may have explained their apparent indifference to Mrs. Burton's obvious injuries. The constable who arrived at the scene simply shrugged his shoulders and advised her to "send for a doctor." When Mrs. Burton was unable to identify her attacker, and objected to the brusque and intrusive questioning of the officers, they concluded that the affair was "nothing but a brawl" and washed their hands of the matter.[10] But it did not rest there.

Edwin Seaborn, a physician who ran a busy medical practice from his residence at 688 Dundas Street, arrived at the Burton row house between 6 and 7 p.m. He examined Mrs. Burton in the front room, making notations of the swelling and multiple bruises. He conducted no internal vaginal examination, although these were routinely done on victims of sexual assault at the time. Noticing that Mrs. Burton's clothes were badly stained with wet spots, he took out his scissors and cut away the stained portions. These he packed up in his bag, and then he went back to his office.

Mrs. Burton's husband, Robert, arrived home to considerable commotion emanating from his house and clusters of curious neighbours gossiping from their porches and stoops. What transpired when Mrs. Burton described her ordeal is unknown, but initially at least, Robert seems to have been supportive of his spouse. The two went looking for her assailant early the next morning, and managed to extract his name from individuals in the neighbourhood. Robert and Mary Ann Burton swore out a criminal complaint of rape against Joseph Gray that evening.[11]

Joseph Gray's Response

JOSEPH GRAY'S VERSION OF what transpired on 8 July 1907 can be pieced together from interviews he gave to the newspapers. From the outset, the accused man seems to have been confident that he had no cause for alarm. He did not wait for the police to execute a warrant for his arrest but simply "walked into the police station" and gave himself up, declaring that he had "nothing to fear," and "demanding a full investigation" into the charges. The *London Advertiser* reported that Joseph Gray took his arrest "coolly," and maintained that he "never was near the Burton residence" on the afternoon in question.[12] Gray professed to have delivered his last load to the dump and left the vicinity at about 4:50 p.m., heading directly to the Britannia House at York and Wellington where he downed a drink or two, after which he went straight home. The coverage in the *London Free Press* was quite partial to the accused. Describing Joseph Gray as "a well-to-do young man," the paper indicated that he was "not averse to talking about the case," and that he told a "pretty straight story to the *Free Press* reporter." Gray's lengthy explanation of his innocence was published in full, under the caption "Declares Charge Case of Blackmail":

> "It is a case of blackmail," he said, "pure and simple, for I was never inside the woman's house in my life. My men were drawing gravel down there, and I was superintending the work when Mrs. Burton came out and asked me for a load of the blocks we were drawing away. I told her that she could have the next load if she wanted it, and when the load came I had the men leave

Left: "Woman Assaulted in West London," *London Advertiser*, 9 July 1907. Right: "Attacked in House," press clipping of Mrs. Burton's attack, *London Free Press*, 9 July 1907

it there. When it was unloaded she asked me if I would come in and have a drink with her as she had some beer in the house. I went up to the back porch and had a drink and then I went back to my work, and that is all I know about it. She was out talking to me and the men the biggest part of the afternoon, and she told me that she knew who I was and that I owned a farm. She asked me several times to come into the house, but I told her I was too busy. I'll have all my men there Tuesday. They saw the whole thing from start to finish."[13]

Later coverage would indicate that Joseph Gray's story was a bit less "straight" than the reporter had surmised. Gray would admit that it was not Mrs. Burton who supplied the beer, but her former boarder, and that Gray had paid him twenty-five cents to fetch the ale. He would also concede that he drank the ale in Mrs. Burton's woodshed, not standing on the porch, although he continued "stoutly" to deny ever having assaulted the complainant. These discrepancies did nothing to detract from the supportive commentary in the newspapers. The *London Advertiser* weighed in with a glowing assessment of Joseph Gray's position, describing him as a "respect-able-looking young man" who bore "a good reputation."[14] He had no trouble securing bail after signing a recognizance for $2000. Gray's father and uncle, Michael and Patrick Gray, both teamsters, each put up a $1000 surety on his behalf as well.[15]

"You Insult Me": The Cross-Examination of Mary Ann Burton

WHEN THE PRELIMINARY INQUIRY commenced on Monday, 15 July 1907, Francis Love was presiding as the police magistrate.[16] Middlesex County Crown attorney James B. McKillop prosecuted.[17] Edmund Allen Meredith, KC, appeared as defence counsel. It was Meredith who stole the show.

Like many elite lawyers of his day, Edmund Meredith had had the good fortune to be born into a remarkably powerful Anglo-Irish legal dynasty. His brother, William Ralph Meredith, served as the Tory Opposition leader at Queen's Park, and went on to become Chief Justice of Ontario. Another brother, Richard Martin Meredith, sat as a judge of the Supreme Court of Ontario. Edmund, practically as well known as his famous younger brothers, had served as London's mayor in the city's boom years during the 1880s and practised as a partner in the firm of Meredith, Judd & Meredith at 365 Richmond Street. His successful defence of the infamous Esther Arscott, a flamboyant madam who ran an east London brothel, had garnered him substantial notoriety some years back, and his stature as one of London's preeminent criminal lawyers only increased with the passage of time. Meredith's contemporaries accorded him high ranking within legal circles, recognizing his advantages of "family, personal appearance and influence."[18]

Meredith's cross-examination of Mrs. Burton was a model for its time. Defence lawyers mounted their attacks upon rape complainants personally, hoping to convince the court that such women were unworthy victims, not the sort who ought to merit putting a good man in jail. They tried to prove that the complainants were sexually promiscuous, rabble-rousing, foul-tongued, ill-mannered, or intemperate in drinking habits. They gave voice to multiple theories why such women might fabricate a rape complaint. Some were alleged to be suffering from delusional fantasies. Others were supposedly protecting their reputations, and caught in an act of consensual extra-marital sex, they "cried rape" to protect their honour and cast blame on the male. Some, it was suggested, had consented to the sex act initially — whether prompted by abundant sexual desire, or swept away by clever masculine wiles — but later recanted and blamed their former paramours. Others were described as cloaked in venomous rage, seeking to wreak revenge upon the hapless men who had scorned their feminine attentions. Some were accused of extortion, denouncing innocent men in order to extract vast sums of money. Few counsel stopped at this point. Most also persistently chipped away at the complainants' testimony, seeking to illustrate inconsistencies in the evidence, and using the most minor factual discrepancies to cast doubt on the entirety of the women's narratives.

The consistency of such defence practices appears through scores of criminal trial transcripts across seventy-five years of the twentieth century from all regions of the country. Questions asked of rape complainants in coastal Halifax, urban Toronto, small towns in southwestern Ontario, and farming districts in rural Saskatchewan were similar.[19] Criminal law texts advised lawyers to "adduce evidence to show that the woman is of notoriously bad character, unchaste, and of indecent habits, or that she is a common prostitute; or to show that she has previously had carnal connection with the defendant of her own free will."[20] All defence counsel, whether criminal law specialist or dabbler, senior or junior at the bar, seem to have defined it as their professional responsibility to make unsavoury assertions about the women and girls who brought charges of sexual assault. That so many of the questions were rooted in misogynistic ideology is striking. The malevolence and relentlessness of their insinuations turned cross-examination into gendered character assassination. And Crown prosecutors and judges generally stood by without objection, their silence a solemn affirmation of sexually discriminatory defence strategies.

Meredith's first set of questions to Mrs. Burton had nothing to do with the rape. "You had a little trouble on Saturday?" he queried, referring to the weekend immediately prior to the preliminary inquiry. Mrs. Burton, characteristically, stood her ground. "The trouble had nothing to do with the case," she replied. "Don't you do all the talking; answer the questions and don't be bold about it," commanded Meredith. This was Meredith's initial signal, a rather heavy-handed one, that he was the party controlling the exchange. He was correct that Mrs. Burton had to "answer the questions" and that he was legally permitted wide range in the conduct of the cross-examination. The rules of evidence allowed him to explore multiple aspects of the rape complainant's "life and conduct" in his attack on her "credibility."[21] But his chastisement of Mrs. Burton for "doing all the talking" seems a bit odd, since

London Central Police Court and Station, 1897

she had uttered one short sentence so far. His depiction of her as "bold" was closer to the mark, and his remonstration against such independence a clear beacon of things to come.

"You had a little trouble on Saturday?" he repeated. "Yes," she answered — briefly, to the point. "With your husband?" continued Meredith. "Yes," agreed Mrs. Burton, again answering the question without more explanation. The examination continued:

Q. And his hands are all tied up now, what was that with?

A. Because my husband turned round and said, "That is through your allowing that man Gray here for people to laugh at me as I am passing on the street," and I said, "Don't bring that up in my face, I could not help that."

Q. What did you do after your husband said that?

A. I threw a shovel at him.

Q. What did the shovel do to him?

A. It grazed his hand.

Q. Cut his hand?

A. No, it is not.

Q. Aren't they tied up?

A. Yes, sure they are tied up.

Q. At all events, you threw the shovel at him. What kind of a shovel was it?

A. A small shovel.

Q. That hit him in the hand?

A. Yes.

Q. Both hands?

A. No, one hand.[22]

It is not fully clear how to interpret this, but it would seem that Meredith had learned about a domestic scuffle between Mrs. Burton and her husband on the weekend preceding the hearing. Robert had complained that his neighbours were making snide remarks to him about the rape. He was accusing his wife of having invited the accused man to her home, insinuating that she was in part responsible for the rape. Mrs. Burton had defended herself verbally, proclaiming her innocence, and then heaved a small shovel at her husband. Meredith was trying to prove that the bandages on Robert's hands were the result of his wife's violent behaviour. She denied this. Meredith must have been satisfied with the exchange, however. He had proven that in the opinion of some of her neighbours, Mrs. Burton was responsible for what had transpired between her and the man being prosecuted for rape. Relations were obviously strained between husband and wife. The whole neighbourhood was joking about the alleged rape, not just behind closed doors, but in public, right to Robert's face. Meredith had also demonstrated that Mrs. Burton was quite capable of dishing out physical abuse to her husband. He moved on.

The next line of inquiry attempted to demonstrate that the witness was inconsistent in her recollection of details. Meredith began by asking Mrs. Burton to describe where she had been on the morning of the alleged rape. She testified that she had been in police court until noon, accompanying a friend whose husband was up on charges, and that the two women had then strolled home, window-shopping along the way for about an hour and a half.[23] Lawyer and witness argued back and forth about the timing of Mrs. Burton's return home. She initially said that she had arrived home "about three to four as far as I can remember." Meredith compared that answer to the mere hour and a half Mrs. Burton had mentioned devoted to window-shopping, and pounced:

Q. You told me you left here [police court] about eleven o'clock?
A. Twelve o'clock.
Q. Then you strolled around for an hour and a half?
A. It may be a little longer.
Q. I thought you did not get home till between three and four?
A. It may have been before that.
Q. You told me between three and four.
A. I cannot tell exactly.
Q. Why did you tell me between three and four?
A. Because I did not take that much notice of the time; I am not on my oath on the time.

Mary Ann Burton was incorrect about the oath, of course. All her testimony was under oath, and her jaunty suggestion that the matter of time was exempt was not well calculated to impress the court. Meredith was pursuing the customary defence tactic of tripping up the witness, getting her to profess inconsistent statements so that he could accuse her of deliberate falsehood or reckless indifference to detail. Meredith was well within his rights to pursue the question of timing, since his client would later maintain he was elsewhere around five o'clock, the time of the alleged attack. However, Mrs. Burton had qualified her initial testimony, careful to refrain from an exact pinpointing of the time she arrived home. She had testified that it was between three and four, possibly earlier, and stipulated that this was only as far as she could "remember." Mrs. Burton did not own a watch. She told time as often as not by the factory whistle from the nearby ironworks shop. In light of this, Meredith's cross-examination on time seems more than a little unfair. He had also, intentionally or unintentionally, misled Mrs. Burton by wrongly giving her time of departure from the courthouse as eleven o'clock. She had testified that it was noon when she left.

The skirmishing over time continued, with Meredith badgering the witness repeatedly over her inability to recollect exactly when certain events had occurred. When she testified that the five o'clock whistle had blown after her former boarder had departed, and then subsequently that it had blown before her former boarder and Gray left, Meredith must have been delighted over the clear inconsistencies. The finale to this protracted interrogation was his pointed assertion: "You are kind of mixed up." "No," replied Mrs. Burton, "I am not." This rather astonishing response exemplifies Mary Ann Burton's confidence and self-conviction. She might have mixed up exactly when the men had left her place, but she was adamant that she was not mixed up about the rape itself.

The presence of alcohol at a rape scene was always helpful to the defence, and Meredith played this card with aplomb. He asked Mary Ann Burton to describe the events that led to the purchase of the beer. Mrs. Burton reminded the court that she had refused to let the men drink their ale inside her house, but sent them instead to the woodshed. She also repeated that she had told them she didn't want any of their beer. Meredith asked: "Did you drink?" "No," replied Mrs. Burton, but "that gentleman there," pointing to Gray, "asked me to drink." "Were you pretty well drunk at the time?" queried Meredith. Apparently astonished at the question, Mrs. Burton asked Meredith to repeat himself, and then replied, "No, sir, I was not drunk at that time." "Did you drink any that day?" persisted Meredith. "No, sir, not a drink the whole of that day." "Do you drink?" was Meredith's next query. "Yes, sir," replied Mrs. Burton.

Meredith had skillfully maneuvered his witness into admitting she was a drinker, and then used her admission that she drank to insinuate that it was implausible that such a woman would sit by while others imbibed the free-flowing alcohol:

Q. You never put it to your lips at all?
A. No, I never had any.
Q. You had not had a drink that morning?

A. No, I never had any.

Q. You had not had a drink that morning?

A. No, Sir.

Q. No drink was supplied at your house that morning?

A. No, Sir.

Q. Did [your former boarder] go out for a drink that morning?

A. No, not for me; he went for himself, I believe.

Q. Did you drink any portion of that drink?

A. No.

The intense interest in Mary Ann Burton's alcohol consumption had little to do with whether she was raped. The defence wished to portray her as an inebriate, an abandoned woman who drank with strangers on a weekday afternoon. The intent was to characterize Mrs. Burton as lacking in respectability, as the sort of woman who was not worth the trouble of convicting a man for rape. London, Ontario, was a heartland for organizations such as the Woman's Christian Temperance Union, which had hosted a spectacularly successful provincial convention in the city in 1906, and it was customary for turn-of-the-century, respectable, middle-class women to shun alcohol and lobby for its prohibition.[24] Women who imbibed alcohol were perceived as a disgrace to their gender. The Royal Commission on the Liquor Traffic had reported in 1895 that "drunkenness among the women" was "ten times worse than in men, because it causes them to lose their maternal instinct and feeling, and they become thoroughly degraded." Newspaper reports fastened upon incidents of women's alcoholism with prurience, portraying the wreckage of their homes and families as deplorably inevitable.[25]

In the final portion of his cross-examination, Meredith also insinuated that Mrs. Burton was a sexually promiscuous woman. He intended to shock the jurors with the following question, which came right upon the heels of the queries about alcohol:

Q. Did you go out and catch some young fellow by the privates and invite him in?

A. No, Sir.

Q. Did anything of that kind occur?

A. No, Sir.

Q. Fiddling with his privates?

A. No, Sir.

CITIZENS AWAKE AND ACT

Pioneer (Toronto), 24 October 1902

"Citizens Awake and Act" Pro-Temperance cartoon

"The Morkin House Bar," J.J. Talman Regional Collection, UWO Archives, RC41578

London bar, circa 1905

Industries of Canada: Historical and Commerical Sketches: London
(Toronto: M.G. Bixby, 1887) at 89

Promotion of Temperance
Coffee House in London

To further intimidate the witness, Meredith professed to be able to back up his assertion with independent evidence:

Q. I am told by a most respectable person that there was a man at your
house and that you took hold of him
and pushed him in the back way. Is
that true?

A. No, Sir.

Q. That you at the back door caught
hold of some man and ran him right
in your back door?

A. It is a story, I did not Sir, I should not
think of doing such a thing.

Q. Upon your solemn oath, about four
o'clock, you were seen by a lady in
the neighbourhood to take hold of a
man who was dressed in black and
shove him through your back door?

A. It is false.

Q. Not a word of truth in it?

A. No, Sir, false, false.

Q. If I put that lady in the box and she
swears you did, that is untrue?

A. I would not care if you put a thousand, it is false.

Q. I have her statement in black and
white?

A. It is false, Sir.

Mrs. Burton held firm throughout, never wavering in her denials of impropriety.
Edmund Meredith did not call the "most
respectable" woman who claimed to have
observed such shenanigans. Although the
defence was entitled to call witnesses to back up its case at the preliminary
inquiry, hearings at this stage usually consisted solely of Crown evidence.
A preliminary inquiry was designed to ascertain whether there was a "suf-

ficient case" against the accused to warrant putting the matter over for a full-fledged trial at the next assizes. It also provided an opportunity for the defence to obtain disclosure of the evidence that would be introduced against the accused at trial, to extract damaging concessions from Crown witnesses, and to figure out the most promising lines of future argument.[26] Meredith seems to have positively revelled in his parry-and-thrust with Mary Ann Burton. At no time was this more evident than when he cross-examined Mrs. Burton on the specifics of the sexual attack.

Q. Gray caught hold of you by the breast?
A. That was when he caught hold of me, and I scrambled for him to let go.
Q. Did you holler out?
A. Yes, about as loud as I could.
Q. At the top of your voice?
A. I do not suppose I could holler at the top of my voice, the way he kept hold of me.
Q. He caught hold of you from the back?
A. Yes.
Q. Did that interfere with your mouth?
A. Could anybody hear and the door shut?
Q. Did you holler at the top of your voice?
A. I could not say whether I hollered at the top of my voice or the bottom, I hollered, I hollered as loud as I could.
Q. Where is the bottom of your voice?
A. I hollered as loud as I could.

Meredith hoped here to plant a seed of doubt over whether the sexual connection had really been against Mrs. Burton's wishes, or perhaps to raise the possibility that it had never happened. Mrs. Burton refused to budge, and the struggle between witness and lawyer intensified as the cross-examination went on:

Q. What did you call out?
A. Let me go, you beast, let me go.
Q. How many times did you holler that out?
A. I could not tell you.
Q. As near as you can?
A. I could not.
Q. Was it ten times?

A. I did not know what I was doing, I suppose.

Q. Was it ten times?

A. I could not count the times.

Q. Was it more than once?

A. Yes.

Q. More than twice?

A. I could not tell you.

This was serious sparring indeed. At an earlier point in the cross-examination, Meredith had accused Mrs. Burton of becoming "wild" over his questions. "I am not getting wild," she retorted from the stand, "but you are asking me such ridiculous questions I cannot give you an answer." "Do not argue with me," was Meredith's next admonition. "I am giving the answers as well as I can," rejoined Mrs. Burton. The determination and forcefulness with which Mrs. Burton resisted Meredith's inquisition seem to have inspired the defence lawyer to escalate his cross-examination. The portion of the transcript that dealt with Mrs. Burton's depiction of the rape itself is typical. Mrs. Burton had described how she and Gray had fallen to the floor scuffling, and how she had tried to escape:

Q. What did he do?

A. He got me around the waist and threw me away on the bed.

Q. How did he get you in the room?

A. He lifted me right up and threw me.

Q. You are sure of that?

A. I should not tell you if I was not sure.

Q. Got you in the bed room door?

A. Yes.

Q. Waltzed you in the hall and then into the bed room?

A. Yes.

Q. You did not invite him in?

A. I did not get as far as the door.

Q. How did he get you in the room?

A. He lifted me right up and threw me in the room.

Q. How much do you weigh?

A. I do not know.

Q. No idea?

A. No.

Edmund Allen Meredith

Later, newspaper accounts would estimate that Mrs. Burton appeared to be "at least fifty pounds heavier" than Joseph Gray.[27] Meredith probably paused to let the physical bulk of the witness register more fully, and then continued:

Q. He caught you and threw you two yards from this door and chucked you on the bed?

A. Yes, Sir.

Q. What were you doing with your hands?

A. Struggling to get away.

Q. How?

A. I do not know how, I was so excited.

Q. Do you know what you were doing with your hands at all?

A. No, I do not know.

Q. Do you mean to tell me this yarn occurred?

A. Yes, as true as God is my judge.

The references to "waltzing" and "yarns" were deliberately calculated to mock Mrs. Burton's testimony.

Next, Meredith attempted to ridicule the witness when she tried to describe how her clothes had been thrown into disarray when Joseph Gray tossed her upon the bed.

Q. He threw you across the centre of the bed?

A. Yes.

Q. Then your legs would just be about the end?

A. Yes, Sir.

Q. What part of your legs would come there?

A. I could not tell you exactly.

Q. Where were your clothes?

A. My clothes were all up, sir.

Q. Did you pull them up?

A. No, sir, they were all up the way he threw me.

Q. He threw you with your clothes up, right exposing your person? Did he throw you that way on the bed?

A. Yes, Sir.

Q. He conveniently threw you with all your clothes off your person; that is what you are swearing to?

A. Yes.

Meredith was insinuating that Mrs. Burton had volunteered some assistance in disrobing. When she denied this, in the final question in this sequence Meredith expressed disbelief that the petticoat, apron, and dress could have come "off" without deliberate effort. Mrs. Burton had initially testified that the clothes had come "up" not "off" as she was thrown to the bed. Now Meredith had tricked her into agreeing to a somewhat less feasible statement, that the clothes were "off" rather than "up."

As his final shot, Meredith demanded: "You were after this man's money?" Mrs. Burton retorted: "You be very careful what you say." "I say you were after this man's money," repeated the lawyer. "If you do say so, you are speaking a falsehood, you are not a man fit to speak to. 'After this man's money,' it is disgusting. I refuse to speak to you any more," exclaimed Mrs. Burton. Strangely enough, the newspaper account of the "blackmail" exchange differed a bit from the official transcript. The *London Free Press* reported that Meredith "had quizzed" Mrs. Burton "for about an hour, during which time he had had her pretty well mixed up several times," and then Meredith had said:

> "Be honest, now; you were after this man's money, weren't you?" "You insult me," cried the witness, and she rained a torrent of her opinion of a man who would ask any woman such a question upon the attorney's head until he was forced to appeal to his worship to stop the onslaught, only to be met with a smiling reply that he had started it. "Isn't it disgusting," said the witness, "that I have to stand for this?" "Oh, I guess it doesn't bother you very much, if the truth were known," replied the lawyer and the case proceeded.[28]

Either the court reporter failed to record this passage in the official transcript, or the newspaper reporter embellished his copy. But both versions captured something of the bitterness of the repartee, and both revealed a witness who stood her ground no matter what accusations were hurled her way.

Early twentieth-century newspapers often used the scandalous testimony of rape trials to bolster sales, and Mrs. Burton's case hit the front pages a number of times. However, the running commentary that accompanied the press coverage of Mary Ann Burton's case was quite unusual. Reporters from this era occasionally interlaced the factual descriptions of court proceedings with their own opinions of the witnesses, but this case inspired even greater journalistic licence.[29] The *London Free Press* reporter clearly thought that Mrs. Burton had been bested by defence counsel Meredith. In one paragraph, he indicated that the "warm wordy tilts" exchanged between the complainant and the lawyer had left Mrs. Burton "mixed up occasionally" and "pretty well mixed up several times." Characterizing the witness as "extremely voluble," the paper noted that Meredith had had "troubles of his own in getting coherent answers from her."[30] The *London Advertiser* advised that "while being cross-examined by Mr. Meredith, Mrs. Burton became greatly enraged by some of the questions asked her, and talked back freely to the attorney for the defence."[31]

It was quite true that Mary Ann Burton's testimony was not wholly consistent. She had been unclear and occasionally inconsistent over timing. She had described her clothes as thrown upwards, and then responded in the affirmative when Meredith characterized them as thrown off her body. But a careful reading of the full examination and cross-examination reveals few other discrepancies in the witness's evidence. The depiction of the complainant as "extremely voluble" is even more bewildering. Mrs. Burton's responses to the lawyers' questions were brief and to the point. She rarely answered a question with more than a one-sentence reply. Meredith's curt upbraiding of the witness for "doing all the talking" rang false at the time, yet the reporters seem to have taken their cue from the defence lawyer, and parroted his caricature. It was almost as if the lawyer and the journalists were astonished that a rape complainant could find the words to resist the onslaught of cross-examination at the hands of an experienced defence lawyer. It was as if any reply struck the observers as too long-winded, too fulsome, too arrogant.

The reference to Mrs. Burton as "incoherent" is equally curious. The reporters, of course, had the advantage of viewing the cross-examination live, whereas one century later, we are restricted to the typed transcript of the proceedings. However, the written record depicts a witness who spoke in sentences and responded logically, if occasionally unhelpfully. It was not that she was "mixed up" or "incoherent," but that she refused to be pushed into testifying to such things as the exact time that certain events took place, the number of times she called for help, the number of pounds she weighed, and other matters that she could not remember with accuracy. She explained that she was not mixed up about the fact of the rape, who had done it, or that the sexual connection was forced upon her. Rather, she insisted that she would not testify beyond her recollection.

The description of Mrs. Burton as "enraged" and "raining a torrent of her opinion" upon Meredith also seems exaggerated. Mrs. Burton continued to address Meredith as "Sir" in her testimony, replying "yes, Sir" and "no, Sir" throughout. When Meredith tried to bait her with queries about what she meant by the "bottom of her voice," her response was simply to repeat her previous answer that she had hollered as loud as she could. The closest she came to responding in kind was when Meredith asked her, several times over, exactly what her former boarder had been "helping" her do before Joseph Gray arrived that afternoon. He had apparently been helping Mrs. Burton wash the dishes at the time, and she replied: "I told you twice, 'wash up.'" "Tell me the third time," mocked Meredith. "Wash up," replied Mrs. Burton. "Don't be so impertinent about it," interjected Meredith. This was the point at which Mrs. Burton exclaimed, in what must be one of the most powerful statements ever voiced by a Canadian rape complainant, "Don't you bully me, I want to speak justice, and justice I want if there is justice to be had."

Meredith's cross-examination utilized virtually every technique designed by defence lawyers to demolish a woman testifying about rape. He insinuated that Mary Ann Burton was an inebriate, drunk all day and swilling beer with strangers in her woodshed. He suggested that Mrs. Burton had been the sexual aggressor, waylaying a man whom she dragged into her home for a sexual tryst. He claimed that Mrs. Burton had not cried out, intimating that her description of the physical act of rape was unbelievable, the fantasies of a woman who had consented to a voluntary sexual liaison or imagined the whole affair. He asserted that the boarding-house keeper was an extortionist, scheming to extract money from a well-to-do working man by charging him with a fictitious incident of rape. He insisted that Mrs. Burton's recollection of the details of the sexual assault was faulty, inconsistent, and ultimately, incredible in a court of law. Throughout the ordeal, Mrs. Burton held to her narrative of the incident, and spoke with conviction about the responsibilities of the justice system towards victims of rape.

Betrayal from Other Quarters

THE CROWN PUT ITS full case before the court in the preliminary inquiry. There were some obvious, gaping holes. Crown attorney James McKillop did not call the police officers who investigated the crime scene, a departure from the usual practice where most prosecutors routinely examined the officers who had interviewed the complainant. McKillop may have been concerned that the antagonistic relationship between Mrs. Burton and the police would render them all too helpful to defence counsel Meredith during cross-examination. However, the police had seen the complainant immediately after the attack, and could testify first-hand to her bruising, her physical exhaustion,

James B. McKillop

and her distraught condition. McKillop's decision not to call them prevented the admission of this valuable evidence.[32]

McKillop did call the physician who had examined Mrs. Burton on 8 July. His replies to the Crown attorney's questions were helpful as far as they went. He testified that he had examined Mrs. Burton's "person and also her clothing very carefully." He discovered "five or six" bruises on her left breast, and a swelling behind her left shoulder joint, all "quite recent." Mrs. Burton would later assert in her re-examination that she had suffered serious bruising around her legs, and that Dr. Seaborn had seen these as well. Perhaps he had forgotten to note the leg injuries in his report, since he said nothing about them in court. Without explaining why, Dr. Seaborn also told the court that he had not conducted an internal vaginal examination, so could give no further details regarding Mrs. Burton's "private parts." This was another serious omission in the Crown's case. In the absence of any proffered rationale, one can only wonder whether Dr. Seaborn had decided that Mrs. Burton was beneath his consideration, unworthy of the full medical examination required for rape victims. When McKillop asked what had been done with Mrs. Burton's clothing, the physician explained that he had taken away pieces of her petticoat and apron "because there were spots of moisture on them that might possibly have been semen." The logical follow-up, as to what examination had been made of the spots since, revealed a surprising answer: absolutely nothing. Contemporary medical journals described the examination of stains that might be "seminal" as "the most important duty that falls to the hand of the physician in a case of alleged rape."[33] Yet no one seemed apologetic about the omission, no one suggested an adjournment to allow testing for semen stains, and Mrs. Burton was left with no idea why Dr. Seaborn had cut up her apron and petticoat that evening.

Edmund Meredith's cross-examination of Dr. Seaborn was masterful. He asked the physician whether Mrs. Burton's bruising might have been caused in "any number of different ways," and Dr. Seaborn's response was yes. He asked the doctor whether the swelling might have been caused by something other than force, and Dr. Seaborn replied: "I could not say anything about it." As for the clothing, he got Dr. Seaborn to state that neither Mrs. Burton's drawers or clothes were torn, and that he could see "no evidence of a struggle at all as far as the clothes were concerned." The two men got into a bit of a spat over the semen stains, with Dr. Seaborn maintaining that it was not too late to run tests upon the stained portions of the clothing, and Meredith insisting that it would be "impossible" to draw any reliable conclusions after such delay. Medical texts of the time maintained th?t seminal stains could be reliably detected on clothing even seven years after the event, but this would remain a moot point.[34] No one pursued the matter, the stains were never subjected to chemical analysis, and a potentially valuable piece of evidence was left festering in Dr. Seaborn's surgery.

Dr. Seaborn's treatment of Mrs. Burton's case was not atypical of medical evidence given in twentieth-century sexual assault trials.[35] Medical textbooks urged doctors to exercise skepticism when examining women and children complaining of rape. A popular treatise on medical jurisprudence asserted as common knowledge that it was doubtful that a rape could be committed "on a grown female, in good health and strength," adding: "For a woman always possesses sufficient power, by drawing back her limbs, and by the force of her hands, to prevent the insertion of the penis, while she can keep her resolution entire."[36] Physicians were cautioned that "false accusations" were "frequently made for the gratification of malice and revenge."[37] One forensic manual urged doctors not to be the "dupes of designing persons," estimating that for every case of "real rape tried on the circuits, there were on average twelve pretended cases."[38] Texts advised doctors to go beyond the simple observation of the vulva, the vagina, and stains on the underclothing. They were told to consider the patient's "walk or attitude, bodily and mental," "bruises and injuries found on the body generally," the "physical development of the limbs for powers of struggling," and whether the woman's story sounded "concocted or genuine."[39]

Many physicians also seem to have believed that physical force was an acceptable part of sexual coupling. One widely circulated treatise advised that signs of the "employment of force, such as contusions on various parts of the extremities and body" were "compatible with final consent on the part of the female."[40] Another text asked physicians to consider whether "the marks of violence found on the genital organs" were "no more than you would expect to find in a girl who had really given consent."[41] The issue of class permeated medical diagnosis. Forensic medical specialists wrote openly about the need to be particularly skeptical of working-class women. One commented: "Women of the lower classes are accustomed to rough play with individuals both of their own and of the opposite sex, and thus acquire the habit of defending themselves against sportive violence. In the majority of cases such a capacity for defence would enable a desperate woman to frustrate the attempts of her intentioned ravisher."[42] Dr. Seaborn's testimony may have reflected his dismissive attitude towards a working-class complainant whose

Dr. Edwin Seaborn

COURT HOUSE.

London Court House

physical injuries failed to meet his own estimation of what was required in a real rape.

The final Crown witnesses were the young boys who had rescued the bound and gagged woman. Percy Sullivan didn't help much when he testified that, at first, he and his friends thought nothing of the smashed window, knowing there had been "trouble there before," and assuming it was "just a quarrel" between Mr. and Mrs. Burton who fought "frequently." James Ingray was a somewhat stronger witness. He described how he and his friend approached the half-open door between 5 and 5:30 p.m., and saw a groaning woman, lying flat on her back, her head between the parlour door and her feet between the street door. Ingray testified that there was a rope tied "pretty tight" around Mrs. Burton's head that had left "a blue line right around her neck." Ingray swore that he had untied the rope with his fingers, but Percy Sullivan also testified that he had cut it off with his knife. According to Sullivan, the rope was loose enough to allow him to get two or three fingers behind it. "That would not be very tight," noted defence counsel Meredith. "You can stretch the flesh," replied Sullivan. "It would be like this handkerchief on my neck?" queried Meredith. "Yes, a little tighter," replied the witness. "Nothing of any consequence?" offered Meredith. "No," stated Sullivan. "It was not necessary to cut it, it was not bothering her very much?" continued Meredith. "I just wanted to cut it," offered Sullivan, without more. The discrepancy between the witnesses made the evening's news, with the *London Free Press* noting that "many of the witnesses varied in their stories more or less materially," one testifying he had "cut the string from Mrs. Burton's neck" and "a moment later" another boy swearing he did the deed.[43] The divergence of opinion on the tautness of the rope was equally damaging.

Both witnesses were consistent, however, concerning the bulky handkerchief stuffed in Mrs. Burton's mouth. Percy Sullivan described how the handkerchief "came up bit by bit" and fell out on the floor as the complainant was struggling to catch her breath. Two girls standing out on the sidewalk screeched out, "It is false teeth," as Mrs. Burton's teeth fell out along with the wad of material. The handkerchief "kept coming out and coming," taking a full two minutes for the complainant to "spue it out," or "gawk it out" as the witnesses described it. Defence counsel Meredith paid little notice to the oversized gag, but made much of the fact that Mrs. Burton's hands were "free" from any rope or binding, demanding of James Ingray:

Q. Her hands were free?
A. Yes.
Q. It didn't occur to you it was a put-up job?
A. I could not say.
Q. Woman's hands free and this thing stuffed in her mouth?
A. I could not tell you.
Q. A big stout woman?
A. Yes, Sir.

Of Percy Sullivan, Meredith asked whether Mrs. Burton had "pretended to be moaning" when he got there. Seemingly without much reflection, Sullivan simply replied, "Yes." "Didn't it look to you like a put-up job, from first to last?" he demanded. "It looked as if somebody tried to choke her," replied

Sullivan. "You thought so?" queried Meredith. "Yes," replied the witness. Neither witness made any effort to explain that Mrs. Burton may have been unable to use her hands to cut the rope and ungag herself because she was nearly asphyxiated, or half-unconscious from the exhaustion of her struggle.

In the final tally, Meredith had scored important points. He had got Dr. Seaborn to testify that the bruising and swelling on Mrs. Burton's body might have been due to multiple unknown causes. The bystanders who had rescued Mrs. Burton were confused over who had cut the rope from the disheveled woman and how tautly it had been tied. "Mr. Edmund Meredith was evidently so well satisfied with the information, and the statements that he elicited in cross-examination of the witnesses for the prosecution," reported the *London Free Press*, "that he will submit no evidence for the defence at all."[44] The standard of proof required at the preliminary inquiry was minimal, necessitating evidence only of a "sufficient case" to send the matter forward for a full trial, and magistrates rarely halted the criminal process at this point.[45] Police Magistrate Love committed Joseph Gray for trial at the fall assizes.

The Trial: "The Case against the Prisoner Gray Is Lamentably Weak"

THE TRIAL UNFOLDED MUCH as the preliminary inquiry had, with Edmund Meredith securely in the ascendancy from beginning to end. He was in his element as he subjected Mrs. Burton once again to an interminable and blistering cross-examination. The *London Advertiser* made much of the "conflicting evidence and obnoxious details" elicited by the defence lawyer, despite admitting that Mrs. Burton's testimony "did not vary to any material extent" from her evidence at the preliminary inquiry. This consistency seems to have counted for little, however, and the newspaper reporter announced that "it was made painfully apparent before the case had proceeded any length that one side or the other was very much in error . . . for prosecution and defence witnesses were in direct contradiction to one another."[46]

The Crown had done little to repair the cracks in its case. The two young boys who had rescued Mrs. Burton continued to claim, each contradicting the other, that he had been the one to remove the rope from the semi-conscious woman's neck. Meredith scored additional points during his cross-examination of Dr. Seaborn, managing to get the medical man to admit that "it was possible for a person to sham excitability in such a manner as to deceive a physician." The Crown again chose not to call the police.

Defence counsel Meredith decided to call his own witnesses at the trial, and Joseph Gray was first. According to the *London Advertiser*, the accused man "denied in toto all of Mrs. Burton's story in reference to the alleged assault, and stoutly maintained that he had never seen the complainant before the day in question and that he had never set foot within her house."[47] Gray conceded delivering a load of kindling and footing the bill for a round of ale for Mrs. Burton, her former boarder, and the workmen in the woodshed. In his opinion, Mrs. Burton had been in a state "of intoxication" when he left her place. He maintained he had downed one lone drink. He swore he left 12 Dundas Street no later than 4:50 p.m., had stopped off at the Britannia House at York and Wellington for "a drink or two" and heard the five o'clock whistle blow as he left the pub for home. Other witnesses took the stand to record their recollections regarding time. A city street inspector testified that Gray had left the Clarence Street job around 4:45 p.m. A fellow teamster put the time closer to 5:00 p.m. Another witness told of having met Gray driving along the road to his home between 5:00 and 5:30 that afternoon.

The contrast between the cross-examination that Edmund Meredith visited upon Mrs. Burton and the one that the Crown attorney used for the accused man was remarkable. Joseph Gray was not subjected to a lengthy and searching inquisition about his recollection of the events of 8 July. He was not badgered about minute matters of timing. He was not asked about his drinking habits, or his sexual proclivities. No evidence was led about the alleged rapist's character and lifestyle. When the Crown ventured to ask Joseph Gray why Mrs. Burton would have brought such a serious charge against him if it were untrue, the question completely backfired. Gray declared that he thought the whole affair was a "trumped-up charge" instigated by a man "fairly high up in street contracting matters." He testified that a "certain man" had advised him that the contractor wanted to "even up" the score with Gray, in return for "some trouble the two had had at one time." The same informant had ostensibly quoted Mrs. Burton as saying: "I sent the message and there was no money forthcoming. I shall have to swear Gray's life away." This last must have referred to the maximum penalty of death that was still on the books for the charge of rape, although such a sentence had not been imposed since before Confederation.[48] Even the judge seems to have been surprised at these allegations, and he instructed Gray that he had "better bring the man up in court who told you that." No such individual ever took the stand. The Crown attorney never objected to the omission.

James Vernall Teetzel

Finally, the defence called a young woman who lived in a boarding house a few doors down from the Burtons. Miss Leon Macpherson testified that she had seen Joseph Gray drive towards the city at 4:30 p.m. This was not a solid beginning, since it underscored the inconsistency of the defence witnesses on the question of timing. Their various estimates for Joseph Gray's departure ranged from 4:30 p.m. through 4:45 p.m., 4:50 p.m., and 5 p.m. But Miss Macpherson had more compelling evidence, for she appears to have been the "most respectable woman" that Meredith had described at the preliminary inquiry. She told the court that she had seen Mrs. Burton "shove some dark complexioned man into the rear door of her house" early in the afternoon of 8 July. Macpherson swore that the man was "not the prisoner," but that she would recognize him if she saw him again. Then she dealt a final devastating blow to the Crown's case. She testified that Mrs. Burton had emerged from her house quite drunk a few minutes after five o'clock, and added that the older woman "bore a very unsavoury reputation." She declared that the Burton home was infamous throughout the neighbourhood for the "noise of drunken brawls." With this final damning opinion, the defence closed its case.

When the trial resumed the next morning, Judge James Vernall Teetzel dispensed with legal submissions from counsel. "Gentlemen of the jury," he announced, "the case against the prisoner Gray is lamentably weak." Under Canadian law, judges ruled on questions of law and juries decided questions of fact.[49] However, judges also maintained a gate-keeping function. They assessed the evidence prior to delivering the case to the jury, to ensure that the Crown had adduced a sufficient case — should the jury believe the prosecution's evidence — to warrant a conviction. If this threshold test was not met, the judge could direct the jury to deliver a verdict of "not guilty."[50] That was what Judge Teetzel did here. "I do not think there is a man on the jury," he declared, "who after hearing the evidence would say, or could say, that this man is guilty of the serious offence that he is charged with." Since the judge gave no reasons for his decision, it is difficult to know fully what motivated the ruling. The burden of proof was upon the Crown to prove the accused guilty beyond a reasonable doubt. The Crown had presented material evidence which, if believed, could have resulted in a criminal conviction. The judge must have disbelieved Mrs. Burton or else preferred the defence witnesses so substantially that he pre-empted the fact-finding exercise generally relegated to the jury.

Born, bred, and educated in southwestern Ontario, Judge Teetzel was proudly claimed by the *London Advertiser* as a local "Middlesex boy." The fifty-nine-year-old judge would have been all too familiar with the unsavoury reputation of the industrial, working-class neighbourhood just down the street from the London Court House in which he presided.[51] Like many affluent Londoners of the time, he seems to have been contemptuous of the manners and morals of the Burtons and their contemporaries. The *London Free Press* reported that before releasing the prisoner, Judge Teetzel "severely scored" Joseph Gray "for the company he had been in on the afternoon in question."[52] His near undoing had come from mixing with the rabble who abutted the dump, rather than from the perpetration of the crime of rape. Teetzel wished Joseph Gray to recognize, in no uncertain terms, that he should have kept his attention confined to his respectable haulage business and restricted his social interaction to a more elevated crowd.

The *London Advertiser* seemed positively jubilant over the outcome, depicting Joseph Gray as a man who had been "honourably acquitted by Mr. Justice Teetzel." This was an odd characterization, since acquittals did not come in categories such as "honourable," "dishonourable," or whatever might have served to define the uncertain ground in between. What was more, the *Advertiser* asserted that the entire prosecution had been a waste of time and resources. It complained that the "taking of the evidence" had "monopolized the entire attention of the assizes." The editorial epilogue rendered a final, dismissive retort: "And another case which, according to the developments, should never have reached the high court of justice, had gone into the annals of London court history."[53]

"Justice I Want if There Is Justice to Be Had"

FEW OF MARY ANN Burton's contemporaries treated her claim of rape as worthy of belief. Passersby stood gawking as the semi-conscious woman attempted to dislodge a filthy, oversize handkerchief from her throat while two young boys doused her with a pail of water in a draconian effort to revive her. The elderly woman's false teeth, expelled along with the gag, seem to have excited as much interest as her bruises. The neighbours concocted their own snide version of the incident, gossiping about Mrs. Burton's sexual habits, and ridiculing her husband with accusations of cuckoldry. Robert Burton, a man with a history of violent domestic altercations, came home to accuse his wife of responsibility for the sexual episode. When called to testify, Mrs. Burton's neighbours gave indifferent or pernicious commentary. The physician who was supposed to conduct the forensic examination botched the job.

The Crown attorney presented the case in a barely passable fashion, without conviction or fortitude. The defence lawyer relished his role of destroying the complainant's credibility, attacking Mrs. Burton's character along with her testimony. The press departed from a standard of objectivity and attached demeaning descriptions to Mrs. Burton and her testimony, all the while portraying Joseph Gray as an exemplary specimen of respectable manhood.

Now a century later, many will argue that it is impossible to determine whether Mrs. Burton was raped at the fork of the Thames in 1907. There were undeniable problems with the case for the prosecution. There were similar problems with the defence. What is most impressive, however, was the testimony offered in the London Court House by Mrs. Burton herself. Despite the forces arrayed against her, she gave her own narrative of rape, the testimony of an elderly, working-class woman who described herself as the unwilling victim of an arrogant, sexually aggressive teamster. In this, she ultimately triumphed, for the official transcript has captured her story for posterity.

Mary Ann Burton's courageous call for "justice" reveals that there were multiple understandings of justice in early twentieth-century Canada. Mrs. Burton's sense of justice incorporated her right to be protected from non-consensual sexual intercourse. Joseph Gray's rendered him astonished that legal charges might ever have been levied. Edmund Meredith understood his cross-examination of Mrs. Burton, in which he parlayed sexist accusations into a relentless barrage, to be his ethical and professional obligation. Mrs. Burton believed Meredith's cross-examination to be the actions of a deceptive and malicious bully. Crown attorney McKillop's sense of justice encompassed Mrs. Burton's right to a criminal trial. In the face of defence counsel's onslaught, however, McKillop stood silently by, his passivity a powerful affirmation of the attack on Mrs. Burton's credibility. The judge accepted that the cross-examination of alleged rape victims should encompass gruelling, sexually biased character assassination. The press applauded the result. The directed verdict for Joseph Gray was a stinging rebuke of Mrs. Burton's dramatic call for justice on her own terms. A century later, as competing notions of justice continue to jockey for position within criminal law, Mrs. Burton might well ask which concept of "justice" will become the most compelling over time.

Chapter 3

"ON PENSAIT QUE LA FILLE ÉTAIT BONNE À RIEN":
Fiola, 1917

NINETEEN SEVENTEEN WAS AN incendiary year in the province of Québec. The First World War, now into its third horrific year, had become a tragic bloodbath sucking up millions of men, munitions, and supplies in the rotting trenches of Western Europe. In Québec, mass protests and anti-conscription riots erupted when English-speaking enlistment officers foraged the countryside for young recruits. In April and May, French crowds pelted troops that were marching through Québec City with rotten vegetables, ice, and stones. While patriotic fervour held steady in English Canada, it evaporated in much of Québec, where the French populace dubbed it "national suicide for a foreign cause," and the explosive issue of conscription took centre stage.[1]

Amidst growing critique that Québec, the province providing the fewest recruits, was the "spoiled child of Confederation," Parliament passed the *Conscription Act* on 28 August 1917. In Ontario, the *Globe* newspaper applauded the "equalization of sacrifice." In Québec City, there was talk of separation and civil war. Increasing numbers of young Québecois took to the woods, preferring to camp out than to risk compulsory wartime service.[2] The tensions were particularly acute in working-class Verdun, a densely populated Montréal district with solid blocks of three-storey tenements and rented flats, southwest along the shores of the St. Lawrence River. Two-thirds of Verdun's 28 000 residents were English speakers, many of them recent immigrants from Britain with pronounced "Old Country" allegiances. The British-born Verdun enlistments were among the highest in Canada,

exacerbating linguistic and ethnic hostilities and making the minority francophone population even more anxious.[3]

Not three weeks after the passage of the *Conscription Act*, a group of
French-Canadian youths took off from Verdun on a sightseeing spree. Perhaps it was another way to rebel against the forces that were mounting to
press them into military service. There were eight of them: Léo Fiola, Albert Lassonde, Georges Mollot, Arsène Lamontagne, Antonio Paquin, Albert
Thivièrge, Henri Perrotte, and Léodore Venne. The youngest was eighteen,
the eldest twenty-three. Amongst them there were two automobile chauf-
feurs, one steam-fitter, one plumber, one apprentice shoe-tack operator, one
journeyman carpenter, one munitions factory worker, and a butcher.[4] They
came from the same small francophone neighbourhood in Verdun, where
they lived side by side and down the street from each other.[5] These were the
sons of skilled working-class families.[6] Only one of them, Léo Fiola, seems
to have been solidly middle class. His father owned a furniture store in Verdun.[7] It was Léo Fiola's car, a Hudson Super Six, that the eight young men
piled into and headed out for Québec City.

The event that drew them was the much-heralded completion of the
Québec Bridge. The towering edifice of concrete and steel designed to span
the banks of the St. Lawrence River had collapsed twice during construction, causing death and injury to nearly a hundred bridge workers. Twenty
years and one royal commission after its first conception, the bridge drew
massive crowds eager to watch the final stage of civil engineering's *"huitième
merveille du monde"* — "eighth wonder of the world." Monday morning, 17
September 1917, the central span was floated out on pontoons, and gigantic
hydraulic jacks tried to haul it up into place between the cantilevered arms.
The operation would take a full three days to complete, and by evening the
eight young men from Verdun were bored watching and took off to see the
town.[8] Their adventures over the next seventeen hours offer a fascinating
insight into the codes of masculinity that governed a group of men looking
for sex, adolescent male attitudes towards female sexuality, the risk-taking
behaviour of young working-class women, and corruption within the criminal justice system.

Sexual Assault in a Hudson Super Six

WOMEN SEEM TO HAVE been uppermost in mind, as the group circled the
streets of the capital city between 7 and 8:30 p.m. on 17 September, looking

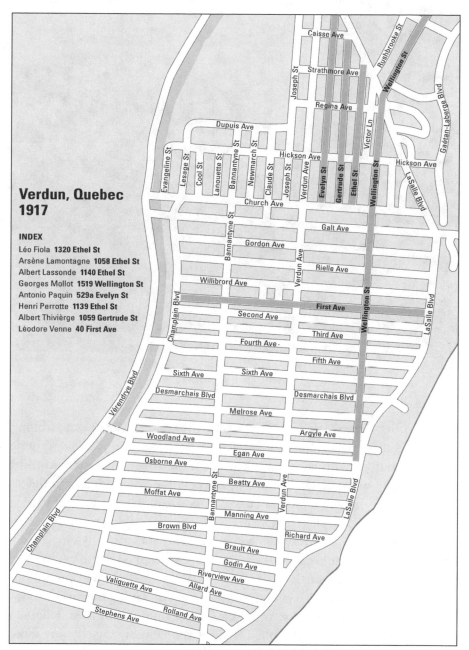

Verdun, Quebec 1917

INDEX

Léo Fiola **1320 Ethel St**
Arsène Lamontagne **1058 Ethel St**
Albert Lassonde **1140 Ethel St**
Georges Mollot **1519 Wellington St**
Antonio Paquin **529a Evelyn St**
Henri Perrotte **1139 Ethel St**
Albert Thivièrge **1059 Gertrude St**
Léodore Venne **40 First Ave**

Map designed by Page One Publishing, copyright held by Constance Backhouse

Map of Verdun, Québec, showing proximity of residence of the accused

Hudson Super Six, circa 1918

for pick-ups. Their attention was caught by a young woman out strolling alone, and they slowed the car. The female was fourteen-year-old Yvonne Collin, who lived with her family just down the street on the rented third floor of 1044½ rue St-Valier. A major artery near the railway tracks in the St-Malo neighbourhood, the street housed a mixture of shops, a lumber yard, a tannery, and working-class tenements. Yvonne was walking towards her father's barbershop on 1100 St-Valier, when she saw the Hudson driving slowly by, and she called out to ask the occupants if they wanted her to get in.[9] The beautiful car with distinctive engraved initials on the side had caught her eye.[10] The young men stopped and told her to get in, saying they were strangers who didn't know the city, and asking if she would show them where to get gasoline. Yvonne Collin replied that she didn't know the city any more than they did, but they told her to get in all the same, and she did.

As she would explain to the court, she told them that she would get in *"pour le fun"* — "for fun." One of the young men would testify that Yvonne Collin

All photos on this page taken from St. Lawrence Bridge Co.: The Québec Bridge carrying the transcontinental line of the Canadian government railways over the St. Lawrence River near the city of Québec, Canada, 1918

The Québec Bridge

Above: The suspended span falling, 11 September 1916

Right: The suspended area half-way up, 18 September 1917

Below: Bridge completed, 1917

agreed to direct them to a neighbourhood where they could find prostitutes. Others, diverging in their stories, made no mention of this, but suggested that Yvonne Collin consented to ride with them if they would drive her to Montréal. They couldn't agree on where Yvonne sat, some saying she was wedged between the boys in the back seat, and others that she sat up front, because "she liked to sit with the driver."[11] The young men also claimed that Yvonne Collin had told them her parents were in the United States, and that she was staying with an aunt who wouldn't mind if she were out late or even absent for a few days. Yvonne frankly admitted on the stand that she had boasted about her freedom, and she replied in the affirmative when defence counsel asked if these statements had been "*sacrées menteries*" — "damn lies."

The Hudson Super Six, bursting to the seams with its nine passengers, drove away from the city along the chemin de la Petite Rivière. Automobiles were unreliable in the early twentieth century and the young men had to stop briefly at the side of the road to repair the Hudson. Still, they described a jovial and pleasant tone among the group. Some claimed that Yvonne was in a "good mood," that they conversed about the amount of "manufacturing" in the region, and that she remarked that the scenery was "beautiful."[12] Others admitted that things quickly got risqué. They conceded that the young men were joking and making "*des paroles grossières*" — "rude remarks," touching Yvonne's legs, breasts, and stomach, and trying to reach between her thighs and legs. Others stoutly denied doing or seeing any such thing. At least one recalled that Yvonne had told them to "*ôte-toi*" — to get off, and had pushed them aside, although he insisted that she didn't push them away each and every time. Yvonne testified that the young men were drinking brandy out of a flask, but they all denied this, except Fiola who conceded they had "*un petit flask.*" Apparently there was general agreement that the automobile was much too crowded, so they drove back to the city to let some people out. When they reached the corner of St-Valier and the cemetery, six of the young men disembarked, leaving Léo Fiola, Albert Lassonde, and Yvonne Collin alone in the front seat. Fiola testified he thought it was Lassonde who determined who got out, but Lassonde swore it was Fiola who made the decision.

Fiola drove to the outskirts of the city, turned off onto a deserted side road, and parked. The two young men put the driver's cushion into the back seat, and told Yvonne to lie down on it. She did. They demanded that she unbutton her "*culottes.*" She did. They lifted her dress, lowered her "*pantalons,*" and then climbed on top of her. Lassonde went first and Fiola second. Yvonne testified that she had never had sexual intercourse before. She told the court she had objected, insisting that she was too young, and complaining that they were hurting her. The young men would later deny that she had objected at all. All agreed that Yvonne Collin did not resist physically. She explained to the court that she was apprehensive that they would dump her out of the car and leave her alone in the dark. She testified that she was afraid "because they were bigger than she was" and she was *"seule, une fille"* — "a girl alone."[13] The standards of resistance expected of girls were lower than for adult women, but as will soon become apparent, consent would never amount to a critical issue in the subsequent proceedings. Nevertheless, the Crown prosecutors made sure to bring out in Yvonne's testimony that she did not understand that the young men meant to have sexual intercourse with her, and that she had no idea of the significance of such an act.[14] According to Yvonne Collin, Lassonde tried, but was not able to achieve full sexual penetration, and emitted semen beside her. Lassonde denied this, and claimed he had successfully completed the sexual act. There was no disagreement that Fiola had managed full sexual intercourse.

Next, Lassonde took the wheel and drove the three of them, Yvonne in the middle of the front seat, back to where the six others had been waiting for about half an hour on the sidewalk. There was protracted debate among the group — with the young men insisting that Yvonne should have sex with all of them, and Yvonne adamantly refusing.[15] All six piled back into the car and they continued to squabble as they drove around. Eventually, they gave up and stopped at the Queen's Hotel in the lower St-Roch neighbourhood, at the corner of rue Du Pont and Des Fossés, where six of them booked rooms for the night. Fiola and Lassonde continued to drive around with Yvonne, trying to convince her to have sex with the others, but she refused. Finally, the two men took the young woman back to the hotel. Yvonne would testify that she wanted to go home, but agreed to stay because it was 11:30 p.m., and she was afraid of what her father might do if she came home so late. Fiola attempted to smuggle her in as his sister, but the woman at the front desk insisted that the young girl be given a separate room. According to Yvonne, when she got up to her room she discovered that there was blood on her undergarments.

The next morning she came down for breakfast, and sat alone at a table separate from the eight. When Lassonde told her to get into the car, she did. They stopped at the "Magazin de 15 cents," and then for gas at a filling station, and then again to change the tires. The young men testified that Yvonne demanded repeatedly that they take her to Montréal with them. Yvonne's evidence was somewhat different. She testified that she did not want to go to Montréal, but was reluctant to disembark because her ring had been taken from her. Earlier that morning one of the boys had asked to see the ring she was wearing, and she had taken it off to show him. He had given it to Fiola, who refused to return it. She insisted that she would not leave without it, even when the young men drove the Hudson Super Six down her own street and told her to get out.

The next thing she knew, the car was back on chemin de la Petite Rivière. As the boys continued to argue, they came to a full stop by a field laden with piles of tree branches. With some sarcasm, the Crown attorney asked whether they might have suggested to Yvonne Collin that it would be a good place for a picnic, or to say some prayers.[16] "*Non,*" replied Antonio Paquin. Albert Thivièrge was more forthcoming: "We all said: '*Tu va gagner ton passage*'" — "You are going to earn your fare."[17] Henri Perrotte remembered this, but attributed the demand only to Thivièrge. Léodore Venne recalled that Yvonne had replied: "I can do that," as if in full consent.[18] They led her to a spot hidden from the roadway by the brush, and took turns lying with her in sequence. Although there was some disagreement about the order, the majority agreed that Thivièrge went first, then Paquin, Mollot, Fiola, Perrotte, and Venne. There was a general consensus that neither Lassonde nor Lamontagne participated.

Asked how they knew the young girl was willing, one testified: "Because when we asked her, she didn't refuse."[19] Another added: "She didn't complain at all."[20] Yvonne Collin claimed that she told Fiola that she was hurt, and that he should "leave her alone," but she admitted that she hadn't spoken loudly enough to be heard by him.[21] Explaining her decision not to fight back more strenuously, Yvonne stated: "They were eight, and they could do to me whatever they wanted. They were older than I was."[22] Some of the young men claimed that Yvonne Collin had been very cooperative. Several testified that she was so eager that she lay down on her back in the field and lifted up her own dress.[23] Two added that she came out from behind the brush to get them, one after the other, challenging them and calling out "*un autre là!*" — "next here!"[24] Léodore Venne testified that after he finished, Yvonne Collin came looking for Arsène Lamontagne, who had not yet taken a turn. He claimed that the young girl stood up, got herself straightened out, and demanded: "*Il y en a encore un à passer*" — "There is still one to go."[25] All of this was expressly denied by Yvonne, who testified in evidence that

would be completely disregarded by the court, that she had not consented at all. There was no disagreement, however, that when the last had finished, the young men unceremoniously dumped Yvonne's hat and scarf out on the side of the road, got back into the Hudson, and sped off for Montréal. Yvonne was left in tears to return on foot, a distance so far that it was afternoon by the time she got home.

Female Risk-Taking and the Sexual Dynamics of Men in Groups

THE HISTORICAL RECORDS INDICATE that men sexually assault all kinds of women, and that it is naive to assume that if women take care to avoid obvious risks, they will be protected against sexual attack.[26] Bearing in mind that women's allegedly "provocative" behaviour ought not to excuse men who coerce them into non-consensual sex, it remains useful to examine the conduct of those involved in this case. Yvonne Collin seems to have been a bit of a daredevil, a young girl out for exploration and adventure. Under cross-examination, she was asked whether she hadn't thought it "a little dangerous" to get into a car alone with eight young men. She replied that she hadn't thought "anything of it," that she only wanted to take a drive in the car.[27]

By the time the danger became apparent, with the young men pawing over her in the car, and then escalated in the back seat with Lassonde and Fiola, she seems to have resigned herself to her fate. She tried to push their hands away, she objected to having sex, but in the end, she was passive, lying down on the back seat and subjecting herself to their sexual attentions. Yvonne Collin's decision to stay the night at the Queen's Hotel was another dangerous step, choosing to face further entanglement with the group of eight over the punishment she feared her wrathful father might inflict. Her decision to get back into the car in the morning, and her insistence that she recover her ring before getting out, may have cost her another round of gang rape in the deserted field. One way to interpret her behaviour is to conclude that she was as interested in sexual contact as the young men were. Another is that she was simply unaware of the gravity of the risk, and once into the fray, was not intellectually, physically, or emotionally able to extricate herself. It was as if her risk-courting decision to get into the car in the first place had left her options circumscribed. As she slid deeper into the morass, even where opportunities for rescue occasionally presented themselves, she followed one bad decision with another, apparently bereft of hope.

UNE AFFAIRE INFAMANTE A QUEBEC

Les autorités policières de Québec et de Montréal saisies d'une affaire des plus graves. Un détective de cette ville est parti pour la métropole à ce sujet. Il s'agirait d'un crime infamant, dont la victime serait une fillette de Québec, âgée de 14 ans. Ceux qui seraient mêlés à cette affaire sont des individus de Montréal, qui sont venus à Québec en auto pour le parachèvement du pont.

"Une Affaire Infamante à Québec"
Le Soleil (Québec), vendredi 21 septembre 1917, at 10

Would any of this have happened if Yvonne Collin had resolutely kept walking towards her father's barbershop? If she had insisted on getting out of the car at the first sign of sexual overture? If she had sought help when she got to the Queen's Hotel? The answers depend greatly upon the motivations and group dynamics of the eight young men. Gang rape has been an all-too-common feature of sexual assault, with groups of three or more men charged regularly in cases that span the century and stretch across the country.[28] However, it was rare to find all the men involved testifying, as occurred here. With the exception of Georges Mollot, each of the seven other young men took the stand and gave his version of the events. While the evidence contained a number of inconsistencies, it is possible to piece together some of the male posturing and psychological interaction that affected their actions.

While it seems uncontested that the young men were already out hunting for women and sex, they told the court that Yvonne Collin's daredevil behaviour marked her as easy prey. Lassonde volunteered that the reason he and Fiola took her out alone in the car was because they thought that *"la fille était . . . bonne à rien"* — "the girl was good for nothing."[29] Asked whether Yvonne had the "air of a girl who was a little free," Lamontagne replied that "she seemed to be an experienced girl."[30] The point was put to Fiola that they must have thought she was *"une putain"* — "a whore," so there was no reason to be afraid.[31] He did not disagree. Their designation of an un-known young woman as *"bonne à rien"* is worthy of reflection. Women can be marginalized by factors such as age, class, race, ethnicity, disability, and prior sexual history, rendering them easier targets for men pursuing sex. Here, Yvonne Collin's youthfulness and working-class status increased her vulnerability. The jaunty conversation she initiated to win herself a drive in the Hudson — which the young men seem to have taken as a sign of sexual "promiscuity" — exacerbated this.

No one gave evidence about whether the decision to engage in sex with Yvonne was taken collectively by the group, or was an idea promoted by one or more instigators. However, Fiola, the owner of the vehicle, and Las-sonde, the second driver by virtue of his occupational qualifications, were clearly the leaders of the group. And while it is difficult to draw a sense of a witness's character from archival transcripts, occasionally some personali-ties shine through. A man of five foot seven, with fair complexion, brown hair, and hazel eyes, Fiola was arrogant and obstinate from the start. Unlike the other accused, he professed not to remember the dates of the events, what streets they drove down, who had said what, or what had been said. He even purported to have forgotten whether he had had sex with Yvonne in the field. Asked if he noticed any blood after having sex with Yvonne, he dismissively retorted that he had seen nothing, even on the handkerchief he had used to wipe himself clean. He had no hesitation about baiting Yvonne with the ring, and refused to return it until it was ultimately filed in court as an exhibit. Some of Fiola's flippancy is apparent from this exchange about Yvonne Collin's age:

Q. You noticed that she wasn't built like a mature woman?
A. She wasn't built like a woman, but she was built like a girl of eighteen.
Q. You saw that she was a child. She was no bigger that evening than she is today?
A. There are many very small children who are older than eighteen.[32]

Given the force of Fiola's personality, that Lassonde was the one who took the first turn at sex suggests that the two ringleaders may have been vying for dominance.

The testimony reveals quite a bit about the young men's attitudes towards sex. Certainly, the eight were completely dismissive of Yvonne Collin's sex-ual desires or pleasure. The half-hour that encompassed the two sexual acts that first evening as well as the round-trip drive could have left little time for preliminaries. And it is hard to imagine that a fourteen-year-old virgin — whose first experience of sexual intercourse had occurred the evening before — would have found the successive six trips behind the bush in the field anything but painful and overwhelming. Indeed, the medical evidence adduced at the trial showed "fresh tears of the hymen membrane," "fresh wounds," and "very inflamed parts."[33] If the eight young men believed that Yvonne Collin had consented to this series of sexual acts, it tells us a great deal about their sense of women's sexuality.[34]

Part of this may have been attributable to their own lack of sexual experience. Both Fiola and Thivièrge admitted on the stand that it was their first sex with a woman, and Perrotte claimed only to have had relations with one "girl" before. Even the language of love-making eluded them. Some professed to be confused by the phrases the lawyers posed, *"des rapports sexuels"* and *"rapports charnels,"* and spoke in more colloquial or street terms such as *"de se mettre une fille"* or *"fourrer"* — to "get a girl" or to "fuck," "cram," "poke," or "butt into" her.

Yvonne testified that some watched as the others took their turns in the field, suggesting a voyeuristic aspect, and that their behaviour had as much to do with competitive sexuality as with male bonding. For some, the pressure to go along with the group seems to have been substantially greater than their own sexual desire. Three told the court that although they tried to penetrate the young girl, they were unable to complete intercourse. One said he wasn't "tempted" and another complained that the girl "wasn't clean enough."[35] Several explained that they were forced to ejaculate outside Yvonne's body. Although Venne denied it, Yvonne testified that he forced her to masturbate (*"crosser"*) him, because he was unable to maintain an erection.[36] Lassonde showed no interest in a repeat of his previous night's performance.

That so many took part without any indication of personal sexual arousal suggests that the desire to match their peers and be part of the gang was an overriding motivation. Individuals who on their own might never have entertained the prospect of sex with an unknown young girl stood by, watched others attempt coitus on top of her, and then tried to take their turn. Only one, Arsène Lamontagne, resisted the compulsion of the group mentality. He not only didn't participate, but according to Yvonne Collin, he also warned the others that they would "have trouble" if they didn't "leave her alone."[37] However, he did not physically intervene, or disassociate himself from the activity further. Yvonne testified that he watched as the others had sex with her in the field.

It would have been helpful to the potential victims of gang rape if the law had made it a crime to stand by and watch one's friends and companions sexually assault a woman, or had penalized those who failed to make reasonable efforts to stop the others in the group. Given the nature of group dynamics, the law could have intervened to encourage every impulse to resist, to promote verbal and physical efforts to terminate the crime, to require at least that non-participants disassociate themselves and walk away. However, neither common law nor legislation had ever established a legal duty to stop others from committing crime, and the courts would give a very narrow interpretation to the offence of "aiding and abetting" with respect to rape. "Passive acquiescence" was not sufficient, and judges refused to convict without clear evidence of "instigation" or the "procurement" of the rape itself.[38]

Why Lamontagne was charged with rape along with the others is unclear. Perhaps the prosecutors thought that this might make Lamontagne a helpful witness. They peppered him with questions when he took the stand. Lamontagne admitted that it was because Yvonne Collin was "too young" that he wasn't interested in her.[39] But getting him to testify that he had told the others to leave her alone was like pulling teeth. He denied it six times. The seventh time the question was put to him, he finally gave in. This was the exchange:

Q. Be careful now. Did you say something of this nature on the night of September 17th, when they wished to screw her and amuse themselves with her? Would you not have said there, like an honest boy, to leave her alone that she was too young?

A. I said, "In the first place, since she doesn't want to do it, leave her alone."[40]

That was the only time he broke ranks with his companions in the courtroom. He may have been a dissenter in the Hudson and out in the deserted field, but once on the witness stand, loyalty to his mates overcame any earlier reticence. Lamontagne went out of his way to mention that Yvonne had wanted to drive to Montréal in the Hudson, that she hadn't complained about maltreatment, that she had come looking for the young men one after another in the field, even looking for him when he failed to come for his turn. Desperately trying to regain lost ground, Crown attorney Arthur Fitz-

Photo from *Le Soleil*, 28 September 1938, at 3

Crown attorney Hon. Louis-Arthur Fitzpatrick

patrick persisted: "Isn't it true that others showed up before she had time to get up?" Lamontagne sabotaged him with his last reply: "I told you what I saw."[41] The Crown called for a recess, and when he returned, demanded to know whether Lamontagne had been properly sworn with his hand on the Bible. When it was revealed that the witness had held his hand under the Bible, rather than upon it, the flustered court clerk made Lamontagne take his oath again. Asked by Fitzpatrick one last time whether all his evidence had been completely true, the newly sworn witness again responded: "*Oui.*"[42]

The group solidarity held fast to the last, with all of the eight swearing that they never discussed among themselves their sexual escapades with Yvonne Collin — not while they waited on the sidewalk on 17 September, not after their two comrades rejoined them, not at the hotel, not on the drive out to the field, and not on the way home to Montréal after they had abandoned Yvonne Collin. To the apparent disbelief of the Crown attorneys who asked them all if they hadn't boasted or swapped details about their sexual conquest, for many their first ever, they replied to a man: "*Non.*" It stretched the bounds of credibility. It was not as if they had gone into the venture furtively, individually. Even more implausibly, they insisted that they had passed the trip home in song. Léodore Venne's reply captured the tenor of the group:

Q. You say that what occurred between this girl and you and your companions never came up from the time that you left her and all the way to Montréal? . . . Yet this is somewhat remarkable, eight boys who go find a girl in a field, this does not happen every day?

A. We started to sing, each one coming up with a song of his own . . .

Q. It made no more impression upon you than that?

A. No, Monsieur.[43]

So was the die cast when Yvonne Collin got into the Hudson that evening? Were there distinct moments when the flow of these events might have been halted? Perhaps if Yvonne had been more prudent, the young men would have tired of looking for action and meekly driven home. However, it seems more realistic to suggest that Yvonne's decision to get into the car probably saved some other young woman from their coercive sexual overtures. Once Yvonne got in, it also seems unlikely that she could have extricated herself without any sexual contact, however much she resisted. But the extent of the sexual activity, and the number of men who had connection with her, might have been reduced had she taken the several opportunities for escape that

Trial judge Hon. Charles Langelier, JSP, c. 1905

presented themselves. And any number of the other young men might have joined Lassonde that morning, taking the high road and balking at the joint venture. One wonders, reviewing the historical records of group rape, how many dissidents it would have taken to dampen the group's enthusiasm and successfully staunch the solidarity that seems to have been so central to the sexual behaviour of men in gangs.

The Crime of Seduction

ALL EIGHT MEN WERE initially charged with rape, an offence that required proof beyond a reasonable doubt that the victim had not consented to the sexual intercourse.[44] Yvonne Collin had testified that all the sexual contact took place without her consent. Arsène Lamontagne had testified that "she didn't want to do it." Reviewing the evidence, it seems quite likely that the young woman had not consented. However rape law required that even young women demonstrate a certain amount of resistance, and Yvonne's passivity led Québec City justice of the peace Charles Langelier to conclude that consent could not be disproved. The rape charge was abandoned after the preliminary inquiry. Nor was there any prospect of charging the men with statutory rape, which set forth a blanket prohibition on men having sexual intercourse with girls younger than a certain age, regardless of their consent. Although the age of consent would go up to sixteen in 1920, at the time of this hearing it took effect once a girl reached her fourteenth birthday, putting fourteen-year-old Yvonne Collin just beyond the reach of protection.[45] Instead, the trial went ahead on the reduced charge of "seduction of a girl between fourteen and sixteen years of age."[46] The crime of "seduction" was first enacted in 1886, when Parliament made it an offence to seduce a girl of "previously chaste character." The penalty was substantially lower than that for rape or statutory rape: a maximum of two years instead of capital punishment or life imprisonment.[47]

The crime of seduction was a curious one, in that the word "seduce" was never defined by legislation. However, the judges who interpreted the statutory language decided that seduction had to be distinguished from the crime of rape. They dismissed charges of non-consensual seduction where the complainant had resisted the sexual intercourse, and where the act was accomplished by means of force.[48] They determined that seduction involved consent, but they also ruled that not all women who "parted with their virtue" willingly could claim to have been seduced. Judges from one coast of Canada to the other issued rulings requiring proof that the accused had "induced," "importuned," "enticed," "bribed," "solicited," "persuaded," "employed artifices," "had connection by allurement," or used some "art, influence, promise or deception" to overcome the woman's objections before they would convict of seduction.[49] Ruminating on the multiple impulses to sexual contact, one Canadian judge explained:

> No matter how chaste a certain girl has been before, it is a possible thing that she will fall in love with a man and give herself away to him without any inducing or enticing on the man's part. Her great, but misguided, love may impel her to do so, or she may do it from lasciviousness, or from the strength of mere natural passion. . . . [Such] is not seduction.[50]

To summarize, seduction was not rape, nor was it lascivious, passionately consensual sex. It was something in between. It was a crime that attempted to chart the impermissible boundaries for lustful male behaviour that stopped short of force, but ventured well beyond the range of gentlemanly courtship. Whether Judge Langelier would have held that Léo Fiola and his companions had "seduced" Yvonne Collin is difficult to know. Before he could turn his mind to the substance of the seduction charge, the case got derailed on the definition of "previously chaste character."

A woman's sexual reputation was always open season in rape trials, but this was especially so with seduction, where it was a legislative precondition that the victim be "of previously chaste character."[51] Answering repeated queries from different Crown prosecutors at different points in the multiple proceedings, Yvonne Collin swore that she had never had sexual contact with other men before.[52] She mentioned one incident when she had been out walking with friends and some young boys tried to get fresh. But she testified that this was the only such incident, and that she and her friends hadn't let the boys do anything. She admitted that the ring Fiola had taken had been loaned to her by a young man named Maranda, who lived on rue St-Valier and often came into her father's barbershop. But she indicated that he was merely a "good friend." Yvonne's father testified that Maranda was a "very polite, reserved young boy," the son of a neighbour who engraved marble headstones, and that there was nothing improper in the friendship — that it was *"une affaire d'enfantillage"* — "a childish affair."[53]

Defence counsel at trial, Jules-Alfred Lane, KC, was highly dubious.[54] He challenged Yvonne to tell him whether she knew that she had "conducted herself like a whore" with the eight accused.[55] Three times he asked, three

Photo taken from Raphael Ouimet, *Biographies Canadiennes-Françaises* (Montréal, 1929) at 443

Crown attorney Arthur Lachance, KC

times Yvonne sat silent. Lane then called on Louis Beaumont, the butcher who lived on the second floor below the Collins. Beaumont told the court that the main floor apartment was rented by Mme Michel Gingras, who had been convicted in September for keeping a brothel. Beaumont testified that Yvonne Collin was often in and out of the apartment, running errands for Mme Gingras, adding that he found it *"curieux"* that André Collin would let his daughter frequent such a place. Crown attorney Arthur Lachance, KC, tried to undo the damage by leading evidence that Yvonne Collin ran errands for many neighbours, including Beaumont's wife, that she had only gone three or four times to Mme Gingras, that no one had known that the place was disreputable, and that Yvonne had never gone back once they learned.[56] But the stain lingered. It was geographical character assassination by virtue of neighbourhood.

The Curious Role of the Police

NEXT, IN A MOST unusual move, Lane called Montréal detective Arthur Gagnon. Gagnon testified that he had taken Yvonne Collin alone into the police chief's office to grill her about her sexual past.[57] He told the court that at first she denied all. Then she started to cry. When he told her crying wouldn't help and that she should confess everything, he claimed that Yvonne admitted that previous to meeting the eight, she had had "an affair with a young man, but not in the same circumstances." Further questioning revealed that this had entailed manual masturbation: *"[E]lle s'amusait avec lui avec sa main, et lui s'amusait avec elle avec son doigt."*[58] Québec City vice-squad detective Joseph Delphis Beaudoin confirmed that Gagnon had passed the information along to him, and he had double-checked it with Yvonne the morning before the preliminary inquiry, when the two were walking outside the courthouse.[59] The Crown attorneys protested that Yvonne Collin's sworn testimony that she had never before committed an indecent act could not subsequently be contradicted by calling other witnesses on a collateral matter of evidence.[60] Judge Langelier disagreed. He ruled that Yvonne's "chastity" was an "essential element" of the seduction offence, which made the reception of the evidence permissible.[61]

The Crown prosecutors were dumbfounded by the detectives' evidence. They had had no inkling that Gagnon and Beaudoin would turn table and testify for the defence. The two detectives had purported to be hot on the trail of the accused, working "without respite" until they could "put their hands on the culprits" who had committed such an "infamous crime."[62] Crown prosecutor Joseph-Abel Rochette, KC, demanded that both men tell him who they had told about Yvonne's alleged sexual past.[63] When Beaudoin testified that they told only counsel for the accused, Rochette exploded: "You are a detective, aren't you? You work for the Crown?"[64] "I didn't have a clear conscience," was how Beaudoin explained it.[65] Crown attorney Fitzpatrick inquired why, as officers of the court, the detectives had told no one connected with the prosecution. Why had they come into court only at the last minute to give evidence on behalf of the accused? Beaudoin replied he didn't think it was "his duty" to do otherwise.[66] It also turned out that the police had been the ones to hunt down Yvonne Collin's neighbour, Louis Beaumont, and tip off the other side that the butcher could give evidence about the young girl's relationship with Mme Gingras. Fitzpatrick accused the detectives of being in league with the accused, but the policemen denied any complicity.

Even more remarkable revelations continued to flow from the mouths of the detectives. Under further questioning from Crown attorney Fitzpatrick, detective Gagnon blurted out that Yvonne's father, André Collin, had been singularly interested to learn that Léo Fiola's father was a successful furniture merchant. Gagnon testified that the young girl's father had vowed to him and Beaudoin that the more money he got from them, the "thicker the pile" would be for the detectives. Both policemen hastened to add that they had straightened Collin out pretty quickly, indicating that their pay came from the force.[67] When Fitzpatrick again asked why none of this had surfaced before the trial, Gagnon quipped: "I wasn't asked."[68] Why, Fitzpatrick asked again, vainly, did the detectives come to discredit the father of the child? "It was weighing on my heart," replied Beaudoin.[69]

Sealing the last nail into the Crown's case, defence counsel Lane called Québec City vice-squad detective Delphis Bussières to expand upon the story of Dame Gingras.[70] To the astonishment of all, Bussières told the court that it had been none other than André Collin who led the police to put a watch on the first-floor apartment, culminating in the arrest of the brothel-keeper last September. When it came time for the Gingras trial, the police anticipated that André Collin would be one of their key witnesses. But when he took the stand, Collin professed to know "absolutely nothing" of the house, and had "nothing bad to say against the woman."[71] Lane tried to get Bussières to give his general opinion of a man who would make such an about-turn on the stand, but the Crown's objection to the question was upheld.

Philippe Gingras, vers 1895, Le Centre de Québec des Archives nationales du Québec, P585, D3, P2. Photo of le poste de police, no. 3 de la ville de Québec, dans la partie commerciale du quartier Saint-Roche. Photo of police headquarters, three uniformed police, two in plain clothes, possibly detectives.

Québec police detectives at St. Roche, c. 1895

L'Action Catholique (Québec), 27 September 1917, at 8

The public furor surrounding the press coverage was such that an unusual follow-up appeared on 27 September 1917 in *L'Action Catholique*. Although the paper had not covered the trial itself, it carried this announcement: *"On nous prie d'annoncer que les enfants de M.J.E. Collin, employé civil de St-Sauveur, ne sont nullement concernes dans la malheureuse affaire d'enlèvement dont il a été question ces jours derniers."*

Astonished at the defence broadside to their case, the most the Crown prosecutors could do was to recall Yvonne Collin and her father. Asked for her version of the police interrogation, Yvonne indicated that detective Gagnon had flatly refused to believe her denial of previous sexual experience: *"Il m'a dit qu'une jeune fille qui passait huit garçons, était pas vierge avant d'avoir commencé"* — "He told me that a young girl who went through eight boys was no virgin beforehand."[72] She denied that she had ever mentioned anything like manual masturbation. Her testimony never deviated that prior to the rape, she had had no sexual experience whatsoever. André Collin had more difficulty trying to extricate himself from the unsavoury financial insinuations. He denied making the statements attributed, but said he was anxious to have the culprits caught, and wanted to pay the detectives "for their troubles."[73] He admitted that there had been discussion of *"cinquante piastres"* with several of the detectives. As for any money for himself, he reluctantly admitted that "someone" — whom he preferred not to name — had offered him *"une couple de cents piastres"* and lawyers' fees to settle the matter, but he had refused.[74]

Why did the police testify for the defence? Their reference to pureness of "heart" and "conscience" is belied by their failure to inform the Crown attorneys. The proper course would have been to tell the Crown, who would have halted the prosecution if there was no realistic prospect of a seduction conviction. Given the one-sided unburdening, it is also equally unlikely that the detectives were simply attempting to make "disclosure" to the other side. In fact, disclosure of Crown evidence to the defence was a concept that had yet to be introduced to Canadian criminal practice. A more likely interpretation is that the detectives were on the take, that their testimony had been purchased by the families of the accused. Financial discussions apparently initiated from several quarters, and perhaps the fifty piastres that André Collin put up was less than other offers. Whether this was a rare occurrence or fairly common practice at the time would require substantially more documentation than has yet surfaced in criminal trial transcripts.[75] Defence counsel Jules-Alfred Lane seemed unembarrassed to admit that it was his initiative to interview the police.[76] It may have been that some defence lawyers were open to acting as a go-between for the accused and Crown witnesses.[77] Whether money was actually involved, and whether Lane took part in such an exchange, is unknown.

As for André Collin, his behaviour on the stand in the Gingras case suggests that he was all too open to selling his testimony. His admission that he had discussed a financial offer in his daughter's case and tried to secure better results by paying off the detectives indicates that he viewed the trial as inextricably tied up with money, whatever the truth of the detectives' assertions. The deep-rooted belief that sexual assault complainants were motivated by financial gain, so often evident from defence counsel's arguments, seems to have developed legs here. But it wasn't the victim of the crime who was wheeling and dealing — it was her father. It was another example of an attack on credibility similar to the "character assassination by neighbourhood" earlier. The sins of the father came home to roost on the shoulders of the daughter. It was character assassination by familial relationship.

Wrestling with the Legal Interpretation of Seduction

SINCE FIOLA AND HIS companions had chosen an expedited trial without a jury, it was solely up to Charles Langelier, Justice of the Court of Sessions of the Peace, to rule on the evidence. Langelier had grown up on a farm in Ste-Rosalie and studied law at Laval University, where he carried off the silver medal. Called to the bar in 1875, he took up practice in Québec City with his brilliant older brother, François, who was also a popular professor of law, and later dean, at Laval. The two brothers became drawn into a powerful circle of Liberal party activists who dominated Québec politics for several decades. A "born politician and orator," Charles Langelier ran successfully for provincial and federal election several times between 1878 and 1892. That year, he was implicated in the Baie des Chaleurs scandal, and accused of having skimmed off for personal use more than $8000 from government funds intended to subsidize railway construction. Langelier went down to crushing electoral defeat, but subsequently employed his considerable talent as a writer to try to rehabilitate himself from the stinging disgrace, publishing lengthy defences of the Liberal party and the Mercier administration.[78]

Langelier also began to lobby for a judicial position as reward for his long-time political service. Prime Minister Wilfrid Laurier balked at the prospect, partly because the memory of the political scandal was still too fresh, and partly because he had already appointed Charles's brother François to the Superior Court. Langelier was left cooling his heels as Québec district sheriff until 1910, when, at the age of sixty, he was finally appointed as magistrate to the lower court, rather than to the higher bench with his brother.[79] Whether Langelier's experience with political scandal made him more sympathetic to the detectives in their remonstrations of innocence is open to speculation. It is interesting to note that at one point, he interrupted Crown prosecutor Rochette's cross-examination of detective Gagnon, telling him he thought whether Gagnon had "done his duty or not" ought not to be pursued further in the trial.[80]

Whatever his predilections concerning police officers potentially on the take, Langelier took his responsibilities as an interpreter of the law most seriously. An editor of legal casebooks and author of publications on "La procédure criminelle," and "La prostitution," Langelier was no stranger to the finer points of criminal jurisprudence.[81] The judgment he rendered on 17 January 1918 was described by the press as "très élaboré" and subsequently published in two law reports, typically reserved for superior and appellate court decisions.[82] And yet Langelier opened his decision with a glaring mistake. He noted that one of the "essential ingredients" of the crime consisted of the "prosecutrix having a previous chaste character," and cited an American and English treatise to the effect that "chastity, like other elements of the offence should be proved by the prosecution in the first instance." If he had referred to the Criminal Code instead, he would have seen that this burden of proof fell to the defence.[83] In 1900, Parliament had altered the rule that customarily placed the criminal burden of proof on the Crown due to a concerted lobby campaign on the part of women's organizations objecting to the very existence of the "previous chaste character" requirement.[84] The extent to which this procedural error affected the verdict can never be evaluated, but it surely was sufficient ground to overrule the judgment on appeal, and send the matter back for a new trial. Inexplicably, the Crown brought no appeal forward, and the case stood, a decision repeatedly cited in later seduction cases.

Langelier next turned to the question of the legal meaning of "previous chaste character," a phrase that had never been defined in the *Criminal Code*. Here he embarked on a wide-ranging jurisprudential search that encompassed cases, evidentiary texts, and dictionaries. Citing decisions from the Northwest Territories in 1903 and Nova Scotia in 1912, he noted that good reputation and physical virginity (*virgo intacto*) were beside the point, if the woman was not of virtuous disposition in mind and "chaste in fact."[85] The question was whether she had "a lewd disposition" or "lascivious character," whether she was "lost to all sense of shame." Quoting from Larousse's *Great Dictionary*, Langelier expanded:

> Chastity is a virtue which makes one abstain from the prohibited carnal pleasures and repel even the thought of it. Purity is the most perfect chastity. As far as the three words *honour, wisdom, virtue* are applicable to woman, *honour* supposes the determination to remain estimable to the eyes of the world; *wisdom* brings the idea of prudence with which a woman must avoid the dangerous occasions; *virtue* suggests the courage with which a woman shall resist the seducer's attacks.[86]

Formula such as these would lead Crown prosecutors to introduce evidence that the victims of seduction had attended Sunday School, participated in Bible class, and sung in the choir. But even this did not always suffice. Expressing doubt over the chastity of a woman who had done all three, but who also got into a motor vehicle with a man she had not known before and allowed him to drive her to a secluded place, the Ontario Court of Appeal would later proclaim:

> In an unmarried woman, chaste character and virginity are not necessarily synonymous. . . . Chaste character means the possession of the qualities and traits of pureness or decency of thought and conduct. It is moral cleanliness in the sense that reasonable, right-thinking persons would say there is an absence of impurity or indecency. That does not imply that type of excessive virtue found in a prude, but it does embody that degree of decency which is found in the average decorous, self-respecting unmarried woman.[87]

"Les Huit Accusés sont Libérés," *Le Soleil* (Québec), vendredi le 18 janvier 1918, at 10

Debates erupted over whether chastity once lost could ever be regained, with some judges valiantly claiming that character was "not a material substance like glass" but something that could "be amended."[88] Although the courts were divided, those who believed in rehabilitation were of the view that there would need to be substantial evidence of swift "repentance," "absolute virtuousness," and "pureness of living" for a significant period of time.[89]

In the end, Langelier acquitted all eight accused. He accepted detectives Gagnon and Beaudoin's evidence that Yvonne Collin had "confessed" to "acts of gross immorality" with another man prior to 17 September, adding: "She has shown a lewd and lascivious disposition by offering herself to prostitution and showing by her manners that she could not be put on the same footing with pure women for the protection of whom the law has been framed."[90] The word of a young girl of fourteen, stacked up against two seasoned police detectives, had gone down to defeat. The alleged acts of manual masturbation had been characterized as "gross immorality." Somehow this had burgeoned into "lewd and lascivious" manners, even an offer of prostitution. Given the state of the law, the result would not have surprised many, although it does seem an exoneration of the predatory behaviour of this gang. Even if the detectives had told the truth, the tragedy was that young women who had experienced almost any degree of non-marital sex were shut off from legal protection. In so doing, the law took some of the women most at risk for coercive sexual male attention, and rendered them more vulnerable still. The verdict assured the eight young men from Verdun that Yvonne Collin was, indeed, *bonne à rien.*

Outside the courtroom, the war casualties continued to climb, and the conscription turmoil raged on. Crown attorney Arthur Lachance, KC, who had vigorously opposed conscription from his Liberal seat in the House of Commons, was so disgusted that he refused to run again in the federal election that took place on 17 December 1917, right in the middle of the trial. Perhaps it was a good thing, because the results produced an overwhelming English-Canadian endorsement of conscription. Charles Langelier presided over the criminal trials arising from the anti-conscription riots in Québec City in the spring of 1918, where he demonstrated his own political views by "freeing most of the participants" and "imposing light fines" on the others. He died unexpectedly in his sleep at his home on 7 February 1920. Lachance was appointed to succeed him on the Court of Sessions of the Peace that year. The year that Lachance retired in 1929, Arthur Fitzpatrick followed him to that bench. There was no judicial elevation for defence counsel Jules-Alfred Lane, KC, who died a mere eight months after the trial, on 25 October 1918, at the age of 50.[91] As for the accused, at least four of them went to war. Within a few months of their acquittals, Léo Fiola, Léodore Venne, and Henri Perrotte were drafted into the army, and Albert Thivièrge voluntarily signed up shortly thereafter.[92] Whatever their crimes, one certainly could not have wished the horrors of overseas military service upon any of them. The muddy, rat-infested, and death-filled trenches of Europe must have made their exuberant, carefree days on the road in the Hudson Super Six but a distant memory.

≈ Chapter 4 ≈

THE PROSECUTION OF HENRY KISSEL IN THE ROARING TWENTIES IN HALIFAX

HENRY KISSEL WAS A young man whose future brimmed with promise. A native New Yorker born in the Bronx, twenty-six-year-old Kissel was in his final year at the prestigious Dalhousie Medical School in Halifax.[1] Only the best students were selected to intern at the city's Victoria General Hospital, and Henry Kissel was one of the favoured few.[2] When he wasn't at the hospital, he shared a comfortable two-room flat in the Westminster Apartments at the corner of Morris and Church streets with another Dalhousie medical student from New York, Irving Marks.[3]

Senior medical students were immersed in classes and rounds at the hospital, but Henry Kissel never let his studies interfere with his social life. His fashionable haircut and eyewear betrayed his dashing sense of style. Round horn-rimmed glasses were much in vogue, meant to produce the "academic look that was *de rigueur* on campus" that year.[4] Trend-setters like Kissel found insufficient scope for revelry at Dalhousie's strictly chaperoned student dances, where smoking was prohibited and a midnight curfew prevailed. Henry Kissel preferred the public dance hall at the Armouries, where he could mix with a looser, more boisterous crowd. That was where, in the late summer of 1925, he met and mingled with women like Ethel Machan.[5]

By 1925, the Roaring Twenties were in full swing, part of an irresistible surge of rebellion sweeping across North America. The First World War had ended, ushering in a bold and vivacious new decade to chase away the horrific memories of the shattered battlefields. The Maritime region was slower to experience the optimism, having been crippled by economic instability

Henry Kissel, Dalhousie Medical School, 1929

Irving Edward Marks, Dalhousie Medical School, 1929

Dalhousie Medical Building, 1929

and serious strikes in the first years of the decade. But even there, by 1925 the desperate times had begun to ease. The romance and drama of Hollywood movies and silent films transformed a population hungry for new fantasies. Musical extravaganzas from New York reached delighted listeners by radio broadcast all the way to Halifax. The hallmark of the decade was the "flapper," who cast off her profusion of petticoats and abandoned wasp-waisted corsets. She bobbed her hair, shortened her skirts, rouged her cheeks, and shadowed her eyelids. She took up competitive sports, smoked in public, carried flasks of bootlegged liquor in her garters, and danced the "Charleston" until dawn. Dr. H.B. Atlee, Henry Kissel's professor of obstetrics and gynecology at Dalhousie, writing in the *Halifax Chronicle* in 1924, described the flapper as "the Bolshevik of the feminine world":

> She displays breezily her maiden charms in public. She draws attention to
> these charms in a hundred naughty little ways, such as powdering her pretty
> nose, touching up her saucy lips, and wearing clothes that combine the ex-
> treme and the bizarre. . . . [She] puts her feet on the mantlepiece, and swigs

hooch. . . . What is more she has had the temerity to do in public those things that we, the superior sex, have long claimed as our sole right.[6]

Flappers disdainfully mocked the old Victorian notions of the "innate passionlessness" of women, and scoffed at the staid pamphlets circulated by Canadian public health officials, with sobering, clinical titles like "Facts on Sex Hygiene for Girls and Young Women," that urged young women to reject "fast" men who tried to "fondle or spoon."[7] An exposé published in 1922 in *Maclean's* magazine, told of young flappers who engaged in necking and petting at unchaperoned "fussing parties" where "each girl sits on a boy's knee and lets him kiss her all he wants to do . . . for hours."[8]

Some of the most notorious flappers were single, working-class women like Ethel Machan, who was employed at the Simpson's Department Store in Halifax. Ethel Machan's age is not mentioned in the court records, but she was probably in her twenties; she had been working at Simpson's for five years. Public anxiety about gender roles had grown in tandem with rising female workforce participation in the 1920s, as young women swarmed into a host of new waged jobs in factories, offices, restaurants, and retail stores.[9] Large department stores were the flagships of the exploding consumer culture, and Simpson's had opened its first Halifax building on Chebucto Road in Armadale in 1919.[10] The position of salesclerk was a much-coveted job, generally restricted to white, native-born, Protestant, high school graduates, whose feminine manners and appearance appealed to wealthier female customers. Despite the long working hours, female salesclerks savoured the stylistic surroundings and "chic" merchandise advertised in full-page spreads in the daily newspapers, and immersed themselves in a culture of heterosexual romance, with endless gossip about boyfriends and evening entertainment.[11] One drawback was the low wages that left most without the wherewithal to pay room and board. Ethel Machan continued to live at home. Her father had been killed in active service near the end of the war, and the family residence at 65 Bilby Street housed Ethel, her widowed mother Blanche, and several siblings.[12]

There are no surviving photographs, and so it is impossible to know how Ethel Machan wore her hair or how she dressed. But accounts from other young white-collar workers in the 1920s suggest that many succumbed to the pleasures of fashion. Writing in 1923, one Toronto downtown office worker confessed: "Seeing girls wearing what looked to me like lovely evening dresses at work went to my head . . . . I got the lowest-necked georgette blouse and the shortest skirt I could find and high heels and silk stockings with roses on

Simpson's Building, Halifax, established 1919

them and hennaed my hair . . . [and] never got to bed before twelve."[13] There was much incentive to splurge. The most attractive salesclerks were sometimes selected as models for department store fashion shows, where they strolled the runways sporting metallic beaded dresses trimmed with velvet and topped with furs, the "last word from Paris."[14]

Ethel Machan and her friend Marjory Hubley, a waitress at the Halifax Hotel, flouted old-fashioned rules of courtship that restricted socializing to the supervised settings of the church, the sheltered residences of friends, and the family home.[15] The two were frequent patrons of the Armouries Park Street dance hall, as often as several nights a week. Both seem to have felt quite comfortable chatting up the young men there, some of whom they permitted to squire them home at the end of the evening.[16] Ethel Machan and Marjory Hubley first met Henry Kissel and his roommate Irving Marks when they stopped to talk to them on Barrington Street one evening in August. As Ethel Machan would later admit in court, there had been no traditional courtship formalities: they "were not introduced."[17] The foursome

NSARM Photographic Collection: Nova Scotia: Places: Halifax Buildings, Nova Scotia Archives

Halifax Armouries, c. 1900

struck up a conversation and then exchanged addresses. Within a week the two young women had agreed to come up to the medical students' bachelor suite in the Westminster Apartments.

Initially, the four spent the evening sitting in the living room. But familiarities progressed over the next weeks. Irving and Marjory took to retiring to the bedroom, while Henry and Ethel "made out" on the living-room sofa. On Saturday, 12 September, Henry phoned to ask Ethel for their fifth date. They met around 9 p.m., and despite the cold and windy weather, watched the Masonic Parade wind its way along Barrington Street through town to the Armouries.[18] When they returned to the apartment, Irving was there, waiting for Marjory to get off work.[19] Henry fried up some meat for dinner, and although the two young men offered to share it with Ethel, she declined. They invited her to join them at the dining table which was set up in the bedroom, and she sat on the bed while they ate. Henry said something to Irving in French, and then asked Ethel if she had understood him. She admitted she did not speak French, and the two men did not translate for her, obviously enjoying the privacy and the superiority that their linguistic facility granted. Irving left to collect Marjory from the hotel, and Henry asked Ethel if she would wash up the dirty dishes. She flatly refused. The dirty plates, frying pan, and cutlery were left lying in the sink.

The Vogue for Women and Girls

Popular Polka Dots

Bust sizes 34, 36, 38, 40, 42, 44, 46
Choice of Tan with Green; Tan with Blue, or
Tan with Rose

78-102 Polka dots are carrying off the
honors as far as patterns go, and
they are closely spaced on this stylish Over-
blouse, buttoned down front in smock fashion.
The material is a highly-mercerized cotton
called Cambridge Dots, and the plain tie
matches dots in color. Little tabs give
the effect of pocket openings at the
sides. Price...................... 3.50

Lovely Evening Frock

Bust sizes   Length down back
34, 36   about 43 inches only
38, 40   about 44 inches only
42, 44   about 45 inches only
Orchid over Peach, Powder Blue over Peach, Elfin
Green (light) over Sunni (yellow), Peach over Sunni
58-182 An enchanting party or dance frock in
two tones of Swiss Georgette
Crepe and gold-colored Tinsel Lace.
Little nosegays at shoulder and waist. 21.50

58-182

82-170

**A Modish and
Girlish Style**
(Illustrated below)

Sizes
8, 10, 12, 13, 14, 14X years
Lengths
33, 36, 39, 41, 42, 43 ins.
Choice of Raisin, Rustic
Brown, Ginger or Navy

86-303 Its handsome
trimming, pleat-
ed sides, puff sleeves and
crush collar of Mandel
(sheared European Lamb)
all vouch for the smartness
of this Girl's comfortable
Coat. It is skilfully fashioned of soft All-Wool
Duvelyne, fully lined with
Striped Venetian and cosily
interlined throughout. Bands
of self and contrasting em-
broidery with wee metal
studs is the very new and
highly - pleasing treatment
that trims sleeves
and pleated sides.
Price 19.75

86-303
19.75

Smart Felt Hat

Chanel (Wine) Red, Jungle (Dark) Green,
Rosewood, Steel (new Saxe) Blue, Wood
Brown, Pearl Grey, Black, or Light
Sand trimmed with Brown
51-237 Very new is the creased and
draped crown featured by this
jaunty Felt Hat. Brim turns up smartly at
back, and ribbon trimming is cleverly applied. Headsize 22¼ ins. only 3.65

39.50

Expertly Fashioned

Bust sizes   Length
34, 36   about 45 inches only
38, 40, 42   about 46 inches only
44, 46   about 47 inches only
Choice of Mole Grey, Castor or Dark
Brown

82-170 Such interesting details as
fancy underarm seaming,
scalloped over-sleeves and triangular
pockets give distinction to this Woman's very smart Coat. Imported All-
Wool Velour is the material used, and
the fur chosen for collar and cuffs is
full-furred American Opossum. Em-
broidery arranged as illustrated adds its
charm to this model that is lined
throughout with Satin de Luxe, a lus-
trous cotton fabric, and is fully interlined to provide extra warmth.
Price........................ $39.50

Fashionable 1920s flapper dresses from a department store catalogue, 1926–27, Toronto

Ethel Machan's Testimony: Raped on a Date in a Bachelor Suite

HENRY KISSEL DID NOT testify in the criminal proceeding, and so we are confined to Ethel Machan's version of what transpired between the two. Her deposition indicated that when Irving and Marjory returned to the apartment, Henry insisted that Ethel accompany him to the bedroom. She told the court that she "did not trust" Henry and that she "did not like the look on his face." In front of the other couple, she told him she "did not want to go in the bedroom," but when he called, "Come here, I want you," she followed. Henry switched off the light by the door of the bedroom, and she chided him to "put it on." When she tried to reach the switch, he stopped her. When she tried to leave, he shut the door. Henry said: "Take off your skirt," and Ethel replied, "No, my skirt stays on."

Situations such as this must have been repeated a thousand times over, as young men and women attempted to renegotiate dating rituals in an era of shifting sexual mores. A bold participant in the sexualized youth culture that was emerging in the 1920s, Ethel Machan was prepared to spend evenings in the bachelor apartment of a man she barely knew. She was prepared to experiment sexually, but still described herself as a "respectable" working woman who meant to protect her virginity. She was well aware that Henry Kissel wanted more than she was willing to offer, and she was trying to draw lines that permitted preliminary love-making while placing sexual intercourse beyond reach. She may also have been worried that a lack of cooperation could spell an end to the dalliance with a man of elevated social status, a medical student who would have been viewed as a "prize catch" by her peers.[20]

Ethel testified that Henry "pushed" her onto the bed, adding "he frightened me terrible." She told the court that she "started to yell" and screamed for "about ten or fifteen minutes." Henry grabbed her by the mouth and throat. Ethel cried that he was hurting her and begged him to leave her alone. Instead, Henry grabbed her left breast and pushed her down on the bed again. He pulled her clothes with his right hand, and covered her mouth with his left. Ethel testified that Henry got on top of her, pulled her skirt up, and "tore" her "drawers down the front." Anything but passive in response, Ethel described for the court her efforts to resist:

> I kicked and screamed and he kept putting his hand over my mouth.... I kicked and did everything possible to get clear of him. I got weak. I said please leave me alone but he would not. I fought so bad my legs ached. I was so weak I could not move. He grabbed me by the nose and I had to gasp for breath.

Ethel's description of Henry's reaction suggests that the young man was somewhat mystified by her resistance. At one point, he tried to calm her down, saying, "Don't be frightened." Ethel indicated that Henry got "heated and perspired," and that he "took out his private" and "had connection" with her. After it was over, Henry even entreated Ethel to "put your arms around me." She refused. When Henry got up, she found there was blood on her "corsets and drawers." Ethel told the court she started to cry, saying: "Look what you have done. What am I going to do? I am ruined." Suddenly the medical man again, Henry attempted to reassure the sobbing young woman that it was "all right," that it was "just your periods." Ethel wasn't convinced. As she explained in court later, she "was frightened something had broken inside and that I might get some disease." The sex hygiene pamphlets being handed out by social purity advocates at public lectures and doctors' offices warned readers that girls who showed a "love of excitement" were prime candidates for the scourge of venereal disease.[21]

In what seems to have been a fairly well-rehearsed response, Henry led the young woman into the bathroom, telling her: "Come with me, I will fix you up. Do as I say and it will be all right." The bathroom was rigged up with what looked like laboratory equipment. There were bottles filled with manure-coloured liquids and glass tubing with rubber knobs on the end. Henry instructed Ethel how to "douche" with the equipment, and waited outside. When Ethel emerged, frightened that she had not carried out the instructions properly, he tried to reassure her that everything was fine.

What Henry Kissel meant the douching to accomplish is not clear. Knowledge about venereal disease had grown in the wake of the First World War, and he probably understood that the bacteria causing venereal diseases were susceptible to mild antiseptics, although medical experts knew that washing after exposure was frequently ineffective.[22] He may also have intended the douching to serve as a contraceptive measure. As a medical student, Henry Kissel would have studied reproduction, pregnancy, childbirth, and possibly the rudiments of birth control, although the latter was not a topic deeply delved into at most schools. In fact, medical journals bemoaned the use of contraceptives, complaining that they "pervert[ed] the highest function of woman's nature," and were associated with prostitutes and the sexually profligate.[23] Canadian law also prohibited contraception, making it a crime for anyone to "offer to sell," "advertise," or possess for "sale or disposal" any "medicine, drug or article intended or represented as a means of preventing conception," or to advertise any means of "curing venereal diseases."[24]

Henry Kissel was flouting both the norms of the medical world and the legal system in equipping his bathroom with glass tubing, bottles, and caustic liquids.

Belatedly solicitous of Ethel Machan's welfare, Henry told her to use the towel that was hanging on the rack to wash herself. Then he gave her one of his carefully folded handkerchiefs and two pins, explaining that he didn't want her to stain her clothes further on the way home. He told her she was not "hurt" and begged her not to cry because she was making him "feel bad." They emerged into the living room, where they waited for Marjory to comb her tousled hair. Henry collected Ethel's hat and coat, and the four-some tiptoed out of the apartment, afraid to waken other residents at such a late hour. Henry hailed a cab to take his date home, and during the drive, Ethel demanded that he give her back the Kodak snapshots that had been taken of the two of them.[25] Henry replied playfully that if she wanted them, she would have to come back up to the apartment, and "if you come you will know what to expect." He kissed her goodnight, and let her out of the cab. Finally home, Ethel went "straight to bed."

The Decision to Prosecute a Dalhousie Medical Student

ETHEL MACHAN TESTIFIED THAT she was "so ashamed" about what had happened in the Westminster apartment that she "did not tell a soul" for a week. When Marjory caught her crying several days later, all she would say was that she had had "a terrible night" with Henry the previous Saturday. Finally, she chose to confide in her sister, Florence. Florence told their mother, Blanche, and then one of Halifax's few policewomen, Mrs. May Virtue, became involved. May Virtue was well known to local working-class mothers, many of whom sought her intervention when they became concerned about their daughters' freewheeling sexual behaviour.[26] The records do not reveal whose decision it was to pursue criminal charges. Left to her own devices, Ethel might have chosen to let matters lie the way so many deeply embarrassed sexual assault victims had always done. It is possible that Blanche Machan and May Virtue took the case out of her hands and became the main impetus behind the prosecution. However, the testimony later given by Ethel Machan suggests that she was clearly of the view that she had been raped, and that she was neither a reluctant witness nor averse to the legal process.

Charges of rape were laid on 23 September 1925. Henry Kissel was arrested the same day, although there is no indication that the police ever searched his apartment, or that they discovered or seized the elaborate equipment rigged up in the bachelor suite.[27] It was unusual to find a medical student charged with rape. During the twentieth century, it was working-class men who typically found themselves on trial for sexual assault, not middle- and upper-class, professional men.[28] Although there is no reason to suspect that rapists were restricted to one class *in fact*, those with wealth and position remained largely immune from prosecution. Rape victims, hesitant to bring forward public complaints in any event, may have been doubly skeptical of the capacity of the criminal law to sanction men of status. The considerable discretion that rested in the hands of police officers and Crown prosecutors may also have resulted in the diversion of complaints against middle- and upper-class men. Men with money and social standing may have had more resources to buy their way out of public exposure, by paying off complainants or their families, or by bribing or otherwise importuning officials.[29]

The unusual decision to carry through with the prosecution of Henry Kissel may be partly explained by his New York background. Anti-American sentiment had a long tradition in Canada, and such feelings may have been exacerbated by the number of American students registered at Dalhousie Medical School. Almost half of Henry Kissel's class was American-born.[30] Another possible clue to Henry Kissel's brush with the criminal justice system was his Jewish identity.[31] His application to Dalhousie University listed "Reformed Hebrew" under the heading "religious denomination." Antisemitism had a long and entrenched history in Canada, and the 1920s witnessed some of the worst excesses. Jews were subjected to discriminatory restrictions in employment, housing, social activities, immigration, and educational opportunities.[32] In fact, Henry Kissel may have come to Dalhousie because it, in contrast to many universities south of the border and in other parts of Canada, still admitted Jewish students.[33]

Halifax appears to have been somewhat sheltered from antisemitism, largely as a result of its small Jewish population.[34] Whereas the Toronto press frequently made reference to Jews who appeared in Police Court as "the Jew" without further designation of name, Henry Kissel was not identified in the press as a Jew, nor was any note made in the court records about his Jewishness.[35] But even in the relatively tolerant environment of Halifax, the evidence that Henry Kissel's prosecution had unsettled the Halifax Jewish community is obvious from the bail records. The bail, set at $2000, was posted in full by four leading Jewish Halifax businessmen.[36] One wonders what the bail guarantors thought about this upstart outsider, dating and

ROBIE ST. SYNAGOGUE

Nova Scotia Archives and Records Management, fonds/collection Jewish Historical Society, reference/accession number 1992-329/13

Robie Street Synagogue in Halifax, established 1920

sexually experimenting with a Halifax Gentile girl, and bringing the full force of the criminal justice system down upon himself.[37] Presumably they were concerned that a young Jewish man charged with rape might bring recriminations upon the wider community in Halifax.[38] The memory of the internationally infamous case of Leo Frank, a Jewish man who had been wrongly accused of raping and murdering a thirteen-year-old girl in the United States, and lynched by a Ku Klux Klan mob in 1913, must have provided a vivid context for their actions.[39]

The Case for the Defence: Cross-Examination of Ethel Machan and Surprise Witnesses

EVENTS MOVED VERY QUICKLY after Henry Kissel's arrest. The preliminary hearing commenced two days later on 25 September, in Halifax Police Court before Magistrate Andrew Cluney, KC.[40] Magistrate Cluney was a native Newfoundlander, who had moved to Halifax some years before he studied at Dalhousie Law School, and then went on to practise as a Crown prosecutor in Halifax for over thirty years. He was new on the bench, having been appointed just one year earlier.[41] Irwin Cahan Doty, a native Nova Scotian with a Dalhousie law degree, who ran a Halifax law office while working as a part-time Crown attorney, appeared for the prosecution.[42] Henry Kissel was represented by thirty-five-year-old Lionel Avard Forsyth, one of Halifax's most charismatic lawyers. Born in Mount Benson, Nova Scotia, Forsyth had spent the first years of his remarkable life sailing around the world on his father's two-thousand-ton square rigger. His subsequent education at King's College and Harvard University provided the intellectual backdrop that spawned a dizzying range of careers. Before taking up legal practice in Halifax in 1918, Forsyth had been a professional baseball player, a railroad surveyor, a streetcar driver, a time-keeper who supervised wharf construction, a banker in Canada and Cuba, a Romance languages professor, a breeder of Jersey cows, and a poet.[43]

Although there is no way of knowing what Henry Kissel paid Forsyth for his legal defence, it must not have come cheap, because the versatile lawyer commanded one of the highest professional incomes in the city. Harnessing legal talent of Forsyth's calibre was undoubtedly a wise decision. Forsyth's shrewd strategy was to demonstrate that whatever might have happened in the bachelor suite, Ethel Machan had been a fully consenting participant. He began his cross-examination with probing questions about how the couple had first met, eliciting the information that they had not been "introduced," that Ethel had visited the apartment four or five times, occasionally without invitation, and that her mother had known nothing of the visits. Trying to dispel any suggestion that Henry might have been Ethel's first boyfriend, Forsyth asked the young woman about her past. Ethel admitted that she had "kept company" with Douglas Fleet, a teamster for the Cunard coal company, for about five months a year earlier.[44]

Next, Forsyth honed in on the Sunday night prior to the alleged rape, when Ethel admitted that she had gone up to the apartment without her friend Marjory Hubley. In her direct examination, Ethel had testified that she and Henry had "wrestled" on the living-room sofa, that her skirt was wrinkled during the tussle, and that she was "mad" about it. In an astonishing display of the risqué flirtatiousness of the modern flapper, under cross-examination Ethel admitted that she had undressed right in the apartment, while Henry and Irving were present, and used their electric iron to press her skirt: "I took my skirt off and pressed it. I took my skirt off in the bedroom." Forsyth seems to have seized gleefully upon the spectacle of a young woman semi-attired in a bachelor apartment, because he asked a series of questions about what underclothing remained. Recognizing that near nudity was perhaps not the best picture for a rape complainant to portray, Ethel insisted that she was wearing a slip under her skirt, a slip that came down past her knees, and that she had put on "a kimona" while she pressed her dress. Flappers had done away with traditional "underbodices," turning them in for racier "chemises, vests and slips" that hung straight down from ribbon-like straps, silhouetting their slim figures.[45] The diverting image of the fashionable lingerie must have overwhelmed Ethel's best efforts to explain.

Forsyth seemed surprisingly conversant with Ethel's recent social life, and his final questions forced the young woman to admit that on Tuesday, 15 September, a mere three days after the events that led to the criminal charge, she and Marjory had gone out to the Armouries where they danced until about eleven o'clock. The duo returned again to the dance hall on Thursday, 17 September. Both nights, Ethel told the court she had been escorted home by a young man named Donald Copp. This sort of behaviour was not what might have been expected of a traditional assault victim, dancing till dawn with other young bachelors before the information was even sworn out against the accused assailant.

Forsyth next called to the stand the taxi driver who had driven Ethel and Henry home on 12 September. Borden Saunders testified that he had picked

Nova Scotia Archives and Records Management, photographer Allan Fraser, c. 1921, reference/accession number 1988-71/8

Lionel A. Forsyth

the couple up shortly after midnight, and that he saw "no signs of Miss Machan having been crying." The driver's attention seems to have been riveted on the physical side of the dalliance taking place in the back seat of his cab, for he added: "He kissed her goodnight. I heard the kiss." None of this was necessarily inconsistent with a rape having occurred. Rape can affect women in different ways, and not all rape victims cry in front of witnesses. Nor was it unusual for rapists to kiss their victims after the assault, and for rape victims not to resist. Some rapists even tried to arrange subsequent dates with women they had accosted, with no apparent recognition that their earlier coercive advances might have marred their prospects.[46] But the taxi driver's evidence was certainly damaging within the context of cultural expectations that all raped women would raise an immediate outcry.

Forsyth's final defence witness was none other than Marjory Hubley. Under Forsyth's skillful questioning, she stated that she had been present in the apartment the entire evening of 12 September. As she recalled, Ethel and Henry had spent "most of the evening" in the bedroom. Directly contradicting her girlfriend's testimony, Marjory testified that the bedroom door had been ajar the whole time, and the light had been on. There was "nothing to indicate that there was anything going on in the bedroom," she indicated. "I heard no screams but I heard Miss Machan laughing. I could have heard her scream. I heard no noise but the laughing." Indeed, she had been completely

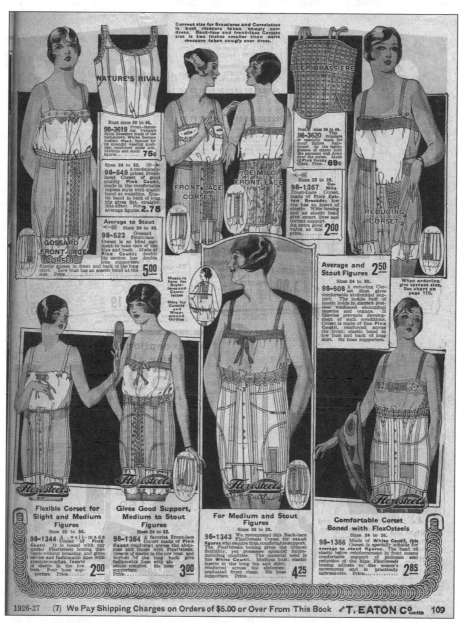

Modern 1920s lingerie from a department store catalogue, 1926–27, Toronto

unaware of any forced sex. "Miss Machan never spoke to me or indicated to me that any man had connection with her that night." This was a startling contradiction of Ethel's version of the events, and suggested that any sexual interaction that had occurred that night had been entirely consensual, even joyful. It was a defence that Henry Kissel might have been expected to make, had he taken the stand himself. That the evidence was proffered through the mouth of Ethel's girlfriend made it even more effective.

The relationship between Ethel and Marjory was a complicated one. For some time the two young women had frequented dance halls and double-dated together. Ethel had taken the lead in bringing Marjory up to the apartment, at Henry's request. On at least one previous occasion, it had been Marjory and Irving cavorting in the bedroom while Ethel and Henry remained in the sitting room. It was common for young women to seek to protect themselves in the uncharted social territory of the Roaring Twenties by travelling in pairs.[47] However, Crown prosecutor Doty believed that Marjory had not only failed to prove a safeguard on the night of 12 September, but that she had also betrayed her friend on the witness stand. And Doty had a theory as to why. He asked Marjory whether she had had any conversation with her boyfriend since 12 September. She admitted that Irving had spoken to her the night before the trial, and conceded that the subject of the conversation was Henry's case. On re-examination, Forsyth got Marjory to state that no one had asked her to come to court and tell "anything that was not so," but Doty had cleverly planted the suspicion that Marjory's loyalty to her boyfriend overrode her loyalty to her friend. With this last witness, the preliminary inquiry drew to a close, and the case moved forward to the Supreme Court of Nova Scotia.[48]

The Crime of Rape: Carnal Knowledge without "Consent"

THE SOCIAL CONTEXT OF the prosecution, in the thick of the tumultuous Roaring Twenties, further complicated the already complex law of rape. The "racy" flapper set was taking issue with traditional feminist complaints about gendered sexual standards. Turn-of-the-century feminists had argued that the double standard ought to be rooted out by forcing men to conform to the restrictive sexual mores prescribed for women. "Votes for women; chastity for men" was the catch-phrase of the movement.[49] The flappers also took aim at the double standard, but they wanted it relaxed in favour of women. They wished to discard the role historically assigned to women as the gatekeepers of sexual purity, hemmed in by rigid Victorian and Edwardian evangelical mores. In cities from Vancouver to Halifax, they sought to mark out greater access to sexual relations not only for men, prostitutes, and "shameless hussies," but for "good times girls" who insisted that so long as they didn't kiss "too many men," sully their "amateur standing," or lose their virginity, they should be able to retain their social respectability.[50]

Ethel Machan had wholeheartedly embraced this bold new ethos. Her sense of independence and bravado is wonderfully conveyed in her retort to Henry Kissel that time he instructed her to wash the dirty dinner dishes. "I said no," she shot back that night, rejecting any notion that she should assume a subordinate domestic role. She was prepared to flout traditional conventions that forbade respectable women from any sexual interaction before marriage. She was eager to discover what there was to learn about fun, romance, and the sexual excitement of youth. Her evidence indicates that she did so in the full expectation that she could experiment like this and still retain her virginity and good character. She testified that she had not consented to intercourse. "I said no," she emphasized. "I said leave me alone. . . . I kicked and screamed."

What Henry Kissel thought about this version of the events is difficult to elicit, for he never took the stand. From what we can tell based on Ethel Machan's testimony, the elaborate set-up in the bachelor apartment and Henry's post-coital routine suggest that the sexual conquest was neither spontaneous nor unplanned, and that she was not his first or only sexual partner. According to Ethel, Henry was dismissive of her repeated "no's," and in the face of her vocal and physical resistance, even asked her to put her "arms around" him. Her objections appeared irrelevant to him, seemingly invisible. He may have experienced a twinge of remorse afterwards, offering her a clean handkerchief and towel, and telling her not to cry because it made him "feel bad." But contemporary perspectives portrayed male sexuality as "lustful, passionate, even bestial, scarcely capable of containment," easily aroused by female invitation.[51] Henry Kissel may have felt that Ethel Machan's consent to sexual preliminaries, especially in the venue of a bachelor apartment, encompassed consent to full sexual intercourse.

The law of rape required that the Crown prove the elements of the crime beyond a reasonable doubt. The *Criminal Code* defined rape as "the act of a man having carnal knowledge of a woman who is not his wife without her consent, or with consent which has been extorted by threats or fear of bodily harm, or obtained by personating the woman's husband, or by false and

Halifax Chronicle, 17 September 1929, at 1

Magistrate Andrew Cluney, KC

fraudulent representations as to the nature and quality of the act."[52] The *Code* sorted sexual encounters into various types. First, wives had no sexual autonomy and no right to withhold spousal consent. Second, if a woman consented to intercourse with someone other than a marital partner, the activity was also free from legal sanction. Third, if she refused to give her consent, it was rape. If her "consent" was extracted involuntarily — due to threats, fear of bodily harm, or trickery of certain specified kinds — it was also rape. It seems rather peculiar to describe the latter transactions as "consensual" at all. Such acts seem better characterized as "submission" or "acquiescence" rather than true "consent." Equally important, the statute did not define "consent" as "the voluntary agreement of the complainant to engage in the sexual activity in question," as the current *Criminal Code* specifies.[53]

In the hands of the judges and jurors who applied the law, the concept of "consent" took on some strange dimensions. Judges and jurors did not take a woman at her word when she testified that her free will had been overcome, but scrutinized her behaviour for overt signs of resistance.[54] They invented the concept of "clandestine consent," and attributed this to rape victims who were too "silent" and failed to make "a spontaneous and irrepressible outcry."[55] Some threats, intimidation, and forms of bodily harm were considered too minimal to count.[56] Judges and jurors seemed to believe that "normal" heterosexual relations often manifested very significant physical and psychological coercion.[57] Bruising to the arms and face, swelling on the neck, cut lips, even possible rib fractures, were depicted as the sort of injuries that might occur after a "mild sort of protest" in which a young woman "willing enough that the action occur" was trying to signal that she didn't want to "surrender her virtue . . . too readily."[58] Courts also searched for evidence of consent well beyond the sexual encounter itself. Women's general reputations, movements, drinking habits, and other behaviour were probed with particular intensity. Class biases permeated the search for signs of consent, with working-class women subjected to greater suspicion than women from wealthier families.[59]

It was the concept of "consent" that had to be interrogated, inspected, and properly probed before the authorities could determine where to draw the line. Ethel Machan's testimony suggests that she had anticipated that the legal system would support her, apparently confident that she was within her rights and would have the protection of the criminal law when she chose to draw the line against sexual intercourse. Henry Kissel's defence suggests that he understood himself to be within his rights when he forged ahead with intercourse upon an adventuresome young woman in his bedroom apartment. The question to be determined was whose perspective would govern the legal definition of "consent." Was it a case of "consensual sex" immune from legal sanction? Or was it a duly proven crime of "rape" that could garner an offender the potential of life in prison?

The Outcome: Prosecution Halted in Its Tracks

ON 5 OCTOBER 1925, the case moved forward to a "grand jury" of twenty-four men.[60] The rules of criminal procedure required that after the preliminary inquiry, the case be screened by a grand jury empanelled to determine whether there was sufficient evidence to lay an indictment and issue a "true bill" that would push the matter on to trial before a "petit jury" of twelve men.[61] It was rare for grand jurors to issue "no bill" verdicts, although rape cases generally provoked such results more than other charges.[62] As it would turn out, the rare occurrence transpired on 8 October 1925, when the Halifax grand jury rejected the bill of indictment, leaving Henry Kissel free to go. The *Halifax Evening Echo* duly reported that "no bill was reported in the case of William Kissell, charged with rape."[63] Henry Kissel may have taken some ironic sense of satisfaction that the newspaper had failed to get the name down correctly.

The dismissal of the charges was probably predictable from the outset. Rape prosecutions achieved very low rates of conviction even where the evidence was substantially less contested.[64] And even if the grand jurors had accepted Ethel Machan's testimony completely, the physical force that Henry Kissel administered was probably too mild for jurors who anticipated certain levels of physical "persuasion" to be a masculine right. The level of resistance Ethel Machan described having mounted would have been equally unimpressive to a criminal justice system that expected heroic efforts. Her apparent composure afterwards, choosing to ride home in a taxi with the accused rather than to latch onto her girlfriend and flee the scene, was insufficiently hysterical for legal authorities who adhered to the belief that raped women should raise a hue and cry at the first possible opportunity.[65] And the wider class and reputation indicia used to assess "consent" militated against a conviction. Ethel Machan's working-class background, her dance-hall affinities, parading about in a slip in a bachelor pad, all made a guilty verdict most unlikely.

Was the result the correct one? The evidence was mixed, and it is impossible to know who was telling the truth so many years ago. Perhaps Ethel Machan had voluntarily consented to intercourse, and then been frightened into asserting that she was forced into it, when confronted with her mother's wrath after the sexual deed was disclosed. Such an interpretation certainly accords with cultural stereotypes that women ventured into sexual liaisons and then regretted them afterwards. It is also possible that Ethel Machan may have exaggerated the level of resistance she put up, in an effort to persuade the court of the merits of her case. But even if one assumes that the defence witnesses were completely truthful about the level of resistance she offered that September evening, it is also possible that she unequivocally refused Henry Kissel's advances in the bedroom, even without the screaming, with the light on, and the door ajar. And that Henry Kissel ignored her repeated "no's" and considered himself licensed to forge ahead to accomplish his objective, and then finished the evening off with a farewell kiss in the taxi cab.

The criminal justice system was accustomed to dividing women into two categories: pure and impure. The former were presumed to know nothing whatsoever of sex prior to marriage; the latter were supposed to accede without coyness to all sexual demands. In the face of Ethel Machan's insistence that she was a respectable woman who "petted," the outcome indicated that there could be no betwixt and between. Judges bemoaned the newfangled dances that went on "into the small hours of the morning" at public dance halls, with "close contact" that "inflame[d] passions." They complained of "young people out all night, practically," with "no chaperonage at all." They professed themselves shocked by the new fashion styles, young girls out in "a skirt and a pair of bloomers only, no underskirt, no petticoat."[66] Modern youth needed to be taught that if the female accepted some liberties, she had crossed the line from pure to impure. The criminal law refused to accept that sexual relations were under transformation in the Roaring Twenties. There could be no sexual adventuring that proceeded by stages, where couples began with kissing, escalated to measured degrees of fondling, and then either took the full plunge or stopped, depending on the reciprocal desires of the two parties. There would be no modifications to the law of rape or the concept of consent.

In the aftermath, the parties slowly returned to their normal lives. The press coverage of the prosecution would undoubtedly have provoked some raised eyebrows back at the university, and Henry Kissel must have continued his studies under a cloud of controversy and uncertainty. A criminal prosecution that began just two weeks into the start of the fall semester must have exacerbated the already stressful student workload. Yet despite a terrifying brush with the law, Henry Kissel's promising career was not significantly jeopardized. He passed his courses and graduated from Dalhousie Medical School with a doctorate of medicine and Master's degree in surgery, along with Irving Marks, on 11 May 1926.[67] He moved back home, where he obtained his licence to practise medicine in New York State in January 1927.[68] Irving Marks was also licensed in New York State two months later.

Ethel Machan may have been slightly better shielded from the publicity than Henry Kissel. She had not been named in the press coverage, but she would have had to justify to her employer the time she took off from work to testify. Sessions with the police, testimony at the preliminary hearing, testimony before the grand jury — all would have combined to increase the difficulty in keeping the matter secret. Given the adverse testimony offered by her friend Marjory, it is quite likely that word leaked out, causing substantial damage to her reputation. Yet Ethel continued to board with her mother and sister, and managed to hold onto her job at Simpson's. She had been a Simpson's employee almost from its opening in 1919, and her relatively long tenure may have offered her a degree of job protection. In 1929, she was promoted to the position of bookkeeper.[69] She moved out of her mother's home one year later, whether to live in her own apartment or to get married is unknown.[70] Ethel's old boyfriend, Douglas Fleet, took up lodgings as a boarder at Marjory's family residence in 1927. In what seems a surprising twist in the tangled relationship between the two women, Marjory Hubley wed Douglas Fleet shortly thereafter.[71]

Lionel Forsyth's future career proved to be as fascinating as his earlier life might have predicted. He left Halifax to take up legal practice in Montréal the year after the Kissel case, where his brilliant practice expanded to include

Dalhousie Medical School Graduating Class, 1926

tax, labour, combines, corporation, and admiralty law, across five provinces. A director of more than forty companies, Forsyth would become known as Canada's highest paid corporation lawyer. He left practice at the height of his success in 1949 to become president of Dominion Steel and Coal Corporation, where his spectacular energies catapulted a company described as a "fossilized debt-ridden giant" with "one of Canada's worst labour records" into a thriving, high-performance organization that employed one-sixth of the Nova Scotia workforce. Famous for his humour, his vinegar-like eloquence, and his delight in deflating official stuffiness, Forsyth was as apt to crawl through the most inaccessible coal and iron-ore drifts to chat with his workers as he was to give mesmerizing after-dinner speeches to well-heeled, cigar-smoking New York financiers. Asked about the incredible range of his career, shortly before his death in 1957 from leukemia, Forsyth apparently mused: "Something I've not yet seen, heard, or experienced awaits me at every corner. I've had many occupations, but I never did anything from which I didn't get sixty minutes of pleasure for every hour of work."[72]

If the parties managed to get on with their lives relatively unscathed, the case itself indicates little appetite for altering the legal rules surrounding sexual assault in response to the 1920s sexual revolution. As Ethel Machan and Henry Kissel were brought to realize, women who dared to dally with male paramours did so at their own risk. The *Kissel* verdict represented a legal staunching of loosened sexual beliefs and practices. It signalled that pleasure-seeking, working-class females who claimed to be trying to protect themselves against aggressive male sexual demands would receive scant support in law.

Chapter 5

SEXUAL BATTERY:
Gynecological Treatment in the Mercer Reformatory, 1939–40

EIGHTEEN-YEAR-OLD VELMA DEMERSON SAT on the edge of her narrow bed, in a locked cell seven by four feet in size, in the Andrew Mercer Reformatory for Women. The cell was lit with a bare bulb. The toilet facilities consisted of an enamel pail and lid. Classified by law as "incorrigible" because she was pregnant out of wedlock and living with a Chinese man, Velma was serving a twelve-month sentence in the women's prison in Toronto. One of the few women profiled in this book who is still living, Velma Demerson generously consented to a series of interviews to supplement the records of her case. As she recalls it, that first night in the Mercer, 28 June 1939, she was overwhelmed by a "premonition" that something dreadful was about to befall her.[1]

The next morning, Velma and forty-six other new inmates were sent to the medical examining room. They filed in, one behind the other, forming a long line from the examining table out into the hall. The female physician who serviced the Mercer was dressed in a white medical coat, with a black band wrapped around her head. She demonstrated how she wanted the girls to mount the table by stepping on a box. The object of the exercise was to conduct an internal gynecological examination of all forty-seven women before noon. There was no assistant present. No one took the trouble to make notes. The pace was so rapid that two examinations were completed every five minutes. One of the earliest to mount the table was a girl in her last trimester of pregnancy. Velma was shocked at her treatment: "The girl was crying, and we had to stand around and watch. We could see everything. There was

Frank W. Micklethwaite Collection, Library and Archives Canada, E0038495555

Above: Andrew Mercer
Reformatory for Women, c. 1895

Right: Velma Demerson (age 15)
and brother Leo (age 17),
Toronto, 1937

Courtesy of Velma Demerson

no privacy at all."[2] When it came Velma's turn, she failed to mount the table quickly enough. The angry doctor ordered her to dismount and stand in the corner as punishment. When she was given a second turn later, Velma leaped onto the examining table for the physician's inspection. The good news was that the young woman successfully cleared her first Mercer internal examination. The bad news was that Velma Demerson had the misfortune to be confined to the Mercer on the eve of the Second World War, when military and medical authorities were deeply engrossed in the effort to eradicate the threat that venereal disease posed to the fighting capacity of Canadian soldiers.[3]

Dr. Edna Guest: Surgeon, Medical Researcher, and Feminist

THE IRONY WAS THAT the physician who conducted the rapid-fire processing of the new prisoners that morning was none other than fifty-six-year-old Dr. Edna Mary Guest, a socially prominent physician and the pride of the Toronto feminist community. Born in London, Ontario, in 1883, Dr. Guest had studied medicine at the University of Toronto, one of three women in a class of 150 graduating in 1910. She did postgraduate studies at Harvard University in 1911, where she interned at the Women's and Children's Hospital, and then spent the next three years as a medical missionary at the Ludhiana Women's Medical College in India. With the onset of the First World War, Dr. Guest served as a military doctor in Huston, England, with the Scottish Women's Hospital in Corsica, and on a base hospital on the Western Front in France. One of the founders of Women's College Hospital in Toronto, she was appointed its Chief Surgeon in 1935. The first woman ever elected to the Academy of Medicine in Toronto in 1931, she was also created an Officer of the Order of the British Empire by King George V in 1935.[4]

An internationally recognized leader of the Canadian feminist movement, Dr. Guest was active in a host of prominent women's organizations: the International Federation of Medical Women, the World Federation of Medical Women, the Federation of Medical Women of Canada, the American Medical Women's Association, the International Council of Women, the National Council of Women, the University Women's Club, and the Council of Canadian Girl Guides. She was an enthusiastic advocate of medical careers for women, and argued for an expanded role for female doctors during the war, insisting that despite the reluctance of the military to hire them, "our women physicians were still standing ready to serve their country when needed."[5]

It was not only Dr. Guest's gender that marked her out as anomalous in the Canadian medical profession, but also her specialization in venereal disease. Most physicians disdained the field, dismissing its victims as "an undesirable class," and expressing apprehension that "success in this department of medicine" would "mark out a physician" and reduce opportunities in other areas.[6] The popular wisdom was that doctors who made a practice of treating such patients would be "gossipped" about, and diminished in professional status.[7] Dr. Guest's interest seems to have commenced with her stint in the army, and it may have been her hope that she could offer patriotic service in a specialty that other physicians, who had more professional options, shunned. In addition, it was a field that offered unique opportunities for scientific research, another career direction that may have attracted the ambitious female doctor.

Dr. Guest was also firmly committed to the eugenics movement, the "science of the improvement of the human race by better breeding."[8] Canadian eugenicists combined notions of public health, psychiatry, social work, and mental hygiene with elitist Anglo-Saxon beliefs about the inferiority of other races and the lower classes, and bemoaned the mental and physical decline of the Canadian population. They sought to increase the birth rate of the "superior" groups, and to curb the procreation of "inferior human stock," ultimately advocating segregation and sterilization of the "socially unfit."[9] Dr. Guest was one of a nucleus of people active with the Canadian Social Hygiene Council and the Health League of Canada, who spearheaded a propaganda campaign against sexual promiscuity and venereal disease, giving public lectures and distributing films, such as *The End of the Road* and *Damaged Lives*.[10] She chaired the Special Department of Venereal Disease at the Women's College Hospital, and in 1921, she secured access to a large pool of potential patients when she was appointed physician to the Mercer, where all the inmates were assumed to be sexually promiscuous, each one a potential carrier. In 1922, her access expanded further when she was appointed Gynecologist for the Family and Juvenile Court, a position she held for several decades.[11]

In keeping with her feminism, Dr. Guest claimed that women doctors had an advantage over male practitioners in treating women, because they had "a better understanding of [women's] ailments and their domestic and other responsibilities."[12] This special sensitivity was nowhere to be seen in Dr. Guest's ministrations to the Mercer women. The class and cultural barriers between the female physician and young women like Velma Demerson were so pronounced that they erased the gender bonds that Dr. Guest espoused in other settings.[13] Dr. Guest had come to believe that women's sexual glands held clues to their anti-social and criminal behaviour, and she was committed to studying the Mercer inmates as research subjects for the advancement of medical knowledge.[14]

From the earliest years at the Mercer, Dr. Guest's medical predecessors had put their incarcerated patients at risk, in part because of an inability to make accurate diagnoses or offer effective treatment for venereal disease, and in part because no one seems to have held them to account.[15] Dr. Guest followed suit, for she often gave the young women doses of medicine far in excess of standards set by the Board of Health, and extended their reformatory terms well beyond the court sentences because she deemed them uncured. Dr. Guest characterized Mercer inmates with venereal disease as "filthy" and turned her considerable research talents and patriotic energies towards "waging war" on sexually transmitted illnesses.[16] Velma Demerson was to become one of her most challenging subjects.

Velma Demerson: Life before the Mercer

VELMA'S UNCONVENTIONAL YOUTH, ALWAYS on the edge of respectability, posed a stark contrast to Dr. Edna Guest's dignified, genteel upbringing. Velma was born in Saint John, New Brunswick, in 1920, where her father, Alexander Demerson, a Greek-born entrepreneur, ran a restaurant, ice-cream parlour, and movie theatre. Although the Mercer admission records would describe Velma Demerson as "Greek Canadian," this was a label she resisted. While still a child, she was incensed when playground bullies jeered that she "wasn't white." Her mother, Alice Clifford Demerson, was English, and she preferred to identify herself through her mother's ethnicity. "I hated it in school when I had to identify myself as Greek on the school register," comments Velma. "My mother was respectably English and all my friends were British." She was convinced that "the terminology of Greek-Canadian didn't fit," because she couldn't speak the Greek language.[17]

Velma's parents' marriage was a stormy one. Her father had a roving eye, her mother took to the dance halls, and the couple divorced in 1928. Velma's father remarried a woman he brought over from rural Greece. Velma's free-spirited, unconventional mother migrated to Toronto, where she earned her living by setting up hair salons and fortune-telling tearooms in her apartment, and presiding over tumultuous rooming houses with an eclectic group

Left: Alice Demerson, 1926

Below: Alice Demerson, circa 1955

All photos on this page courtesy of Velma Demerson

of tenants she dubbed "the poor, the welfare recipients, and the escapees from bureaucracy." When finances became too stretched to handle, Alice lit clandestine fires in her quarters to collect insurance money. Velma lived with her mother until her mid-teens, when she moved back to Saint John, quit school, and went to work behind the soda fountain of her father's ice-cream parlour. Her father refused to allow her to wait tables at the restaurant, because he did not want his attractive, young daughter serving male patrons. A slim, hazel-eyed brunette who had grown to her full stature of five foot and one-half inches and one hundred and two pounds, Velma was undeniably a beauty.[18]

Chafing at the restrictions her father imposed, at age sixteen Velma decided to go on a date with a twenty-seven-year-old chemist who frequented her father's restaurant and often went out with the waitresses. The chemist picked Velma up in his car, and drove her to a secluded spot. He told her he wanted to have intercourse. She protested that she was a virgin. His response was, "Well, I'm going to find out." Velma tried to resist, but her date was athletic in build and much stronger than she was. He forced her to have sexual intercourse, and then proudly announced that he believed she had indeed been a virgin. He told Velma that he would have no need to go to his laboratory to "get fixed up," as he usually did.[19]

Velma told no one about the rape:

I didn't tell anybody about what had happened. I didn't even tell my best friend. Why not? If I'd gone to the police, I would have been disgraced. You don't have any proof. Your word would mean nothing. It would have been my fault, of course, because I went out in the car. When you think about it, thousands and thousands of us got raped this way, and never told anybody. Once a girl got into an automobile, she couldn't escape, and then she couldn't tell anybody afterwards.[20]

In fact, Velma went out with the chemist again, motivated by what turned out to be an illusory hope that he might offer to marry her. He took her to his room, had sex with her a second time, and then told her that he was Catholic, separated from his wife, and in no position to marry anyone. Velma recalls that she was devastated, especially when the chemist absolved himself from all responsibility. "I remember him saying, 'Well, I thought you enjoyed it as much as I did,'" she notes. "Which of course was ridiculous. It hurt. I never went out with him again."[21]

If Velma's experience with the chemist, and her decision to keep the matter private with no legal intervention, were as common as she believed, this underscores the risk of relying upon public or legal records to explain the history of sexual assault. It means that Velma's story is probably more representative of twentieth-century rape than the other cases in this book. Modern-day experts all agree that far more women hide the fact that they have been sexually assaulted than disclose the crime. Canadian researchers estimate that 94 percent of women refuse to report their sexual victimization to the legal authorities.[22] It is difficult to know whether the current-day estimates are accurate for the first three-quarters of the twentieth century. Certainly, the factors that Velma describes as influential in 1936 seem familiar still: self-blame, women's reluctance to bring public focus upon their private sexual lives, and a sense that others would not understand their experiences as coercive or unlawful. At the root of this is women's recognition that they are unlikely to be viewed as "credible" complainants. They suspect that family, friends, community, and the legal authorities will probably interpret their actions as equivalent to "consent." As in Velma's case, they may even have doubted whether they had the right to withhold consent once they had agreed to let their male partners take certain liberties.[23]

After breaking off with the chemist, Velma moved back to her mother's in Toronto, where she dated several older men, some of them Alice's boarders. With two of them, she had consensual sexual relations. Then in 1937, she met the man who would become her fiancé, Yip Kum Kuey. Known by his Canadian name, Harry Yip was almost fifteen years Velma's senior. He had come to Canada in 1919 at the age of fourteen, before the 1923 *Chinese Exclusion Act* put a stranglehold on immigration, leaving the predominantly male community without opportunity to bring over Chinese wives and families.[24] Harry was working at the Commodore Restaurant on Yonge Street when Velma, her mother, and a friend stopped in for dinner. The three women struck up a friendly banter with the handsome Chinese waiter. A man of medium height and slender build, Harry was impeccably dressed in starched white shirt and tie. When he asked Velma for a date, she agreed to meet him at the restaurant the next day.

There were few public places where Chinese men and white women could socialize comfortably in the racist environment of the late 1930s in Toronto. Most often Velma met Harry in his room in the back of the third floor of a house on Walton Street. An exceptional chef, he cooked Velma Chinese delicacies and steamed custard, and served her tea, Chinese biscuits,

City of Toronto Archives, Series 372, subseries 33, item 178

Chinatown, 1937

and tiny whisky glasses of vermouth. Velma found herself entranced by the quiet orderliness of the Walton Street room, worlds apart from the chaos of Alice Demerson's building where bedbugs, alcohol, and boisterous roomers were omnipresent. Velma was equally impressed by Harry's patience. Unlike the other men of her acquaintance, he did not push her to have sexual relations immediately. The first night she slept over, he kissed her, asking nothing more. When their sexual relationship did begin, she was struck by his gentleness and the respect he exhibited towards her.[25]

Velma was conflicted about crossing racial boundaries. She clung to her mother's British heritage, and resisted being classified along with others from southern Europe as "racially" inferior. She recognized that her efforts to hold onto "white" status would be jeopardized by her relationship with Harry. "Outcasts" is the word she uses today to describe the white women who partnered with Chinese men. "We all knew we had to hide away. We were just like criminals. You couldn't walk down Yonge Street with a Chinese." But Velma was falling in love with Harry Yip, a man who epitomized "dependability, peace, and security" for her. By the spring of 1939, Harry and Velma were engaged to be married, something Velma had yet to disclose to her family because she expected resistance. Harry's financial precariousness put the wedding plans on hold, and when he accepted a job at a Hamilton restaurant, Velma decided to elope with him. The ever-resourceful Alice Demerson tracked them down, marched into Harry's new place of employment, and staged a spectacular scene. "I guess she tried to hit him," recalls Velma. "My mother could be pretty devastating." Harry lost his job on the spot. The couple returned to Toronto, and took a room with a shared kitchen and bath in the back of a storefront building on Church Street, below Dundas.[26]

Now truly worried, Alice Demerson contacted Velma's father in Saint John to advise that his daughter was living with a Chinese man. Alexander Demerson was furious at what he took to be a mortal blow to the reputation of his new family. He travelled to Toronto and alerted the police. They would have advised him that they could not charge Harry with rape, because Velma was of full age of consent and living with her fiancé voluntarily. There was no option to prosecute for "seduction under promise of marriage," because this offence only protected women "of previously chaste character," something Velma undoubtedly was not.[27] Instead, the legal focus shifted to Velma herself. On the morning of 3 May 1939, Velma's father stormed over to Harry's room with two burly policemen. The lovers were still in their nightclothes. The policemen ordered Velma to dress, herded her into the police car, and locked her in a barred cell in the Don Jail. Her valuables, confiscated by the guard, consisted of an empty purse, one pin, five keys, and a watch. The charge — "incorrigibility" — had been laid by Alexander Demerson.[28]

Branded as "Incorrigible": The Criminal Justice Process, or Lack Thereof

VELMA WAS BROUGHT TO police magistrate's court, charged under the *Female Refuges Act*, which authorized a parent to make allegations of "unmanageability" or "incorrigibility" against a daughter under the age of twenty-one years.[29] The policeman who had arrested Velma took the stand and testified that he had found the young woman in Harry Yip's apartment. He stated that Velma had been wearing pyjamas and Harry a bathrobe. Magistrate R.J. Browne asked Velma if she were pregnant. Although she was uncertain, Velma suspected she might be, and replied in the affirmative. She hoped this might incline the judge to let her go, so that she could marry her lover. In fact,

Velma Demerson, 1949, age 29

she was four months' pregnant and the information did nothing to promote lenience. Judge Browne convicted her of "incorrigibility" and sentenced her to one year.[30]

The "incorrigibility" section of the *Female Refuges Act* had first been enacted in 1919, at the culmination of the First World War when anxieties about the disruption of gender roles and working-class female sexuality were running high. That year the *Royal Commission on the Care and Control of the Mentally Defective and Feeble-Minded in Ontario* had equated extramarital sexual behaviour with female mental deficiency, and called for the incarceration of promiscuous young women in the interests of the wider society.[31] There was little that could be recognized as "due process" under the Act. The magistrates conducted all hearings "in private." "No formal information" was required, but the judge was instructed to "have the person brought before him," to "take evidence in writing under oath of the facts charged," and to "make reasonable inquiry into the truth."[32] The police officer in Velma's case had probably given his evidence under oath, but the "reasonable inquiry" had stopped there. No one asked for evidence of the young woman's life history, character, or deportment. Velma was not given the opportunity to cross-examine the police officer, nor to present her own witnesses. There was no way to contact Harry. There were no lawyers present to contest the meaning of the term "incorrigibility." To her knowledge, no pre-sentence report was ever compiled, and Velma was not asked to speak to sentence. The hearing was over in the blink of an eye. There was no right of appeal under the Act until 1942. In retrospect, Velma explained she must have been "in shock." "I really didn't have any idea what was going on. I felt dead. Funny you ask me about my feelings. We didn't think we were important enough to have feelings."[33]

Hundreds of women were arrested under the *Female Refuges Act* during the decades that it was in force. The peak of the prosecutions came during the 1930s and with the onset of the Second World War. Like Velma, most of the women were young, Canadian-born, and working-class. Few had finished high school. Almost half had an illegitimate child or were pregnant when they appeared in court. Although most were imprisoned on the flimsiest of evidence, their "incorrigibility" appears to have been constructed from extramarital sexual activity and illegitimate pregnancies. There was no equivalent statute governing the behaviour of heterosexual young men: the law was gender-specific.[34] Many of the women who ran afoul of the Act were involved in inter-racial relationships with Asian, Black, and Aboriginal men.[35] Although there were no laws against "miscegenation" in Canada, several provinces had passed legislation making it a crime for Asian men to hire white women, and there were many extra-legal pressures brought against inter-racial couples.[36] In keeping with the long-standing Canadian pretension to racial neutrality, the law did not articulate on its face that inter-racial sexual relationships constituted "incorrigibility."[37] But the criminal justice authorities knew precisely what they were about when they arrested and locked up white women who were crossing the colour bar.

From the earliest days of its enactment, the *Female Refuges Act* had also been used to detain women who had contracted venereal disease. By the time of Velma's admission, medical practitioners were required to screen all inmates within three days of admission, and every six months thereafter. If found to be infected, women could be held well beyond their term of detention, until certified healthy.[38] A sister statute passed in 1918, *An Act for the Prevention of Venereal Disease,* allowed medical authorities to inspect anyone committed to a prison, or merely charged with an offence. If individuals were diagnosed with venereal disease, the statute authorized their forced treatment and continuing detention.[39]

"Unbelievable Pain": Inmates at the Mercy of Dr. Guest

VELMA WAS SUMMONED BACK to Dr. Guest's clinic again on 4 July and 11 August, and subjected to additional internal examinations long before the statutory six-month interval had passed. Again, the serological tests for venereal disease came back negative. But by mid-August, she began to experience vaginal burning and itching. On 21 August, she returned to the clinic and mounted the examining table with trepidation, too intimidated to describe her symptoms or ask any questions. She simply spread her legs and waited for the doctor to examine her. Dr. Guest was not inclined to make small talk. She made only one curt comment: "I see you have warts."[40]

The condition would be diagnosed today as "human papilloma virus," a sexually transmitted infection that causes genital warts. It is not uncommon for genital warts to increase considerably in size during pregnancy, and then to diminish or disappear entirely thereafter. It is also the case that such warts often clear up without any medical intervention.[41] At the time, Dr. Guest diagnosed the condition on Velma's medical chart as "gono warts."[42] Although the medical literature of the time expressed uncertainty, Dr. Guest believed that warts were caused by gonorrhea. She had encountered the infection in many Mercer inmates, a number of whom had previously had gonorrhea

Collection of Miss Margaret Robins, Archives of Women's College Hospital

Dr. Edna Mary Guest, 1928

but seemed cured, and then manifested genital warts. It is now generally accepted that although patients with human papilloma virus frequently suffer from other sexually transmitted diseases, there is no causal connection.[43] It is also now known that the length of time between sexual exposure and symptoms varies between three and six months or longer, suggesting that Velma had caught the infection prior to her detention. However, in Dr. Guest's era, doctors were unaware of the lengthy latency period. Thinking that the incarcerated inmates could not have been infected by intercourse, Dr. Guest erroneously surmised that the cause must be masturbation. As a fervent proponent of moral hygiene, she would undoubtedly have found the very thought reprehensible.[44]

Dr. Guest turned to a metal box beside the table, and removed a pair of scissors from a steamer. Seconds later, Velma experienced an excruciating pain. There was a moment of respite and the pain recurred with even greater intensity. Then she was brusquely ordered down from the table. The notes Dr. Guest made on Velma's medical file that day read: "Numerous gono warts clipped from inside labia minora. Clinically G.C. Metaphen to cer." She had snipped the genital warts with surgical scissors without any anesthetic, although the use of anesthesia for such procedures was customary medical practice at the time.[45] She had applied metaphen, a burning liquid, to the cervix. And she had diagnosed the young woman as "clinically gonococcus." All of Velma's previous tests for venereal disease — Kahn tests, Hinton tests, smears, and serological reports — had come back negative. Dr. Guest made a clinical diagnosis of gonorrhea regardless.[46]

When she hobbled out of the clinic, Velma was led to a solitary isolation cell with an iron-barred window. There was a thick layer of dust over the iron bedstead and coiled bedspring. Walking would be almost impossible for three days. She was seven months pregnant. For the next week, the only contact Velma had with another human being was the matron who delivered her meals. On 28 August 1939, she was briefly released from the isolation cell to return to the medical clinic, where the painful treatment was repeated. Dr. Guest clipped more warts, and then swabbed silver nitrate over the wounds. There seemed to be no end to the scissoring, chemical burning, and agony, which continued each day Dr. Guest's schedule brought her to the Mercer: 11 September, 18 September, 25 September, 29 September, 2 October, 11 October, and 16 October. A woman of few words, Dr. Guest only once looked up from her notes to declare, "This is the worst case of gonorrhea warts I've ever come across!"[47]

The first month of treatment was spent in solitary confinement, where the only other inmate Velma ever saw was fifteen-year-old Helga, a pregnant inmate with a hearing defect. When their paths crossed at the medical clinic some days later, Velma discovered that Helga was also being treated for genital warts. Lying awake in her cell at night, Velma was tortured by the thought that she, the expectant mother of a mixed-race baby, and Helga, a pregnant woman with a physical disability, had been singled out for the abusive treatment.[48]

Next, drugs were added to the regimen. "Sulfanilamide," the "wonder drug" that had been introduced in 1937 on a trial basis in some of the provincial venereal disease clinics despite its deadly side effects, was one.[49] The other was "Dagenan," an experimental and highly toxic sulfanilamide derivative introduced as a treatment for gonorrhea in 1939. The drug trial did not go smoothly. Dr. Guest noted on Velma's medical record that Dagenan did not cause any "blueness of lips or other reaction" on 25 September, but by the 29th, her patient was experiencing "drowsiness." She continued varying doses of Dagenan, interspersed with multiple doses of sulfanilamide. By 4 October, Velma was definitely worse. Her medical chart shows her "sick to her stomach," "dizzy," "jumpy," "nervy," sleeping "poorly," and looking "pale." Dr. Guest seems to have chalked this up to the fact that her patient was "nine months pregnant," which she noted on the record. Ultimately, she dismissed Velma as "not a good subject," and discontinued the Dagenan.[50] The drug trials were in disregard of the medical literature of the time, much of which advised against the administration of sulfanilamide to pregnant women.[51] Conventional medical wisdom also insisted that patients receiving these drugs be monitored daily or every forty-eight hours by a physician, a regimen that could not be maintained at the Mercer where Dr. Guest came to the clinic on an irregular schedule.[52]

On 16 October 1939, the day Velma went into labour, Dr. Guest packed the pregnant woman's vagina with cotton saturated with a cauterizing chemical, and left her on the examining table, feet entwined in the steel stirrups, in such pain that she felt as if her "entire body had caught fire," for more than an hour. With the onset of contractions later that night, Velma was transported to the Burnside Hospital, where her labour lasted seventeen hours.[53] In retrospect, Velma is convinced that Dr. Guest's motivations were malevolent:

> I'm positive she was conducting experiments. She [may have felt] justified in her experiment because [she thought my] baby was going to be feeble-

minded anyway, defective. Was her main objective to kill the baby all along? This really plagues me. I still don't know the answer and [Dr. Guest is] dead. She may have been afraid that if I got to the hospital, if the baby was born, that it would have something wrong with it and she'd be open to question. Maybe that's why she wanted to do it in. Or, on the other hand, she may just have been plain racist and had to make sure that baby died.[54]

Velma's baby did not die, but almost immediately after his birth, little Harry Demerson developed severe eczema, a condition that was serious enough to require lengthy hospitalization during infancy, and would plague him, along with debilitating asthma, into adult life. Velma later concluded that he suffered from an uncommon blood condition called methemoglobinemia, linked to sulfanilamide.[55]

The night before she was due to be returned to the Mercer to serve the remainder of her term, Velma escaped from the hospital. She hitchhiked to her mother's home, where she begged not to be returned to the clutches of Dr. Guest. She blurted out the horrendous details of the genital cutting, swabbing and burning, the side effects of the drugs. But Alice Demerson, who seems not to have known what else to do, sent Velma back to the Mercer. Locked in detention because of her attempted escape, Velma took a dinner fork and stabbed it into her upper body, working it deeper and deeper into her flesh. Miss Milne, the Mercer superintendent, sat for several hours with the distraught young woman, rubbing iodine into the wound. Velma sobbed as she tried to explain that she could not withstand any further medical attention from Dr. Guest. The memory of the scissors dominated the discussion. Miss Milne promised Velma that she would have one month to recover from the birth before the venereal treatments would continue.[56]

Although Superintendent Milne did not question Dr. Guest's medical techniques, she seems to have recognized that the treatment was painful. She wrote to the Deputy Provincial Secretary of the Reformatories and Prisons Branch, arguing that Velma's term of detention should not be increased because of her attempted escape:

> Velma Demerson was admitted to this Institution on June 28th . . . and, before being sent to hospital for the birth of her child, it was necessary from the time of her admission here to give her intensive and quite painful treatment for a social disease. In talking with her on her return yesterday, I found that it was fear of this medical treatment being continued that had made her run away. I was able to reassure her that there would not be any immediate treatment,

Courtesy of Velma Demerson

Velma Demerson, age 33

and today Dr. Edna Guest reported that no further treatment of the rather severe kind would be required, in the meantime at any rate.

The Deputy agreed that no punishment should be imposed.[57]

The month's dispensation did not apply to the drug treatment. Dr. Guest resumed the administration of sulfanilamide and Dagenan on 29 October 1939, Velma's first day back, ignoring the fact that Velma was now nursing her baby. The infant's "dark and tawny" complexion inspired Dr. Guest to remark that Harry was "not quite an English baby," rekindling Velma's fears that the doctor's racism was animating her medical decisions. The eczema that had appeared shortly after birth worsened to the point that the baby had to be transferred to the Hospital for Sick Children on 3 February 1940.[58]

Next, Velma became a participant in a new experimental drug trial. She was invited into Dr. Guest's office, and asked if she would agree to take some "white pills." She was not told the name of the drug, only that it would "make her better." This was the only time that Velma was asked to consent to medical treatment, and it was the first time that Dr. Guest's interactions with her young patient were pleasant and polite. The departure from the ordinary protocol caused Velma some anxious moments. "Why is the doctor asking me? Why am I not being told what to do?" she wondered. Despite her uncertainty, the young patient agreed to cooperate. "To refuse would be unthinkable," she noted in retrospect. "Besides how dare I say no." For three days, Velma was met by a matron outside the dining room after each meal, who watched as she downed the prescribed pills. Extreme nausea and dizziness ensued. When Superintendent Milne remarked on Velma's inability to finish a meal without bolting for the toilet to vomit, she was sent back to see Dr. Guest. The experiment was cut short, and Dr. Guest's brief period of affability halted equally abruptly.[59]

Most of the medical treatment remained seared into Velma's memory. However, some treatments were so unbearable that her conscious mind appears to have blotted them out for decades. It was not until the mid-1990s that a flashback brought back the most harrowing treatment of all. As the memories came flooding back, Velma remembered being stretched out on Dr. Guest's examining table, and feeling a sharp and "unbelievable pain," unlike anything she had ever known before. Reliving the incident, Velma recalled with horror that Dr. Guest had used a hypodermic needle to inject her clitoris, and then swabbed a burning liquid over the whole area.[60]

Velma's clear memory is that the injection was done more than once, always without anesthetic. The medical records confirm one instance in early December, and indicate that novocaine was administered as well. This does not accord with Velma's recollection that the injections were done repeatedly, both before and after childbirth. And it is Velma's recollection that an anesthetic was used only once, the first time she reappeared on Dr. Guest's examining table after the month's respite following the birth. The written records indicate that silver nitrate was again applied externally on 11 December, four times in January 1940, and one final time in February. Dr. Guest left her post at the Mercer around this time, and was replaced by another physician. Velma was not required to undergo any further treatment.[61]

Velma Demerson was discharged from the Mercer on 1 March 1940. She was given time off for good behaviour despite her botched escape, and another month was knocked off her term as a celebratory gesture to honour the royal visit to Toronto. She rejoined Harry Yip and the two were married by a Chinese Protestant minister on 21 June 1940.[62] The couple successfully reclaimed their son from the hospital, but life as an impoverished mixed-race family in a racist city was not easy. Harry worked long, tiring shifts in the restaurant. Velma found herself shunned and the object of scandalized and prurient attention from white neighbours, storekeepers, and passersby when she ventured out with her son. The baby's eczema worsened, and his abscesses, infections, asthma, and multiple allergies necessitated extensive further hospitalization. In 1942, Velma and Harry Yip separated. As a consequence of the baby's continuing physical ailments and the parents' financial stress, little Harry became a permanent ward of the Children's Aid Society in 1953. Velma lost contact with her estranged husband, and made a new life for herself in Vancouver. Little else is known about Harry Sr., except that he unsuccessfully contested the Children's Aid application for permanent wardship, with the aid of his lawyer cousin, Kew Dock Yip. Velma speculates that the failure of the marriage and the loss of custody of his son left him "humiliated" and "completely beaten down." Their son Harry died in an accidental drowning in 1966.[63]

The Question of (Il)legality

VELMA DEMERSON FIRMLY BELIEVES that the gynecological treatment Dr. Guest administered to her constituted a form of non-consensual sexual assault. Thinking back upon the invasive procedures, she finds uncanny parallels between the rape she suffered from the chemist and Dr. Guest's ministrations:

> It's the helplessness, of course. The chemist was physically stronger in the car, but Dr. Guest had so much power over me. I was incarcerated. She left me in solitary confinement for a month. I couldn't stop the chemist. And I couldn't say to Dr. Guest, "Stop." I had no right to say, "Don't inject, don't cut these warts." When you think about how I got raped in the car . . . I never told anybody. There's a parallel with Dr. Guest, I guess. I didn't have a right to complain about the doctor. People accept that the doctor has the right to inflict that pain. In terms of pain, the medical treatment hurt much more than the sexual assault by the chemist. And Dr. Guest was different from the chemist because her medical treatment was repetitive. The chemist only did it once.[64]

A poem that Velma Demerson wrote many years after her release from the Mercer begins and ends with the phrases "Save me! Save me from the state! I've never known such hate!"[65] The concept of "state sexual assault" is a characterization also used by other prisoners, who argue that the intrusive internal examinations and strip-searches that prisoners undergo repeatedly

Harry Yip, Jr., in Cub Scout uniform

Left: Harry Yip, Jr., Age 5

All photos on this page courtesy of Velma Demerson

Right: Harry Yip, Jr., age 23, died age 26.

in penal institutions constitute forcible sexual assaults. They object that penal authorities are vested with the power to carry out acts which, if done outside working hours without the uniform, would be defined as sexual assault. They argue that the state, which purports to abhor sexual assault, administers its own sexual assault as a means of institutional control.[66]

Efforts to attack such practices through legal challenge have proven problematic. At age eighteen, imprisoned in the Mercer Reformatory without the support of family or friends, there was simply no opportunity for Velma Demerson to attempt to convince the courts of what she knew in her heart. Even if she had tried, it is unlikely that any judge or jury at the time would have construed Dr. Guest's actions criminally as an "indecent assault." Although it is difficult to reconstruct Dr. Guest's mental perspectives from the available evidence, it seems improbable that a court would have characterized her treatment of Velma Demerson as "sexual" in motivation or substance.[67]

It took Velma Demerson more than sixty years to try to frame her interpretations legally. In the spring of 2002, she hired a lawyer and brought a civil action against the Ontario government, seeking both an apology and financial compensation. The claim was broadly drafted to encompass wrongful confinement for the entire term at the Mercer; Dr. Guest's medical treatments were included as part of the wider injury.[68] The decision to shift the focus to civil law was an interesting turn. Civil actions differ from criminal prosecutions in several ways. First, the lawsuit is initiated and controlled by the injured person, rather than the state. Instead of a passive role as the Crown witness in a criminal trial, the plaintiff in a civil suit is a full and active participant in the action. Second, the standard of proof is the "balance of probabilities" rather than the more difficult criminal burden "beyond a reasonable doubt." Third, the result of a successful suit is typically an order for the party who caused the injury to make financial redress to the victim. The court is asked to consider the damages suffered by the victim, and to attempt to put her back into the position she would have been before the civil wrong, insofar as money can do. It is a considerably more positive outcome than the punitive incarceration of the accused under criminal law.

Would a civil lawsuit have held any prospects of success in 1940, if Velma had been able to pursue her claim then? The effort to seek compensation through civil "tort" for sexual "battery," although less frequent than criminal prosecution for rape, was not unprecedented historically. In 1904, a wife who was joined by her husband in the suit, claimed damages against another man for attempting to rape and indecently assault her. A civil jury in

Peterborough scrutinized the plaintiff's conduct, found her testimony that she had not consented to be credible, and awarded damages.[69] In 1945, the father of a twelve-year-old girl brought a civil action on behalf of himself and his daughter, against a man who had indecently assaulted her when she was delivering milk. Despite the defendant's acquittal in criminal court, the Alberta judge cited the lower standard of proof in civil actions, and found the defendant liable on the same facts, awarding the child $1000 in damages, and the father $100 and costs.[70] In 1950, a judge in Lauzon, Quebec, awarded damages under the Quebec *Civil Code* to a father whose child had been indecently assaulted by the male defendant. This time it was only the parent who claimed compensation, and he was awarded $300 based on the damage to the family's reputation, and the fact that the public humiliation had forced him to remove his child from public school and seek private tutoring.[71] In 1957, a father, mother, and daughter brought a tort action for "intentional assault and battery," claiming damages against the man who had raped the five-year-old daughter. The defendant, who was in prison for the rape, did not defend the action. The Manitoba judge awarded $2000 to the child, and $133 to the father for his daughter's hospital bills.[72] In 1969, a fifty-one-year-old widow brought an action for assault and battery against a married male friend who had forcibly sought to have sexual relations with her, and beat her quite severely when she resisted. The Ontario court awarded her $1500 and costs.[73] In 1975, a Quebec court ordered a group of men to pay $2400 to an epileptic woman they had raped in a motel.[74]

Few of the civil cases during this era were launched by the sexual assault victim alone, and the number of husbands and parents who joined the action as co-plaintiffs suggests that their presence may have offered necessary weight and credibility. Velma would have been at a disadvantage here, for it seems unlikely she would have been able to call upon the support of Alice or Alexander Demerson. Furthermore, it appears that in many of these civil lawsuits, the defendants did not dispute that the sexual assault had occurred, whether because they were in prison or otherwise impecunious and unable to appear at trial. It seems most unlikely that Dr. Guest or the penal authorities at the Mercer would have sat back and let an action against them go undefended. They would have insisted that Dr. Guest's medical procedures could not be equated with the types of sexual assault that gave rise to damages in these civil actions.[75]

Equally problematic would have been the requirement to prove that the gynecological procedures took place without "consent." Velma Demerson

Courtesy of Velma Demerson

Velma Demerson, circa 2004

undoubtedly understood the medical treatment to be administered under coercive duress, without her consent. At law, however, the question was considerably more complicated. It is true that for any consent to be valid, it needed to be informed and freely given, without duress,[76] and where medical treatment was experimental, the standards of disclosure and voluntariness were scrutinized more critically.[77] However, in the early twentieth century, the law had barely begun to conceptualize the disclosure expected of physicians. Doctors were viewed as authority figures who operated with paternalistic benevolence and ought not to be intricately supervised by law.[78] The defence would also have argued that Velma had no capacity to withhold her consent, because she was still a "minor" under the age of majority, and with her detention in a penal facility, her "guardianship" had been transferred to the superintendent of the Mercer.[79] Furthermore, the *Act for the Prevention of Venereal Disease* authorized medical authorities to treat individuals diagnosed with venereal disease, with or without their consent.[80] Once Dr. Guest had diagnosed Velma's genital warts as "gono warts," they clinically fell within the conditions classified as "gonorrhea" and gave the Mercer physician complete licence to force Velma to undergo treatment.[81]

Velma Demerson's attempts to challenge her confinement and treatment sixty years later have taken place within a quite different cultural, social, and legal context. Her efforts to have the defunct *Female Refuges Act* declared unconstitutional, and an apology issued to all of the women imprisoned under it, faced an uphill battle given the passage of time and sweeping nature of the claim. What the courts would ultimately have ruled is unknown, because the case did not reach trial. However, she did obtain a public apology from the Ontario government in January 2003, and a substantial payment of damages in May 2004, in consideration for the withdrawal of further legal claims. The government insisted, as part of the settlement, that the amount of compensation not be publicly disclosed. Velma's own assessment was that after several years of protracted and difficult negotiations, she got "the most possible" she could. The eighty-one-year-old advocate for social justice has begun to speak in public about her case, hoping to encourage others who experienced similar abuse to come forward. She receives standing ovations wherever she speaks.[82]

⊳ Chapter 6 ⊲

SEXUAL ASSAULT AND
DISABILITY: Saskatchewan, 1942

BEATRICE IRENE TISDALE WAS born in 1918 on the family homestead near Torquay, thirty-seven miles west of Estevan, Saskatchewan, the fourth in a family of seven children.[1] In 1920, her father's ill health forced the family to give up the farm and move to Midale, midway between Estevan and Weyburn. They bought the former dentist's house at 219 Main Street, where the family would reside into the next generation. Beatrice's father worked on neighbouring farms when his health permitted, until his death in 1933. Beatrice's mother, famous for her cooking, earned some income by baking "mounds of loaves" for the many bachelors who homesteaded in the area. She also did domestic work in other Midale homes, and laboured in the "cook cars," to meet the voracious appetites of the threshing crews that travelled from farm to farm for the annual harvests. Somehow, with the help of the children, the family eked out a living.[2]

Midale, where Beatrice spent the early years of her childhood, was in the southeast corner of Saskatchewan. It was a typical Prairie town, with three grain elevators and fewer than two hundred inhabitants, where the farmers tended cattle and sowed unpredictable crops of wheat, oats, barley, and rye. The first white homesteaders in Midale had arrived in 1903, taking up farms along the Soo Line of the Canadian Pacific Railway that connected Moose Jaw with Minneapolis, Minnesota. The area was hard-hit during the Depression of the 1930s and with severe drought in 1934. That year the besieged rural municipality dealt with 273 applications for relief in a seven-day period. The winter of 1935–36 was the coldest on record. One year later, in July 1937,

From *Plowshares to Pumpjacks: R.M. of Cymri: Macou, Midale, Halbrite*(Midale: R.M. of Cymri History Book Society, 1984) at 547.

Bertha and Henry Tisdale (Beatrice's parents) with her older siblings (left to right)
Leona, Mabel, and Howard

Atlas of Canada, atlas.gc.ca 2005 — produced under licence from Her Majesty the Queen in Right of Canada, with permission of Natural Resources Canada

Map of the Prairies

From *Plowshares to Pumpjacks: R.M. of Cymri: Macou, Midale, Halbrite* (Midale: R.M. of Cymri History Book Society, 1984) at 94.

Farmers at threshing time

From *Plowshares to Pumpjacks: R.M. of Cymri: Macou, Midale, Halbrite* (Midale: R.M. of Cymri History Book Society, 1984) at 608.

Fair time at Midale

Midale's thermometers reached 113 degrees Fahrenheit, tying with Yellow-grass, Saskatchewan, for the hottest temperature ever recorded in Canada.[3]

A Deaf Childhood

BEATRICE TISDALE'S CHILDHOOD WAS a little different from that of her six sib-lings during these tough times, in that she was one of many children across Canada who grew up deaf.[4] In the absence of a Saskatchewan school for the deaf, Beatrice's family sent her on a three-day journey by train to Montréal, to board at the Mackay Centre for Protestant Deaf Children, probably at the age of eight in 1926. Families were asked to pay tuition as well as transpor-tation costs, but the Tisdales were likely among the 25 percent of Saskatch-ewan families who needed public assistance to cover the costs. The sadness that must have welled up at the prospect of leaving parents, brothers, and sisters from September to June may have been offset, in part, by the excite-ment and anticipation of moving to a residential school with a community of deaf children who could learn to communicate with each other.[5]

Beatrice's first sight of the Mackay school, where she would study for the next five years, must have been both inspiring and intimidating. Construct-ed in 1878 on the Décarie Road property of Montréal philanthropist Joseph Mackay, the school was a beautiful Gothic structure with towering turrets. It must have seemed like a fairytale castle to the newly arrived, small-town, Prairie pupils. Residential school would offer Beatrice her first opportu-nity for sustained contact with peers. Deaf children who had deaf parents shared their language and culture with those who came from hearing fami-lies, and the schools emerged as the "nucleus" of what would become a rich cultural and educational heritage of the "capital-D Deaf."[6] Deaf advocates have long taken the position that capital-D Deaf people do not have a "dis-ability" but belong instead to a "cultural minority." Their language, *Sign*, is capitalized in common with other recognized languages. Deaf communi-cators describe Sign as worlds apart from written languages, and explain that trying to write Sign would be an "effort to transcribe in two dimen-sions a language whose syntax uses the three dimensions of space as well as time."[7] The elusiveness of capturing the beauty of Sign through written accounts is vividly brought home by one commentator, describing the ani-mated conversation between two Deaf signers in the 1830s, as "a thousand changing motions through which every thought of the mind flashes and disappears."[8]

Courtesy of the Mackay Centre for Deaf Children (Montreal, Québec)

Exterior of the Mackay Institution for Protestant Deaf Children, 1950s

Courtesy of the Mackay Centre for Deaf Children (Montreal, Québec)

Staff and students on the front steps of the Mackay Institution, 1893

Saskatchewan School for the Deaf, 1930s

Yet the development of Deaf culture and Sign had a troubled history, even in the residential schools. The Mackay Centre, like all schools for the deaf, had experienced serious internal struggles over methods of instruction. "Manualism" — teaching students by sign language — favoured the development of a sophisticated Deaf culture, and seems to have been preferred by most of the students and Deaf advocates. "Oralism" — teaching students by lip-reading and speech training — was the choice of many hearing parents and teachers, who hoped that it would enable greater integration with the hearing world. Deaf advocates complained that oralism reduced students' communication skills, by demanding that they achieve a level of speech that few could master, while the more culturally appropriate Sign education languished, leaving students with low levels of literacy and an impoverished vocabulary. By the time that Beatrice arrived at the Mackay school, although oralism was in the ascendancy, some vestiges of manualism remained and a rudimentary sign language using "natural signs" and the "double-handed alphabet" was still being taught.[9]

In 1931, thirteen-year-old Beatrice was able to return to her home province, when the Saskatchewan School for the Deaf opened in Saskatoon. The school was the product of unremitting lobbying efforts by the Deaf educator R.J.D. Williams, who would serve as its chief supervisor of resident students for more than thirty years. Williams advocated a combined system of manualism and oralism, as well as the employment of Deaf teachers. His position was bolstered by the new principal, Edwin Gallaudet Peterson, who would preside over the school for the next seven years of Beatrice's residence.

Peterson was the hearing son of two Deaf parents, and had grown up next to the Minnesota School for the Deaf, where his parents taught. Between the two men, for nearly a decade they managed to buck the trend towards oralism that was sweeping through most of the schools for the deaf in the 1930s.[10]

When Beatrice arrived on 22 September 1931, she joined a class of sixty-five boys and fifty-three other girls, all between the ages of six and eighteen, some of whom she would already have known from Mackay. Of the fourteen staff members, 25 percent of the teachers and 33 percent of the residential staff were Deaf. Beatrice was taught the one-hand manual alphabet often called "finger spelling" and writing, primarily by Deaf teachers, and she must have communicated primarily by signing

From Carolyn Beally, *et al.*, *The First Fifty Years, 1935–1982: R.J.D. Williams Provincial School for the Deaf* (Saskatoon, Prairie Graphics, 1983) at 77.

Beatrice Tisdale (middle row, far right) and her class at the Saskatchewan School for the Deaf

both in and out of class. The boys were instructed in printing, bookbinding, etching, tailoring, shoe repair, and carpentry. The girls were taught domestic science, advanced laundry work, and home nursing. Boy Scout and Girl Guide troops, dramatic theatre productions, concerts, lessons in dance and calisthenics, publication of a school newspaper, and a host of sporting teams rounded out the extracurricular events. Although schools for the deaf often went to "extraordinary lengths to prevent boy-girl social relations," parties and dances were occasionally organized for the students at the Saskatchewan school.[11] Institutional schools for children, as Canadians have come to know painfully well, often breed conditions where emotional, physical, and

Anderson Café, 215
Railway Avenue, Weyburn,
Saskatchewan, c. 1940s

Courtesy of the Soo Line Historical Museum, Weyburn

sexual abuse flourish. Schools for the deaf were no exceptions in this regard, although there is no evidence that Beatrice experienced abuse of any kind while at school.[12]

Employment after Graduation and the Circumstances of the Sexual Assault

UPON HER GRADUATION FROM grade 9 in 1937, nineteen-year-old Beatrice Tisdale probably returned to help her mother in Midale. The Depression was in full tilt and jobs were scarce.[13] It was not until the Second World War broke out in 1939, and women workers came into greater demand, that opportunities improved. Some of the top Saskatchewan graduates, such as Maureen Mitchell Donald, who had given the valedictorian address for Beatrice's class, obtained teaching positions at other schools for the deaf. Other deaf women who graduated in the same era took jobs in bakeries, hairdressing salons, seamstress shops, the laundry departments of hospitals, the federal civil service, libraries, photography shops, book binderies, and typewriting and mimeographic offices.[14]

In January 1942, at the age of twenty-four, Beatrice moved by train to nearby Weyburn, to take a job as a chambermaid at the Anderson Café, a hotel and restaurant operated by Blair and Minnie Louise Weismiller at 215 Railway Avenue. Minnie Louise had grown up in Midale. Business was brisk at the café, with all of the rooms full most of the time, a result of the growing economy of the early 1940s and the presence of Royal Air Force personnel stationed for training at the Weyburn Airport. Although Beatrice's wages would have been low, she did have the advantage of room and board at the hotel. She worked a nine-hour shift, seven days a week, except for Saturday, when she put in an even longer split-shift from 7 a.m. to 4 p.m., and 8 p.m.

Courtesy of the Soo Line Historical Museum, Weyburn

Leader Department Store, Weyburn, Saskatchewan, c. 1940s

to 11 p.m. The monotonous work involved making beds, dusting floors, and cleaning out the rooms.[15]

Beatrice's social life outside of work consisted of visiting another former Midale resident, Carol Peterson, who had moved to a farm on the outskirts of Weyburn when she married Joseph Probe two years earlier. Carol and Beatrice had both attended the First Baptist Church in Midale, and they would have joined the Calvary Baptist Church in Weyburn, where the visionary Rev. Tommy Douglas was the pastor.[16] Joe Probe, the youngest son of Hungarian immigrants, had been born in 1914 on the family farm near Weyburn, and he and his siblings continued to farm in the district after they married. Carol and Joe Probe had just had their first child, Richard, in March, and they occasionally invited Beatrice for dinner, or to babysit when they wanted to go out dancing or to parties. Joe, who owned a Pontiac sedan, would transport Beatrice to and from the Anderson Café and the farm.[17]

On Saturday afternoon, 22 August, Beatrice got off work early, around 2 p.m. She went shopping at the Leader Department Store, and as she left she saw Joe Probe waving to her from his car. He asked if she could come up to his house to look after the baby. Beatrice lip-read Joe's question and nodded her assent. She got into the car, but instead of driving home, Joe headed out to the countryside. While he drove, he uncapped two bottles of beer and offered one to Beatrice. She told him she wanted to get out of the car, but he kept driving, and finished his beer, and then her beer as well. Several miles south of Weyburn, according to Beatrice, Joe Probe stopped the Pontiac and forced her to have sexual intercourse in his car. He then drove on a bit further, and forced her to have intercourse again on a blanket outside of the car. Before he returned Beatrice to Weyburn, he had intercourse with her a third time in the sedan.[18]

Joe let Beatrice out near the CPR station around 5:30 p.m., and she walked back to the Anderson Café. Tearful and shaking, she went upstairs briefly to clean herself, and then came down to the parlour, where she wrote a note to one of the waitresses asking if she could speak with Mrs. Weismiller. The waitress passed the note on, and Mrs. Weismiller returned from the front of the café to the parlour. Still in tears, Beatrice told her — through a mixture of spoken words, gestures, and written notes — what had happened, and showed her employer the red, swollen marks and bruises on her neck, wrists, hip, and leg. Mrs. Weismiller called the police, and Beatrice was taken for medical examination that evening to Dr. Harry Aaron Brookler's office, and later Sunday morning to Dr. James E. McGillivray's office. Joe Probe was arrested and charged that day. Granted bail on Monday, 24 August 1942, the accused man appeared at the preliminary inquiry in Regina on 31 August, where he was bound over for trial in Weyburn.[19]

The Courtroom Challenges of a Deaf Witness

IT WOULD BE SOMETHING of an understatement to note that Beatrice Tisdale's ability to give evidence in the courtroom was seriously disrupted because

From Carolyn Beally, et al., *The First Fifty Years, 1935–1982: R.J.D. Williams Provincial School for the Deaf* (Saskatoon, Prairie Graphics, 1983) at 18.

Staff of the Saskatchewan School for the Deaf, Saskatoon, June 1941.
Miss Molland, Beatrice's teacher and court interpreter, shown in the third row,
sixth from the left, in the white dress with puff sleeves

of the legal failure to accommodate her deafness. Crown attorney Donald James Mitchell seems to have had little or no appreciation of the needs of his key witness.[20] In his opening address, he introduced Beatrice Tisdale to the court as "a deaf mute" who had obtained her education at "deaf and dumb schools." Both terms "mute" and "dumb" had long since fallen into disfavour within the Deaf community and with those at all familiar with their lives. Most North American schools for deaf students had eliminated the word "dumb" before the First World War. "Mute" had never properly described deaf people, most of whom had nothing wrong with their voice apparatus, but simply chose not to use it.[21]

The *Saskatchewan Evidence Act* provided that a witness who was "unable to speak" could give evidence "in any other manner in which he can make it intelligible."[22] But there was no legislative requirement that deaf witnesses be afforded accurate interpretation.[23] Beatrice had had so much difficulty giving evidence in the earlier preliminary inquiry that written interrogatories and responses were substituted for oral testimony.[24] For the trial, Mary Ellen Molland, a young hearing woman who had been one of Beatrice's teachers at the Saskatoon school, was sworn in to interpret.[25] It is not fully clear from the transcript what means of communication Mary Molland and her former student used, although there is reference to some signing, bodily gestures, and speech. There is also no doubt whatsoever that the pace of the proceeding, the complexity of the questions, and the insensitivities of the legal personnel made it impossible for Beatrice Tisdale to give her testimony fairly and fully.

One of the first problems was Mary Molland's capacity as an interpreter. There were no courses, standards, or certification processes to qualify hearing persons as interpreters for the deaf.[26] Mary Molland taught the younger grades at the school, her specialty was oralism, and she probably had at best a marginal knowledge of Sign.[27] Even in the hands of experts, translating spoken language into precise Sign language is extremely complex. Simultaneous presentation of Sign and speech results in the deletion of significant portions of the spoken message. This is partly because there are many words for which there are no formal signs, and these must be fingerspelled, slowing the normal rhythm of communication. Sign language also has a limited vocabulary when it comes to verbs and tenses. Sign and English have such distinct grammar that it is not possible to speak one while signing the other without sounding incoherent in at least one version. Proper lighting is required to minimize glare and shadows that interfere with lip-reading and Sign. Visual background distractions, speakers who confuse signers by using their arms and body when speaking, distance from the speaker, and obtuse angles of view also impede communication.[28] The cut and thrust of the courtroom setting would have created even further difficulties. The interpretation process flounders when speakers ask a series of questions at once, when answers are detail-laden, when more than one person speaks at a time, and when speakers use long sentence constructions, sophisticated terminology, or legal words for which there may be no Sign equivalent. Legal language is challenging to understand at the best of times, as it often contains unusual prepositional phrases, metaphors, similes, and a degree of formality based on courtroom protocol that is rarely found in ordinary conversation.

Crown attorney Mitchell began by asking Beatrice Tisdale whether she could "speak or hear." Through the interpreter, she replied, "I can speak a little but can't hear." In answer to the question of how long this had been the case, the interpreter translated: "Since she was a baby." Deaf individuals who have been unable to hear from birth usually have difficulty learning how to articulate all of the different sounds, and modulating tone and volume in ways that mimic hearing people when they speak.[29] Beatrice Tisdale's efforts to speak in the courtroom that morning quickly became a topic of pejorative comment. She started by trying to explain, through the interpreter, how Joe Probe had physically forced her to have sexual intercourse. She was telling the court how she had resisted, that she had threatened that she would tell his wife and the police, and that she had said, "Shame on you." Trial judge H.V. Bigelow interrupted almost immediately to ask: "I don't understand how you told Probe all these things. Does Probe speak the deaf and dumb language?" Mary Molland replied: "He doesn't speak the deaf and dumb language, no."

The transcript records the next exchange:

Q. Well, how did you tell him these things then?
A. She spoke it.
Q. She spoke?
A. Yes.
Q. Well, let her speak now the same way as she spoke to Probe.
A. (Witness makes some guttural sounds.)
Q. If Probe could understand that, I can't. What was she trying to say there?
A. (Interpreter.) Shame on you.
Q. Repeat it again, please?
A. (Witness.) Shame on you.
Q. Oh yes. I understand it when we know what it is.

THE COURT: I think in the conversation she had with Probe she had better tell us just what she said to him, expressing herself in our language.

MR. MITCHELL: — The way that she tried to make herself . . .

THE COURT: Probe couldn't speak the deaf and dumb language.

MR. MITCHELL: No.

THE COURT: I would just like to know how it was communicated to him.

A. (Witness.) I want to go home.

MR. MITCHELL: Well, we will go on and anything she said from then on, have her give it as she gave it, you see?

INTERPRETER: Yes.

The court reporter's choice of the word "guttural" to describe Beatrice's speech seems particularly disparaging, a judgmental dismissal of the deaf woman's effort to communicate across languages. The judge's demand that

Saskatchewan Archives Board, R-B768

Weyburn, Saskatchewan, looking north east, 1937

Saskatchewan Archives Board, R-B128

Weyburn, Saskatchewan, grain elevators and railyards, date unknown

Beatrice should express herself "in our language" is a stark reminder of how dominant the hearing and speaking culture remained in the courtroom, and in the cars and fields outside of Weyburn, Saskatchewan. The court was consumed with the question of whether the deaf woman had properly communicated her rejection of a hearing man's sexual advances — "in our language" — in terms that Joe Probe had understood. No one seemed inclined to consider the equally important question of whether the hearing man had made any particular effort to inquire whether a deaf woman had really consented. The criminal law always dwelled on what the accused man thought. There was no exploration into what obligation the law should place upon a hearing man wishing to consummate consensual sex with a deaf woman. The question should have been "Did Beatrice Tisdale understand Joe Probe?" not just "Did Joe Probe understand Beatrice Tisdale?"[30] And although in both cases, Beatrice's words "Shame on you" and "I want to go home" were efforts to give voice to statements she had earlier made to Joe Probe, they leap out of the typed transcript as words that might just as well have been directed to the lawyers, judge, and jurors who surrounded her that day.

Crown attorney Mitchell appears to have been impatient with Beatrice when she was unable to spell the names of the police officers and physicians who had examined her. Defence counsel Murdoch Alexander MacPherson took issue with her inability to clarify in words the passage of time, the distinction between "main" or "side" roads, or precise distances travelled in miles. He scoffed at Beatrice, sarcastically observing: "Oh well now, she has taken grade nine in school, she has lived in this country all her life. Point this out to her." Interpretation floundered when words that Beatrice did not know, such as the "heater" in a car, popped up. Often this became obvious only later in the examination, long after the witness had been recorded as assenting to a question. She was repeatedly asked whether a radio was on — at the Probe farm, in the car — and whether she could hear it, in complete disregard of her deafness. Counsel made the same mistake with other witnesses, continually asking them what Beatrice had "told" or "said" to them, heedless of her reluctance to use speech.[31] Both counsel had an annoying habit of asking the same question twice, and repeating the previous answer before asking their next question. Their mannerisms of speech undoubtedly doubled Mary Molland and Beatrice Tisdale's problems. The interpreter also took some liberties with the translation, sometimes turning the question around so that something that should have generated a "yes" answer brought forth a "no" from the witness.[32]

The trial judge repeatedly expressed his concern at the slowness of the testimony, intervening at regular intervals to announce his increasing frustration. Over and over again, he admonished counsel to "shorten it up." He chided counsel for their apparent difficulties in making use of Beatrice's written notes from the preliminary inquiry. And throughout the trial, he demonstrated palpable disdain for the difficulties of a deaf woman attempting to testify, at one point complaining: "It takes long enough to get an answer out of this witness." Towards the end of Beatrice's evidence, the testimony had become so unravelled that the two lawyers and the judge halted the inquiry — which Crown attorney Mitchell denounced as "a garbled mess." They moved the proceeding into an evening meeting where the lawyers, Mary Molland, and Beatrice could try to "straighten it all out" and put "the record" in a way that it could be given "in some logical sequence" that would be "satisfactory to the court."

Being the only deaf person in the room must have made it particularly difficult for Beatrice. The presence of even one deaf juror would have required the proceeding to slow down, and would have necessitated a much fuller accommodation of her efforts to testify. But that would have been wishful thinking. Deaf persons were legislatively barred from serving as jurors, because deafness was thought to be "incompatible with the discharge of the duties of a juror."[33] Undeniably, deafness did complicate the giving and receipt of testimony. But the absence of Deaf jurors, lawyers, and judges privileged the hearing culture over Deaf culture, in ways that rebounded to the extreme detriment of members of the Deaf community who dared to enter the legal forum.

Courtroom Skirmishing over Evidence of Physical Force

FORTUNATELY, BEATRICE TISDALE WAS not the only witness for the prosecution; there were others who corroborated her evidence. Minnie Louise Weismiller testified that when she first set eyes on the young woman in the café that Saturday, Beatrice was hysterical and her hair was disheveled and hanging in strings. Mrs. Weismiller observed red marks and substantial bruising around her employee's wrists, neck, and hip area. The police officers testified that they too noticed the complainant's red marks and her distraught condition. Dr. James E. McGillivray testified that Beatrice had "multiple bruises on her body" over her chest, arms, wrists, hips, thighs, and shins, as well as red marks on her neck. The RCMP Crime Detection Laboratory had found semen and spermatozoa stains on Beatrice's coat and undergarments.

There was nothing in the language of the *Criminal Code* to stipulate that rape victims must be physically overwhelmed by their assailants. However, judges and juries were historically loath to convict without evidence of substantial force and spirited resistance. Even in cases with extensive bruising and torn clothes, courts could conclude that despite her initial resistance, a woman might "ultimately yield" to a man's advances.[34] Beatrice's testimony indicated that Joe had "grabbed her arm" and "twisted it behind her back and up against the door" of the car. She had fallen over the side of the seat, and he had ripped the tie off her coat while opening it up. He had pulled up her dress, "torn off her bloomers," "lain on top of her," and "opened up the front of his pants." In the words of the interpreter, Joe Probe then "intercoursed with her." Afterwards, she "slapped his face." Disregarding Beatrice's plea to be taken home, Joe drove down the highway and stopped again at the side of the road. He "grabbed her out of the car" and "took a blanket." He took his pants off and had another beer. Communicating through Mary Molland, Beatrice described the second and third rapes:

> He threw her down on the blanket and he started playing with her breasts and after that she shoved him away, when he started doing that she shoved him away, and then he started playing with her privates just like a dog. And then intercoursed. After that he took her back into the car and went to a small field. She thought she could run away then and from this small house to where people lived not very far, but she felt so very weak she didn't think she could run, so she stayed in the car.
>
> He heard the whistle and he said it was five o'clock and she said, "Take me home now," and she wanted her sleep before she started work again, and he said "What time do you start work?" and she said seven o'clock and then he moved over and intercoursed her again. Then he started the car back to town again.

Crown attorney Mitchell asked Beatrice about her injuries, and she indicated that she had been bruised on her left side, arms, shoulders, wrist, and knees. Finally, he produced Beatrice's coat as an exhibit to show that the tie was torn off.

Defence counsel Murdoch Alexander MacPherson next cross-examined Beatrice on what he clearly believed to be insufficient resistance on her part.[35] The difficulties faced by deaf witnesses were still further exacerbated on cross-examination, where defence lawyers typically try to put witnesses "off their centre," hoping to make them angry, get them to admit to certain facts, and appear confused. To do this, counsel often spring questions swiftly, demanding answers before witnesses have time to reflect. They want to be able to see the witness at all times, and object to the interference with their sight lines when the interpreter stands between them and their quarry, disrupting their efforts to "control the witness."[36]

MacPherson signalled his skepticism with his opening salvo: "And you slapped him once — that was all? Slapped him once. You didn't scratch him once?" He then turned to the timing of the slap, where there appeared to be some inconsistency in the evidence. MacPherson read from the handwritten notes Beatrice had provided at the preliminary: "But he held me so tight he tore my panties off and I told him I would tell Carol but he didn't seem to care for anything but do it to me. I slapped his face hard. He then put his organ in me." Beatrice and Mary Molland were at pains to stress that the key thing was that Beatrice had demonstrated her resistance, emphasizing: "She slapped his face." MacPherson retorted: "Yes, I know she did, but when was it? This woman who was protecting her virtue." Beatrice responded that she "slapped his face and then he intercoursed her." MacPherson jumped on what he perceived to be continuing inconsistency. How could Beatrice have slapped Joe if he was holding her hand behind her back? The exchange reveals the difficulties in interpretation:

Q. Well, how did she get that hand loose?
A. The hand was behind her back and she was struggling.
Q. Now she understands what that word "struggling" means; I am glad she mentioned that.
A. Pardon me, she didn't say struggling.
Q. Oh, she didn't?
A. She was going like that. (Indicating.)
Q. She didn't use the word?
A. No.
Q. Now I want to show her this from that examination and ask her if the stenographer got this wrong. 'Q. You slapped him before the first intercourse?' 'A. After.' Ask her that.
A. She said she slapped him before the first intercourse.
Q. Now I am asking you if she got that wrong at the other trial.
A. She says it is true that is wrong.
Q. Well, did the stenographer get it wrong? Did you say that at the other trial or is that a mistake?

MR. MITCHELL: — I think she is mixed up between what she wrote and —

MR. MacPHERSON: — Well, did she say it then? She can say yes or no to that. Did she say it?

THE COURT: — Can't she say yes or no to that?

A. No, she didn't say yes or no. She is really mixed up.[37]

MacPherson then suggested it was highly unlikely that any woman could be raped in the front seat of a car. "It was just an ordinary car, wasn't it. . . . Was it custom made for this purpose, do you suppose?" It was only after the interpreter replied that Beatrice had not understood what "custom made" meant, that he backed off.[38] Any concern he offered over Beatrice's communication difficulties was designed to undermine her. When she was trying to explain how she had lip-read what Joe had said to her in the car, he admonished: "But she was crying terribly; her eyes were full of tears. How could she see anything?" Beatrice did her best to answer: "She said he poked her in the arm and she looked to see what he wanted to say and he told her then." MacPherson belittled Beatrice's efforts to resist the advances, repeatedly asking her why she had not run off into the fields when Joe had her out on the blanket. Her reply, that "she was scared," that she "knew that he could get in the car and chase her," and that "she was weak," did little to satisfy him. "And for strength she went back to the blanket — is that right?" was his sarcastic retort. When Beatrice testified that she cried when she sat on the blanket, he replied: "She cried. Well, of course. What else did she do? Point out to her that she is a woman who is being outraged, a woman whose virtue is being taken from her, against her will." He made much of the fact that Dr. Harry Aaron Brooker, the first physician who had examined Beatrice after the alleged rape, had found her "private parts quite unbruised," with "no laceration, no tearing, no contusions, and no signs of violence."

The *Criminal Code* defined "rape" as "the act of a man having carnal knowledge of a woman . . . without her consent." It did not stipulate that the non-consensual sexual act had to occur by force and violence, or that the victim was required to fight back. This was a gloss that the lawyers, judges, and jurors had added to the straight-forward words of the legislation, that gave defence counsel more leeway to attack rape victims on the witness stand. It also made it substantially more difficult to obtain convictions in cases where the victim had not consented, but had not resisted up to the standard that the authorities expected she should have.[39]

Insinuations of Sexual Promiscuity

IN THEORY, SEXUALLY EXPERIENCED women were to be protected from rape as much as any other. In practice, defence lawyers insinuated that women who were not "chaste" could not be trusted when they testified they had been raped. The Supreme Court of Canada had ruled as early as 1877 that evidence of extramarital sexual relations was "manifestly calculated to affect the character, and as a consequence, the credibility of the prosecutrix in a case of rape."[40] A women's prior sexual history was also deemed relevant to the issue of consent. As the Nova Scotia Supreme Court pronounced in 1906, "a strumpet would more likely consent than a virgin."[41] The British Columbia Court of Appeal added that previous sexual acts with other men went to show "what kind of girl she was" and raised the question of whether she was telling the truth when she denied consent.[42] Stereotypical assumptions that divided women into "sexually pure" and "promiscuous" categories were manifestly unfair to non-virginal rape victims. Such thinking also betrayed peculiar conceptions about when and why women consent to sexual relations. Prior heterosexual experience might just as well convince some women to reject future sexual attention as to implicate them in further consensual activity. But the masculinist world-view held complete sway over the Weyburn courtroom that day, and there were no objections when defence counsel MacPherson asked Beatrice, twice, if she had had sexual intercourse before 22 August. "Never before," she responded.

Defence counsel were permitted to put such questions, and the complainant was entitled to deny sexual activity or to refuse to answer, which was supposed to be the end of the matter.[43] However, MacPherson went on to elicit further testimony from Carol Probe regarding a Corporal Roberts, who had accompanied Beatrice "two or three times" when she was babysitting at the Probe residence. Beatrice had earlier admitted to attending an "airport dance," where she had drunk a bottle of beer. Socializing with the air force personnel stationed in the city was not unusual. The community had set up a "hostess club" for visiting servicemen, and the women of Weyburn "catered monthly to the RAF 'Wings' graduation." Beatrice had two brothers serving in the war and was undoubtedly interested in others who had enlisted. She may also have been introduced to some of the air force men at the Anderson Café. But MacPherson would have known that attention shown by the air force trainees to the Weyburn women had stirred up some local jealousy. MacPherson's line of questioning meant to infer that Beatrice had a foreign boyfriend with

Murdoch Alexander
MacPherson, 1929

Saskatchewan Archives Board, R-A4994

whom she might have been sexually involved. Amplified with the mention of beer and an airport dance, his insinuation took firm root.[44]

The law also permitted counsel to put questions to Beatrice about previous sexual acts with the accused. Any denial was open to full rebuttal and contradiction. She testified that prior to 22 August there had been no sexual connection. MacPherson was unconvinced. He got Beatrice to admit that she had drunk beer with Carol and Joe Probe the first night she arrived to babysit. Further questioning revealed that Joe had danced with Beatrice that evening, to a tune on the radio in the kitchen. Even more damaging, MacPherson got Beatrice to admit that she had driven with Joe to the neighbouring town of Yellowgrass in April, that Joe had taken a room in a hotel there, and that she had stayed in his room for about an hour. Vainly did Beatrice try to explain that she had agreed to the drive because she thought

Joe wanted her to accompany him to pick up his wife in Yellowgrass, and that she thought she could trust him because he was "married to a friend of hers." She explained that Joe had left her alone for a long time in the freezing car when he went into the hotel alone. When he returned visibly drunk, he insisted she come into the hotel to warm up. Joe told the lady at the front desk that the car had frozen up and that they needed a room. He was so drunk that he vomited and then passed out on the bed. Beatrice eventually managed to wake him up, and they drove back home, slowed to a snail's pace by a broken car radiator. Beatrice insisted repeatedly that she had not had intercourse with Joe in the hotel room, that all he had done was to kiss her once on the cheek.

MacPherson also questioned Dr. Brookler, who testified that although Beatrice's hymen was torn, this did not appear to be "of recent origin." Dr. Brookler indicated that one would expect to find bruising, tearing, or blood in a virgin who had been forced sexually. MacPherson emphasized that there was none of this, concluding: "And is this not true also, that a woman who has been in the habit of sexual intercourse is much less subject to injury to her vaginal organs than one who is having that experience for the first time?" Dr. Brookler agreed. No one thought to comment on the physician's evidence in light of Beatrice's earlier testimony. When asked earlier whether Dr. Brookler had examined her, Beatrice had replied "not very well."

MacPherson wanted to paint Beatrice as a worldly young woman, and demanded that the interpreter translate a question: "She wasn't innocent to the point that she didn't know what the relationship between men and women was. She was quite acquainted with that. . . . She knew what the relations between men and women under those circumstances might be when they went to a room in a hotel alone. Does she understand that?" Mary Molland responded: "I am afraid not," and MacPherson seems finally to have sensed he should go no further. He replied: "Well, I won't press it." Mary Molland would have been aware that most of the young girls who graduated from her school had had no instruction in sex education and were woefully unaware of the nature and consequences of sexual activity.[45]

Joe Probe's Version

JOE PROBE TOOK THE stand to testify that he had had a flirtatious and consensual sexual relationship for several months with Beatrice Tisdale. It began, he told the court, the evening that Beatrice had come to his home to babysit.

Carol was still upstairs getting ready, and Joe "had a dance or two with her to the radio." Joe added that when his wife was out of the room, he had held Beatrice "a little closer." Beatrice had "laughed a little bit and laid her head against my head." Joe then ran his leg "up between hers," which suggested to him that he "might be able to take her out some time." After he and his wife returned from the party, he drove Beatrice home, but first parked the car by the snow fence and "made love" to her "for about half an hour or so." When MacPherson asked whether Beatrice had consented, Joe replied: "She did not write me a note and say: go ahead, diddle me — no." However, he insisted she had not "objected."

Joe Probe's lawyer repeatedly asked questions that assumed that Beatrice and Joe could communicate with each other through oral speech, and Joe rarely disabused him of the notion. Crown attorney Mitchell did little to correct the misapprehension. He asked once: "Did she always carry a pencil and paper with her?" Joe agreed, and the Crown followed up with: "Did she talk to you as well? Can you understand her?" "Yes, I can understand some things," was Joe's reply. With this answer, Mitchell took a leaf from MacPherson's book, and began himself to make reference to uninhibited spoken conversation back and forth between the two. Neither counsel nor the judge sought to explore whether Beatrice had understood Joe.

According to Joe, after the first act of intercourse by the snow fence, he and Beatrice met many times for sex. He told the arresting officer that he had "diddled" Beatrice "thirty or forty times." This was the number he cited when he confessed to his wife, in the company of a police officer, later that day. When he and his wife drove to Midale a few days later to speak with Mabel Tisdale, Beatrice's older sister, Joe had moved his estimate up to "forty or fifty times." At that meeting, according to Mabel, Joe demanded that she prevail upon Beatrice to drop the charges. "It will be her that suffers," he threatened Mabel, "not me, because everything will be brought out and her name will be just as black as mine in Weyburn." He had offered to pay Beatrice $500, so that she could "take a trip to Vancouver and forget it." He threatened to have Beatrice charged with perjury if she continued the prosecution.

On the stand, Joe reduced the number of times he had had consensual intercourse with Beatrice to eleven. He told the court they had had sex in his Pontiac on the side road going out to the airport, in the countryside on the way to Yellowgrass, in the hotel room at Yellowgrass, on the way home from Yellowgrass, in his own home when his wife was away at a Midale funeral,

Victory Loan Parade, Weyburn, Saskatchewan, 1941

and when Beatrice had accompanied him one afternoon to babysit while he swam in the dug-out on his farm. They "put the little fellow in the back and I took off my trunks and we had intercourse in the car," he told the court. Asked about the discrepancy between the count of eleven and the "thirty to forty" and "forty to fifty" times he had reported earlier, Joe conceded he might have exaggerated. Beatrice continued to deny all sexual activity except for the three rapes on 22 August.

It was Joe's contention that Beatrice had concocted the story of the rapes, because she had become suspicious that Joe was bragging about his sexual conquest. In this transcript extract, Joe and his lawyer move back and forth from reference to written notes to reference to speech. Both are too anxious to insinuate that Beatrice was intimate with another man, and to create a speculative motive for fabrication, to pay any attention to the potential for errors in comprehension between a young deaf woman and a man who has earlier admitted that he can understand only "some things" when Beatrice communicates with him:

A. She wrote and asked me if I had ever told anyone she was a tough girl, and I wrote or stated — I don't know which it was — back, that I hadn't told anyone about us.

Q. Yes — what did she write then?

A. She then said, well, it must have been Bill.

Q. Who is Bill?

A. He is an Air Force fellow that come [*sic*] up there once in a while. She and him watched the baby too sometimes together.

Q. Yes?

A. Well, she said, it must have been Bill, and have you seen him for maybe two or three weeks, I haven't seen him. I says, no, I haven't seen him. Well, she says, if I see him I am going to give him the devil. Well, I says, I don't know anything about Bill but I haven't told anyone.

Q. Did she say anything else?

A. Well, she says, if you ever tell anyone I am going to tell that you made me do it.

Q. Did she write that?

A. Yes.

Q. You haven't got that note?

A. No, I haven't.

As Crown attorney Mitchell was able to confirm later, Joe Probe was caught in an outright lie here. An earlier witness, Weyburn machine agent Wilbur W. Thompson, had testified that Joe had boasted to him about having sex three times with Beatrice, in his house and after swimming. He was not only a man cheating on his wife, but he was bragging about it to "one or two" people, as he was later forced to admit on the stand. Mitchell was also able to attack Joe Probe's reputation by showing him to be a heavy drinker, who kept beer and whisky in the house, drank beer every time he took Beatrice out in the car, and consumed half a thirteen-ounce bottle of scotch on the drive to Yellowgrass, and four more bottles of beer in the hotel.

Mitchell's effort to shake Joe's insistence that Beatrice had consented was less successful. The best he could muster was this exchange:

Q. Now then you say that all these acts of intercourse took place with her consent. Is that correct?

A. That is correct.

Q. Would you tell us how she got these bruises? If she was a consenting party?

Weyburn Courthouse, c. 1930

A. I don't believe she had very many — any bruises.

Q. You were going to say she didn't have very many?

A. She didn't have any bruises.

Q. Why did you say she didn't have very many?

MR. MacPHERSON: — I do object to the method he is now adopting in jumping at the witness.

THE COURT: — You must let him answer one question before you ask another.

MR. MITCHELL: — Did you start out to say she didn't have very many bruises?

A. No.

Q. You won't admit that? You won't admit that you even used those words now?

A. I didn't finish it.

Q. No, but up to that point. I don't think she had very many — did you say that?

A. No.

Q. You didn't say that?

A. No.

Q. You know perfectly well she had bruises, don't you?

A. No, I don't.

All of this went squarely to the issue of consent, which was a complete defence to the charges of rape and indecent assault. Trial judge Bigelow would charge the jury that he was suspicious about the Yellowgrass hotel incident, about Beatrice's failure to use her fingernails to fight back, and about the evidence that she sat down on the blanket at the side of the car, which he equated with walking "humbly to the slaughter."[46] He reminded the jury that they knew "how motor cars are constructed and the small spaces in the front seat." He would leave it to their good sense to say "whether it was a possibility or not, for a man to rape a woman on the front seat of a motor car." The male jurors agreed with the judge that these factors overwhelmed any evidence of bruising or Beatrice's assertions of non-consent. They brought in a verdict of not guilty on the first two charges.[47]

Unlawful Carnal Knowledge of a "Deaf and Dumb Woman"

THE THIRD CHARGE THAT had been laid against Joe Probe — "unlawful carnal knowledge of a deaf and dumb woman" — was more complicated. This offence had been introduced in 1892, when the first *Criminal Code* was enacted. It appears to have been grafted onto an 1886 law that had made it a crime to "unlawfully and carnally know" any "idiot," "imbecile," or "insane" woman "under circumstances which [did] not amount to rape" but where it could be proven that the offender "knew" of the disability.[48] In 1900, the law was amended to ensure that men who had "good reason to believe" that a woman was disabled could also be convicted. In 1922, "feeble-minded women" were added to the list.[49] Thus, the exact wording of the offence with which Joe Probe was charged read:

> Every one is guilty of an indictable offence and liable to four years' imprisonment who unlawfully and carnally knows, or attempts to have unlawful carnal knowledge of, any female idiot or imbecile, insane or deaf and dumb or feeble-minded woman or girl, under circumstances which do not amount to rape but where the offender knew or had good reason to believe, at the time of the offence, that the woman or girl was an idiot, or imbecile, or insane or deaf and dumb or feeble-minded.[50]

The definition did not contain the usual reference to lack of consent found in so many other sexual assault provisions. In fact, the phrase "under circumstances which do not amount to rape" suggested that the legislators meant to distinguish this from rape. One interpretation of the charge would have been that sexual intercourse with any women in the categories listed was prohibited, as an exploitative act of male sexual aggression, whether the facts indicated consent or lack of consent. Such an interpretation would have resulted in an open and shut case against Joe Probe, whose admissions of intercourse would have concluded the issue.

Recognizing this, defence counsel MacPherson made a series of arguments to pre-empt the conviction. First, he took the position that Beatrice Tisdale was not "deaf and dumb." He began by suggesting that because this phrase was twinned with the language of insanity, imbecility, and feeble-minded-ness, that it implied that only "deaf mutes" who were "mentally unbalanced" were included. Judge Bigelow dismissed this suggestion, noting the repeti-tion of the word "or" between the phrases. Next, MacPherson claimed that Beatrice was not "dumb" because she could talk. Judge Bigelow interjected that although the court had heard Beatrice speak, "I wouldn't call that talk-ing." In the end, the trial judge proposed to leave this to the jury's decision.

The problem that perplexed the lawyers more was the use of the word "unlawfully" in the provision. MacPherson claimed that this meant that the Crown must prove the absence of consent. Noting that Beatrice was twenty-four years old and not feeble-minded, MacPherson insisted that she could marry and lawfully have connection with a man. Rather hesitantly, Crown attorney Mitchell pointed out that this would have meant equating the crime to rape. In the legal skirmish that followed, the lawyers and the judge con-cluded that they would have to disregard one or the other of the two phras-es — "unlawfully" or "under circumstances which do not amount to rape." Crown attorney Mitchell admitted that he was quite "floored" with the di-lemma and had no definite submission to make to the court.[51]

Judge Bigelow finally ruled that the Crown was required to establish non-consent, because the charge "really amounts to a charge of rape . . . ex-cept that it alleges that he raped this deaf and dumb girl — that is all." In his charge to the jury, he stated:

> [I]f she consented to the carnal knowledge it was not unlawful. And my rul-
> ing on that was and I so instruct you that this deaf and dumb woman, who
> is in possession of her senses, has just as much right to consent to sexual
> intercourse, carnal knowledge, as anybody and if she consents there is noth-
> ing illegal about it. It is quite all right from a legal standpoint. It may not be
> morally all right, as has been pointed out to you. You are not here trying a
> question of morals.

Saskatchewan Archives Board, R-D1404

Judge Henry V. Bigelow

The jury returned their verdict of not guilty on the final charge of unlawful carnal knowledge of a deaf and dumb woman.

The Crown appealed the acquittal to the Saskatchewan Court of Appeal. Judge Philip Edward Mackenzie quickly grasped the dilemma of the "deaf and dumb" provision. He could see why the legislators might wish to distinguish the crime from rape, because the "gravamen of the offence" was having sex with a woman who was "mentally or morally incapable of resisting." As Mackenzie put it more colloquially, the object was to prevent such women from being "easy marks" for morally unscrupulous men.[52] For this reason, consent would not unequivocally immunize the accused, and the court was bound to inquire into the nature of the woman's "incapacity." Mackenzie equated this with a much-quoted nineteenth-century precedent directing a court to consider whether an insane woman was really incapable of consenting to sex. If she had given her consent, even "from mere animal instinct or passion," there could be no conviction.[53] Mackenzie was dismissive of the suggestion that a "deaf and dumb" person was "presumed to be no more mentally competent than an idiot," adding:

> It would seem to me unreasonable to hold however that just because a woman is proved to be deaf and dumb she is *ipso facto* incapable of lawfully consenting to carnal knowledge. Common experience tells us that not infrequently women and girls so afflicted are unquestionably moral and highly intelligent with the ability to take and utilize an advanced education.[54]

In the case of Beatrice Tisdale, Judge Mackenzie pointed to her age, her education, her good handwriting, her ability to hold a respectable job, and concluded that "she had the will-power to direct her own conduct as she saw fit," that she "had a considerable understanding of what are commonly known as 'the ways of the world.'" He faulted trial judge Bigelow for failing to leave the matter of Beatrice's "mental and moral competence" to the jury, rather than deciding it for them. But in the end, speaking for a unanimous court, Judge Mackenzie concluded that there was no need to order a new trial because there had been no substantial error.[55]

There is much to admire in Judge Mackenzie's refusal to relegate all deaf women to the status of incompetence. His conclusion that morality and high intelligence could accompany deafness was clearly correct, even progressive for the time. Deaf people had long argued that inability to hear was not to be equated with disability.[56] Judge Mackenzie was an unusual judge in many ways. He had distinguished himself in 1921, by overruling a racially discrimi-

Philip Edward Mackenzie

natory decision of the Regina City Council to deny a restaurant licence to a Chinese-Canadian businessman, Yee Clun, who had sought permission to employ a "white woman." Objecting that the council had rejected the application solely "upon racial grounds," he ordered the councillors to grant the licence.[57] A judge widely respected for his "politeness," Mackenzie appears to have been a staunch defender of individual human rights — whether relating to race or disability.[58]

However, there are aspects of this decision that are problematic. Judge Mackenzie's use of the word "afflicted" reflects his acceptance of the wider social stigmatization of the deaf community. His endorsement of the nineteenth-century language of "animal instinct or passion" as explanatory of the sexuality of women with disabilities is alarming, and reflects stereotypical assumptions that such women were "overly sexual" as a result of "diseased lusts."[59] It was this sort of reasoning that often made women with disabilities particular targets for coercive and exploitative sexual assault. His linking of mental and moral incapacity also did a serious disservice to individuals labelled disabled.

In his desire to support the sexual autonomy of deaf women, Judge Mackenzie had shorn the law of much of its potential power to protect them from sexual violence, and penalized the woman at the core of the inquiry, who had insisted all along that she was forcibly raped. Sexual agency can be elusive, especially when it takes place in a vacuum without sex education, assertiveness training, and assistance in learning how to develop meaningful relationships. Judge Mackenzie's emphasis on mental capacity left the evidence of force and coercion to languish. Once he concluded that Beatrice Tisdale was mentally capable of consenting, he failed to pursue how the issue of *deafness* had affected the sexual interaction between the two, and how it had affected the courtroom examination of that interaction.

The failure to accommodate a Deaf witness in the Weyburn courtroom was probably no worse than other Canadian courtrooms of the era, and as Deaf advocates would argue, many current-day courtrooms as well.[60] However, a legal system that wished to protect deaf women from sexual assault would have started by ensuring that there was full and accurate Sign interpretation at the trial, and that the complainant was entirely satisfied with the communication process. It would have insisted that Beatrice Tisdale be asked what she understood by Joe Probe's efforts to seduce her. Had she comprehended his intent when he asked her to dance to the radio that first babysitting evening? If it was true, as Joe Probe alleged, that he had run his leg up between Beatrice's legs while dancing, had she understood that to be a sexual signal? Had she been able to communicate to Joe what she thought of the gesture? If it was true that when Joe drove Beatrice home that first evening, he continued his sexual overtures while parked by the snow fence, what efforts had he made to communicate to her what he was doing and why? Joe's testimony that "she did not write me a note and say: go ahead, diddle me — no," but that he had assumed consent because of the absence of objection, leaves open a wide vista for exploration. When Joe asked Beatrice to drive to Yellowgrass, had she understood that he intended to pursue his sexual agenda? Did she realize that they would end up in a hotel room? Had she understood Joe's sexual intentions when he told her to go into the hotel and to follow him upstairs to the room? Drawing inferences and conclusions based on what two hearing people might have understood or meant in similar exchanges is difficult enough. For a hearing man, lawyers, jurors, and judge to draw similar inferences about the comprehension and behaviour of a deaf woman who was being sexually importuned by a hearing man seems palpably unjust.

This was not the first or last time that sexual assault charges involving women with disabilities would flounder. In 1916, a man charged with carnal knowledge of a thirty-four-year-old female "idiot" in Alberta was acquitted because the court found that the woman's "imbecility" was insufficiently severe.[61] In 1924, a prosecution for carnal knowledge of a "feeble-minded girl" failed in Nova Scotia.[62] In 1931, the Crown had put a "feeble-minded woman" on the stand to testify against a man who had sexually assaulted her. She was apparently "unable to give any evidence," and a Manitoba court later quashed the conviction for lack of evidence.[63] In 1941, a British Columbia court objected that a jury in a rape trial had wrongly substituted a conviction for "carnal knowledge of a feeble-minded woman," with respect to a woman the court described as a "high grade mental defective." The court concluded that the carnal knowledge offence was not a "lesser and included offence" to rape, because the essential elements of the two offences were dissimilar.[64] In 1954, a Nova Scotia prosecution for carnal knowledge of a "retarded girl" with a "mental age of seven or eight" was unsuccessful.[65] In 1958, a prosecution for sexual intercourse with a "feeble-minded woman" faltered in Quebec.[66] In 1960, a Saskatchewan rape prosecution involving a complainant who was described as a "mental defective," with the "mentality of a child of eight years" went down to defeat.[67] In 1962, an Ontario court quashed a conviction where the complainant was described as "mentally retarded" and of a "mental age near ten." The Crown psychiatrist had testified that such individuals could "tell us a story in their simple way" but were "not imaginative enough to concoct stories." The appellate court concluded that it was improper to lead evidence suggesting the witness was truthful simply because of her mental classification.[68] Although there were occasional convictions, it is evident that the difficulties that ordinarily beset prosecutors in sexual assault trials were greatly magnified for victims with disabilities.[69]

Aftermath

THE TISDALE FAMILY HISTORY recounts that Beatrice subsequently moved to Winnipeg, where she married in 1947. After her husband's death in 1952, she and her young son moved back to Midale to live with her mother and older sister, Mabel, for two years. Then Beatrice got work at the Wascana Hospital in Regina, where she stayed for fifteen years before moving to take a job at the Shaunessey Hospital in Vancouver. Ill health forced her early retirement, and she died on 25 September 1990.[70]

Joe Probe's later life stayed true to character. In February of 1962, he rented a car in Calgary, and drove it to the Royal Bank in Plenty, Saskatchewan. He pulled a sock over his head, and entered the bank carrying a shoebox and a .38 calibre revolver. He told the manager that he had nitroglycerine with him, and that he was "not afraid to use it since he only had one year to live." The "jittery" bank robber, "continually roaring and swearing," forced the staff to turn over $19 901 from the vault, and dashed out the back door. His getaway was foiled when the car rolled over into a snow-filled ditch on the gravel road between Loverna and Coldwell. He exited the car, took a few steps, and shot himself in the right temple. The *Saskatoon Star-Phoenix* reported that "he must have figured the game was up." By the time the RCMP arrived at the scene, Joe Probe was dead.[71]

Chapter 7

Michelle - FOR
Michael Against

CHILD WITNESSES — "BY PSYCHOLOGICAL DEFINITION ... A DISSERVICE TO THE TRUE END OF JUSTICE": Soulière, 1951–52

MARIE TREMBLAY (WHOSE NAME has been changed to protect her privacy) was barely five years old. She bravely stood up as tall as she could muster, but her slight frame must have been dwarfed by the witness box in the imposing courtroom in Hull, Québec, on 14 December 1951. The tale she had to tell was shocking but sadly commonplace. She pointed to forty-seven-year-old Ovila Soulière, and identified him as the man who had sexually assaulted her in the late summer of 1950. Few records survive for this case, making it difficult to reconstruct the narrative in detail. However, the result is known. Ovila Soulière was convicted at trial, a verdict that was later quashed by the Québec Court of Appeal.[1] Despite the skeletal factual record, Marie Tremblay's case provides a useful illustration of the difficulties facing child victims, and an opportunity to explore the "doctrine of corroboration," one of the most significant hurdles facing sexual assault complainants. It is also fascinating for what it reveals about the perspectives of judges, jurors, legal theorists, and so-called experts about the credibility of women and children who claimed to be sexually assaulted. ———

At least some of the facts can be discerned. Marie Tremblay's parents were separated. She shared a two-storey house in South Hull with her mother and Ovila Soulière. The French phrase *"vivant maritalement"* was translated in the English report of the decision to describe the couple as living "in concubinage." Whether Ovila Soulière's status as Mme Tremblay's lover predated or postdated her marital breakdown was a matter of speculation. Whatever the situation, as the judges would note, it left little Marie Tremblay *"dans un très mauvais milieu"* — "in a very bad environment."[2]

Ovila Joseph Soulière was himself married to Adrienne Côté, whom he had wed in nearby Deschênes in 1930. A working-class labourer from an Outaouais family of unskilled labourers, Ovila held down a variety of jobs that occasionally took him across the river to Ottawa, as a labourer with the federal district commission, and as a shipping clerk with an instrument repair firm.[3] He denied Marie Tremblay's assertions that he had awakened her in her bedroom on the ground floor of the house, and abused her sexually: *"J'ai rien à dire du tout sur le sujet de la petite; je suis innocent de la chose. Je connais rien de la chose parce que la petite fille je lui ai jamais touché."* — "I have nothing at all to say on the subject of the little girl; I am innocent of the affair. I know nothing about the matter because I have never touched the little girl." Marie's mother sided with her paramour, insisting that Ovila had never sexually molested her daughter. She claimed that Marie slept in a bedroom next to hers and not on the ground floor as the little girl had said, and that Ovila had never left his bed to go to Marie's.

Hull was a blue-collar, predominantly francophone town on the north shore of the Ottawa River, across from the national capital of Ottawa. Initially settled by anglophone New Englanders, it altered its composition in the mid-1800s when French-Canadian industrial workers displaced the early agricultural settlers. A series of catastrophic fires wreaked devastation upon Hull's architectural pretensions, culminating with the Great Fire of 1900, which levelled two-thirds of the predominantly wooden buildings. New saw mills, steel foundries, lumbering, meat-packing, and textile industries blossomed, crowned by the E.B. Eddy factories perched on the edge of the river. During Prohibition, working-class Hull developed a "beer town" reputation, and was dubbed "Little Chicago" by revellers from Ontario, who crossed by ferry to drink and gamble in speakeasies on Jacques-Cartier Street. But the city's industrial infrastructure began to crumble by the 1930s, and inferior housing and worker tenements reflected the stark poverty and unemployment of most residents. In 1951, Hull was stagnating, a city that had seen, and would see, better days.[4]

Child Sexual Abuse

SEXUAL ABUSE HAS ALWAYS been a terrifying reality for Canadian children, both male and female.[5] Contrary to the opinion of modern commentators,

Courtesy of Ville de Gatineau, H012/0193

Aerial view of Hull, 1940

Courtesy of Ville de Gatineau, H012/0225

Hull on fire, 1946

who often suggest that the legal prosecution of child sexual abuse is a recent phenomenon, the historical record proves otherwise.[6] The law reports and judicial archives are filled with records that demonstrate an extraordinary degree of child sexual abuse throughout Canadian history.[7]

Although some of the children were assaulted by strangers, most were violated by men they knew. Fathers, stepfathers, grandfathers, uncles, brothers, boarders, neighbours, farm labourers, teachers, school-janitors, shopkeepers, and supervisors of training-school facilities all appear as men accused between 1900 and 1975.[8] Charges included rape, indecent assault, carnal knowledge of a girl under the age of consent (statutory rape), incest, and contributing to juvenile delinquency. In Marie's case, it is surprising that Ovila was not charged with statutory rape, which created a blanket prohibition on men having sexual intercourse with girls younger than a certain age, regardless of their consent. Instead, the charge of indecent assault was selected, possibly because the authorities may have thought that it would be less difficult to show sexual touching than to prove full sexual intercourse with a child witness.[9]

Canadian courts dealt with prosecutions involving children as young as three, although these were often cases in which the accused had confessed, or other witnesses had observed the assault, and so the child was not required to testify.[10] Four-year-old children occasionally testified, but at age five, Marie Tremblay was among the youngest of sexual assault complainants to appear in court.[11] The first question was whether she could qualify to testify as a child witness. It was a cumbersome process that was even less supportive of children than of adult female complainants.

Sworn and Unsworn Testimony from a Child Witness

ALL WITNESSES WERE CUSTOMARILY asked to swear upon the Bible, based on the belief that perjured evidence would provoke divine punishment. Very young children could theoretically be sworn, but judges screened everyone under fourteen before administering an oath. Judicial failure to determine whether the child understood that hellfire and damnation would follow false testimony constituted irreversible error.[12] Although we have no record of what questions Québec Superior Court trial judge Paul Ste-Marie asked Marie Tremblay when she first took the stand, the inquiries that greeted other young sexual assault victims may help to fill in the gap.

Nine-year-old Alice Wright answered "yes" when asked by a Vancouver magistrate in 1946 whether she understood "about swearing on the Bible to tell the truth," and then was ordered to kiss the Bible, which she obediently did. She was asked to swear that her evidence should be "the truth, the whole truth, and nothing but the truth," which she also did. Her sworn evidence was later rejected when an appeal court concluded that there had been "nothing to show that she knew the consequences of an oath."[13] Six-year-old Gary Whittington of Galt, who told the magistrate in 1950 that he went to a "separate school" where he was reading "in the First Book," that he knew what it meant to tell a lie, and that boys and girls who told lies got "put in jail," also failed.[14] Little wonder then, that ten-year-old Fred Moland was disqualified when he admitted in 1951 that although he used to go to church and Sunday School in Halifax, he had not attended for some months after he moved to Chester. His answer about what it meant to tell a lie, that "you are something bad, or something like that," and that the consequences were that you "go to jail," did little to redeem him.[15] Twelve-year-old Frances Anne Cumming would do no better in Toronto in 1959. Although she indicated that she attended Sunday School "sometimes" and knew what the Bible was, and what it was to tell the truth, she failed miserably when asked what would happen if you tell a lie. "You are punished," her answer, was lacking in religious rigour.[16] Judge Ste-Marie ruled that Marie too had failed to answer the questions he put that morning in Hull. She was rejected as a proper candidate to swear an oath.

Barring young victims of sexual assault from testifying because of their sketchy sense of the catechism created obvious problems. Consequently, the *Canada Evidence Act* and the *Criminal Code* had been amended to provide that children could give unsworn testimony even though they did not "understand the nature of an oath." But first the judge was required to ascertain that the child was "possessed of sufficient intelligence to justify the reception of the evidence" and understood "the duty of speaking the truth."[17] Judge Ste-Marie's questions led him to conclude that Marie was a *"fillette intelligente"* — "an intelligent little girl" who could give *"un témoignage d'une très grande clarté"* — "very clear testimony."[18] To have secured such confidence, little Marie Tremblay must have impressed the courtroom greatly that day. She was permitted to give unsworn testimony. She described for the court what her house in South Hull looked like, and explained that she slept on the ground floor, while her mother and Ovila Soulière shared an upstairs bedroom. She testified that Ovila had come down to her room while she slept, awakened her, and penetrated her sexually.

Although it appears that Marie was a forthright and convincing witness, there was another legal impediment to finding her credible. The *Canada Evi-*

Courtesy of Andrée Ste-Marie

Trial Judge Paul Ste-Marie

dence Act warned that no case should be decided upon the unsworn testimony of a child, but must be "corroborated by some other material evidence."[19] The *Criminal Code* was even stricter, insisting that in prosecutions for many sexual assault offences the complainant's testimony — sworn or not — must be "corroborated by some other material evidence in support thereof implicating the accused."[20] This was a substantial deviation from the general principles of evidence, in which the assessment of credibility was left to the discretion of the jurors who heard the witness testify in court. Ordinarily, the testimony of a single witness sufficed, providing the jury believed the individual beyond a reasonable doubt.[21] The very high standard of proof in criminal trials, much higher than in civil proceedings, was meant to protect individuals from wrongful convictions.[22] Adding the requirement for corroboration created an evidentiary hurdle that made it far more difficult to prosecute sexual assault cases, no matter how convincing the victim's testimony.

The Dubious Rationale for the Doctrine of Corroboration

THE REQUIREMENT FOR CORROBORATION was imported from English common law, where it had been attached to allegations involving sexual violence, exploitation, or immorality made by women and children both.[23] The idea that women and children were inherently untrustworthy when they testified about sexual matters had deep roots in Anglo-Canadian legal traditions. Most authorities credited seventeenth-century English jurist Sir Matthew Hale as the source, citing his famous adage that rape "was an accusation easily to be made, and hard to be proved, and harder to be defended by the party accused, though never so innocent." The inaccuracy of Hale's comment appears to have provoked no critique until after 1975.[24] Under common law, although corroboration was not mandatory, judges were obliged to warn juries in rape and similar cases that it was dangerous to convict without it.[25] Similarly, there was a common law duty to warn juries in all cases where a child was sworn as a witness.[26] Canadian legislators then expanded upon the common law rules, fortifying many of their statutes with mandatory provisions that insisted that juries *must not* convict without corroboration.[27] Poor Marie Tremblay's evidence required corroboration as a result of common law rules because she was a child witness, and again because she was a child complaining of indecent assault. Legislation then mandated corroboration as well, because as a child she gave unsworn testimony. The wonder of it was that the court didn't require triple corroboration.

Despite the multiple demands for corroboration, no one ever troubled to cite research that would have laid a factual foundation for the skepticism. It was simply, as was said frequently, "a matter of common sense and common experience."[28] Further explanation came wholly from the armchair musings and anecdotal memories of elderly male judges, jurists, and politicians. Lord Hale mustered all of two cases of "malicious prosecution" that had "come within his own knowledge."[29] John Henry Wigmore, the leading twentieth-century American expert on the law of evidence, made sweeping claims about the pathology of female psychology without discernible justification.[30] Canadian politicians drew upon these ill-founded speculations to justify their own suspicions. John Diefenbaker erroneously cited Lord Coke rather than Lord Hale, musing in Parliament:

> If my recollection is correct, Lord Coke pointed out a long time ago that this type of charge is often laid through motives of malice, revenge, jealousy and so on. . . . Trial judges have found necessary [to warn jurors] to protect the innocent from probable blackmailing activities of those who through the ages have invariably chosen this means to secure their revenge for wrongs done to them, imagined or actual.[31]

Others displayed deep-rooted anti-female sentiments, describing complainants as "designing girls," "libidinous women," and "brazen females" who might "entrap" the "vigorous, active" and "foolish" young men of the country. The efforts of women's reform groups to remind everyone that "false charges of this kind" were of "very rare occurrence" failed.[32]

The theorizing about children was equally discriminatory. Wigmore claimed that children made poor witnesses because of their reduced capacities of observation, recollection, abilities to understand questions and frame intelligent answers, and lack of moral responsibility.[33] Equating "child-nature" with the "disposition to weave romances and to treat imagination for verity," Wigmore offered no research in support. Instead he footnoted to "Child's Play," an essay by the Scottish author Robert Louis Stevenson, adopting literary images of children pretending to construct castles in the air amidst mists and rainbows. The images were playful enough, but the passages Wigmore selected from Stevenson's essay soon shifted from happy nursery scenes to descriptions of children's sensations as "dim," their lives as "vain," and their personalities as resting "in open self-deception."[34]

Rupert Cross, a mid-twentieth-century English expert often cited in Canada, argued that children were "more susceptible to the influence of third persons, and may allow their imaginations to run away with them."[35] Sidney Phipson, a barrister who wrote a text on the law of evidence in Canada in 1911, stated that children's "habits of romancing" often led them "to state as facts circumstances having no existence but in their own imaginations." He added that the "suggestions or threats of grown-up persons" could induce children to act "on their fears and unformed judgments."[36] The editors of *Tremeear's Criminal Code of Canada* in 1944 elaborated upon the suggestibility point: "Small children are possibly more under the influence of third persons — sometimes their parents — than are adults, and they are apt to allow their imaginations to run away with them and to invent untrue stories."[37] *Kenny's Outlines of Criminal Law*, published in 1952, added: "It has been said that 'Children are a most untrustworthy class of witnesses; for, as our common experience teaches us, they often, when of a tender age, mistake dreams for reality, repeat glibly as of their own knowledge what they have heard from others, and are greatly influenced by fear of punishment, by hope of reward, and by drive for notoriety.' They are both 'suggestible' and even 'auto-suggestible.'"[38] This unsavoury list of attributes — glibness, mistakenness, suggestibility, proclivity to grasp for reward and to seek notoriety — is attributed to none other than "common sense." Canadian judges repeated such homilies, equally failing to ground such speculations in research.[39]

The Narrow Construction of "Corroboration"

SIMPLY STIPULATING THAT CORROBORATION was required did not answer the next question: precisely what did the term "corroboration" mean? Dictionaries defined the word as "strengthening," "fortifying," and "confirming."[40] Putting aside the debate over whether corroboration should have been demanded in the first place, there was much in Marie Tremblay's case that should have qualified, if the ordinary sense of the word had been adopted.

Fortifying her evidence of sexual assault was unequivocal medical testimony that the little girl's hymen was broken, and that her genitalia were red and inflamed. Dr. Church of Aylmer, Québec, who had examined Marie on 29 August, testified that "something" must have "entered her vagina" to cause this.[41] Judge Ste-Marie conceded that the doctor's evidence "demonstrated that an offence had been committed," but the *Criminal Code* demanded that the corroboration must also "implicate the accused." His conclusion was inevitable under the mandatory statutory rule: "The doctor's examination, the things that he ascertained, do not prove it was the accused who did that.

Judge Ste-Marie on the bench, centre

Courtesy of Andrée Ste-Marie

It may have been others." His ruling joined a long line of Canadian cases that rejected medical evidence confirming a sexual assault because the doctor could not prove *whose penis* had caused the tearing and inflammation.[42]

The testimony of Marie's grandmother also appeared to confirm the young girl's story. She advised the court that when Marie came to stay with her in mid-August, she was alarmed to discover that her granddaughter was in tears for much of the time, hid herself away whenever adults were around, and cried whenever she had to urinate. Marie's grandmother tried to find out what was wrong, but Marie kept insisting that she was "not telling." "*Je ne te le dis pas, j'aime mieux pas te le dire,*" she repeated. For three days Marie refused to divulge further information. Finally, the grandmother conducted "*l'examen des organes sexuels de l'enfant*" and discovered the inflammation. Marie broke down and told her grandmother what Ovila had done.[43]

Under the wording of the statute, this would seem to suffice as evidence "implicating the accused." But the question of whether the complainant's first disclosure could legally qualify as corroboration was not so straightforward. The courts were prepared to admit evidence of "recent complaint," as it was called in law, even though this was a departure from the rules against hearsay evidence, because judges anticipated that women who were truly raped would raise a "hue and cry."[44] However, Canadian courts had created certain restrictions on the admissibility of "recent complaints." It was the "duty of a woman who had been sexually attacked" to complain "at the first reasonable opportunity." If the victim delayed her disclosure, the evidence could be excluded.[45] Such thinking stemmed from the wider skepticism that greeted allegations of sexual assault, for women

Paul Ste-Marie's family.
Left to right: Marcel Ste-Marie
(brother, surveyor); J. Wilfrid (father,
lawyer); Robert LaFleur (brother-in-
law, married to his sister Gabrielle);
Paul Ste-Marie; Joseph Ste-Marie
(brother, lawyer)

Courtesy of Andrée Ste-Marie

and children who failed to raise an immediate "hue and cry" were thought to be shamming. None of this took into account the multiple reasons why victims might not divulge their sexual violation to the first person they met — fear, embarrassment, and disorientation, to name but a few.[46] Courts also refused to admit evidence of recent complaint where the complaint was not offered in a voluntary and spontaneous fashion, but extracted by suggestive, leading, or intimidating questions.[47]

Fortunately, for Marie Tremblay, the judge did not exclude her recent complaint to her grandmother, even though it had not been made immediately after the assault, and was elicited by pointed questioning. This may have been the only point in the trial when Marie's youth operated to her relative advantage, allowing the court to excuse her delay and her reticence.[48] But whatever assistance the admission of the complaint may have offered to the prosecution evaporated when the judge turned to the legal impact of the evidence. "The fact that she has told her grandmother" would definitively *not* qualify as corroboration, announced Judge Ste-Marie. Earlier courts had occasionally accepted recent complaint as corroboration, but by the mid-century it was clear that it no longer met the increasingly stringent tests.[49] In the words of the Ontario Court of Appeal in 1951, a recent complaint was "not evidence which corroborates in the slightest degree the complainant as to the facts of the offence charged, but can merely be used to assist in determining whether or not the complainant is a credible witness."[50] The Supreme Court of Canada elaborated in 1952: "In cases where a sexual offence is charged, evidence of the making of a complaint is not corroborative of the testimony of the complainant . . . . It must be made plain to the jury that the witness whose testimony requires corroboration cannot corroborate herself."[51] According to the collective wisdom of the Canadian judiciary, recent complaints may have been *"confirmatory"* but they could not be *"corroborative."*[52]

Judge Ste-Marie was less dismissive of Marie Tremblay's grandmother's testimony that her granddaughter had been in tears from the pain of urination, and that she was frightened and had taken to hiding. In his charge to the jury, he allowed that this might, if believed, constitute legal corroboration:

> I was telling you a little while ago that this corroboration may result from circumstantial evidence. Here is one of these circumstances: the little girl leaves the house in which the accused Soulière was living; she is taken to her grandmother's home; the grandmother finds that she was hiding and crying — there is something the matter with that child. That is where there is some corroboration. Not in the facts that she has told her grandmother, but in the fact that she cries, that she has pain in urinating; there is something wrong somewhere. That is a circumstance; it is an element corroborative of the little girl's testimony.

Judge Ste-Marie also suggested that opportunity could constitute corroboration:

> There is also another circumstance — the fact that Soulière was living in the same house. That is a circumstance that you may take into account in order to see whether, in your judgment, it was indeed he or another who did that. He was living in the same house, upstairs.

Judge Ste-Marie's interpretation of these last pieces of evidence was generous. Trial judges were privy to the painful, heart-rending, first-person testimony of the victims of child sexual abuse. Some of them seem to have taken a more expansive definition of corroboration than the appellate judges.

Born in 1904 in Hull, Judge Paul Joseph Hormidas Ste-Marie was only one month older than Ovila Soulière. Like the litigants, he was also a long-time resident of the Outaouais. His father Joseph-Wilfrid Ste-Marie, QC, had practised law there since the turn of the century. When Paul Ste-Marie was admitted to the bar in 1929, he took up practice in the dynastic family firm with his father and brother. His legal ties expanded still further when he married Lucile Rinfret in 1934, the daughter of Chief Justice Thibaudeau Rinfret of the Supreme Court of Canada, and the sister of G. Édouard Rinfret, Chief Justice of Québec. Named to the Superior Court of Québec in August 1951, Judge Ste-Marie had sat on the bench for only four months prior to the Soulière case.[53]

Above: Paul Ste-Marie's daughters, Lise and Andrée
Below: The Ste-Marie home, 126 Laurier, Hull (now demolished)

Author unknown, 1933, Le Centre de l'Outaouais des Archives nationales du Québec, P45,S1,D153

The paddy wagon, city of Hull, 1933

At the time of the appointment, Paul Ste-Marie and his wife were living in a large and stately home on 261 Laurier with their three daughters: Andrée, Lise, and Paule, aged sixteen, fifteen, and ten. Decades later, Andrée recalled that although she did not remember the Soulière trial specifically, she had watched her father preside over one of his early murder trials. "In a small town," she noted, "*un procès* always attracted a lot of people ... the whole town wanted to attend." She reflected that her father had found criminal cases challenging: "I think he was more comfortable with civil causes than criminal causes, because his practice as a lawyer had been in the civil area." She described her father as "a very calm and patient man" who "didn't talk much" during the trial. Asked to reflect upon his attitudes towards children, she characterized him as "very attentive," a father who "spent time" with his daughters, and an avid amateur photographer, who took many photos, including some of his daughters at play. In an era when many in the province of Québec did not pursue their studies beyond grade seven, all three of his daughters went on to complete post-secondary education, with the enthusiastic support of Judge Ste-Marie.[54]

Judge Ste-Marie's decision, at the conclusion of the trial, was that the grandmother's testimony about Marie's tears, her fears, and her hiding, as well as the evidence of opportunity, taken collectively, had legally satisfied the statutory test of corroboration. The twelve male jurors who had been empanelled to try the case agreed. They retired to consider their findings and returned with a verdict of guilty. They had found Marie Tremblay's testimony true beyond a reasonable doubt, and the corroborating evidence equally credible. Judge Ste-Marie pronounced a sentence of eighteen months' imprisonment, admonishing the prisoner: *"J'espère que les mois passés en prison vous feront réfléchir sur votre conduite afin que vous ne recommenciez jamais."* — "I hope that your months in prison will make you reflect upon your conduct so that you never reoffend."[55] Ovila Soulière was taken back to the Prison de Hull, where he had been jailed since his arrest on 5 December 1951.[56] His defence counsel applied for bail, and he was released on a bond of $2000 on 12 January 1952, pending appeal to the Québec Court of Appeal. Although Ovila personally posted the $2000 in cash, there is no indication how an impoverished labourer was able to raise such a sum.[57]

Corroboration under Scrutiny in the Court of Appeal

THE APPEAL CAME BEFORE all five judges of the Québec Court of Appeal on 25 March 1952. Their decision, issued on 29 May 1952, unanimously quashed the conviction. This was not for want of believing Marie Tremblay. The appellate judges could understand why the jury had found Marie Tremblay to be telling the truth beyond a reasonable doubt. They reviewed the trial record and agreed that she was "an intelligent little girl" who "remembered well," and gave "clear" and "impressive" testimony. But no matter how convincing she had been as a witness, without corroboration there would be no legal finding of guilt.

Chief Justice Antonin Galipeault agreed with the trial judge that the definition of corroboration excluded the doctor's report.[58] It undoubtedly proved that "the little [Tremblay] girl was the victim of an indecent assault," but the "findings of the professional man" did not "implicate the accused." He dismissed the recent complaint as equally unhelpful. Even had the court been inclined to be as generous as the trial judge in ignoring "the lapses of time" between the offence and the complaint, the most the complaint could do was to give "credence to the victim's testimony." It did not count as corroboration in law.[59] Unlike Judge Ste-Marie, the appeal judges did not find the testimony of the grandmother as to Marie's painful urination, crying, and hiding to be corroborative. In fact, they dismissed these points without comment. It was surprisingly common for appellate courts to overrule convictions without addressing all of the items labelled corroborative at the lower court.[60] We are

Antonin Galipeault

left to diagnose on our own why the judges found this testimony unhelpful. Perhaps it was because they felt it did not "implicate the accused."

Another clue may lie in Chief Justice Galipeault's subsequent statement that corroboration had to be "independent testimony" linking the accused to the crime. The demand for *independent* corroborative evidence is one of the most troublesome features of this judgment. The legislation only required that the complainant's testimony be "corroborated by some other material evidence."[61] The word "independent" did not appear. It is debatable whether the phrase "some other" should have been equated to "independent." Undoubtedly, if Marie Tremblay had testified herself that she was having pain on urination, that she was crying, and that she was hiding from adults, this would not be "some other" testimony. However, if Marie's grandmother testified that she had personally observed these things, that could conceivably constitute "some other" testimony that affirmed the little girl's evidence. The grandmother was an individual who was someone other than the complainant, and her assessment of Marie's behaviour was separate from Marie herself. Although such evidence could not be characterized as "independent," because it was tied to behaviour exhibited by the complainant, it might well have constituted "some other" testimony.

If the extra requirement for "independent" corroborative evidence did not come from the statutory language, then where did it originate? The source appears to have been *Rex v. Baskerville*, where the English Court of Appeal had introduced the concept of "independent" corroboration in 1916, specifically overruling earlier decisions that disavowed the idea, and without any discussion as to why this new feature was to be required.[62] The Supreme Court of Canada imported the "independence" concept in the rape case of *Hubin v. The King* in 1927, dismissing a long list of potentially corroborative items because they had not emanated "independently" of the complainant.[63] Subsequent cases picked up the new rule, still without analysis or rationale.[64] In 1952, the Supreme Court of Canada would confirm, again without explaining why, that the "independence" standard that had perused common law should now be understood as a prerequisite for all statutory corroboration tests as well.[65] The "independent" criterion set the evidentiary burden for sexual assault victims one step beyond where the legislators had already gone. It practically necessitated third-party evidence in crimes where the judges must have known that separate witnesses would rarely exist. To import the criteria of "independent" evidence constituted a rude and unnecessary dismissal of the veracity of sexual assault victims. Not only were they

Division des archives, Université de Montréal, fonds bureau de l'information (D37).1FP03444. Fête des anciens de la Faculté de droit, 12 décembre 1955.

Bernard Bissonnette at the Faculty of Law, University of Montréal,
front row, second from right

rejected as trustworthy witnesses, but everything that stemmed from their evidence was also summarily disregarded.

The final item that Judge Ste-Marie had found corroborative in the Soulière trial was "the opportunity" the accused had had to commit the crime. Chief Justice Galipeault rejected this as well: "The fact that . . . the child lived under accused's roof, that the latter had the opportunity or occasion to commit the crime, is still not sufficient." One might be forgiven for wondering why this was so self-evident. Certainly opportunity was "some other material evidence," and it "implicated the accused." Judge Garon Pratte tried to explain:

> I had thought at first that I might find this corroboration in the fact that the accused seemed to have been the only one to have the opportunity to commit the offence. But after a minute examination of the evidence, that does not appear possible to me. In fact, if it is clearly demonstrated that appellant had had the opportunity to do that with which he is charged — since he was living under the same roof as the child — it remains that others may have had the same opportunity. Under these conditions, I would say that the child's

evidence is not sufficiently corroborated to warrant a reasonable conclusion that the accused is guilty.[66]

If it seems unfair that the law insisted upon corroboration for children's evidence as well as for sexual assault cases, it seems doubly unfair that the courts were then so restrictive in their assessment of what qualified. Here, the court was demanding that corroborative evidence not only strengthen the narrative of the alleged victim, but also that it not arguably suggest the guilt of anyone else. Judge Bernard Bissonnette stated: "To be sufficient, to be legal and admissible, this corroboration must bear upon the facts that in some way are constituents of the offence. The dominant fact is, without doubt, the evidence of a group of circumstances which connect the accused with the victim and tend to prove that the offence can have been committed only by him." An offence committed *only by him* seems an extraordinarily high hurdle for the prosecution to leap, and a barrier that placed demands far beyond what the legislators had stipulated.

The most outspoken of the appellate judges in his critique of child witnesses, Judge Bissonnette must have had at least some personal experience with children as he was a father of two. He was born in St. Esprit, Montcalm County, in 1898, the son of a physician who was a member of the Legislative Assembly. Educated at L'Assomption College, with a B.A. from Laval, and an LL.B. from the Université de Montréal, he was called to the bar in 1920, and later served as secretary to the Montréal bar. A distinguished politician who was elected to the legislative assembly in 1939, he was unanimously elected its speaker and president in 1940. At the time, *La Presse* attributed the honour to Bissonnette's genial personality, depicting him as "courteous," "affable," and "generous." During his first year as speaker, he presided over the legislative approval of women's suffrage. In 1941, he was appointed a professor of constitutional law at the Université de Montréal, an institution he would later head as dean, and in 1942 he was elevated to the bench. He would later become the author of the distinguished *Essai sur la Constitution du Canada*, a text that spoke proudly of the place of the French-speaking minority within the delicate balance of the federal Canadian political system.[67]

Judge Bissonnette was not content to let the Soulière matter rest with an exposition on legal doctrine. He felt moved to write an additional passage to explain his dismissal of children's evidence. Noting that in this case, "quite apart from the question of corroboration, it would have appeared to me imprudent to accept the child's testimony," Bissonnette ventured further: "It is

HON BERNARD BISSONNETTE
PRÉSIDENT DE L'ASSEMBLÉE LEGISLATIVE

Archives nationales du Québec, P560,S2,R300303,P18, J.E. Livernois, 1940

Bernard Bissonnette in the Speaker's chair

with great circumspection that the testimony of a child should be admitted. It has been said and written that it is error, not truth, that comes naturally from the mouth of the child. To this may be added the statement by a great Canadian psychiatrist, the lamented Dr. Antonio Barbeau, that a child before the Court is, by psychological definition, a witness to be regarded with suspicion and that he can do only a disservice to the true end of justice."

The Lamented Dr. Antonio Barbeau

"BY PSYCHOLOGICAL DEFINITION . . . a disservice to the true end of justice." It was quite a summation. Dr. Barbeau, deceased in 1947, had neither testified at the trial nor been cited by the lawyers in their appellate briefs, but Judge Bissonnette may have known him personally, as his wife's mother was a Barbeau. Or he may simply have been familiar with the doctor's writings. The above quotation, although not acknowledged as such in the decision, came from a chapter titled *"L'enfant et la criminologie"* in Dr. Barbeau's book, *Sous les platanes de Cos*, published in Canada in 1942.[68]

Born in 1901 in Montréal, Dr. Barbeau was educated in classical studies at Collège Sainte-Marie. He had obtained his *"licence en philosophie,"* his doctorate in medicine, and his doctorate in philosophy, all from the University of Montréal. He studied psychiatry and physiology as a Rockefeller Fellow at Harvard, and then pursued neurophysiology in France at Montpellier and the Sorbonne. Upon his return to Montréal in 1928, he married Rachel Jodoin. Like Judge Bissonnette and his wife, they would have one son and one daughter. Dr. Barbeau began his teaching career at the University of Montréal's Faculty of Medicine, and also served as the chief of the neurology department at Hôtel-Dieu.[69]

The many eulogies that were published upon Dr. Barbeau's premature death from kidney failure depict him as something of a Renaissance man, who combined a love of literature, music, art, religion, and philosophy, with science and medicine. He was a zealous proponent of French and Québecois culture, and wrote passionately against the spectre of assimilation with American and English culture. Dr. Barbeau was not a scholar who developed ideas by simply importing European or American psychological theories. While willing to learn from other cultures, he was insistent that French-Canadians consciously fashion a distinctive and nationalist medical science.[70]

Dr. Barbeau's wide-ranging academic publications encompassed writing on malaria, eugenics, sterilization of the unfit, early dementia, syphilis, men-

Centre hospitalier de l'Université de Montréal, photographed by Albert Dumas

Antonio Barbeau, professor, 1939

tal hygiene, neurology, criminal insanity, epilepsy, neuroses, and psychoses.[71] He appears to have done substantial empirical research. His articles and books on these topics described multiple studies, complete with charts, bars, and graphs, conducted on sample populations, many at the Bordeaux Prison where he was the superintendent of the criminally insane wing.[72] His famous publication "*L'enfant et la criminologie*," which was reprinted numerous times, was a complete contrast. He opened this with the comment that "*le médecin [est un] continuel observateur de la nature humaine*," — "the doctor is a continual observer of human nature." Then he apologized that what followed was devoid of empirical study: "*Négligeant systématiquement tout étalage de statistiques, de citations, d'interprétations quantitatives, je voudrais aujourd'hui montrer l'enfant face à Justice*." — "Systematically neglecting to provide supporting statistics, references, and quantitative observations, today I wish to show the child facing Justice."[73]

The absence of research did not deter Dr. Barbeau from issuing pejorative generalizations about child witnesses. He claimed that error, and not truth, flowed naturally from the mouths of children. He stated that children lived in a world of dreams, rather than reality; that they had a horror of real absolutes, of which they were blissfully ignorant; that they had an instinctive tendency to create myths; and that they were supremely suggestible. He added that they loved only themselves, and were subject to capricious sentiments and irrevocable hatreds.[74] Such characteristics made them a menace in court:

> *Il suit de là que, devant le tribunal, l'enfant est, par définition psychologique, un témoin suspect. L'ambiance intimidante de la cour n'est pas de nature à conférer à ses dires une objectivité plus grande. Inhibition complète ou inexactitude représenteront ses perspectives les plus probables. Les témoignages sérieux donnés par des enfants ne peuvent être qu'exceptionnels. En résumé, à moins qu'il ne s'agisse de faits ultra-simples et corroborés par d'autres témoins sérieux, l'enfant devant le tribunal n'est pas à sa place. De par sa psychologie même, il ne peut que desservir la fin véritable de la Justice qui est de connaître la Vérité, toute la Vérité, rien que la Vérité.*

It follows that, before a court of law, the child is by psychological definition a suspect witness. The intimidating environment of the court is not of the sort to confer greater objectivity on his statements. Complete inhibition or inaccuracy represent more likely prospects. Serious testimony given by children can only be exceptional. To summarize, unless the facts reported are ultra-simple and corroborated by other serious witnesses, the child's place is not before a court

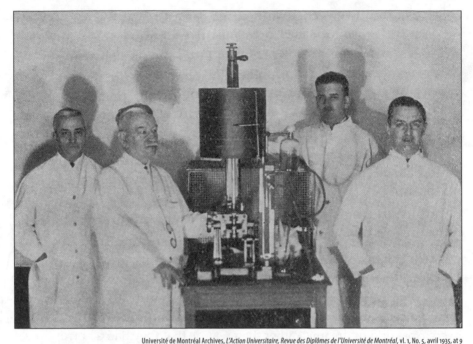

Université de Montréal Archives, *L'Action Universitaire, Revue des Diplômes de l'Université de Montréal*, vl. 1, No. 5, avril 1935, at 9

University of Montréal Physiology Lab, 1935. Left to right: M.M. Lapointe, E.G. Asselin, Gaston Gosselin, Antonio Barbeau

of law. By reason of his psychology, he can only disserve the true end of Justice, which is to know the Truth, the full Truth, and nothing but the Truth.[75]

Although Dr. Barbeau was prepared to concede that some adults did victimize children, the fear of false accusations, especially against parents and guardians, loomed throughout his writing:

> *Tous, nous avons lu ces effrayantes histoires d'enfants, accusateurs de leurs parents devant les tribunaux. Il n'y a jamais eu de plus infamante accusation portée devant la justice que celle du Dauphin contre sa mère Marie-Antoinette. Il n'y en a peut-être pas de plus banales dans les romans feuilletons appelés annales judiciaires, que les accusations des pseudo-enfants-martyrs. Victimes fictives: nous venons de le signaler. C'est le rôle du magistrat de faire la part du vrai et du fantastique dans le mille forfaits que certains enfants, anormaux et pervers, imputent à leurs parents ou à leurs protecteurs.*

We have all read frightening stories of children accusing their parents in a court of law. There has never been a more infamous charge than that filed by the Dauphin against his mother Marie-Antoinette. There may be no accusations as commonplace in the serialized novels called judicial annals than that of false child-martyrs. Fictional victims: as we just pointed out. It is the judge's role to distinguish truth from fantasy in the thousand crimes that some children, abnormal and perverse, impute to their parents or their guardians.[76]

What are the sources for these sweeping statements about falsehoods told by so many "abnormal and perverse" children? Stories we have all read (unreferenced), serial novels, and Marie-Antoinette. It is all the more surprising, coming from a highly reputed scientist, who in other scholarly endeavours was well versed in research techniques and rational empirical inquiry. In the complete absence of supporting social science data, the tendency of adults to fear the recriminations of children seems remarkable. The marked power imbalance that attends parent–child relations, and those of other adults who come into a care-giving situation with youngsters, ought more logically to lead to the conclusion that most abused children will not disclose their mistreatment. It is denial of abuse that ought, more realistically, to be viewed with skepticism.

Had Dr. Barbeau felt it helpful to cite any research apart from his own musings, there was little material extant. The two leading theorists of child development at the time, Freud and Piaget, had also drawn sweeping generalizations about the untrustworthiness of children, speculating well beyond their sources.[77] Trying to account for the reluctance to credit disclosures about violence against women and children more generally, some observers have concluded that the "reality in question is too unseemly to stomach."[78] It would take decades before researchers began to try to measure empirically the reliability of such generalizations. Studies from the late 1970s into the present have produced contradictory findings, leaving most to conclude that the only certainty is that more research is needed. In the words of two leading researchers: "Our knowledge about children and truth in legal proceedings is so limited that few conclusions that can be useful in the legal arena can be drawn."[79]

But neither Dr. Barbeau nor Judge Bissonnette seem to have had any concern that the flagrant generalizations they pronounced had no factual foundation. After his ringing endorsement of Dr. Barbeau, Judge Bissonnette closed his judgment with a final rumination. "There are in this case some facts that one suspects, but we can go no further. Did the child's mother perjure herself? She could have thrown some light on this affair. If she preferred protecting her concubinage with appellant to defending the honour of her little daughter, she will always bear the redoubtable responsibility for so doing." This remarkable passage suggests that Judge Bissonnette had his own suspicions, and this time not only against child evidence. If Judge Bissonnette's hunches were correct, no apologies can be made for Mme Tremblay's role in this very sad case. However it seems odd that his tongue-lashing was directed solely at the mother. For if Mme Tremblay had perjured herself, so had her paramour, Ovila Soulière. The man who had perpetrated the sexual crime, if one had been committed, came in for no reproach whatsoever. The full responsibility was shifted to the shoulders of the little girl's mother: away from the perpetrator of the crime, and equally away from the appellate court judges who had dismissed the child's evidence with such dispatch.

The Consequences of the Corroboration Doctrine

THE QUÉBEC COURT OF Appeal concluded that there was no point in sending the parties back for a new trial, because it was unlikely that would "bring out new facts." The judges conceded that it was "undeniable" that "this little girl of five years was outraged," using the language of sexual assault then in vogue. Yet their refusal to offer any legal protection to Marie Tremblay provoked not a moment's hesitation. Ruling that there was no corroboration in law, they quashed the conviction and discharged the prisoner.

The credibility of witnesses rests at the foundation of the legal system. It is beyond debate that some witnesses tell the truth, while others do not. However, the manner in which the trustworthiness of witnesses is assessed reveals a great deal about the judiciary, the legislators who shape the statutory framework of evaluation, and the wider society within which such findings of credibility are constructed. Deeply suspicious of the testimony of women and children, Canadian authorities parlayed their unsubstantiated anxieties into a thicket of rules that demanded confirmatory evidence that went well beyond the ordinary tests for veracity. Instead of allowing fact-finders to scrutinize each witness, observe their demeanour under cross-examination, and draw appropriate conclusions, the law created an almost irrebuttable presumption of incredibility.

Psychiatrists published weighty tomes speculating about the untrustworthiness of women and children, undeterred by the absence of empirical research or inquiry. Legislators laid down statutory enactments that insisted upon corroboration, setting forth parameters that were substantially narrower than the ordinary usage of the word might have suggested. In the hands of the judiciary, the boundaries of what qualified constricted still further. The confusing complexity of the doctrine led to multiple errors on the part of trial judges, many of whose most valiant attempts to do justice to the restrictive rules went down to defeat.

Judge Ste-Marie was no anomaly. The records are filled with cases of appeal courts critiquing the performance of trial judges in their rulings on corroboration. Trial judges who failed to warn jurors of the dangers of convicting without corroboration, even where corroboration existed, were overturned.[80] Trial judges who warned the jury that "many years of painful experience" had taught them the lesson that "complaints of sexual misconduct unfortunately are often untrue and unfounded," but forgot to warn them specifically about the danger of convicting on uncorroborated evidence, were overruled.[81] Trial judges who failed to explain what the term "corroboration" meant were overturned.[82] Trial judges who warned of the importance of corroboration, but did not tell jurors which pieces of evidence they might look to as possible corroboration, were reversed.[83] Trial judges who tried to instruct the jury on which pieces of evidence might constitute corroboration, but made mistakes as to which did and which didn't, were reversed.[84] Trial judges who failed to spell out "with exactitude and precision" what evidence constituted corroboration were also overruled.[85] Trial judges who charged jurors that specific items of evidence were corroborative were overturned because they should have told the jurors only that the evidence *could* have been corroborative, leaving it to the jury to decide whether it "ought to be so regarded."[86] Trial judges who failed to clarify that corroboration was required both as to the fact that the sexual assault occurred, and that it had been committed by the accused, and to distinguish between the two, were reversed.[87]

Speaking for the Newfoundland Supreme Court in 1960, Justice Sir Brian Dunfield would complain heartily about the idiocy of the rules:

> One cannot help feeling that the common sense warning that an unscrupulous, or untruthful, or an hysterical woman can bring grave charges against a man, and force him to try to prove a negative, has been blown up into too technical a matter. It would surely be an extremely stupid jury to which, or to some members of which, the point would not occur anyway. Part of the very purpose of juries is to bring in the practical man-of-the-world point of view, as against technicality. To assume that if the judge does not mention the point they will not think of it really does seem going rather far. Every practical judge knows that for every one person wrongly convicted by a jury, very

many who ought to be convicted go free; and rather exaggerated fears are often expressed as to the risk of unsound conviction. . . . To say that there is a rule that a judge must willy-nilly indicate certain classes of evidence, seems to me to go too far.[88]

While Judge Dunfield's *cri de coeur* is certainly a welcome indication that not all judges complacently complied, his comment is intriguing as well for what it indicates about the biases of jurors. Judge Dunfield's mention of the suspicions that would naturally arise in most "man-of-the-world" jurors is telling. The doctrine of corroboration was only the top layer of barriers facing women and children who attempted to seek legal protection against sexual assault. It rested upon another layer of misogynistic skepticism that ran far deeper into the male psyches of judges and jurors.

Fashioning corroboration as the *sine qua non* for conviction was calculated to ensure that the testimony of guilty men would receive more credence on the scales of justice than the testimony of female and child victims of sexual assault. The restrictive definition of corroboration tilted the balance still further. The application of such doctrines in the hands of the judges whittled down the scope of qualifying evidence and served to skewer the credibility of women and children who complained of sexual abuse. The doctrine of corroboration made a mockery of the ideals of evenhanded justice, and left Marie Tremblay vulnerable to exploitative sexual assault. One can only wonder what the days and months after the appeal ruling held for her, abandoned by the legal system, and left to the mercies of her mother and Ovila Soulière.

Chapter 8

CANADA'S FIRST CAPITAL "L" LESBIAN SEXUAL ASSAULT: Yellowknife, 1955

THERE WERE THOUSANDS OF prosecutions for sexual assault during the twentieth century, but the 1955 case of *Regina v. Moore* appears to have been the first in Canadian history where the complainant and the accused were both female.[1] Same-sex relationships had not gone unnoticed, of course. Police had used nuisance by-laws and vagrancy charges to harass women cross-dressing as men for years.[2] Prosecutions against gay men for "buggery," "indecent assault upon a male," and "acts of gross indecency" also stretched back many years.[3] But this seems to have been the first prosecution of a woman for "indecent assault upon a female." The presiding judges, who characterized the case as highly "unusual," described the behaviour as "Lesbianism" with a capital "L."[4]

A Newcomer in Yellowknife

THERE IS VERY LITTLE information about Willimae Moore, the woman at the centre of this unprecedented prosecution. Like many of the residents of Yellowknife, she was new to the town. An American citizen by birth, she had flown into the northern mining community on 1 September 1954. Her travelling companion was Beatrice Gonzales, who had been hired as the vice-principal for the Yellowknife High School. Willimae had found work as a "casual" and temporary typist with the federal government's Department of Northern Affairs and Natural Resources. The two women lived together in the schoolteacher's house on Franklin Road. Although her age is uncertain, it seems that Willimae was in her forties.[5]

Yellowknife, aerial view, 1961

Giant Mine, Yellowknife, aerial view, 1947

The town into which Willimae Moore and Beatrice Gonzales flew at the start of the freezing season was on the edge of the Arctic Circle next to Great Slave Lake. Travellers arrived by plane, mostly Canadian Pacific Airways DC3s, flying 700 air miles north from Edmonton on flights priced at $210 return. Because the routes were generally milk runs, with stops at every town along the way, it could take seven hours to reach Yellowknife, even if the plane was on time. Although it was often described as "a child of the air age," Yellowknife was sustained during the brief summer by water freight transport, which ferried in materials ordered a year ahead. Residents dined on dehydrated and canned vegetables and fruits, supplemented with caribou steak and ptarmigan. Those who lived there in the fifties recalled Yellowknife as memorable for its small houses, board sidewalks, and absence of long distance phones.[6]

As the travel-weary Willimae Moore and Beatrice Gonzales disembarked from the plane with their dog, they must have been struck by the stark landscape: stunted spruce trees clinging to the glacier-scarred, rocky outcropping of the Canadian Shield, and wild mosses growing in the bush. Newcomers were usually staggered by the weather. The harsh winters produced light snow for months on end, and temperatures that varied between four and minus fifty-eight degrees Celsius. As one of the bush pilots reminisced: "When it was a mere twenty below . . . we'd think, 'Boy, this is a great day; we can push back our parka hoods.'" The colourful aurora borealis, also known as the "Northern Lights," made the night sky magical.[7]

The population had reached 2000 in 1954, in a community that was overwhelmingly white after racial tensions forced the Aboriginal people to move to Detah, across the bay. More than half the workforce was employed in the Con and Giant gold mines. Virtually all the white residents of the isolated town came from somewhere else. Their unifying characteristic was a strong streak of "individuality and non-conformity." The townspeople took pride in their "camaraderie" and the "thrill of isolation," referring to areas other than Yellowknife as "the outside."[8] Social norms were substantially looser than in the south. A stenographer who arrived in 1946 recorded her surprise when she discovered that some of the couples were "shacked-up" (a new term to her) without benefit of marriage. And many of the single women who came after her described fending off amorous assaults from drunken miners, taxi drivers, and pilots, who seemed to take a licence for wayward behaviour from the boisterous drinking culture.[9]

Beatrice Gonzales's apartment, 1950s

The Sexual Overture

SHORTLY AFTER SHE STARTED in the typing pool, Willimae Moore was introduced to Laura White (whose name has been altered to protect her privacy). Laura had worked as a stenographer for the federal government in Ottawa until she moved up to Yellowknife in the summer of 1953. Both women were typing "land and game documents" under the supervision of Harold James Mitchell, the sub-district administrator and mining recorder. They became friendly and socialized in each other's homes. The relationship altered on Saturday, 22 January 1955, when Laura found a brown envelope on her desk. The letter inside would become Exhibit A in the ensuing criminal prosecution:

My dear Laura;

I suppose some people just go all through life knocking their heads against that proverbial stone wall. I certainly should know because I seem to be doing a pretty good job of it myself right through here.

Bea stayed at home on Monday, Tuesday and Wednesday, because she was honestly ill; Thursday she went back to work. Yesterday it was another story altogether. She stayed at home because she knew I had every intention of taking that afternoon plane out of here. She knows there is some woman in Yellowknife "bugging" me, but who the woman is, she doesn't know. She has a good idea it may be Alice. If she only knew how wrong she is!

You made it quite clear to me that my type of life is quite foreign to you and, even if it were not, you'd not have any interest in it. That I can understand very well. It's certainly not the first time I've had to buck this particular type of situation. The big difference is that prior to this, I have been able and willing to bow out gracefully. This time I am not finding it very easy. I'm particularly sorry because I know that if I don't leave you alone, I am taking a chance on losing your friendship. I'd be very sorry for that; I value your friendship very highly.

I wish there was some way of making you understand just how I feel. You probably feel that women with me are just a weakness which, like most weaknesses, can be gotten over with a bit of will power on my part. That's not true. Women to me are as important — in many cases more important — than the food I eat or the water I drink. They are a vitally important part of my life and, should the time ever come when I might be denied any relationship with them, I may as well just stop breathing. That may sound like just so much hog-wash to you but, believe me, it's been tried before, a fact to which Bea can swear, and I almost lost my mind.

I would never ask you to try to change. That would be very foolish. Any such thought or desire would have to come from your side. I do ask, though, that you be a bit tolerant of me. Even though it may seem as though you will be catering to a person's weakness, it certainly won't be for long. As a matter of fact, the Spring in which you are planning on leaving is coming much quicker than I care to think about. What will happen after you go, I don't know. In any case, you surely have nothing to lose, nothing I could do to you would phase you in one way or another and would certainly leave you unblemished. How many men can say that?

I suppose you have noticed long since just what part of a woman's body I am weakest for. If I get no more than that, believe me, I can be very happy. If I ever went any further than that, it would be entirely up to you.

If you feel at this point you simply don't want to have anything to do with me whatsoever, you need only say. I'll understand and keep my distance.

WILLIE.

Despite the anguish evident in the letter, this was a bold overture. The word "lesbian" was never voiced, but Willimae appears to have taken great pride in her love for women. Her query, "How many men can say that?" reveals an awareness of the dangers that heterosexuality posed for women, and a resounding dismissal of this in her own life.

Laura White would later testify that the letter had not come entirely out of the blue. Willimae had asked her earlier what she thought of "women wanting other women," and Laura had replied that "she didn't know a great deal about it," but believed "it was an illness" and "an abnormality." Her negative characterization of lesbianism was in keeping with the times. The chaos of the Second World War had briefly opened up new space for gays and lesbians, but post-war retrenchment demanded strict compliance with compulsory heterosexuality.[10] In 1952, Canadian immigration law had been amended to bar all "homosexuals" from entry.[11] And during the late 1950s and early sixties, the RCMP would recruit psychologists and psychiatrists to oust gay and lesbian "perverts" from the civil service.[12] Dr. Alfred Kinsey's research on the prevalence of same-sex relations, released in Canada a few years earlier, had sparked accusations of Communism and demands for suppression.[13] Anti-vice campaigners disparaged *Batman* and *Robin* comics as "a wish dream of two homosexuals living together" and *Wonder Woman* as a dangerous role model, whose lesbianism was "psychologically unmistakable."[14]

Lesbians searching for positive images in popular culture found little there. Lurid pulp fiction distributed in the 1950s under titles such as *Daytime in Suburbia, Black Nylon Lovers,* and *Satan Was a Lesbian,* titillated readers with stories of alcoholism, violence, suicide, and heterosexual conversion. In 1952, the dime-store novel *Women's Barracks* was found criminally obscene in an Ottawa court, because of its portrayal of lesbian sexual attraction during the war.[15] *Queer Patterns* was typical of the genre. A female theatrical director and an actress in New York City fall in love, a lesbian nurse complicates the plot, and all three find themselves stalked by ugly gossip, "its fetid breath" trailing "slimy fingers dipped in the filth of rumour and scandal." The nurse is killed in a car accident as she "walks in a daze," causing the author to pause briefly to note: "Death is the only release from certain hopeless maladies." The actress saves herself from strangulation, but dies violently pages later, and the novel ends with the director sobbing over her female lover's coffin. The back cover urges readers to buy "this book and gain an enlightened understanding of the lost women whose strange urges produce one of the great problems of modern society."[16]

The few Canadian medical researchers and clinicians who wrote about homosexuality in the 1950s characterized it as "a mental hygiene problem," "a personality disturbance," and "a matter of neurotic conflict," possibly linked to "hereditary susceptibilities" and triggered by "faulty training and environment." Although the literature focused primarily on male homosexuality, there were isolated references to "homosexual females." Canadian medical journals noted that it had "been thought that homosexual females are masculine in appearance and movement" and are "interested in more masculine occupations." However, it was not always possible to pick them out "by appearance and manner alone." Speculating on the causes of lesbianism, one Saskatchewan psychologist put the blame on mothers who might have made girls "believe that all men are evil wolves and that sex relations are bestial."[17] Even the most progressive of physicians, who pleaded for sympathy from the medical profession, the clergy, and the law, defined homosexuality as an "affliction" in need of a "solution."[18] Electroshock, chemical intervention, hypnotism, aversion therapy, and other forms of behaviour modification were prescribed as "treatment" for lesbians incarcerated in prison or mental institutions.[19]

Although Laura White seems to have accepted the homophobia of the culture that surrounded her, she was ambivalent about what to do about the letter. When Willimae asked if the two of them might lunch together at Laura's home next Tuesday, she agreed. Laura testified about what happened next:

Q. What did you do when you got there?
A. We both took our coats off.
Q. Was there any conversation between you?
A. Yes, I asked her what she wanted for lunch.
Q. She said, "I'll have you," and I said, "Don't be ridiculous, will you have a drink?" and she answered, "Yes." I then asked her if she would have anything to eat, and she said, "No." I asked her if she would have a cup of coffee and she said, "Yes." I poured her the drink and I went into the kitchen and made sandwiches and coffee.

Laura seated herself on the armchair, Willimae sat on the sofa, and they ate lunch. They talked about Willimae's inclination to take the plane out the next day, about Beatrice's efforts to dissuade her. At two o'clock, Laura left for work, resolving to tell Beatrice about Willimae's overture. Later that afternoon, she found Beatrice in her classroom and showed her the letter. When Beatrice returned home, she found a note from Willimae:

My dearest Beatrice —

"Greater love hath no man." There have not been many battles in the last 2–3 years for which you have not gone to bat for me. Yet, it was inevitable that the time should come when I would have to face the forces alone.
    The time has come —

"W"

Beatrice left for Laura's apartment where, to her surprise, she found Willimae. Willimae started to cry and she and Beatrice collapsed into each other's arms. Then, in another surprising turn of events, Willimae suggested a game of Scrabble, and Beatrice left for home because she "couldn't stand Scrabble."

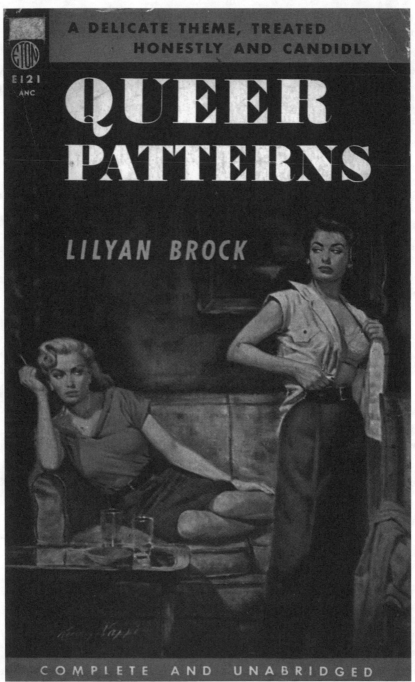

The front cover of *Queer Patterns*, a novel by Lilyan Brock (New York: Eton Books, 1935)

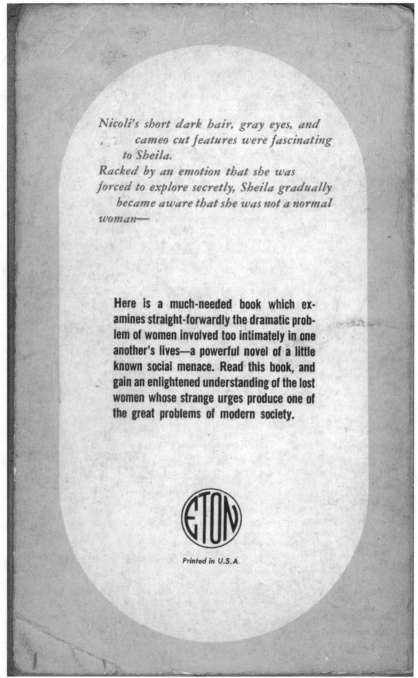

Nicoli's short dark hair, gray eyes, and cameo cut features were fascinating to Sheila.
Racked by an emotion that she was forced to explore secretly, Sheila gradually became aware that she was not a normal woman—

Here is a much-needed book which examines straight-forwardly the dramatic problem of women involved too intimately in one another's lives—a powerful novel of a little known social menace. Read this book, and gain an enlightened understanding of the lost women whose strange urges produce one of the great problems of modern society.

ETON

Printed in U.S.A.

The back cover of *Queer Patterns* by Lilyan Brock (New York: Eton Books, 1935)

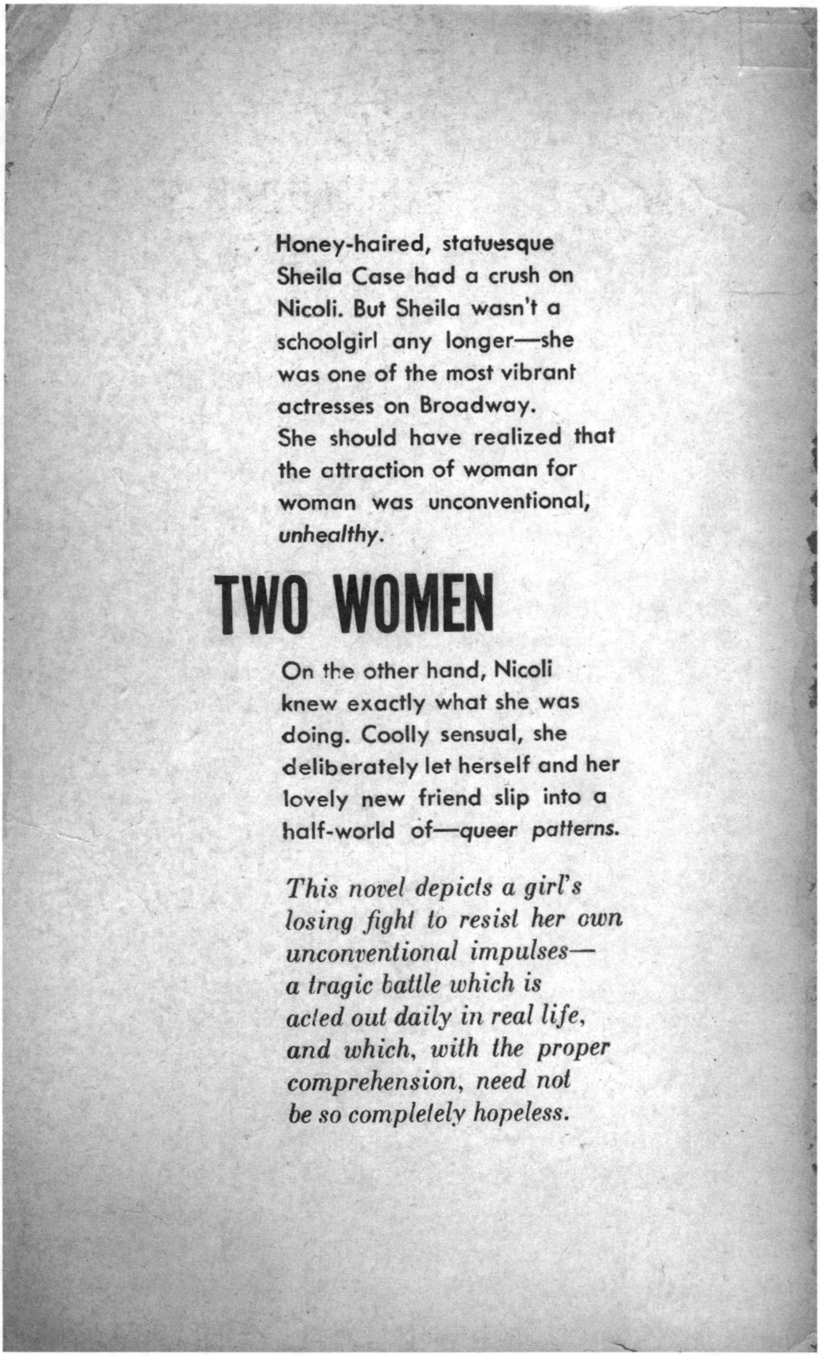

Honey-haired, statuesque Sheila Case had a crush on Nicoli. But Sheila wasn't a schoolgirl any longer—she was one of the most vibrant actresses on Broadway. She should have realized that the attraction of woman for woman was unconventional, *unhealthy*.

TWO WOMEN

On the other hand, Nicoli knew exactly what she was doing. Coolly sensual, she deliberately let herself and her lovely new friend slip into a half-world of—*queer patterns.*

This novel depicts a girl's losing fight to resist her own unconventional impulses— a tragic battle which is acted out daily in real life, and which, with the proper comprehension, need not be so completely hopeless.

Courtesy of Bruce Ryder, Osgoode Hall Law School, York University

The description of *Queer Patterns* by Lilyan Brock (New York: Eton Books, 1935)

Laura pulled the hassock up to the coffee table, and the two women opened up the board game. The trial transcript gave Laura's version of what transpired next:

Q. Did the game commence?

A. After about four or five moves I looked up and Miss Moore was looking at me very strangely.

Q. Can you tell the Court about her appearing to be strange?

A. It was a rather concentrated look.

Q. What did you do?

A. I immediately looked down.

Q. What happened then?

A. She grabbed hold of me and attempted to kiss me.

Q. Was anything said?

A. I can't recall too much other than — I know there were words between us and then she said to me, "You are cruel," and I started to cry.

Q. Were you permitting her to do this?

A. I tried to push her away. She is very strong.

Q. Had you ever invited any attention of this matter?

A. Not to my knowledge.

Q. What do you mean, "Not to my knowledge"?

A. I never took it as that.

The Laying of Criminal Charges

THE NEXT MORNING LAURA reported the situation to her boss, Harold James "Mitch" Mitchell. Mitchell had been in the North longer than many, working first as a federal government accountant in Hay River, and then in Yellowknife for some years. He had an outgoing personality and a reputation as a comedian at parties.[20] It was Mitchell who made the decision to turn over the letter and Willimae's Underwood typewriter to Corporal William George Campbell, the RCMP officer stationed in Yellowknife. Campbell forwarded the whole package to the Crime Detection Laboratory in Regina. The crime lab confirmed that Willimae's typewriter had typed the letter, and that the signature was identical to signatures on Willimae's bank records and order forms from the Yellowknife Liquor Store. Corporal Campbell charged Willimae Moore with "unlawfully and indecently assaulting [Laura White] a female."

Courtesy of Ralph Moyle

Department of Northern Affairs,
Yellowknife, 1955–56. Harold
Mitchell, first row, far left.

What was there about Yellowknife, a town that had seen more than its share of sexual unconventionality, that marked it out for this first lesbian prosecution? As one observer has suggested, in the historical construction of gay and lesbian identity and spaces, "place mattered."[21] In some ways, it seems an unlikely location. Yellowknife was filled with non-conformists, many of them hoping to "escape the scrutiny of others." The North held a lure for those who chafed at the confines of heterosexuality, and some moved there precisely because they believed it would bring a safe haven.[22] But the sheer number of gays and lesbians seeking isolation and anonymity in the North may, ironically, have increased the likelihood of prosecution. With the Cold War crackdown on homosexuality, in Yellowknife in 1955, neither Harold Mitchell nor Corporal Campbell was prepared to look the other way.

The decision to prosecute Willimae Moore sent a buzz through the town, with rumours rife over what this might mean about the nature of the accused's relationship with the high school vice-principal. Many in Yellowknife seem to have been aware that the trial was a novelty.[23] An attempted kiss would have been trifling if the gesture had involved a man and a woman. What Willimae Moore was accused of doing to Laura White was very different from the evidence in most male-to-female "indecent assault" trials. The latter cases encompassed feeling a woman's breasts and reaching under her skirt,[24] touching a thirteen-year-old's "private parts,"[25] rubbing a seven year old's vagina,[26] the forced insertion of a penis in a young girl's mouth,[27] the ripping of underpants and the placing of a penis on a woman's genitals,[28] a sexual assault short of penetration that left visible bruising on a woman's thighs,[29] another committed while dragging a woman from a car and badly ripping her clothes,[30] and still another while tearing off the underpants of a seven-year-old girl who was screaming and trying to get out of a car.[31] In one case, the court described the man's conduct as "sadistic," noting that he had inflicted "painful and serious injuries on the sexual organs of the little girl either by the use of his hands or otherwise."[32] In another, a judge found the

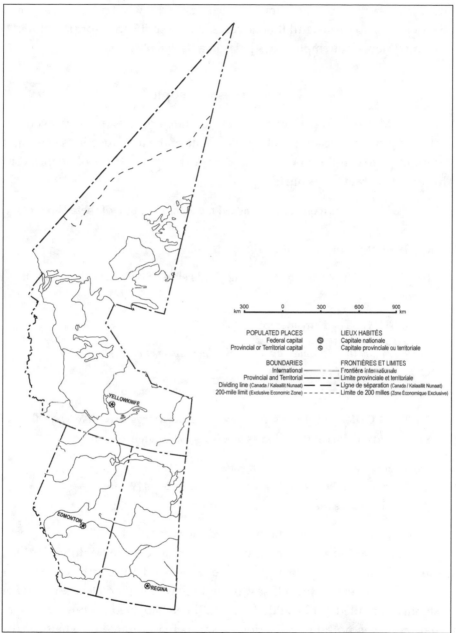

Map of the Northwest Territories, Saskatchewan, and Alberta, showing Yellowknife, Edmonton, and Regina.

indecent assault committed upon a hitchhiker who was trying to get home to a sick child so distasteful that he refused to describe the "sordid details."[33] Willimae Moore's attempted kiss pales in a list such as this.[34]

"These Types of People"

WILLIMAE MOORE'S TRIAL COMMENCED on 10 March 1955, after she waived her right to a jury and pleaded "not guilty."[35] One of the first questions was what terminology to use. Laura White tried the phrase "these types of people," but this only frustrated the court:

A. Well in the office one day she asked me what I thought of these types of people.

Q. Types of people — that's alright.

BY THE COURT: We are not mincing words either, you must call a spade a spade.

BY MISS [WHITE]: I am attempting to.

Direct examination continued by Mr. Parker [the Crown attorney]:

Q. What types of people?

A. She asked what I thought of women wanting other women.

BY THE COURT: Where possible give the exact words used. We want the exact words of the conversation as nearly as you can remember.

Direct examination continued by Mr. Parker:

Q. Do you recall how she phrased the question, Miss [White]?

A. I couldn't give the exact words.

It was Harold Mitchell who first used the word "lesbian," when he testified that Laura had told him "she had reason to believe [Willimae] was a Lesbian." As if to denote the significance of the word, the court stenographer capitalized the term. Mitchell seems not to have been too clear about what lesbianism entailed, for he added that Willimae had tried to convince Laura "that there was nothing too serious about being intimate or whatever the equivalent was." Exactly what lesbians did with each other seems to have mystified many. An Ontario trial judge expressed as much seventeen years later, when trying to explain to a jury terminology related to sexual practices other than heterosexual intercourse: "Frankly gentlemen, I had to get the dictionary to know what it was about. I venture to say most of you are the same."[36]

The real sparks flew when Beatrice took the stand, and was cross-examined on her knowledge of same-sex sexuality. Willimae never testified at the trial, and it was Beatrice, in keeping with her history of "going to bat" for Willimae, who advanced the defence. Beatrice claimed that Willimae had never typed the letter, that the signature was forged, and that the entire affair was a nasty hoax. But first, Beatrice was asked to give evidence about her life history. And thus we come to learn about an extraordinary individual, whose life story underscores yet again how many hidden treasures lie buried in legal archives. It is worth pausing to examine the experiences of a woman who must have been one of the most accomplished Canadians of her generation.

The Education and Work History of Beatrice Gonzales

BEATRICE MARGARET GONZALES was born in Vancouver on 15 June 1907.[37] George C. Gonzales, her father, was a skilled mill-mace. Her mother, Lilly Rae Gonzales, was a dressmaker.[38] Beatrice lost her father while she was still a student, and her mother remarried George Wellington, a Welsh-born machinist, who worked for automobile repair garages. Lilly ran a dress shop under the name "Madame Wellington" on Alma Street near Broadway.[39] The couple had another child, William, when Beatrice was fourteen years old.[40] Beatrice took her stepfather's surname, and enrolled as a student at the University of British Columbia under the name of Beatrice Wellington. While there, she came under the mentorship of the Dean of Women, Mary Louise Bollert, who took a special interest in the promising pupil. Beatrice graduated with a bachelor of arts in history and economics in 1927.[41]

Although many women from working-class families would have been justifiably proud of completing one degree, Beatrice continued on. The Crown attorney's long list of questions kept eliciting more degrees:

Q. You have told us that you have a degree from the University of British Columbia, that is a B.A. degree?

A. Yes.

Q. Is there a degree from California?

A. Summer school.

Q. Leading to a degree?

Beatrice Gonzales, 1948

A. Yes.

Q. Do you hold an M.A. degree?

A. I do.

Q. From where?

A. University of London.

Q. England?

A. Yes.

Q. What year did you get that?

A. 1944.

Q. And in what subjects — what was it granted for, in what field?

A. Slavonic studies and peasant agriculture.

Q. M.A. degree from the University of London, London, England?

A. Yes.

Q. And you went to Columbia University in New York?

A. Yes.

Q. What degree?

A. Master of arts.

BY MISS GONZALES: I would like to ask if I am on trial by Mr. Parker?

BY THE COURT: This is cross-examination.

CROSS-EXAMINATION CONTINUED BY MR. PARKER:

Q. You hold a degree from Columbia University, New York?

A. Yes.

Q. What year did you obtain that?

A. 1935.

Q. And in what subjects was that obtained?

A. That was totalling up my credits from the University of California plus
the study of peasant agriculture.

Crown attorney John Parker appeared astonished, even skeptical, about the list of degrees spanning two decades and four universities.[42] Parker did not move in circles where women received such education. His own wife, Claire, was a homemaker who was raising their three children. Parker had come to Yellowknife in 1944, the first lawyer to live and practise in the Northwest Territories. In 1945, he married Claire, who had come to Yellowknife to visit her sister, who was married to a bush pilot. John's office hours were lax, but his practice involved drawing up options and agreements, business incorporations, criminal work, and a part-time Crown attorney appointment.

Courtesy of Claire Parker, published in Susan Jackson, ed., *Yellowknife, N.W.T: An Illustrated History* (Sechelt: Nor'West, 1990) at 101

Lawyer brothers John and Peter Parker

Described as a "fiery speaker who came straight to the point," and a "visionary and a sparkplug," Parker was elected in 1954 to the Council of the N.W.T., a post he would continue to hold for years by acclamation. In 1958, he would be appointed to sit as a judge of the Yukon Territory, in Whitehorse.[43]

Parker's amazement must have grown as it became clear that Beatrice Gonzales had done more than just study. Asked to describe her occupation, she responded: "I am an economist, social worker, and teacher." The stipendiary magistrate, seemingly bewildered, intervened: "May I have some further information as to Miss Gonzales' qualifications? Economist, social worker, and teacher?" Beatrice Gonzales would have drawn their full attention as she began to describe her employment history. A forty-seven-year-old woman, stout with greying hair and conservatively dressed, she had "a presence about her" that, according to her students, "commanded an immediate respect." As one recalled: "You paid attention when she walked into a room. You were very aware of her. You knew that she was somebody."[44]

Beatrice had entered the workforce as a teacher from 1929 to 1936, at Vancouver's Edith Cavell School and Point Grey Junior High, and then at Chilliwack High School.[45] In 1936, the League of Nations Society in Ottawa

John and Claire Parker

Courtesy of Claire Parker, James Whyard, photographer. Published in Susan Jackson, ed., *Yellowknife, N.W.T.: An Illustrated History* (Sechelt: Nor'West, 1990) at 100

nominated Beatrice as Western Canada's delegate to the First World Youth Conference in Geneva. The consensus was that it was here that her "exceptional organizing and executive ability" were first recognized.[46] While she pursued postgraduate work in Geneva, Beatrice worked as administrative assistant to the Peace Disarmament Committee of the Women's International Commission, and then with the Women's Service of the International Labor Office. Described as a "university graduate with a fine record of work with young people," who was "clever," "versatile," and "friendly," she was seconded by the international YWCA to organize a camp for girls in Rezek, Czechoslovakia, in the summer of 1938.[47]

Thoughts of recreational camps were soon to recede from the agenda. The world was careening towards war, and Beatrice was in the thick of the European maelstrom. In September 1938, Germany occupied part of Czechoslovakia under the Munich Pact. That month the Czech government hired Beatrice to help survey the tragic consequences. Although Beatrice could speak only English, she hired translators in Prague and immersed herself in refugee work, helping to resettle the Sudetenland refugees and evacuate Jewish Czechs to England and Canada. Her effectiveness led to an appointment as the head of the British Refugee Commission in Prague.[48] Years later, one of the families she helped gratefully recalled Beatrice's efforts to warn Jews of the impending German invasion, her ingenious strategies to secure visas, and her successful plot to include their family among a group of forty to fifty Jewish children she was assisting. All this, one refugee related, was at "great risk to everyone involved, especially herself." The danger was not lost on Beatrice, who confessed that "when she saw people off at the station, her knees were like boiled macaroni."[49] The first her family learned of this was when a Czech physicist, who had escaped through Beatrice's efforts, tried to track her down years later to express his thanks. His search led him to Beatrice's brother at the University of British Columbia, who was startled to hear of his sister's heroic work under the Nazi regime.[50]

Beatrice's notoriety eventually resulted in her arrest by the German Gestapo. Detained a second time in April 1939, she was "subjected to Gestapo third degree" questioning, but managed to secure release a week later. She continued her evacuation efforts until the final days before war broke out in August 1939, when she was forced to relocate to London. By this time, Beatrice had helped thousands of Czechs flee the country, including Dr. Julie Matouskova, the general secretary of the YWCA in Prague.[51]

In London, she came perilously close to losing her life twice during the bombing. She also took on a host of new positions: chief welfare officer of the Czech Refugee Trust Fund, labour liaison officer and secretary to the Minister of Production, research assistant to the Royal Institute of International Affairs, and the head of the secretariat of the European regional office of the United Nations Relief and Rehabilitation Administration (UNRRA). At the war's close, UNRRA promoted her to the post of chief supply officer in Warsaw, to coordinate all foreign voluntary relief agencies in Poland. She trekked to outlying areas, often through blizzards and subzero weather, pushing her uncooperative automobile up even the slightest incline, to report on population, housing, transportation, and industry.[52] She was quoted in the *Vancouver Sun* in January 1947, as saying: "Polish children have forgotten Christmas. They know it only as a time of year that brings greater cold into the earthen cellars dug under the ruins of houses and buildings that they must call their homes."[53]

Beatrice's correspondence stressed her concern about the gender inequality of Polish women, and the need to include women's organizations in postwar relief. She lamented that "so much is being done for the men and boys that it almost seems that there is some force at work to restrict women's organisational activities and to relegate women to the home." She also reported new Jewish pogroms in the Kiece area, adding that it passed her comprehension how, "after all the Poles have been through, they can recommence this activity."[54] Observers described Beatrice's reconstruction work as "outstanding," noting that she had "real ability, initiative, brilliance."[55] The Polish government awarded her its highest civilian award, the "Polonia Restituta" medal.[56]

Eventually, the pace took a toll on Beatrice's health. She succumbed to typhoid and returned briefly to England to recover. Fourteen years after she began work in Europe, in the spring of 1949, she returned to North America to take up a posting in New York City with the World YWCA. She had been asked to make a report about the negotiations with the Polish government, the Catholic Church, and Polish women's organizations to create a Polish YWCA. The New York typist she hired to assist her was none other than Willimae Moore, who came recommended by the personnel department of the American YWCA.[57]

Beatrice's Testimony at Trial

ASKED ABOUT HER RELATIONSHIP with Willimae Moore, Beatrice told the court that they had become friends as a result of working together, and that Willimae had accompanied her when she left New York City in November 1952. The two travelled to San Francisco, Portland, Seattle, and then Vancouver, where they stayed with Beatrice's family and a lawyer friend. In the fall of 1953, Beatrice accepted a half-year teaching position in Burn's Lake in northern British Columbia, and finished out the year at a school in Barrhead, northern Alberta. Willimae came with her, at Beatrice's "invitation," for part of the school year. Then the two women moved together up to Yellowknife in the fall of 1954.

Crown attorney Parker probed further: "You and Miss Moore were living together in Yellowknife? Just the two of you?" "Yes," replied his witness. He continued: "For several years you and Miss Moore have been very close together?" Beatrice answered: "Yes, very friendly." "Miss Moore is a woman, there is no doubt about that?" was the next question. "I believe her birth certificate would give that," replied Beatrice. "Have you ever seen her without her clothes on?" asked Parker. "No." "Have you seen her in a slip?" "Yes." "Have you seen her with some clothes off?" "Yes." One interpretation of this is that the Crown hoped to establish that Willimae was a lesbian involved with Beatrice. Another is that the Crown wondered whether Willimae Moore was a cross-dressing man. Whatever the case, the judge's own notes, later typed and archived, reveal his suspicious reaction: "I took note of

UBC Co-ed Talked Back To Gestapo In Czecho-Slovakia

● THE MOST POPULAR woman in Czechoslovakia, who talked back to the Nazi Gestapo and aided 3500 Czecho-slovakian refugees to escape from Hitler's wrath—such is the record of Miss Beatrice M. Wellington, graduate of the University of British Columbia and former Vancouver school teacher.

At present Miss Wellington is general secretary of a British Government com-mittee for in-terned refugees in London. Most U.B.C. co-eds will envy her the thrilling and dangerous experi-ences which have been her lot since the outbreak of war.

In Czechoslo-vakia she was affectionately cal-

"dangerous" refugee cases before the war broke out..

Twice captured by the German secret police and subjected to Ges-tapo third degree methods for 12 hours, the former U.B.C. co-ed talked back to her oppressors who were forced to release her. As head of the British Refugee Com-mission she helped 3500 Czechs flee the country.

It was Miss Wellington who aid-ed Dr. Julie Matouskova, general

"UBC Co-ed Talked Back to Gestapo," 1941 article about Beatrice (Wellington) Gonzales

The Ubyssey, 15 May 1941, at 2

the evasive attitude of the witness Gonzales, particularly in cross-examina-tion. She seemed reluctant to admit that the accused was a female."

Parker asked Beatrice why she was using the surname "Gonzales" when she had studied and worked in Europe and New York as "Beatrice Welling-ton." He seemed to suspect she had assumed a new name to hide from past indiscretions. Beatrice did not explain why she was using her birth father's surname again, except to retort: "That's my correct name. That's the name on my birth certificate."[58] Parker did not ask Beatrice why she had left the YWCA office in New York to teach in tiny northern posts. But some must have wondered why an internationally renowned woman with multiple graduate degrees had applied to be vice-principal at Yellowknife High. Bea-trice would later explain that she had "returned to teaching as a very tem-porary measure with no desire to make it my profession again." Parker then asked Beatrice if the letter that had been filed in court was Willimae's. "It is not her signature," replied Beatrice. Asked if she was aware that an RCMP handwriting expert had testified that it was, Beatrice responded: "I'm not responsible for his opinion. That is mine."

Sparring over definitions of sexuality followed. The capitalization and hyphens appeared in the transcript.

Q. Is Miss Moore a Homo-sexual?

A. No.

Q. Would you swear to that?

A. As far as the interpretation goes I have had no experience of it.

Q. Do you mean to say, Homo-sexual practices with yourselves?

A. With myself or any knowledge.

Q. You exclude all of those?

A. I exclude the term to Miss Moore.

Q. Homo-sexuality is some sort of sexual relationship between two women?

A. Frankly that was not my understanding of the term Homo-sexual, which I have always understood to mean a relationship between two men.

This was precisely the dilemma that underlay the prosecution. Criminal law had always concentrated on gay male sexuality. Canadian medical experts sourced biology as the explanation for the maleness of "sex delinquency," suggesting that "for anatomical reasons" many of the acts "were only possible of male indulgence," and noting that the law took "no cognizance of female inversion."[59] The lore was that criminal law had neglected lesbians because when asked, Queen Victoria replied that "ladies did not do such things."[60] The Canadian military prosecuted male homosexuals with rigour, but the Second World War court-martial records contain no files about female same-sex behaviour.[61] Even the Nazis, who forcibly interned homosexuals, defined illegal homosexuality as same-sex relations between men.[62] This case was proceeding in uncharted waters. The transcript continued:

Q. Is there any word by which you understand sex relationship between two women?

A. The word explained to me was Lesbian.

Q. Let's use that word, it is more clear than the word I use. Is Miss Moore a Lesbian?

(Pause)

A. No.

BY THE COURT: Why the hesitation?

A. I was just thinking of the question, Your Worship. "Is Miss Moore a Lesbian"? The thought in my mind is that Miss Moore is a married woman with three children.

There had been no warning that Willimae's former life included a husband and children. Parker cleverly followed with, "A Lesbian can be married and have three children?" to which Beatrice replied: "I suppose." It was rare for court stenographers to record pauses in testimony, so Beatrice's marked pause must have been a long one. The judge's intercession, "Why the hesitation?" presaged the notes he would write on the file: "[W]hen asked the direct question 'Is Miss Moore a Lesbian?' there was a noticeable hesitation before the answer 'No.' Where the evidence of the witness Gonzales was in conflict with that of the complainant, I accepted that of the complainant."

How had the judge interpreted this pause? As an evasive reluctance to answer? Did he think that Beatrice had lied when she denied that Willimae Moore was a lesbian? It seems reasonably clear that Willimae was a lesbian, and that Beatrice knew it. Presumably the criminal charge was a compelling deterrent to truth-telling. The homophobic environment would have been another. Beatrice was not asked whether she herself was a lesbian. She had denied being a homosexual, but had qualified that to mean relationships between two men.[63]

In the end, Beatrice denied that the signature was Willimae's, that Willimae was a lesbian, and that the letter was anything but a "hoax and silliness." This stood in contrast to the experts at the crime lab, the bank accountant, and the liquor store

Woman UBC Graduate Carves Amazing Career in Europe

By RON THORNBER

A strange and tragic contrast between the Christmas which the children of Vancouver enjoyed, and that which children in Poland endured as another day in the unceasing struggle for existence itself, was drawn here by a Vancouver woman who knew all too well the grim subjects whereof she spoke.

Beatrice M. Wellington charted an amazing career for herself. Born in this city, she graduated from University of British Columbia and taught in Edith Cavell School, Point Grey Junior High School and Chilliwack High School, and then in August 1936, set out on the path towards the realization of her highest hopes.

WENT TO GENEVA

In that year she was nominated by the League of Nations Society in Ottawa to go as Western Canada's delegate to the First World Youth Conference in Geneva. It was here that her exceptional organizing and executive ability was first recognized.

When the youth conference ended, the Vancouver girl was directed to serve as an administrative assistant on the Peace Disarmament Committee of the Women's International Commission and then, still in Geneva, was appointed to the Women's Service of the International Labor Office.

This position carried her into Czechoslovakia in September, 1938, to conduct a survey there for the Czech government of the tragic consequences of the Munich agreement. From this point onward, the story of her career assumes the proportions of a saga.

NAZI ARREST

On April 14, 1939, Miss Wellington was arrested by the Gestapo for aiding in the evacuation to England and Canada of several thousand Polish refugees and their dependents who were sheltering within the Czech republic.

Released after a week of intense and exhausting questioning, she kept quietly on with her work until the outbreak of war in September when she made her return to England to serve as chief welfare officer in the administration of the Czech Refugee Trust Fund established by the British government.

In England during the war years she held many official capacities including labor liaison officer for the Minister of Production, research assistant in the Postwar Reconstruction Section of the Royal Institute of International Affairs, secretary to the minister of production on matters of supplies to liberated areas, and as an advisor on the problems of Britain's requirements and methods of procuring needed supplies.

WON PROMOTION

Appointed by UNRRA in November, 1943, to head the secretariat of the European regional office, involving close co-operation with the Committee of the Council of Europe, Miss Wellington was promoted in 1945 to be chief supply officer in the Warsaw office of UNRRA.

In this post she was responsible for the co-ordination of all foreign voluntary relief agencies operating in Poland, but as an UNRRA official was unable to accept the Polish government's highest civilian award, the "Polonia Restituta" medal. She will receive it at the termination of her work with that organization.

Home a short while ago, Miss Wellington noted the gay preparations for Christmas being made throughout the city, and made a remark about the Polish

BEATRICE WELLINGTON

children as poignant as a line from Dickens:

"Polish children have forgotten Christmas. They know it only as a time of year that brings greater cold into the earthen cellars dug under the ruins of houses and buildings that they must call their homes. Happiness is a part of a child that cannot live with constant hunger, misery and cold —and an awful loneliness."

Miss Wellington is going back to Poland now. Vancouver has lost its appeal for her because its troubles are as lines on a kindly face compared to the deep grooves on a visage contorted with suffering.

Vancouver Sun, 7 January 1947, at 11

"Woman UBC Graduate Carves Amazing Career in Europe"

NWT Archives, N-2003-004:0053

Game Wardens' conference, 1960s. Harold Mitchell is in the second row, far left.

clerk, who verified the signature as Willimae's and the typing as that of her Underwood machine. Harold Mitchell testified for the Crown about the recent complaint that Laura had made to him.[64] Yet Mitchell's description of the conversations in Laura's apartment was later contradicted, when Laura testified that he had misconstrued some of what she had told him. And Mitchell's confirmation that Willimae's typewriter could have been used by anyone in the office weakened the Crown's case.

Elsie Smith and Lillian Crate, two social acquaintances of Beatrice, Willimae, and Laura, also pointed out discrepancies in Laura's testimony. They noted that Laura had been at Beatrice and Willimae's home for dinner on American Thanksgiving, 27 November 1954, although Laura had testified that the first time she was entertained there was in mid-December. Laura had also testified that several days after receiving the letter, she had joined a small group for Scrabble and tea at Beatrice and Willimae's place. Laura had told the court that when she put on her galoshes to leave, Willimae asked for her answer to the letter, and she had replied, "No." Elsie Smith testified that she had been present all evening, and heard no such conversation. Lillian Crate told the court that she had phoned Willimae on 25 January, the evening of the alleged assault, and that Willimae was at home, not at Laura's apartment.[65]

The Trial Verdict: An "Invitation to Lesbianism"

JOHN EDWARD (JACK) GIBBEN was the stipendiary magistrate whose interventions and notes left little doubt about his inclinations in this case. He was sixty years old, an English-born immigrant who had come to Canada with his family as a young boy. He served with the infantry in the First World War, and studied law at the University of Manitoba upon his return. Called to the bar in 1921, Gibben practised law in Winnipeg until his appointment as stipendiary magistrate for the Northwest Territories in 1938. He lived in Yellowknife with his wife and daughter from 1938 until 1941 and then in Dawson, where he served as stipendiary magistrate for the Yukon. In 1947, he was appointed controller of Yukon Territory, and in 1950, he became a judge of the Territorial Court. Those who knew him well described him as "courteous and gentlemanly," "serious and thoughtful," but a figure "of the old school, which enabled him to remain politely above much of the hurly-burly of small town life."[66] One of his court clerks left a memorable impression of the man. "Gibben, John E., was a little man, physically not much over five foot, chubby, rosy, well-scrubbed. Immaculate in dress. The last is a key word. The first impression of Gibben was that he had just emerged from a shower, parboiled and pink, barbered with extreme care, then clothed in fresh linen. Sordid cases, I think, left him with a feeling of having been personally besmirched. At the end of a day's sitting, he would shower interminably – as though to wash away the stains."[67]

Magistrate Gibben concluded that the infamous letter had been typed and signed by Willimae Moore. He stated that while Laura White's testimony at times "appeared vague and indirect, particularly as to dates," she had "impressed" him "as being truthful" in the crucial points. This gentle treatment of a complainant's factual inconsistencies was something of a sea-change from how most other sexual assault victims fared in Canadian courtrooms. Mary Ann Burton in London, Ontario in 1907, Ethel Machan in Halifax in 1925, and Beatrice Tisdale in Weyburn in 1942, had all been pilloried over factual inconsistencies in their testimony.[68] Not so Laura White. Gibben's notes reflect none of the customary suspicion about sexual assault complaints:

> I cannot conceive of the witness [White] falsifying the account of what transpired that evening. We find her the following morning seeking out Mr.

John (Jack) Edward Gibben,
stipendiary magistrate,
Northwest Territories

Yukon Archives, John Gibben fonds, #82/253 #1

Mitchell — and the question arises — Did she invent this incredible story? The complaint is of course not evidence of the facts alleged but it does show consistency of conduct on the part of the complainant. . . . I believed the evidence of the witness [White] as to what transpired at her apartment on the evening of January 25th after Gonzales had left.

This response was a far cry from Sir Matthew Hale's famous dictum about the dangers of trusting women who claimed sexual assault. And in cursory treatment of the need for corroboration, Gibben simply indicated that the letter would suffice.[69] The judge paid no attention to the features of this case that might have lent themselves to the legal defence of consent, as it was defined at the time. If Laura had objected seriously to the overture in the letter, why had she continued to socialize with Willimae, dropping over to her home for Scrabble and tea after she received it? Why had she permitted Willimae to come to her apartment for lunch? Why had she allowed Willimae to linger in the apartment later that night after Beatrice had gone home? Mary Ann Burton had been subjected to a blistering cross-examination alleging consent when there were no facts to support such a theory. Young Yvonne Collin's passivity had been interpreted as an undeniable consent to sex with eight strange men. Ethel Machan's multiple visits to Henry Kissel's bachelor apartment had sealed her fate, despite the changing sexual mores during the 1920s. The court had scoffed at the single slap Beatrice Tisdale delivered to her assailant.[70] Yet here, Laura White was simply asked whether she had "ever invited any attention of this matter." Her reply, "no, not to my knowledge; I never took it as that," was accepted at face value. "The Crown has adequately negatived consent," concluded Gibben. It was as if it were unthinkable that a woman would consent to a sexual overture from another woman.

As for Beatrice, Gibben summarily dismissed her evidence: "Miss Gonzales' testimony was, to say the least, unconvincing. I am satisfied that the letter was written by the accused and no one else, and I do not believe that the witness Gonzales thinks otherwise." In contrast, Gibben did "not question the bona fides" of Lillian Crate's evidence denying that Laura and Willimae had had a conversation about the letter. The discrepancy between Lillian and Laura's evidence, he concluded, must have been caused by "an unconscious mistake on her part, or indeed perhaps on the part of Miss [White], as to the exact time in question."

Gibben moved on to his analysis of the law. "An assault," he read out, was "an act of intentionally applying force to the person of another directly or indirectly without the consent of the other." The *Criminal Code* contained no definition for "indecent assault," because the phrase was "deemed to be self-explanatory."[71] In its "most obvious form," he explained, the term encompassed "the touching or attempting to touch the private parts of another," although there were other "less obvious" examples. "The offence has been described as an assault accompanied by circumstances of indecency on the part of the accused." He continued:

> It is not necessary that the act constituting the assault be in itself indecent in its nature. The act though itself ambiguous, may be interpreted by the surrounding circumstances. Having in mind the letter which indicates that the accused is a sexual invert, I find that the "Grabbing hold," accompanied by the "Attempt to kiss" constituted an indecent assault.

The grabbing and the attempt to kiss were the "assault" elements here, and the letter from the "sexual invert" provided the circumstances of indecency. Gibben rejected the defence argument that the letter did not constitute a threat, and that "the writer went out of her way to approach the matter gently and assure the recipient that the resultant conduct would be by the recipient's own will." Crown attorney Parker's theory had overridden a benign interpretation: "Crown Counsel submits that the letter with its definite reference to the physical is an invitation to Lesbianism. I am in agreement." Gibbon convicted Willimae Moore and rejected the request that she be given a suspended sentence since this was her first criminal conviction. He imposed a three months' sentence, to be served in the RCMP Guardroom at Fort Smith, noting that although the "accused in many respects is more to be pitied than blamed . . . the public must be protected in cases like this."

Appeal to Edmonton

THE CASE WAS APPEALED to Edmonton, where the Alberta Court of Appeal reviewed decisions of Yellowknife magistrates. Willimae's bail was extended upon the filing of $250 in cash and a surety in the same amount. Beatrice continued to orchestrate the case for the defence, although she was deeply worried about the cost. She wrote several anxious letters to the court clerk in Edmonton, explaining that the defendant had "NO resources with which to engage a lawyer." Beatrice sought the advice of the clerk for the "names of lawyers noted in Edmonton for their experience in criminal matters and for their skill in handling appeals." She explained that "individuals" she had approached for funding had told her "that if they are to be asked to contribute they wish to have definite assurance that the appeal will be taken by the best criminal lawyers available in Edmonton."[72]

Court registrar Michel Dubuc wrote back to recommend Frank Dunne of the firm Maclean and Dunne, but either Dunne's fees were too high, or Beatrice was unable to raise the money she had hoped. Instead, Willimae and Beatrice flew to Edmonton and retained Lewis Bernstein. A thirty-year-old English lawyer who had graduated from Oxford in 1949, Bernstein had tried but failed to establish a barrister's practice there, and then moved to Edmonton. He was called to the Alberta bar in January 1955, and this was one of his first cases. As he recalls: "I don't know how I got this case. They came to see me, and didn't want to pay the big fees of the other lawyers. I didn't charge them very much."[73]

Despite his low fee, Lewis Bernstein prepared a first-class appellate argument. He claimed that Gibben had misdirected himself on the meaning of "consent," that he had mistakenly found corroboration when none existed, and that he had wrongly admitted the letter and other hearsay evidence. He argued that the judge had erred in principle in passing sentence, ignor-

Legal Archives Society of Alberta, 5-G-71

Edmonton Courthouse, 1916

ing that this was Willimae's first conviction, and wrongly deciding that the public needed protection when there was no evidence of this. But it was his argument about the definition of indecent assault that ultimately carried the day. Crown counsel Edward W. Sully, who had unwisely restricted his argument to the alibi evidence, failed to engage on this issue at all.[74] Bernstein referred the court to a 1951 English case, *Beal v. Kelley*, in which the judge had stated: "If there is a hostile act with every circumstance of indecency, I cannot see why it is not an indecent assault. If a man assaults a woman, at the same time exposing his person to her, I have no doubt that it is an indecent assault."[75] Bernstein seized on the phrase "a hostile act," arguing that Gibben had "misled himself by not directing his mind that, to constitute assault, the act complained of must be a hostile act."[76]

Two of the three judges who sat on the appeal used this case to reverse the conviction. They rejected Gibben's opinion that the letter with its "invitation to commit acts of Lesbianism" could be classified as a "hostile act." Chief Justice George Bligh O'Connor, who wrote the opinion for himself and Judge Horace Gilchrist Johnson, was known for his "brief and concise" decisions. After reciting the facts, O'Connor simply stated: "On the evi-

Courtesy of the Court of Appeal of Alberta, Office of the Registrar   Courtesy of the Court of Appeal of Alberta, Office of the Registrar

Left: Hon. Clinton J. Ford, Chief Justice of Alberta, 1951–61
Right: Hon. Horace G. Johnson, Court of Appeal of Alberta, 1954–73

dence of the complainant there was no hostile act with the circumstances of indecency."[77]

The ruling was not unanimous. Judge Clinton James Ford dissented, noting ominously that he took "a serious view of the evidence." Ford characterized Willimae Moore's letter as "an invitation to acts of indecency." He noted that the trial judge had accepted the evidence of the complainant, and properly found that there had been an assault. The assault was linked with the letter, giving contextual meaning to the grabbing and the attempted kiss. "The object was an act of indecency on the part of the accused, who made unsolicited advances to the complainant, and who on her part, found it necessary to ward off the accused and so escape her intended unlawful embraces." Although he did not use the terminology of "lesbianism" or "sexual invert," the linkage was clear. The letter was "an invitation to indecency." The embraces were "unlawful." The conviction was warranted. Judge Ford would have preferred to affirm the conviction.[78]

In 1954, Parliament had amended the definition of "gross indecency," to permit charges to be laid against women as well as men, in what later judges would describe as a "modern recognition of equality between sexes."[79] However, most understood the new gender-neutral definition of "gross inde-

NWT Archives, N-1979-052:4060

Yellowknife High School, c. 1940s

Courtesy Joan Greaves, published in Susan Jackson, ed., *Yellowknife, N.W.T.: An Illustrated History* (Sechelt: Nor'West, 1990) at 141

Yellowknife Public School students, 1953–54

cency" to be aimed at non-coital heterosexual practices rather than lesbianism, and so far no one has discovered any other sexual prosecutions against same-sex female activity prior to 1975. Other Canadian judges would profess to be confused and disgusted by a range of non-coital sexual practices, consensual or otherwise, but Willimae Moore's prosecution would remain in a category of its own.[80]

Postscript

REGARDLESS OF THE LEGAL exoneration in Edmonton, the damage had been done. Beatrice Gonzales was summarily discharged from her post as vice-

Edmonton Public Schools Archives, Accession #2000.13.2.

McNally High School yearbook composite, 1965–66. Miss Gonzales, centre

principal of Yellowknife High School. A group of students put together a petition to have her reinstated, because they were upset to lose a highly re-spected teacher at a critical time in the school year. The school refused to reconsider the decision, admonishing the students that they "didn't know all the facts."[81]

Beatrice left Yellowknife for "outside" directly after the criminal pros-ecution. Six years later in 1962, she surfaced in Edmonton, teaching with the Edmonton School Board.[82] Willimae Moore was not apparently living with her, and whether she kept in touch with Beatrice, the friend who always "went to bat" for her, is unknown. But Beatrice had dealt with sadness in her life before, and if her letters to friends were any indication, she could find solace by putting down stakes in a new place.[83] Edmonton turned out to be a satisfactory venue, and when her younger brother visited her there in 1968, she was living with another female teacher.[84] Although she had testified ear-lier in Yellowknife that teaching was only a temporary vocation, Beatrice remained a teacher either by choice or necessity. She taught English, social studies, sociology, biology, chemistry, and French, and directed the debating club, in a series of Edmonton high schools from 1963 to 1971.[85]

Beatrice Gonzales died in Edmonton on 4 April 1971, less than two years after the Stonewall Riots in New York City spawned the emergence of wider gay liberation movements throughout the Western world.[86] Her brother, who was then a professor of Plant Science and Resource Ecology at the University of British Columbia, established the "Beatrice Wellington Gonzales Memori-al Scholarship" to be awarded annually to a deserving senior undergraduate student in social work. In making the donation, Dr. William G. Wellington indicated that it was "in memory of Beatrice's unflagging service to others, both as an inspired teacher in Canada, and as a resourceful social worker in Europe where she was a field officer in various League of Nations and United Nations Agencies, [and] her strenuous and successful efforts to protect and salvage the lives of political refugees in Europe prior to and following World War II." The initial gift was augmented by donations from dozens of former students from Edmonton, who wrote to describe the extraordinary influence Beatrice had had on their education and lives.[87]

Library and Archives Canada, PA-166272

Duke de Coursey, editor and publisher of *News of the North*, the only newspaper in the Northwest Territories, September 1945

According to the local paper, *News of the North*, Laura White left Yellowknife for "outside" almost directly after the trial convicting Willimae Moore. Her final destination was not noted.[88]

Willimae Moore also left Yellowknife immediately after the trial. Whether she returned to her family, went back to the United States, or continued to travel is unknown.[89] Her lawyer, Lewis Bernstein, reflecting years later on this very unusual case, offered the startling *coup de grâce*. She probably would never have been prosecuted, he mused, "if she hadn't been Black."[90]

me—for
Lisa—against [handwritten annotation]

"SORDID" BUT "UNDERSTANDABLE UNDER THE CIRCUMSTANCES":
Kohnke, Croft, and Wilson, 1967

THE TRAGIC DISCOVERY OF the body of an Aboriginal woman on 9 April 1967 set in motion a train of events that displayed Canadian criminal justice at its most callous core. It was a frosty Sunday morning when the body of Rose Marie Roper, a seventeen-year-old member of the Esketemc First Nation Alkali Lake Band, was found. Small in stature, she weighed less than a hundred pounds. Her battered and nude body was lying face down on the ice and mud, near a garbage dump on a lonely logging road between Williams Lake and Lac La Hache, in Cariboo County, central interior British Columbia. The RCMP indicated that Rose had suffered "a broken neck," "bruises," and "cuts." They had yet to determine whether she was sexually assaulted as well.[1]

Sexual assault culminating in homicide was not uncommon in Canada. Some men choked, suffocated, stabbed, beat, or strangled women and girls in an effort to facilitate rape or indecent assault. Other times they killed their victims in a violent frenzy after the sexual attack, or in an effort to avoid being caught.[2] Such acts could lead to charges of murder, which, if proven, could result in capital punishment or mandatory life imprisonment.[3]

A murder conviction required proof that the accused had intended to cause death, or intended to cause bodily harm that he knew was "likely to cause death" and was "reckless whether death ensued."[4] Even if the assailant had no desire to cause death or bodily harm, he could be convicted if he did something "for an unlawful object" that was likely to cause death.[5] The law also recognized an offence of "constructive murder." If an accused was in the process of committing a serious criminal offence, such as rape

Courtesy of the Esketemc Land Settlement Office, PO Box 4479, Williams Lake, BC, V2G 2V5.

Panoramic view of the Alkali Lake Reserve

or indecent assault, and intentionally caused bodily harm to facilitate that crime, he could be convicted even though he had no wish to kill his victim, and had no idea that death was likely to result.[6]

Where the Crown was unable to prove murder, but the court was still of the view that there had been a culpable homicide, the accused could be convicted for the lesser crime of manslaughter, for which life imprisonment was the maximum sentence.[7] Where the evidence did not establish culpable homicide, reduced verdicts could include rape, indecent assault, assault causing bodily harm, common assault or, in extreme cases, accidental homicide resulting in an acquittal.

The Fraser River landscape between the Alkali Lake and Dog Creek reserves

A Tragic Childhood

ROSE ROPER'S YOUNGEST SISTER, Sandra Archie, has written: "In our culture, the greatest honour to bestow on anyone is to tell stories about them. Should you decide to tell Rose's story, she will be honoured that most people will hear the truth of her short life."[8] Rose Marie Roper was the eldest child of Jacob B. Roper and Patricia (George) Roper. Her paternal grandmother was Christine Haines, and the family traced its heritage to Shuswap, Chilcotin, and Scottish ancestry.[9] The Roper family lived at Alkali Lake, an isolated reserve located 52 kilometres south of Williams Lake, in hauntingly beautiful, mountainous ranching land covered with forests and fed by the Fraser River.[10]

The lands around Alkali Lake and Williams Lake had traditionally belonged to the Shuswap people. After two-thirds of the Shuswap population were wiped out in smallpox epidemics, the white settlers who followed the Cariboo Gold Rush in the mid-nineteenth century helped themselves to the land, despite the absence of treaties and in blatant disregard of Aboriginal title. Aboriginal resistance proved futile. Five men from the neighbouring Chilcotin community were convicted and hanged when their efforts to pre-

Courtesy of Sandra Archie and Dianne Crosina

Roper family home at Alkali Lake Reserve where Rose grew up (now demolished)

Courtesy of Constance Backhouse

St. Theresa Roman Catholic Church, Alkali Lake Reserve

vent the trespass of a crew of white men building a road over their territory resulted in the death of some of the white intruders. Subsequent provincial legislation prohibited "Indians" from pre-empting land, at the same time that white settlers were invited to apply for free grants of up to 320 acres.[11]

By the 1880s, the Shuswap survivors were relegated to small reserves on the most marginal lands. The first white male settlers had intermarried with Aboriginal women, but as the white immigrants grew in number after the fur trade and the gold frenzy died down, racial divisions continued to harden. By the late nineteenth century, residential schools run by Christian churches in combination with the state took control over Aboriginal children, who were forcibly removed from their homes and families. The Shuswap community was thrown into further economic upheaval as the expanding forest industry intruded upon their traditional lands and their subsistence hunting and fishing. Alcohol, introduced in the 1940s, created social crisis, family breakdown, and violence on the reserves.[12]

Rose Roper was born on 24 September 1949, into these troubled and despairing times. Four of her younger siblings survived infancy: Mary, born 1950; Dianne, born 1953; Sandra, born 1954; and Jake, born 1963. The home the Roper family lived in was a one-storey, decrepit wooden shack. Rose's grandparents were the last generation to speak their traditional language. At residential school, the nuns had stabbed needles into Rose's grandmother's tongue whenever they caught her speaking Salishan.[13] Rose's grandparents had refused to teach their descendants their native language for fear they would be punished too. Catholicism had taken deep root in the Alkali Lake community, and Rose's family was particularly religious. Rose's baptism was duly recorded on the Oblate Register, and the children were faithful parishioners of the St. Theresa Roman Catholic Church on the reserve. Rose's sister Sandra remembers that the girls had strict instructions always to stop and genuflect in front of the church, and to say the rosary when they passed the statue of the Crucified Christ.[14]

Some recall Rose's father, Jacob, to have been a kind man. However, he was also violently abusive, drank to excess, and terrorized his family and neighbours. The children remember their father engaged in too many fights and acts of sexual assault to count, many of which they witnessed personally. He brutalized his wife and sexually assaulted other women. One of the men he assaulted died. Sometimes he was charged criminally; occasionally he spent time in jail. He verbally abused his children, cursing and calling them "dirty Indians," "bitches," and "whores." Once he tied wire around the family pet

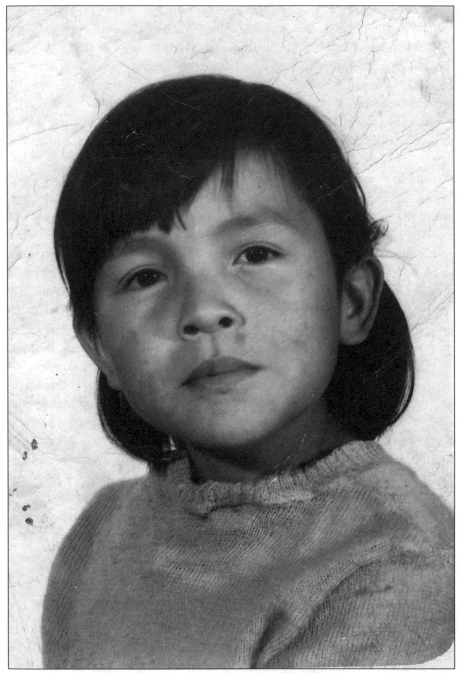

Residential school photograph of Rose Roper, age unkown

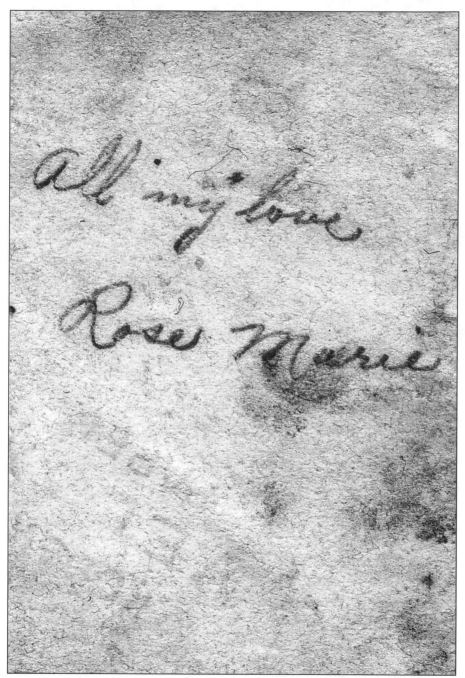

Rose Roper's signature on the back of the photograph, opposite

dog's mouth and legs, and drove it away and shot it. He told the girls it was because they had fed the dog a bologna sandwich. The deeply dysfunctional man locked up food in his room, and "pounded" the girls' heads into the wall if they took food without asking. Reflecting upon their home life years later, Rose's sister Sandra described it as "traumatic" and "hateful."[15]

In 1964, Jacob Roper beat his wife so severely that she miscarried and died shortly afterwards in hospital. Fifteen-year-old Rose and fourteen-year-old Mary were left to clean their mother's blood and two near-term twin male fetuses from the outhouse. In this terrifying household, Rose assumed the "mother figure" role, serving as her younger siblings' "protector." She stole food and clothes in a desperate attempt to meet their needs. When their father was in a violent rage, she rounded up the children and hid them under the bed, in the barn, or high on the hillside, reminding them to bring sticks for self-defence. After her father sexually abused her, as did other male relatives, Rose taught her younger sisters to sleep with all of their clothes and shoes on. Most of all, she stressed they should sleep with their "belts on backwards." Despite her efforts, she was not able to protect her younger sisters, who were also sexually abused in turn. No criminal charges were ever laid despite the multiple sexual assaults. In this tragic home, Rose also tried to introduce some amusement. Sandra remembers how Rose would play "dress up" with her, and polish her nails. Despite everything, Rose had "a great sense of humour," laughed a lot, and loved music and dancing. She sang her favourite song, "A little bit of me, a little bit of you," by the Monkees, over and over again.[16]

Residential Schooling

THE FIRST SCHOOLING ROSE received began in 1955 at the Cariboo Indian Residential School at St. Joseph's Mission, near 150 Mile House.[17] Opened in 1891, the "Mission" was managed until 1969 by the Roman Catholic Church, financed by a small sum paid annually by the federal government for each pupil registered.[18] The Indian residential school program was designed "to kill the Indian in the child," and to destroy Aboriginal cultures through the brainwashing of children.[19] In addition to cultural destruction, St. Joseph's Mission's legacy of abuse and neglect included starvation, excessive corporal punishment, and punitive confinement. Some students committed suicide or attempted to do so. Runaways occasionally died of exposure and exhaustion. Complaints of contaminated water, unheated buildings that served as per-

Library and Archives Canada, with permission of the Minister of Public Works and Government Services Canada (2006)

Old building of St. Joseph's Cariboo Indian Residential School

Library and Archives Canada, with permission of the Minister of Public Works and Government Services Canada (2006)

New building of St. Joseph's Cariboo Indian Residential School, front view, c. 1961–65

ilous firetraps, epidemics, overcrowding, and scandalously deficient class-room instruction spanned the school's history.[20]

In 1946, a police report documented the violent beating of a fourteen-year-old student by a religious brother at the school; the brother was subsequently removed.[21] In 1952, the nuns threatened to leave the dilapidated school en masse because they refused to "live and teach under the deplorable conditions." In 1953, the federal government finally ordered the construction of a new school. Before the project was complete, the old boys' dormitory was destroyed by fire. The new school was officially opened in 1955, the year Rose arrived.[22]

The September she started at the Mission, Rose was one of three hundred Aboriginal students from forty-three reserves. Like all the other students, Rose was assigned a number. The number 133 was sewn into each item of her clothing, appeared on her classroom seat, and was how she would be called by the school staff, who preferred numbers over names. Despite the new building, the overcrowding, understaffing, and water problems continued. The food was terrible. Breakfast consisted of "mush" and Fry's Cocoa, an unappetizing mixture of water, baking chocolate powder, and sugar. There was soup for lunch, and not much more for dinner. A serious outbreak of measles occurred in 1956, and epidemics of influenza, measles, and chicken pox in 1960.[23]

The culture of the school was severely authoritarian. Students were punished for not brushing their teeth or washing properly, not eating appropriately, not folding their clothes or making their beds properly, talking in school or church, failing to stand straight in the interminable line-ups, answering schoolwork incorrectly, losing track of belongings, and bed-wetting. Since the children were not permitted to use the bathroom at night, the latter posed considerable challenges. Sanctions ranged from public humiliation and verbal abuse to being forced to stand or kneel while holding arms outstretched for protracted periods of time. Corporal discipline included hair-pulling, ear-pulling, and strapping with rulers, yardsticks, and long black straps fashioned out of conveyor belts. Although her family knew Rose to be very "smart," she did not distinguish herself academically at residential school, and was frequently struck over the head and knuckles with a wooden ruler. She gained a reputation as a fighter when she intervened while one nun was hitting another of the girls. When Rose pulled off Sister Juliette's black veil before the astonished gasps of her classmates, she was forced to scrub the stairs with a toothbrush.[24]

They won the hearts of a nation, played from coast to coast and provided life-long memories for both the players and those who heard them. (N. Buchanan photo)

From Irene Stangoe, *Looking Back at the Cariboo-Chilcotin* (Surrey: Heritage House, 1997) at 137. Permission for use granted by Irene Stangoe, 2007.

Cariboo Indian Girls' Pipe Band, Williams Lake, British Columbia. Rose is in the middle of the back row. She played the bass drum shown in front of the group.

However bleak the conditions at the residential school, Rose found it a relief from the brutal conditions at home. Her sisters who followed her to St. Joseph's suspected that they may have had less trouble than other students because of their strict religious upbringing. "We knew the catechism," recalled Sandra. "The priests and nuns were happy with us." All three girls were selected to play in the Girls' Pipe Band, the pride of St. Joseph's Residential School. In 1958, a Williams Lake chiropractor had come up with the idea to train the Aboriginal girls to form a marching pipe band. The nuns and students sewed kilts and shawls from a grey-blue "air force" tartan, and purchased sets of bagpipes. The juxtaposition of Aboriginal pupils and ancient Scottish Highland traditions struck many as an "unlikely premise," but the novelty of the combination drew acclaim. One observer, watching the band perform at Stampede parades, commented: "As they marched along, their tartan skirts swinging, their faces beaming as they puffed and blew on a musical instrument that was so foreign to their culture, they were an instant hit wherever they went." Rose, who was selected to carry the big bass drum despite her diminutive stature, was almost dwarfed by her instrument.[25]

Indian residential schools were rife with sexual abuse, and St. Joseph's was no exception. Three Oblate priests at the school would later face crimin-

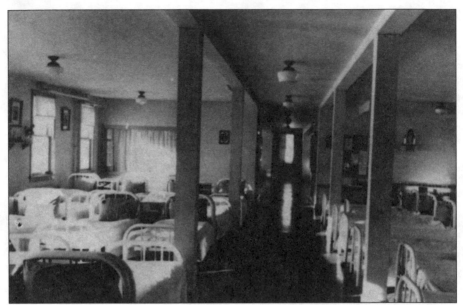

Library and Archives Canada, with permission of the Minister of Public Works and Government Services Canada (2006)

Dormitory of St. Joseph's Cariboo Indian Residential School, c. 1961–65

al sanctions. Rev. Harold McIntee and Brother Glen Doughty were convicted of sexually abusing male students, and Bishop Hubert Patrick O'Connor was prosecuted for sexually abusing female students and former female pupils who were employed at the school.[26] Hubert O'Connor had been appointed principal of the residential school in 1961. He was an enthusiastic sponsor of the Cariboo Indian Girls' Pipe Band, and fund-raised to assist them to perform in Ottawa on Parliament Hill. During the mid-1960s, Principal O'Connor was also having multiple sexual relations with Aboriginal teenagers who were former female pupils living in residence and working as office staff under his supervision. O'Connor claimed to have been "seduced" by the young women in hotel rooms when they toured with the pipe band, in trains, in his automobile during driving lessons, and on school premises. One of his defences to the six charges against him was that the young women had "consented." In contrast, the women took the position that they did not want to have sex, but were afraid that O'Connor would fire them from their office jobs or "kick [them] off" the pipe band if they did not comply.[27]

The courts never finally resolved the matter. The initial trial was derailed after the judge determined that the Crown had not fully disclosed evidence. Lengthy appeals resulted in an order to start the criminal trial over again.

"Bishop beats sex charge," *Vancouver Province*, 25 March 1998, A39, photo of Hubert O'Connor.

The rape and indecent assault convictions that emerged from the second trial were set aside on another appeal. O'Connor avoided a third trial when he pleaded for mercy due to a "serious heart condition" and his victims indicated they had "had enough" of the courts, and agreed to accept his public apology at a traditional healing circle instead.[28]

By the time the complaints against Principal O'Connor surfaced publicly, Rose Roper had been dead for years. But the women who testified that O'Connor had sexually assaulted them were her contemporaries. Like several of them, Rose had briefly left residential school to complete grade 9 at Williams Lake Public High School, and grade 10 at Prince George Catholic High School, where the Aboriginal students faced racist bullying from their white classmates, and were relegated to the stigmatized "occupational skills" program. Along with the other sexually abused women, Rose had returned to St. Joseph's to live in the staff quarters on the fourth floor and to work in the kitchen and laundry room.[29]

No one can now know with certainty whether O'Connor also sexually abused Rose. Her sister Sandra thinks not. Sandra believes that the principal left the Roper girls alone because of their father's reputation. Once all his daughters were living at St. Joseph's, Jacob Roper had followed them to live in a bunkhouse on school property and work as a "jack of all trades" doing carpentry and driving the bus, tractor, and caterpillar at the school. The irony was that if Rose was protected from sexual abuse by Principal O'Connor, it may have been because her tyrannical father's presence loomed over her night and day. Equally tragically, it seems that Rose's father may have continued to perpetrate sexual abuse upon Rose and her sisters at the residential school.[30]

While she worked at St. Joseph's from 1965 to 1967, Rose continued to look after her siblings as best she could. She went back to Alkali Lake often, to bring clothes and food to her little brother. In the summers when her sisters were back on the reserve, she gave the younger children money and told them to walk the sixteen-mile round trip to the 150 Mile Store for groceries. Her sisters remember Rose standing at her window on the fourth floor, rolling up a dollar bill into a little ball, and throwing it down to them. Rose found the endless laundry interminable, and she started to drink on the weekends. That led to a public altercation with her father, who discovered her drunk at a dance at Alkali Lake one weekend. Sandra remembers Rose "cussing" when Jacob Roper picked her up, threw her over his shoulder, and hurled her into his station wagon. "She was so tiny," recalls Sandra, "but I was always scared of her when she was drunk because she had so much anger. She was so unhappy and had no way out. I want you to understand why Rose drank. I want you to understand that she was not an alcoholic. She needed to forget, like we all did."[31]

A Ride That Culminated in Death

THE WEEKEND OF ROSE Roper's death she had gone AWOL from the residential school. As her irate father later told the press, she "left the Mission Friday night for no good reason." She either walked or hitchhiked to Williams Lake, where she was arrested that evening for being intoxicated in a public place. Released on Saturday morning, 8 April 1967, she was let off with a ten-dollar fine because it was her first offence.[32]

In the 1960s, Williams Lake was a predominantly white, burgeoning "cow town," sitting on land that the Shuswap people had made their wintering area for thousands of years. It was named after Chief William, the baptismal name of Wesemaist, a Shuswap leader from the fur-trade era. In the middle of a building boom, Williams Lake had paved its first roads, and constructed a new hospital, schools, and modern hotels. TV service had made its first appearance, and in keeping with the rest of the country, town leaders were preparing to celebrate Canada's 100th birthday on 1 July 1967. A substantial wooden archway had been erected to span the highway south of town, engraved with the motto "Welcome to Williams Lake: The Heart of Cariboo."[33]

The evening of 8 April, after Rose was released onto the streets of Williams Lake, she walked or hitchhiked back to 150 Mile House. There she met up with a white youth, Alfred William Kohnke, whom she knew from school in Williams Lake. Williams Lake residents often drove to neighbouring towns in search of drinking partners, dances, and parties, and that night,

All photos on this page courtesy of the Museum of the Cariboo Chilcotin, with permission of Bridget Dan and Joan Gentles

Above: Williams Lake Stampede beauty queens, 1957. Bridget Dan (left) and Joanne Dunaway (segregated pageant)

Left: Joan (Palmantier) Gentles, the first Aboriginal woman to win in "open" pageant, 1966

Alfred had begun his evening at 150 Mile House.[34] There had been some previous attraction between Rose and Alfred, who had "hung out" a bit, but never "dated."[35] Racial intermixing was frowned upon in the town, where there was a "background of Jim Crowism as far as Indians were concerned." Restaurants refused to serve Aboriginals, and stampede dances and other social events were racially segregated.[36] Even the beauty pageants had traditionally been separate. Two Williams Lake Stampede queens were selected each year — one white, one Aboriginal — both posing in their own distinctive costume — white cowgirl outfits, and Aboriginal buckskin with beads and feathers. The year 1966 marked the first time an Aboriginal girl had won the title in an "open competition" with whites.[37]

Twenty-year-old Alfred came from a well-known family of Williams Lake residents, whose renown came primarily from wrestling. Alfred's uncles Bill and Felix Kohnke were "champion wrestlers" who, along with Alfred's father Walter, sponsored hospital fund-raisers by waging professional wrestling matches at the local Elks Hall. The Kohnke brothers also had operated the Williams Lake Maple Leaf Hotel and beer parlour for some years, and Felix Kohnke chaired the school board. Alfred was employed by his father, Walter Kohnke, in logging.[38] That Saturday night Alfred had arrived at a pub at 150 Mile House with two white friends, Stephen Arthur Croft, aged twenty, and Robert (Bob) Leslie Wilson, aged twenty-three. Stephen, whose parents were deceased, was employed as a carpenter. Bob worked as a printer at the *Williams Lake Tribune*. His mother and stepfather lived in North Burnaby.

According to the recollection of the Alkali Lake Aboriginal community, the three young men met up with Rose on the highway as she was hitchhiking to Lac La Hache, about 60 kilometres down the road.[39] The white witnesses quoted by the press suggested, in contradiction, that the three young men first bumped elbows with Rose in the pub that Saturday evening. Beer parlours had begun to serve Aboriginal patrons some years earlier, and according to later testimony from a young white male who had been at the pub, Rose "was feeling pretty good and went roaming from table to table."[40] The press added that Alfred, Stephen, and Bob had told Rose that they were on their way to a dance at Lac La Hache. Apparently she asked them for a lift, because she wanted to visit an aunt who lived at Lac La Hache.

The four departed in Bob Wilson's car, with Alfred in the back seat beside Rose. How Rose might have described what ensued next will never be known. Instead, we are left with the boys' version of the facts. Their statements suggest that Alfred and Rose were "necking," and that Alfred then switched places with Stephen, who began to make sexual advances. Stephen undid and removed some of Rose's clothes. The boys had no intention of driving straight to Lac La Hache, and Bob turned off the highway near 126 Mile House, onto a deserted logging road that led to a garbage dump. Bob parked and opened up bottles of beer for the four of them. As they consumed the beer, the trio "took off all Rose's clothes." Rose was resisting Stephen's efforts to have intercourse, and he decided to switch places with Bob. Bob would later testify that he was "petting" with Rose, but she then "failed to co-operate" and said: "Don't touch me."

Instead, according to Bob Wilson, he used his fingers to penetrate Rose vaginally, only to discover that she was menstruating. He "got mad" and

Courtesy of Constance Backhouse

Sideroad to dump near 126 Mile House, 2006

"remonstrated" with Rose for not having told them, and ordered her to get her clothes back on. Rose grabbed a bottle of beer and poured it over Bob and the backseat of his car, all the while "screaming and swearing." Bob "cuffed" Rose on the face with his hand "once or perhaps twice" and "told her to smarten up." He ordered her out of the car. Stephen admitted to the police that he opened the door and "kicked her posterior" and she "landed on the ground." Subsequently testifying on the stand, he changed his mind and said he "pulled her out" instead. Asked to explain the discrepancy, Stephen replied that he had "lied" to the police earlier. All three swore that Rose was "sitting on the road freely cursing them" and muttering, "You are going to die, Kohnke." The boys tossed Rose's clothes out after her, except for her "panties." They hung those on the radio aerial and drove off to the dance at about 11:15 p.m., abandoning Rose on the ice and mud.

The aerial caused a flurry of interest when the trio arrived at the dance. Rose's undergarment was removed from Bob Wilson's car and transferred from one car aerial to another, almost as a point of pride. The three white boys continued to drink as they danced with the white girls. Two of these, nineteen-year-olds Diane Lamothe and Karen McFadden of Williams Lake, offered to drive Alfred and Stephen home. Forty-two kilometres south of Williams Lake, Diane's car plunged down a fifteen-foot embankment, sheared off a telephone pole, and split in half. Miraculously, all four passengers survived with minor injuries, and Bob Wilson, who was following behind, ferried all of them to the Cariboo Memorial Hospital for treatment.

Back on the lonely logging road, Rose Roper's nude body was discovered Sunday morning by a white fisherman. Her clothes were heaped about one hundred feet from her corpse. The *Vancouver Province* quoted the police as indicating that death appeared to be due to "exposure" and that there were "no indications of foul play."[41] Reconsidering this shortly after, the police began to investigate further. First, they went down to Lac La Hache and arrested Rose's aunt's common law husband, but further inquiry revealed him to be unconnected to the crime.[42] A search of the death scene turned up money, rings, and two buttons near where the clothes had been found, along with empty beer bottles and cigarette butts. The police looked for fingerprints, and took photographs of the shoe prints, bare footprints, and tire tracks around the scene. When Alfred Kohnke and Stephen Croft happened to arrive at the RCMP station Monday morning to file a traffic accident report along with the two white girls, one of the officers showed the group a photograph of Rose. The boys denied knowing her, a lie they later explained in court because they had not wanted "to embarrass the two (white) girls."

They left the traffic office, but after receiving legal advice, all three young men returned to the police station that day to give voluntary statements. It was probably only a matter of time before the police traced the crime to them. Witnesses had reported seeing Alfred Kohnke leaving with Rose Saturday evening, the tire tracks at the scene matched those of Bob Wilson's 1956 sedan, the fingerprints on his dashboard matched those on the beer bottles, and the butts at the scene were the same brand that Alfred smoked. The boys professed to wish to "tell everything." They confessed that they had "intended to have intercourse with the girl," but denied that they had done so. All three boys swore that Rose had been a willing sexual partner, and that it was they who had lost interest in her. Yet even their own version of the facts indicated that Rose had resisted Stephen's advances, and that she had "failed to co-operate" with Bob too. In fact, she had explicitly objected, saying: "Don't touch me." The evidence of Rose's full consent seems dubious at best. However, the police apparently concluded that they could not make out a case of sexual assault.

They were less convinced of the veracity of the boys' insistence that they were mystified by Rose's death, and that she had been alive when they drove

Field near 126 Mile House where Rose Roper's body was found

Alkali Lake cemetery, 2006. Rose Marie Roper's burial place, grave unmarked.

off. The police arrested all three, and transferred them to police cells at 100 Mile House. The charges became a matter of some contest. The initial charge of manslaughter was raised to murder by the time of the preliminary inquiry, and then dropped to double charges of manslaughter and assault at the trial. The changes may have reflected debates between police and the prosecutor's office regarding the likelihood of proving the required degree of intent and causation for a conviction.[43]

A Prosecution Infected with Racism

RACISM HAS BEEN DEEPLY embedded in sexual assault law throughout Canada's history. Although the legal records often fail to record racial identities, there are sufficient notations to suggest that race was a central feature of many prosecutions.[44] Past research has tended to focus on the racialized men brought before the courts charged with rape, where more privileged white men probably would have gone free. Racism often made it easier for victims assaulted by racialized men to report the crime, for police to lay charges, for Crown attorneys to prosecute, and for judges and juries to convict. Racist overtones are often evident in the prosecution of Aboriginal, Asian, and African-Canadian men.[45] There has been less attention to the ways that discrimination may have an impact on the victims of sexual assault, some of whom seem to have been marked for sexual abuse by white men specifically because of their presumed racial inferiority.[46] Circumstances of racism combined to make them more vulnerable targets, and to suggest to perpetrators that there was little risk in sexually assaulting individuals with so little power. If criminal prosecution did ensue, the disparity in status between the assailant and victim continued to work against the latter throughout the courtroom proceedings.

The records from the preliminary inquiry held at 100 Mile House and the trial in Quesnel have not survived, and newspaper coverage is sometimes inaccurate, but the press clippings reveal much about the racial perspectives that suffused the case. As the press portrayed it, the prosecution was as much a contest of character as an inquiry into the events that led to Rose's death. Much was made of the unblemished past of the three accused. They had no previous criminal convictions. They were steadily employed. The families of two were members of the Masonic Lodge. Their friends and relatives crowded the courtroom. One white friend testified that none of the trio was drunk when they arrived at the dance in Lac La Hache. A string of other white witnesses spoke to the "reputation for truthfulness" of Alfred Kohnke, Stephen Croft, and Bob Wilson. Nothing was said about their reputation for drinking and carousing.[47]

In contrast, on 12 April 1967 the front page coverage of the *Williams Lake Tribune* reported that Rose had been convicted of intoxication in a public place the night before her death. Other articles quoted two white witnesses who described Rose as "feeling pretty good" and "roaming from table to table" at the pub on Saturday night. The paper repeated Alfred Kohnke's observation that she was "fairly gassed up." The press also advised that Alfred Kohnke and Stephen Croft had "flipped a coin" to see which one would "go back into the beer parlor and get the girl who had asked them for a ride." The one who went, Alfred, testified: "I lost."

The press highlighted Alfred's assertion that Rose had "offered to sell herself for $500." No one contested this statement even though the amount, which would be $2981.65 today in inflation-adjusted dollars, seems highly unrealistic in comparison to the financial means of the blue-collar accused.[48] The press added that the physician who had conducted the autopsy had pronounced Rose "not a virgin," and stressed that there was no physical evidence of sexual force. Apparently, the autopsy also indicated that "there

"Trio Arrested After Death," *Williams Lake Tribune*, 12 April 1967, at 1

were no medical signs of any coition or attempted coition, whether enforced or not, but it would seem that the deceased had anticipated such activity as she had fitted herself with a makeshift contraceptive device."[49] The written report noted that this was a "plug of paper."[50]

Principal O'Connor, Rose's employer, was the only individual to speak positively of her character. The press noted that O'Connor had been called to the RCMP station to identify the body, and quoted him as saying that Rose was "a pleasant, outgoing girl" who was "steady at her work." O'Connor was never called to testify at the trial, but it was probably he who gave the newspaper a photograph of Rose, which the *Williams Lake Tribune* published a few days later. The picture is a heart-rending image of a beautiful young woman, her eyes almost covered by her bangs and her mouth tentatively hidden by her hand, with an unforgettable, direct gaze. The caption, "Rose Marie Roper . . . found nude and battered," must have struck some readers as sad and shocking, despite the character attacks that filled the press.

The written autopsy report filed by Dr. Douglas Bilbey, a white physician from 100 Mile House, described the body as that of a "young Indian woman" in her "late teens," with "small" hands and feet and "juvenile" features. The

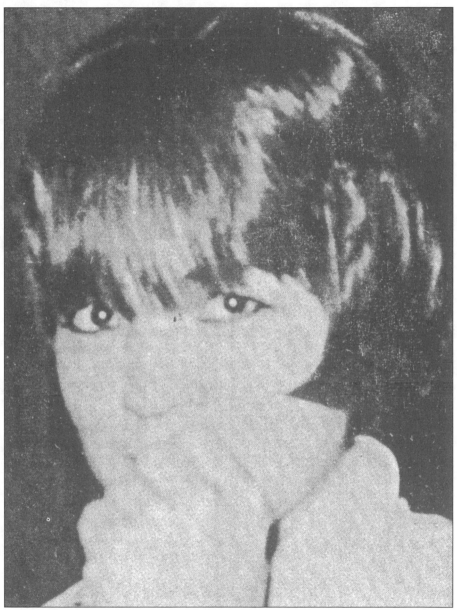

Williams Lake Tribune, 12 April 1967, at 1.

Close up of Rose Marie Roper.

girl's arms were "held across [her] chest," and her fingers were "clenched." Her hair, which was "dishevelled," was "black with auburn dye." "Mud and fine sand" and a "few pine needles" covered the whole body except the hair and scalp. There was also "mud washed into [the] vulva and natal depression." Dr. Bilbey concluded that "death was caused by asphyxia coma due to a broken neck and paralysis of the muscles of respiration, with extra-dural hemorrhage in the cranial area as a contributing factor." In addition, Rose had "slight bruising behind her left ear," a "bruise underneath her chin," and "superficial abrasions." There was "bleeding in to the skull and the upper end of the spinal column, and a displacement of vertebrae." According to the report, "all injuries were received simultaneously."[51]

Dr. Bilbey estimated that the original force that caused Rose's death had occurred "about half an hour before she died." His diagnosis offered a bewildering range of possibilities. The injuries could have been sustained "by applied force" or by "being pushed from a car" or "from falling on a blunt object," and "a bruise under the chin could result in the head tilting back and injuring the neck." Dr. Bilbey also testified that after receiving these injuries, Rose might have remained alive, able to "scream and shout and even walk about not longer than one hour and anywhere between fifteen to thirty minutes." Speculating on what might have occurred during this time, Dr. Bilbey added that "a person could be stunned but not act abnormally, be able to move, then become irrational, collapse, and die." Moreover, under such circumstances, a person "wouldn't worry about putting clothes on or keeping warm." He added that it was even "possible, though unlikely, that the victim could remove her own jeans" during the interval before death.

Dr. Bilbey's testimony seemed designed to exonerate the accused young men. He stated that the abrasions and scratches "would have been more prominent if she had fallen," and that if Rose had been struck by a "hard blow," it would have "caused more serious exterior marks." Asked if Rose might have sustained a broken neck "whilst alighting or being ejected from the car," Dr. Bilbey replied that "this theory was not tenable because of the extra-dural haemorrhage having to occur while she was still breathing" and because "all the injuries had been sustained simultaneously." Dr. Bilbey also gave his opinion that Rose had died "while on her back" and that since she was found face down, "unless the victim was on an incline and rolled over after death, someone must have turned her."

Before he left the stand, the trial judge thanked Dr. Bilbey "for his fairness in giving opinion evidence," but it was a confusing welter of testimony that must have left the jury wondering. He had ruled out death by exposure, for there were bruises, abrasions, bleeding, and a broken neck. Yet the autopsy report curiously severed Rose Roper's death from anything the boys had done. Dr. Bilbey almost seemed to be suggesting that Rose had broken her neck entirely on her own after the boys left. Years later, H. Lee Skipp, the white Williams Lake defence lawyer who represented the three boys, described the autopsy report as "the most fortuitous medical evidence that could possibly be imagined." He added that Dr. Bilbey, who was "a bit of a character," might have been "absolutely wrong for all I knew, but I wasn't about to question it."[52] Capitalizing on this testimony, Skipp posed the question to the jury: "Is not the cause of her death still a bit of a mystery?"[53]

Skipp was also confident that his three clients possessed no criminal intent. Even though the murder charge, with its high requirements for proof of intent, had been withdrawn by the time of trial, Skipp argued that his clients were innocent of *any* criminal intent. "These young men were driving around with the girl's panties appendaged to the aerial of the car. They were completely brazen about it. Their actions were not consistent with a surreptitious crime. It fit with the medical evidence, that the injury was such that they wouldn't have realized it would cause death."[54] Skipp insisted that "the girl met her death by accident with no intention that this should happen."

Skipp was correct that accidental homicide was not a criminal offence. However, if the accused had "unlawfully caused" Rose's death, this on its own could amount to manslaughter. If the boys had been sexually assaulting Rose at the time, this might have qualified, so Skipp was quick to insist that any sexual contact with Rose had been consensual:

> [T]he three went out in the lighthearted manner of 23-year-olds . . . they were not averse to female companionship . . . she was there . . . approached them . . . went with them of her own free will. It is a fair assumption they were going to have intercourse . . . they didn't have difficulty in approaching that . . . no terrific struggle . . . with the clothing intact except for two buttons off a blouse. I would ask if a charge of indecent assault has a chance of succeeding and I would say no.

He continued:

> The picture that emerges is that one pushed her . . . she fell out . . . they put her clothes out of the car . . . she was screaming . . . they left her there not far from the highway. The only single bit of evidence is pushing her out of the

Page 2

Robert L. Wilson   Alfred W. Kohnke   Stephen A. Croft

More about murder

(continued from page one) of us took off all her clothes." He added "Bob got mad and slapped her. Steve pushed her. She stumbled onto the road. She mumbled about me dying. We left her about 11 p.m.

gave her a shove and she landed on the ground She had jeans, blouse and shoes on."

Other witnesses were Marvin Bates, 20, of Deep Creek, who said he saw Miss Roper in a beer parlor before she went

ynavich, all of whom gave evidence concerning the co-operation of the three who appeared at Williams Lake Police station the day after Miss Roper's body was found.

The officers said the accused

"More about murder," photos of Wilson, Kohnke, and Croft,
Williams Lake Tribune, 13 September 1962, at 2

car with subsequent injury, unbeknown to these boys, and the tragic result. It is hard to justify morally and it is not my intention to cast any aspersions on the deceased, but it is my duty to bring out the facts.

Anticipating the jurors' feelings, Skipp urged them to wipe disapproval from their minds:

> This address is a delicate job because I have to speak [of] a young Indian girl being taken advantage of, — I agree. But there is no crime in taking advantage. Don't let the things you disapprove of govern your decision. I can't get up and say they're saints — they are not. . . . It was wrong to go away and leave this girl. They made a mistake and a bad one. It doesn't excuse them. [But] there was no common intention to do anything unlawful. There is nothing unlawful about intercourse if there is consent.

Crown attorney Harry Thomas of Kamloops, who prosecuted at the preliminary inquiry, did not object to the portrayal of the sexual acts as consensual. Instead, he fell back on the pushing, which he argued demonstrated "ample evidence of an assault" and "considerable force." The definition of manslaughter might encompass pushing a person, if the unlawful assault subsequently caused death. Stephen and Bob had both admitted using physical force, and the prosecution argued that Alfred should be held equally responsible because he had formed a "common intention" with the others to carry out the "unlawful purpose." The prosecutor who took over at the trial, S.J. Hardinge of Prince George, noted that the Crown was "not alleging intent" to murder, but that the boys had used "unlawful means" to cause Rose's death.[55]

Neither of the white prosecutors took serious objection to the disparagement of Rose Roper. "It was cold that night," Harry Thomas argued, and "they left her stark naked, whatever her manners or morals." Crown attorney Hardinge was equally insensitive. Questioning Bob Wilson at trial, he asserted: "I suggest you thought you had a bit of Indian trash." According to the press, "there was a pause and Wilson replied: 'Yes, you could say that.'" Presumably Hardinge meant to demonstrate Bob Wilson's contemptuous disregard of Rose Roper, but the phrase, introduced first from the mouth of the Crown attorney, was highly derogatory.

In his summation to the jury, Crown attorney Hardinge addressed the racial issues directly. Although he insisted that Rose Roper deserved to live as much as any human being, he did so with words that belied his argument:

> It is undisputed that a native girl died. Rose Roper was a human being and entitled to protection. She may have been injudicious. It may not be the thing you'd want your daughter to do. They treated her with utmost callousness . . . flipped a coin . . . . I suggest they were ashamed to be seen with a drunken native girl . . . ashamed when with the white girls to admit to being in her company.

Defence counsel Skipp was quick to respond to the label "Indian trash." He argued that his client's use of the term should not be held against him. "Indian trash is an emotional term to make a jury act on emotion," he asserted. "Don't go in there (the jury room) thinking about exploitation of Indians, but a twenty-year-old girl who had been drinking. Are boys to be more blamed than girls?" Seventeen-year-old Rose Roper had suddenly turned twenty, and the lawyer for the accused not only wanted to blame her for her own death, but was urging that the "exploitation of Indians" was irrelevant to Canadian criminal law.

Thomas Anthony Dohm, the white Vancouver judge who presided over the trial, summed up for the jury.[56] An admonition that the jurors "should not be moved by sympathy or prejudice" was his only reference to the racial issues. Then he pointed out that Rose had been picked up in a beer parlour, where she was drinking. He noted that none of the accused had intercourse with her, as one of them "gained the impression that she was menstruating." He reminded the jurors that "a crude contraceptive device was found in her private parts."[57] He stressed that Rose "was alive" when the three accused left her that night, and that they had voluntarily given themselves up to the police after the body was found. On the causation of death, Judge Dohm's charge to the jury was as confusing as the physician's testimony had been. He indicated that "all the injuries could have been caused by a blow or by falling," but added that the Crown's theory that Rose had sustained the broken neck "whilst alighting or being ejected from the car and being kicked on the posterior" was "not tenable," because of the "extra-dural haemorrhage having to occur while she was still breathing, and also because [Dr. Bilbey] felt that all the injuries had been sustained simultaneously."

He instructed the jury that if they found the accused not guilty of manslaughter, they should consider "assault causing bodily harm," and failing that, "common assault," and lastly, "not guilty." Findings of attempted rape or indecent assault were not on the list. Judge Dohm reminded the jury that "there was no case against Kohnke" even for common assault, unless they found that the three boys had formed a "common intention" to have "forcible sexual intercourse" with Rose and to "assist each other to that end." Answering a question from one of the jurors, he added: "The Crown must absolutely prove to you that there has been a common intention to pursue the unlawful purpose." In Judge Dohm's opinion, as he indicated after the trial, "there was no evidence on which a jury could reasonably convict any of these accused of causing her death or of causing her actual bodily harm."[58]

After ten hours of deliberation, a weary set of white jurors brought in their verdicts at 2:30 a.m. on Friday, 15 September.[59] Alfred Kohnke was found not guilty, and discharged from custody. Stephen Croft and Bob Wilson were found guilty of common assault. Judge Dohm thanked them for their service, adding that they constituted "the most conscientious jury I've ever encountered." In sentencing, Judge Dohm emphasized that the verdict demonstrated that the boys were "not responsible for the death of the girl," and that the case should be treated like "any other case of common assault." The only evidence against the accused was that "one slapped her" and "the other kicked her or pulled her out of the car." Given that neither Stephen Croft nor Bob Wilson had previous criminal records, he fined each one $200.[60]

The outcome struck many in the Aboriginal community as outrageous.[61] Rose Roper was dead, and no one was held to account. Had Rose really been alive when the three boys drove off? How had she broken her neck? Had the jurors thought that some other person had happened upon the young Aboriginal girl and attacked her after the three accused left the scene? Surely that was a most unlikely prospect on a deserted logging road in the dead of night in frosty weather. Even if the three boys had never intended to kill Rose, their own testimony indicated that they had assaulted and abandoned her on that isolated road. If the boys had been engaged in an indecent assault or attempted rape, and had intentionally caused bodily harm to facilitate their crime, the doctrine of constructive murder permitted a conviction even if the culprits had no wish to kill and no idea that death was likely to result from their actions. The law also permitted a conviction for culpable homicide when a person caused the death of a human being "directly or indirectly" "by means of an unlawful act," or "by criminal negligence." Criminal negligence was defined in law as showing "wanton or reckless disregard for the lives or safety of other persons."[62] The decision to drop the verdict to common assault seemed inexplicable to many in Rose's community. On the other hand, Skipp was "elated" over the result, and remembers thinking that the accused never fully realized "how lucky they were." They were "very unhappy being convicted at all," he noted, adding: "It's just in the business however . . . you don't expect gratitude."[63]

Appealing the Outcome and the Sentence

CROWN ATTORNEY GEORGE L. Murray, QC, of Vancouver, one of the province's pre-eminent criminal lawyers, took carriage of the case after the trial.[64] The white prosecutor appealed the verdicts to the British Columbia Court of Appeal on 15 February 1968. Murray argued first that the jury had erred in acquitting all three of manslaughter. He noted that the Crown was required to prove criminal cases "beyond a reasonable doubt." However, Murray complained that Judge Dohm had told the jury that the Crown had to prove the existence of common intention "absolutely." It was this excessive burden of proof, claimed Murray, that must have misled the jury, because "no jury, properly instructed as to the applicable law, could reasonably have acquitted."[65] The white appeal judges made short shrift of the argument. Chief Justice Herbert William Davey, and Justices Hugh Alan MacLean and Bruce Robertson, unanimously dismissed the appeal.[66] They noted that the prosecutor had not objected to the judge's remarks at the time, and that the trial judge had earlier made reference to the proper standard of proof. While use of the word "absolutely" was "unfortunate," the appellate bench concluded that the charge "as a whole" contained no misdirection.[67]

Undeterred, Murray pressed ahead to appeal the sentences. Fines of $200 were inadequate to deter others or to protect the public, he argued, and the penalty had failed to take into account "the particular circumstances." This time, he drew a different bench. Chief Justice Davey was still sitting, but he was joined by Justices Meredith Milner McFarlane and Ernest Bolton Bull. Justice McFarlane wrote the unreported majority decision, in which the Chief Justice concurred.[68] He summarized the evidence, emphasizing different facts than the previous judges. He noted that the assault "occurred late at night," and "in the vicinity of a garbage dump." He added that "the deceased native Indian girl" was "of small stature, weighing about 100 pounds." He did not mention the so-called contraceptive device. He did not discuss Rose's whereabouts before the crime, although he did note that she was "in a state of intoxication" by the time she was thrown out of the car. He noted that Rose had been "completely undressed in the car by the three men," and that "her panties were taken and attached to the car aerial." He described how the accused "drove away leaving the deceased, as they said, sitting on the ground screaming and cursing." He referred to the "patches of snow on the muddy ground." Then he briefly rejected the trial judge's sentence:

> [T]he learned Judge ... failed to give proper consideration to the circumstances which I have described briefly, and in particular to the callous indifference shown by the respondents to the girl by leaving her exposed to the elements as they did. In my opinion this has resulted in the imposition of a sentence which I can only regard as entirely inadequate and inappropriate. I think leave to appeal should be granted, the appeals allowed, and a sentence of one year's imprisonment imposed upon each respondent.[69]

Judge Bull wrote a dissenting opinion that summarized the evidence differently.[70] He emphasized that Rose had met up with the three men "in a beer parlour." He described the sexual activity in the back seat as "a certain amount of love play or necking" to which "the deceased was a willing partner." On Rose's state of undress, he stressed that "she cooperated in this regard." He indicated that Rose had anticipated sexual activity "as she had fitted herself with a makeshift contraceptive device." He noted that Rose poured beer over the car, and was screaming and cursing. He mentioned that Bob Wilson had only "slapped her face with his open hand once, or perhaps twice." As for Croft, he had only "kicked her posterior" or "pulled her out." Bull reiterated that the three accused had surrendered themselves to the police. He stressed that the jury had found the accused not responsible for causing Rose's death.

In conclusion, Bull believed that the $200 fines should be upheld:

[T]he greatest care must be taken to avoid at all costs any invidious temptation to punish a person indirectly for that of which he has been found not
guilty. The circumstances here are sordid, and the after conduct of the young
men perhaps callous, notwithstanding the drunken abuse they received, but
the only crimes which they committed were the unlawful slaps and ejection
from the car, neither of which were shown to have caused harm or damage.
There is just no question but that the deceased girl was a willing party to the
debauchery present and planned, and the assaults of the respondents Wilson
and Croft, although by no means justified, were, in my respectful opinion,
modest and at the least understandable under the circumstances.[71]

Skipp told the press that the dissenting judgment had demonstrated that there was at least some "reason for optimism." But years later, he recalls that he "wasn't surprised" at the majority decision, because even for Judge Dohm, who was known to be a light sentencer, the initial fines had been "lenient." Despite the revised sentence, he added: "I still think they were lucky boys. . . . Cariboo had racial attitudes . . . that surfaced in these trials involving Indians. I think it's improved since then."[72]

Lee Skipp was appointed a county court judge in 1973, and elevated to the British Columbia Supreme Court in 1989. Although he enjoyed his career on the bench, he "missed the small town feeling of Williams Lake" after he moved to Vancouver.[73] George Murray was appointed to the British Columbia Supreme Court in 1976, and went on to become its Chief Justice.[74] Stephen Croft and Bob Wilson served their one-year terms at the Oakalla Prison Farm. What happened after their release from prison is unknown. Although Alfred Kohnke was spared a term in prison, his life settled into decline, which some attributed to a belated sense of guilt. According to his testimony, Alfred had been the only one of the three who thought to suggest that night that they might return to the spot where they had abandoned Rose. He raised the question in Lac La Hache when the dance ended, two

hours after Rose had been ejected from the car. Both Stephen and Bob rejected the idea, because they suggested "she might be hitchhiking," and Alfred
made no further effort to convince them. Even though he had been legally
exonerated, after the trial Alfred Kohnke's alcoholism worsened, and he ran
afoul of the law on other matters. Ultimately, he became a recidivist, "in and
out of jail."[75]

Rose Roper's death was neither the first nor the last such case. In 1889,
a Cree woman identified in the press only as "Rosalie" a "prostitute," was
brutally murdered by William "Jumbo" Fisk, a white Calgarian. The Crown
prosecutor apologized for having to charge the "genial accommodating and
upright young man" who had admitted to the killing.[76] In 1969, a seventeen-
year-old Aboriginal woman from Kapuskasing was dragged out of a laundromat at 3 a.m. by two white male strangers, who drove her to an isolated
location and raped her. Although they were subsequently convicted, the
defence counsel and the judges made comments during the trial that were
painfully reminiscent of the Roper prosecution.[77]

In 1974, an eighteen-year-old Aboriginal girl had come to Williams Lake
to meet friends at the Ranch Bar, and to go to a dance at an outdoor facility
locally known as "Squaw Hall." Four white men grabbed her, forced her into
the back of a red Ford Mustang, and drove her to an isolated spot where they
raped her. Three were convicted, but not without similar racialized commentary.[78] That same year, a sixteen-year-old Aboriginal girl was raped by
two white men in Port Alberni. She had arrived in the city with a friend who
abandoned her around 12:30 a.m. without funds. She tried futilely to contact
people she knew, unsuccessfully hailed taxis to see if she could charge a
ride, and then stopped two police officers in desperation to ask if they would
drive her to some place she could stay for the night. They refused, even after
she begged them to arrest her for vagrancy. She finally accepted a lift from
the two male accused who drove her to a basement apartment, threatened
her, and then raped her.[79]

In 1971, Helen Betty Osborne, a nineteen-year-old Cree student from Norway House who was boarding away from home to attend high school, was
walking along a downtown street in The Pas, Manitoba. It was common for
white men in the town to go "cruising for sex" on weekends, "attempting to
pick up [often underage] Aboriginal girls for drinking parties." Such practices were apparently "well known to and ignored by the RCMP." As one later
testified, they hoped to "pick up [a] squaw" and take her for a "gang bang."
Helen Betty Osborne was accosted by four young white men who forced her

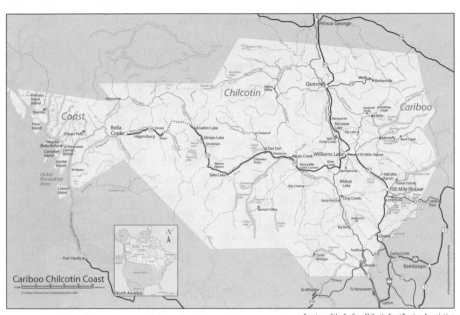

Map of the Cariboo Chilcotin region of British Columbia

into their car, drove her to a secluded spot, and then indecently assaulted and stabbed her more than fifty times. When her body, nude except for boots, was later discovered on the snow in the bush, it appeared she had suffered massive puncture wounds to the head and torso, a broken skull, cheekbones, and palate, damaged lungs, and a torn kidney. Twenty years later, an Aboriginal Justice Inquiry would conclude:

> Her attackers seemed to be operating on the assumption that Aboriginal women were promiscuous and open to enticement through alcohol or violence. It is evident that the men who abducted Osborne believed that young Aboriginal women were objects with no human value beyond sexual gratification. . . . Her murder was a racist and sexist act. Betty Osborne would be alive today had she not been an Aboriginal woman.[80]

The perverse sentiments of the white men who sexually assaulted and murdered so many Aboriginal women were given sustenance in Canadian courtrooms. The spectre of insensitive white courts, ruling upon the racist acts of white men, was to become a feature of the Canadian criminal justice landscape.

The Aftermath

THE TRAGEDY OF ROSE Roper's death left "a big hole in our family," according to Sandra Archie. "I was twelve years old when Rose died. . . . Our mother died when I was six and Rose took the role of a mother. I guess we always wondered if life could have been different or better had she lived. When she died, we all fell apart." Dianne (Roper) Crosina, one year older than Sandra, remembers that their father claimed Rose's body, and drove it "all over the place" displaying her remains to relatives and strangers. He brought her body to the residential school and forced Rose's sisters Dianne and Mary to "take a damn good look," threatening that "if they wanted to drink, this is how they'd end up." In despair, Jacob even tried to drive into the lake with Rose's body in the car. Rose's sisters recall their inconsolable sadness at the funeral service in the Alkali Church, and the grim burial in the Alkali Lake graveyard above the hill.

In retrospect, Sandra Archie notes that the Aboriginal community expected betrayal from the white criminal justice system. "I always expected that we'd never see justice. All your life you'd hear from grandparents, parents, nuns, priests, you're just not good enough. Even justice wasn't good enough for you. We'd faced so much loss and violence that for some it just didn't matter anymore." Yet the trial verdicts sparked rancour from many. Dianne Crosina was shocked at the $200 fines, and found the newspaper articles that "said she asked for it" very upsetting. Sandra Archie added: "All of the students from residential school who knew her were very angry. I think there was outrage from some of the chiefs. The murder of Rose Roper in Williams Lake sparked organizing that began to lead to the shut down of residential schools."[81] In what may also have been a related development, the Indian Friendship Society was formed in 1969, to offer a welcoming place and drug and alcohol counselling for Aboriginal people who came into Williams Lake.[82]

Reflecting years later, Sandra Archie adds with sadness:

> Rose's good qualities outweighed her weaknesses. She was so smart and she was our teacher and protector. She wasn't one to sit back and take it. When they started in on her, I bet she was probably swearing. We had learned from our dad to cuss worse than a mule-skinner. If they started in on her, she would have cussed and fought. She would have made them angry enough to go after her. She wouldn't have gone down without a scratch. I know that she fought hard to live! It must have been very painful for her knowing that we

Courtesy of Constance Backhouse

Sandra Archie with her granddaughter Saidra Rose (namesake of Rose Roper)
and husband Eric Archie

Courtesy of Sandra Archie

Rose Roper's younger sisters as adults at Alkali Lake (date unkown).
Left to right: Dianne Crosina, Sandra Archie, Mary Garman.

would always be unsafe with my dad. Rose would tell you that she did the
best she could, and I know that she did.[83]

Reviewing this chapter before its publication, Sandra suggested one addition: "Is it possible to note that our life experiences have made us stronger, I
guess have made me stronger?"[84] As for the criminal justice system, Sandra
Archie's final comment is searing: "I have forgiven the men who raped and
strangled her. What hurts is the way they portrayed my sister in order to win
this case. They used their beliefs about us to win."[85]

❧ Chapter 10 ❧

"IMPRISONMENT WOULD BE OF NO ASSISTANCE TO THE ACCUSED": Angione, 1974

THREE MEN WERE SEATED in judge's chambers, trying to hammer out a settlement for the attempted rape case set for trial downstairs in the Windsor Courthouse. Ontario Supreme Court judge Edson Livingstone Haines had called the lawyers into his private chambers to discuss a plea bargain. Frank Joseph Montello, the defence lawyer, was keen on the idea; his client was probably "facing two to three years of penitentiary time" if he were convicted of the sexual assault he was charged with perpetrating upon his female employee. Raymond J. Houlahan, the Crown prosecutor, was a bit more reluctant because Montello was proposing a very unusual resolution. He was offering a guilty plea to the less serious offence of indecent assault, on the condition that his client pay "restitution" of $1000 to the victim instead of going to jail. Montello had brought the cash with him, to demonstrate his client's sincerity, and was counting out hundred-dollar bills on Judge Haines's desk. He paused, peered up at the big window alongside the judge's desk, and queried: "Should that fellow be looking at us?" Haines and Houlahan looked up, startled, to an empty window, and only then realized that Montello was kidding. They continued to discuss the plea bargain. Judge Haines had a reputation as a "maverick" who liked to settle cases. It was 25 September 1974, and innovation was in the air.[1]

Montello and Houlahan were no strangers to each other. They had squared off before a different judge earlier in September in a ten-day trial for gang rape. Houlahan had accused Montello then of trying to "blacken the complainant's reputation." Montello, who described Houlahan as "a very feisty Crown," lost

First law firm strike launched

By GORD HENDERSON

The first law firm strike in Ontario history, and possibly the first ever in Canada, was launched today by two employees of the Windsor law office of Weingarden and Hawrish.

Mary Anne Fox, 22, and Janet Martin, 25, began picketing at 8.30 a.m. at the Ouellette Avenue entrance of the Canada Building where the law firm has its offices.

The women, members of the Office and Professional Employees International Union, were joined on the picket line by three men, including Blaise Robinet, a volunteer negotiator for OPEIU.

"We're not going to shut them down. Let's face it—this is a two-girl office," said Mr. Robinet.

He said the picket line has been set up, "for information purposes," and leaflets will be distributed, "to let the public know what the score is."

Mr. Robinet said he expects one of the other law firms in the Canada Building will seek an injunction to prevent picket action on the grounds it interferes with business.

The major contract issues in dispute, according to the firm and the union, are management's opposition to a union shop and insistence on the right to discharge employees for any reason.

Mr. Robinet described the law firm's stand as "an attempt to break the backbone of the (organizing) movement right off."

He said he suspects collusion among city lawyers. "It is quite apparent a good majority have common interests in seeing the movement broken.

A lengthy strike is expected, he said, and he believes the two employees will need strike support from other Windsor unions, "to put some teeth in it."

The two secretaries have been promised 100 per cent support from OPEIU and both have husbands who work.

Arthur Weingarden, a partner in the law firm, today said arrangements have been made for other staff and he doesn't anticipate "any slowdown."

The firm issued a press release which stated the partners feel "the nature and size of our business operation does not make a union shop practicable or beneficial to all those concerned."

The release pointed out that the staff consists of only six persons who are required to work together very closely.

Photo by BEV MACKENZIE

FIRST EVER — Two Windsor legal secretaries made labor history this morning when they began a strike against the law firm of Weingarden and Hawrish. It is believed to be the first strike ever undertaken by law firm employees in Canada. Mary Anne Fox, a striker and president of the Windsor law firm units of the Office and Professional Employees International Union, pickets in front of the Canada Building while Arthur Weingarden crosses the picket line to go to his office.

Americans say they're on time with Great Lakes cleanup . . .

(See Also Page 32)

TORONTO (CP) — An official of the United States Environmental Protection Agency (EPA) said Wednesday he thinks the U.S. is on schedule in its cleanup of the Great Lakes.

EPA administrator Russell Train was replying to Ontario government complaints that the U.S. is so slow in its cleanup that it is near the point of violating the U.S.-Canada Great Lakes Water Quality Agreement in 1972.

Mr. Train was here to address the International Public Works Conference.

He told a news conference Wednesday that each side of the border interprets the treaty "a little differently."

The treaty, signed by Prime Minister Trudeau and former U.S. president Richard Nixon, requires that both countries complete or start adequate treatment of pollution dumped into the Great Lakes by 1975.

The U.S. view is that paperwork planning is enough while Ontario thinks this means starting actual construction.

Mr. Train described progress on both sides of the border as commendable.

He said there is a "very dramatic change" on the U.S. side,

"First law firm strike launched," *Windsor Star*, 19 September 1974, at 1.

that case. His client was convicted by the eight-man-four-woman jury, and sentenced to four and a half years.[2] Jury composition was one thing that had begun to change sexual assault trials. Since 1951, women had been permitted to sit on juries in Ontario, and with establishment of the first rape crisis centres and the growth of the feminist movement in the 1970s, lawyers had begun to spar over gender in the jury selection process.[3] As Montello put it, "the Crowns were always trying for the 8–4 female-packed jury. It was making a difference in the verdicts."[4] The data do not substantiate Montello's observation, with records showing a mere 33 percent conviction rate for rape in 1970, in comparison with 56 percent in 1920, 43 percent in 1950, and 54 percent in 1960, for example. The rates also compared unfavourably to average conviction rates between 1900 and 1975 for burglary 90 percent, theft 87 percent, assault 81 percent, robbery 72 percent, and murder 51 percent.[5] But Montello's sense that feminists hoped to change sexual assault law was undeniably correct.

In 1974, Windsor was Canada's southernmost "City of Roses," a vibrant manufacturing metropolis perched on the busy Detroit River at the hub of the voluminous traffic flowing across the U.S. border. The Big Three auto manufacturers were investing heavily in new plants, and the city's image as a militant union town was in high profile. In mid-September, workers at Hiram Walker's massive distillery were out on strike, and Ontario NDP leader Stephen Lewis walked the picket lines with "a cigar clenched in his fist," denouncing the company for "cynical" bargaining. The papers were filled with demands for better working conditions for migrant farm workers, and two female secretaries were making history with the "first strike ever" at a law firm in Canada. One day later, the male lawyers at Weingarden and Hawrish replaced the strikers with their wives.[6]

Almost simultaneously with the meeting in Judge Haines's chambers, the University of Windsor law school was staging a public seminar on sentencing. Panelists reviewed a brand-new report of the Law Reform Commission of Canada recommending the "diversion" of criminal cases into the community, and the need for a "fresh consideration" of victims' needs for compensation. The Windsor police inspector and the spokesman for the John Howard Society both agreed that for minor offences, the adversarial courtroom setting had "got to go," and suggested that where the offender acknowledged his guilt, it would be "better to bring the victim and offender together in some sort of conciliatory process." Regina lawyer Morris Schumiatcher disagreed vehemently, arguing that prisons were already too "comfortable" and suggesting prisoners be put on "humiliating [public] exhibit"

Osgoode Hall Legal and Literary Society executive, 1955–56.
Back row: Donald Reid, Gerald FitzHenry, Donald Hudson, Richard Piner
Front row: Robert Law, Frank Montello, Patricia Bagwell, Leonard Braithwaite

instead. It was an invigorating time, when radical ideas circulated about victims' rights, offenders' responsibilities, workers' rights, and gender equality, all sparking considerable backlash.[7]

A Cast of Three: Montello, Houlahan, and Haines

VERY DIFFERENT PATHS BROUGHT the three men together in judge's chambers that September morning. Frank Montello was born in Windsor in 1931, the only son of immigrant parents. His father had come to Canada from Catanzaro, Italy, in 1914, never having seen the inside of a school, and unable to sign his name. His mother was of German descent from Syracuse, New York. Montello described his father as doing "everything he could to make a dollar," and for more than forty years his parents ran the Paradiso Spaghetti House at the corner of Wyandotte and Mercer. Montello recalled the war as

Courtesy of the *Windsor Star*, 18 October 1977

Frank Montello, 1977

a frightening time for Italians in Windsor, when the police would drive by in the "Black Mariah" scooping them off the street to be sent to detention camps. His father was lucky. "Not only did we have the spaghetti house, but we had an 'unlicensed' spaghetti house, serving 'Calabrese tea,' a beverage made from grapes. We had all sorts of people who would hide him."[8]

Montello did his first degree at Assumption College (now University of Windsor), and then moved to Toronto to study law at Osgoode. "My mother wanted me to become a priest, my dad wanted me to run the Spaghetti House, and I didn't want to do either," explained Montello. "I took the easy route out. At that time, if you had $400 and weren't convicted of anything, you could go to law school." From the outset, Montello knew he wanted to practise criminal law. It was an unusual career choice, for criminal law had an "unsavoury connotation" and many of the more prominent counsel and judges looked down on criminal lawyers. A small but distinguished cohort of brilliant criminal barristers had slowly started to turn things around, following a path forged by the renowned G. Arthur Martin. Montello admired Martin enormously, and was fortunate to be able to benefit from Martin's mentorship while he was a student and later in practice.[9] Although Montello admitted that in his first years in Toronto there was a bit of a stigma attached to being "an Italian from wicked Windsor," he got himself elected as class representative and president of Osgoode's Legal and Literary Society, where he could "rub shoulders" with elite lawyers and be "wined and dined" with Law Society benchers. He used his Windsor connections to get the governor of Michigan to give a guest lecture at Osgoode, and at the luncheon afterwards, Ontario Premier Leslie Frost expressed his amazement that a law student could get the governor to come to Toronto when the legislature had tried and failed before.

Montello articled with the Toronto firm of Beaton, Bell, and Leake, where he managed to avoid most of the title searching he dreaded by plying the secretary with "a bottle of Hiram Walker Canadian Club." Offered a position at the firm after his call to the bar in 1956, he opted to return to Windsor. There he landed a part-time job as assistant Crown attorney, due primarily to the intervention of his newfound friend Premier Frost. Montello loved the courtroom experience, but hated the low salary, and worked nights at the Paradiso to make ends meet. In 1960, he left to open his own criminal practice because he "wanted three meals a day." He soon began to attract paying clients, garnering a reputation during his forty-three-year career as "the dean of Windsor's criminal defence lawyers."[10]

Courtesy of the *Windsor Star*, 27 May 1977

Raymond J. Houlahan, 1977

Edson Haines and family. Left to right: Paul Haines, Vera Haines, Edson Haines, Barbara Haines, Bruce Haines.

Born in 1935, Ray J. Houlahan was only four years younger than Montello, but much newer at the bar. He didn't start law school until age thirty, and would have been senior to many of his classmates when he graduated from the University of Toronto in 1968. Called to the bar in 1970, he too began his criminal law practice with the Crown attorney's office. But by this time the positions were full-time and much better paid. Houlahan was named the assistant Crown attorney in Windsor directly after his call. He never switched over to the criminal defence side, and thrived in the prosecutorial work.

A mark of his distinction as a prosecutor, Houlahan would be promoted three years after this case to become the Crown attorney for Bruce County. Later, he would make international headlines as the lead prosecutor in the 1995 trial of Paul Bernardo for the sexual assaults and murders of Leslie Mahaffy and Kristen French. The press described Houlahan as "low-key" and "methodical," "well prepared," and well versed in the intricacies of criminal law. Montello characterized him as a "fighter," a rough and ready type who would physically challenge defence counsel who upset him to "see him outside" after court. "Ray would be the first one to approach you for a deal if he didn't have a case, but he was a courageous individual in the courtroom and ready to fight. Bernardo wouldn't have scared Ray in the courtroom at all."[11]

Judge Edson Haines was a man with a polished exterior, known for his "erect bearing," "immaculate suits," "silvery hair," and "aristocratic appearance." A man of formidable intellect and forceful personality, he had been sitting as a judge for twelve years. Reputed to be an "innovator," his hallmarks were "efficiency," "speed," and "supreme confidence." He moved in socially elite circles, as a member of the Royal Canadian Yacht Club, the Albany Club, and the Granite Club. Yet Haines's own roots were modest. Born into a millwright's family with German and Scottish heritage in 1907 in Hamilton, he rejected his mother's wish that he become a Methodist minister and decided to become a criminal lawyer instead. He took the matriculant route into the profession, because he was unable to afford university. He started his legal apprenticeship right out of high school with Hamilton criminal lawyer M.J. O'Reilly, where he gained a wealth of experience in Hamilton Police Court. He took classes at Osgoode Hall, and later switched his articles to Thomas Phelan, a litigator who specialized in insurance defence work. It took five years, but Haines was called to the bar in 1930, and joined Phelan's practice. Phelan convinced him to abandon criminal law because there was "no money in it." Three years later, he set up his own office which expanded to become the powerful Bay Street law firm of Haines, Thomson & Rogers, where he conducted a busy and lucrative practice as the senior founding partner until his appointment to the bench in 1962.[12]

Law Society of Upper Canada, photographer Lynde & Sons

Edson Haines, Call to the Bar

His stature within the legal profession was signified by his election as a bencher to the Law Society from 1951 to 1962, his leadership in continuing legal education programs, his work to create the first Ontario legal aid program, his chairmanship of the Insurance Section of the Canadian Bar Association, his early membership in the American Trial Lawyers' Association and as the only Canadian member of the American Law Institute, and his founding of the Medico-Legal Society. He was the first Ontario lawyer to put together a "structured settlement" to pay out compensation over time in a large damages award. As a practitioner, he "settled fast and quick," usually for the amount he had quoted opposing counsel at the outset. On the bench, he was similarly "noted for his skill and firm guidance in pre-trial conferences with counsel."[13]

He could also be controversial. He was an outspoken critic of the right to remain silent, claiming that to allow crime suspects to refuse to answer police questions was a "luxury" society could "no longer afford," that it frustrated the police, comforted criminals, and encouraged "disrespect for the law."[14] Judge Bertha Wilson long remembered a conversation she had had with him, when he critiqued her idealistic concept of the role of a trial. "A trial is a search for proof," Haines had told her, "not a search for truth."[15] Counsel who appeared in his courtrooms often described him as flinty in temperament. He once threatened a lawyer in a trial that had gone on too long with contempt of court if he tried to call another defence witness. Defence counsel occasionally joked among themselves that they needed to bring their own personal bail money when they appeared before Haines.[16]

The Case That Spawned the Plea Bargain

THE WOMAN AT THE centre of the case, Ana Tesla (whose name has been altered to protect her privacy) had come to Windsor from Eastern Europe five years earlier. Her English had improved dramatically, but she was still not fluent. A twenty-three-year-old hairdresser by occupation, she had been working for a year and a half at the beauty salon at 415 Ouellette Avenue, where the sexual assault took place. Beauty salon businesses burgeoned in the 1970s, as women left behind the "Joan Baez look" of long, straight hair for the "feathered big hair look" of the *Charlie's Angels* star, Farrah Fawcett. Warren Beatty's star-studded movie *Shampoo*, released in 1975, would offer a racy Hollywood version of the business, depicting a charismatic playboy hairdresser, a "sexual opportunist" who slept his way through his female clientele, in a wildly successful satire of late 1960s sexual mores.[17]

The salon where Ana Tesla worked was a little less glamorous than the L.A. salon in *Shampoo*. "Franco's Hairstyles" was a two-person shop, staffed by the owner, Francesco Angione, and Ana. A part-time beautician came in on Saturdays. The salon was comprised of one large room with a curtained window, front and back doors, and a bathroom. It was nestled between a small jewellery store and a dress shop, near the Laura Secord candy store and the Seaway

All photos on this page courtesy of Diana Backhouse

415 Ouellette, July 2006, streetscape and close up

Inn.[18] Ana had testified at the earlier preliminary inquiry that her employer Franco began to make unwelcome overtures on New Year's Eve 1972, when he asked her for a kiss at the close of work. She refused, but the advances accelerated thereafter: "When I bring some customers he pass by me all the time and pull my dress or something and I told him leave me alone. Don't touch me anymore." On 4 June 1973, Ana was getting ready to leave at 6 p.m., closing time. She told the court that as she was putting on her coat, Franco locked the front door and barred her way: "I was going to go out and he was . . . following me and that's when we start fight. And he grab my waist and told me to make sex with him. I said, no, because I'm married, I don't want."

According to Ana, the two struggled and fell to the floor. A hairdryer toppled over on top of them. As Franco began to pull off her coat and undergarments, Ana fought back, twisting her body around. She hit him on the head, scratched him in the face with her nails, and bit him on the shoulder. His blood streamed down over her coat. She was badly bruised on her right knee, and scratched and bruised on her left wrist and elbow. Her assailant ejaculated on her leg. She fled for home, where she waited alone in shock until 1 a.m., when her husband returned from his evening shift at the auto plant. She told him that she would never go back to work for Franco again, and explained what had happened. The two filed a complaint with the police the next morning. Ana's blood-stained coat, torn pantyhose, and several coloured photographs of her scratches and bruises were introduced as exhibits at the preliminary hearing.

The accused was Franco Angione, a forty-year-old married man, and father of two. He had come to Windsor from Salerno, Italy, about nine years earlier, part of a large influx of immigrants that doubled the size of the Italian population in one decade, and eventually led them to become the third largest ethnic community, after the English and French, in the city. A respectable businessman, Franco Angione was actively involved in his community as a member of the Giovanni Caboto Club, the largest Italian organization in Windsor. Although the provincial human rights commission had reported complaints from Italians about "unfair treatment by policemen, judges, court officials and lawyers" in Windsor in 1965, the discrimination was apparently less than that towards the Chinese and African-Canadians. By the mid-1970s, the hostility towards Italians had lessened substantially, and in Montello's opinion, his client's ethnicity had "no effect" on his case. Montello, who had many clients from the Italian community, could converse with Franco in Italian. Like Ana, Franco was not yet fluent in English, and Montello arranged for an interpreter to assist in all the court proceedings.[19]

Montello initially assessed the case using "the shotgun approach," which he described as "your opportunity to take a look in their eyes and test what will go and what won't. You get everything you can at the preliminary hearing, and then use what you think might be credible." In his questions to Ana at the preliminary hearing, he had suggested that Franco fired her on 4 June, and that she had retaliated physically, going after her employer with her purse to scratch him out of spite. She denied it. He tried to portray Ana and Franco as involved in a consensual sexual relationship, and suggested to Ana that Franco often drove her home after work. She denied his estimate of "fifteen to twenty times," admitting he had done so twice. Montello asked whether she had gone with Franco to hair-styling conventions in Toronto, and to the Holiday Inn in Windsor. Ana denied any Toronto trips, and said she had attended a demonstration on false eyelashes once in Windsor, with Franco and another female employee, but had never gone to the Holiday Inn. Montello suggested she had been at Franco's apartment, that the two had gone to Alexander Park and Memorial Park together; she said no. Montello asked whether she had gone out for drinks with her boss after work; she said no. He asked if screwdrivers were her favourite drink; she replied she never drank alcohol. He asked if she had ever received gifts from her employer; she said he had brought two capes back from a European vacation, one for her and one for the other female hairdresser. Franco apparently intended to explain the scratches on his face, which Ana's husband had observed the day following the assault, as razor cuts from shaving, or injuries from an evening soccer game. Montello planned to call the other hairstylist who worked for Franco, to give evidence in her employer's defence.

All thoughts of such strategies collapsed when Montello discovered that the case had been scheduled before Judge Haines. Montello recalled that he and Haines had had "many battles in the past," and that Haines was notorious for being "very pro-Crown" and for "detesting criminal defence counsel." In Montello's view, "with Haines, a reasonable doubt never factored into his decisions; [my client] would have done penitentiary time." He called in Franco Angione and told him: "The draw is against you, you didn't win the lottery, you got the worst judge to try you, he will obviously believe the Crown's evidence." Montello reviewed the Crown's case to satisfy himself that a sexual assault had occurred: "While there was no vaginal penetration, I was satisfied by what he and the police officers told me that there was indecent assault." Montello advised his client to try to plea bargain his way out of jail, recalling that one of the positive things about Judge Haines was that "he was the type of judge that if you wanted to try something out for size, you could go ahead and do so without being hurt if he disagreed with you."[20]

Before any plea bargain could be sealed, the three men had to agree on a statement of facts. Crown attorney Houlahan would have insisted that the statement should closely reflect the testimony his complainant had given in the preliminary. Defence counsel Montello wanted to minimize any reference to matters that put his client in a bad light. Judge Haines was there to broker a deal he felt satisfied the needs of justice. Montello tried to downplay the struggle that took place in the beauty salon. He thought Ana's injuries were insignificant in comparison to other rape cases, noting: "My god, in order for a woman to get a conviction back then, she'd almost have to be dead, into the hospital." Montello preferred to characterize Ana's response as "some resistance at the outset, but nothing beyond that." Montello called the rip in the pantyhose "a little tiny hole," and the bruise "a little tiny red spot." During the preliminary hearing, Ana had admitted under cross-examination that the struggle lasted only "ten or fifteen minutes." She had also admitted that although she screamed, no one on the street seemed to have heard. But ultimately, Houlahan was more successful than Montello in his advocacy about the facts that morning. Montello was not that happy with the compromise statement that found its way into the final decision:

> The accused is a businessman, 40 years of age, married, and living with his wife and two teenaged children. He was the employer of the complainant who had worked for him in his shop for many months. He had made advances to her previously and they were rejected. On the evening in question she was the last employee to leave and thereupon the accused locked the door and attacked her. She resisted vigorously and finally escaped. Her clothing was damaged, she sustained bruises to various parts of her body. She went home at once, related her traumatic experience to her husband who called the police. They investigated and charged the accused with attempted rape. The accused has no criminal record. There was no evidence of any previous attacks by him on other employees.

Sexual Assault in the Workplace

Judge Haines's factual summary emphasized that the sexual assault took place in a workplace setting, perpetrated by an employer upon an employee. The vulnerability of women in the labour force to coercive sexual overtures from male supervisors and employers was a problem of long standing. The workplace, with its juxtaposition of physical proximity and economic power differentials, created an explosive potential for sexual exploitation. However, it seems that the employment nexus was not often recognized in the criminal sexual assault records. The few cases that specified the existence of an employment relationship included housekeepers employed on a Saskatchewan farm, and in Saanich and Vancouver, British Columbia,[21] waitresses and cashiers working in Winnipeg and Vancouver restaurants,[22] and babysitters in Manitoba and Ontario.[23]

The spectre of sexual assault in the workplace had prompted Canadian legislators to create a separate offence, "seduction of a servant," in 1890. This made it a crime for an employer to seduce or have "illicit connection" with any female employee under "his control or direction." Only females under the age of twenty-one, who were of "previously chaste character" were protected, and only employees in factories, mills, and workshops were initially included.[24] Shops and stores were added in 1900, and the section was expanded to cover all areas of employment in 1920. Some male legislators expressed hesitation about criminalizing sexuality in the workplace, repeatedly raising concerns about false complaints and the lamentable prospects for blackmail. Consequently, the enactments contained the usual requirements for corroboration, and set out a limitation period of one year. The legislators also emphasized that the court might find the accused not guilty if the evidence did not show that "as between the accused and the female person, the accused [was] more to blame." Oddly, it was also a full defence for the seducer to subsequently marry the employee.[25] The scope was narrowed still further in 1935, when a British Columbia court held that married women were excluded from coverage.[26] In 1941, another British Columbia court drew a distinction between "seduction" and "rape," suggesting that where there was evidence that the female employee had not consented, it was wrong to use the "seduction" charge.[27] A Quebec court dismissed one of the few prosecutions of a male employer in 1964 for lack of corroboration.[28]

But there were strong winds of change sweeping through North America in the 1970s. The phrase "sexual harassment" was first coined in 1975 at a "speak-out" rally in Ithaca, New York, when hundreds of women publicly denounced the sexual intimidation and violence they had suffered at work. *Ms. Magazine*, an influential new feminist periodical, put the topic on its front cover in 1977. Lin Farley published the first book on sexual harassment in 1978, and Canada was not far behind with the second in 1979. Feminists had conceptualized sexual harassment as a systemic barrier for working women who were striving to obtain equality, and were demanding a level playing field.[29] In the 1980s, the law of sexual harassment would take several new directions under revised human rights statutes, collective agreements in unionized work settings, newly promulgated employer "sexual harassment policies," and lawsuits demanding compensation in tort. What was most surprising, however, was that in 1974, the criminal law was ahead of this, already beginning to move in step with these radical new directions. Judge Haines's decision continued:

> This accused as an employer owed a duty to his female employees. If another employee or an intruder attacked a female employee, the employer would be expected to come to her defence. How much more must an employer restrain his own impulses for the protection of his female employees, especially where their duties often bring them in close bodily proximity, often alone. Employers have a position of trust. They owe it to their employees and it is expected they will discharge it not only by the female employee herself but by the members of her family who permit them to work there in confidence.[30]

Judge Haines's decision was couched in paternalistic language. His focus was the higher obligation of a woman's employer and the expectations of her family. His comments provoke images of weak women, physically in need of protection from their more powerful male employers, and women who are first and foremost daughters, wives, and mothers. There was little recognition of women's demands for personal sexual autonomy, and the need to eliminate sex discrimination from the workplace as a matter of gender equality. Nevertheless, it acknowledged the harm of sexual assault in the workplace in no uncertain terms.

Sentencing: "Restitution for Wrong Done"

THE HAINES DECISION WAS equally remarkable for its concern about the sexual assault victim. "All too often she is ashamed, embarrassed and suffers in silence," he noted. "Our system of corrections spends substantial sums on the correction of the offender, and quite properly so. But what of the victim?" Haines recognized that victims could seek some governmental compensation under the "Criminal Injuries Compensation" scheme, first launched in 1969, but concluded that sexual assault victims were more likely to want "to forget the nightmare of the event" than to apply.[31] Haines believed that the criminal law should play an important new role in compensating the victim. He cited the recently released Law Reform Commission report, and characterized as "refreshing" its recommendation for "indemnification of the victim as an alternative to imprisonment."

The Law Reform Commission of Canada, chaired by Judge E. Patrick Hartt, had floated the idea of putting more emphasis upon the "injury" done to the victims of crime, and encouraging "restitution" rather than "simple vengeance."[32] This was a far cry from the caution urged by the federal government's 1967 Ouimet Report on Corrections. It had emphasized the "difficulty likely to be experienced by a criminal court in assessing damages which arose from personal injury" and the "difficult constitutional questions" that would arise if the award of damages were vested in a criminal court. The Ouimet Report had not supported restitution except to say that the "correctional possibilities" should be "kept under review."[33] But the concept of restitution was not new. Legislation had been on the books since 1921 authorizing courts to order a convicted offender to "make restitution and reparation" to any person "aggrieved or injured" by the offence for the "actual damage or loss thereby caused."[34]

The Ouimet Report noted that the restitution provision had been only "rarely invoked."[35] This may have been accurate as far as reported judgments went, but underneath the formal gaze of the law, it was a different picture. Compensation payments were sometimes utilized behind the scenes, before the case got into court, when defence counsel approached an investigating officer to see if they could resolve the matter before charges were laid, through payment to the victim or her family.[36] Frank Montello admitted that it was something they got "criticized for," but argued that compensating victims was "often a very humane thing to do," helping them "reconstruct their lives" instead of "ruining lives" by taking it into the courtroom. He had come into this case far too late to negotiate such a result. His only chance now, in judge's chambers, was to convince the prosecutor and the judge that court-ordered restitution was appropriate. He recalled Houlahan as the more reluctant, possibly concerned that Franco Angione could be perceived as trying to "buy his way out of the crime," but eventually he conceded. Although Montello did not know it at the time, Haines may have been the best judge he could have drawn for this.[37] Eight months earlier, Haines had decided in a theft case that it was constitutionally valid to provide for restitution under the *Criminal Code*, and that criminal courts were fully authorized to quantify damages for "pain and suffering."[38] He took little further convincing. Mon-

Edson Haines at a Canadian Bar Association meeting in Windsor, 1953.
Left to right: Edson Haines, John J. Robinette, John Arnup, George L. Mitchell,
Stanley Lount Springsteen, G. Arthur Martin.

tello thought the matter was best left at a simple plea bargain, but Haines wanted to justify the result fully, in a reasoned decision that could stand as future precedent.[39] His written judgment on sentence follows:

> Imprisonment would be of no assistance to the accused. It is likely it would ruin his one-man business. To him the conviction itself forms a substantial portion of the punishment. . . . While the solution I propose to follow here cannot be adopted in all cases, because the offender is usually without funds, here the offender is a man of modest means. I could fine him and the money would be transferred to Her Majesty's treasury. I do not propose to do that. Rather I propose to make compensation of the victim part of the process of rehabilitation. After all it has long been recognized that restitution for wrong done is rehabilitation. . . . I am going to suspend sentence on the accused and direct that . . . the accused pay the victim forthwith the sum of $1000.

Haines's novel attempt to impose compensation as the end result of a sexual assault trial ran contrary to the bulk of sentencing law in the twentieth century. Most Canadian judges imposed prison terms. The death penalty, although it remained a potential punishment for rape until 1954, was never administered to rapists in the twentieth century.[40] Rape and "carnal knowledge of a girl below the age of fourteen" carried a potential for life imprisonment, but that was rarely imposed either.[41] Five to ten years was a more common sentence, although occasionally judges dispensed terms as high as twenty-five years and as low as three months.[42] Courts could also impose corporal punishment for some sexual assault offences, requiring that the offender be whipped with a specified number of lashes.[43] Up to thirty lashes had been ordered in some instances, although the propriety of corporal punishment was hotly contested and such penalties became much rarer over time.[44] After 1948, individuals found to be "criminal sexual psychopaths," and later "dangerous sexual offenders," could be sentenced to "indeterminate periods" in a penitentiary.[45]

The maximum penalties set for the lesser sexual assault provisions varied between two and fourteen years.[46] Individuals sentenced for crimes such as indecent assault typically received a few months to several years.[47] More rarely, suspended sentences and fines were substituted. These lighter penalties were usually bestowed on men of financial means, who could claim a "respectable family background" and steady skilled employment. They often retained private psychiatrists to produce favourable prognostic reports, offering plans for supervised treatment and rehabilitation within the community.[48] Franco Angione, a successful salon proprietor, fit squarely within this privileged class. Haines had justified his ruling that "imprisonment would be of no assistance" on the basis that it would "ruin" Angione's business.

What was not pursued in Canadian courtrooms was the crucial question of whether imprisonment was an effective punishment for any perpetrator of sexual assault, regardless of class. Judges agreed that "retribution in the sense of revenge" was of "little or no importance" in sentencing.[49] So presumably putting someone in jail just to inflict harm was not a rationale. All courts stressed that "reform of the offender" was an important objective. However, there were no demonstrably effective treatments for sexual assault offenders, and no one even attempted to argue that a prison term was rehabilitative.[50] "Deterrence" of the offender and others, along with "protection of the public," were often cited by judges as the overriding factors that led them to impose prison terms.[51] Yet psychiatrists and criminologists claimed that deterrence was elusive, and many offenders came out of prison posing more risk of violence than before they entered.[52]

Feminist activists from rape crisis centres, battered women's shelters, and women's centres, whose numbers grew through the 1970s, expressed dismay over the many injustices they encountered with sexual assault law. Out of a desire to have the destructiveness of rape fully recognized in law, many advocated longer jail sentences.[53] It may not have equalled Morris Schumiatcher's complaint at the University of Windsor seminar that prisons were "too comfortable" and that criminals should be publicly humiliated, but it was an undeniable endorsement of prisons. And it was in stark contrast to feminist demands pertaining to female criminal offenders, where the campaigns were for less punitive regimens within jails and fewer terms of imprisonment. Few considered the dangers of locking up large numbers of violent sex offenders in institutions that were dehumanizing, racist, homophobic, and inherently violent themselves. Few advocated resources to search for treatments that would reduce coercive sexual behaviour. The advocacy of jail as an appropriate remedy for rape was, in retrospect, neither carefully considered nor humane. It failed to recognize that sexual assault originated within a deeply rooted culture of sexism, and that individualized penalties could never address systemic problems. Judge Haines's decision to opt for restitution was by no means a panacea, but it was a step in an interesting new direction, and appears to have been ahead of much feminist analysis at the time.

Haines's efforts to refocus the sentencing process upon the victim's needs was short-lived. A Manitoba appellate court would strike down three orders for $250 to victims of indecent assault in 1976, because the Crown had failed to prove "actual loss or damage sustained such as torn clothing." The court stressed that the "complainants' injured feelings could not be compensated for in monetary terms."[54] In 1977, another Ontario court would refuse to follow the *Angione* decision, holding that Haines was wrong to think that Parliament had authorized criminal courts "to make financial awards to compensate victims for pain and suffering." The restitution provision was to be restricted in future to damages that were "relatively concrete and easily ascertainable," ruling out "vague, amorphous and difficult matters" such as "pain and suffering."[55] The practice of having a judge discuss a plea bargain in his chambers would also become the subject of adverse comment. In 1975, an Alberta court admonished that all such discussions should take place "in open Court," and that there was "no place in the sentencing procedure for hole-and-corner bargaining."[56] Haines's reputation as a "maverick" continued to hold.

The Glare of the Media Spotlight

THERE REMAINED ONE OTHER matter that set the *Angione* case apart. Frank Montello advised Judge Haines in his chambers that his client had been able to keep the charge secret from his family, and that any publicity would "cause untold anguish to his wife and children" and would "ruin him in his business." He requested a court order to ban the press from naming the accused. Montello had long been of the view that individuals accused of crime should be shielded from the scrutiny of the press. On his retirement, he spoke proudly of the many people he had defended, still refusing to name clients he felt were "entitled to avoid the glare of the media spotlight."[57]

The matter of publicity had also occupied Canadian legislators. But their main worry was that the unsavoury details of sexual assault might have a detrimental influence on general readers. The *Criminal Code* was amended in 1900 to allow judges to foreclose media coverage by excluding the public from a trial "in the interests of public morals."[58] Most trials remained open, however, and in the early decades newspapers had few qualms about publishing the names of both the accused and the sexual assault victim.[59] By the 1970s, it was common practice that the press no longer mentioned the name of a rape victim. There was no such privacy for anyone accused of rape. This was a position that would provoke Frank Montello to argue that it was unjust not to extend equal treatment to his clients. His equation of abuser and victim was not particularly fair, but his sentiment, that we should treat a sexual offender "like a human being," was compelling.[60]

Judge Haines expressed astonishment that Franco Angione had kept the matter hidden so far, and he sympathized with the man's plight, to the extent that he filed his decision using Angione's initial: *Regina v. A.* was the title that would appear in the formal law report. But an order barring Angione's identification in the press was not something he was prepared to grant:

> I sympathize with the plight of the wife and children. So often they are the real sufferers. Teenagers can be unwittingly very cruel in dealing with each other, and idle gossip in the community may well break up a home. Nevertheless, I do not think I should make such an order. Without considering whether I have such power . . . I prefer to leave the matter to the sound discretion of the responsible news media. Daily they balance what has been called the public's right to know against the great damage that would be done by disclosure. For example, it is common practice not to mention the name of the

Victim gets $1,000 award

By TOM McMAHON

A city businessman, who indecently assaulted a female employee, was ordered by a Supreme Court judge Wednesday to pay the woman $1,000 compensation.

In what is believed to be the first case ever of a criminal trial judge compensating a complainant, Mr. Justice Edson Haines ordered Franco Angione, 40, to pay the money to a former employee.

Of the decision to grant compensation Mr. Justice Haines and Assistant Crown Attorney Ray Houlahan said they believed it to be unprecedented.

In speaking on behalf of Angione, who pleaded guilty to the charge, lawyer Frank Montello told the court the woman was not hurt in the assault.

Mr. Justice Haines, who made the paying of the money part of a three-year probation order, told Angione, of Goyeau Street, "were it not for your wife and children I would have sent you to jail."

The judge said this is a case of an employer assaulting an employee after hours

He added, we spend enormous amounts of money trying to rehabilitate the accused," however, "we tend to forget the victim."

Many cases like this go unreported because the complainants feel "ashamed" and "dirty," he said. The victim can go to the Criminal Injuries Compensation Board, but few do in these cases.

The case of an employer taking advantage of a female employee after hours is "not new," the judge said. However, he added, "why shouldn't we provide for some compensation for this young woman?"

Mr. Justice Haines told the man because of the employer-employee relationship he had a duty to protect the woman. He said the man had violated that trust.

In passing sentence the judge told the man if he had any character at all the conviction itself would be enough punishment. However, he said, "I don't think the victim in appropriate cases should be forgotten."

Mr. Justice Haines said he could not have made the compensation order directly under the Criminal Code but was able to do so as part of a probation order as stipulated in the Code.

Rochester Township man acquitted on arson charge

A 27-year-old Rochester Township man was acquitted on a charge of arson by a county court jury that deliberated less than 15 minutes before returning its verdict.

Ansley Scott Grant, of Lot 7, West Ruscom River Road, was charged with arson after his house was destroyed by fire Oct. 4, 1972.

Donald Campbell, a fire investigator with the Ontario Fire Marshal's Department said the blaze which destroyed the two-bedroom frame house started in the one of the bedrooms.

He said it looked like it was started by a petroleum product and an empty petroleum can was found about 75 feet from the scene.

Gordon Coombes, a plumbing contractor from Tilbury, said Grant had joked with him about burning the house down and that there was quite a bit of insurance on it. This conversation occurred shortly before the fire when Coombes was installing a toilet fixture.

Grant's counsel, Ted Perfect, called no defence evidence.

"Victim gets $1,000 award," *Windsor Star*, 26 September 1974, at 5.

victim of a rape, and in appropriate cases I am confident they would exercise the same discretion in regard to those found guilty where the sins of the accused fall heavily on the shoulders of his family.

The *Windsor Star* was not moved. Reporter Tom McMahon consulted with his senior editor, and both concluded that there was no reason to grant the judge's informal request. The case was significant because neither could recall an instance where a criminal judge had ordered restitution to a sexual assault victim. "We like to deal in specifics," McMahon advised, "and the more information we provide the more complete the story. There was some compassion for the man's family, but in the end he was the author of his own misfortune." The paper carried a full article on the case, titled "Victim gets $1,000 award." The sexual assault victim was not identified, but Franco Angione was named no less than three times, along with his age and address. Reflecting upon the case years later, McMahon remembered that Franco Angione, or his lawyer, he couldn't recall who, had been so upset about the article that he had called the reporter afterwards. McMahon added: "He wanted to tell me I had ruined his life."[61]

> Chapter 11 <

CONCLUSION

EACH OF THE NINE cases profiled here against the backdrop of the larger collection demonstrates that injustice was deeply rooted in sexual assault law.
Mary Ann Burton's case displayed misogynistic assumptions about the
venality of women as well as class bias that infected police investigations,
doctors' testimony, and defence cross-examinations. Women who made
complaints of sexual violation were stereotyped as incredible. Skepticism
and disbelief interspersed all their interactions with the legal system. It was
one thing for the criminal law to demand that the Crown prove its case "beyond a reasonable doubt," the highest standard of proof known in law. It was
quite another then to tilt the playing field still further against the victims of
sexual violence with double standards in the courtroom. Mary Ann Burton's
response, "Don't you bully me," indicates that she knew the treatment to
be unfair, and that her sense of "justice" would have required a dramatic
refashioning of the trial.

Police and physicians should have been instructed to conduct full investigations free from sexism and class discrimination. Criminal law should
have been enforced to ensure that all women were protected from sexual
assault, regardless of their class, family history, sexual past, use of alcohol,
or lifestyle. Rules of professional ethics should have restrained lawyers from
lines of cross-examination that played on the discriminatory biases of judges
and juries. Just as it has long been recognized that counsel must not tell jurors that they can disregard the law, neither should they have been allowed
to suggest that some women were not worthy of legal protection.

The sexual assault that eight men perpetrated upon Yvonne Collin was one of a large number of gang rapes in this era. Yet the sexual behaviour of men in groups was a matter almost completely unaddressed in the law. As a point of criminal procedure, every sexual assault was treated as a discrete and individualized act, and each accused was charged and tried separately. Consequently, the law failed to respond to the many ways in which homosocial group dynamics affected the actions of young men out looking for sexual conquest. Given that competitive posturing led a number to join in without any evidence of personal sexual arousal, it suggests an increased responsibility for ring-leaders who set the stage for such group displays of aggressive masculinity. Equally, it raises questions about those who stood furthest to the margins, reluctant to participate personally. Why did the criminal law adopt a rigidly narrow concept of "aiding and abetting," choosing to exonerate those who stood and watched? Those who stood by lent their force to the sexual assault by their very presence. Victims of gang rape suffered inordinately due to the sheer number of sexual assaults visited upon them. If the men on the edges, who were disinclined to participate, had intervened, objected, even walked away expressing disgust, the group dynamics might have shifted and the number and extent of gang rapes might have diminished. To conclude that only those guilty of active instigation were legally responsible was short-sighted. There were obvious difficulties inherent in prosecuting mere bystanders. But there was no need to immunize those who were part of a group that was engaged collectively in a gang rape. To do so was to assume mistakenly that the law had no role to play in motivating group members to stop their comrades.

The crime of seduction with which the eight were charged, restricted to females "of previously chaste character," was fundamentally misconceived. Enacted partly out of recognition that rape law as historically interpreted covered only a minuscule portion of coercive sexual acts, the offence should never have been premised on prior chastity. Feminist organizations recognized this from the outset. In the hands of lawyers, judges, and jurors, an unjust provision was applied even more unfairly, with women labelled "unchaste" because of the neighbourhoods they lived in, their poverty, and the sexist rumours and innuendo that defence counsel managed to dig up about them. The role of the police in Yvonne Collin's case also seems to have been problematic. The testimony the officers gave at trial on behalf of the accused shocked the Crown prosecutor, and the evidence of monetary discussions suggests that they were "bought" by the defence. Whether this was an isolated turn of events or part of wider-ranging police practices, it indicates that at times the criminal justice system was up for sale.

The sexual relationship between Henry Kissel and Ethel Machan reminds us that date rape is not a particularly recent phenomenon, and that it appeared in Canadian courtrooms many decades before it became a term of art. The case also permits an intriguing glimpse into cultural mores undergoing major shift. On the heels of the tragedy of the First World War, the Roaring Twenties swept in on winds of change. Young women cast off their corsets at the same time that they embraced sexual experimentation. But they hoped to do so within limits. Many desired to explore sexual contact prior to marriage, while still protecting themselves from the loss of virginity, venereal disease, and pregnancy. Some young men who participated in these emboldened sexual adventures considered it their masculine right to press female partners well beyond the parameters that women tried to negotiate.

In the face of such cultural transformation, this was an important opportunity for the law to intervene, to assess the expectations of the parties, as well as the benefits and costs of these new sexual mores, and to work out the fairest rules of engagement possible in such uncertain times. Instead, the criminal courts cast young women to the winds, insisting that flappers who chose such risky behaviour were no longer entitled to draw boundaries beyond which their dates could not go. Judges and jurors interpreted the concept of consent in ways that privileged male perspectives, and made nonsense of women's experiences. Women who unequivocally said "no" were deemed to be shamming. Their paramours were licensed by law to use both psychological and physical coercion to extract submission.

The devastation caused by such distorted definitions of "consent" is ably demonstrated in Velma Demerson's case in 1936. Physically forced into sexual intercourse while on a date with an older man, young Velma believed herself completely without options. She understood recourse to the law to be futile. She knew she had been raped, but concluded that her "word meant nothing," and that public disclosure would bring only "disgrace." Her estimate that "thousands and thousands" similarly chose to hide their violation indicates that the legal system betrayed far more women than those whose court cases were preserved in the archives. It is a stunning indictment of the injustice of law, one that seems to have been widely recognized at the time and openly condoned.

The law was equally unhelpful in responding to the repeated internal gynecological examinations and experimental medical treatments that Velma

Demerson equated with "state sexual assault." Dr. Edna Guest's humiliating and painful ministrations to her young reformatory patient were marked by racism and class bias. In her eugenically motivated desire to root out venereal disease, Dr. Guest disregarded many of the medical norms of the time, and intrusively examined and operated upon a patient she dismissed as practically inhuman. Although in Velma's opinion, Dr. Guest's treatments constituted sexual assault equivalent to the date rape she had suffered earlier, neither the criminal law nor the civil law respected her view. Women incarcerated by the state were deemed to "consent" to all such treatment, by social expectation and via legislation. They represented the lowest echelon of the female population, and could be dealt with at whim. Velma Demerson's successful effort to extract an apology and some compensation from the government decades later offers a singularly unusual, but decidedly positive, outcome in her long and tenacious battle to obtain justice.

For women with disabilities, the law offered little respite. Beatrice Tisdale's efforts to communicate with Joe Probe, as well as with the legal authorities in the Weyburn courtroom, were disparaged by hearing people who refused to treat deafness with respect. The dominance of the hearing culture, and its impatient response to Beatrice's deafness, betrayed any hope for honest communication in the wheat fields, motor vehicles, hotels, and courtrooms of small-town Saskatchewan. Provisions of the *Criminal Code* that had purportedly been passed in recognition of the particular vulnerability of women with disabilities were applied in ways that neutralized any potential to protect them from coercive sexual attack. That Beatrice Tisdale courageously chose to continue communicating throughout this lamentable criminal trial, despite the disdain with which her testimony was received, should have kindled amazement and admiration. Her case punctures all illusion that law represented universal justice.

Although the legal definition of rape contained no requirement that victims exhibit physical resistance, judges and jurors demanded evidence that women had forcefully fought off their assailants' advances, preferably to the point of serious injury. Beatrice Tisdale's bruises, disheveled appearance, torn coat-tie, and single slap to Joe Probe were deemed too inconsequential to count. Why did the law choose to demand such evidence of resistance? Such rules deliberately precluded less combative women from protection, in a culture that constructed meekness and gentility as a hallmark of femininity. And for courts to suggest that bruising, swelling, cut lips, and possible rib fractures constituted only "mild protests" exhibited by women who later saw the error of their ways and "consented" to sexual relations was patently in error. What did this say about the legal understanding of masculine sexuality? About women? It was to endorse a version of sexual practice that bore no resemblance to genuine, freely offered, mutually reciprocal sex. Similarly, although the definition of rape did not overtly exclude women who had had previous non-marital sexual experience, in practice, courts dismissed cases where there was any suspicion of this, even when there was little other than rumour to substantiate the claim. Non-virginal women faced the risk of rape as much, if not more, than other women. The division of women into categories of "sexually pure" and "promiscuous" was calculated to exonerate rapists who preyed upon the latter.

The large number of child victims in court on sexual assault cases is overwhelming evidence of the exploitation of the most vulnerable. Although many believe that the public disclosure of child sexual abuse is a relatively new phenomenon, nothing could be further from the truth. It was not a topic that was too shameful to discuss, that was kept from all public gaze. Police, lawyers, judges, and jurors dealt with such trials on a daily basis throughout Canada. Sadly, the response of the legal system was not to meet the trauma of sexually abused children with special efforts to enforce the criminal law, but to step back in panic. Lacking any systemic evidence that children were less truthful than adults, legislators and judges forged ahead to create presumptions of unreliability. The doctrine of corroboration could defeat even the most compelling child witnesses. In Marie Tremblay's case, it seemed that almost nothing would suffice to secure a conviction for her assailant. Equally unfairly, the rules surrounding "recent complaint" demanded that sexual assault victims report their violation spontaneously and immediately, and then unaccountably found such evidence to be "confirmatory" rather than "corroborative."

While children were taken to be particularly lacking in credibility, similar apprehensions greeted all women who claimed to have been sexually assaulted. No one ever produced any empirical evidence that sexual assault complainants were less truthful than other victims of crime. Indeed, all logic would have pointed the other way. There was so much to deter victims from making official complaints. Women were forced to report to male police officers who often treated them disparagingly, as Mary Ann Burton and Yvonne Collin had discovered to their dismay. Then they had to endure the humiliation and embarrassment of a painful public trial. Even at the end of a gruelling process, the outcome was anything but certain, with conviction rates substantially lower than for other crimes. The doctrine of corroboration, tapping into the deep suspicions that juries and judges already carried into the courtroom, reinforced misogynistic proclivities, jettisoning convictions even in some cases where the triers-of-fact believed the victim's testimony beyond a reasonable doubt.

Willimae Moore's prosecution for indecently assaulting another woman may have been the first lesbian criminal trial in Canada. Choosing to move to the northernmost reaches of the country to evade the dictates of compulsory heterosexuality, Willimae Moore and her illustrious travelling companion Beatrice Gonzales ran smack into a frenzied Cold War homophobia that reached as far as Yellowknife in 1955. Prosecuted for an attempted kiss, Willimae Moore's sexual overture was almost laughably trifling in comparison with the sexual acts of men accused of indecently assaulting women. The complainant, Laura White, received none of the customary hostility and suspicion that greeted most other female victims of sexual assault. The rules of corroboration and the definition of consent were relaxed, and her testimony was taken at face value. Although the conviction was eventually overturned by a divided appellate court, this anomalous case presents a remarkable contrast to the male-to-female sexual assault prosecutions. At the same time it also reveals the racism that suffused Canadian society and the criminal justice system. Willimae Moore's own lawyer believed that the charges would never have been laid, and that no conviction would have been registered, if his client's non-white racial identity had not factored into the situation. There is here an uncanny resemblance to Henry Kissel's earlier prosecution, where his Jewish identity seems to have altered the class-based protection his status as a medical student might otherwise have provided.

The issue of race also dominated the tragic events surrounding Rose Marie Roper's sexual assault and death. To trace the events that occupied her brief life is to weep. Born into an Aboriginal community that had been wrested from its lands, livelihood, language, and culture, Rose grew up in a home that was a microcosm of the violence and despair that follow upon the heels of such destruction. Deprived of her own childhood, she withstood physical, emotional, and sexual abuse while she tried to shelter the younger children around her. The numbingly punitive residential school regime, where she was neither fed nor educated properly, struck her as "a relief." Through all of this, in a remarkable testament to the resilience of the human spirit, Rose Roper laughed often and danced to music she loved. Her seventeen-year-old life was snuffed out by three white boys out for a night of carousing, who looked upon her as nothing more than a disposable sex object they could toss out like garbage when they were finished. Rose did not go quietly, raging against this callous treatment to the end.

Put to the test again, the criminal justice system revealed itself to be saturated with racism. At the start, the police classified the death as one of simple exposure. The authorities turned to the white principal of the residential school, a man busy having multiple sexual relationships with Aboriginal teenagers, to identify Rose's nude body at the morgue. When the police began to investigate further, they tried to pin the killing on an innocent Aboriginal man. After the culprits turned themselves in, police and prosecutors dithered about what charge to lay. They abandoned any claim of sexual assault, because they apparently could not imagine that an Aboriginal woman who had been drinking with her assailants would ever refuse consent to indiscriminate acts with multiple partners. Verdicts of murder, manslaughter, and assault causing bodily harm all collapsed after the lawyers, judges, jurors, and newspaper reporters were finished eviscerating Rose Roper's life. A local physician who was "a bit of a character" paved the way with a curious autopsy report that offered multiple explanations for Rose's death, none of which mystifyingly traced the death to the acts of her assailants. How, precisely, did the doctor think Rose Roper came to her death? Quite possibly the three boys never intended to murder Rose Roper. More probably, they just didn't think about the consequences of their actions. But we are left wondering how anyone could honestly maintain that her death was not criminally connected to their acts that night. The legal proceeding left so many questions unresolved. Yet it left no doubt whatsoever that Rose Roper's death was a racist and sexist act, one that was squarely condoned by Canadian criminal law.

Franco Angione was the only accused person in these nine cases to plead guilty. Not surprisingly, the relatively low conviction rates for sexual assault led most accused to take the risk of proceeding to trial rather than pleading to a lesser and included offence. Angione's decision to plea bargain was prompted by the reputation of a single judge, who was regarded as overly partial to the Crown. This too is evidence of injustice, since erratic results based on the personality of the judge did little to resolve the wider imbalances that afflicted sexual assault law. Judge Haines's decision to impose restitution rather than imprisonment was unusual within a criminal justice system that preferred the draconian penalties of jails occasionally twinned with corporal punishment for most sex offenders. The class privilege that allowed Franco Angione to escape jail was more evidence of unfairness, but the punitive and ineffective sentences typically meted out to sex offenders were even more so. Although the courts spoke the language of rehabilitation, societal protection, and deterrence, there was no evidence that prisons worked. There were no laws to protect rape complainants or the accused from the glare of publicity. The victims were at the mercy of the press, although reporters and editors appear to have chosen not to disclose their names most of the time in later decades. The accused had no such protection, formal or informal. The stigma of sexual assault was such that both groups suffered from public gaze.

What has changed since 1975, when the law of sexual assault began to undergo dramatic legislative reform? Other researchers are better situated to conduct detailed reviews of what progress has occurred in the last thirty years. I offer only cursory comments here. Most observers continue to believe that the bulk of sexual assault remains unreported; Velma Demerson's claim that "thousands and thousands of us . . . never told anybody" remains as true today as at the outset of the last century. What this suggests is that in assessing the criminal justice system, the vast number of victims vote with their feet. This is a searing indictment of the law, and should make us shake our heads every time lawyers and judges proclaim pride in the "rule of law."

Some changes are observable, but typically the reforms accomplished far less than their proponents had hoped. The requirement for corroboration was removed, but the suspicion that greeted women and children who complained of sexual assault lingers. Police remain reluctant to charge without corroboration, Crown attorneys are reluctant to prosecute, and judges and juries are reluctant to convict. Concepts such as "previous chaste character" have been eliminated, and the scope for questioning about "prior sexual history" somewhat reduced, but convictions are still elusive with respect to sexually active women, those involved with substance abuse, and those who are marginalized by poverty, ethnicity, race, or disability. Incarcerated women remain at the bottom of the heap. Defence counsel still cross-examine sexual assault complainants intrusively, and they attempt to procure private personal records to assist them. The immunity for spousal rape was eliminated, but few such cases ever make it to trial.

The search for vigorous physical resistance and concomitant injury has scaled back somewhat. However, as soon as the legal authorities stopped demanding definitive proof that victims had fought to the bitter end, the focus shifted to the mindset of the accused. New hurdles presented themselves as courts began to ruminate upon *"mens rea"* — the guilty mind. Trials would become an intricate search into the *mens rea* of the accused, to try to elicit whether he could subjectively have understood that the woman he assaulted had not really consented. The concept of "honest mistakes" surfaced, something that had never been articulated in earlier sexual assault law. Debates took place over whether "unreasonable" mistakes could also serve as a full defence. The use of alcohol as a legal explanation for the accused's failure to possess the requisite *mens rea* also appeared; although alcohol was often present in these earlier cases, with few exceptions, it does not appear to have been understood as legally significant. The most recent round of statutory revision, which attempted to redefine "consent" to begin to take some account of the victim's perspective, potentially holds some promise for addressing these new problems in the future.

The law of rape was redefined and restructured to encompass three tiers of "sexual assault" with the possibility of shorter prison sentences for those convicted of the lower tiers. These tiers of sexual assault replaced the older offences of rape, attempted rape, indecent assault, and seduction. The objective was to emphasize the violent aspects of the assault, to reduce the focus on the sexual features of the crime, and to secure more convictions for lesser offences. It is not clear that the reclassification accomplished any of these goals. The new sexual assault laws were "gender-neutralized" so that both men and women can now be charged with all these offences. There has been no upsurge in prosecutions of women, although concerns have been expressed within the feminist movement that sexual coercion within the lesbian community exists and remains problematically hidden from view.

The evidence suggests that women with disabilities continue to experience a disproportionately high rate of sexual assault. The particular criminal laws that ineffectually attempted to address this problem historically have been repealed, but there has been no further legal reform in this area. Courtrooms are now theoretically more accommodating for witnesses with disabilities, but most disability rights activists insist that full inclusivity is a distant dream. The rules of evidence were altered to attempt to make courtrooms more responsive to child witnesses. But most child sexual assault now seems to be diverted from the criminal setting, and treated as a mental health and social welfare problem. There has been no legal recognition of how gang rape complicates the practice of sexual assault, except that it is one of the factors that moves a sexual assault up to a higher tier in the new classification scheme. There has been no change whatsoever to the problematic interpretation of the concept of "aiding and abetting." The law has been amended to prohibit media publication of the names of sexual assault complainants, or evidence that would otherwise identify them, if they so request. Where the publication of the name of the assailant might identify the victim, his name too has been protected from public disclosure.

The racism, class bias, and discrimination on the basis of ethnicity, disability, and sexual identity that historically disadvantaged large numbers of sexual assault victims continue to affect the outcomes of trials. In 1995 Pamela George, a young Saulteaux woman from the Sakimay Reserve, was sexually assaulted and brutally murdered in Regina by two white male university students in a fact situation eerily reminiscent of the Rose Roper case. The subsequent prosecution was riddled with racism, and gender and class bias.[1] The Sisters in Spirit Campaign was launched in 2004 by the Native Women's Association of Canada to document the appalling number of Aboriginal women who have gone missing or been murdered without criminal redress, as a result of sexualized and racialized violence. The flip side of this is that the same factors also disadvantage certain accused. Men with privilege are rarely prosecuted for sexual assault. Men without are the overwhelming targets of the criminal justice system.

There has been virtually no progress in searching for more humane and rehabilitative criminal remedies for sexual assault. Some have begun to argue that until we find more promising treatments, it is folly to advocate reforms that will result in more convictions. More victims have begun to seek compensation through tort lawsuits outside the criminal justice system, although the injury of sexual assault is typically devalued in comparison to other forms of damage. Criminal injury compensation schemes dole out scanty awards. Very occasionally, creative new "alternative dispute resolution" (ADR) agreements are used to provide hearings and compensation for groups who have suffered sexual abuse in institutional settings. While these show potential promise, they have also come under nasty critique. Most frequently the accusation is that the ADR programs fail to screen out fabricated claims. The roots of the skepticism run deep.

I came to write this book as a feminist who is part of the second wave of the Canadian women's movement, who believes that sexual assault could be completely eradicated in a radically transformed society. The law should be of great assistance in this quest. So far it has failed abjectly. Others will evaluate the thirty years of reform more optimistically than I have done.

The next thirty years await. Although I understand why some have argued that the flaws within the legal system render it useless, I am not prepared to abandon the efforts to hold it to account. We owe it to the courageous individuals, who tried so valiantly to harness the potential for legal assistance in the past, not to give up hope.

NOTES

Acknowledgments

1   Velma Demerson, *Incorrigible* (Waterloo, ON: Wilfrid Laurier University Press, 2004).

Chapter 1: Introduction

1   Constance Backhouse, *Petticoats and Prejudice: Women and Law in Nineteenth-Century Canada* (Toronto: The Osgoode Society and Women's Press, 1991).

2   In 1975, the *Criminal Law Amendment Act, 1975*, S.C. 1974–75–76, c.93, s.8 repealed some of the statutory corroboration requirements, provided that questions about the sexual conduct of the complainant with persons other than the accused could not be asked unless they were pre-screened by a judge in camera, and stipulated that newspapers should not refer to the holding of such hearings. In 1982, *An Act to amend the Criminal Code in relation to sexual offences and other offences against the person*, S.C. 1980–81–82–83, c.125, s.19 redefined "rape" as "sexual assault" with three tiers and a range of penalties, set forth a definition of consent and reasonable mistake, removed additional statutory corroboration requirements, stipulated that judges "shall not instruct the jury that it is unsafe to find the accused guilty in the absence of corroboration," abrogated the common law rules of recent complaint, abolished the marital rape exemption, prohibited the disclosure in the press of the identity of a complainant if she so requested, began to restrict the scope of questioning on prior sexual activity with persons other than the accused, and stipulated that evidence of sexual reputation was not admissible to challenge the credibility of the complainant. In 1987, S.C. 1987, c.34, ss.1–8 revised the sexual assault law with respect to young persons, anal intercourse, bestiality, and prior sexual history. In 1992, S.C. 1992, c.38, ss.1–3 redefined consent and mistake of fact, and revised the provisions regarding prior sexual history. In 1997, S.C. 1997, c.30, ss.1–3 attempted to restrict the production and disclosure of some personal records regarding the complainant.

3　The most extensive archival research was done in Ontario, Québec, and Nova Scotia.

4　See, for example, the case of *Rex v. Auger*, Archives of Ontario, RG22-392-0-998, Box 26; *Rex v. Auger* (1929), 52 C.C.C. 2 (Ont. S.C.); *Rex v. Auger* (1930), 54 C.C.C. 209 (Ont. S.C.), selected for its discussion of corroboration law. Press coverage later revealed that Louis Auger was the first member of Parliament ever charged with sexual assault, that the assault had been perpetrated in his office in the House of Commons, and that he was subjected to five full trials, an unparalleled prosecutorial frenzy that seems to have been motivated by anti-francophone sentiment. Details of this unusual case were published separately as Constance Backhouse, "Attentat à la dignité du Parlement: Viol dans l'enceinte de la Chambre des communes, Ottawa 1929" (2001–2) 33 *Ottawa Law Review* 95; "Rape in the House of Commons: The Prosecution of Louis Auger, Ottawa, 1929" in Jim Phillips, R. Roy McMurtry, & John Saywell, eds., *Essays in the History of Canadian Law*, vol. 10: *A Tribute to Peter Oliver* (Toronto: The Osgoode Society and the University of Toronto Press, forthcoming 2008). A marvellously creative, fictional interpretation of the case has also been published: Marguerite Andersen, *Doucement le bonheur* (Sudbury: Prise de parole, 2006).

5　Benjamin Karpman, *The Sexual Offender and His Offenses* (New York: Julian Press, 1954) at 477.

6　David Abrahamsen, *The Psychology of Crime* (New York: Columbia University Press, 1960) at 165.

7　Menachem Amir, *Patterns in Forcible Rape* (Chicago: University of Chicago Press, 1971) at 262–69.

8　Susan Brownmiller, *Against Our Will: Men, Women and Rape* (New York: Bantam, 1975) at 5.

9　See, for example, Diana E.H. Russell, *The Politics of Rape* (New York: Stein & Day, 1975); Diana E.H. Russell, *Rape in Marriage* (New York: Macmillan, 1982); Diana E.H. Russell & Rebecca Morris Bolen, *The Epidemic of Rape and Child Sexual Abuse in the United States* (Thousand Oaks, CA: Sage Publications, 2000).

10　Robin Morgan, *Going Too Far* (New York: Vintage, 1978) at 163–65.

11　Andrea Dworkin, *Our Blood* (New York: Harper and Row, 1976) at 32.

12　Lorenne Clark & Debra Lewis, *Rape: The Price of Coercive Sexuality* (Toronto: Women's Press, 1977) at 124.

13　Catharine A. MacKinnon, *Sexual Harassment of Working Women* (New Haven: Yale University Press, 1979) at 161–62; Catharine A. MacKinnon, *Feminism Unmodified: Discourses on Life and Law* (Cambridge: Harvard University Press, 1987) at 85–92.

14　Ann Snitow, Christine Stansell, & Sharon Thompson, eds., *Powers of Desire: The Politics of Sexuality* (New York: Monthly Review Press, 1983); Carole S. Vance, ed., *Pleasure and Danger: Exploring Female Sexuality* (Boston: Routledge & Kegan Paul, 1984); and Gayle Rubin, "Thinking Sex: Notes for a Radical Theory of the Politics of Sexuality" in Vance, *Pleasure and Danger, ibid.* at 267. See also Brenda Cossman, "Sexuality, Queer Theory, and 'Feminism After': Reading and Rereading the Sexual Subject" (2004) 49 *McGill Law Journal* 847; Kathryn Abrams, "Sex Wars Redux: Agency and Coercion in Feminist Legal Theory" (1995) 95 *Columbia Law Review* 304.

15　Clark & Lewis, *Rape: The Price of Coercive Sexuality*, above note 12.

16 She noted that "laws against sexual violation express what men see and do when they engage in sex with women." MacKinnon, *Feminism Unmodified*, above note 13 at 92; see also MacKinnon, "Feminism, Marxism, Method and the State: An Agenda for Theory" (1982) 5 *Signs* 515.

17 Christine Boyle, "Married Women — Beyond the Pale of the Law of Rape" (1981) 1 *Windsor Yearbook of Access to Justice* 206; Christine Boyle, *Sexual Assault* (Toronto: Carswell, 1984) at 6–7.

18 Elizabeth Sheehy, "Feminist Argumentation before the Supreme Court of Canada in *R. v. Seaboyer*; *R. v. Gayme*: The Sound of One Hand Clapping" (1991–92) 18 *Melbourne University Law Review* 391; Elizabeth Sheehy, "Canadian Judges and the Law of Rape: Should the Charter Insulate Bias?" (1990) 21 *Ottawa Law Review* 741; Elizabeth Sheehy & Susan Boyd, "Feminist Perspectives on Law: Canadian Theory and Practice" (1986) 2 *Canadian Journal of Women and the Law* 1; see also Julian Roberts & Renate M. Mohr, eds., *Confronting Sexual Assault: A Decade of Legal and Social Change* (Toronto: University of Toronto Press, 1994).

19 Carol Smart, *Feminism and the Power of Law* (New York: Routledge, 1989) at 49 and 71, added that "it is unfortunate that working within the discourse of law seems to produce [tendencies to recreate existing hierarchies of knowledge and dogmatic certainties] — it is as if law's claim to truth is so legitimate that feminists can only challenge it and maintain credibility within law by positing an equally positivist alternative." See also Carol Smart, "Law's Power, the Sexed Body, and Feminist Discourse" (1990) 17 *Journal of Law and Society* 194; Carol Smart & J. Brophy, "Locating Law: A Discussion of the Place of Law in Feminist Politics" in J. Brophy & Carol Smart, eds., *Women-in-Law: Explorations in Law, Family and Sexuality* (London: Routledge & Kegan Paul, 1985) 1 at 18.

20 Katherine Franke, "Theorizing Yes: An Essay on Feminism, Law and Desire" (2001) 101 *Columbia Law Review* 181.

21 Dianne L. Martin, "Retribution Revisited: A Reconsideration of Feminist Criminal Law Reform Strategies" (1998) 36 *Osgoode Hall Law Journal* 151.

22 She adds that as the "institutional arm of punishment, criminal justice systems [consist] of a subset of bodies and practices that were never designed to provide remedies, or to offer alternatives to the victimized." Laureen Snider, "Feminism, Punishment and the Potential of Empowerment" (1994) 9 *Canadian Journal of Law and Society* 75 at 77; Laureen Snider, "The Potential of the Criminal Justice System to Promote Feminist Concerns" (1990) 10 *Studies in Law, Policy, and Society* 143.

23 Elizabeth V. Spelman, *Inessential Woman: Problems of Exclusion in Feminist Thought* (Boston: Beacon Press, 1988); Angela Davis, *Women, Race and Class* (New York: Random House, 1981); bell hooks, *Black Looks, Race and Representation* (Boston: South End Press, 1992); bell hooks, *Teaching to Transgress* (New York: Routledge, 1994); Patricia Monture-Angus, *Thunder in My Soul: A Mohawk Woman Speaks* (Halifax: Fernwood, 1995); Sherene H. Razack, *Looking White People in the Eye* (Toronto: University of Toronto Press, 1998); Himani Bannerji, *Returning the Gaze* (Toronto: Sister Vision, 1993); Philomena Essed, *Understanding Everyday Racism* (London: Sage, 1991); Richard Delgado, ed., *Critical Race Theory* (Philadelphia: Temple University Press, 1995).

24 Adrienne Rich, "Compulsory Heterosexuality and Lesbian Existence" (1980) 5 *Signs* 631.

25 Terry Chapman, "Sex Crimes in Western Canada, 1890–1920" (Ph.D. Thesis, University of Alberta, 1984); Lesley A. Erickson, "'A Very Garden of the Lord'? Hired Hands, Farm Women, and Sex Crime Prosecutions on the Prairie, 1914–1929" (2001) 12 *Journal of the Canadian Historical Association* 115; Lesley Erickson, "The Unsettling West: Gender, Crime, and Culture on the Canadian Prairies, 1886–1940" (Ph.D. Thesis, University of Calgary, 2003); Dorothy E. Chunn, "Secrets and Lies: The Criminalization of Incest and the (Re)Formation of the 'Private' in British Columbia, 1890–1940" in John McLaren, Robert Menzies, & Dorothy E. Chunn, eds., *Regulating Lives: Historical Essays on the State, Society, the Individual and the Law* (Vancouver: University of British Columbia Press, 2002) at 120; Jim Phillips, "Women, Crime and Criminal Justice in Early Halifax, 1750–1800" in Jim Phillips, Tina Loo, & Susan Lewthwaite, eds., *Essays in the History of Canadian Law*, vol. 5: *Crime and Criminal Justice* (Toronto: The Osgoode Society and University of Toronto Press, 1994) at 174; Marie-Aimée Cliche, "Un secret bien gardé: l'inceste dans la société traditionnelle québécoise, 1858–1938" (1996) 50 *Revue d'histoire de l'Amérique française* 201; Marie-Aimée Cliche, "Du péché au traumatisme: l'inceste, vu de la Cour des jeunes délinquants et de la Cour du bien-être social de Montréal, 1912–1965" (2006) 87 *Canadian Historical Review* 199.

26 Ruth Olsen, "Rape: An 'Un-Victorian' Aspect of Life in Upper Canada" (June 1976) 68 *Ontario History* 75; Patrick J. Connor, "'The Law Should Be Her Protector': The Criminal Prosecution of Rape in Upper Canada, 1791–1850" in Merril D. Smith, ed., *Sex without Consent: Rape and Sexual Coercion in America* (New York: New York University Press, 2001) at 103.

27 Carolyn Strange, "Patriarchy Modified: The Criminal Prosecution of Rape in York County, Ontario, 1880–1930" in Phillips *et al.*, eds., *Essays in the History of Canadian Law*, above note 25 at 207; Carolyn Strange, *Toronto's Girl Problem: The Perils and Pleasures of the City, 1880–1930* (Toronto: University of Toronto, 1995).

28 Karen Dubinsky, *Improper Advances: Rape and Heterosexual Conflict in Ontario, 1880–1929* (Chicago: University of Chicago Press, 1993).

29 Joan Sangster, *Regulating Girls and Women: Sexuality, Family, and the Law in Ontario 1920–1960* (Don Mills, ON: Oxford University Press, 2001); Joan Sangster, "Masking and Unmasking the Sexual Abuse of Children: Perceptions of Violence against Children in the Badlands of Ontario, 1916–30" (2000) 25 *Journal of Family History* 504.

30 Becki Ross, *The House That Jill Built: A Lesbian Nation in Formation* (Toronto: University of Toronto Press, 1995); Mary Louise Adams, *The Trouble with Normal: Postwar Youth and the Making of Heterosexuality* (Toronto: University of Toronto Press, 1997); Elise Chenier, "Stranger in Our Midst: Male Sexual Deviance in Postwar Ontario" (Ph.D. Thesis, Queen's University, 2001); Elise Chenier, "Tough Ladies and Troublemakers: Toronto's Public Lesbian Community, 1955–1965" (M.A. Thesis, Queen's University, 1995).

Chapter 2: "Don't Bully Me . . . Justice I Want if There Is Justice to Be Had"

1   Details of the legal proceeding have been drawn from Rex v. Joseph Gray, (1907) Middlesex C.A. and C.P. Criminal Court Records, accessed in 1999 at D.B. Weldon Library, University of Western Ontario, J.J. Talman Regional Collection, Box 559 [records now removed to Archives of Ontario], and the press coverage: *London Free Press* 9, 11, 12, 16, 24, and 31 July; 8, 10, and 11 Oct. 1907; *London Advertiser* 9, 10, 11, 15, 23, 30 July; 7, 9, 10 Oct. 1907.

2   Where surviving records include the testimony of the women alleging rape, it is common that the female witnesses appear to have been intimidated into submission and frequently into complete silence during their court appearances. They answered questions put to them by counsel haltingly, often tearfully, without reference to their own ideas and feelings. They rarely challenged defence counsel either directly or indirectly.

3   Sir Matthew Hale, *Historia Placitorum Coronae*, vol. 1 (London: Nutt and Gosling, 1734, published posthumously) at 635–36. The full statement read: "[Rape] is an accusation easily to be made, and hard to be proved, and harder to be defended by the party accused, though never so innocent."

4   S.F. Harris, *Principles of the Criminal Law*, 7th ed. (London: Stevens and Haynes, 1896) at 164 noted that Hale's opinion was quoted at "almost every trial." For other references adverting to the enshrinement of Hale's views in legal thought and practice, see Roscoe's *Digest of the Law of Evidence in Criminal Cases*, 12th ed. (London: Stevens and Sons, 1898) at 775; *Russell on Crimes*, 6th ed., vol. 3 (London: Stevens and Sons, 1896) at 235. Cornelia Dayton Hughes, *Women before the Bar: Gender, Law and Society in Connecticut* (Chapel Hill: University of North Carolina Press, 1995) describes how Hale's opinions overtook the earlier seventeenth-century Puritan understandings of female credibility, replacing a previous skepticism over the credibility of men accused of rape with a presumption as to the unreliability of women.

5   Carolyn Strange, "The Criminal Prosecution of Rape in York County, Ontario, 1880–1930" in Jim Phillips, Tina Loo, & Susan Lewthwaite, eds., *Essays in the History of Canadian Law*, vol. 5: *Crime and Criminal Justice* (Toronto: The Osgoode Society, 1994) 207 at 212.

6   The term "prosecutrix," the feminine of "prosecutor" was a carry-over from the time when criminal complaints were all laid privately, with the injured victim responsible for the legal prosecution and the costs associated therewith. A more professionalized system was instituted in Canada by the early nineteenth century, when law officers of the Crown conducted proceedings at all assizes: Paul Romney, *Mr. Attorney* (Toronto: The Osgoode Society, 1986) at 239. The characterization of the rape complainant as the "prosecutrix" was thus incorrect. It was also anomalous, since no witnesses in other criminal proceedings were so labelled.

7   Mary Ann Burton was not listed in *Vernon's City of London Directory* (1906, 1907, 1907–8, and 1908–9), but her husband, Robert Burton, was. His occupational designations varied, with listings shifting from "tanner" to "labourer." Mary Ann Burton's lack of education is obvious from the grammatical errors in her speech; ref-

erence to her weight is found in the preliminary inquiry transcript; her age is never given in the legal documentation although the press referred to her several times as "elderly." On the nature and location of the rental dwelling at 12 Dundas Street, see Fire Insurance Plans for London, Ontario, 1881–1970, J.J. Talman Regional Collection, University of Western Ontario, M720, Sheet 4. The couple had been living there only nine months, and boarded previously at 394 Ridout Street. On the wealth and gentrification of turn-of-the-century London, see Frederick H. Armstrong, *The Forest City: An Illustrated History of London, Canada* (London: Windsor Publications, 1996); Orlo Miller, *This Was London: The First Two Centuries* (Westport, ON: Butternut, 1988); Wayne Paddon, *"Steam and Petticoats" 1840–1890* (London: Murray Kelly Ltd., 1977) at 106–25.

8 The involvement of Harry Wilkinson, the former boarder, is more fully described in my earlier version of this material, published as Constance Backhouse, "Don't You Bully Me . . . Justice I Want if There Is Justice to Be Had: The Rape of Mary Ann Burton, London, Ontario, 1907" in Jonathan Swainger & Constance Backhouse, eds., *People and Place: Historical Influences on Legal Culture* (Vancouver: University of British Columbia Press, 2003) at 60–94. In the interests of brevity this is removed.

9 Gray seems to have been previously employed as a cigar-maker, although by the time of the trial the *London Advertiser* described him as a "contracting teamster" who worked his own team of horses. *Vernon's City of London Directory* (1906) and (1907) shows Joseph M. Gray as a homeowner at 444 Hill. The same *Directory* (1907–8) and (1908–9) has no listing for Joseph Gray. The blocks the men were unloading were probably cedar blocks, used after 1880 to pave the city streets. The blocks rotted quickly and absorbed malodorous horse urine, and were slowly replaced by asphalt resting on a concrete foundation; see Armstrong, *The Forest City*, above note 7 at 133.

10 The London police force typically enforced petty infractions of municipal ordinances in a city renowned for its lawfulness. In 1899, the chief gave the force a full week's leave "in view of the recent quietness of the city." Little is known about Constable James Highstead from the Carling Street police station, who first attended the scene, but historical records reveal that recruits had to be at least five feet, ten inches tall, between twenty-one and thirty-five years old, and have a "fair education." Detective Thomas Nickle, who arrived second, was renowned for his tracking — across 12 000 miles of the United States and Canada — and arrest in 1899 of Marion "Pegleg" Brown, an escapee from a Texas jail who had murdered London constable Michael Toohey when Toohey attempted to arrest him for vagrancy. Brown's subsequent hanging at the County Court House, up the street from the Burtons' dwelling, marked the culmination of the most expensive trial ever held in Middlesex County. See Charles Addington, *A History of the London Police Force* (London: Phelps, 1980). See also "Elderly Woman Falls out of House with Gag in Mouth" *London Free Press* (9 July 1907) 10, which focused on Mary Ann Burton's resistance to the police officers' mode of investigation. She "would say no more," noted the reporter, "giving the officer to understand that he was entering on other people's business," with the upshot being that it was "not likely that any further steps [would] be taken in the matter."

11 Charges were also laid against Charles Burton (no relation), the hired hand who had initially helped Joseph Gray unload wood at Mrs. Burton's home. He was charged with being an accomplice to the rape, and was alleged to have stood guard at the door while Joseph Gray committed the sexual assault. These charges were treated as secondary to those against Gray, and were not pursued after Gray's acquittal.

12 *London Advertiser* (10 July 1907) 1.

13 *London Free Press* (11 July 1907) 13.

14 *London Advertiser* (10 Oct. 1907) 1.

15 *Vernon's City of London Directory* (1907) lists Michael J. Gray as a teamster who owned his home at 446 Hill. Patrick Gray, a drayman, owned his home at 198 York Street.

16 There is little biographical detail available on Police Magistrate Love. *Vernon's City Directory* (1907–8) notes that he resided at 562 Wellington Street, along with Miss Irene C. Love, Miss Isabel C. Love, and Miss Mary A. Love.

17 McKillop's appointment as Crown attorney was a part-time one; he also practised law with Thomas G. Murphy at McKillop & Murphy, 413 Richmond Street. McKillop resided at 326 St. James Street.

18 Edmund Meredith's law partners were Joseph C. Judd, the current mayor of London, and William Ralph Meredith, his younger brother. William Ralph Meredith's views on women and law were publicly disclosed in the late nineteenth century, when he vigorously opposed the admission of women to the profession of law from his position as provincial Opposition leader. Edmund resided with his brother William at 504 Colborne Street. For biographical details, see "Meredith, Edmund Allen"; "Meredith, Richard Martin"; "Meredith, William Ralph" in Henry Morgan, *Canadian Men and Women of the Time*, 2d ed. (1912) at 796–98; David J. Hughes & T.H. Purdom, *History of the Bar of the County of Middlesex* (London: 1912) at 33 and 50; Peter Oliver, *"Terror to Evil-Doers": Prisons and Punishments in Nineteenth-Century Ontario* (Toronto: University of Toronto Press, 1998) at 285 and 295–302. On Meredith's representation of Esther Arscott in 1884–85, see Constance Backhouse, *Petticoats and Prejudice: Women and Law in Nineteenth-Century Canada* (Toronto: The Osgoode Society and Women's Press, 1991) at 244–59.

19 The themes and lines of argument in the Burton case accurately reflect the larger sample of transcripts reviewed. The only difference is that most other cases tended to pose fewer questions covering a narrower range of issues.

20 James Crankshaw, *The Criminal Code of Canada* (Toronto: Carswell, 1915) at 320–21; Seymour F. Harris, *Principles of the Criminal Law*, 9th ed. (London: Stevens & Haynes, 1901) at 168–69. If the complainant denied this, the defence could adduce evidence to prove it. See also Sir William Oldnall Russell, *A Treatise on Crimes and Misdemeanors*, 7th ed. (London: Stevens & Sons, 1909) at 945: "The character of the prosecutrix, as to general chastity, may be impeached by general evidence, as by shewing her general light character. . . . And the prosecutrix may be cross-examined as to particular discreditable transactions." Crankshaw added at 320–21: "If asked on cross-examination whether, outside of the prisoner, she has had carnal connexion with other men, named to her in the questions, and if she deny having had any such inter-

course with them, her answer will be conclusive and those men cannot be called to contradict her."

21 See, for example, *Rex v. Bell*, [1930] 1 W.W.R. 433 (Alta. C.A.), quashing a conviction because the trial judge had refused to allow an intensive cross-examination of the complainant upon her previous life and conduct, even though "the matter had nothing to do with the particular facts of the charge in question." In *Regina v. Muggli* (1961), 131 C.C.C. 363 (B.C.C.A.), the trial judge and Crown attorney made serious efforts to protect the rape complainant from invasive cross-examination; the appellate court (with one dissent) quashed the subsequent conviction, ruling that this had deprived the accused "of a fair trial." One of the statements the trial judge had made in his charge to the jury was: "Then [the defence counsel] says, 'Women are guilty of telling strange tales.' I wonder. That is a matter for you. Are you prepared to arrive at the conclusion that women are greater liars than men? That is what is suggested to you, that women are given to telling strange tales." This was juxtaposed with a comment about the accused's obvious "interest in the outcome and the temptation to go into the witness box and perjure himself." Both of these statements were the subject of explicit condemnation by the appellate court. In *Regina v. Makow*, [1974] 13 C.C.C. (2d) 167 (B.C.C.A.), defence counsel asked the married rape complainant if the accused had asked her whether his penis was bigger than her husband's. The trial judge upheld her refusal to answer, indicating that she did not have to explain to the court what her answer was, or whether it was complimentary to her husband or the accused. The majority of the appellate court overturned the conviction, because the trial judge had precluded a "relevant line of questioning." For decisions allowing somewhat more latitude to a trial judge, see *Regina v. Jensen and Waithe* (1957), 119 C.C.C. 314 (B.C.C.A.); *Regina v. Boucher*, [1963] 2 C.C.C. 241 (B.C.C.A.); *Regina v. Basken and Kohl*, [1975] 21 C.C.C. (2d) 321 (Sask. C.A.).

22 This, and the extracts that follow, are all drawn from the court reporter's transcript of the preliminary inquiry. In the interest of succinctness, in a very few instances I have made minor changes to the order of the questions in order to combine related queries in a single passage.

23 Meredith quizzed her about the identity of the accused, but did not pursue this. He must have been unaware that Daniel Rodgers, the husband of Mrs. Burton's friend, was on trial for "drunk and disorderly" behaviour on a street car. The *London Free Press* (9 July 1907) 10 indicated that Rodgers appeared in the "Monday morning assortment of drunks and disorderlies" but that the street railway officials did not pursue the charge, and he was released on suspended sentence.

24 Sharon Anne Cook, *Through Sunshine and Shadow: The Woman's Christian Temperance Union, Evangelicalism, and Reform in Ontario, 1874–1930* (Montréal: McGill-Queen's University Press, 1995) describes the strong appeal of temperance for middle-class women in Ontario, who established 222 unions with 5521 members by 1900. On the successful London 1906 convention, see S.G.E. McKee, *Jubilee History of the Ontario Woman's Christian Temperance Union 1877–1927* (Whitby: Goodfellow & Son, 1927) at 69.

25 See statement of J.J. Kelso, superintendent of the Toronto Children's Aid Society, in Canada, *Royal Commission on the Liquor Traffic* (Ottawa: Queen's Printer, 1895) at 529. For press discussion, see, for example, "Pitiable Case of a Ruined Fireside: A Young Woman of Thames Street Has Little Regard for Her Three Children" *London Advertiser* (23 Sept. 1909). See also Cheryl Krasnick Warsh, "Oh, Lord, pour a cordial in her wounded heart: The Drinking Woman in Victorian and Edwardian Canada" in Cheryl Krasnick Warsh, ed., *Drink in Canada: Historical Essays* (Montréal and Kingston: McGill-Queen's University Press, 1993) at 70.

26 The *Criminal Code*, S.C. 1906, c.146, s.679 provided: "A justice holding a preliminary inquiry may in his discretion, (a) permit or refuse permission to the prosecutor, his counsel or attorney, to address him in support of the charge, either by way of opening or summing up the case, or by way of reply upon any evidence which may be produced by the person accused; (b) receive further evidence on the part of the prosecutor after hearing any evidence given on behalf of the accused." Section 682(1) provided: "When the accused is before a justice holding [a preliminary] inquiry, such justice shall take the evidence of the witnesses called on the part of the prosecution." Section 686(1) provided that after the prosecution witnesses were called, "the accused shall be asked if he wishes to call any witnesses."

27 *London Advertiser* (10 October 1907) 1.

28 *London Free Press* (16 July 1907) 3.

29 See also Paul Craven, "Law and Ideology: The Toronto Police Court 1850–80" in David H. Flaherty, ed., *Essays in the History of Canadian Law*, vol. 2 (Toronto: The Osgoode Society, 1983) at 248, on the florid and irreverent newspaper reporting of the proceedings of the mid-nineteenth-century Toronto Police Court.

30 *London Free Press* (16 July 1907) 3.

31 *London Advertiser* (15 July 1907) 8.

32 The *London Advertiser* (23 July 1907) 8 erroneously reported that Constable Highstead had testified. There is no record of his appearing as a witness in the official transcript or in Police Magistrate Love's handwritten notes. This was not the only error; on 30 July 1907, the paper reported that Gray and Burton had appeared for sentence. Since the trial would not be held until 9 October 1907, this was clearly inaccurate.

33 Sir Francis W. Anthony, "Rape" (1895) 132 *Boston Medical and Surgical Journal* 29 at 58.

34 J. Dixon Mann, *Forensic Medicine and Toxicology*, 2d ed. (London: Charles Griffin, 1898) at 113–14. Clark Bell Taylor's *Manual of Medical Jurisprudence*, 12th ed. (New York: Lea Brothers, 1897) at 693 noted that the detection of dead or motionless spermatozoa in stains could be made long after emission, citing cases in which this was accomplished eighteen years later.

35 In *Rex v. Edmond Lemieux* (2 February 1914) Archives nationales center, Archivo-Histo, Thémis II - TP12, S1, SS1, SSS1, Cont. 1960-01-357/601 Enquête #16 & TP12, S1, SS1, SSS1, Cont. 1960-01-357/217, DOCS. 261454 to 261458, Cour des Sessions de la Paix, District de Québec, Cité de Québec, several physicians testified that sperm was found in the six-year-old victim's vulva. However, under questioning from the defence counsel, they were side-tracked into discussing whether the girl's enlarged

clitoris might have been caused by self-masturbation, and giving their opinions about whether children aged three to five practised masturbation, and whether hysteria was linked to masturbation. For other cases where medical testimony demonstrated skepticism, see *Rex v. Francis Moisan*, Archives nationales du Québec, Cour des Sessions de la Paix, District de Québec, Cité de Québec, 23 July 1911, Côte: TP12, S1, SS1, SSS1 Cont. 1960-01-357/600 Enquête #13, Dossier judiciaire 365; *Rex v. Drew* (1932), 60 C.C.C. 37 (Sask. C.A.); *Regina v. Muise*, [1975] 22 C.C.C. (2d) 487 (N.S.C.A.).

36 Thomas Romeyn Beck & John B. Beck, *Elements of Medical Jurisprudence*, vol. 1 (Philadelphia: J.B. Lippincott, 1860) at 201–3. See also C.C. Mapes, "A Practical Consideration of Sexual Assault," (1906) 24 *The Medical Age: A Semi-Monthly Journal of Medicine and Surgery* 928 at 928–29.

37 Beck & Beck, *Elements of Medical Jurisprudence*, above note 36 at 212. See also Mann, *Forensic Medicine and Toxicology*, above note 34 at 107: "The circumstances under which the crime is usually committed are such as to render it easy for a designing person to make a charge of rape, and difficult for the accused to rebut the accusation. The crime is one so thoroughly and so universally detested that the victim, or supposed victim, obtains immediate sympathy. It is unfortunately a fact that accusations of rape are very frequently groundless, and in such cases the accused and innocent person suffers from this proneness on the part of the public to accept without question the statements of the prosecutrix. False accusations are not only made by women, and by girls of responsible age, but cases occur from time to time in which mere children are instructed by their mothers to accuse an individual selected for some special reason — extortion of money, or for the sake of revenge — and are not only taught what tale to tell, but are manipulated in such a way as to produce physical indications resembling those caused by criminal assaults, so as to bear our their statements." See also Anthony, "Rape," above note 33 at 31: "The story of the victim is, of course, to be heard — simply as a story. She may be after blackmail; she may be self-deceived, insane or coached by others."

38 Bell Taylor, *Manual of Medical Jurisprudence*, above note 34 at 670. See also Mapes, "Sexual Assault," above note 36 at 936–37: "It is safe to state that Jackson State Prison (Michigan) contains more innocent men convicted of rape (sexual assault) than all other innocents there multiplied together, for the reason that in such cases there are usually but two witnesses to the crime, and the man's evidence counts for nothing as a rule, while the woman's testimony is accepted verbatim without regard to previous standing of either person. . . . Not only innocent men but those who have been actually seduced have 'danced at the rope's end' on account of the woman's swearing away the life of the man in order to shield her priceless reputation! . . . Adult females often accuse innocent men, particularly physicians, surgeons, and dentists."

39 Fred J. Smith Taylor, *Principles and Practice of Medical Jurisprudence* (London: Churchill, 1905) at 123–26.

40 Beck & Beck, *Elements of Medical Jurisprudence*, above note 36 at 197.

41 Smith Taylor, *Principles and Practice*, above note 39 at 139. See also Mapes, "Sexual Assault," above note 36 at 934.

42 Mann, *Forensic Medicine and Toxicology*, above note 34 at 102.

43 *London Free Press* (24 July 1907) 3.

44 *Ibid.*

45 The *Criminal Code*, S.C. 1906, c.146, s.687 provided: "When all the witnesses on the part of the prosecution and the accused have been heard the justice shall, if upon the whole of the evidence he is of opinion that no sufficient case is made out to put the accused upon his trial, discharge him." Section 690 provided: "If a justice holding a preliminary inquiry thinks that the evidence is sufficient to put the accused on his trial, he shall commit him for trial." Sir James Fitzjames Stephen, *A History of the Criminal Law of England*, vol. 1 (London: 1883) at 220, indicated that justices were to commit for trial if the evidence raised "a strong or probable presumption of guilt." See also Seymour F. Harris, *Harris's Principles of the Criminal Law*, 9th ed. (London: Stevens & Haynes, 1901) at 326: "If, when all the evidence against the accused has been heard, the magistrate does not think that it is sufficient to put the accused on his trial for an indictable offence, he is forthwith discharged. But if he thinks otherwise, or the evidence raises a strong or probable presumption against the accused, he commits him for trial." Douglas Hay, "Controlling the English Prosecutor" (1983) 21 *Osgoode Hall Law Journal* 165 at 169 discusses the low frequency with which nineteenth-century English magistrates dismissed charges at preliminary hearings.

46 *London Advertiser* (10 Oct. 1907) 1.

47 *London Free Press* (10 Oct. 1907) 1.

48 The *Criminal Code*, S.C. 1906, c.146, s.299 provided: "Every one who commits rape is guilty of an indictable offence and liable to suffer death or to imprisonment for life." In his earlier charge to the grand jury, Judge Teetzel had declared that "although the laws of this country allow the imposition of capital punishment" for the crime of rape, "it has never been done in my recollection."

49 S.R. Clarke, *A Treatise on Criminal Law as Applicable to the Dominion of Canada* (Toronto: Carswell, 1872) at 598.

50 The procedure for directed verdicts would be outlined in *R. v. Comba* (1938), 70 C.C.C. 205 (S.C.C.); *R. v. Robichaud* (1950), 98 C.C.C. 86 (N.B.C.A.).

51 *London Advertiser* (7 October 1907) 1; "Teetzel, Hon. James Vernall" in Morgan, *Canadian Men and Women of the Time*, above note 18 at 1090; W. Stewart Wallace, *Macmillan Dictionary of Canadian Biography*, 4th ed. (Toronto: Macmillan, 1978) at 823. Born in Elgin County in 1853, Teetzel had been educated at Woodstock College, Galt Collegiate Institute, and Osgoode Hall Law School. Called to the bar in 1877, Teetzel practised with the illustrious firm of Osler, Teetzel, Harrison & Osler. He served as Hamilton's city mayor from 1899 to 1901, and ran unsuccessfully for federal election as a Liberal in 1900. Appointed to the bench in 1903, Teetzel developed a reputation as "one of the most popular members of the Ontario judiciary." Teetzel was awarded an honorary doctorate by McMaster University the year of Mrs. Burton's trial.

52 *London Free Press* (11 Oct. 1907) 3.

53 *London Advertiser* (10 Oct. 1907) 1.

Chapter 3: "On pensait que la fille était bonne a rien"

1   Susan Mann Trofimenkoff, *The Dream of Nation: A Social and Intellectual History of Québec* (Toronto: Gage, 1983) at 203 and 212; Arthur R.M. Lower, *Colony to Nation: A History of Canada* (Toronto: McClelland and Stewart, 1977) at 467; Janet Morchain & Mason Wade, *Search for a Nation: French–English Relations in Canada since 1759* (Toronto: J.M. Dent, 1967) at 58–61. See also Hugh MacLennan's *Two Solitudes* (Toronto: Macmillan, 1959) at 71–87 for a fictional account.

2   Mann Trofimenkoff, *The Dream of Nation*, above note 1 at 208–13; Lower, *Colony to Nation*, above note 1 at 469–70; Morchain & Wade, *Search for a Nation*, above note 1 at 61.

3   Verdun had the highest per capita enlistment rate of any city in the British empire, with a high percentage of the enlistees British-born. Serge Marc Durflinger "Owing Allegiance: The British Community in Verdun, Québec, during the Second World War" (2004) 36 *Canadian Ethnic Studies* 4 at 4–9; Lloyd G. Reynolds, *The British Immigrant: His Social and Economic Adjustment in Canada* (Toronto: Oxford University Press, 1935) at 120–4 and 138–40. On the population of Verdun, see *Lovell's Montréal City Directory* (1917–18) (Montréal: John Lovell and Sons, 1917).

4   The information about this case is drawn from the Archives nationales du Québec, Cote: TP12, S1, SS1, SSS1 Cont. 1960-01-357/603 Enquête # 13, Dossiers judiciaire: 1012–1019. Le Roi vs Léo Fiola, Cour des Sessions de la Paix, District de Québec, Cité de Québec, No. 1013 (viol) 25 sept., 13 nov., 10 and 18–20 déc. 1917; and No. 949 (séduction) 19–20 and 27 sept., 7 and 12 nov., 1 and 15 déc. 1917, 17 jan. 1918. The case files contain the *"denonciation et plainte," "mandat pour l'arrestation," "acte d'accusation et plaidoyer,"* release on bail, *"cautionnement,"* consent to *"procès expéditif"* without a jury, plea, subpoenas, *"preuve de la défense"* and the *"dépositions des témoins"* taken at the *"instruction préliminaire"* and the *"procès expéditif."*

   Le Roi vs. Arsène Lamontagne, Cour des Sessions de la Paix, District de Québec, Cité de Québec, No. 1012 (viol et séduction d'une fille mineure âgée entre 14 et 16 ans) 21 and 25 sept., 13 nov., 10, 20–21, and 26 déc. 1917, 17 jan. 1918.

   Le Roi vs. Georges Mollot, Cour des Sessions de la Paix, District de Québec, Cité de Québec, No. 1014 (viol et séduction d'une fille mineure âgée entre 14 et 16 ans) 13 nov., 10 déc. 1917; and No. 1014 (séduction) 20–21 déc. 1917, 17 jan. 1918.

   Le Roi vs. Albert Lasonde (also *Lassonde*), Cour des Sessions de la Paix, District de Québec, Cité de Québec, No. 1015 (viol et séduction d'une fille mineure âgée entre 14 et 16 ans) 25 and 27 sept., 13 nov., 10, 20–21, and 26 déc. 1917, 17 jan. 1918.

   Le Roi vs. Antonio Paquin, Cour des Sessions de la Paix, District de Québec, Cité de Québec, No. 1016 (viol et séduction d'une fille mineure âgée entre 14 et 16 ans) 25 sept., 13 nov., 10, 20–21, and 26 déc. 1917, 17 jan. 1918.

   Le Roi vs. Henri Perrote (also *Perrotte* and *Perrot*), Cour des Sessions de la Paix, District de Québec, Cité de Québec, No. 1017 (viol et séduction d'une fille mineure âgée entre 14 et 16 ans) 13 nov., 10, 20–21, and 26 déc. 1917, 17 jan. 1918.

   Le Roi vs. Léodore Venne, Cour des Sessions de la Paix, District de Québec, Cité de Québec, No. 1018 (viol et séduction d'une fille mineure âgée entre 14 et 16 ans) 21 and 25 sept., 13 nov., 10, 20–21, and 26 déc. 1917, 17 jan. 1918.

Le Roi vs. Albert Thivièrge, Cour des Sessions de la Paix, District de Québec, Cité de Québec, No. 1019 (viol et séduction d'une fille mineure âgée entre 14 et 16 ans) 21 and 25–26 sept., 13 nov., 10 and 25–26 déc. 1917, 17 jan. 1918.

5 Fiola lived at 1320 Ethel St., Lamontagne at 1058 Ethel, Lassonde at 1140 Ethel, Perrotte at 1139 Ethel. Paquin lived at 529a Evelyn St., Thivièrge at 1059 Gertrude, Venne at 40 Première Ave., and Mollot at 1519 Wellington St. *Lovell's Montréal City Directory* (1916–17), (1917–18), (1918–19), and (1920–21) (Montréal: John Lovell and Sons, 1916, 1917, 1918, and 1920).

6 Mollot's father, Abel, was a contractor. Lassonde's father, Charles, was a butcher. Perrotte's father, Ovila, was a locksmith. Paquin's father, Alfred, was an entrepreneur paint contractor. Thivièrge's father, Joseph, was a labourer. Venne's father, Alfred, was a blacksmith. There is no further information about Lamontagne. *Lovell's Montréal City Directory* (1916–17), (1917–18), (1918–19), and (1920–21) (Montréal: John Lovell and Sons, 1916, 1917, 1918, and 1920).

7 Léo Fiola's father, Aimé Victor Fiola, is listed as a furniture dealer, a director of "A.V. Fiola & Co. Ltd.," which sold furniture, carpets, tarpaulins, and stoves, at 1357–1359 Wellington St., Verdun. The Wellington Street neighbourhood contained several banks, a post office, a wood and coal yard, an ice company, several churches, a Chinese laundry, and the office of the Verdun Council of the Knights of Columbus. The Fiola family had previously resided at 1357b Wellington St., but both father and son had moved by the time of the legal proceedings to 1320 Ethel St., Verdun. *Lovell's Montréal City Directory* (1916–17), (1917–18), (1918–19), and (1920–21) (Montréal: John Lovell and Sons, 1916, 1917, 1918, and 1920).

8 Regarding the bridge and its earlier collapse in 1907 and 1916, see Michel L'Hébreux, *Le Pont de Québec* (Sillery: Éditions du Septentrion, 2001). The reference to the "eighth wonder of the world" is at 11.

9 The details and quotes that follow have been drawn from the archival court records listed earlier, and from the press coverage: "Une affaire infamante à Québec" *Québec Le Soleil* (21 sept. 1917) 10; "Les huit prevenus comparaissent" *Québec Le Soleil* (25 sept. 1917) 10. Yvonne Collin lived with her father, André Collin, and his wife, Adéline Langlais. It is unclear whether Adéline was Yvonne's mother or stepmother. Yvonne, who had quit school the year before, was fourteen years and eight months old. Her father had worked at the barbershop at the Château Frontenac before he took a position in Thomas Beaulieu's barbershop on St-Valier.

10 The distinctive initials would provide the clue that led the police to identify and arrest the accused some days later.

11 *"Elle aimait à s'asseoir avec le chauffeur."* Testimony of Antonio Paquin, 20 déc. 1917.

12 *"Elle était de bonne humeur. . . . Elle nous parlait, le long du chemin, que c'était beau. . . . On parlait . . . s'il y avait bien des manufactures par ici."* Testimony of Henri Perrotte and Léodore Venne, 20 déc. 1917.

13 *"Parce qu'ils sont plus grands que moi et j'étais seule, une fille."* Testimony of Yvonne Collin, 27 sept. 1917.

14 *"Q. Connaissiez-vous ce que c'était que de faire ces choses là? R. Non. Q. Faire l'acte du mariage? Non. Q. Vous ne connaissiez pas quels pouviez en être les résultats et les effects de*

cela? R. Non." Questions of Greffier de la Paix, J.A. Rochette, KC, and testimony of Yvonne Collin, 27 sept. 1917.

15 *"Q. Elle vous a parlé roughment quand vous lui avez demandé de vous mettre? R. Oui. Q. Elle n'a pas voulu? R. Non."* Questions by Crown attorney Fitzpatrick and testimony of Albert Thivièrge, 20 déc. 1917.

16 *"Q. Non, on a pas dit que c'était un pique-nique . . . que vous feriez sous les arbres? [. . .] C'était pas pour dire ses prières qu'il allait là?"* Questions posed by Crown attorneys Lachance and Fitzpatrick, 20 déc. 1917.

17 *"On a dit tous ensemble: 'Tu va gagner ton passage.'"* Testimony of Albert Thivièrge, 20 déc. 1917.

18 *"La demoiselle s'est mise à dire: 'Je suis capable,' pareil comme si elle était consentante à ces fins-là."* Testimony of Léodore Venne, 20 déc. 1917.

19 *"Parce que, quand on lui a demandé, elle n'a pas refusé."* Testimony of Antonio Paquin, 20 déc. 1917.

20 *"Elle ne se plaignait pas du tout."* Testimony of Albert Thivièrge, 20 déc. 1917.

21 *"Q. Avez vous dit, le matin du dix-huit, que ça vous faisait mal et de vous laisser tranquille? R. Oui, je l'ai dit à Fiola. Q. L'avez vous dit assez fort pour que l'accusé vous entende? R. Non, monsieur."* Questions by Crown attorney Fitzpatrick and testimony of Yvonne Collin, 20 déc. 1917.

22 *"Ils étaient huit and ils auraient pu me faire bien de quoi, ils étaient plus vieux que moi."* Testimony of Yvonne Collin, 27 sept. 1917.

23 *"C'est elle-même qui a levé sa robe, c'est elle-même qui s'est couchée sur le dos."* Testimony of Henri Perrotte, 20 déc. 1917. *"Q. Elle vous avait montré ses parties, elle? R. Oui, elle avait levé sa robe."* Question by Crown attorney Lachance and testimony of Léodore Venne, 20 déc. 1917.

24 *"Elle nous appelait comme ça, elle disait: 'Un autre là!'"* Testimony of Antonio Paquin, 20 déc. 1917. *"La demoiselle est venue nous chercher, chacun notre tour."* Testimony of Léodore Venne, 20 déc. 1917.

25 *"Là, elle s'est levée, elle s'est arrangée . . . toujours bien, elle dit: 'Il y en a encore un à passer,' en parlant de Arsène Lamontagne, qui était le dernier."* Testimony of Léodore Venne, 20 déc. 1917.

26 The cases reviewed for this research include rape victims younger than five years of age and elderly widows. They were sexually assaulted by family members, friends, and strangers, in their homes, on the street, in barns, in fields, in garages, in cars, in theatres, in medical offices, and dental chairs, at Girl Guide camps, in schools, and outside of dance-halls and bars.

27 *"Je n'ai pensé à rien, j'ai pensé rien qu'à faire un tour d'auto."* Testimony of Yvonne Collin, 27 sept. 1917.

28 The records do not reveal the full extent of gang rape, because men were often charged or tried individually in cases where they had committed the assault in groups. However, for examples of reported cases demonstrating group sexual assault with more than two accused, see *Rex v. De Young, Liddiard, Darling* (1927), 60 O.L.R. 155 (Ont. C.A.) with four accused; *Rex v. Hewston & Goddard* (1930), 55 C.C.C. 13 (Ont. C.A.) with three accused; *Holmes et al. v. The King* (1949), 7 C.R. 323 (Que.

C.A.) with four accused; *Regina v. Jumbo Singh* (1955), 112 C.C.C. 289 (B.C.C.A.) with four accused; *Regina v. Adams, MacAllister & Stables* (1956), 117 C.C.C. 93 (N.S.S.C.) with three accused; *Regina v. Smith & Gilson* (1956), 115 C.C.C. 38 (Ont. C.A.) with three accused; *Regina v. Fennell* (1957), 119 C.C.C. 344 (B.C.C.A.) with four accused; *Regina v. McLean et al.* (1957), 119 C.C.C. 297 (B.C.C.A.) with three accused; *Regina v. Gerald X* (1958), 121 C.C.C. 103 (Man. C.A.) with three accused; *Regina v. Huffman, Huffman and Davignon* (1958), 120 C.C.C. 323 (Ont. C.A.) with three accused; *Regina v. Hibbit & Ward* (1959), 125 C.C.C. 1 (Ont. C.A.) with four men involved and two identified and charged; *Regina v. Hay* (1959), 125 C.C.C. 137 (Man. C.A.) with three men; *Kribs v. The Queen* (1960), 127 C.C.C. 1 (S.C.C.) with four accused; *Regina v. Lakatos* (1961), 129 C.C.C. 387 (B.C.C.A.) with three accused; *Regina v. Kyselka* (1962), 133 C.C.C. 103 (Ont. C.A.) with three accused; *Regina v. Boucher*, [1963] 2 C.C.C. 241 (B.C.C.A.) with three men; *Regina v. Laurier Deschenes et al.*, [1963] 2 C.C.C. 295 (Que. C.A.) with four accused; *Regina v. Zamal et al.*, [1964] 1 C.C.C. 12 (Ont. C.A.) with five accused; *Regina v. Patzer, Clark & Warren*, [1965] 3 C.C.C. 142 (Man. Q.B.) with three accused; *Regina v. Dick, Penner & Finnigan*, [1965] 1 C.C.C. 171 (Man. C.A.) with four men involved and three charged; *Regina v. Starr*, [1965] 50 W.W.R. 125 (Man. Q.B.) with four men involved; *R. v. Sigmund, Howe, Defund & Curry*, [1967] 60 W.W.R. 257 (B.C.C.A.) with four men; *Regina v. Kohnke, Croft & Wilson*, [1968] 3 C.C.C. 333 (B.C.C.A.) with three accused; *Regina v. Stewart & Johnson*, [1969] 2 C.C.C. 244 (B.C.C.A.) with three accused; *Ex Parte Hill*, [1970] 2 C.C.C. 264 (Ont. H.C.) with four men; *Regina v. Salajko*, [1970] 1 C.C.C. 352 (Ont. C.A.) with fifteen men involved and three identified and charged; *Regina v. Cross, Cassell, Bryan & Foley*, [1970] 1 C.C.C. 216 (Ont. C.A.) with four accused; *Regina v. Morrissette*, [1970] 75 W.W.R. 644 (Sask. C.A.) with three accused; *Regina v. Harbison, Harbison & Gerz*, [1973] 9 C.C.C. (2d) 259 (B.C. Prov. Ct.) with three accused; *Regina v. Mercier*, [1973] 12 C.C.C. (2d) 377 (Que. C.A.) with four men and the wife of one of them charged; *Regina v. Fisico et al.*, [1974] 15 C.C.C. (2d) 20 (Ont. C.A.) with six accused; *Regina v. Wedge, Peltier, Peters & Lachance*, [1974] 1 W.W.R. 626 (Man. C.A.) with four accused; *Regina v. Bear, Bear & Tinker*, [1974] 13 C.C.C. (2d) 570 (Sask. C.A.) with three accused; *Regina v. Bell, Christiansen, Coolen & MacDonald*, [1974] 14 C.C.C. (2d) 225 (N.S.C.A.) with five accused; *Regina v. Simmons, Allen & Bezzo*, [1974] 13 C.C.C. (2d) 65 (Ont. C.A.) with three accused; *Regina v. Woodworth, Stutt & Giles*, [1974] 17 C.C.C. (2d) 509 (Ont. C.A.) with three accused; *Regina v. Lieberman, Teaney, Legault & Cosgrove*, [1974] 17 C.C.C. (2d) 536 (Ont. C.A.) with four accused; *Regina v. White, Dubeau & McCullough*, [1974] 16 C.C.C. (2d) 162 (Ont. C.A.) with three accused; *Regina v. Warkentin, Hanson & Brown*, [1975] 20 C.C.C. (2d) 321 (B.C.C.A.) with four men and three accused; *Regina v. Plummer & Brown* (1975), 31 C.R.N.S. 220 (Ont. C.A.) with three accused; *Regina v. Cosgrove*, [1976] 29 C.C.C. (2d) 169 (Ont. C.A.) with four men involved.

29　Testimony of Albert Lassonde, 20 déc. 1917.

30　"Q. *Ça avait-il l'air d'une fille libre un peu? R. Ça avait l'air d'une fille accoutumée.*" Question by defence counsel Lane, and testimony of Arsène Lamontagne, 20 déc. 1917.

31　"*Vous pensez que c'était une putain, vous n'avez pas raison d'avoir peur?*" Question put by Crown attorney Fitzpatrick, 20 déc. 1917.

32 "*Q. Vous avez constaté qu'elle n'était pas faite comme une femme d'un certain âge? R. Elle n'était pas faite comme une femme, mais elle était faite comme une fille de dix-huit ans. Q. Vous voyez que c'était une enfant, elle n'était pas plus grande ce soir-là qu'aujourd'hui? R. Il y a bien des enfants tout petits qui ont plus que dix-huit ans.*" Questions by Crown attorney Fitzpatrick and testimony of Léo Fiola, 20 déc. 1917. Antonio Paquin later admitted that Yvonne Collin had no female body hair, an obvious sign of immaturity, but that this made no difference to him. Testimony 20 déc. 1917. On the physical description of Fiola, see Archives Canada RG 150, Accession 1992–93/166, Box 3098-32, Regimental #3086688.

33 "*Il y avait déchirure, des déchirures fraiches de la membrane hymen à la partie intérieure et latéro-inférieure . . . les parties étaient très inflamées . . . les plaies étaient encore fraiches. C'est habituellement ce qui arrive chez les nouvelles mariées, une déchirure comme ça.*" Testimony of Dr. Charles Oscar Samson, 20 sept. 1917.

34 Further indication of the perspectives on sexuality held by men accused of sexual assault can be seen in several other much later cases. In *Regina v. Craig*, [1975] 11 N.B.R. (2d) 646 (N.B.C.A.), the trial court convicted the accused upon evidence that a fourteen-year-old virgin was dragged from the street to a car, threatened with death, and forced to have oral sex and intercourse with a stranger, causing vaginal tearing and bleeding as well as vomiting. The accused told the police that the girl had waved to him from the sidewalk, and agreed to go for a drive, and then immediately dropped her hand "down on my privates" and continued to rub him until he parked. He described her as "more willing than I was," and the initiator of the oral sex. He said she was the one who removed both their clothes, and that she sat on his lap facing him when she demanded he "bawl" her. When he was ready to remove his penis, he said she "told me to leave it there that I would ruin the best part of it if I took it out." The appellate court overturned the conviction because the trial judge had failed to put the theory of the defence properly to the jury.

In *Regina v. Muise (2)*, [1976] 23 C.C.C. (2d) 422 (N.S.C.A.), a twenty-eight-year-old male accused talked a sixteen-year-old high school student, who was waiting for the bus and initially refused, into accepting a ride home, although he later testified that she was hitchhiking. Her evidence was that when they neared her home, she tried to get out, but he grabbed her by the head, slapped her on the face, and speeded up the car. When she tried to strike him with a milk bottle that was in the back seat, he grabbed it from her and hit her over the head with sufficient force to render her unconscious. When she came to, her clothes were off, and he forced her to perform fellatio and had intercourse. He drove her back and let her out, first asking if she would shake hands with him. She testified she did shake hands, because she was afraid if she didn't he'd come after her with the car. The accused's version was that the girl had consented. He testified that although he broke the bottle over her head, she had got "all upset for some reason" and held the bottle, and he "just . . . shot [his] hand out . . . and it hit her on the side of the temple." He testified that she then told him that "some son of a bitch had screwed" her, and she thought she was pregnant. He told the court that when she eventually got out of the car, she "shook his hand

and said, 'Well, thank you Joe. I feel you've comforted me to some extent.'" The jury convicted, and the verdict was upheld on appeal.

35 *"Parce que ça ne me tentait pas. . . . Parce que je voyais qu'elle n'était pas assez propre."* Testimony of Thivièrge and Perrotte, 20 déc. 1917.

36 *"Il dit qu'il n'était pas capable de rentrer. Il m'a dit de le crosser. C'est lui qui m'a montré comment faire."* Testimony of Yvonne Collin, 21 sept. 1917. On the use of the word *"crosser"* in the vernacular — *"dans le language usuel,"* see testimony of Detective Beaudoin, 13 nov. 1917.

37 *"Il a dit de me débarquer, qu'ils étaient pour avoir de trouble. . . . Il a dit, le soir, de me laisser tranquille."* Testimony of Yvonne Collin, 21 and 27 sept. 1917. Léodore Venne also testified that he tried to stop the sexual incidents, claiming that he told Yvonne to lower her dress in the field, *"Baissez votre robe, je viens pas dans l'intention de faire ça,"* that it did not make good sense for a girl to be with eight young men like that, *"Tu sais, il n'a pas de bon sens pour une fille d'être avec huit jeunes gens comme ça,"* and that he would not be responsible for this affair, *"Tu sais, je ne veux pas être responsable pour cette affaire-là."* Testimony 20 déc. 1917. Venne was probably stretching the truth here. His testimony was expressly refuted by Yvonne Collin, not corroborated by any of his companions, and under further questioning about what he meant by "responsable," he responded that there might be a car accident on the way home to Montréal.

38 In *Rex v. Hewston & Goddard* (1930), 55 C.C.C. 13 (Ont. C.A.), three men took a young woman out in a car, and one raped her. A second, who confessed to holding his hand over her mouth when she was trying to scream during the rape, was convicted of aiding and abetting. The third was the driver who had stopped his car on an isolated country road for thirty minutes while this occurred. The second accused's confession implicated the third, saying the driver had "come around and grabbed [hold]" of the complainant. The complainant testified that the driver had grabbed her ankle to push open her legs, but the driver denied this, and said that he had not noticed what was going on until he heard the girl's screams, and then he ordered his companion to stop, got out of the car, and almost immediately thereafter got back in because the rape was over. At trial, the jury convicted the driver of aiding and abetting, after the judge stated: "He [drove his car] far enough to be out of sight and sound and he stopped there for half an hour. [. . .] Do you think that staying there for half an hour, while within touch of him almost, [and] this diabolical act was going on and he did nothing . . . was that because he had lost his way, or was it because he was a party to what was going on?" The appellate court set aside the conviction of the driver, on the ground that "there was no direct evidence" that he had "committed any overt act" in aiding the rapist. "If he had no knowledge of the intention of [the rapist and his accomplice] to commit rape when they arrived at the place, then his not seeking to prevent it would not make him a party to the offence. . . . No overt act of wrongdoing against him was legally established."

In *Ex Parte Reid* (1954), 110 C.C.C. 260 (Ont. H.C.), Reid and a male companion drove the complainant in Reid's car to an isolated area. Reid's companion got out of the car while Reid "attempted to indulge in familiarities" with the complainant. The complainant resisted verbally. When she got out of the car, Reid's companion told her: "The sooner you get back in the car, the sooner you get home." The two men stood behind the car and conversed, and then Reid's companion got back in the car and raped the complainant. Charged with aiding and abetting, Reid was discharged, with the court holding that there was no evidence of "combining or conspiring, no aiding or abetting by Reid."

In *Regina v. Salajko*, [1970] 1 C.C.C. 352 (Ont. C.A.), Chief Justice Gale and judges Schroeder and Bora Laskin overturned the conviction of an accused who stood near the victim with "his pants down" while she was being raped by fifteen men in "frightful circumstances" in a "lonely field," holding that this did not constitute aiding and abetting. In *Regina v. Cosgrove*, [1976] 29 C.C.C. (2d) 169 (Ont. C.A.), the accused testified that he was asleep in the car while three of his friends raped the victim in a nearby corn field. The victim testified he was one of a group of four men who held her "arms and legs while the other took turns having sexual intercourse with her." She also testified that the accused twice "kicked [her] in the ribs." The trial judge charged the jury that "if Miss Strong was raped by any one and the accused persons did anything or omitted to do anything which assisted the rape, then they are equally guilty of rape as the person who actually committed the act of rape." The conviction was overturned on appeal: "A possible interpretation of this instruction was that if the jury believed that the appellant had not entered the corn field and was in fact asleep in the car a short distance away, his failure to assist the complainant could nevertheless make him a party to the offence. In our view, the suggestion to the jury that there was an obligation on the appellant to do something to rescue, assist or help the complainant, and that failure to do so constituted a participation in the rape, was a serious misdirection." See also *Regina v. Gerald X* (1958), 121 C.C.C. 103 (Man. C.A.); *Regina v. Sekyer & Simon* (1962), 133 C.C.C. 98 (B.C.C.A.); *Regina v. Zamal*, [1964] 1 C.C.C. 12 (Ont. C.A.); *Regina v. Starr*, [1965] 50 W.W.R. 125 (Man. Q.B.); *R. v. Sigmund, Howe, Defund & Curry*, [1967] 60 W.W.R. 257 (B.C.C.A.); *Regina v. White, Dubeau and McCullough*, [1974] 16 C.C.C. (2d) 162 Ont. C.A.); *Regina v. Lieberman, Teaney, Legault & Cosgrove*, [1974] 17 C.C.C. (2d) 536 (Ont. C.A.); *Regina v. White, Dubeau & McCullough*, [1974] 16 C.C.C. (2d) 162 (Ont. C.A.).

39 "*Q. Vous la trouviez trop jeune cette enfant-là, n'est-ce pas? R. Oui, monsieur.*" Question by Crown attorney Fitzpatrick and testimony of Arsène Lamontagne, 20 déc. 1917.

40 "*Q. Je vous mets sur vos gardes, là. Avez vous dit quelque chose à cet effect-là, le soir du dix-sept septembre, quand ils voulaient la taponner, et s'amuser avec elle? Est-ce que vous n'auriez pas dit là, comme un honête garçon, de la laisser tranquille, qu'elle était trop jeune? R. J'ai dit: 'D'abord, puisqu'elle ne veut pas, laissez-la donc tranquille.'*" Questions by Crown attorney Fitzpatrick and testimony of Arsène Lamontagne, 20 déc. 1917.

41 "*Q. N'est-il pas vrai qu'elle n'avait pas le temps de se lever, que les autres arrivaient et, que ce n'est pas vrai ce que vous dites là? R. Ce que j'ai vu, je vous dis ce que j'ai vu. Q. Je vous demande ça, moi? R. Quand un avait fini, il s'en venait avec, elle disait: 'C'est à toi, c'est à ton tour à venir.' Elle me l'a demandé à moi-même, je le sais.*" Questions by Crown attorney Fitzpatrick and testimony of Arsène Lamontagne, 20 déc. 1917.

42 Arthur Fitzpatrick was born in Québec in 1884, the son of the Hon. Sir Charles Fitzpatrick, the lawyer who had represented Louis Riel and become minister of justice,

Québec lieutenant-governor, and chief justice of the Supreme Court of Canada. His mother, Corinne Caron, was the daughter of René-Edouard Caron, minister, judge of the superior court and the court of appeal, and second lieutenant-governor of the province. Fitzpatrick studied at the Seminaire de Québec and the Faculté de Droit de Laval. He married Blanche Preston. Admitted to the bar in 1909, Fitzpatrick practised first with Taschereau, Roy, Cannon, Parent & Fitzpatrick. In 1916, he switched to practise with Fitzpatrick, Dupré & Gagnon at 105-107 Mountain Hill. He was deputy public prosecutor in Québec for several years, and became a KC in 1918. He resided at the Château Frontenac, and died in 1938. His obituary described him as a lover of books, who read widely in the sciences, literature, history, economics, and social problems. *Québec Adresses* (1917–18), 29th ed. (Québec: Edouard Marcotte, 1917); Ignace-J. Deslaurier, *Les cours de justice et la magistrature du Québec*, vol. 2 (Québec: Gouvernement du Québec, 1991) at 229; "L'hon. Arthur Fitzpatrick, décédé à l'âge de 54 ans" *Québec Le Soleil* (28 sept. 1938) 3 and 19.

43 "*Q. Vous dites qu'il n'a pas été question de ce qui s'était passé entre cette fille-là et vous et vos compagnons, depuis le moment où vous l'avez quittée en vous en allant à Montréal? . . . C'est pourtant assez remarquable, huit garçons qui vont trouver une fille dans un champs, ça ne se fait pas tous les jours ça? R. On a commencé à chanter chacun notre chanson . . . . Q. Ça ne vous avait pas fait plus d'impression que cela? R. Non, monsieur.*" Questions by Crown attorney Lachance and testimony of Léodore Venne, 20 déc. 1917.

44 S.C. 1892, c.29, s.266; R.S.C. 1906, c.146, s.298; R.S.C. 1927, c.36, s.298; S.C. 1953–54, c.51, s.135.

45 See, for example, S.C. 1892, c.29, s.269, which provided: "Every one is guilty of an indictable offence and liable to imprisonment for life, and to be whipped, who carnally knows any girl under the age of fourteen years, not being his wife, whether he believes her to be of or above that age or not." See also R.S.C. 1906, c.146, s.301. A new provision was added in S.C. 1920, c.43, s.8, which provided: "s.301(2). Every one is guilty of an indictable offence and liable to imprisonment for five years who carnally knows any girl of previous chaste character under the age of sixteen and above the age of fourteen, not being his wife, and whether he believes her to be above the age of sixteen years or not. No person accused of any offence under this subsection shall be convicted upon the evidence of one witness, unless such witness is corroborated in some material particular by evidence implicating the accused." Section 17 added: "the trial judge may instruct the jury that if, in their view the evidence does not show that the accused is wholly or chiefly to blame for the commission of said offence, they may find a verdict of acquittal." See R.S.C. 1927, c.36, s.301. Another provision was added in S.C. 1934, c.47, s.9: "Proof that a girl has on previous occasions had illicit connection with the accused shall not be deemed to be evidence that she was not of previously chaste character." The language of "carnal knowledge" was changed for "sexual intercourse" in S.C. 1953–54, c.51, s.138. See also ss.131, 133, and 134. For additional clarity, s.132 provided that "Where an accused is charged with an offence under section 138 . . . in respect of a person under the age of fourteen years, the fact that the person consented to the commission of the offence is not a defence to the charge."

46 *An Act respecting the Criminal Law*, R.S.C. 1906, c.146, s.211: "Every one is guilty of an indictable offence and liable to two years' imprisonment who seduces or has illicit connection with any girl of previously chaste character, of or above the age of fourteen years and under the age of sixteen years." All eight were originally charged with seduction as well as rape. They all chose to waive their right to a jury trial on 11 déc. 1917 and to proceed before a single justice in the Court of the Sessions of the Peace.

47 *An Act to punish seduction and like offences, and to make further provision for the Protection of Women and Girls*, S.C. 1886, c.52 earlier specified the ages as between twelve and sixteen, and used the conjunctive phrase "seduces and has illicit connection" rather than the disjunctive "seduces or has illicit connection." See also S.C. 1892, c.29, s.181. In 1920, the upper age limit would be raised to eighteen: S.C. 1920, c.43, s.4 provided: "s.211. Every one over the age of eighteen years is guilty of an indictable offence and liable to two years' imprisonment who seduces any girl of previously chaste character of or above the age of sixteen years and under the age of eighteen years. Proof that a girl has on previous occasions had illicit connection with the accused shall not be deemed to be evidence that she was not of previously chaste character." The 1920 amendment also removed the phrase "seduces or has illicit connection," substituting the word "seduces." It amended the fourteen-to-sixteen-year provisions in s.8, providing: "s.301(2). Every one is guilty of an indictable offence and liable to imprisonment for five years who carnally knows any girl of previous chaste character under the age of sixteen and above the age of fourteen, not being his wife, and whether he believes her to be above the age of sixteen years or not. No person accused of any offence under this subsection shall be convicted upon the evidence of one witness, unless such witness is corroborated in some material particular by evidence implicating the accused." The parliamentary debates indicate that the male legislators were gravely concerned over the potential for allowing girls "of vicious habits" to entrap innocent men. To prevent this, they added s.17, stipulating that "the trial judge may instruct the jury that if, in their view the evidence does not show that the accused is wholly or chiefly to blame for the commission of said offence, they may find a verdict of acquittal." One member of Parliament seems to have hoped that the proviso would eviscerate the law, stating: "I cherish this view that where two young people have misconducted themselves, as a rule the girl is just as much to blame as the boy." *House of Commons Debates* (10 May 1918) 1st Sess., 13th Parl., vol. 3 at 1702. See also R.S.C. 1927, c.36, s.211; S.C. 1953–54, c.51, s.138(3). The first reported decision to consider what this meant was *Regina v. Wiberg* (1955), 113 C.C.C. 257 (Alta. C.A.). The judges pronounced themselves confused: "The two words have quite different meanings. It seems to me that either one word or the other should have been used but not both, even disjunctively. Considering first the word 'wholly,' if the girl was only very slightly to blame then the accused would not be 'wholly' to blame. The girl, however, would have to be more than 50% to blame before the accused would not be chiefly to blame." The court determined that the terminology must require something beyond just showing that the accused was "more to blame than the girl seduced," adding that the surrounding circumstances

were critical and even slight conduct encouraging the accused might be sufficient to infer that the accused was not "wholly" to blame." S.C. 1959, c.41, s.9 removed the words "wholly or chiefly to blame" and substituted "more to blame."

Separate provisions made it a crime to seduce under promise of marriage an unmarried female of previously chaste character under the age of twenty-one, to seduce wards or servants of previously chaste character under the age of twenty-one, or for a master, officer, or seaman to seduce a female passenger. A subsequent marriage to the accused, except for a ward, constituted a full defence to the charge. See S.C. 1892, c.29, ss.182, 183 & 184; as amended by S.C. 1900, c.46, s.3; R.S.C. 1906, c.146, ss.212, 213, & 214. See also S.C. 1917, c.14, s.2, adding step-children and foster-children to the list, and S.C. 1920, c.43, s.5 broadening the category of "servants" to include more female employees. All provisions were governed by a limitation period of one year: see S.C. 1892, c.29, s.511; R.S.C. 1906, c.146, s.1140; R.S.C. 1927, c.36, s.1140; S.C. 1953–54, c.51, s.133. The seduction provisions were reduced in 1953, leaving in force only seduction of a girl between sixteen and eighteen, seduction under promise of marriage, and seduction of female passengers on vessels. See S.C. 1953–54, c.51, ss.143, 144, and 146.

48 *The Queen v. Doty* (1894), 25 O.R. 362 (Ch. Div.); *Rex v. Zambapys and McKay* (1923), 32 B.C.R. 510 (B.C.C.A.); *Rex v. Schemmer*, [1927] 3 W.W.R. 417 (Sask. Dist. Ct.); *Rex v. Blanchard* (1941), 75 C.C.C. 279 (B.C.C.A.). See also *Rex v. Dubuyk* (1920), 35 C.C.C. 32 (Sask. C.A.); *Rex v. Jones*, [1935] 3 D.L.R. 237 (B.C.C.A.).

49 *Rex v. Zambapys and McKay* (1923), 32 B.C.R. 510 (B.C.C.A.); *Rex v. Schemmer*, [1927] 3 W.W.R. 417 (Sask. Dist. Ct.); *Rex v. Gasselle* (1934), 62 C.C.C. 295 (Sask. C.A.); *Rex v. Landry* (1935), 64 C.C.C. 104 (N.B.C.A.); *Rex v. Blanchard* (1941), 75 C.C.C. 279 (B.C.C.A.). Courts also took a restrictive interpretation of seduction "under promise of marriage": see *R. v. Walker* (1893), 5 C.C.C. 465 (N.W.T.S.C.); *Rex v. Lougheed* (1903), 8 C.C.C. 184 (N.W.T.S.C.); *Rex v. Daun* (1906), 12 O.L.R. 227 (Ont. C.A.); *Rex v. Romans* (1908), 13 C.C.C. 68 (N.S.S.C.); *Rex v. Comeau* (1912), 5 D.L.R. 250 (N.S.S.C.); *Rex v. Spray* (1914), 24 C.C.C. 152 (B.C.C.A.); *Rex v. Seymour* (1931), 57 C.C.C. 95 (Sask. K.B.); *Rex v. McIsaac*, [1933] O.W.N. 251 (Ont. H.C.). For a similarly restrictive interpretation of seduction of an employee, see *Rex v. Jones*, [1935] 3 D.L.R. 237 (B.C.C.A.).

Although rarely acknowledged as such, it appears that the seduction terminology was drawn in large measure from American cases; see references listed in James Crankshaw, *The Criminal Code of Canada and the Canada Evidence Act, as amended to Date, with Commentaries, Annotations, Forms* (Toronto: Carswell, 1915) at 200–1. Historians who have reviewed American seduction law have suggested that United States' judges "obsessed" over the definition of seduction, utilizing sources ranging from dictionaries to foreign texts. Lea VanderVelde has noted that "the judicial proclivity to define and redefine seduction makes it appear as if the judges would not, or perhaps could not, reason from any understanding of human experience and hence turned to the dictionary for authority." See Lea VanderVelde, "The Legal Ways of Seduction" (April 1996) 48 *Stanford Law Review* 817 at 884. Some of the Canadian criminal decisions also referred to *Gibson v. Rabey* (1916), 9 Alta. L.R. 409 (Alta. C.A.), a civil suit for seduction based upon a 1903 Ordinance (2d Sess., Ord.

No. 8, s.4). No analysis was offered as to why the elements of the civil tort ought to be imported into the criminal jurisdiction, an omission that seems odd in view of the reference in the tort case to an earlier criminal prosecution for seduction arising out of the same facts that had resulted in an acquittal. Some decisions also referred to *The King v. Moon* (1910), 1 K.B. 818 (C.A.), an English case defining "seduction" under the *Children Act*, 1908, 8 Edw. 7, c.67, s.17. Since this was a distinctive statute not duplicated in Canada, and the English Parliament had not criminalized seduction, this also seems anomalous.

50 *Rex v. Schemmer*, [1927] 3 W.W.R. 417 (Sask. Dist. Ct.).

51 R.S.C. 1906, c.146, s.211.

52 *"Q. Il n'y a pas d'homme qui s'était mis sur vous jamais? R. Non. Q. Est-ce qu'il y en avait qui vous avait déshabillée ou touchée? R. Avant, non."* Questions of Greffier de la Paix Rochette and testimony of Yvonne Collin, 27 sept. 1917. *"Q. Maintenant, Mademoiselle, vous savez ce que c'est qu'un serment? R. Oui, monsieur. Q. Jurez-vous que vous ne vous êtes jamais fait toucher, par qui que ce soit, avant la nuit du dix-sept septembre dernier? R. Je me suis jamais fait toucher, jamais."* Questions of Crown attorney Fitzpatrick and testimony of Yvonne Collin, 21 déc. 1917.

53 *"C'est un petit garçon réservé . . . un gentil petit garçon, d'une honnête famille . . . un jeune homme bien poli . . . Je m'en suis pas beaucoup occupé de ça parce que c'était une affaire d'enfantillage."* Testimony of André Collin, 27 sept. 1917. Zéphirin Maranda, the young man's father, lived at 1129 St-Valier, and ran his business from 1089 St-Valier. *Québec Adresses* (1917–18), 29th ed. (Québec: Edouard Marcotte, 1917).

54 Lane was born in Hull in 1868, the son of Alfred Lane and Zénaide Lauzon. He graduated from the Collège de l'Assomption and Laval University where he received the Prince-de-Galles prize. He was married in 1897 to Marie-Albertine Lauzon, the daughter of a lumber merchant. Admitted to the bar in 1894, Lane was elected to the provincial legislature for Québec-Est in 1900, and received a KC in 1906. He practised law with Antonin Galipeault, François-Xavier Lemieux, and Marc Aurèle Lemieux. At the time of the trial, his firm was Lane & Lemieux at 93 St Pierre, and he resided at 202 St-François. See www.assnat.qc.ca/fra/Membres/notices/j-l/LANEJA.htm; *Québec Adresses* (1917–18), 29th ed. (Québec: Edouard Marcotte, 1917).

55 *"Sais-tu ma fille que tu t'es conduite comme une petite putain?"* Question of defence counsel Lane, 27 sept. 1917.

56 Born in Quebéc City in 1868, Marie-Arthur Lachance was the son of François-Xavier Lachance, a master blacksmith and manufacturer, and Eulalie Jobin, daughter of a gardener. He studied at the Séminaire de Québec and Laval University, was admitted to the bar in 1894, and practised with the Hon. M. Adélard Turgeon (president of the legislative council), Michael Joseph Ahern, KC (secretary of the public utilities commission), and M. Maxime Morin, at 111 Côte de la Montagne. He was named KC in 1903 and elected to the legislature as a Liberal in 1905, 1908, and 1911. He married Marianne Routhier in 1903, and resided at 79 d'Aiguillon and later 10 av. des Erables. He served as deputy public prosecutor for Montmagny and Beauce from 1899 to 1905, and for Québec from 1905 to 1920. Lachance also taught criminal law at Laval,

where he received a doctorate. He would retire in 1929, and died in 1945. *Québec Adresses* (1916–17), 29th ed. (Québec: Edouard Marcotte, 1917); Pierre-Georges Roy, *Les avocats de la région de Québec* (Lévis: n.p., 1936) at 234–35; Ignace-J. Deslaurier, *Les cours de justice et la magistrature du Québec*, vol. 2 (Québec: Gouvernement du Québec, 1991) at 233; "L'honorable Arthur Lachance" in *Biographies Canadiennes-Françaises* (Montréal: Editions biographies canadiennes-françaises, 1929) at 443.

57   Gagnon, age forty, resided at 226 Mercier. *Lovell's Montéal City Directory* (1917–18) (Montréal: John Lovell and Sons, 1917).

58   *"Elle m'a répondu que non, jamais, et elle s'est mise à pleurer, et je lui ai dit que ça servait à rien de pleurer qu'il faillait qu'elle dise la vérité, et là elle m'a avoué qu'elle avait déjà eu affaire avec un jeune homme, mais pas dans les même circonstances, que l'homme avec qui elle avait eu affaire, elle s'amusait avec lui avec sa main, et lui s'amusait avec elle avec son doigt."* Testimony of Arthur Gagnon, 13 nov. 1917.

59   Beaudoin, age twenty-nine, resided at 23 Langevin. *Québec Adresses* (1917–18), 29th ed. (Québec: Edouard Marcotte, 1917).

60   See chapter 2 for further discussion of the general rules of cross-examination with respect to rape and prior sexual history.

61   *Rex v. Fiola* (1918), 29 C.C.C. 125 (Que. Sess. Peace) at 129–30. For similar rulings, see *Rex v. Pieco* (1916), 27 C.C.C. 435 (Alta. C.A.); *Rex v. McPherson* (1922), 37 C.C.C. 315 (Sask. C.A.).

62   "Une Affaire Infamante à Québec" *Québec Le Soleil* (21 sept. 1917) 10: *"Les autorités policières tant de Québec que de Montréal viennent d'être saisies d'une affaire excessivement grave. Il s'agirait d'un crime infamant."* "Les Huit Prévenus Compairissant" *Québec Le Soleil* (25 sept. 1917) 10: *"Le détective . . . commençait immédiatement les recherches . . . presque sans répit . . . Ils étaient de ne pas prendre de repos tant qu'ils n'auraient pas mis la main sur ceux qu'ils recherchaient."*

63   Joseph-Abel Rochette, KC, was born in Québec in 1865, the son of Marcel Rochette and Adéline Langlois. He was admitted to the bar in 1888, conducted his legal practice from 4 St-Pierre, and resided at 627 St-Valier. He would die in 1931. He was described by contemporaries as *"probe, averti, renseigné,"* a lawyer *"conscient de sa mission"* who had *"toujours le respect de sa robe d'avocat."* *Québec Adresses* (1917–18), 29th ed. (Québec: Edouard Marcotte, 1917); Pierre-Georges Roy, *Les avocats de la région du Québec* (Lévis, n.p.: 1936) at 381–82.

64   *"Vous êtes détective, vous-même, n'est-ce pas? Vous travaillez pour la Couronne?"* Question of Greffier de la Paix Rochette, 13 nov. 1917.

65   *"Moi, j'avais pas le coeur net de cette affaire-là . . ."* 19 déc. 1917.

66   *"Je pense pas que c'était mon devoir."* 19 déc. 1917.

67   *"À la porte du magasin du père Fiola, à Verdun, le père m'a demandé si c'était du monde en moyens. J'ai dit: 'Oui.' Ensuite, il m'a fait la remarque, en présence de Beaudoin, que plus il aurait d'argent d'eux autres, que plus mon magot serait gros. Je lui ai dit que, nous autres, on était payé par la Corporation."* Testimony of Gagnon, 19 déc. 1917. For almost verbatim phrasing, see testimony of Beaudoin, 19 déc. 1917.

68   *"Il y a bien des choses que je n'ai pas dites à l enquête préliminaire, qui ne m'ont pas été demandées."* 19 déc 1917.

69 *"C'est parce que j'avais ça sur le coeur . . ."* 19 déc. 1917.

70 Bussières, age forty-six, resided at 260 d'Aiguillon. *Québec Adresses* (1917–18), 29th ed. (Québec: Edouard Marcotte, 1917).

71 *"Il a dit qu'il connaissait absolument rien de cette maison-là, qu'il n'avait rien à dire de mal contre cette femme-là."* 19 déc. 1917.

72 *Ibid.*

73 *"J'étais anxieux de trouver les jeunes gens, j'ai fait signe que oui, que si on trouvait les jeunes gens, qu'on verrait à récompenser le détective, pas dans le dessein d'avoir de l'argent des jeunes gens, mais dans le dessein de lui payer ses troubles."* 19 déc. 1917.

74 *"Q. Maintenant, y a-t-il eu des offres de règlement à vous, que vous avez refusées? R. Pas directes. On m'a dit, quelqu'un m'ont dit que je pourrais avoir une couple de cents piastres, les honoraires de mon avocat, payées; alors j'ai refusé."* Question put by Crown attorney Lachance and testimony of André Collin, 19 déc. 1917.

75 Such discussion rarely surfaced in open court, but three years later, there would be widespread public dissatisfaction over the failure of the Québec City police force to locate the rapist/murderers in the Blanche Garneau case. The body of a young, working-class woman who had been violently raped and strangled was discovered in Victoria Park, in July 1920. Detective Delphis Bussières, the first officer on the case, was asked by Garneau's adoptive parents to search for her after she went missing. Arthur Fitzpatrick was counsel for the early stages of the coroner's inquest, and Arthur Lachance, then chief justice of the Court of Sessions of the Peace, presided over a trial of two accused who were subsequently acquitted after it was determined that they both had water-tight alibis. No others were ever charged. A Royal Commission was held in 1922 to investigate many complaints that the authorities had been less than diligent in pursuing the case, and that police and others had covered up the responsibility of the real culprits, alleged to be sons of two influential members of the Legislative Assembly. Reviewing the affair sixty years later, one author described the findings of the Royal Commission as a "white wash" [*les conclusions de la Commission royale . . . ont blanchi le gouvernement, le procureur general et les corps policiers*] and their conclusions about the police in particular as "bizarre." See Réal Bertrand, *Qui a tué Blanche Garneau?* (Montréal: Quinze, 1983) at 29, 37–38, 53–54, 64–68, 118, 141, 152, and 181–82. There had also been complaints previously about corruption in the Montréal police force, and abysmal police wages in both forces. The 1909 Cannon Commission of Inquiry found that the Montréal force was letting untendered contracts for kickbacks, and revealed administrative incompetence, corruption, and tolerance of commercial vice. Greg Marquis, *Policing Canada's Century: A History of the Canadian Association of Chiefs of Police* (Toronto: University of Toronto Press, 1993) at 85.

The Montréal morality squad was first established in 1909, and given a mandate to investigate disorderly houses, as well as the unlawful trade in alcohol, cocaine, and morphine — all areas rife with the potential for bribery. In 1917, a first-class constable in Montréal earned $1150 per annum. Jean Turmel, *Le Service de Police de la cité de Montréal (1909–1971)* (Montréal: La Section Recherche et Planification du Service de Police de la C.U.M., 1974) at 6, 29, and 38.

Gérald Gagnon, *Histoire du service de police de la ville de Québec* (Québec: Publications du Québec, 1998) documents at 107 and 137 complaints from Québec City police officers about their low wages in 1888, 1905, 1907, 1917, and 1919, culminating in a strike in 1921. He also notes that Québec City constables earned less than carpenters in 1922. In an ironic after-note, it seems that Arthur Fitzpatrick represented the Québec police as their lawyer during the 1919 salary negotiations (*ibid.* at 137).

76 "*Q. Vous avez dit à M. Rochette que vous aviez raconté ces faits-là à moi; vous rappelez-vous que c'est moi qui vous ai demandé de me raconter ces faits-là, si elle vous avait fait quelques déclarations? R. Oui, monsieur. Q. Et que c'est en réponse à ma question que vous m'avez déclaré ça? R. Oui, monsieur.*" Questions by defence counsel Lane, and testimony of Detective Beaudoin, 13 nov. 1917.

77 See chapter 10 for further discussion.

78 Langelier was born in 1850, the son of Louis-Sébastien Langelier and Julie-Esther Casault. Prior to law, he studied at the Séminaire de Ste-Hyacinthe and the Petit Séminaire de Québec. He was named a QC in 1880. He married Marie-Louise-Georgiana-Lucille La Rue, daughter of a tax-collector, in 1882, and they had one daughter. Despite six electoral defeats, Langelier was elected to the provincial legislature from 1878 to 1881, the House of Commons from 1887 to 1890, and again to the provincial legislature under the Mercier government from 1890 to 1892, where he served as president of the executive council and provincial secretary. From 1897 to 1901, Langelier served as MLA for Lévis. His residence was at 111 Grande-Allée. The quote is from "Langelier, Charles" in *Dictionary of Canadian Biography* [*DCB*], vol. 14 (Toronto: University of Toronto Press, 1998) at 592. See also "Langelier, Charles" in W. Stewart Wallace, *DCB*, 2d ed., vol. 2 (Toronto: Macmillan, 1945) at 337–38; J.-A. Fortier, "Charles Langelier" in *Biographies Canadiennes-Françaises*, vol. 1 (Montréal: Editions biographiques canadiennes-françaises, 1920) at 52; Pierre-Georges Roy, *Les avocats de la région de Québec* (Levis: n.p., 1936) at 245–46; *Québec Adresses* (1919–20), 31st ed. (Québec: Edouard Marcotte, 1919). On the Baie des Chaleurs scandal, see Québec, *Royal Commission Inquiry into the Baie des Chaleurs Railway Matter* (Québec: Queen's Printer, 1892) at 110–31 and 170–76, where two members of the commission concluded that Langelier knowingly received money for his personal use out of funds fraudulently obtained from the government by his close friend, journalist, and fellow Liberal, M. Pacaud. The third member of the commission concluded that the evidence against Langelier was purely circumstantial. For details on Sir François Langelier, see *DCB*, vol. 14 at 593–94.

79 *DCB*, vol. 14 at 592–93; Wallace, *DCB* at 337–38; J.-A. Fortier, "Charles Langelier" in *Biographies Canadiennes-Françaises*, vol. 1 (Montréal: Editions biographiques canadiennes-françaises, 1920) at 52.

80 "*Que M. Gagnon ait fait son devoir ou non, je n'ai pas à y voir dans cette enquête-ci, et je m'objecte à cette preuve.*" Intervention by Judge Langelier, 13 nov. 1917. Langelier also upheld Lane's objection to Crown attorney Fitzpatrick's subsequent grilling of Gagnon, ruling that the witness did not have to answer the question as to whether he had done his duty: "*Q. Croyez-vous que vous faites votre devoir en examinant un témoin*

de la poursuite, comme vous l'avez fait . . . OBJECTE de la part de l'accusé à cette question. OBJECTION maintenue," 19 déc. 1917.

81 *"La procédure criminelle d'après le Code civil et la jurisprudence"* (Québec, 1916); *"La prostitution: ses dangers, son remède; lettre ouverte à son honneur le maire et à MM. les échevins de la cité de Québec"* (Québec, 1916) as cited in *DCB*, vol. 14 at 593. See also Ignace-J. Deslaurier, *Les cours de justice et la magistrature du Québec*, vol. 2 (Québec: Gouvernement du Québec, 1991) at 234.

82 *"Les huit accusés sont libérés"* *Québec Le Soleil* (18 jan. 1918) 10; *"Ne pas confondre"* *Québec L'Action Catholique* (27 sept. 1917) 8. For the legal reports, see *Rex v. Fiola* (1918), 41 D.L.R. 73 (Que. S.P.); *Rex v. Fiola et al.* (1918), 29 C.C.C. 125 (Que. S.P.).

83 R.S.C. 1906, c.146, s.210. Langelier indicated that the crime of seduction did "not exist" in England, and therefore English jurisprudence was not helpful, so it seems odd that he turned first to an American and English encylopedia: "vol. 25 Am. & Eng. Ency., p.240, sec. 7." Had he examined *Rex v. Wakelyn* (1913), 21 C.C.C. 111 (Alta. S.C.); *Rex v. Rioux* (1914), 8 Alta. L.R. 47 (Alta. C.A.); or *Rex v. Pieco* (1916), 27 C.C.C. 435 (Alta. C.A.), he would have realized that other courts had recognized that the burden of proof lay with the defence.

84 From the earliest enactment of the phrase, Canadian women's organizations had ineffectively lobbied to have it removed entirely as inherently unfair. Feminists also argued that the character clause could present an almost insurmountable barrier, because it was "easy for the kind of men who [were] liable to be indicted for this offence to get a friend or friends to prove that this girl [had] been previously unchaste." They complained that it was unfair to force women to prove their previously chaste character when no one "question[ed] the man as to his previous character." Appendix to *Women Workers of Canada*, Third Annual Meeting of the National Council of Women of Canada (Montréal: 1896) at 313–25; *House of Commons Debates* (1886) vol. 1 at 442; Constance Backhouse, *Petticoats and Prejudice: Women and Law in Nineteenth-Century Canada* (Toronto: Women's Press, 1991) at 69–80. Responding in 1900, Parliament refused to remove the phrase, but shifted the burden of proof "as to previous unchastity" to the accused. See S.C. 1900, c.46, s.3; R.S.C. 1906, c.146, s.210; R.S.C. 1927, c.36, s.210; S.C. 1953–54, c.51, s.131(3). Several legislators tried to prevent the change, arguing that it was a "drastic change," "monstrous," and a "perfectly stupendous thing to put the burden of proof on the accused." See *House of Commons Debates* (4 May 1900) at 4716–18.

Three years after Yvonne Collin's case, Parliament would also stipulate that prior sexual acts with the accused could not be offered as proof of previous unchastity. See S.C. 1920, c.43, s.4; R.S.C. 1927, c.36, s.211; S.C. 1953–54, c.51, s.131(4). Before this, some judges had ruled that evidence of a prior sexual connection with the accused warranted an acquittal, noting that the offence was one which could "only be committed once with the same girl." See *Rex v. Lougheed* (1903), 8 C.C.C. 184 (N.W.T.S.C.); *Rex v. Lacelle* (1905), 10 C.C.C. 229 (Ont. C.A.); *Rex v. Comeau* (1912), 19 C.C.C. 350 (N.S.S.C.). In *Rex v. Hauberg* (1915), 24 C.C.C. 297 (Sask. S.C.), the court found that the complainant had been seduced by the accused in Norway prior to immigrating with him to Canada, and quashed the initial conviction, stating that the presumption of "illicit intercourse" in Canada would not support a charge unless there was evidence that "between the two acts of seduction there was such conduct and behaviour on her part as to imply reform and self-rehabilitation in chastity." *Rex v. Farrell* (1916), 26 C.C.C. 273 (Ont. C.A.) took a different approach. The trial judge determined that the victim "was under the influence of liquor" and might have been "mistaken as to what occurred" when she had earlier sexual intercourse with the accused. Since this was the only previous act of carnal connection, he concluded that the evidence did not necessarily disprove chastity, a ruling upheld on appeal. Similarly, in *Rex v. Magdall* (1920), 34 C.C.C. 244, the Supreme Court of Canada upheld the conviction of an accused who had had intercourse with the complainant once previous to the incident that spawned the charge. Although Justices Duff and Brodeur dissented, Chief Justice Davies stated: "I am not able to accept the argument that such a single fall from grace of a woman, engaged to a man to whose solicitations she yields, either because of a weaker will than his or that combined with affection and a hope of their prospective marriage under his promise, necessarily stamps that woman as one of an unchaste character for all time. That surely cannot be so. There must come a time when repentance or pureness of living can rehabilitate her as a chaste character within the meaning of the statute." Justice Idington added: "Indeed, to meet the possibility of such a case as of this class again arising, enabling the offender to set up his own wrong as a means of defence, I submit the law might well be so amended as to prevent the possibility of such a curious means of defence." The legislative amendment carried that year. See also *Rex v. Stinson* (1934), 61 C.C.C. 227 (B.C.C.A.), where the majority, with one dissent, held that submitting to prior sexual intercourse with the accused while under duress did not deprive the complainant of the status of chaste character. Feminist demands to eradicate the entire concept of "previous chaste character" never ceased; see Canada, *Royal Commission on the Status of Women in Canada* (Ottawa: Queen's Printer, 1970) at 373.

85 *Rex v. Loughood* (1905), 8 C.C.C. 184 (N.W.T.S.C.); *Rex v. Comeau* (1912), 19 C.C.C. 350 (N.S.S.C.).

86 *Rex v. Fiola* (1918), 29 C.C.C. 125 at 125–27.

87 *Rex v. Johnston* (1948), 5 C.R. 320 (Ont. C.A.). In *Regina v. Shaw*, [1964] 1 C.C.C. 104 (N.S.S.C.), the appellate court quashed a conviction because the trial judge had failed to put fully to the jury the theory of the defence that although the complainant was a virgin, she was not of previously chaste character due to her allegedly profane and indecent language, and indecencies with boys in a tent, a bowling alley, and a theatre. But see *Rex v. Rioux* (1914), 8 Alta. L.R. 47 (Alta. C.A.), where the trial judge heard evidence that the complainant (a young runaway virgin) had discussed sex and "how to avoid trouble" with an older woman, that a man had "grabbed at her private parts" in a second-hand store several days earlier, and that she had gone to a hotel with the accused after he promised to pay her ten dollars. The ruling that the complainant had not been "of previously chaste character" was overturned on appeal, where the court held that the financial "bait" was only successful because the girl was "absolutely without money," and that the chaste character of a woman

could not be affected by the "nature of the motive which impels her, whether it be the lure of money or the excitement of passion."

88 *Rex v. Comeau* (1912), 19 C.C.C. 350 (N.S.S.C.). This view was expressed by three judges, but not concurred in by Justice Drysdale, who determined that previous acts of illicit intercourse disposed of the complainant's reputation for chastity. The judges were unanimous, however, in upholding the acquittal given the evidence that the injured woman had had intercourse with the accused ten or twelve times previously.

89 In *Rex v. Comeau* (1912), 19 C.C.C. 350 (N.S.S.C.), Justice Ritchie stated that a young girl who "goes wrong, quickly repents and is absolutely virtuous for the next twenty years" could reacquire a chaste character. In *Rex v. Magdall* (1920), 34 C.C.C. 244 (S.C.C.), the court held that a "single fall from grace" did not necessarily stamp a woman as one of unchaste character for all time. "There must come a time when repentance or pureness of living can rehabilitate her as a chaste character within the meaning of the statute," noted the court, declining to fix a "statutory limit of time." In *Rex v. Johnston* (1948), 5 C.R. 320 (Ont. C.A.), the court held that "chastity may be lost and later regained." For examples of judicial opinions that seem to have rejected the rehabilitation thesis, see *Rex v. Lacelle* (1905), 10 C.C.C. 229 (Ont. C.A.) and the minority decision of Justice Drysdale in *Rex v. Comeau*.

90 *Rex v. Fiola* (1918), 29 C.C.C. 125 at 128 and 130.

91 "L'honorable Arthur Lachance" in *Biographies Canadiennes-Françaises* (Montréal: Editions biographies canadiennes-françaises, 1929) at 443; on Charles Langelier, see *DCB*, vol. 14 at 592–93; on Arthur Fitzpatrick, see Ignace-J. Deslaurier, *Les cours de justice et la magistrature du Québec*, vol. 2 (Québec: Gouvernement du Québec, 1991) at 229; on Jules-Alfred Lane, see www.assnat.qc.ca/fra/Membres/notices/j-l/LANEJA.htm; *Québec Adresses* (1917–18), 29th ed. (Québec: Edouard Marcotte, 1917).

92 Henri Perrotte's "Particulars of Recruit" records show him drafted as Class 1, 2d Québec Regiment, with a medical examination done 18 Feb. 1918; Archives of Canada, RG 150, Box 7745 - 50, Regimental #3156289. Léodore Venne's "Particulars of Recruit" records show him drafted as Class 1, 2d Québec Regiment, with a medical examination done 1 March 1918; Archives of Canada, RG 150, Accession 1992–93/166, Box 9929 - 2, Regimental #3156526. Léo Fiola's "Particulars of Recruit" records show him drafted as Class 1, 1st Québec Regiment, with a medical examination done 11 July 1918; Archives of Canada RG 150, Accession 1992–93/166, Box 3098 - 32, Regimental #3086688. Albert Thivièrge's "Attestation Paper" shows he enlisted on 21 April 1919; Archives of Canada, Canadian Over-Seas Expeditionary Force, No. 1284399. Although two of Georges Mollot's brothers, Albert and Harry Victor, were drafted in 1918, we have found no other records for the rest of the group.

Chapter 4: The Prosecution of Henry Kissel in the Roaring Twenties in Halifax

1 Details of the case have been drawn from the Public Archives of Nova Scotia, The King v. Henry Kissell, RG 39 "C", vol. 708, #278 [Kissell, P.A.N.S.]. The Archival record contains the information, the arrest warrant, commitment to jail, depositions of testimony in chief and cross-examination for the Supreme Court, Crown Side,

and "no bill" from the grand jury. The legal records use "Kissell" but the Dalhousie records, probably more reliable, use "Kissel." The Dalhousie University Archives list Henry Kissel as born 10 June 1899, with a home address of 1048 Brigaut Ave., Bronx, New York. His father was Samuel Kissel. Application No. 144, 9 Sept. 1925; Order of Proceedings at the 62d Spring Convocation, 11 May 1926. Students were admitted to the six-year medical school program directly out of high school. The Halifax Medical College had merged with the non-denominational Dalhousie University to form the Faculty of Medicine in 1912. This was, in part, due to a critical rating in the American-based Flexner report in 1909, which ranked Canadian medical schools as follows: "Western University (London) is as bad as anything to be found on this side of the line; Laval and Halifax Medical College are feeble; Winnipeg and Kingston represent a distinct effort toward higher ideals; McGill and Toronto are excellent." After substantial reorganization and grants from the Carnegie and Rockefeller Foundations, by 1925 the Dalhousie M.D. was given an A1 rating by the American Medical Association. On the history and prestige of Dalhousie's Faculty of Medicine, see P.B. Waite, *The Lives of Dalhousie University*, vol. 2: *1925–1980, The Old College Transformed* (Montréal and Kingston: McGill-Queen's University Press, 1994–98) at 8–23; J.A. MacFarlane, *Royal Commission on Health Services: Medical Education in Canada* (Ottawa: Queen's Printer, 1965) at 21, quoting Abraham Flexner, *Bulletin Number Four*, at 150 and 325; N. Tait McPhedran, *Canadian Medical Schools: Two Centuries of Medical History 1822 to 1992* (Calgary: Harvest House, 1993). In 1925, forty-three students graduated with an M.D.; see "Dalhousie Professional Faculties at Work" *Halifax Herald* (14 Sept. 1925) 14. In 1925, the annual tuition rate at Dalhousie of $225 ranked second in the country, after $232 at McGill, and ahead of Montréal, Alberta, Toronto, Manitoba, Western, Queen's, and Laval: Dr. Clare Robinson, *Financial Background of Canadian Medical Students* (rpt. Camsi Journal, Oct. 1946). The first woman to graduate from Dalhousie Medicine was Annie Isabella Hamilton, in 1894. There were no women in Kissel's graduating class, but two in the preceding year, and three in the following year: Enid Johnson MacLeod, *Petticoat Doctors: The First Forty Years of Women in Medicine at Dalhousie University* (Lawrencetown Beach, NS: Pottersfield Press, 1990). See also R.D. Gidney & W.P.J. Millar, "Quantity and Quality: The Problem of Admissions in Medicine at the University of Toronto" (Fall 1997) 9 *Historical Studies in Education* 165.

2   Colin D. Howell, *A Century of Care: A History of Victoria General Hospital in Halifax, 1887–1987* (Halifax: The Hospital, 1988) at 65–66, described the significant role of students, interns, and medical faculty, and the increasingly sophisticated treatment, diagnosis, and medical education delivered within the expanding hospital during the inter-war years.

3   On the lack of residence facilities, see Waite, *Dalhousie University*, above note 1 at 30. Dalhousie University Archives list Irving Edward Marks as a former resident of New York City, registered in his final year of medical studies.

4   On the trendiness of horn-rimmed glasses adopted by medical students among others in the 1920s, see Kevin Boyle, *Arc of Justice: A Saga of Race, Civil Rights, and Murder in the Jazz Age* (New York: Henry Holt, 2004) at 100.

5 On the strictly regulated Dalhousie dances, see Waite, *Dalhousie University*, above
note 1 at 27. The Armouries served as a drill centre for the military, and a location
for public concerts, dances, and community events; Canadian Heritage, *Halifax Armoury* (Author: Historic Sites & Monuments Board of Canada, 1996).

6 On the influence of the Roaring Twenties at Dalhousie, including the presence of
women with "bobbed hair and silk stockings (with seam)" in 1925 at Shirreff Hall,
the female residence, see Waite, *Dalhousie University*, above note 1 at 4–7 and 30–31;
Thomas H. Raddall, *Halifax: Warden of the North* (Toronto: McClelland and Stewart,
1971) at 257–66. For general discussions of the flapper, see Alison Prentice et al., *Canadian Women: A History* (Toronto: Harcourt, Brace, Jovanovich, 1988) at 244; Angela J.
Latham, *Posing a Threat: Flappers, Chorus Girls and Other Brazen Performers of the American 1920s* (Hanover: University Press of New England, 2000); Kathy Peiss, *Hope in a
Jar: The Making of America's Beauty Culture* (New York: Henry Holt, 1998) at 97–202;
Lois W. Banner, *American Beauty* (New York: Knopf, 1983) at 271–80; Jenna Weissman
Joselit, *A Perfect Fit: Clothes, Character, and the Promise of America* (New York: Henry
Holt, 2001) at 58–73. For reference to the *Halifax Chronicle* article, and life and career
of Dr. Atlee, see Wendy Mitchinson, "H.B. Atlee on Obstetrics and Gynaecology: A
Singular and Representative Voice in 20th-Century Canadian Medicine" (Spring
2003) 32 *Acadiensis* 3–30; Harry Oxorn, *H.B. Atlee M.D.: A Biography* (Hantsport, NS:
Lancelot Press, 1983).

7 National Archives of Canada, Dominion Department of Health, RG29, vol. 217
(1920); Carolyn Strange, *Toronto's Girl Problem: The Perils and Pleasures of the City
1880–1930* (Toronto: University of Toronto Press, 1995) at 205–6.

8 Gertrude E.S. Pringle, "Is the Flapper a Menace?" *Maclean's* (15 July 1922) at 19.
Waite, *Dalhousie University*, above note 1, refers at 28 to the growing evidence of sexual innuendo in the student *Gazette* of 1922:

> "What shall we do?" she asked, bored to the verge of tears.
> "Whatever you wish," he replied gallantly.
> "If you do, I'll scream," she said coyly . . .

9 Prentice et al., *Canadian Women*, above note 6 at 218–32. Suzanne Morton, *Ideal Surroundings: Domestic Life in a Working-Class Suburb in the 1920s* (Toronto: University of
Toronto Press, 1995) at 132 noted that in Halifax, women composed 25.5 percent of
the labour force in 1921, and 26.9 percent in 1931.

10 Between 1871 and 1929, Toronto merchant Robert Simpson built multi-storey, retail
operations in Toronto, Regina, Halifax, and Montréal. The demise of local businesses and the growth of national chains were exemplified in Halifax by the opening of
Simpson's mail-order operation in 1919, its expansion to retail premises in 1924, and
the opening of Eaton's in 1929. Ethel Machan may have worked first as a mail-order
employee, answering customer letters and sending out invoices for customer orders
across the Maritime provinces and Newfoundland. See n.a., *Simpson's Mail Order
Division* (1952) n.p., Hudson's Bay Company, RG17/1T/11; Morton, *Ideal Surroundings*,
above note 9 at 146; Donica Belisle, "Civilising the Nation: Department Store Publicity in English Canada, 1890–1930," unpublished manuscript, June 2004; n.a., *Simp-*

son's (1949) n.p., Hudson's Bay Company, RG17/1Q/31; n.a., *The Story of Simpson's: 68 Years of Progress* (Wood, Gundy & Co., 1940) n.p., Hudson's Bay Company, RG17/1Q/2; n.a., *Historical Notes re Simpson's Halifax Store* (1963) n.p., Hudson's Bay Company, RG17/1T/12.

11   Simpson's prided itself on its fashionable merchandise, advising clients of the latest styles available from their "salons" in full-page advertisements in the *Globe and Mail* and the *Toronto Sunday World*; see, for example, "Sportive Chic in Smart Frocks from the West End of London" *Globe and Mail* (20 Nov. 1926) 17; Belisle, "Civilising the Nation," above note 10; Eileen Collard, *Women's Dress in the 1920s: An Outline of Women's Clothing in Canada during the 'Roaring Twenties'* (Burlington: Eileen Collard, 1981) at 27. On the need to obtain high school education and to adopt the standard grammar, speech, tones, and dress of the middle class in order to obtain jobs in department stores, and on the culture of "heterosexual romance," see Morton, *Ideal Surroundings*, above note 9 at 144–47, citing Veronica Strong-Boag, *The New Day Recalled: 1919–1939* (Toronto: Copp Clark Pitman, 1988). See also Susan Porter Benson, *Counter Cultures: Saleswomen, Managers, and Customers in American Department Stores, 1890–1940* (Urbana: University of Illinois Press, 1988) at 6, 26, 135, 211, and 266; Kathy Peiss, *Cheap Amusements: Working Women and Leisure in Turn-of-the-Century New York* (Philadelphia: Temple University Press, 1986) at 39; Mary-Eta Macpherson, *The Eatons: Shopkeepers to a Nation* (Toronto: McClelland & Stewart, 1963) at 83.

12   On the low wages, see Morton, *Ideal Surroundings*, above note 9, who noted at 140–43 that employees in the Halifax Simpson's warehouse were paid five dollars a week, while the average board in Halifax was between five and six dollars a week. On the propensity of the T.E. Eaton Company and Robert Simpson Company to flout minimum wage regulations, see Prentice et al., *Canadian Women*, above note 6 at 229. Ethel's father, Henry Machan, was on "active service" in 1917, and Blanche was widowed the year after. Ethel's brother, H. Machan, was employed as a labourer at the Halifax Shipyards, and her sister Florence also resided with the family. Miss Annie Machan, presumably another sister, who was also an employee at Simpson's, had moved out in 1924. *McAlpine's Halifax City Directory 1925* (Halifax: Royal Print & Litho, 1925) at 42 and 295; *Halifax City Directory 1923* at 353; *Halifax City Directory 1917* at 355; *Halifax City Directory 1916* at 362. Working-class, single women who were employed in the same cities as their families generally lived at home, and turned over much of their wages to families; see Prentice et al., *Canadian Women*, above note 6 at 228. This was particularly true in Halifax, where non-familial lodging was not widely available; Morton, *Ideal Surroundings*, above note 9 at 138.

13   Ontario, Provincial Board of Health, Division of Industrial Hygiene, *Health Confessions of Business Women by Business Women* (Toronto: 1923) at 157, cited by Strange, *Toronto's Girl Problem*, above note 7 at 190.

14   See, for example, the description of the "Season's Most Spectacular Fashion Show" featuring Simpson's and Eaton's salesclerk models, staged at the Royal York in Toronto, in the *Toronto Evening Telegram* (4 Oct. 1929).

15   For Marjory Hubley's occupation, see *McAlpine's Halifax City Directory 1925* (Halifax: Royal Print, 1925) at 257. On the traditional strictures governing courtship, see Peter

Ward, *Courtship, Love, and Marriage in Nineteenth-Century Canada* (Montréal: McGill-Queen's University Press, 1990).

16 On the practice of "picking up" unknown partners in amusement resorts and the streets, see Peiss, *Cheap Amusements*, above note 11 at 106–7: "Such social customs as 'picking up' . . . suggest the paradoxical nature of dance hall culture for women. Women enjoyed dancing for the physical pleasure of the movement, its romantic and sensual connotations, and the freedom it allowed them. The commercial dance halls were public spaces they could attend without escorts, choose companions for the evening, and express a range of personal desires. Nevertheless, the greater freedom of expression . . . occurred in a heterosocial context of imbalanced power and privileges. Picking up women and breaking dancers were more often male prerogatives in a scenario where women displayed themselves for the pleasure of male eyes." See also Strange, *Toronto's Girl Problem*, above note 7 at 120; Beth L. Bailey, *From Front Porch to Back Seat: Courtship in Twentieth-Century America* (Baltimore: Johns Hopkins University Press, 1988).

17 Details of the testimony and the quotes that follow have all been drawn from the archival depositions of the examination-in-chief and cross-examination of the witnesses who testified: Kissell, P.A.N.S.

18 The parade set off a week-long series of other parades, drills, booths, and tea tables in connection with the Masonic Fair of Nations; see "Girls to Parade This Afternoon" *Halifax Herald* (19 Sept. 1925) 20.

19 Halifax waitresses often worked seventy or eighty hours in a seven-day week at this time. See Morton, *Ideal Surroundings*, above note 9 at 142.

20 Morton, *Ideal Surroundings*, above note 9 notes at 147 that for working-class Halifax women in the 1920s, "men were necessary to provide financial access to popular entertainment." Peiss, *Cheap Amusements*, above note 11 describes at 108–14 the concept of "treating" in which women bargained their flirtatious companionship and occasionally sexual acts for male attention, tickets to dance halls and amusement parks, and often simply a good time. In New York, those who did so were dubbed "charity girls," a term that differentiated them from prostitutes because they would not accept money in their sexual encounters with men.

21 Ontario, Provincial Board of Health, Division of Preventable Diseases, Sex Hygiene Pamphlets, PAO RG62, Box 467 (1923). Information about the perils of venereal disease had been widely disseminated in post-war Canada. The full list of titles prepared in 1923 was: "Facts on Venereal Disease — General"; "Facts for Boys and Young Men"; "Facts for Girls and Young Women"; "Short Description of Venereal Diseases"; and "Instructions to those Having Venereal Diseases"; see Strange, *Toronto's Girl Problem*, above note 7 at 205–6.

22 Jay Cassel, *The Secret Plague: Venereal Disease in Canada 1838–1939* (Toronto: University of Toronto Press, 1987); Angus McLaren, *Our Own Master Race: Eugenics in Canada 1885–1945* (Toronto: McClelland & Stewart, 1990).

23 On the content of medical journals, see Angus McLaren & Arlene Tigar McLaren, *The Bedroom and the State* (Toronto: Oxford University Press, 1997) at 21. Dalhousie Medical School may have been somewhat unusual, in that Kissel would have been

instructed in obstetrics and gynecology by Professor Harold Benge Atlee, widely regarded as a brash but brilliant young upstart. Atlee apparently had some sympathy
for the "new" woman of the interwar years who had left the Victorian code of behaviour behind, although he never challenged the belief that women were confined
by their "reproductive destiny." Atlee was perceived as a maverick in medicine, in
part, because he supported birth control and the use of tampons during menstruation. Some of his female medical students would later recall that he taught at least
some information about birth control. Waite, *Dalhousie University*, above note 1 at
19–23; Wendy Mitchinson, "H.B. Atlee on Obstetrics and Gynaecology: A Singular
and Representative Voice in 20th-Century Canadian Medicine," above note 6.

Although physicians were not often held out as experts in such matters, people
had resorted to douching with spermicidal solutions for centuries, to mixed results.
French prostitutes had been using syringes to douche since 1600, although the Massachusetts physician Charles Knowlton was the first to publish information about
this method in his *Fruits of Philosophy* in 1832. He advocated douching with concoc-
tions of vinegar, alum, astringent vegetables, zinc, baking soda, sugar and lead, all
intended to create a hostile environment for sperm. In *The Bedroom and the State*,
McLaren & McLaren note at 21 that information about douching was in circulation
in Canada, and that those who believed in the prophylactic benefits of douching
would have been able to read between the lines in the early twentieth-century advertisements for "Every Woman Marvel Whirling Spray," which appeared in publications such as the T. Eaton Company catalogue, the *Toronto Daily Mail and Empire*,
and the *Dominion Medical Monthly*. Post-coital douches were of limited effectiveness,
however, because the transport of sperm from the site of ejaculation to the site of
fertilization was too rapid, and because douches with spermicidal properties tended
to be caustic agents which could seriously irritate the epithelial lining of the female
reproductive tract. The first "scientific" knowledge about the efficacy of "morning-
after" contraception appears to have originated in veterinary circles in the 1920s,
when researchers initially demonstrated that estrogenic ovarian extracts could
interfere with pregnancy in mammals. Despite scattered reports of clinical use of
post-coital estrogens in humans as early as the 1940s, the first documented cases
were not published until the mid-1960s. Early proponents of birth control in Canada
recommended barrier methods such as diaphragms and contraceptive jellies during the 1930s. See B.E. Finch & Hugh Green, *Contraception through the Ages* (London:
Peter Owen, 1963) at 28–37; James W. Knight & Joan C. Callahan, *Preventing Birth*
(Salt Lake City: University of Utah Press, 1989) at 20; Charlotte Ellertson, "History
and Efficacy of Emergency Contraception: Beyond Coca-Cola" (1996) 28 *Family Planning Perspectives* 44–48; Dianne Dodd, "Women's Involvement in the Canadian Birth
Control Movement of the 1930s: The Hamilton Birth Control Clinic" in Katherine
Arnup et al., eds., *Delivering Motherhood: Maternal Ideologies and Practices in the 19th
and 20th Centuries* (London: Routledge, 1990) at 150–72.

24 First enacted with the introduction of the *Criminal Code* in 1892, as S.C. 1892, c.29,
s.179, the section in force in 1925 was S.C. 1913, c.13, s.8, which made it a criminal
offence for anyone who "offers to sell, advertises, publishes an advertisement of, or

has for sale or disposal any means or instructions or any medicine, drug or article intended or represented as a means of preventing conception or of causing abortion or miscarriage; or advertises or publishes an advertisement of any means, instructions, medicine, drug or article for restoring sexual virility or curing venereal diseases or diseases of the generative organs." An earlier enactment, still in force, provided that no one could be convicted if he could prove that "the public good was served by the acts alleged to have been done, and that there was no excess in the acts alleged beyond what the public good required." R.S.C. 1906, c.146, s.207(2). Section 207(4) provided that the motives of the manufacturer, seller, exposer, publisher or exhibitor should "in all cases be irrelevant." For an account of a prominent Ottawa trial in 1936, in which Dorothea Palmer of the Parents' Information Bureau was acquitted under the "public good" clause, see Dianne Dodd, "The Birth Control Movement on Trial, 1936–1937" (Nov. 1983) 16 *Histoire sociale/Social History* 411–28; Gerald J. Stortz & Murray A. Eaton, "Pro Bono Publico: The Eastview Birth Control Trial" (Spring 1983) 8 *Atlantis* 51–60.

25 "Kodaks" were all the rage with the flapper set, which used the new cameras to take photographs of their dancing and cavorting. Gertrude E.S. Pringle, "Is the Flapper a Menace?" *Maclean's* (15 June 1922) at 19, described a "close view of the American flapper" in Buffalo: "There were two young, short-skirted, giggling girls, walking with their admirers who were armed with kodaks. One of the young men threw a girl over his shoulder with her legs straight out, while the other photographed them."

26 Morton, *Ideal Surroundings*, above note 9 at 141.

27 "Medical Student Is Arrested Here" *Halifax Herald* (24 Sept. 1925) 12; "Student Faces Serious Charge" *Halifax Morning Chronicle* (24 Sept. 1925) 7.

28 Not all case files permit an assessment of the class of the accused, but those that do rarely suggest wealth or status. The few examples that do include Rex v. F.J. Bateman (1906) Middlesex County Crown Attorney and Crown Prosecutor Criminal Court Records, #866 (1906), UWO Regional Room, Box 558, where a Strathroy physician who was purporting to remove a woman's ovary was charged with attempting to rape her while she was on his medical examining table; he was found not guilty. Rex v. Samuel Schennery (1923) Nova Scotia Provincial Archives RG 39 "C" [Halifax] vol. 706 #B193 involved a schoolteacher charged with raping several of his female pupils; no verdict is recorded. Louis Auger, a student-at-law and member of Parliament, was convicted of seduction of a seventeen-year-old female constituent in 1929; see Constance Backhouse, "Attentat à la dignité du Parlement: Viol dans l'enceinte de la Chambre des communes, Ottawa 1929" (2001–02) 33 *Ottawa Law Review* 95–145. *White v. The King* (1947), 89 C.C.C. 148 (S.C.C.) involved a dentist accused of indecently assaulting a patient while she was at the dental clinic. He was acquitted, but the appellate court sent the case back for a new trial due to a misdirection relating to the assessment of evidence. In *Regina v. Collerman*, [1964] 46 W.W.R. 300 (B.C.C.A.), the manager of a drive-in restaurant was convicted of indecently assaulting a female employee. In *Regina v. Bolduc & Bird*, [1967] 2 C.C.C. 272 (B.C.C.A.), a physician who misrepresented a lay friend to be a medical intern and permitted him to watch as

he conducted a vaginal operation upon a patient was convicted of indecent assault. In *Regina v. D.*, [1972] 5 C.C.C. (2d) 366 (Ont. C.A.), a schoolteacher was convicted of pedophilic assaults on young girls. In *Regina v. A.*, [1976] 26 C.C.C. (2d) 474 (Ont. H. Ct.), a businessman who ran a hairdressing shop was convicted of indecent assault on a female employee; see chapter 10 for more details.

Some of the cases involving charges of "contributing to juvenile delinquency" show more accused with means. In *Rex v. Christakos* (1946), 87 C.C.C. 40 (Man. C.A.), an employer who owned a chain of restaurants was convicted of contributing to juvenile delinquency by "debauching" his female employees. In *Regina v. Cairns* (1960), 128 C.C.C. 188 (B.C.C.A.), an elementary school principal was convicted of contributing to the delinquency of a fifteen-year-old female pupil. In *Regina v. Horsburgh*, [1968] 2 C.C.C. 288 (S.C.C.), a United Church minister was convicted of contributing to the juvenile delinquency of teenage members of his church. On appeal, a new trial was directed because the trial judge had failed to warn of the importance of corroboration.

Records outside the criminal realm occasionally reveal more. *Re G. and College of Dental Surgeons of B.C.* (1908), 9 W.L.R. 650 (B.C.S.C.) refers to a dentist struck from the register of practitioners for "infamous or unprofessional conduct" involving sexual relations with his office staff. The *Saskatoon Daily Star* (27–28 Aug. 1912), mentions that the police were laying charges of indecent assault against a businessman named John Harper, and an architect named Neil MacKinnon, but no outcome was reported. In *Latimer v. College of Physicians and Surgeons* (1931), 55 C.C.C. 132 (B.C.C.A.), a physician was erased from the register of the college for administering narcotics to a female patient in a successful attempt at seduction. *Re Peraya and College of Dental Surgeons for B.C.*, [1970] 1 C.C.C. 73 (B.C.S.C.) refers to a dentist found to have committed infamous and unethical acts against female patients. *Kerster v. College of Physicians and Surgeons of Sask.*, [1970] 72 W.W.R. 321 (Sask. Q.B.) involved a successful appeal from a doctor who had been found guilty of indecent advances against female patients; his "long and high standing in the profession" was noted when the court overturned the college's disciplinary decision.

The court records relating to sexual assaults upon male victims contain more cases involving accused men of means. See, for example, the indecent assault case of Rex v. Lionel Beaupré, (13 Oct. 1916) Archives nationales du Québec, Cote: TP12, S1, SS1, SSS1 Contenant 1960-01-357/602 Enquête # 17, Dossier judiciaire: 1169, Cour des Sessions de la Paix, District de Québec, Cité de Québec, which involved an accused described by the young male complainants as a "Doctor Beaupré," a "rich" man. He was acquitted on summary process. *Rex v. Elliott* (1928), 49 C.C.C. 302 (Ont. C.A.) involved a superintendent of a Children's Aid Shelter in Oshawa, charged with a sexual offence upon one of the young male inmates. The conviction was quashed on appeal, in part due to the "good reputation of the accused." In *Rex v. S.*, [1946] 2 C.R. 191 (Man. C.A.), a man convicted of contributing to juvenile delinquency by "corrupting boys" was described as "a professional man with a good record as a naval medical officer in the late war." *Regina v. Neil* (1957), 119 C.C.C. 1 (S.C.C.) involved a high school teacher charged with gross indecency with teenage boys; his sentence as a criminal sexual psychopath was set aside on appeal. *Regina v. Johnston*, [1965] 3 C.C.C. 42 (Man. C.A.) involved a schoolteacher convicted of sexual offences upon young male students. *Regina v. F.*, [1969] 2 C.C.C. 4 (Ont. H. Ct.) involved a public school teacher convicted of contributing to the juvenile delinquency of his four-teen-year-old pupil by homosexual acts. Reversing the conviction and directing an acquittal, the appellate court made reference to "the unusually high character and reputation" of the accused.

29 See, for example, the evidence suggesting bribery in the case of Fiola in chapter 2.

30 Of the thirty-five medical students in Kissel's class, fifteen were from Chicago, De-troit, Hartford, Connecticut, New York City, and Cicero, Illinois. Two came from the British West Indies, two from India, and one from the Philippines. The enrollment of American students would increase further during the Depression of the 1930s, when financial pressures peaked, and medical school administrators decided to register American students at double the fees, a move that barely saved the school from closure. In comparison, the 1926 arts, science, engineering, and law students came primarily from Nova Scotia, New Brunswick, and P.E.I.; N. Tait McPhedran, *Canadian Medical Schools: Two Centuries of Medical History 1822 to 1922* (Calgary: Harvest House, 1993) at 17 and 221. Waite, *Dalhousie University*, above note 1, notes at 23 that the State Medical Board of New York gave recognition to Dalhousie Medical School degrees.

31 Strange, *Toronto's Girl Problem*, above note 7, notes at 156–67 and 167–79 that racism motivated the police force, who gave keen attention to the "sexual depredations of Asian, black, and Jewish men" and that "widely held assumptions about sexually designing Jews" could outweigh prevailing gender-biased suspicions against female complainants.

32 On the use of the term "antisemitism" rather than "anti-Semitism," see Lynne Pearlman, "Through Jewish Lesbian Eyes: Rethinking Clara Brett Martin" (1992) 5 *Canadian Journal of Women and the Law* 317 at 319. On antisemitism in Canada, see Louis Rosenberg, *Canadian Jews: A Social and Economic Study of Jews in Canada in the 1930s* (Montréal: McGill-Queen's University Press, 1993); Ira Robinson & Mervin Butovsky, eds., *Renewing Our Days: Montéal Jews in the Twentieth Century* (Montréal: Véhicule Press, 1995); Irving Abella & Harold Troper, *None Is Too Many: Canada and the Jews of Europe 1933–1948* (Toronto: Lester Publishing, 1983); David Rome, *The Immigration Story I, The Jewish Times* (Montréal: National Archives Canadian Jewish Congress, 1986); Alan Davies, ed., *Antisemitism in Canada: History and Interpretation* (Waterloo, ON: Wilfrid Laurier University Press, 1992) at 67–91; Esther Delisle, *The Traitor and the Jew* (Montéal: Robert Davies Publishing, 1993); Mordecai Richler, *Belling the Cat: Essays, Reports and Opinions* (Toronto: Alfred A. Knopf, 1998) at 32.

33 On Dalhousie Medical School's continuing admission of Jewish students, see Sheva Medjuck, *Jews of Atlantic Canada* (St. John's: Breakwater Press, 1986) at 41. Many of the American students who graduated in Henry Kissel and Irving Marks's class were Jewish. The Order of Proceedings at Dalhousie's 62d Convocation, 11 May 1926, listed American-born students named Samuel Berkowitz, Louis Dworkin, Jacob Joseph Goldenberg, Edwin John Mittleman, Ralph Jack Rosenthal, and Harry

Maurice Levin. Although names are not fully reliable in discerning Jewish identity, it would appear that adding Kissel and Marks to this list, there were at least eight Jewish-Americans in the group. During the interwar years, quotas on Jewish students were in place at major North American medical schools and universities, such as Columbia, Harvard, Yale, and Cornell, Manitoba, Queen's, McGill, and Montréal. In 1926, McGill adopted a policy to reject all "Hebrew" applicants from outside the province of Québec. By 1928, the arts faculty began to require higher high school matriculation grades for Jewish applicants than for Christians; Jewish enrollment came down by half in ten years. The McGill medical school then adopted a 10 percent ceiling on the Jewish candidates who had met the higher matriculation requirements. In the summer of 1934, a dozen medical interns at the francophone l'Hôpital Notre-Dame, an institution affiliated with the University of Montéal, called a general strike in response to the admission of a Jew. The strike spread to other hospitals, forcing the Jewish intern to resign after three days. The extent of quotas at the University of Toronto remains in dispute. See Pierre Anctil, "Interlude of Hostility: Judeo-Christian Relations in Québec in the Interwar Period, 1919–39" in Alan Davies, ed., *Antisemitism in Canada: History and Interpretation* (Waterloo, ON: Wilfrid Laurier University Press, 1992) 135 at 140–49; W.P.J. Millar, "We wanted our children should have it better: Jewish Medical Students at the University of Toronto 1910–51" (2000) *Journal of the Canadian Historical Association* 109 at 110–13 and 124; R.D. Gidney & W.P.J. Millar, "Medical Students at the University of Toronto 1910–1940: A Profile" (1996) 13 *Canadian Bulletin of Medical History* 29; Charles Levi, "The Jewish Quota in the Faculty of Medicine, University of Toronto: Generational Memory Sustained by Documentation" (Spring 2003) 15 *Historical Studies in Education* 130 at 131–38. On the use of "personal interviews" and admissions tests to screen out Jews, Italians, Catholics, and working-class applicants in the United States, see Charlotte G. Borst, "Choosing the Student Body: Masculinity, Culture, and the Crisis of Medical School Admissions, 1920–1950" (Summer 2002) 42 *History of Education Quarterly* 181. On the pervasiveness of antisemitism in Canadian universities generally, see David Zimmerman, "'Narrow-Minded People': Canadian Universities and the Academic Refugee Crises, 1933–1941" (June 2007) 82 *Canadian Historical Review* 291.

34 By 1931, more than 80 percent of all Canada's Jews were living in Montréal, Toronto, and Winnipeg. The Halifax Jewish population grew slowly, reaching 593 or .6 percent of the population by 1921. In 1894, the Halifax community was large enough to establish the small Starr Street Synagogue, used until 1917. In 1920, the Robie Street Synagogue replaced it. Jews in smaller communities like Halifax were more likely to integrate into the wider society with respect to politics, economics, friendship networks, and intermarriage. See Canada, Dominion Bureau of Statistics, *Sixth Census of Canada, 1921* (Ottawa: 1921) Bulletin II at 2, Bulletin XII at 2, 3, and 10; Abella & Troper, *None Is Too Many*, above note 32 at xi; Sheva Medjuck, "Jewish Survival in Small Communities in Canada" in Robert J. Brym et al., *The Jews in Canada* (Toronto: Oxford University Press, 1993) at 363–78; Medjuck, *Jews of Atlantic Canada*, above note 33 at 6 and 32.

35   Toronto rabbis often protested such press coverage in the early 20th century; Stephen A. Speisman, *The Jews of Toronto: A History to 1937* (Toronto: McClelland and Stewart, 1979) at 119.

36   Although the handwritten entries are difficult to make out, it appears that Joseph Arron, president of Brager's Ltd., a house-furnishing business, who resided at 323 South St., put up $500. Charles Zwerling, who operated a clothing business at 141½ Gottingen and resided at 274 Gottingen, put up $400. Morris B. Fineberg, who operated a grocery at 184 Quinpool Road in the West End Fish and Meat Market and resided at 181 Quinpool Road, put up $400. Isaac Tarshis, a tobacconist who also ran a stationery business on 537 Barrington, and resided at 263 Brunswick, put up $400, and a fifth individual (illegible) put up $400. Why the total amounted to $2100 when bail had been set at $2000 is unclear. See *McAlpine's Halifax City Directory 1925* (Halifax: Royal Print & Litho, 1925) at 111, 205, and 458; *Halifax City Directory 1924* at 464; *Halifax City Directory 1927* at 139; *Halifax City Directory 1930* at 41. I am indebted to Chief Justice Constance Glube of the Nova Scotia Court of Appeal, for confirming that Arron, Zwerling, and Fineberg were Jewish, and that Tarshis probably was as well, and for information confirming that all would have been members of the Robie Street Synagogue. Although Kissel had identified himself as a Reform Hebrew, the only synagogue available to him would have been the Robie Street Synagogue, which served all members of the Jewish community in this era, regardless of their religious perspectives.

37   The probability that Ethel Machan was not Jewish is underscored by the barriers to employment of Jewish women as salesclerks in Canadian department stores in this era.

38   On the fragility of the Jewish community in the Maritime region, and the necessity of maintaining a "good image" with Gentiles, see Alison Kahn, *Listen while I Tell You: A Story of the Jews of St. John's, Newfoundland* (St. John's: Memorial University of Newfoundland, 1987) at 173. In 1912, leading Toronto Jewish businessmen had supported the appeal of two Jewish brothers charged with procuring an abortion for a young woman, for fear that a conviction would become a "stain on their community's reputation." In 1915, two Jewish merchants were convicted of forgery, in a case where the Crown attorney refused to accept sureties from well-to-do Jewish citizens, stating in open court that he "would not accept the bond of any Jew in town in this matter." See Strange, *Toronto's Girl Problem*, above note 7 at 167–69; Archives of Ontario, Attorney-General's Department, RG4-32 (1915) f.1699; Lita-Rose Betcherman, "Clara Brett Martin's Anti-Semitism" (1992) 5 *Canadian Journal of Women and the Law* 280 at 295.

39   Mary Phagan, a thirteen-year-old girl, was found murdered in Atlanta, Georgia, in 1913, and a local Jewish factory owner, Leo Frank (who had been raised in Brooklyn, and educated at Cornell University) was wrongly accused of the crime. Months of international publicity attended the spectacular trial and appeals, during which intense antisemitism infected the guilty verdict. After the sentence of death by hanging was commuted, a Ku Klux Klan mob stormed the jail in which Frank was held and lynched him. Witnesses later revealed that another man had been the real

culprit, and Frank was granted a posthumous pardon in 1986. Leonard Dinnerstein, *The Leo Frank Case* (Atlanta: University of Georgia Press, 1987); Albert S. Lindemann, *The Jew Accused* (Cambridge: Cambridge University Press, 1991).

40 "Hearing of Case against Student" *Halifax Morning Chronicle* (25 Sept. 1925) 7. The court chose to hold the inquiry "in camera," with public and press excluded. *An Act respecting the Criminal Law* R.S.C. 1906, c.146, s.645 provided that the court might order the public "excluded from the room or place in which the court is held" during a rape trial, if this was "in the interests of public morals." First enacted in S.C. 1900, c.46, s.550A, the provision applied to a series of sexual offences.

41 Cluney had articled with Foster, Foster, and Mills, and was admitted to the bar in 1887. He was married to Elizabeth Murphy, and was known to be a "quiet" barrister, who was never known "to badger a witness." Famous for his "rich baritone voice" in the choir at Anglican St. Paul's, Cluney developed a reputation on the bench for merciful judging, and "always manifested a keen interest in the real welfare of even the most degraded criminal brought into his court." He died suddenly in 1929. "Magistrate Cluney Dies after Illness of Only Week's Duration" *Halifax Herald* (17 Sept. 1929) 8; "Andrew Cluney Dies Suddenly at Halifax Home" *Halifax Chronicle* (17 Sept. 1929) 1 and 4.

42 Doty was born in Hebron, Nova Scotia, and graduated from Dalhousie University with an LL.B. in 1921. He conducted his private law practice from the McCurdy Building, 183 Hollis, and resided at 75 Jubilee Road. *Halifax City Directory 1925* at 188; Dalhousie Law School Register, as described in correspondence from Anne Watling, Library Services, Nova Scotia Barristers' Society, 17 Dec. 2003.

43 Forsyth, B.A., M.A., D.C.L., LL.D., KC, commenced his public schooling in grade 2 at the Windsor Academy in 1897, graduated in arts from King's College in Windsor, N.S., in 1909, and then did a graduate degree at Harvard in French and German. He took an appointment as Associate Professor of Romance Languages at Trinity College in Durham, North Carolina, now Duke University, and then worked as a banker in Toronto and in Havana, Cuba. In 1915, he took a post as a modern languages professor at King's College in Nova Scotia. That same year, he married his public school sweetheart, Elsie Maie Dimock. While at King's, Forsyth began teaching himself law after classes, and took his Nova Scotia bar examinations in 1918. James M. Davison, KC, his partner in the law firm of Davison and Forsyth, was the Swedish vice consul. Forsyth's multi-faceted practice included everything from collections to divorce law, and some of his most famous cases in the early 1920s involved representing striking miners against Halifax coal and shipyard employers. By 1926, Forsyth's law practice earned him thirty thousand dollars a year. See *Halifax City Directory 1925* at 180, 211, and 522; "Forsyth, Lionel Avard" *The Canadian Encyclopedia*, 2d ed., vol. 2 (Edmonton: Hurtig, 1988) at 818–19; Peter C. Newman, *Flame of Power: Intimate Profiles of Canada's Greatest Businessmen* (Toronto: McClelland and Stewart, 1959) at 131–46.

44 For Douglas Fleet's occupation, see *Halifax City Directory 1927* at 141 and 108. There is no listing for Fleet in 1924 or 1925, but in 1926 he was boarding at 1 Lockman Ave: *Halifax City Directory 1926* at 239.

45 On the latest fashions in undergarments in the 1920s, see n.a., *Canada's Illustrated Heritage: The Crazy Twenties 1920/1930* (Toronto: Natural Science of Canada, 1978) at 86; Collard, *Women's Dress in the 1920s*, above note 11 at 45.

46 In Rex v. Moisan (23 July 1911), Archives nationales du Québec, Cote: TP12, S1, SS1, SSS1 Cont. 1960-01-357/600 Enquête # 13, Dossier judiciaire: 365, Cour des Sessions de la Paix, District de Québec, Cité de Québec, the accused rapist asked the complainant to marry him after the sexual assault. The complainant refused, stating that the accused did not "respect" her. In *Regina v. Bursey* (1957), 118 C.C.C. 219 (Ont. C.A.), the accused rapist suggested that he would meet the complainant "the following night with a view to going together to a moving-picture show." In *Regina v. Wyatt*, [1969] 1 C.C.C. 136 (N.S.C.A.), the complainant testified that she was forced to have sex with the accused in his car on a dirt road, and submitted because "she thought she was in great danger." Afterwards, she testified that she told the accused she had enjoyed the act of intercourse, and held his hand and sang while she drove, because she "felt she was still in danger." The accused gave her his phone number before he left. In *Regina v. Lawrence*, [1974] 16 C.C.C. (2d) 404 (N.S.C.A.), after indecently assaulting a seventeen-year-old girl, the accused asked her for a date. He was later apprehended in the vicinity of the store where she had agreed to meet him. The appellate court used this to justify quashing the conviction, noting that his apprehension where he thought he was meeting her for a date "hardly strikes me as being conduct consistent with a previous unconsented-to act of intercourse." In *Regina v. Muise (2),* [1976] 23 C.C.C. (2d) 422 (N.S.C.A.), after raping a high school student whom he had cajoled into taking a ride home, the accused asked her to have a cigarette and to shake hands with him. She did, testifying she was scared that if she didn't he would come after her in the car. For other examples from sociological research, see Diana E.H. Russell, *The Politics of Rape: The Victim's Perspective* (New York: Stein & Day, 1984).

47 Peiss, *Cheap Amusements*, above note 11, notes at 113 that it was a pattern for working-class dance hall girls to try to exert control over their interactions with men by socializing in pairs.

48 The standard of proof at the preliminary inquiry stage was merely that there be "sufficient evidence" to warrant putting the accused on trial, and few cases were dismissed at this point; *The Criminal Code* R.S.C. 1906, c.146, s.690.

49 Sheila Jeffreys, *The Spinster and Her Enemies: Feminism and Sexuality 1880–1930* (London: Pandora, 1985) at 47, citing British suffragist Christabel Pankhurst.

50 Strange, *Toronto's Girl Problem*, above note 7; Strong-Boag, *The New Day Recalled*, above note 11; Beth Light & Ruth Roach Pierson, eds., *No Easy Road: Women in Canada 1920s to 1960s* (Toronto: New Hogtown Press, 1990); Karen Dubinsky, *Improper Advances: Rape and Heterosexual Conflict in Ontario 1880–1929* (Chicago: University of Chicago Press, 1993); Kathy Peiss & Christina Simmons, *Passion & Power: Sexuality in History* (Philadelphia: Temple University Press, 1989).

51 Dubinsky, *Improper Advances*, above note 50 at 132–33.

52 R.S.C. 1906, c.146, s.298. The definition was the same as in the original *Criminal Code*, S.C. 1892, c.29, s.266(1). Subsection (2) added that "no one under the age of

fourteen years can commit this offence," and subsection (3) that "carnal knowledge is complete upon penetration to any, even the slightest degree, and even without the emission of seed." See also R.S.C. 1927, c.36, s.298. The wording was altered slightly by S.C. 1953–54, c.51, s.135: "A male person commits rape when he has sexual intercourse with a female person who is not his wife, (a) without her consent, or (b) with her consent if the consent (i) is extorted by threats or fear of bodily harm, (ii) is obtained by personating her husband, or (iii) is obtained by false and fraudulent representations as to the nature and quality of the act." R.S.C. 1970, s.143 made no changes.

53 R.S.C. 1985, c.C-46, s.273.1.

54 See, for example, *Rex v. Jones*, [1935] 3 D.L.R. 237 (B.C.C.A.), where the court rejected the rape complainant's testimony that she had "submitted to force and fear," adding: "It is not enough for a woman to say, 'I was afraid of serious bodily harm and therefore consented'; she must prove in evidence that she had dire reason to be afraid, and that she took every reasonable precaution to avoid the outrage." Indeed, it was difficult to tell who was on trial — the accused or the complainant — from the following passage: "Therefore I think she has failed to make out a case calculated to convince a jury of reasonable men of the appellant's guilt and of her own innocence."

55 *Rex v. Jones* (1944), 84 C.C.C. 299 (P.E.I.S.C.) rejected a complainant's testimony that she did not make an outcry when the accused raped her in an outhouse because he told her "to keep quiet" and she was in a "state of fear," noting: "The girl's acquiescence in this request and her continued silence, are consistent with clandestine consent. . . . [A] resisting victim would be expected to make a spontaneous and irrepressible outcry." See also *Rex v. Lovering* (1948), 92 C.C.C. 65 (Ont. C.A.), in which the complainant "did not sound the motor horn or make any outcry" when the accused had sexual intercourse with her in a car in the country. The court found nothing to indicate "lack of consent" despite evidence that she told the accused she "was scared and didn't want to [have sex] as she was afraid of getting into trouble," that she told him "she wanted to go home" and spoke of "poisoning herself," and that she began "snivelling" during the sexual act. In *Descoteau v. The Queen* (1952), 104 C.C.C. 299 (Que. C.A.), the appellate court quashed a conviction for rape upon a thirteen-year-old girl, because "she made no outcry" and was "not threatened"; a verdict of indecent assault was substituted instead. In *Regina v. Jesseau & Breen* (1961), 129 C.C.C. 289 (B.C.C.A.), the trial judge acquitted on charges of rape on the basis of consent, despite evidence that the two accused had threatened the complainant with knives and lighted cigarettes, tore off her clothing, and that she had run screaming and naked out into the street on a winter morning at 4 a.m., where she was found by a motorist. The appellate court belatedly concluded that this evidence might constitute corroboration of lack of consent and ordered a new trial. In *Regina v. Aubichon*, [1965] 1 C.C.C. 215 (Sask. C.A.), there were physical injuries sufficiently severe that a physician ordered X-rays to ensure there was no skull fracture, and an admission from the accused that he "roughed her up a bit" when she objected. The trial judge depicted this as "the usual love-making" and held that the complainant's injuries

and bruises were not capable of constituting corroboration of non-consent. The appellate court overturned the acquittal and ordered a new trial, concluding that the trial judge's comments regarding "aroused passion" and the "usual love-making" were without foundation. In *Regina v. Plummer & Brown* (1975), 31 C.R.N.S. 220 (Ont. C.A.), Plummer asked a fourteen-year-old girl to come to his apartment, and when she got there told her he wanted to have sex and she could "take it the easy way or the hard." When he told her he would "beat the ass off" her, she submitted to sexual intercourse. Brown arrived after Plummer had raped the girl, and saw her in the bedroom crying, naked except for a jacket. He entered and had intercourse without speaking to her or threatening her. The complainant testified she was in a state of fear because of the earlier threats and made no resistance to Brown's advances, except for crying. The appellate court upheld Plummer's conviction but quashed Brown's, holding that the judge had failed to charge the jury that if the Crown had failed to prove Brown "could not have honestly believed her participation was voluntary," he must be acquitted.

56 There was no conviction in *Rex v. Moisan* (23 July 1911), Archives nationales du Québec, Cote: TP12, S1, SS1, SSS1 Cont. 1960-01-357/600 Enquête #13, Dossier judiciaire: 365, Cour des Sessions de la Paix, District de Québec, Cité de Québec, despite medical evidence of marks of violence including bruising and an abnormally red, torn hymen. *Rex v. Landry* (1935), 64 C.C.C. 104 (N.B.C.A.) insisted on "some degree of physical force." *Rex v. Arnold* (1947), 87 C.C.C. 236 (Ont. C.A.) distinguished "threats" from "inducements," noting that if consent was obtained as a "result of inducements," there was no rape. In *Regina v. Bursey* (1957), 118 C.C.C. 219 (Ont. C.A.), an accused man forced a female ballet instructor to have sex in his car on a dark side road, telling her that she might "never get home" unless she did what he wanted, and leading her to fear that he would "attack" her and then "just leave [her] in the ditch" unless she obeyed. She kept asking him to stop, told him it was hurting her, hit him on the cheek with her hand, and cried. The court concluded that "her nervous state and her fright were occasioned to a great extent, if not wholly, by what might happen to her after the [accused] had intercourse with her," and this was irrelevant to the issue of consent. The court added that it was true that the "complainant testified that the [accused] said she might never get home unless she did what he wanted, but one must know the tone and inflection of voice with which those words were spoken to be certain that they were in the nature of a threat of bodily harm and that the use by him of those words extorted her consent." Lacking evidence of "any struggle resulting in the tearing of any of the complainant's clothing" or "any bruise or bodily injury," the "proper view of the evidence is that the complainant consented to the act of intercourse." In *Regina v. Craig*, [1975] 11 N.B.R. (2d) 646 (N.B.C.A.), an accused was convicted of rape upon the testimony of a fourteen-year-old girl who said he dragged her off the street into his car, threatened to kill her, compelled her to have oral sex, and then forced her to commit sexual intercourse and "further indecent acts." There was medical evidence of a vaginal tear and blood. When the accused ejaculated, she vomited. The appellate court quashed the convic-

tion, on the basis that the judge had "failed adequately to instruct the jury that the burden of proving lack of consent was on the Crown."

57 In *Rex v. Mudge* (1929), 52 C.C.C. 402 (Sask. C.A.), the appellate court quashed a rape conviction despite evidence of torn clothes and bruising, noting that the trial judge failed to "take proper account of the possibility that notwithstanding any resistance made by her at first, as evidenced by those matters, she may have ultimately yielded to the prisoner's advances to the extent of giving a real consent." See also *Rex v. Lastiwka* (1945), 61 B.C.R. 450 (B.C.C.A.), in which the court discusses how "evidence of resistance" such as torn clothing and bruises might be "followed by submission held to amount to a real consent." In *Regina v. Harrison* (1956), 115 C.C.C. 347 (Ont. C.A.), the court explicitly accepted as a fair "generalization" the notion that "a woman in the earlier stages will resist a man's attempts to have connection with her" and that "torn clothing" and "bruises" did not alter that inference, but added that on occasion "violence to the person of a complainant and torn clothing and bruises" could be corroborative of lack of consent. In *Regina v. Rivera*, [1975] 22 C.C.C. (2d) 105 (B.C.C.A.), the accused broke into the complainant's ground floor apartment, threw his coat over her head, fell on top of her, and had sexual intercourse with her twice. She testified that she struggled for five minutes, and then stopped, hoping he would get it over with and leave. The accused was convicted of break and enter and acquitted of rape at trial. On appeal, the court stated: "The jury may have come to the conclusion that the accused entered the suite through a window with the intent of raping the complainant, but that she, having a healthy liking for 'sex,' lost her fear of him under the influence of his reasonably gentle caresses and was a consenting party." The court ordered a new trial on the rape acquittal due to errors in the jury charge relating to corroboration.

58 *Rex v. Cullen* (1948), 93 C.C.C. 1 (Ont. C.A.); (1949), 94 C.C.C. 337 (S.C.C.). The trial judge acquitted on this evidence, adding: "The mere fact the girl puts up some resistance it seems to me doesn't necessarily indicate that she has not consented." The appellate courts took no issue with this definition of consent, but ordered a new trial because consent was not an element of the crime with which the accused was charged: assault with attempt to commit rape and indecent assault.

59 See, for example, *Rex v. Dubuyk* (1920), 35 C.C.C. 32 (Sask. C.A.), in which the court quashed a conviction at trial, noting: "these people are foreigners, who possibly have not been accustomed to look upon affairs of this kind in the same light as people of greater refinement would look upon them." See also Note "Forcible and Statutory Rape: An Exploration of the Operation and Objectives of the Consent Standard" (1952) 62 *Yale Law Journal* at 55–57, adding: "Many threats other than direct bodily harm, such as loss of a job or suitor, may coerce a girl into submission; and though she may consider herself opposed to the act, the law does not treat these situations as rape." Canadian criminal law texts that made reference to the factors that influenced decisions on issues of consent include Alan Burnside, *Harvey Tremeear's Annotated Criminal Code of Canada*, 5th ed. (Toronto: Carswell, 1944) at 338–40; A.E. Popple, *Crankshaw's Criminal Code of Canada*, 7th ed. (Toronto: Carswell, 1959) at 186; Hon. William Renwick Riddell et al., eds., *An Abridgment of Criminal Cases*

(Toronto: Burroughs, 1938) at 397–401; J.W. Cecil Turner, *Russell on Crime*, 10th ed. (London: Stevens & Sons, 1950) at 806–11.

60 "Supreme Court Chambers" *Halifax Evening Echo* (25 Sept. 1925) 2; "Criminal Trials" *Halifax Evening Echo* (5 Oct. 1925) 2; "Supreme Court Criminal Trials Open at Halifax" *Halifax Evening Echo* (6 Oct. 1925) 1.

61 The grand jury system was introduced into Canada (with the exception of the provinces of Saskatchewan and Alberta) as each province introduced English law. Proceedings were held *in camera,* and the prosecutor called witnesses for the Crown, who were sworn by the foreman of the jury. If a majority of the grand jurors decided that there was "sufficient and properly received evidence" to send the case to trial before a petit jury, a "true bill" was issued. If the majority was in favour of discharging the accused, the foreman endorsed the words "no bill" on the indictment. See Roger Salhany, *Canadian Criminal Procedure,* 2d ed. (Agincourt, ON: Canada Law Book, 1972) at 96–102; P. Michael Bolton, "Criminal Procedure" (Vancouver: Unitrend Industries, 1970) at 40–44; *Criminal Code,* R.S.C. 1906, c.146, ss.874–47 and 921.

62 The *Halifax Grand Jury Book,* which recorded charges, witnesses, and outcomes, reveals that the grand jury reported a "no bill" only three times in the session of October 1925 (on the charge of rape in Kissel's case, in one carnal knowledge case, and in one perjury case), and twice in the spring session of 1926 (in one carnal knowledge case, and one rape case). Correspondence from John Macleod, Nova Scotia Archives and Records Management, 7 October 2003. The witnesses who appeared before the grand jury in Kissel's case were Ethel Machan, Blanche Machan, Marjory Hubley, and Irving Marks.

63 "Grand Jury Reports on Gammon Case" *Halifax Evening Echo* (8 Oct. 1925) 1.

64 Nationwide data compiled by Statistics Canada in 1930 show rape convictions running at 34 percent, compared with robbery at 75 percent, assault at 75 percent, theft at 85 percent, and burglary at 91 percent. Convictions on charges of murder (including offenders detained for insanity) registered 44 percent (Canada, Dominion Bureau of Statistics, *Annual Report of Statistics of Criminal and Other Offences,* Ottawa, 1930). On the low conviction rates for rape in nineteenth-century Canada, see Constance Backhouse, *Petticoats and Prejudice: Women and Law in Nineteenth-Century Canada* (Toronto: Women's Press, 1991) at 99–100. Carolyn Strange, "Patriarchy Modified: The Criminal Prosecution of Rape in York County, 1880–1930" in Jim Phillips et al., *Essays in the History of Criminal Law: Crime and Criminal Justice,* vol. 5 (Toronto: The Osgoode Society, 1994) 207 at 215 found a rate of conviction averaging 20 percent. Jim Phillips concludes in the same volume that 28 percent of men indicted for rape were convicted in late eighteenth-century Halifax: see Jim Phillips, "Women, Crime, and Criminal Justice in Early Halifax, 1750–1800" at 174. For more discussion of conviction rates, see chapter 10.

65 For more information on the doctrine of "recent complaint," see chapter 7.

66 *Rex v. Steele* (1923), 33 B.C.R. 197 (B.C.C.A.). For a later case, in the midst of the 1960s sexual revolution, see *Regina v. Parish,* [1967] 59 W.W.R. 577 (B.C.C.A.), where the Crown asked the court to find that evidence that the accused was at a "necking party" in which he was observed lying on a hotel bed with a female under fourteen,

could constitute corroboration that he later had sex with her. The majority of the court held that it could not: "Until fairly recent times . . . evidence of love-play occurring over several hours in a bed in a hotel room would have been treated as a situation so shocking [as to raise] firm conclusions of ultimate coition. But times and view do change. . . . [Mo]dern youth considers necking as a common social experience which can be indulged without fear or expectation . . . of ultimate intercourse." Here, while the judges gave legal recognition to freer sexual mores, the result did not expand women's sexual autonomy, but led to the acquittal of a man charged with sexual intercourse with a female under fourteen. A further appeal resulted in the direction of a new trial: [1968] 64 W.W.R. 310 (S.C.C.). See also *Regina v. Wright*, [1971] 4 C.C.C. (2d) 220 (Ont. C.A.), in which the trial judge noted that the complainant and the accused along with another couple were out for a "protracted evening drive in an automobile," that they parked "in a secluded place" and exchanged "intimate caresses" by "mutual consent." "You may also feel that this is too much to expect of a lusty young buck, as the accused obviously is" said the trial judge in his charge to the jury. The jury acquitted of rape, but convicted of the lesser offence of indecent assault. Even this less serious conviction was set aside on appeal.

67 Order of Proceedings at the 62d Spring Convocation of Dalhousie University, 11 May 1926. The academic transcripts for Kissel and Marks remain confidential, but neither won any awards when they graduated; correspondence of Kelly Casey, Dalhousie University Archives, 18 December 2003.

68 Communication from the New York State Education Department, Office of the Professions, 14 February 2003, indicating that Henry Kissel obtained Licence No. 021278, dated 01/27/27. Communication from the College of Physicians and Surgeons of Nova Scotia, 27 January 2003, indicated that Dr. Henry Kissel was never listed on their records.

69 *Halifax City Directory 1929* at 220.

70 *Halifax City Directory 1930* at 201.

71 *Halifax City Directory 1927* at 141 shows Fleet as a boarder with the Hubley family at 71 West Street; on the marriage, see *Halifax City Directory 1930* at 384.

72 In 1926, Forsyth left Halifax to join the Montréal law firm of Montgomery, McMichael, Common, Howard and Ker, where he practised until he became the president of Dominion Steel in 1950. *Halifax City Directory 1925* at 180, 211, and 522; "Forsyth, Lionel Avard," *The Canadian Encyclopedia*, above note 43 at 818–19; Peter C. Newman, *Flame of Power: Intimate Profiles of Canada's Greatest Businessmen*, above note 43 at 131–46.

Chapter 5: Sexual Battery

1 On 28 February 2000, Velma Demerson wrote to me in connection with her public legal campaign to obtain an apology and compensation for her detention in the Mercer. When she learned that I was writing a book on the history of sexual assault law, she agreed to have her story constitute one of the chapters. Details of her experience are drawn from my Interviews with Velma Demerson, Toronto, 26 March, 3 May, and 22 May 2001, supplemented by her autobiography: Velma Demerson, *Incorrigible*

(Waterloo, ON: Wilfrid Laurier University Press, 2004), an earlier unpublished version *The Spirit of Hygeia* (edited version received March 2001), and the many additional documents she shared with me. She generously reviewed the draft chapter on 27 October 2006. The court records for this case no longer exist: correspondence from Jim Lewis, archivist, Justice Portfolio, Ontario Ministry of Culture and Communications, 21 Dec. 1990. A further search of Domestic Files from the Provincial Court (Family Division) was unsuccessful.

2   Interview, 26 March 2001; Demerson, *Incorrigible*, above note 1 at 10–11.

3   Velma Demerson, Serological Report, Public Health Laboratories, Department of Health, Mercer Reformatory Records, 29 June 1939 ["Serological Report"]; Clinical Records, Mercer Reformatory ["Clinical Records"]. On the connection between war and venereal disease, see Jay Cassel, *The Secret Plague: Venereal Disease in Canada 1838–1939* (Toronto: University of Toronto Press, 1987); Ruth Roach Pierson, *"They're Still Women after All": The Second World War and Canadian Womanhood* (Toronto: McClelland & Stewart, 1986), chapters 5 and 6; D.H. Williams, "Canada's National Health and Venereal Disease Control" (June 1943) 34 *Canadian Journal of Public Health* 261; D.H. Williams, "A Six-Point Attack against Venereal Disease" (Summer 1943) 2 *Health* 6; Mary Louise Adams, "In Sickness and in Health: State Formation, Moral Regulation and Early VD Initiatives in Ontario" (Winter 1993–94) 28 *Journal of Canadian Studies* 117.

4   Dr. Edna Guest was the daughter of John and Elizabeth Scott Guest. Her siblings included Professor Walter Scott Guest of the Electrical Engineering Department of the University of Toronto, Ernest A. Guest, Miss Emily Jane Guest (lecturer and writer), Mrs. Earle M. Grose, and Miss Elena Guest (librarian). "Guest, Edna Mary" *Canadian Who's Who 1949–51* (Toronto: Trans-Canada Press, 1951) at 415; *Who's Who in Canada 1951–52* at 134; *Toronto Star* (2 Jan. 1935) 22; Women's College Hospital Archives, Chronology of Edna Guest's Achievements; Shabir Bhimji & Rose Sheinin, "Dr. Edna Mary Guest: She promoted women's issues before it was fashionable" (15 Nov. 1989) 141 *Canadian Medical Association Journal* 1093–94; Leah Leneman, *In the Service of Life: The Story of Elsie Inglis and the Scottish Women's Hospitals* (Edinburgh: Mercat, 1994) at 143 and 209; Eileen Crofton, *The Women of Royaumont: A Scottish Women's Hospital on the Western Front* (East Lincoln: Tuckwell Press, 1997) at 176–77, 274–76, and 281; "King Honors Worthy Women Serving Canadian People" *Toronto Mail* (1 Jan. 1935).

5   John Henderson & Alfred H. Allen, eds., *Trails to Success* (Toronto: Macmillan, 1931) at 82–83; Edna Guest, "Maude Abbott, 1869–1940: Her Contribution to Cardiology" (Feb. 1950) 5 *Journal of the American Medical Women's Association* 74–75. Dr. Guest's "Medical Women in Canada" (1946) 1 *Journal of American Medical Women's Association* 254–55, lamented that the services of women physicians had been rejected by the Armed Forces because "the time was not yet when it was felt the services of women physicians could be utilized," adding: "We were not sure that we entirely agreed." In the same article, however, she dismissed allegations of discrimination: "In Canada the woman physician has no frustration. All that is required of her is that she do her work well — as well as the best men in the profession. Fortunately, this is the

standard that has been set for her, and she must measure up if she is to be worthy of the degree that has been conferred upon her, and worthy of her predecessors, those earnest women who have continued to break trails since Dr. Emily Stowe led the way after her graduation in 1868. Perhaps our best allies in accomplishing this high ideal is [*sic*] the faith and encouragement given to us by the Canadian men in our profession. One feels they are willing to encourage women physicians to go to the top, and to give them their place." Dr. Guest was an admirer and good friend of Dr. Augusta Stowe-Gullen, Emily Stowe's daughter. Both Stowes were famous Canadian suffragists; Emily was the first woman to practise as a physician in Canada, and Augusta was the first woman to graduate as a medical doctor from a Canadian university. See Scrapbook, University of Toronto Library and Thomas Fisher Archives, "Dr. Edna Guest Honored by Doctors," "Dr. Edna Guest, Dr. Stowe Gullen, Mrs. A. Primrose and Lady Falconer received the many guests" *Toronto Star* (5 June 1930); "Council of Women Officially Opens New Health Exhibit" *Toronto Globe* (27 Aug. 1928); "Will Organize U. of T. Alumnae" *Toronto Globe* (25 Oct. 1929); "Arranged Exhibit" *Toronto Globe* (24 Aug. 1928); "Plans Health Day" *Toronto Globe* (17 Aug. 1929); "Ontario News: Address of Dr. Edna Guest on Presentation of Portrait of Dr. Augusta Stowe Gullen" (March 1930) 22 *Canadian Medical Association Journal* 449–50.

6   The Hon. Frank Egerton Hodgins, "Report on Venereal Diseases" *Royal Commission on the Care and Control of the Mentally Defective and Feeble-Minded in Ontario* (Toronto: Wilgress, 1919) at 19–20.

7   See, for example, the novel written by Ethel Chapman, *With Flame of Freedom* (Toronto: Thomas Allen, 1938) at 107–8, where a young woman cautions a young male doctor who treats "girls at the Refuge" that "he had a brilliant career" ahead of him, and could not "afford to do anything that might be misunderstood." He was told that he should let "some other doctor do the work" for the "girls at the Refuge" because he had his "future to think of" and knew "what gossips can do." Chapman, whose novel was acclaimed as "one of the Canadian books of the season," was familiar with Dr. Guest's career. She co-authored with Dr. Edna Guest "An Experiment in Applied Nutrition for Canadian Communities" prepared in 1943 as a Summary Report of the Swift Fellowship.

8   The term "eugenics" was coined in 1881 by the British naturalist and mathematician Francis Galton; for details on the spread of this "scientific movement," see Daniel Kevles, *In the Name of Eugenics: Genetics and the Uses of Human Heredity* (Berkeley: University of California Press, 1985); Angus McLaren, *Our Own Master Race: Eugenics in Canada, 1885–1945* (Toronto: McClelland and Stewart, 1990); Kathleen McConnachie, "Science and Ideology: The Mental Hygiene Movement and Eugenics Movements in the Inter-War Years, 1919–1939" (Ph.D. Thesis, OISE, University of Toronto, 1987); Horst Biesold, *Crying Hands: Eugenics and Deaf People in Nazi Germany* (Washington, DC: Gallaudet University Press, 1999) at 2.

9   The National Council of Women, of which Dr. Guest was a prominent member, advocated such sterilization in 1925; McLaren, *Our Master Race*, above note 8 at 94. See also Clarence M. Hincks, "Canada Needs a Vital Mental Hygiene Plan" (Summer 1943) 2 *Health* 9. The *Report of the Royal Commission on Public Welfare, 1930* (Toronto:

Queen's Printer, 1930) recommended at 41 and 45 that sterilization be carried out on those diagnosed as mentally defective or "immoral defectives." *The Sexual Sterilization Act*, S.A. 1928, c.37 authorized the sterilization of mental defectives in Alberta on the recommendation of a Eugenics Board with the consent of the patient or guardian. In 1937, the legislation was amended to remove the consent provision; S.A. 1937, c.47. Gerald E. Thomson, "'Not an Attempt to Coddle Children': Dr. Charles Hegler Gundry and the Mental Hygiene Division of the Vancouver School Board, 1939–1969" in (2002) 14 *Historical Studies in Education* 247–78 indicates at 250–52 that the advocacy of Canadian eugenicists was linked to the enactment of sterilization laws in Alberta and British Columbia, noting that between 1928 and 1971, Alberta sterilized 2822 people, many of them "from minority backgrounds." *An Act Respecting Sexual Sterilization*, S.B.C. 1933, c.59, set up a Eugenics Board consisting of a psychiatrist, a judge, and a social worker to order the sterilization of any inmate of a British Columbia provincial institution who "would be likely to beget or bear children who by reason of inheritance would have a tendency to serious mental disease or mental deficiency." Bill No. 142, titled "An Act concerning Operations for the Prevention of Procreation," was introduced into the Second Session of the Thirteenth Legislature in Ontario on 24 February 1913, but not passed. It would have permitted the Lieutenant-Governor in Council to appoint two surgeons to provincial institutions for the care of the insane, feeble-minded, and epileptic, to examine "such persons as are reported to them by the Superintendent or the physician or surgeon in charge, to be persons by whom procreation would be inadvisable." If it was determined that "procreation by any such person would produce children with an inherited tendency to crime, insanity, feeble-mindedness, idiocy or imbecility," and if there was "no probability that the condition of any such person so examined [would] improve to such an extent as to render procreation . . . advisable," the performance of the operations of vasectomy or oophorectomy was directed. On comparable eugenics movements in the United States and England, see Daniel J. Kevles, *In the Name of Eugenics* (New York: Alfred A. Knopf, 1985).

10 "Healthy Immigrants Urged in Resolution of Hygiene Council" *Toronto Globe* (30 May 1928). On Dr. Guest's social and professional connections with the champions of social hygiene and eugenics, see the Health League of Canada, Woodwards Library, University of British Columbia, WD1-X02A, Health 4–14, 1936–46, Report of the Toronto Social Hygiene Club at 21–22, which notes that "among the many delightful functions held by the Club" in 1935 was a "reception, musical and tea in honor of Lady Gooderham and Dr. Edna Guest OBE, at the home of Mr. Justice Riddell." William Renwick Riddell, of the Supreme Court of Ontario, was one of the leaders of the eugenics movement in Canada. Dr. Guest gave public lectures regularly: "Diseases Affecting Young Women," *Health League Activities*, April 1940 (Toronto) at 14–16; Toronto Health League, *Speakers' Service* (1935); "Dr. Guest Commended Highly Work of Social Hygiene Council" *Toronto Globe* (27 March 1925); Bhimji & Sheinin, "Dr. Edna Mary Guest," above note 4.

11 Women's College Hospital Archives, Chronology of Edna Guest's Achievements; "Edna Mary Guest" obituary, unmarked clipping. The *Report of the Royal Commission*

on Public Welfare, 1930 (Toronto: Queen's Printer, 1930) noted at 82 that a percentage of the persons committed to the Mercer were "mentally defective." Christabelle Sethna, "The Cold War and the Sexual Chill" (Winter 1998) 17 *Canadian Woman Studies* 57 notes that "the female juvenile delinquent came to be seen as synonymous with the amateur prostitute who infected soldiers and civilians thereby compromising allied war aims at home and abroad."

12 Henderson & Allen, eds., *Trails to Success*, above note 5 at 82–83; Guest, "Maude Abbott, 1869–1940," above note 5 at 74–75; Guest, "Medical Women in Canada," above note 5 at 254–55.

13 Dr. Guest seems to have been typical of women physicians of her generation and earlier. See, for example, the description of the insensitivity demonstrated towards an unwed pregnant, working-class patient by Dr. Emily Stowe and Augusta Stowe, in Constance Backhouse, *Petticoats and Prejudice: Women and Law in Nineteenth-Century Canada* (Toronto: The Osgoode Society and Women's Press, 1991) at 140–66. Dianne Dodd, "Helen MacMurchy, MD: Gender and Professional Conflict in the Medical Inspection of Toronto Schools, 1910–1911" (Autumn 2001) 93 *Ontario History* 127, considers the contradictions that beset Dr. MacMurchy, a physician and social reformer of the same era, who espoused legal and social control of the "feeble-minded" from the ideology of maternal feminism.

14 Scrapbook, University of Toronto Library and Thomas Fisher Archives, "Glands Link with Crimes: Disorders Associated with Criminal Acts by Mercer Physician" (undated clipping, circa March 1928). At a 1931 Ontario Department of Health conference for clinicians working in venereal disease clinics, Dr. Guest gave an address titled "Treatment of Gonorrhoea in Female." Seventh Annual Report of the Department of Health, Sessional Paper No. 14 (Toronto: Herbert H. Ball, 1932) at 33–34.

15 A ward for syphilis had been set aside in the Mercer as early as 1881. Although diagnosis techniques were then rudimentary and inaccurate, the reformatory physicians took to their task with abandon. Dr. King, the first physician assigned to the Mercer, administered mercurial salves and pills that frequently failed to staunch the syphilis, but destroyed tissue in the mouth, stomach, and intestines. During the tenure of Dr. Algae, who took over in 1915, the Wassermann blood test provided a more reliable clinical diagnosis of syphilis, and salvarsan, an organic arsenic, a more specific therapy. However, even when the test results came back negative, the doctor often initiated treatment "just to be safe." "She did not test positive," noted one report, but "we gave her three months of vaginal treatment anyway." In some cases, as many as forty doses of salvarsan were given over a period of a year. The inter-muscular injections were painful and frequently supplemented with mercury or other chemicals applied internally and externally. Those diagnosed as victims of gonorrhea were required to undergo daily douches and weekly applications of silver nitrate and agyrol to the cervix. Some women were treated for both syphilis and gonorrhea despite negative tests for both. Those diagnosed with syphilis, correctly or incorrectly, were not considered cured until three Wassermann tests, each taken three months apart, came back with negative results. This extended the terms of imprisonment for many of the women involved. See Carolyn Strange, "The

Velvet Glove: Maternalistic Reform at the Andrew Mercer Ontario Reformatory for Females 1874–1927" (M.A. Thesis, University of Ottawa, 1983) at 87–88 and 119–22; Wendy Elizabeth Ruemper, "Formal and Informal Social Control of Incarcerated Women in Ontario: 1857–1931" (Ph.D. Thesis, University of Toronto, 1994) at 188 and 223; Joan Sangster, "Incarcerating 'Bad Girls': The Regulation of Sexuality through the Female Refuges Act in Ontario, 1920–1945" (1996) 7 *Journal of the History of Sexuality* 239 at 262–63.

16 In "Velvet Glove," *ibid.*, Strange reviewed the medical files from 1918 and 1927, and concluded at 122–25:

> Dr. Guest prided herself on her ability to diagnose and treat venereal disease in women. She gave inmates doses of medicine far in excess of standards revised by the Board of Health in 1920. Officials noted that it was often impossible to obtain a negative Wasserman test and that, as long as inmates had received six salvarsan and six mercury injections, they should not be held beyond their terms since they were not infectious after the primary stage of syphilis. Despite the acknowledged weaknesses and potential dangers of venereal detection and treatment, Guest proceeded undaunted. She gave one inmate twenty-six injections of mercury, twenty-two of salvarsan, and ten of bismuth. For Ruth R., she prescribed applications of fifty percent silver nitrate, ten times the strength recommended by the Board, because Ruth was in 'such a filthy condition.' (See 37th Annual Report of the Provincial Board of Health of Ontario (Toronto: King's Printer, 1919) at 12 which prescribed 'the application of 5% silver nitrate solution to the vaginal walls' for female venereal disease patients.) Guest defended her decisions as courageous responses to a formidable problem. Concerned with upholding her reputation, she tried to remove all manifestations of impurity even when this meant risking inmates' health. Between 1918 and 1927, more than fifty inmates remained in the Reformatory longer than two years because their Wassermann tests were positive. Only Dr. Guest could determine whether there was an improvement and she rendered the final verdict in all petitions for parole, basing her decision on the inmate's physical condition. Guest thus proceeded unmindful of the Board of Health's recommendation that inmates not be detained simply on account of their Wassermann test results.

Despite her efforts, Dr. Guest sometimes despaired of results. On 18 October 1926, she wrote to Dr. Hunt at Spadina House: "[M]ine is a hopeless task at the Mercer, slogging to get these women cured of disease, only to have them go home and in a week be as bad as when they came in six months to two years previously." Archives of Ontario RG 62 Series C-2-C, Box 467a, Provincial Board Health Division Preventable Diseases Special Clinical Reports 1921–1926. For the comment on the "waging of war," see Ruemper, "Formal and Informal Social Control," above note 15 at 224.

17 Velma Demerson's birth name was Athena Mary Demerson. Alexander Demerson had anglicized his Greek name, Themopoulos, to Demerson shortly after immigrating. He ran the Paradise restaurant, on Charlotte Street across from King's Square,

with a staff of twelve waitresses. Alice Demerson was born near Manchester and immigrated to Canada with her family. She left the family farm on the Saint John River for domestic work in Saint John, and met Alexander Demerson when she wandered into his ice-cream shop at the age of nineteen. Interview, 2 May 2001; Demerson, *Incorrigible*, above note 1 at 51 and 89; Mercer/Vanier Prison Register 1933–42, E-13, vol. 4.

18 Adultery was the ground for Velma's parents' divorce. Interview, 26 March 2001; Interview, 3 May 2001; Demerson, *Incorrigible*, above note 1 at 19–24, 28, 32, and 48; Mercer/Vanier Prison Register 1933–42, E-13, vol. 4; Mercer Medical Examination Record, 25 May 1939.

19 Interview, 26 March 2001; Interview, 3 May 2001; Demerson, *Incorrigible*, above note 1 at 33.

20 Interview, 3 May 2001; Interview, 22 May 2001.

21 Interview, 3 May 2001.

22 Melanie Randall, "Agency and (In)Subordination: Victimization, Resistance and Sexual Violence in Women's Lives" (Ph.D. Thesis, York University, 1996) at 200; Lori Haskell & Melanie Randall, "Private Violence/Public Fear: Rethinking Women's Safety" (Solicitor General of Canada, March 1994) found that 6.8 percent of sexual assaults were reported to the police. These data were consistent with a national telephone survey (Statistics Canada, 1993) that found 6 percent of sexual assaults reported to the police.

23 Randall, "Agency and (In)Subordination," above note 22, notes at 201–4 that a 1994 survey of Canadian women who did not report sexual assault elicited the following reasons: they thought the police either would not have believed them, or would have done nothing about the problem; they believed their experiences of sexual violence were not worthy of police intervention, they did not think that what had happened to them qualified as socially or legally recognized "crimes"; shame; and fear of being blamed.

24 S.C. 1923, c.38. On the discriminatory legal measures enacted against the Chinese, see Constance Backhouse, *Colour-Coded: A Legal History of Racism in Canada 1900–1950* (Toronto: University of Toronto Press, 1999); Constance Backhouse, "Gretta Wong Grant: Canada's First Chinese-Canadian Female Lawyer (1996) 15 *Windsor Yearbook of Access to Justice* 3–46; Constance Backhouse, "The White Women's Labor Laws: Anti-Chinese Racism in Early Twentieth-Century Canada" (Fall 1996) 14 *Law and History Review* 315–68. On the estimated date of Harry's arrival in Canada, see Demerson, *Incorrigible*, above note 1 at 34.

25 Demerson, *Incorrigible*, above note 1 at 32–37; Interview, 26 March 2001; Interview, 3 May 2001.

26 Demerson, *Incorrigible*, above note 1 at 36–38; Interview, 26 March 2001; Interview, 3 May 2001.

27 On the inapplicability of rape and statutory rape charges in the *Criminal Code*, see R.S.C. 1927, c.36, ss.292, 298. The definition of "procuring" in s.216 required that the accused procure a woman to have unlawful carnal connection with another person, or endeavour to bring a woman to a common bawdy house for the purpose of pros-

titution. Section 212, "seduction under promise of marriage," prohibited seduction and illicit connection with any unmarried female of previously chaste character. Velma had had previous sexual engagements, and given the outcast status that descended over any white woman involved with a Chinese man, the police would have assumed that she was "unchaste." On the interpretation of this phrase, see chapter 3. The *Juvenile Delinquents Act*, R.S.C. 1927, c.108, s.30 was not an option either, since before an adult could be charged with contributing to juvenile delinquency, the child had to be under the age of eighteen years (s.2). It was Velma's supposition that Harry was not charged because her father would have resisted any efforts to prosecute. "The last thing my father would want to do was charge him with seduction, because then everybody would know I went out with a Chinese. It was a disgrace to the girl of the family. My father wouldn't have made trouble for Harry. The whole thing was to ensure that I wouldn't cause any problems for his Greek family." Interview, 4 May 2001.

28 Demerson, *Incorrigible*, above note 1 at 41–48; Interview, 26 March 2001; Interview, 3 May 2001; Warrant of Commitment for a Conviction under the Female Refuges Act, #8129, 10 May 1939.

29 R.S.O. 1937, c.384, s.18.

30 Demerson, *Incorrigible*, above note 1 at 44–61; Interview, 26 March 2001; Interview, 3 May 2001; Warrant of Commitment, 10 May 1939. The *Female Refuges Act*, s.15(4) gave magistrates the authority to commit "incorrigible" women "to an industrial refuge for an indefinite period not exceeding two years." Velma was committed to the Belmont Home for Girls on 10 May, and transferred to the Mercer on 29 June, when the Belmont was closed. See "Girls Cry When Leaving Refuge for Reformatory" *Toronto Daily Star* (19 July 1939) 23.

31 Justice Frank Egerton Hodgins, *Royal Commission on the Care and Control of the Mentally Defective and Feeble-Minded in Ontario* (Toronto: Wilgress, 1919); Sangster, "Incarcerating 'Bad Girls,'" above note 15 at 246.

32 S.O. 1919, c.84, ss.15(2) and (3), 18. The statute expanded upon the earlier S.O. 1893, c.56, which provided for the transfer of women from common gaols to houses of refuge for women convicts only. *The Female Refuges Act*, S.O. 1913, c.79, s.3(1) allowed women between the ages of 15 and 35 years who were committed to an industrial refuge to be detained for an indefinite period of up to five years. The categories of women who could be so imprisoned were spelled out in more detail in the 1919 statute. In addition to the "unmanageable or incorrigible" women under twenty-one, women under the age of thirty-five were also vulnerable. Section 16(1) provided: Any person may bring before a judge any female under the age of thirty-five years who, (a) is found begging or receiving alms or being in any street or public place for the purpose of begging or receiving alms; (b) is an habitual drunkard or by reason of other vices is leading an idle and dissolute life. Section 16(4) stated: If the judge is satisfied on inquiry that it is expedient to deal with such person under this Act instead of committing her to a gaol or reformatory, he may commit such person to an industrial refuge for an indefinite period not exceeding two years. The 1919 reduction in penalty from five to two years apparently followed a coroner's inquest into

the death of an inmate who was trying to escape from a refuge in Toronto by jump-
ing from a window: *Globe and Mail* (12 April 1919); Joan Sangster, "'Race', Gender and
Class in the Operation of Ontario's Female Refuges Act, 1930–1960" in Wendy Chan
& Kiran Mirchandani, *E-Raced Connections: Racialization and Criminalization in Canada*
(Toronto: Broadview Press, 2001). See also R.S.O. 1937, c.384, s.15(1)(2)(3) and (4), 17.

33 Interview, 26 March 2001; Interview, 3 May 2001. S.O. 1942, c.34, s.13 added the right
of appeal: s.15(5). "Any order made under this Act shall be subject to an appeal to
the Court of Appeal." For discussion of a rare example of litigation under this provision, *Re Bowyer* (1930), 66 O.L.R. 378 (Ont. H. Ct.), see Constance Backhouse, "'Pleasing Appearance . . . Only Adds to the Danger': The 1930 Insanity Hearing of Violet
Hypatia Bowyer" (2005) 17 *Canadian Journal of Women and the Law* 1–13.

34 Sangster, "Incarcerating 'Bad Girls,'" above note 15 at 246, 248–52, and 256–58. Sangster reviewed 327 cases from 1920 to 1960, and found that just over 60 percent of all
incarcerations took place during the Depression and war years. See also Joan Sangster, *Regulating Girls and Women: Sexuality, Family and the Law in Ontario, 1920–1960*
(Don Mills, ON: Oxford University Press, 2001). The committal provisions of the Act
were repealed in S.O. 1958, c.28, s.3; see also R.S.O. 1960, c.140. The full statute was
repealed in S.O. 1964, c.323.

35 Joan Sangster, "Defining Sexual Promiscuity: 'Race,' Gender, and Class in the Operation of Ontario's Female Refuges Act, 1930–1960" in Wendy Chan & Kiran Mirchandani, eds., *Crimes of Colour: Racialization and the Criminal Justice System in Canada*
(Toronto: Broadview Press, 2002) at 45.

36 Sangster, "Incarcerating 'Bad Girls,'" above note 15; Sangster, "'Race,' Gender and
Class," above note 35; Carolyn Strange, *Toronto's Girl Problem: The Perils and Pleasures
of the City, 1880–1930* (Toronto: University of Toronto Press, 1995). On the legal and
extra-legal pressures brought to bear on inter-racial couples and the "white women's
labour law," see Backhouse, *Colour-Coded*; James W. St. G. Walker, *"Race," Rights and
the Law in the Supreme Court of Canada* (Waterloo, ON: Wilfrid Laurier University
Press, 1997).

37 For discussion of the legal roots of the Canadian mythology of "racelessness," see
Backhouse, *Colour-Coded*, above note 24 at 12–14.

38 S.O. 1893, c.56, s.1, provided that "no prisoner shall be discharged . . . at the termination of her sentence, if then labouring under any contagious or infectious disease
. . . but she shall be permitted to remain . . . until she recovers . . . and any prisoner
remaining from any such cause . . . shall be under the same discipline or control as
if her sentence were still unexpired." *The Female Refuges Act*, S.O. 1913, c.79, s.9 provided that "no inmate shall be discharged . . . if she has syphilitic or other venereal
disease . . . but she shall remain . . . until a legally qualified medical practitioner
on the staff of the Refuge gives a written certificate that such inmate has fully re-
covered from the disease . . . and any inmate remaining from any such cause in the
Industrial Refuge shall continue to be under its discipline and control." For the provisions in force during Velma Demerson's term, see S.O. 1919, c.84, s.9; R.S.O. 1937,
c.384, ss.8, 9, and 10.

39 S.O. 1918, c.42, s.3(1) provided that "Whenever any person is under arrest or in custody charged with an offence against The Criminal Code of Canada or against any Statute of Ontario or any by-law, regulation or order made under the authority thereof, or has been committed to a gaol, reformatory or other place of detention upon conviction of such offence, and the medical officer of health for the municipality or district believes that such person is, or may be, infected with . . . venereal disease, the medical officer of health may cause such person to undergo such physical examination as may be necessary, or as may be prescribed by the regulations, in order to ascertain whether or not such person is infected with venereal disease." Section 3(2) provided that if the person examined was found to be infected, "the medical officer of health shall give such directions for the treatment of the patient, and if necessary, for his detention and isolation and the prevention of infection from him as may be deemed proper and as may be authorized by the regulations, and he is hereby empowered to do and authorize any act necessary to effect the carrying out of such treatment, detention, isolation and prevention." See also R.S.O. 1937, c.301, s.2; S.O. 1941, c.62; S.O. 1942, c.38, ss.6, 7, and 8.

40 Demerson, *Incorrigible*, above note 1 at 63–64; Interview, 26 March 2001; Interview, 3 May 2001; Interview, 22 May 2001; Serological Reports, 4 July, 11 August 1939; Clinical Records.

41 Naomi Jay & Anna-Barbara Moscicki, "Human Papilloma Virus Infection in Women" in Marlene B. Goldman & Maureen C. Hatch, eds., *Women and Health* (San Diego: Academic Press, 2000) 324 at 326; Peter J. Lynch & Libby Edwards, *Genital Dermatology* (New York: Churchill Livingstone, 1994) at 121. The propensity of genital warts to increase in size during pregnancy and to disappear thereafter was known around the time of Velma's treatment; see Harry Dover, "Condyloma Acuminata or Genital Warts in the Female" (August 1944) 51 *Canadian Medical Association Journal* 132; C.E. van Rooyen & A.J. Rhodes, *Virus Diseases of Man* (New York: Thomas Nelson, 1948) at 150. That it was common for such warts to disappear without medical treatment was also known during this period; see Donald M. Pillsbury et al., *Manual of Dermatology* (Philadelphia: W.B. Saunders, 1943) 342.

42 Clinical Records, 21 Aug. 1939.

43 The medical literature of the time was divided over the connection between genital warts and gonorrhea or syphilis. J.F. Wilson, "Genital Warts" (Jan.–June 1937) 68 *Journal of the Royal Army Medical Corps* at 229 noted that "as with syphilis it has been found that the presence of the warts may be entirely independent of a gonococcal infection." See also Rooyen & Rhodes, *Virus Diseases of Man*, above note 41, who noted at 150 that "many venereologists and others still contend that gonorrhea may cause some of these [genital warts], but it is more likely, however, that the only effect of gonorrhea is that the purulent discharge causes irritation of the wart with consequent increase in size, and perhaps superficial ulceration." The medical files Dr. Guest kept at the Mercer indicate that she disagreed. For example, she noted that "when a girl is apparently cured clinically of Gono, and has had perhaps six or eight negative smears, she will suddenly grow a great crop of Gono warts on labia, or occasionally around the rectum."Archives of Ontario, RG 62 Series C-2-C, Box 467A,

Provincial Board Health Division Preventable Diseases, Special Clinical Reports, 1921–1926, Correspondence from Dr. Guest to Dr. Hunt, 18 Aug. 1926. For the modern conclusion that there is no causative connection, see Tsieh Sun, *Sexually Related Infectious Diseases: Clinical and Laboratory Aspects* (New York: Field, Rich & Associates, 1986) at 129.

44 Jay & Moscicki, "Human Papilloma Virus Infection," above note 41 at 326; Lynch & Edwards, *Genital Dermatology*, above note 41 at 121. On Dr. Guest's suspicion of a causal link to masturbation, see her notation about "gono warts" in 1926: "Were she not in an Institution I would feel convinced that she had been re-infected by intercourse. Knowing that to be impossible here, and that it is quite impossible for girls to be immoral with each other under their strict supervision here, I can only explain this by their having a dormant infection of the glands of the labia, which is lit up by masturbation. . . . I put this down to possible irritation of a low lying infection caused by masturbation." Archives of Ontario, RG 62 Series C-2-C, Box 467A, Provincial Board Health Division Preventable Diseases, Special Clinical Reports, 1921–1926, Correspondence from Dr. Guest to Dr. Hunt, 18 Aug. 1926.

45 Clinical Records, 21 Aug. 1939. On the need for anesthetic during electrocoagulation with the use of scissors or scalpel, see Dover "Condyloma Acuminata," above note 41 at 132–33, who advised: "The small warts can be treated under local anaesthetic, while the very large ones may be done under pentothal intravenously." See also "Venereal Warts" (May–Aug. 1948) *Journal of American Medical Association* 1640, where it was suggested that electrosurgery be used only in the most difficult cases, and then only after the patient had been anesthetized.

46 It was not uncommon for physicians to make clinical diagnoses of venereal disease without positive test results at this time, and such decisions were supported by Regulation No. 6 (1939) of the *Prevention of Venereal Disease Act*, which stated: "every doubtful case of communicable disease shall be classed and dealt with as if it were a case of communicable disease until such is disproved." Treatment of human papilloma virus today would consist of application of various chemicals to cause wart necrosis, to destroy warts by chemical coagulation, or to induce tissue sloughing. Laser vaporization and cyrosurgery (the topical application of liquid nitrogen) are also frequently used. All current treatments potentially cause ulceration, local irritation, and discomfort, but local anesthetic would routinely be administered unless treatment was being applied to very small areas; see Jay & Moscicki, "Human Papilloma Virus," above note 41 at 331.

47 Clinical Records, 28 Aug. 1939–16 Oct. 1939; Demerson, *Incorrigible*, above note 1 at 64–68 and 72. Silver nitrate is a caustic chemical compound used as a general antiseptic. It irritates any tissue with which it comes in contact and causes considerable pain; see Cassel, *The Secret Plague*, above note 3 at 47.

48 Demerson, *Incorrigible*, above note 1 at 68–70; Interview, 26 March 2001.

49 Clinical Records, 28 Aug. 1939–16 Oct. 1939; Demerson, *Spirit of Hygeia*, above note 1 at 122–23. Sulfanilamide was listed as a standard treatment for gonorrhea for the first time in the *Thirteenth Annual Report of the Department of Health, Ontario, 1937* Sessional Paper No. 14, 1938 (Toronto: T.E. Bowman, 1938) at 50, which added: "Dur-

ing the year encouraging reports having been made in the literature in the use of sulfanilamide for the treatment of gonorrhea it was decided to place this drug in five of the [government-funded, public health venereal disease] clinics in order that a thorough clinical trial could be given this newer form of therapy. Although complete results have not as yet been received from all of these clinics, it would appear that for a certain percentage of cases this drug had resulted in cure of the infection without development of complications. In most instances local irrigations were discontinued." Cassel, *The Secret Plague*, above note 3, notes at 68 that Canadians tried sulpha drugs within a year of their introduction (1937) but used them "only experimentally in the treatment of gonorrhea until the very end of the 1930s." Although Velma apparently did not develop any adverse reactions to the sulfanilamide, the medical literature of the time indicated that it "often cause[d] nausea and vomiting," and had a number of major toxic effects including acute haemolytic anaemia, agranulocytosis, peripheral neuritis, toxic hepatitis, exfoliative dermatitis, severe methaemoglobinaemia and sulphaemoglobinaemia; see E.H. Bensley, "The Toxic Effects of Sulfanilamide and Related Compounds" (Jan. 1940) 42 *Canadian Medical Association Journal* 30; Harold Orr, "Sulfanilamide in the Treatment of Gonorrhoea" (Oct. 1937) 34 *Canadian Medical Association Journal* 364. For additional references to serious side effects, see Perrin H. Long, "Sulfanilamide and Its Derivatives" (July 1939) 37 *The American Journal of Nursing* 719. "The Toxicity of Sulphanilamide and Allied Compounds" in (Nov. 1937) 37 *Canadian Medical Association Journal* 493 noted at 494 that at the time of publication, "some twenty deaths [had] been recorded from the use of a pharmaceutical preparation of sulfanilamide." A follow-up editorial in December (1937: 37) indicated that the number of deaths reported in the United States up to 6 November was seventy-one.

50 Clinical Records, 28 Aug. 1939–16 Oct. 1939. Dagenan, a sulfanilamide derivative named for the town in England at which the substance was first prepared (Dagenham, Essex), was first listed as a treatment for gonorrhea in the provincial venereal disease clinics in 1939: *Fifteenth Annual Report of the Department of Health, Ontario, 1939* Sessional Paper No. 14, 1940 (Toronto, T.E. Bowman, 1940) at 104; "Editorial Comments" (June 1939) 40 *Canadian Medical Association Journal* 596. Contemporary medical literature indicated that "toxic manifestations were present in some degree in all patients" who took Dagenan, and that symptoms included haematuria and skin rashes; see D.R. Mitchell et al., "The Treatment of Gonorrhoea by Chemotherapy" (June 1940) 42 *Canadian Medical Association Journal* 533. A.W. Bagnall, "The Use and Abuse of Dagenan" (Nov. 1940) 18 *University of Toronto Medical Journal* 5 described Dagenan as "a dangerous drug" with "many toxic manifestations."

51 James C. Goodwin, "Venereal Disease in Relation to Pregnancy" (May 1938) 38 *Canadian Medical Association Journal* 447 at 455, noted that the traditional medical view was to defer therapy entirely until after childbirth. He expressed concern that some physicians were reconsidering this in light of the new treatments. He reported on a major study at the Toronto General Hospital, which had concluded that sulfanilamide should not be given prenatally "because of possible toxic effects." Dr. Edna Guest, a recognized expert on venereal disease practising at a neighbour-

ing hospital, would presumably have been familiar with the study and the results. Even had she not, she would have been familiar with the *CMAJ*, the pre-eminent medical journal of the time, and its medical findings. This medical advice was in accord with prevailing American opinion; see P.S. Pelouze, *Gonorrhea in the Male and Female: A Book for Practitioners*, 3d rev. ed. (Philadelphia: W.B. Saunders Co., 1943 [orig. pub. 1928]), who noted at 389 and 391 that "[s]ulfanilamide should not be used in pregnancy nor immediately following delivery," and that "too vigorous treatment should be avoided during pregnancy for fear of causing abortion or premature delivery." For a contrary view, suggesting that sulfanilamide could be administered during pregnancy, see E.N. East & S.A. McFetridge, "Gonorrhoea in the Female" (Sept. 1941) 45 *Canadian Medical Association Journal* 250 at 251–52. The modern perspective is against the use of sulfonamides in pregnant women near term or in nursing mothers; see Division of Drugs and Toxicology, American Medical Association, *Drug Evaluations Annual 1994* (AMA 1993) 1504. The Canadian Pharmacists Association, *Compendium of Pharmaceuticals and Specialities*, 33d ed. (Toronto: Webcom, 1998) notes at 1591–92 that sulphapyridine (Dagenan) "readily crosses the placenta" and is "distributed into breast milk." Physicians are advised that dagenan is "known to cause kernicterus in neonates" (jaundice of newborns) and that its use is not recommended during pregnancy or for nursing mothers.

52 "Health in the Publications" (Oct. 1940) *Health* 77 urged that physicians administering "sulfa-miracle" drugs should see their patients "at least once a day." Dr. R.H. Flett, "Results of Sulphanilamide vs. Dagenan Treatment," *Proceedings of Venereal Disease Conference*, 10 Oct. 1939, Archives of Ontario, RG10-163, Ministry of Health Ontario, Printed Materials, File #25, noted at 2: "In view of the possible reactions to both Sulfanilamide and Dagenan, combined with the fact that the early withdrawal of the drug when a reaction takes place, seldom leads to a permanent or serious result, makes it imperative that the patient be seen every twenty-four or forty-eight hours during the administration of either drug." Dr. Guest was scheduled to work at the Mercer once a week.

53 Clinical Records, 28 Aug. 1939–17 Oct. 1939; Toronto General Hospital, Social Service Department, Report on Childbirth of Velma Demerson, 21 Oct. 1939; Demerson, *Incorrigible*, above note 1 at 78–81; Interview, 26 March 2001.

54 Demerson, *Incorrigible*, above note 1 at 159–60; Interview, 26 March 2001; Interview, 22 May 2001.

55 Demerson, *Incorrigible*, above note 1 at 81–86; Interview, 26 March 2001. Velma Demerson's Complaint to the International Court of Justice, 14 Dec. 1998, alleges that the methemoglobinemia was caused by the sulfanilamide that was administered to her during pregnancy and postpartum, while she was breast-feeding her child. On the link between sulfanilamide and methemoglobinemia, see Ernest Beutler, "Methemoglobinemia and Other Causes of Cyanosis" in Ernest Beutler et al., *Hematology*, 5th ed. (New York: McGraw-Hill, 1995) at 654–55.

56 Demerson, *Incorrigible*, above note 1 at 82–85.

57 Clinical Records, 28 Oct.–27 Nov. 1939; Correspondence, 30–31 Oct. 1939 between C.F. Neelands, deputy provincial secretary, and Miss Milne.

58 Demerson, *Incorrigible*, above note 1 at 81–86; Interview, 26 March 2001. Clinical Records, 28 Oct.–27 Nov.1939; Andrew Mercer Case History File, 10 May 39–1 March 1940.

59 The Mercer medical records contain no reference to this experimental regime of drugs, but Velma Demerson believes that due to the experimental nature of the treatment, no records were kept in the reformatory charts. Demerson, *Incorrigible*, above note 1 at 91–92; Interview, 22 May 2001. The Report of the Provincial Department of Health, Division of Venereal Disease Control, Ontario Sessional Papers, No. 14 (1939) at 103 notes that Mapharsen, Novarsan, tryparsamide, and sulphapyridine were administered on a trial basis to clinic patients at the government-funded clinics during this period, prior to distribution to the profession. Janice Dickin McGinnis, "From Salvarsan to Penicillin: Medical Science and VD Control in Canada" in Wendy Mitchinson & Janice Dickin McGinnis, *Essays in the History of Canadian Medicine* (Toronto: McClelland and Stewart, 1988) notes at 128 that "Canadian doctors and scientists experimented continually" on venereal disease during the 1920s and 1930s, and that "patients were the organisms on which drugs and methods of application were perfected." For recent disclosures of other scientific experimentation on Canadian female inmates, see "LSD 'guinea pig' wins in court" *Ottawa Citizen* (23 June 2001), detailing the testimony of federal government officials and prison psychologists that female inmates were administered LSD as part of a 1961 study at the Prison for Women in Kingston.

60 Interview, 26 March 2001; Interview, 22 May 2001.

61 On 27 Nov. 1939, Dr. Guest wrote: "Two large Sascile Gono Warts on Clitoris to be injected next week." On 5 Dec. 1939, she indicated that she "injected a bunch of gono warts" at the same time as she removed warts from "around the clitoris" and from the "inside labia." According to the medical charts, this was the last snipping or injection. Clinical Records, 27 Nov. 1939–5 Feb. 1940. For Velma's different recollection, see Demerson, *Spirit of Hygeia*, above note 1 at 115–16; Interview, 22 May 2001.

62 Andrew Mercer Case File, 10 May 1939–1 March 1940; Interview, 26 March 2001; Interview, 3 May 2001.

63 Interview, 26 March 2001; Interview, 3 May 2001; Family Court Records, Child Welfare Branch, Harry Yip B41352, (1953); Correspondence from Children's Aid Society of Metropolitan Toronto, 16 July 1991; Correspondence from Office of the Chief Coroner of Ontario, 23 Dec. 1998, including Coroner's Statement, 7 June 1966. Velma Demerson believes that her son's lifelong illnesses may have contributed to his drowning. His eczema and asthma prevented him from learning to swim as a child, and his inexperience with swimming may have caused his death. The drowning may also have been precipitated by an asthmatic attack; see correspondence between Velma Demerson and Office of the Chief Coroner, 9 Nov. 1998.

64 Interview, 3 May 2001; Interview, 22 May 2001.

65 Velma Demerson, "Feebleminded Woman's Plea," *Our O.W.N. Words* (n.p.: Older Women's Network, Feb. 2001):

Save me! Save me from the state!
I've never known such hate!
Danger's spell is cast
They've really got me at last
The scientific method was ill-conceived in hell
A feebleminded woman is locked within a cell
I may be used for other things
That you could never guess
The needles that will puncture me
May never be the best
Save me! Save me from the State!
I've never known such hate.

66 See, for example, Angela Y. Davis, *Are Prisons Obsolete?* (New York: Seven Stories Press, 2003) at 81–83: "Without the uniform, without the power of the state, [the strip search] would be sexual assault." She quotes Australian lawyer and activist Amanda George: "At the same time as the state deplores 'unlawful' sexual assaults by its employees, it actually uses sexual assault as a means of control. In Victoria, prison and police officers are vested with power and responsibility to do acts which, if done outside of work hours, would be crimes of sexual assault. If a person does not 'consent' to being stripped naked by these officers, force can lawfully be used to do it. . . . These legal strip searches are, in the author's view, sexual assaults within the definition of indecent assault."

67 The *Criminal Code*, R.S.C. 1927, c.36, s.290 defined "assault" as "the act of intentionally applying force to the person of another . . . without the consent of the other." Section 292 made it a crime to "indecently assault any female" or to "do anything to any female by her consent which but for such consent would be an indecent assault, if such consent [was] obtained by false and fraudulent representations as to the nature and quality of the act." Indecent assault was not defined in the *Code*, and the courts were left to decide when an assault that fell short of intercourse was sufficiently sexual to prove the offence. Occasionally, acts that seemed more sadistic than sexual resulted in conviction. See, for example, *Rex v. Robertson* (1946), 2 C.R. 222 (Ont. C.A.), where the accused man stripped a twenty-one-year-old university student of her clothes, used rope to tie her wrists to water pipes in the basement, beat her with a rubber hose, and burnt her with a heated poker. He was convicted of indecent assault as well as assault causing bodily harm. Although in retrospect we could characterize Dr. Guest's gynecological procedures as sadistically motivated, it seems unlikely that a court at the time would have equated her actions with those in the case above. For a more detailed discussion of the crime of "indecent assault," see chapter 8. In addition, the *Criminal Code*, R.S.C. 1927, c.36, s.65, stated that criminal charges could not be pursued against individuals who performed a surgical operation "upon any person for his benefit," assuming that the operation was "reasonable, having regard to the patient's state at the time, and to all the circumstances

of the case," and as long as the operation was performed "with reasonable care and skill."

68 Wojtek Dabrowski, "Woman, 81, Sues Ontario for Alleged Wrongful Imprisonment in 1939" Canadian Press NewsWire (5 April 2002); Michelle Landsberg, "Plight of Incorrigible Woman Demands Justice" *Toronto Star* (6 May 2002).

69 *Hopkinson v. Perdue* (1904), 8 C.C.C. 286 (Ont. Div. Ct.). The reported case does not disclose the amount of damages. The defendant's appeal was unsuccessful.

70 *Davis and Davis v. Quayle* (1945), 86 C.C.C. 192 (Alta. S.C.). The judge based his finding on the child's testimony, and evidence that the police had found the grass pressed down, a handkerchief "impregnated with male spermatazoa at the scene of the assault," and sperm stains on her garments and the defendant's trousers.

71 *L. v. G.,* [1950] Que. C.S. 133 (Que. S. C.) alleged a "délit" under article 1053, perpetrated against a fourteen-year-old male child. The removal from school was based, in part, on the embarrassment that ensued when a teacher made insensitive remarks about the assault, and when others suggested that the sexual act might have been consensual. The defendant admitted the assault, but argued unsuccessfully that the father should not be personally compensated for injuries to another. Although it appears that the child had undergone a change in character, and was suffering from worry and anxiety, there was no separate claim on behalf of the child.

72 *Radovskis et al. v. Tomn,* [1957–8] 65 Man. R. 61 (Man. Q.B.). The judge found liability for trespass to the person for "assault and battery," noting that although this could be committed intentionally or negligently, there were "deliberate" acts here. The court noted that the act "must be done against the will of the person who sues for the wrong," which was proven here. The girl's injuries were extensive. In addition to bruising and cuts to her body, she required a three-day hospital stay and operation to repair the tear from the vagina to the rectum. The judge was dismissive of the child's injuries, noting that they "present no real problem," and had "healed well." He added: "[T]he hymen would almost certainly be broken if it had not already been. In addition it is, I think, common knowledge that hymens can be and are broken by many means other than intercourse with a male. . . . She now hides from the neighbours and embarrasses her father by the questions she asks about the happening. . . . The way in which the father and mother deal with this problem is a matter of great importance and a heavy responsibility rests upon them. I can quite see that some of the neighbours might be ignorant enough or inconsiderate enough to cause emotional disturbance in the child for a period, which however would be likely to be short; a 'nine days' wonder.'" He concluded that the injuries here did not result in a "deformity," unlike the more serious case of *Gray v. La Fleche* (1949), 57 Man. R. 396 (Man. K.B.), involving damage to the future life and marriage prospects of a six-year-old boy whose glans penis was injured in a circumcision operation. The judge also refused to consider exemplary damages since this would constitute a double punishment after the criminal sentence. The parents' additional claims for personal compensation for worry and nervous shock were dismissed.

73 *S. v. Mundy,* [1970] 1 O.R. 764 (Ont. Co. Ct.). The plaintiff was attempting to raise three children on a small veterans' allowance, and the defendant, a real estate sales-

man who had known the plaintiff's family for years, offered to help her find cheaper accommodation. Instead, he drove her to a deserted road and attempted to rape her. She suffered abrasions and bruises to her face, throat, and lower abdomen. When the defendant admitted to the police that the plaintiff had not consented or encouraged him, the police recommended criminal charges be laid, but the plaintiff disagreed, and brought a claim for exemplary damages. Given the "wanton," "wilful," and "outrageous" conduct, the court awarded $1500 in exemplary damages. The court indicated in *obiter* that it would have been difficult to determine the amount of compensation owed had general damages been claimed, given that the damage "in the eyes of her children and the public" could not be adequately compensated "by a sum of money."

74 *Pie v. Thibert*, [1976] C.S. 180 (Que. Sup. Ct.). The court rejected the defence that the plaintiff had consented, pointing to her coherent testimony, extensive hospital treatment for genital injuries, and severe psychiatric trauma. Although the plaintiff had sought $25 500, the court only awarded $400 for temporary total incapacity, $1000 for physical, moral, and psychological suffering, and $1000 for damage to reputation, honour, and integrity.

See also *Topolinski v. Harkness and Bland* (1956), 19 W.W.R. 571 (Man. Q.B.); aff'd (1957), 22 W.W.R. 335 (Man. C.A.), and *King (King Estate) v. Hommy and D'Aoust* (1962), 38 W.W.R. 231 (Alta. S.C.), rev'd (1962), 39 W.W.R. 209 (Alta. C.A.), where damages were awarded in negligence to teenage girls (or her estate in the latter case) who had jumped from moving vehicles out of fear of sexual assault. On the *King* case, see an excellent unpublished paper by Ella Forbes-Chilibeck "Jean Elizabeth King" (permission to cite granted by the author July 2004.) See also *Lapalme v. Beaudoin*, [1948] R.P.Q. 363 (Que. Sup. Ct.).

75 For a more recent judicial analysis, see *E.(D.) (Guardian ad litem of) v. British Columbia*, (2005) 252 D.L.R. (4th) 689 (B.C.C.A.), where a majority of the court concluded, in the context of a claim for damages for abuse of public office resulting from the state-ordered sexual sterilization of mental patients, that "where a surgeon operates on a reproductive or sexual organ without lawful authority, I see no injustice in fixing liability for sexual assault." The dissenting judge disagreed, claiming that there must be "a degree of personal moral failure." She preferred to distinguish sexual assault from "medical battery" or "medical negligence."

76 J.-G. Castel, "Nature and Effects of Consent with Respect to the Right to Life and the Right to Physical and Mental Integrity in the Medical Field: Criminal and Private Law Aspects" (1978) 16 *Alberta Law Review* 297–98; *Mulloy v. Hop Sang*, [1935] 1 W.W.R. 714 (Alta. C.A.); *Winn v. Alexander*, [1940] O.W.N. 238 (Ont. H. Ct.); *Murray v. McMurchy*, [1949] 2 D.L.R. 442 (B.C.S.C.); *Male v. Hopmans* (1965), 54 D.L.R. (2d) 592 (Ont. H. Ct.).

77 The heightened scrutiny directed at medical experimentation was first judicially articulated in *Halushka v. University of Saskatchewan* (1965), 53 D.L.R. (2d) 436 (Sask. C.A.).

78 Robert Hayward, *Informed Consent from a Medical Viewpoint* (Kingston, ON: Queen's University Faculty of Medicine, 1982) at 33–34. In *Kenny v. Lockwood*, [1932] O.R. 141

(Ont. C.A.), the court held that a surgeon had a duty to disclose the importance of the proposed operation, as well as its character and the necessity for performing it, but that the duty did not extend to discussing "the dangers incident to, or possible in, any operation, nor to details calculated to frighten or distress the patient." See also *Marshall v. Curry*, [1933] 3 D.L.R. 260 (N.S.S.C.).

79 On the capacity of individuals younger than the full age of majority of twenty-one to give valid consent to medical treatment if they were old enough to appreciate its nature and consequences, see Allen M. Linden, *Canadian Tort Law: Cases, Notes and Materials* (Toronto: Butterworths, 1999) at 124–25; *Booth v. Toronto General Hospital and I.H. Cameron* (1910), 17 O.W.R. 118 (Ont. H. Ct.); Lorne Elkin Rozovsky, "Consent to Treatment" (1973) 11 *Osgoode Hall Law Journal* 103 at 110. See also Ellen I. Picard & Gerald B. Robertson, *Legal Liability of Doctors and Hospitals in Canada*, 3d ed. (Toronto: Thomson Canada, 1996) at 75.

80 S.O. 1918, c.42, s.3(1) authorized a "medical officer of health" to examine penal inmates whenever he or she "believes that such person is, or may be" infected with venereal disease. Section 3(2) provided that if the person examined was found to be infected, the medical officer could "give such directions for the treatment of the patient, and if necessary, for his detention and isolation and the prevention of infection from him as may be deemed proper and as may be authorized by the regulations, and he is hereby empowered to do and authorize any act necessary to effect the carrying out of such treatment, detention, isolation and prevention." See also R.S.O. 1937, c.301, s.2; S.O. 1941, c.62; S.O. 1942, c.38, ss.6, 7, 8. Regulation (q) of the Provincial Board of Health, Ontario, Respecting Venereal Diseases, No. 17, Order in Council 16 April 1920: "Whenever any person in custody under the circumstances mentioned in subsection 2 of section 3 of the Act is found as a result of the examination therein mentioned to be infected with venereal disease the medical officer of health of the district or municipality in which such person is, may direct that such person undergo the treatment prescribed by regulation (b) . . . and that he be detained in custody until cured or until he is no longer a possible source of infection, notwithstanding that his term of imprisonment may have expired." Copy of Order in Council 229/396, dated 9 Nov. 1939, amending Orders in Council 20 June 1918, 16 April 1920, and 28 Dec. 1922, Regulations Respecting Venereal Diseases under the Venereal Diseases Prevention Act, Department of Health, printed in the Annual Report of the Ontario Department of Health for the year 1939 at 50. The legal rights of prisoners had as yet received none of the protection that would come with the *Corrections and Conditional Release Act*, S.C. 1992, c.20, s.88, which provided that prisoners incarcerated in federal penitentiaries had the same right to refuse medical treatment as any other person. See Picard & Robertson, *Legal Liability of Doctors and Hospitals*, above note 79 at 44.

81 Physicians had wide licence to treat patients in detention, and the regulations would seem to have encompassed all that was done to Velma Demerson. "Regulations Respecting Venereal Diseases," Order in Council 26 Jan. 1943, published in (6 Feb. 1943) 76 *The Ontario Gazette*: "The following shall be deemed approved methods and remedies for the treatment, alleviation and cure of venereal diseases: (1) Gonor-

rhoea: (a) sulphonamide compounds, or other approved chemical therapy; (b) local treatment by instillations, irrigations, massage and topical applications; (c) fever therapy." See also "Venereal Diseases Prevention" R.R.O. 1950, Regulation 508, Ontario Regulations 62/44.

82 "Apology Not Enough Jailed Woman Says" *Ottawa Citizen* (8 Jan. 2003); Correspondence between Velma Demerson and Constance Backhouse, 3 July 2003; 6 Oct. 2003; 16, 19, and 29 May 2004; 9 Sept. 2004. Velma Demerson was represented initially by Harry Kopyto, and later by David Midanik.

Chapter 6: Sexual Assault and Disability

1   Henry Alfred Tisdale, Beatrice's father, was born in 1885 in Orangeville, Ontario. He came west around 1902 to follow his brothers who had settled in the Macoun district. Bertha Marie Krueger, Beatrice's mother, came to Saskatchewan from Menomonie, Wisconsin, with her parents in 1904. Henry and Bertha's children were Leona, Howard, Mabel, Beatrice, Laura (deceased age one in the Spanish flu epidemic), Hazel (deceased age eight), and Gordon. See R.M. of Cymri History Book Society, *Plowshares to Pumpjacks: R.M. of Cymri: Macoun, Midale, Halbrite* (Midale, SK: Friesen Printers, 1984) at 547–79.

2   *Ibid.* at 20 and 547–49. Correspondence from the Midale Library, 19 May 2005, indicated that Mabel Tisdale, now in her nineties, still lived in the family home. Beatrice's mother, the eldest of eleven children, had trained as a young cook in Macoun restaurants, where she learned "the art of breadmaking" and "tossed salads" as well as "other valuable tips on keeping people well fed."

3   Midale is 50 km from both Estevan and Weyburn, and 155 km southeast of Regina. The town was initially named "Mitchell" after Dr. R.M. Mitchell of Weyburn, who provided medical services from Moose Jaw to Estevan single-handedly between 1899 and 1903. When the residents learned that there was another town named "Mitchell" in the Territory of Assiniboia, they decided to combine the first two letters of "Mitchell" with "Dale," after Ole Dale, the first homesteader. The name "Midale" pronounced "My-dale" emerged. Population reached 156 in 1911, and 180 by 1921, peaking at 800 after oil was discovered in 1953. Current population is 540. Canada, Dominion Bureau of Statistics, *Sixth Census of Canada, 1921: Population,* vol. 1 (Bulletin 8) at 6 and "Midale Saskatchewan" www.sasktelwebsite.net/jawe/index. htm, accessed 11 July 2005; Bill Waiser, *Saskatchewan: A New History* (Calgary: Fifth House, 2005) at 294; Cymri History, *Plowshares to Pumpjacks,* above note 1 at 3, 19–26, and 61.

4   It is unknown whether Beatrice Tisdale was deaf at birth, or became so in later childhood as a result of accident or diseases such as measles, mumps, spinal meningitis, and whooping cough. Figures from the Saskatchewan School for the Deaf in 1932 show that 42 percent of the pupils were born deaf, 31 percent became deaf at age three or younger, and 27 percent after reaching age three; Allan Peter Torgerson, *The History of the Saskatchewan School for the Deaf* (M.Ed. Thesis, University of Saskatchewan, 1983) at 54.

5   A Saskatchewan School for the Deaf opened in Regina in 1915, but was closed by the
    government in 1916. Deaf children started in residential schools as early as age six in
    this era, but deaf pupils from Saskatchewan were admitted to the Mackay School for
    the first time during the 1926–27 school year, so Beatrice cannot have been younger
    than eight when she started there; Torgerson, *The History of the Saskatchewan School
    for the Deaf*, above note 4 at 18, 52–53. In 1926 there were ninety deaf children in
    Saskatchewan: forty-six went to Manitoba, twenty-five to Québec, one to British Col-
    umbia, and eighteen were kept home by their parents. For the "annual railway trek"
    to Montréal, about fifty deaf children, accompanied by two adult chaperones, slept
    in two special tourist cars that were converted into compact eating, sleeping, and
    living quarters. Many of the younger children acquired a working sign language for
    the first time during the train trip. Clifton F. Carbin, *Deaf Heritage in Canada* (Toron-
    to: McGraw-Hill Ryerson, 1996) at 83–87, 155, 161, 164, and 403–5. For a fictional por-
    trayal of the loss of family as well as the positive aspects of residential deaf school
    experience during the early twentieth century, see Frances Itani, *Deafening* (Toronto:
    HarperCollins, 2003).

6   Carbin, *Deaf Heritage in Canada*, above note 5 at 320; R.A.R. Edwards, "Speech Has an
    Extraordinary Humanizing Power: Horace Mann and the Problem of Nineteenth-
    Century American Deaf Education" in Paul K. Longmore & Lauri Umansky, eds.,
    The New Disability History: American Perspectives (New York: New York University
    Press, 2001) 58 at 65. On the capitalization of Deaf, see James Roots, *The Politics of
    Visual Language: Deafness, Language Choice, and Political Socialization* (Ottawa: Carleton
    University Press, 1999), who notes at 1–2 that the "lower-case *d* 'deaf' is a medical
    label encompassing all individuals in whom the sense of hearing is non-functional
    for the ordinary purposes of living. The upper-case *D* 'Deaf' is a sociological identi-
    fier referring only to those deaf people who are recognized and accepted as mem-
    bers of the Deaf Culture. The language of this culture is Sign. 'Deaf people' and
    'deaf people' . . . are not interchangeable terms."

7   *Sign* uses building blocks of designators (handshape), tabulators (location of the
    sign), signifiers (movement and action of the hands), orientation (the spacial relation
    of the hands to each other and to the body), and affective markers (completely non-
    manual, such as twitching of the nose to communicate colloquialisms). It has taken
    a number of distinct regional forms in Canada: Maritime Sign Language (MSL) in
    eastern Canada, La Langue des Signes (ou Sourdes) du Québec (LSQ) in Québec,
    and even an Inuit dialect. No Canadian Sign Language emerged as a national ver-
    sion, and American Sign Language (ASL) became the "predominant sign language"
    preferred by English-speaking Deaf Canadians. Roots, *The Politics of Visual Language*,
    above note 6 at 3–4; Susan Burch, *Signs of Resistance: American Deaf Cultural History,
    1900 to World War II* (New York: New York University Press, 2002); Harlan Lane,
    "Constructions of Deafness" (1995) 10 *Disability and Society* 171–89; Jill Branson &
    Don Miller, *Damned for Their Difference: The Cultural Construction of Deaf People as
    Disabled* (Washington, DC: Gallaudet University Press, 2002); Carbin, *Deaf Heritage in
    Canada*, above note 5 at 319.

8   Christopher Krentz, ed., *A Mighty Change: An Anthology of Deaf American Writing, 1816–1864* (Washington, DC: Gallaudet University Press, 2000) at xxiii.

9   Mackay Principal Ida I. McLeod, a hearing woman, had fired all the deaf teachers and supervisors by 1897, and by 1934 the Mackay school would move completely to oralism. Carbin, *Deaf Heritage in Canada*, above note 5 at 83–87; Margaret Winzer, "Historical Perspectives on Education of the Deaf in Canada: One More Triumph" (1980) 6 *The ACEHI Journal* 50–53; Margaret Winzer, "An Examination of Some Selected Factors That Affected the Education and Socialization of the Deaf in Ontario, 1870–1900" (Ph.D. Thesis, Ed. D., University of Toronto, 1981); Roots, *The Politics of Visual Language*, above note 6 at 31. Helen Isabell (Briggs) Rayner, who attended the Mackay school along with Beatrice in 1930, recalled being taught to "sign, read and write" by a dedicated teacher, Miss Anderson; see Hilda Marian Campbell, *Deaf Women of Canada* (Edmonton: Duval House, 2002) at 209–10.

10 Rupert Jabez Duncan Williams was born in 1893 in Fort Frances, Ontario, and deafened by spinal meningitis at the age of five. He was educated at the Manitoba Institution for the Education of the Deaf and Dumb in Winnipeg, which combined the "manual method" with speech reading. Williams worked in the printing trade in Winnipeg, Toronto, and Sioux Lookout, and then became a dormitory supervisor at the Manitoba School in 1922, gradually taking over teaching responsibilities as well. He moved to Saskatoon in 1927 to work for the Modern Press, and founded the Western Canada Association of the Deaf to lobby for educational improvements. He was aided by Saskatoon's Chief of Police, George Mitchell Donald, who had two deaf daughters (Maureen and Sheila) and Violet Clara McNaughton, a feminist editor of *The Western Producer*. When Williams retired in 1963, "students would sneak out of classes to make their way to his home to talk and share their problems." In 1982, he was posthumously honoured when the name of the school was changed to the R.J.D. Williams Provincial School for the Deaf, nine years before its closure by the provincial government. Carbin, *Deaf Heritage in Canada*, above note 5 at 140 and 161–67; Institution for the Deaf and Dumb (Winnipeg), (15 May 1894) 3 *The Canadian Mute* 6; Carolyn Beally et al., *The First Fifty Years, 1932–1982: R.J.D. Williams Provincial School for the Deaf* (Saskatoon: Prairie Graphics, 1983); Torgerson, *The History of the Saskatchewan School for the Deaf*, above note 4 at 10 and 62. Burch, *Signs of Resistance*, above note 7, asserts in chapters 1 and 2 that even within an increasingly hostile environment, members of the Deaf community always found ways to transmit their Sign culture.

11 The information that Beatrice was assigned to the "Manual Department" rather than the "Oral Department," is based on communication from Dr. Carol Patrie, director of Curriculum and Instruction at EIPES Language Matters Inc., dated 4 September 2005, whose mother had studied at the Saskatchewan school with Beatrice. It appears that only students who could not "profit by oral instruction" were designated "manual students." Both manual and oral students were permitted to use Sign language in opening exercises and assemblies, and in all the domestic science classes taught by Jean Paterson, a Deaf teacher. Even after the oralism policy took hold in 1938, some students at the Saskatchewan school managed to learn to communicate

fluently in ASL from the Deaf adults at the school and in the community; see biography of Mary Joan (Kohlman) Gauthier, who attended from 1938 to 1946, in Campbell, *Deaf Women of Canada*, above note 9 at 98. *The Annual Report, 1931* reported that thirty children in grades 4 to 6 were enrolled in the Oral Department, and twelve in the Manual Department. The high proportion of Deaf teachers continued through most of the school's first decade, but diminished thereafter. Edwin G. Peterson, *The Annual Report of the Saskatchewan School for the Deaf, 1931* (Saskatchewan Department of Education); Torgerson, *The History of the Saskatchewan School for the Deaf*, above note 4 at 51, 68, and 90; Carbin, *Deaf Heritage in Canada*, above note 5 at 163–64; Margaret A. Winzer, *The History of Special Education: From Isolation to Integration* (Washington, DC: Gallaudet University Press, 2002) at 219; Beally et al., *The First Fifty Years*, above note 10.

12 Carbin, *Deaf Heritage in Canada*, above note 5 at 57–61 chronicles the unfortunate histories of the New Brunswick Institution for the Deaf and Dumb in Saint John and Portland, New Brunswick (open 1873–1890), the Fredericton Institution for the Education of the Deaf and Dumb (open 1882–1902), and the New Brunswick School for the Deaf, Lancaster (open 1903–18), surrounded by allegations of violence, cruelty, and sexual abuse. In 1939, it was discovered that one of the oldest girls in the Saskatchewan school had had sexual intercourse with one of the male students. It was unclear whether this was consensual or coercive; the boy was expelled and increased supervision was instated. Saskatchewan Archives Board, R-234.9, "Enquiry commenced 23 March 1939 under and by virtue of the provisions of Section 14 of the Public Service Act, Chapter 4 1934–35 Statutes of Saskatchewan, to investigate credible information received concerning alleged irregularities at the School for the Deaf, Saskatoon before Col. F.W.G. Miles, Public Service Commissioner," Part II, at 398–406. Winzer, *The History of Special Education*, above note 11, notes at 218 that institutional records of schools for the deaf were "relatively silent about punishment," but that they were likely to have been severe as in the common schools, if not more severe. She adds that the use of corporal punishment declined rapidly by the late nineteenth century, when deprivation of privileges or segregation in "reflection chambers" increased. Marlene Anne ("Mac") (Cole) Olson, who attended the Saskatchewan School for the Deaf from 1947 to 1960 fondly recalled the sports, friends, and classes, but added "how mean the punishments were." See Campbell, *Deaf Women of Canada*, above note 9 at 195–96. Thomas R. Berger, "Report of Special Counsel regarding Claims Arising out of Sexual Abuse at Jericho Hill School" (British Columbia Ministry of the Attorney General, March 1995) notes at 13–14 a "condition of widespread and pervasive sexual abuse of children" at British Columbia's now-closed Jericho Hill Provincial School, from the 1950s to the 1980s. Office of the Ombudsman of British Columbia, "Abuse of Deaf Students at Jericho Hill School" Public Report No. 32 (Nov. 1993) notes at 4–6 that at Jericho Hill, staff inflicted sexual, physical, and emotional abuse on students, and older students abused younger students. Subsequent to more than one hundred allegations of sexual and physical abuse at the Amherst School for the Deaf, which operated in Halifax, Nova Scotia, from 1961 to 1995, and the Halifax School for the Deaf, which operated from 1856 to

1961, Ross Joseph Chappell, a former employee at Amherst, pleaded guilty to charges of indecently assaulting two students. Tom McCoag, "Man Gets House Arrest for Assaults" *Halifax Herald* (3 June 2004) B4 and Kevin Cox, "RCMP Probe Allegation of Abuse at Nova Scotia Schools" *Globe and Mail* (4 July 2002) A11.

13   While I am uncertain what Beatrice Tisdale did between 1937 and 1942, several of her classmates, Helen Isabelle (Briggs) Rayner and Hendrika ("Sis") Conrad, returned to assist their families on the farm until jobs opened up with the outbreak of the war. Campbell, *Deaf Women of Canada*, above note 9 at 50 and 209–10.

14   Maureen Mitchell Donald, the daughter of Saskatoon's chief of police, attended the Manitoba School for the Deaf from 1925 to 1931, and the Saskatchewan School from 1931 to 1937. She became the first Deaf teacher hired by the British Columbia Jericho Hill Provincial School for the Deaf, where she taught from 1945 to 1978. She became the first female president of the Vancouver Association of the Deaf in 1965, and received an honorary doctorate from the University of British Columbia in 2000. Campbell, *Deaf Women of Canada*, above note 9 at 30, 46, 50, 68, 78, 92, 98, 109–11, 123, 163–64, 192–93, 209–10, and 258; Carbin, *Deaf Heritage in Canada*, above note 5 at 151–55 and 208; Beally et al., *The First Fifty Years*, above note 10 at 77 and 90.

15   Transcript of the trial, "His Majesty the King and Joseph Probe" King's Bench, Judicial District of Weyburn, No. 297, 20–21 October 1942, Saskatchewan Archives Board at 9, 109, and 115. The café was one lot removed from the Royal Hotel, and contained eleven hotel rooms, two toilets, and a bathtub at the rear of the second floor. The hiring of Beatrice Tisdale was not indicative of a wider policy of inclusive employment. In 1947, the Anderson Café ran an advertisement in the *Regina Leader Post* stating that it employed "all white help." For reference to the ad, see Carmela Patrias, "Socialists, Jews, and the 1947 Saskatchewan Bill of Rights" (June 2006) 87 *Canadian Historical Review* 265 at 287. See also Neil Overgard, *The Last of the Buffalo, The Soo Line and Its People* (Regina: Overgard, 1956) at 163; Weyburn Writer's Association, *Hey, Seeds!* (Weyburn, SK: Soo Line Historical Society, n.d.) at 101; description of the café from a former resident, who lived there in the 1950s with his parents, but asked not to be identified; n.a., *Weyburn 75 Years* (Weyburn, SK: City of Weyburn, 1987) at 21; Waiser, *Saskatchewan*, above note 3 at 334–37.

16   Carol Peterson was the youngest child of Peter Bernard Peterson and Ester (Anderson) Peterson, who had moved from Minnesota to farm northeast of Midale. The First Baptist Church was known as the "Swedish Baptist" in its early years, when Swedish was still the language spoken during the services. Carol worked at the Saskatchewan Mental Hospital in Weyburn for four months before her marriage to Joe Probe. The Rev. Tommy Douglas would become the premier of Saskatchewan in 1944, a member of the House of Commons in 1956, and leader of the New Democratic Party of Canada in 1963. See Cymri History, *Plowshares to Pumpjacks*, above note 1 at 475–76 and 548; Henri Paul Chatenay, *Echoes of Silence: The Chronicles of William Graham Mainprize, M.D., 1911–1974* (n.p., First Baptist Church & Town of Midale, 75th anniversary addition, 1978) at 117; Isabel Eaglesham, *The Night the Cat Froze in the Oven: A History of Weyburn and Its People* (Weyburn, SK: Weyburn Review Ltd., 1963) at 139.

17 Joseph Probe was the youngest child of Mathias Probe and Elizabeth (Young) Probe. His parents, born in Budapest, Hungary, had immigrated to Indian Head, Saskatchewan, in 1897. In 1899, they homesteaded at Weyburn, moving to another farm a mile from Prospect School in 1907. In 1916, his parents moved to Kelowna, B.C., and in 1917 to Salem, Oregon, where they maintained a fruit orchard. Weyburn R.M. #67 History Book Committee, *As Far as the Eye Can See: Weyburn RM 67* (Regina: Focus Publishing, 1986) at 691–94.

18 Transcript of the trial, at 6–7.

19 This summary comes from the Crown attorney's opening address. This and all further references to the evidence are drawn from Transcript of the trial, "His Majesty the King and Joseph Probe," King's Bench, Judicial District of Weyburn, No. 297, 20–21 October 1942, Saskatchewan Archives Board. Archivist Rebecca Friesen at the Saskatchewan Archives Board indicated that two searches, in June 2000 and in May 2005, failed to locate records from the preliminary inquiry; correspondence 16 May 2005. Nothing appeared in the *Saskatoon Star Phoenix*, the *Regina Leader-Post*, or the *Estevan Mercury*. The *Weyburn Review* reported on 3 September 1942, at 8, that Joseph Probe had appeared before Regina police court magistrate, James Graham, KC, represented by M.A. MacPherson, KC, and A.W. McNeel, and prosecuted by D.J. Mitchell. The case had "occupied practically the whole day and was held in camera."

20 Crown attorney Mitchell was the son of Margaret McKinnon and Dr. R.M. Mitchell, the man after whom "Midale" had been named. Born in Dundalk, Ontario, in 1895, Donald moved to Weyburn with his parents in 1899. He attended St. Andrews College in Toronto from 1909 to 1911, studied at the University of Saskatchewan from 1913 to 1915, and articled with J.C. Martin and W.M. Rose. In 1918, he married Margaret Marshall of Kingston, Ontario. He was admitted to the bar in 1920, and began practice in Weyburn in partnership with J.C. Martin until 1957, when T.L. Geatros became a partner. He was appointed attorney-general for the judicial district of Weyburn in 1941, Queen's Counsel in 1951, and became a provincial magistrate in 1952. Mitchell was a keen sportsman, a civic leader, and an avid horticulturalist whose home garden, at 447 Qu'Appelle St., won numerous prizes. See Weyburn Writer's Association, *Hey, Seeds!*, above note 15 at 28–29.

21 Carbin, *Deaf Heritage in Canada*, above note 5 at 121; Henry Vlug, in Mike King, "A Dialogue with Deaf Lawyers" *Canadian Lawyer* (June 2003) at 35.

22 R.S.S. 1940, c.67, s.39. This provision was introduced in Saskatchewan's first evidence statute: S.S. 1907, c.12, s.33.

23 The *Revised Rules of Court of the Province of Saskatchewan* (Regina: King's Printer, 1942) provided for translators only for non-English speaking witnesses in s.301: "When a witness does not understand the English language, the examination shall be taken with the aid of an interpreter nominated by the examiner and sworn to interpret truly the questions to be put to the witness and his answers thereto, and the examination shall be taken in English." The right to an interpreter may have arisen through common law. An earlier English case, *Rex v. Lee Kun*, [1916] 1 K.B. 337 (C.C.A.) at 342, had compared deaf witnesses to non-English speakers: "If the accused is fit to plead it may yet be that no communication can be made in the ordin-

ary way; it may be that he is deaf and can only be approached by writing or signs, or dumb, and can only make his views known by writing or signs, or a foreigner who cannot speak English and requires the assistance of an interpreter to understand the proceedings and make answer to them. In such cases the judge must see that proper means are taken to communicate to the accused the case made against him and to enable him to make his answer to it." Henry Vlug, "The Right of the Deaf to the Assistance of Interpreters" (unpublished paper, April 1984) at 12; Isaac Lewis Peet, "The Legal Relations of Deaf-Mutes to the Hearing Community" *Columbia Law Times* 2 (November 1888) at 45–51; n.a., "A Deaf and Dumb Witness" (1890) 7 *Cape Law Journal* 235–37.

24 Initial attempts to take testimony through an interpreter named Mrs. Johnson had proven so unwieldy that the proceedings came to a halt, and the interpreter was discharged.

25 Molland was one of a growing number of young hearing women hired by deaf schools, in a trend that was described as "the feminization of oralist teachers." It was cheaper to hire women, who earned about half the pay of men, and who stayed only until marriage. Upon their resignations, the schools could hire new, lower-paid women. Their employment displaced Deaf men and Deaf women from career opportunities. Susan Burch, "Reading between the Signs: Defending Deaf Culture in Early Twentieth-Century America" in Longmore & Umansky, eds., *The New Disability History*, above note 6, 214 at 218–20.

26 Carbin, *Deaf Heritage in Canada*, above note 5, notes at 326 that the early interpreters were usually employees of the provincial schools for the deaf, and/or individuals who had deaf relatives, typically "volunteers who lacked any professional training in sign language interpreting." Interpreter training programs did not appear in community colleges and universities until the early 1980s. See Debra L. Russell, "Interpreting in Legal Contexts: Consecutive and Simultaneous Interpretation" (Ph. D. Thesis, University of Calgary, Sept. 2000), for a modern critique of the accuracy of American Sign Language interpretation in the courtroom.

27 Margaret Sarah (Perkins) Christenberry was taught by Mary Molland in her first year at the Saskatchewan school, in 1939: Campbell, *Deaf Women of Canada*, above note 9 at 46. Beally et al., *The First Fifty Years*, above note 10 at 22 and 24 shows Molland photographed with the younger students.

28 Roots, *The Politics of Visual Language*, above note 6 at 55–56; "Deaf People in Court," presentation by Nathalie Dufour, a Deaf woman from Montéal, LEAF/NAWL Conference, Vancouver, 29 April 2005; King, "Dialogue with Deaf Lawyers," above note 21; Law Society of Upper Canada, "Providing Legal Services to Persons with Disabilities," Bar Admission Course 2003 at 11–13; Winifred H. Northcott, *Oral Interpreting: Principles and Practices* (Baltimore: University Park Press, 1984); Kathryn Woodcock & Miguel Aguayo, *Deafened People: Adjustment and Support* (Toronto: University of Toronto Press, 2000) at 121.

29 Burch, *Signs of Resistance*, above note 7, notes at 33 that speech ability depends on the age at which deafness occurred, the degree of residual hearing, and the length of speech training.

30 Woodcock & Aguayo, *Deafened People*, above note 28, note at 92 that for deaf lip-readers, oral communication is often composed of guessing, and works best with people who are familiar with their context, who have the situational power to control their conversations.

31 See, for example, defence counsel's insistent questioning of Dr. McGillivray as to whether the complainant had "complained of terrible pains" associated with the allegedly forced intercourse. "She didn't complain of terrible pains," responded the physician. "She didn't talk at all to me."

32 See, for example, when Beatrice answered "yes," and counsel asked: "She means 'no,' doesn't she?" The interpreter admitted, "Well, I turned that question around." Vlug, "Right of the Deaf," above note 23 at 26, refers to an unpublished American case, *Commonwealth v. Edmonds*, Cir. Ct. Staunton, Va. (1975), involving a deaf rape victim. The interpreter at the preliminary hearing misinterpreted the sign for "forced intercourse" as "made love" and "blouse" as "short blouse," to the significant detriment of the deaf witness.

33 *The Jury Act*, R.S.S. 1940, c.66, s.4(19) provided: "The following persons shall be exempt from being returned and from serving as jurors: Persons who are affected with blindness, deafness or other mental or physical infirmity incompatible with the discharge of the duties of a juror."

34 *Rex v. Mudge*, [1930] 1 D.L.R. 617 (Sask. C.A.). For a more detailed discussion on the requirements of resistance, see chapter 4.

35 MacPherson was born in 1891, in Grande Anse, Nova Scotia, the son of Margaret (Campbell) and Alexander MacPherson, both second-generation Scots. He studied at St. Peter's Academy, and received his LL.B. from Dalhousie in 1913. He began his law career in Swift Current, Saskatchewan, where he met and married Iowa Briggs. After being wounded in the First World War, he came back to Regina to practise law in 1919. He was elected as a Conservative member of the Saskatchewan legislature in 1925, and appointed attorney-general in 1929 on the eve of the stock market crash. In 1931, he also took on the office of provincial treasurer. His bid for the leadership of the national Conservative party failed twice, in 1938 and again in December 1942. He became the senior partner in the firm of MacPherson, Leslie, and Tyerman, and was known as a sharp adversary of the railways and an advocate of the Western cause of low freight rates on Prairie grain export. In 1959, he would be chosen by Prime Minister Diefenbaker to serve on the MacPherson Royal Commission on Transportation. A bencher of the Saskatchewan Law Society, he was given an honorary degree by the University of Saskatchewan in 1961. "Noted Regina Lawyer Dies" *Regina Leader Post* (13 June 1966) 1 and 5; "MacPherson, Hon. Murdock Alexander" in *The Canadian Parliamentary Guide, 1934* (Ottawa: 1934) at 592–93.

36 Russell, "Interpreting in Legal Contexts" above note 26 at 142 and 169–77.

37 The reference to "struggling" was related to the preliminary inquiry, in which the interpreter had advised MacPherson that Beatrice did not understand the word "struggling."

38 See also *Rex v. Lovering* (1948), 92 C.C.C. 65 (Ont. C.A.), in which defence counsel argued that given the cramped conditions in the front seat of an automobile, it

would be impossible for an accused to accomplish sexual intercourse if the female resisted. The appellate court noted: "That would have been a very fitting argument to address to the jury."

39 R.S.C. 1927, c.36, s.298 defined rape as "the act of a man having carnal knowledge of a woman who is not his wife without her consent, or with consent which has been extorted by threats or fear of bodily harm, or obtained by personating the woman's husband, or by false and fraudulent representations as to the nature and quality of the act."

40 *Laliberté v. The Queen* (1877), 1 S.C.R. 117.

41 *The King v. Bishop* (1906), 11 C.C.C. 30 (N.S.S.C.).

42 *Regina v. Dyment*, [1966] 55 W.W.R. 575 (B.C.C.A.). See also *Regina v. Makow*, [1974] 13 C.C.C. (2d) 167 (B.C.C.A.); *Regina v. Ovcaric*, [1973] 11 C.C.C. (2d) 565 (Ont. C.A.). Such rules facilitated the fabrication of evidence. In *Regina v. Cross, Cassell, Bryan & Foley*, [1970] 1 C.C.C. 216 (Ont. C.A.), the complainant testified that she had had no sexual experience prior to her gang rape by four men. The court discovered that one of the accused had attempted to bribe another man (McWilliams, who was not accused in the case) to testify falsely that he had had previous sexual relations with the complainant.

43 *Rex v. Muma* (1910), 22 O.L.R. 225 (Ont. C.A.) explained that evidence about "improper acts" with persons other than the accused was "collateral," and could require that the court give the complainant notice and an "opportunity to meet the charge," which might then result in the trial of a host of additional distracting issues. Intriguingly, the court added: "If it were open to the defence to prove every separate improper act in the life of a . . . prosecutrix, why not also every such act of the accused?" See also *Rex v. Finnessy* (1906), 10 C.C.C. 347 (Ont. C.A.). There was no rule requiring anyone to advise rape victims that they need not answer questions about their sexual history with other men; see *Laliberté v. The Queen* (1877), 1 S.C.R. 117: "the Judge may tell the witness she is not obliged to answer, if he thinks proper, though not bound to do so." For a rare instance in which the trial judge advised the complainant that she could refuse to answer such questions, and if she did answer yes or no, that was the end of it and counsel could not ask any further questions, see *Regina v. Basken & Kohl*, [1975] 21 C.C.C. (2d) 321 (Sask. C.A.). But in *Regina v. Muggli* (1961), 131 C.C.C. 363 (B.C.C.A.), the appellate court chastised a trial judge for having advised a rape complainant that she didn't have to answer the question of whether she had had "sexual intercourse before with men."

44 The Weyburn Commonwealth Training School received 100 British pilot trainees in December 1941 and more cadets from Britain, New Zealand, Australia, France, and India in 1942, to train on Harvards and four Ansons-twin engined planes. Weyburn R.M. #67 History Book Committee, *As Far as the Eye Can See*, above note 17 at 199. Waiser, *Saskatchewan*, above note 3, notes at 334–37 that the romances that were struck between the airmen and local girls "bred jealousy and resentment." In 1944, isolated brawls escalated to a full-blown rampage between RAF members and the local youth in Moose Jaw. On the military service of Beatrice's two brothers, Murray

and Gordon, see Cymri History, *Plowshares to Pumpjacks*, above note 1 at 117; n.a., *Weyburn 75 Years*, above note 15 at 21 and 40.

45 A public enquiry had been called two years after Beatrice's graduation after a deaf boy and girl were discovered to have had sexual intercourse at the school. The conclusions of the chair of the inquiry were that "the girls at the Saskatchewan School for the Deaf were as ignorant as could be" and "hadn't one idea in the world of what it [sex] was all about." See Saskatchewan Archives Board, R-234.9, above note 12 at 406.

46 Judge Henry V. Bigelow was born in 1874 in Lynn, Massachusetts, the son of Henrietta Agnes and James E. Bigelow. He studied at Dalhousie University, and practised law in Truro, N.S., before coming to Regina in 1906. His wife was Mary Tupper, from Dartmouth, N.S. He was appointed a Justice of the Court of King's Bench for Saskatchewan in 1918. He was active in the Regina Conservative Association, in the Anglican Church, with the Knights Templar for Manitoba and Saskatchewan, and as a curler and tennis player. See "Bigelow, The Hon. Henry V.," *Who's Who in Canada, 1947–48* (Toronto: International Press) at 158.

47 "Probe Found Not Guilty Rape Charge" *Weyburn Review* (22 October 1942) at 1 listed the names of the jurors: H.B. Milne, Tils Reynolds, W.A. Findlay, A.L. Geatros, Jack Cruden, and Art Humby. According to the recollections of a former Weyburn resident who asked to remain unidentified, Howie Milne "played for the Roughrider football team, then refereed football," and was later put in the Saskatchewan Sports Hall of Fame for his prowess in football and hockey. See also Ivol Krueger, *In His Hands* (Weyburn, SK: Weyburn New Horizons Book Committee, 1978) at 86–87. W.A. Findlay was a music teacher, and the organist for the Presbyterian Church. A.L. Geatros ran a restaurant on 3d Street. Jack Cruden was a commercial traveller for a meat wholesale company. Art Humby ran the local taxi.

48 Nothing in the parliamentary debates reveals the motivation of the legislators regarding the introduction of deaf females to the prohibited act. Earlier versions had made reference to women with mental disabilities only. See S.C. 1886, c.52, s. 1(2); S.C. 1887, c.48, s.1; S.C. 1892, c.29, s.189. The eugenics movement often equated physical and mental disability during this era: see Horst Biesold, *Crying Hands: Eugenics and Deaf People in Nazi Germany* (Washington, DC: Gallaudet University Press, 1999). An earlier provincial statute, of doubtful constitutionality given its criminal law focus, was S.O. 1887, c.45, which provided: "No person shall at any time or place within the precincts of any institution to which *The Prison and Asylum Inspection Act* applies, unlawfully and carnally know any female who is capable in law of giving her consent to such carnal knowledge while she is a patient or is confined in such institution." See also R.S.O. 1897, c.260; S.O. 1913, c.80; R.S.O. 1914, c.232; R.S.O. 1927, c.283; R.S.O. 1937, c.317.

49 S.C. 1900, c.46, s.189; S.C. 1922, c.16, s.10. The definition was contained in s.14A: "'feeble-minded person' means a person in whose care there exists from birth or from an early age, mental defectiveness not amounting to imbecility yet so pronounced that he or she requires care, supervision and control for his or her protection and for the protection of others." Unlike the introduction of "deaf and dumb

women," the feeble-minded category prompted fulsome debate on the floor of the
House of Commons. Several legislators objected that the amendment was too broadly worded, and might penalize innocent men who had sex with prostitutes. Mr.
Jacobs cited statistics he claimed showed that "at least four-fifths of fallen women
are found to be feeble-minded," and queried: "Take the case of a fallen woman who
has become an ordinary street-walker, and who, in the course of her peregrinations,
meets a man and takes him to a house of assignation. How is this man, on a mere
cursory acquaintance with this woman, to know that she is feeble-minded?" Mr.
Blake added: "I think it is conceded by medical experts that all the girls in the red
light district can be classified as nympho-maniacs. They are feeble-minded — mentally defective — and this clause here could be construed by any severe magistrate
to ban illicit intercourse entirely." Mr. Thomson from Qu'Appelle agreed, noting
that "there is a certain amount of mental defectiveness about everybody," and "you
might almost assume that almost any of these women are persons who require
care, supervision, and control. I think it is probably because they have not had the
amount of care, supervision and control that they should have that they have gone
astray." These sentiments did not carry the day, and the majority voted in favour of
the amendment. *House of Commons Debates* (25 May 1921) at 3896–99. On the gender,
class, race, and ethnic stereotypes that infected the term "feeble-minded," see Jen-
nifer Stephen, "The Incorrigible, the Bad and the Immoral: Toronto's Factory Girls
and the Work of the Toronto Psychiatric Clinic" in Louis Knafla & Susan Binnie,
eds., *Law, Society and the State* (Toronto: University of Toronto Press, 1995) at 405. S.C.
1938, c.44, s.1 revised the definition of "feeble-minded person" to remove the female
pronouns, presumably because the use of generic male pronouns was preferred and
interpreted as inclusive of female: s.2(1)(15) "'feeble-minded person' means a person
in whose case there exists from birth or from an early age, mental defectiveness not
amounting to imbecility yet so pronounced that he requires care, supervision and
control for his protection and for the protection of others."

50 R.S.C. 1927, c.36, s.219. This provision remained until 1954, when the reference to
"deaf and dumb" was deleted. Just as the politicians had said nothing about why
they first brought deaf women into the provision, there was nothing recorded in
the parliamentary debates as to why they took them out. S.C. 1953–54, c.51, s.140 left
the provision to read: "Every male person who, under circumstances that do not
amount to rape, has sexual intercourse with a female person (a) who is not his wife,
and (b) who is and who he knows or has good reason to believe is feeble-minded,
insane, or is an idiot or imbecile, is guilty of an indictable offence and is liable to
imprisonment for five years." The entire offence was abolished in the 1983 reforms:
R.S.C. 1970, c. C-34, s.148 [repealed, 1980–81–82, c.125, s.8.]

51 Neither counsel referred to *The King v. Karn* (1909), 14 O.W.R. 1215 (Ont. C.A.) in
which the accused was charged with being an owner or occupier who had knowingly suffered a girl between the ages of fourteen and sixteen to resort to the premises for the purpose of unlawful carnal knowledge. The young women had been
importuned to go to the accused's place of business to have sexual intercourse with
himself and his clerk. The defence counsel had argued that "unlawfully" must

mean something such as incest or seduction, and noted that adultery was not an offence at common law. The court concluded that "unlawfully" meant "not sanctioned or permitted by law and as distinguished from acts of sexual intercourse which are not regarded as immoral." Determining that the intercourse that took place in this instance could be described as unlawful, the court held that it was not improper to apply the word to the act itself, and affirmed the conviction.

52 *Rex v. Probe*, [1943] 2 W.W.R. 62 (Sask. C.A.).

53 *Regina v. Connolly* (1867), 26 U.C.Q.B. 317. See also Samuel Robinson Clarke & Henry Pigott Sheppard, *A Treatise on the Criminal Law of Canada*, 2d ed. (Toronto: Hart & Co., 1882) at 213: "In the case of rape of an idiot, or lunatic woman, the mere proof of the act of connection will not warrant the case being left to the jury. There must be some evidence that it was without her consent, e.g., that she was incapable of expressing assent or dissent, or from exercising any judgment on the matter, from imbecility of mind or defect of understanding, and if she gave her consent from animal instinct or passion, or if from her state and condition he had reason to think she was consenting, it would not be a rape."

54 *Rex v. Probe*, [1943] 2 W.W.R. 62 (Sask. C.A.).

55 *Ibid.*

56 Burch, *Signs of Resistance*, above note 7 at 122–24 and 138 indicated that the Deaf community, whose members often "passed," emphasized their identity as separate from other disabled communities. Deaf leaders felt affiliation with other populations considered dangerous and inferior would harm their own image and status. They also viewed disabled activists as hearing people first, then as disabled.

57 *Yee Clun v. City of Regina*, [1925] 4 D.L.R. 1015 (Sask. K.B.). For a fuller description of the case, and the history of the laws prohibiting Asian men from hiring white women, see Constance Backhouse, *Colour-Coded: A Legal History of Racism in Canada, 1900–1950* (Toronto: University of Toronto Press, 1999), chapter 5.

58 Judge Mackenzie (also MacKenzie) was born in London, Ontario, the son of Philip and Elizabeth MacKenzie. He was educated at the London Collegiate Institute and the University of Toronto where he received his B.A. in 1983, and LL.B. in 1895. He "read law" with Mowat, Donney, and Langton in Toronto, and received his call to the Ontario bar in 1896. He practised law for a few years in London with Magee, McKillop, and Murphy, and then moved his practice to Kenora, where he was appointed the Crown attorney of the district of Rainy River until 1910. That year he moved to Saskatchewan, and opened his law practice with McCraney, Mackenzie, and Hutchinson in Regina. He married Agnes Strickland of Toronto in 1902. Appointed to the Court of King's Bench in 1921, he was elevated to the Court of Appeal in 1926. In 1939, he was appointed chancellor of the University of Saskatchewan. He died in 1946. See *Who's Who in Canada, 1938–39* (Toronto: International Press, 1939) at 1476; *Who's Who in Canada, 1945–46* (Toronto: International Press, 1946) at 918; W.H. McConnell, *Prairie Justice* (Calgary: Burroughs, 1980) at 217.

59 See Sherene Razack, "From Consent to Responsibility, from Pity to Respect: Subtexts in Cases of Sexual Violence Involving Girls and Women with Developmental Disabilities" (1994) 19 *Law & Social Inquiry* 819 at 906.

60 For a modern critique, see Russell, "Interpreting in Legal Contexts," above note 26.

61 Provincial Archives of Alberta, Attorney General Papers, Procedure Books and Civil and Criminal Action files from Wetaskiwin Supreme and District Court 1907–1979, R. v. Kowell, File #244, Accession No. 81, 198, 85, 13, as cited in Terry L. Chapman, "Sex Crimes in the West, 1890–1920" (Autumn 1987) 35 *Alberta History* 6–21.

62 *The King v. Simms* (1924), 57 N.S.R. 476 (N.S.S.C.).

63 *Rex v. Baschuk*, [1931] 2 W.W.R. 713 (Man. C.A.).

64 *Rex v. Reeves* (1941), 77 C.C.C. 89 (B.C.C.A.).

65 *Simpson v. The Queen* (1954), 109 C.C.C. 366 (N.S.S.C.).

66 *Dupont v. The Queen* (1958), 123 C.C.C. 386 (Que. C.A.).

67 *Regina v. Taillon* (1960), 127 C.C.C. 275 (Sask. C.A.).

68 *Regina v. Kyselka* (1962), 133 C.C.C. 103 (Ont. C.A.). Similarly, see *Regina v. Burkart; Regina v. Sawatsky*, [1965] 3 C.C.C. 210 (Sask. C.A.), where the court held it was improper to admit evidence from a doctor that the complainant was mentally incapable of fabricating a lengthy story in detail.

69 A conviction was registered in Rex v. Lee Westhaver, Public Archives of Nova Scotia, RG39 Series D, v.715, #874, Nova Scotia Supreme Court, Halifax, October Criminal Term, 17 October 1932, when a jury found there had been unlawful carnal knowledge of Maud Johnson, an eighteen-year-old "feeble-minded woman." The surviving records indicate little about Maud Johnson, except that she had left school in third grade at the age of sixteen. The conviction was assisted by the evidence that Maud's father had caught the accused lying on top of his struggling daughter in a deserted roadway. In *Regina v. Huffman, Huffman & Davignon* (1958), 120 C.C.C. 323 (Ont. C.A.), three accused men from Detroit brutally assaulted a young unmarried woman, who worked in the bottling plant of Hiram Walker's distillery in Windsor. She was described as "quiet," "retiring," and a "virgin," as well as "not bright mentally" and "less than average in matter of appearance or female attractiveness" with a "slight deformity referred to as a wryneck, which she or her mother attempted to camouflage by dress patterns." The injuries inflicted were "so severe" that the victim had to be given general anesthetic before she could be examined. The physician testified that he had never seen such severe and extensive injuries to the sexual organs of any female. There were convictions for rape and indecent assault. In *The King v. Walebek* (1913), 21 C.C.C. 130 (Sask. S.C.), the initial charge of carnal knowledge of an "idiot or imbecile" was dropped at trial because of lack of evidence that the "accused had knowledge of the mental condition of the girl" at the time. However, the court discussed whether the complainant was in such a state of "imbecility" that she was "incapable of giving her consent." The judge found that although the complainant was twenty-one years old, she had never gone to school, could not dress herself or comb her hair, could not cook or do anything around the house, got mixed up when she talked, and liked the company of small children. Noting that the accused had promised her 25 cents to have sex with him, the court concluded that "she did not consent from mere animal passion, and that the very nature of the bargain goes to shew that from mere imbecility on her part she was incapable of exercising any judgment on the matter." The court held that the jury

could have found imbecility incapacitated consent. *Regina v. Moore and Grazier*, [1971] 1 W.W.R. 656 (B.C.C.A.) upheld the conviction of two men for raping a deaf woman. The complainant, a "27-year-old unmarried deaf-mute" was waiting at a bus stop, when two strange men drove up in a car. They testified that they were trying to pick her up, and that she entered their car voluntarily. She testified that she "indicated by facial expressions and gesticulations" that she wished to wait for the bus, but they forced her into the car. The men testified that the complainant voluntarily had sexual relations with both of them, but objected when they tried to force her to participate in fellatio. She testified that she was raped, and that she eventually threw herself out of the vehicle, which was travelling at 50 mph. She was found on the highway, nude from the waist down, suffering from a fractured skull. On the hospital bed, she tried to tell the police officers in writing what had transpired, and then responded in writing to the officer's question: "Did the two boys try to take your clothes off or make advances towards you." She wrote back: "Yes, the boy forced to take and cried and then they do me." The accused argued that this was inadmissible as a recent complaint because it had been induced by a leading question. The appellate court disagreed, in what appears to be a rare occasion of judicial sensitivity to the communication difficulties of deaf women: "At the outset, it is well to recognize the unusual situation that existed. We have a deaf-mute woman found injured on . . . a highway in a semi-nude condition, in circumstances that make it clear that she had fallen, jumped, or been thrown or pushed from a moving vehicle. Shortly afterwards she is receiving attention in a hospital and is approached by a police officer who asks a quite proper question as to what happened. She writes, from a difficult supine position, a short statement that, to my mind, can only be interpreted, despite its imperfect language, as meaning that two boys forced her into a car and forced her to do something . . . that she did not want to do. . . . The statement, unusual as it was in language, was clearly a recent complaint of a sexual act . . . and properly admitted in evidence."

70 Cymri History, *Plowshares to Pumpjacks*, above note 1 at 549.

71 "Suspect in Bank Robbery Shoots Self after Crash" *Saskatoon Star-Phoenix* (24 Feb. 1962) 3; "Inquest into Probe Death" *Weyburn Review* (11 March 1962) at 1; Death certificate, 1 March 1962, Department of Vital Statistics, Regina, #1961-07-002319. He was forty-seven years old.

Chapter 7: Child Witnesses

1 The court repeatedly referred to the diminutive stature of the complainant, describing her as "the little one," "the little girl," and "the little [Tremblay] girl." All of the details that follow were drawn from the English version of the reported decision, *Soulière v. The Queen* (1952), 104 C.C.C. 339 (Que. C.A.), along with the French summary [1952] *Rapports Judiciaires de Québec* (Court du Banc de la Reine) 480, and the press coverage: "Ovila Soulière écope de 18 mois de prison à Hull" *Ottawa Le Droit* (14 déc. 1951) 17; "Une vingtaine de causes aux assises criminelles" *Ottawa Le Droit* (2 nov. 1951) 15. The surviving archival records contain the notice of appeal, documentation regarding bail, facta, and appellate judges' decisions, but no transcript of the

1 preliminary inquiry, trial, or depositions of witnesses. Dossier #774 de la Cour d'appel du Québec, Ovila Soulière v. La Reine (1951–52); Centre d'archives de l'Outaouais in the Superior Court Registry for Hull.

2 The trial was held in French, and except for the judgment of Judge George Miller Hyde, the appellate decision was originally delivered in French, and then translated to English.

3 Ovila Soulière was born 6 November 1904. His parents from Aylmer were Cyrille Soulière, a labourer with the Capital Brewing Company Ltd., and Delia Bourgeau. Institut de la statistique du Québec (ISQ), Bibliothèque, Société de généalogie de Québec, c.p. 2234, Québec, 2E, G1K 7N8; Mariages du comté de Gatineau (du début des paroisses à 1964 inclusivement), vol. 2 L–Z, compilé par Lucien Rivest, c.s.v., Montréal, 1971, p.1261–62; compilé par Jean-Paul Chamberland à partir des deux tomes des Mariages du comté de Gatineau (du début des paroisses à 1964 inclusivement), de Lucien Rivest (Montréal, 1971), Répertoire des mariages du comté du Gatineau, juillet 1996, Index onomastique des épouses: Adrienne Côté, p. 51; Index onomastique des époux: Ovila Soulière, p. 231; *Ottawa City Directory 1922* (Ottawa: Might Directories, 1922) at 793.

4 Chad Gaffield, *History of the Outaouais* (Québec: Presses de l'Université Laval, 1997); Lucien Brault, *Hull: 1800–1950* (Ottawa: Éditions de l'Université d'Ottawa, 1950); E.E. Cinq-Mars, *Hull: son origine, ses progrès, son avenir* (Hull: Bérubé Frères, 1908); Bruce S. Elliott, "The Famous Township of Hull: Image and Aspirations of a Pioneer Québec Community" (1979) 12 *Social History/Histoire sociale* 339; Raymond Ouimet, *Hull: Mémoire vive* (Hull: Éditions Vents d'Ouest, 2000); Raymond Ouimet, *Une ville en flammes* (Éditions Vents d'Ouest, 1996); "Hull," *The Canadian Encyclopedia* (Toronto: McClelland & Stewart, 2000) 1113–14.

5 Dorothy E. Chunn, "Secrets and Lies: The Criminalization of Incest and the (Re)Formation of the 'Private' in British Columbia, 1890–1940" in John McLaren, Robert Menzies & Dorothy E. Chunn, eds., *Regulating Lives: Historical Essays on the State, Society, the Individual and the Law* (Vancouver: UBC Press, 2002) 120; Joan Sangster, "Masking and Unmasking the Sexual Abuse of Children: Perceptions of Violence against Children in the Badlands of Ontario, 1916–30" (2000) 25 *Journal of Family History* 504; Robert Adamoski, "Their Duties towards the Children: Citizenship and the Practice of Child Rescue in Early Twentieth Century British Columbia" (Ph.D. Thesis, Simon Fraser University, 1995); Marie-Aimée Cliche, "Un secret bien gardé: l'inceste dans la société traditionnelle québécoise, 1858–1938" (1996) 50 *Revue d'histoire de l'Amérique française* 201.

6 John C. Yuille & Gary L. Wells, "Concerns about the Application of Research Findings" in John Doris, ed., *The Suggestibility of Children's Recollections* (Washington, DC: American Psychological Association, 1991) noted at 120 that "the rate of appearance of children in courts (both family and criminal) has grown exponentially in just a few years," giving us a "recent and growing understanding of the extent of the sexual abuse of children." Margaret A. Jackson, "Researching Child Sexual Abuse: A Case Study" in Joan Brockman & Dorothy Chunn, eds., *Investigating Gender Bias: Law, Courts, and the Legal Profession* (Toronto: Thompson Educational Publishing, 1993) 97

noted at 100 that "historically speaking, the rise in awareness of child sexual abuse cases [occurred] in the late 70s and 80s." The inaccuracy of this is attested to by historical medical periodicals. See, for example, Sir Francis W. Anthony, M.D., "Rape" (1895) 132 *Boston Medical and Surgical Journal* 29, citing at 31 a mid-nineteenth-century study in France by Tardieu showing 17 657 child rape victims, and cases reported by Brady and Taylor with victims aged nine months, eighteen months, and two years. Anthony noted at 58 that one of the symptoms of senile dementia was an uncontrollable sexual desire, resulting in assaults "by old men on children." C.C. Mapes, "A Practical Consideration of Sexual Assault" (1906) 24 *The Medical Age: A Semi-Monthly Journal of Medicine and Surgery* 928 noted at 933 that "sexual assault is far more common on children than on adult females" and cited a study by Casper of 109 rape cases, with over 75 percent of the victims under the age of twelve. Mapes added at 936 that "adolescent boys not infrequently commit sexual assault on young female children." It is not possible to assess the methodology and accuracy of these studies, but they indicate that child sexual abuse was historically understood to be pervasive.

7   The 1900–75 cases span the country, and include children as young as three. For some examples, see *The King v. De Wolfe* (1904), 9 C.C.C. 38 (Halifax Co. Ct.), unlawful carnal knowledge of a seven-year-old girl; *The King v. Wright* (1905), 10 C.C.C. 461 (N.B.S.C.), rape of an eight-year-old girl; *The King v. Barron* (1905), 9 C.C.C. 196 (Halifax Co. Ct.), indecent assault of a seven-year-old girl; *The King v. Armstrong* (1907), 12 C.C.C. 544 (Ont. C.A.), carnal knowledge of an eleven-year-old girl; *Rex v. Elzear Pailleur* (1909), 15 O.W.R. 73 (Ont. C.A.), attempt to commit incest upon a seven-year-old daughter; *Rex v. Bowes*, [1910] 20 O.L.R. 111 (Ont. C.A.), attempt to have carnal knowledge of a girl aged seven; *Rex v. Whistnant* (1912), 20 C.C.C. 322 (Alta. S.C.), indecent assault upon a twelve-year-old girl; *Rex v. McGivney* (1914), 22 C.C.C. 222 (B.C.S.C.), indecent assault upon a six-year-old girl; *Rex v. McMillan*, [1916] 9 W.W.R. 1181 (Alta. S.C.), rape of a girl aged four; *Shorten v. The King* (1918), 42 D.L.R. 591 (S.C.C.), carnal knowledge of a girl of seven; *Rex v. Turnick* (1920), 33 C.C.C. 340 (N.S.S.C.), rape upon a girl of seven; *Rex v. Landlow* (1922), 38 C.C.C. 54 (Halifax Police Ct.), attempted gross indecency with a boy of twelve; *Rex v. Parkin* (1922), 37 C.C.C. 35 (Man. C.A.), carnal knowledge and indecent assault of a twelve-year-old girl and indecent assault of a ten-year-old girl; *Rex v. Horn* (1923), 40 C.C.C. 117 (Alta. C.A.), indecent assault on a boy aged four; *Rex v. Creamer* (1923), 40 C.C.C. 283 (Alta. S.C.), indecent assault upon a girl aged six; *Rex v. Kramer* (1924), 20 Alta. L.R. 244 (Alta. C.A.), indecent assault upon a six-year-old girl; *Rex v. Gemmill* (1924), 43 C.C.C. 360 (Ont. C.A.), indecent assault upon a girl of six; *Rex v. Girone* (1925), 34 B.C.R. 554 (B.C.C.A.), carnal knowledge of a four-year-old girl; *The King v. John Turnick* (1925), 58 N.S.R. 286 (N.S.S.C.), rape of a seven-year-old girl; *Rex v. Everitt* (1925), 45 C.C.C. 133 (N.S.S.C.), carnal knowledge of an eight-year-old girl; *Rex v. Rump* (1929), 51 C.C.C. 236 (B.C.C.A.), attempt to have carnal knowledge of a girl aged eleven; *Rex v. Fitzpatrick* (1929), 40 B.C.R. 478 (B.C.C.A.), indecent assault upon a seven-year-old girl; *Rex v. Marcus and Richmond* (1931), 55 C.C.C. 322 (Ont. C.A.), rape of a twelve-year-old girl; *Rex v. Silverstone*, [1934] O.R. 94 (Ont. C.A.), indecent assault upon a nine-year-old boy; *R. v. Kirkham* (1935), 64 C.C.C. 255

(B.C.C.A.), indecent assault on a nine-year-old girl; *Rex v. McKevitt*, [1936] 3 D.L.R. 750 (N.S.S.C. *in banco*), indecent assault on a twelve-year-old girl; *Rex v. Hober* (1943), 80 C.C.C. 332 (B.C.C.A.), indecent assault on a six-year-old girl; *Rex v. Hand* (1946), 62 B.C.R. 359 (B.C.C.A.), carnal knowledge of a four-year-old girl; *Rex v. Yates* (1946), 62 B.C.R. 307 (B.C.C.A.), indecent assault on a ten-year-old girl; *Rex v. Antrobus* (1946), 63 B.C.R. 372 (B.C.C.A.), procuring a nine-year-old girl to have unlawful carnal connection with another person; *Rex v. Cowpersmith* (1946), 62 B.C.R. 401 (B.C.C.A.), indecent assault on an eight-year-old girl; *Rex v. Tillitson* (1947), 89 C.C.C. 389 (B.C.S.C.), indecent assault on a girl of eight; *Rex v. Pawlyna* (1948), 91 C.C.C. 50 (Ont. C.A.), attempting to have carnal knowledge of a six-year-old girl; *Rex v. Smullin* (1948), 91 C.C.C. 274 (N.B.C.A.), indecent assault on a girl aged nine; *The King v. Dumont* (1950), 26 M.P.R. 387 (N.B.C.A.), indecent assault upon a boy aged five; *The King v. Brown* (1951), 99 C.C.C. 305 (N.B.C.A.), indecent assault on an eleven-year-old girl; *Rex v. Lebrun* (1951), 100 C.C.C. 16 (Ont. C.A.), indecent assault on a six-year-old boy; *Rex v. Larochelle* (1951), 102 C.C.C. 194 (N.S.S.C. *in banco*), indecent assault on a ten-year-old boy; *Rex v. Tilley* (1951), 101 C.C.C. 223 (Ont. C.A.), indecent assault on a seven-year-old girl; *Regina v. Willaert* (1953), 105 C.C.C. 172 (Ont. C.A.), rape of an eight-year-old girl; *Regina v. Hoyt* (1953), 107 C.C.C. 59 (Ont. C.A.), attempted rape upon a twelve-year-old girl; *Regina v. Allen* (1954), 108 C.C.C. 102 (Sask. C.A.), indecent assault on a three-year-old girl; *Regina v. Gillingham* (1955), 112 C.C.C. 78 (Nfld. S.C.), carnal knowledge of girls aged seven and nine; *Regina v. Johns* (1956), 116 C.C.C. 200 (B.C. Co. Ct.), carnal knowledge of a nine-year-old girl; *White v. The Queen* (1956), 115 C.C.C. 97 (S.C.C.), carnal knowledge of a twelve-year-old girl; *Regina v. Jones* (1956), 115 C.C.C. 273 (Ont. C.A.), indecent assault on girls aged six, seven, and eight; *Regina v. Backshall* (1956), 115 C.C.C. 221 (Ont. C.A.), indecent assault on a girl aged seven; *Radovskis v. Tomm* (1957), 65 Man. R. 61 (Man. Q.B.), rape of a five-year-old girl; *Regina v. Stone* (1960), 127 C.C.C. 359 (Ont. C.A.), indecent assault upon a twelve-year-old girl; *Regina v. Jones*, [1964] 2 C.C.C. 123 (N.S.S.C. *in banco*), indecent assault upon a twelve-year-old girl; *Regina v. Wilband*, [1965] 51 W.W.R. 251 (B.C.C.A.), indecent assault upon a twelve-year-old girl; *Regina v. DeClercq*, [1966] 2 C.C.C. 190 (Ont. C.A.), indecent assault upon an eleven-year-old girl; *Regina v. Mullen*, [1968] 1 C.C.C. 320 (B.C.C.A), indecent assault upon an eight-year-old girl; *Regina v. Resener*, [1968] 64 W.W.R. 257 (B.C.C.A.), indecent assault upon a seven-year-old girl; *Regina v. Grant*, [1968] 4 C.C.C. 346 (Que. Ct. of Sess. of Peace), carnal knowledge of a girl aged ten; *Regina v. Bain*, [1970] 2 C.C.C. 49 (N.S.C.A.), indecent assault upon a girl aged twelve; *Regina v. Hulan*, [1970] 1 C.C.C. 36 (Ont. C.A.), carnal knowledge with an eleven-year-old girl; *Regina v. Baney*, [1972] 6 C.C.C. (2d) 75 (Ont. C.A.), indecent assault upon a four-year-old boy; *Regina v. DeWinter*, [1974] 16 C.C.C. (2d) 491 (B.C.C.A.), contributing to juvenile delinquency by exposing his private parts to a five-year-old girl; *Regina v. Muise*, [1975] 22 C.C.C. (2d) 487 (N.S.C.A.), carnal knowledge of a twelve-year-old girl; *Regina v. Wood*, [1976] 26 C.C.C. (2d) 100 (Alta. C.A.), gross indecency and buggery of a nine-year-old girl; *Regina v. McKeachnie*, [1976] 26 C.C.C. (2d) 317 (Ont. C.A.), indecent assault of a nine-year-old girl.

8 For charges of sexual assault involving children by **fathers,** see, for example, *Rex v. Elzear Pailleur* (1909), 15 O.W.R. 73 (Ont. C.A.); *Leroux v. The King* (1927), 49 C.C.C. 111 (Que. K.B.); *Rex v. J.* (1929), 38 Man. R. 144 (Man. C.A.); *Bergeron v. The King* (1930), 56 C.C.C. 62 (Que. K.B.); *Rex v. Pegelo* (1934), 48 B.C.R. 146 (B.C.C.A.); *Rex v. Droux* (1936), 44 Man. R. 75 (Man. C.A.); *Rex v. Guilbault* (1939), 72 C.C.C. 254 (Que. K.B.); *Rex v. Wyatt* (1944), 60 B.C.R. 255 (B.C.C.A.); *Charest v. The Queen* (1957), 119 C.C.C. 197 (Que. C.A.); *R. v. Fargnoli* (1957), 117 C.C.C. 359 (S.C.C.); *Regina v. Huebschwerlen*, [1965] 3 C.C.C. 212 (Yukon C.A.); *Regina v. Verlaan*, [1972] 6 C.C.C. (2d) 160 (B.C.C.A.); *Regina v. DesLauriers*, [1973] 10 C.C.C. (2d) 309 (Ont. C.A.); *Regina v. Scott*, [1974] 15 C.C.C. (2d) 234 (N.S.C.A.); **stepfathers,** see, for example, *Rex v. Donovan* (1947), 88 C.C.C. 86 (N.B.C.A.); *Regina v. Hulan*, [1970] 1 C.C.C. 36 (Ont. C.A.); *Regina v. Williams*, [1973] 12 C.C.C. (2d) 453 (Ont. C.A.); *Regina v. Wood*, [1976] 26 C.C.C. (2d) 100 (Alta. C.A.); **grandfathers**, see, for example, *The Queen v. Garneau* (1899), 4 C.C.C. 69 (Que. K.B.); **uncles,** see, for example, Rex v. George West (1924), Archives of Ontario, RG22-392-0-3603, Box 85B; *White v. The Queen* (1956), 115 C.C.C. 97 (S.C.C.); **brothers,** see, for example, Rex v. Fearn (1925), Saskatchewan Archives Board, District Court Judges Criminal Court, Judicial District of Arcola, 10 February 1925); **boarders,** see, for example, *Rex v. Lamond* (1925), 29 O.W.N. 297 (Ont. Div. Ct.); **a labourer on the family farm**, see, for example, *Rex v. Paul* (1912), 21 W.L.R. 699 (Alta. S.C.); **superintendents of training school facilities for boys held as inmates**, see, for example, *Rex v. Elliott* (1928), 49 C.C.C. 302 (Ont. C.A.); **shop-keepers**, see, for example, *Rex v. McKevitt*, [1936] 3 D.L.R. 750 (N.S.S.C. *in banco*); **school janitors**, see, for example, *Rex v. Hober* (1943), 80 C.C.C. 332 (B.C.C.A.); **teachers,** see, for example, *Regina v. Johnston*, [1965] 3 C.C.C. 42 (Man. C.A.); *Regina v. D.*, [1972] 5 C.C.C. (2d) 366 (Ont. C.A.); **Sunday School teachers**, see, for example, *Rex v. Cowpersmith* (1946), 62 B.C.R. 401 (B.C.C.A.); **drivers of home-delivery bread wagons**, see, for example, *Regina v. Allen* (1954), 108 C.C.C. 102 (Sask. C.A.); **apartment neighbours**, see, for example, *Regina v. Mullen*, [1968] 1 C.C.C. 320 (B.C.C.A); *Regina v. Baney*, [1972] 6 C.C.C. (2d) 75 (Ont. C.A.).

9 Indecent assault did not require proof of vaginal-penile penetration, and it was no defence to show that a victim under fourteen years had consented: *Criminal Code*, R.S.C. 1927, c.36, ss.292 and 294. For more details regarding the history of the statutory rape provisions, see chapter 3.

10 For a three-year-old complainant, see *Regina v. Allen* (1954), 108 C.C.C. 102 (Sask. C.A.); for four-year-old complainants, see *Rex v. Hand* (1946), 62 B.C.R. 359 (B.C.C.A.); *Regina v. Baney*, [1972] 6 C.C.C. (2d) 75 (Ont. C.A.); *Rex v. McMillan*, [1916] 9 W.W.R. 1181 (Alta. S.C.); *Rex v. Horn* (1923), 40 C.C.C. 117 (Alta. C.A.).

11 A younger child, aged four, testified in a carnal knowledge prosecution in *Rex v. Girone* (1925), 34 B.C.R. 554 (B.C.C.A.), although her evidence was not sworn. The trial judge gave an "unusual testimonial" to the child's "exceptional intelligence and veracity," but the appellate court overturned the conviction because the child's evidence contained inconsistencies. A four-year-old girl gave unsworn testimony in R. v. McLees in 1914, on a carnal knowledge prosecution; the verdict was not guilty: Provincial Archives of Alberta, Attorney General Papers, Criminal and Civil Supreme and District case files pertaining to Southern Alberta from the Supreme

Court of Alberta in Calgary, 1905–1971, File No. 334, Accession No. 29, 285, 85, 249, as cited in Terry L. Chapman, "Sex Crimes in the West, 1890–1920" (Autumn 1987) 35 *Alberta History* 6–21. In *The King v. Dumont* (1950), 26 M.P.R. 387 (N.B.C.A.), a charge of indecent assault, the five-year-old male complainant gave unsworn evidence in court. The appellate court quashed the conviction because the judge had failed to ensure that the child's evidence met the statutory prerequisites for unsworn child testimony.

12 Simon Greenleaf, *A Treatise on the Law of Evidence*, 4th ed. (London: Stevens and Norton, 1848–57) §441; *Omychund v. Barker* (1744) 26 Eng. Rep. 15 (Ct. of Chancery); W.M. Best, *The Principles of the Law of Evidence* (Toronto: Carswell, 1911) at 145; *Regina v. Duguay*, [1966] 3 C.C.C. 266 (Sask. C.A.).

13 *Rex v. Antrobus* (1946), 63 B.C.R. 372 (B.C.C.A.). See also *Rex v. Pawlyna* (1948), 91 C.C.C. 50 (Ont. C.A.).

14 *Rex v. Lebrun* (1951), 100 C.C.C. 16 (Ont. C.A.).

15 *Rex v. Larochelle* (1951), 102 C.C.C. 194 (N.S.S.C. *in banco*).

16 *Regina v. Stone* (1960), 127 C.C.C. 359 (Ont. C.A.). The increasing secularization of society eventually brought change, first in dissent in *Rex v. Larochelle* (1951), 102 C.C.C. 194 (N.S.S.C. *in banco*), and *Regina v. Horsburgh*, [1966] 3 C.C.C. 240 (Ont. C.A.), and later in majority decisions accepting a wider range of answers from child witnesses: *Regina v. Bannerman*, [1966] 55 W.W.R. 257 (Man. C.A.); *Regina v. Taylor*, [1970] 75 W.W.R. 45 (Man. C.A.).

17 *Canada Evidence Act*, R.S.C. 1927, c.59, s.16(1) provided: "In any legal proceeding where a child of tender years is offered as a witness, and such child does not, in the opinion of the judge . . . understand the nature of an oath, the evidence of such child may be received, though not given under oath, if, in the opinion of the judge . . . such child is possessed of sufficient intelligence to justify the reception of the evidence, and understands the duty of speaking the truth." Earlier versions included S.C. 1893, c.31, s.25, and R.S.C. 1906, c.145, s.16. These provisions were duplicated almost exactly in the *Criminal Code*, R.S.C. 1927, c.36, s.1003(1). For earlier versions, see S.C. 1890, c.37, s.13; S.C. 1892, c.29, s.685; R.S.C. 1906, c.146, s.1003. Emphasizing the importance of these provisions in 1890, Justice Minister Sir John Thompson noted that he had seen "very gross offenders escape, on the simple plea of not guilty, in clear cases of assault on children, for the simple reason that there was no possibility of taking the child's statement without the sanction of an oath, and the simple taking of that statement would have been sufficient to put the prisoner on his defence and procure conviction." *House of Commons Debates* 4th Sess., 6th Parl., vol. 30 at 3163.

18 Failure to complete such an inquiry could be fatal. See, for example, *The King v. Dumont* (1950), 26 M.P.R. 387 (N.B.C.A.); *Rex v. Pawlyna* (1948), 91 C.C.C. 50 (Ont. C.A.).

19 R.S.C. 1927, c.59, s.16(2). Earlier versions included S.C. 1893, c.31, s.25, and R.S.C. 1906, c.145, s.16. The parliamentary debates surrounding the initial enactment of these provisions contain no discussion regarding the rationale: *House of Commons Debates* (1893) 3d Sess., 7th Parl., vol. 36 at 435, 1674–1704, and 3482–86.

20 R.S.C. 1927, c.36, s.1002, 1003(2). Earlier versions included S.C. 1890, c.37, s.13; S.C. 1892, c.29, ss.684–85; R.S.C. 1906, c.146, s.1002, 1003. The parliamentary debates do not

provide a rationale specifically for this section, but contain a great deal of discussion about the propensity of women to "blackmail" men with claims of sexual assault, and the difficulties of "young men" who are "led into trouble improperly": *House of Commons Debates* (1890) 4th Sess., 6th Parl., vol. 30 at 342–44, 3162–86, and 3442–60.

21 E. Jowitt & C. Walsh, eds., *The Dictionary of English Law* (London: Sweet and Maxwell, 1959) vol. 1 noted at 504: "The general rule of English law, unlike that of other systems, is that the evidence of a single witness is sufficient to prove any case, civil or criminal." See also Ernest Cockle, *Cases and Statutes on the Law of Evidence*, 7th ed. (London: Sweet and Maxwell, 1946) at 156. Sidney L. Phipson, *Law of Evidence* (London: Sweet and Maxwell, 1942) 8th ed. noted at 476: "As a general rule, Courts may act on the testimony of a single witness, even though uncorroborated. . . . In Anglo-Saxon and Norman times, proof was, according to the importance of the case, made six-handed, twelve-handed, etc.; he who had the greater number of witnesses prevailing. Attempts were not lacking to import this system into the common law; but though various statutes were passed requiring two or more witnesses in particular cases the attempts failed, and from about the middle of the sixteenth century onward the present rule began to be more or less effectively recognized."

22 The civil burden of proof was merely a preponderance of evidence. J.W. Cecil Turner, *Kenny's Outlines of Criminal Law* (Cambridge: Cambridge University Press, 1952) defined reasonable doubt at 417: "Whenever, therefore, an allegation of crime is made, it is the duty of the jury — to borrow Lord Kenyon's homely phrase — 'if the scales of evidence hang anything like even, to throw into them some grains of mercy'; or as it is more commonly put, to give the prisoner the benefit of any reasonable doubt. Not, be it noted, of every doubt, but only of a doubt for which reasons can be given; for everything relative to human affairs and dependent on human evidence is open to some possible or imaginary doubts. It is the condition of mind which exists when the jurors cannot say that they feel an abiding conviction, a moral certainty, of the truth of the charge. For it is not sufficient for the prosecutor to establish a probability, even though a strong one according to the doctrine of chances; he must establish the fact to a moral certainty — a certainty that convinces the understanding, satisfies the reason, and directs the judgment."

23 Corroboration was attached to criminal proceedings for a variety of sexual offences and civil proceedings for affiliation, breach of promise to marry, divorce, and claims against a dead person's estate. In addition, criminal prosecutions for perjury, treason, blasphemy, and personation required corroboration. Two types of witnesses were also singled out: children of "tender years" who had not been sworn, and accomplices. See Cockle, *Cases and Statutes on the Law of Evidence*, above note 21 at 156–57; Constance Backhouse, "The Doctrine of Corroboration in Sexual Assault Trials in Early Twentieth Century Canada and Australia" (Spring 2001) 26 *Queen's Law Journal* 306–7. Even where a child was sworn as a witness, it was customary for judges to warn juries not to convict an accused on the uncorroborated evidence of a child "except after weighing that evidence with extreme care"; Alan Burnside Harvey, *Tremeear's Criminal Code of Canada*, 5th ed. (Toronto: Carswell, 1944) at 1264.

24 Sir Matthew Hale, *Historia Placitorum Coronae*, vol. 1 (London: Nutt and Gosling, 1734) 635–36. Most of the statement was inaccurate. On the difficulty of making accusations of rape, see chapter 5. The very low conviction rates obtained in sexual assault prosecutions support Hale's opinion that the charge was hard to prove, but destroy his conjecture that it was "harder to be defended." On the low conviction rates, see chapter 10. Hale is also cited as the originator of the marital rape exemption; see Jill Elaine Hasday, "Contest and Consent: A Legal History of Marital Rape" (Oct. 2000) 88 *California Law Review* 1373. For discussion of Hale's reputation as a misogynist and his role in convicting women accused of witchcraft, see G. Geiss, "Lord Hale, Witches and Rape" (1978) 5 *British Journal of Law and Society* 26; Jocelynne Scutt, "Law Reform and Child Sexual Abuse in Australia" in Penelope Hetherington, ed., *Incest and the Community: Australian Perspectives* (Nedlands: Centre for Western Australian History at the University of Western Australia, 1991) 117 at 125–26 and 134.

25 A.E. Popple, *Crankshaw's Criminal Code of Canada*, 7th ed. (Toronto: Carswell, 1959) at 172; *Halsbury's Laws of England*, vol. 9 (London: Butterworths, 1909) at 388; E.H. East, *Pleas of the Crown*, vol. 1 (Abingdon, Oxon: Professional Books, 1987 rpt.) at 445; Harvey, *Tremeear's Criminal Code*, above note 23 at 340. On the extension of this rule to gross indecency, see *R. v. Cullen*, [1976] 26 C.C.C. (2d) 79 (B.C.C.A.). Although some sources described the warning as "advisable" rather than mandatory, the distinction was frequently blurred; see Turner, *Kenny's Outlines of Criminal Law*, above note 22 at 420 on the duty to warn about corroboration in sexual offences: "Corroboration, though not essential in law, is always required in practice."

26 Harvey, *Tremeear's Criminal Code*, above note 23 at 1264; *Kendall v. The Queen*, [1962] S.C.R. 469.

27 *An Act to Amend the Criminal Code*, S.C. 1925, c.38, s.26. The parliamentary debates do not provide a rationale for introducing the corroboration requirement; *House of Commons Debates* (1925) 4th Sess., 14th Parl., vol. 14 at 3997–4015. Under R.S.C. 1927, c.36, ss.1002–3, crimes requiring statutory corroboration included seduction of girls between ages sixteen and eighteen (s.211); seduction under promise of marriage (s.212); seduction of a stepchild, foster child, or ward (s.213); seduction of a female employee under age twenty-one (s.213); seduction of a female passenger on a vessel (s.214); parent or guardian procuring defilement of a female (s.215); procuring (s.216); householder permitting defilement (s.217); conspiracy to defile (s.218); carnal knowledge of a female idiot, imbecile, insane, deaf and dumb, or feeble-minded female (s.219); offences involving the prostitution of Indian women (s.220); carnal knowledge of a girl under fourteen years (s.301); carnal knowledge of a girl between ages fourteen and sixteen (s.301); attempted carnal knowledge of a girl under fourteen years (s.302); abortion (ss.303–5); killing an unborn child (s.306); communicating venereal disease (s.307); bigamy (s.308); procuring feigned marriage (s.309); treason (s.74); perjury (s.174); forgery (ss.468–70). There were also mandatory corroboration requirements if the testimony of the child of tender years was not sworn (s.1003). Under S.C. 1953–54, c.51, s.131 and 184(3), crimes requiring statutory corroboration included sexual intercourse with a feeble-minded, insane, idiot, or imbecile woman (s.140); incest (s.142);

seduction of a female between ages sixteen and eighteen (s.143); seduction under promise of marriage (s.144); sexual intercourse with a female ward or employee (s.145); seduction of female passengers on vessels (s.146); procuring (s.184(1)). Section 566 added: "No person shall be convicted of an offence upon the unsworn evidence of a child unless the evidence of the child is corroborated in a material particular by evidence that implicates the accused."

28   See, for example, *Rex v. Cullen* (1948), 93 C.C.C. 1 (Ont. C.A.): "speaking as a matter of common sense and common experience and observation and practice in the courts, it is the duty of the judge to tell you that it is dangerous, it is unsafe, to convict on the evidence of the girl alone."

29   J.W. Cecil Turner, *Russell on Crime*, 6th ed., vol. 3 (London: Stevens and Sons, 1896) at 235. For discussion of the absence of empirical foundation, see Jocelynne Scutt, "Sexism and Psychology: An Analysis of the 'Scientific Basis' of the Corroboration Rule in Rape" (1979) 5 *Hecate* 35–48.

30   Wigmore (1863–1943), a law professor and dean at Northwestern University, was arguably the most famous legal scholar of his day; William R. Roalfe, *John Henry Wigmore: Scholar and Reformer* (Evanston, IL: Northwestern University Press, 1977). One of Wigmore's most frequently quoted passages is in his *Evidence in Trials at Common Law*, 3d ed., vol. 1 (Boston: Little Brown, 1940) at 9: "Modern psychiatrists have amply studied the behaviour of errant young girls coming before the courts in all sorts of cases. Their psychic complexes are multifarious, distorted partly by inherent defects, partly by diseased derangements or abnormal instincts, partly by bad social environment, partly by temporary physiological or emotional conditions. One form taken by these complexes is that of contriving false charges of sexual offenses by men."

Judith Lewis Herman, *Father-Daughter Incest* (Cambridge: Harvard University Press, 1981) noted at 11 that in his original *Treatise on Evidence* (1934), Wigmore unfairly purported to draw upon the "pronouncements of eminent psychiatric authorities," adding: "Where their published case reports suggested the possibility of real sexual abuse, Wigmore, like Freud, falsified or omitted the evidence. For example, in his discussion of incest, Wigmore cited case reports of two girls, ages seven and nine, who accused their fathers of sexual assault. In both cases, the original clinical reports documented the fact that the children had vaginal infections. The seven year old had gonorrhea and the nine year old's vagina was so inflamed and swollen that the doctor could not make a physical examination. This and other corroborating evidence was systematically omitted in Wigmore's presentation, and the cases were discussed as examples of pathological lying in children."

Leigh Beinen, "A Question of Credibility: John Henry Wigmore's Use of Scientific Authority in Section 924a of the Treatise on Evidence" (Spring 1983) 19 *California Western Law Review* 235–68, explored the misrepresentation Wigmore made of the four other sources upon which he relied. The first, William Healy and Mary T. Healy, *Pathological Lying, Accusation, and Swindling* (Boston: Little, Brown, 1915), was a study of juveniles characterized as "abnormal" or "delinquent." Beinen explored the gender, class, and racial biases of the Healy research and critiqued the use of data from a population defined as pathological to draw generalizations about all women. She also noted that Wigmore repeatedly deleted facts from the Healys' monograph of objective evidence corroborating that the young children described had actually been sexually abused. The second source, a 1937–38 American Bar Association Committee report, had been written primarily by Wigmore himself, although misleadingly, no indication of his authorship appeared in the evidence text. She critiqued the third source, O. Monkemoller, *Psychology and Psychopathology of Testimony*, a 1930 German monograph, as a "racist and misogynist" text, "typical of its time" and location. Beinen quoted select passages, including references to the "inferiority of female testimony" as a "matter of common knowledge among judges," and a series of discriminatory and contradictory statements about the "erotically explosive atmosphere" of "institutions where intellectually and morally inferior elements share daily life," and references to menstruation: "Menstruation has always been considered a physiological process which might very well exercise a detrimental influence on female testimony" (at 258–61). The fourth source consisted of three letters written to Wigmore by practising physicians. Beinen critiqued the substance of the physicians' conclusions and the use Wigmore made of their comments (at 261–62).

Wigmore, *A Student's Text on the Law of Evidence* (Brooklyn: Foundation Press, 1935) at 303–4, added that there was "always the risk of the jury's being misled by an attractive face and a plausible tale of woe. Modern psychiatry has further revealed that types of women are found whose unchaste temperament or diseased imagination lead them to the concoction of false charges of sexual offences." In a typical illustration of his propensity to base evidentiary analysis upon speculation, he described the case of "C, a girl of 12" who was a witness in a prosecution of "D, being a janitor in the apartment house" for "rape under age." Wigmore continued: "[C] testifies that D on a certain afternoon took her into his room and did the act. D testifies that he was indeed in his room at that time, but that the girl never came into his room then or at any other time. The local law does not require corroboration. If the jury believe from the girl's age and innocent appearance and plausible manner that her story is true, D will go to the penitentiary for several years (in some States for life). But if proper inquiry were allowed, it could perhaps be shown that the girl has been brought several times before the juvenile court for spending the night away from home, that she has often solicited men on the street, and that the psychiatrists have pronounced her to be a nymphomaniac. This evidence might save an innocent man."

31 *House of Commons Debates* (1954) 1st Sess., 22d Parl., vol. 2 at 2050.
32 For the legislative debates, see Constance Backhouse, "Nineteenth-Century Canadian Rape Law, 1800–92" in David H Flaherty, ed., *Essays in the History of Canadian Law*, vol. 2 (Toronto: Osgoode Society, 1983) at 206; Constance Backhouse, *Petticoats and Prejudice: Women and Law in Nineteenth-Century Canada* (Toronto: Women's Press, 1991) at 69–80. *Horsburgh v. The Queen*, [1968] 2 C.C.C. 288 (S.C.C.) noted that "the danger to be guarded against in cases of sexual offences is that the complainant, through a motive of spite, vengeance, hysteria or perhaps gain by way of blackmail, may make false accusations against which the accused, by reason of the nature of the charges, has no means of defence except his own unsupported denial."

33 John Henry Wigmore, *Evidence*, 2d ed., vol. 1 (Boston: Little, Brown & Co. 1923) at 922–23. These passages were highly influential in Canada; A.E. Branca, "Corroboration" in Roger E. Salhany & Robert J. Carter, eds., *Studies in Canadian Criminal Evidence* (Toronto: Butterworths, 1972) 133 at 178.

34 Wigmore, *Evidence*, above note 33 at 509. "Child's Play" was a chapter in Stevenson's *Virginibus Puerisque: Familiar Studies of Men and Books* (orig. pub. 1881, reprt. London: J.M. Dent & Sons, 1925). Described as a "layman's contribution to a philosophy of youth," it was based upon an upper-class model of care-free childhood, with depictions of youngsters playing enchantingly for hours in imaginary castles, and entertaining each other with stories over tea-drinking. Stevenson's comment that "the doings of grown folk are only interesting as the raw material for play," was certainly off the mark as far as victims of child sexual abuse were concerned. His conclusion, that a child "cares no more for what you call truth, than you for a gingerbread dragon," was meant to relieve innocent children from the burdens of testimony, as his final statement clarified: "They will come out of their gardens soon enough, and have to go into offices and the witness-box. Spare them yet a while, O conscientious parent! Let them doze among their playthings yet a little!" This seems little justification for Wigmore's attack on the credibility of child witnesses.

35 Rupert Cross, *Evidence* (London: Butterworths, 1958) at 135.

36 Sidney L. Phipson, *The Principles of the Law of Evidence by the Late W.M. Best with Full Notes of the Canadian Decisions*, 11th ed. (Toronto: Carswell, 1911) at 149.

37 Harvey, *Tremeear's Criminal Code*, above note 23 at 1264.

38 Turner, *Kenny's Outlines of Criminal Law*, above note 22 at 420. The quotation is cited to Mr. Inderwick, KC, without further details.

39 In *Rex v. McInulty* (1914), 22 C.C.C. 347 (B.C.C.A.), a prosecution for indecent assault, the court referred to "the known danger that children of tender years and immature minds are peculiarly susceptible to suggestions from parents or others." In *Rex v. Parkin* (1922), 37 C.C.C. 35 (Man. C.A.), a case of carnal knowledge and indecent assault, the court noted that young children were "possibly more under the influence of third persons . . . than are adults and they are apt to allow their imaginations to run away with them and to invent untrue stories." In *Horsburgh v. The Queen* [1968] 2 C.C.C. 288 (S.C.C.), a charge of contributing to juvenile delinquency by encouraging sexual conduct, the court described the unreliability of child evidence as due to four factors: "1. His capacity of observation. 2. His capacity of recollection. 3. His capacity to understand questions put and frame intelligent answers. 4. His moral responsibility."

40 *A New English Dictionary*, vol. 2 (Oxford: Oxford University Press, 1893) at 1020.

41 "[L]e vagin et les lèvres étaient rouges; que l'hymen était ouvert; que le vagin était enflammé etc. La cause . . . était quelque chose qui était entré dans son vagin."

42 *R. v. Turnick* (1920), 33 C.C.C. 340 (N.S.S.C.); *R. v. Hubin* (1927), 47 C.C.C. 237 (Man. C.A.); *Hubin v. The King* (1927), 48 C.C.C. 172 (S.C.C.); *R. v. Drew* (1932), 60 C.C.C. 37 (Sask. C.A.); *R. v. Jones*, [1935] 3 D.L.R. 237 (B.C.C.A.); *R. v. Droux* (1936), 44 Man. R. 75 (Man. C.A.); *R. v. O'Hara* (1946), 88 C.C.C. 74 (B.C.C.A); *R. v. Yott*, [1946] 1 D.L.R. 683 (Ont. C.A.); *R. v. Terrell*, [1947] 3 D.L.R. 523 (B.C.C.A.); *R. v. Johns* (1956), 116 C.C.C. 200

(B.C. Co. Ct.); *R. v. Smith & Gilson* (1956), 115 C.C.C. 38 (Ont. C.A.); *R. v. Fennell* (1957), 119 C.C.C. 344 (B.C.C.A.); *R. v. Ball* (1957), 117 C.C.C. 366 (B.C.C.A.); *R. v. St. Hilaire*, [1966] 3 C.C.C. 31 (Que. C.A.); *R. v. Schmidt and Gole*, [1973] 9 C.C.C. (2d) 101 (Ont. C.A.); *R. v. Scott*, [1974] 15 C.C.C. (2d) 234 (N.S.C.A.).

43 Marie Tremblay had also testified that she disclosed the abuse to her mother the day after it happened. Nothing further was made of this in the legal proceeding, possibly because Mme Tremblay later testified that her daughter had never complained to her about the abuse.

44 *Hopkinson v. Perdue* (1904), 8 C.C.C. 286 (Ont. Div. Ct.) described the exception as a survival of an "ancient practice" allowing courts to hear evidence of previous statements of witnesses not under oath, similar to their testimony in court, for the purpose of "confirming" that testimony. Inadmissible as a general rule, such evidence had survived as an exception in sexual assault causes. See also *R. v. Schraba* (1921), 31 Man. R. 275 (Man. C.A.).

45 *Thomas v. The Queen* (1952), 103 C.C.C. 193 (S.C.C.). See also *The Queen v. Riendeau* (1900), 9 Que. B.R. 147 (Que. K.B.); *Regina v. Kribs* (1960), 127 C.C.C. 1 (S.C.C.); *The King v. Akerley* (1918), 46 N.B.R. 195 (N.B.C.A.); *The King v. Trenholme* (1920), 30 Que. B.R. 232 (Que. K.B.); *Rex v. Proteau* (1923), 33 B.C.R. 39 (B.C.C.A.); Rex v. Andrew McLeod (1924) Middlesex Co. Ct. Records, Judge's Notebooks, Judge Judd, 1921, at 31–44, UWO Regional Room, Box 165; *The King v. George Hubley* (1925), 58 N.S.R. 113 (N.S.S.C.); *Rex v. Hall* (1927), 49 C.C.C. 146 (Ont. C.A.); *Rex v. Elliott* (1928), 49 C.C.C. 302 (Ont. C.A.); *Bodechon v. The Queen*, [1965] 50 M.P.R. 184 (P.E.I.S.C.).

46 See *Kribs v. The Queen* (1960), 127 C.C.C. 1 (S.C.C.), where a woman who had been raped multiple times by four men was escaping across a field, and hailed an approaching truck when she arrived at the highway. It stopped, and she got in and tearfully told the driver what had happened. According to the testimony, he said, "Oh you poor kid, I will drive you back to London." He then put his arm around her and said, "You will have to give me a kiss before I will." She jumped out of the truck, thus escaping what might have been an additional sexual assault.

47 *The King v. Bishop* (1906), 11 C.C.C. 30 (N.S.S.C.); *Rex v. Dunning* (1908), 1 Sask. L.R. 391 (Sask. K.B.); *Rex v. Stonehouse and Pasquale* (1927), 39 B.C.R. 279 (B.C.C.A.); *Regina v. Hunt*, [1964] 1 C.C.C. 210 (Ont. H. Ct.).

48 For similar holdings, see *The King v. Barron* (1905), 9 C.C.C. 196 (Halifax Co. Ct.); *Rex v. Bowes*, [1910] 20 O.L.R. 111 (Ont. C.A.); *Rex v. McGivney* (1914), 22 C.C.C. 222 (B.C.S.C.); *Shorten v. The King* (1918), 42 D.L.R. 591 (S.C.C.).

49 See, for example, *The Queen v. Riendeau* (1900), 9 Que. B.R. 147 (Que. K.B.) accepting recent complaint "as corroborative evidence to confirm her [the complainant's] testimony." Constance Backhouse, "Skewering the Credibility of Women: A Reappraisal of Corroboration in Australian Legal History" (March 2000) 29 *University of Western Australia Law Review* 79–107 describes the retreat from this position in Australia. For Canadian decisions refusing to take recent complaint as "corroboration," see *The King v. De Wolfe* (1904), 9 C.C.C. 38 (Halifax Co. Ct.); *Rex v. McMillan*, [1916] 9 W.W.R. 1181 (Alta. S.C.); *Rex v. Everitt* (1925), 45 C.C.C. 133 (N.S.S.C. *in banco*); *Hubin v. The King* (1927), 48 C.C.C. 172 (S.C.C.); *Rex v. Mudge* (1929), 52 C.C.C. 402 (Sask. C.A.); *Rex*

v. Stinson (1934), 61 C.C.C. 227 (B.C.C.A.); *Rex v. Tolhurst* (1939), 73 C.C.C. 332 (Sask. C.A.); *Regina v. Smith & Gilson* (1956), 115 C.C.C. 38 (Ont. C.A.); *Regina v. Nightingale* (1957), 124 C.C.C. 214 (N.B.C.A.); *Regina v. Plantus* (1957), 118 C.C.C. 260 (Ont. C.A.); *Regina v. Ball* (1957), 117 C.C.C. 366 (B.C.C.A.); *Regina v. Cross, Cassel, Bryan and Foley,* [1970] 1 C.C.C. 216 (Ont. C.A.).

50 *Rex v. Lebrun* (1951), 100 C.C.C. 16 (Ont. C.A.).

51 *Thomas v. The Queen* (1952), 103 C.C.C. 193 (S.C.C.).

52 *Rex v. Lebrun* (1951), 100 C.C.C. 16 (Ont. C.A.). In *Regina v. Kribs* (1960), 127 C.C.C. 1 (S.C.C.), the court stated: "The purposes for which it is admissible are (a) to rebut any inference adverse to the prosecution which might otherwise be drawn by the jury in the absence of evidence that a complaint was made and (b) to show the consistency of the conduct of the prosecutrix with the evidence given by her at the trial. The latter purpose, when the details of the complaint are given, is to strengthen the credibility of the prosecutrix."

53 Judge Ste-Marie traced his family roots in Hull back to 1867. His father practised with Ste-Marie & Ste-Marie in Hull. His mother, Lidwine Legris, was the daughter of Senator Joseph-Hormidas Legris. The Ste-Marie Hull legal dynasty of father and two sons (Paul and Joseph) would expand still further in the third generation to include Michel and Jean. Paul Ste-Marie studied at the Collège Notre-Dame de Hull, at the Collège Sainte-Marie de Montréal, and at the Université de Montréal. He was named a QC in 1944. He was elected to executive office in the Barreau de Hull in 1940, and elevated to Bâtonnier in 1949 and 1950. His judicial appointment in the newly created district of Hull made him the first resident judge from Hull on that court for over thirty years. He later became, along with Gérald Fauteux, Guy Favreau, and Charles Stein, one of the founders as well as the first vice-dean of the Faculty of Law, University of Ottawa, which subsequently awarded him an honorary doctorate. He was also one of the co-founders of the Cercle universitaire d'Ottawa, and the first president of the Fédération des oeuvres de charité de Hull et de sa région. Ignace-J.Deslauriers, J.C.S., *La Cour supérieure du Québec et ses juges, 1849–1er janvier 1980* (Dépot légal — 4e trimestre 1980, Bibliothèque nationale du Québec) at 136–37; E.E. Cinq-Mars, *Hull,* above note 4; Chantal Berniquez & Luc Villemaire, *Histoire du Barreau de Hull, des origines à nos jours (1889–1989)* (Dépôt légal: Bibliothèque nationale du Québec, 1989) at 110, 114–16, and 169–70; Société des éditions montréalaises inc., *Hull d'aujourd'hui, 1875–1975* (n.p., n.d.) at 72; *Hull City Directory, 1949* (Hull: Royal Publishing, 1949) at 130; Interview with Andrée Ste-Marie Tellier, daughter of Paul Ste-Marie, Town of Mount Royal, 24 May 2004, by Constance Backhouse.

54 Interview with Andrée Ste-Marie Tellier.

55 "Ovila Soulière a écopé de 18 mois de prison à Hull" *Ottawa Le Droit* (14 déc. 1951) 17.

56 Prison de Hull Écrous 1949, No. Écrou 855, 15 déc. 1951, Archives nationales du Québec — Outaouais, E17, S1, établissement de détention de Hull.

57 Defence counsel J. Harold Maloney, QC, a bilingual lawyer, was a leader within the Hull bar. He sat on the executive committee of the Barreau de Hull in 1936, 1943–44, 1946–48, and 1955–56. Lionel Mougeot, who prosecuted at both the trial and appeal,

also sat on the executive committee of the Barreau de Hull, serving as *vérificateur* in 1949, *sec-trésorier* in 1955, *syndic* in 1960, *conseiller* in 1961 and 1967, and *bâtonnier* in 1966. Berniquez & Villemaire, *Histoire du Barreau de Hull*, above note 53 at 142 and 169–73; Dossier #774 de la Court d'appel du Québec, Ovila Soulière v. La Reine (1951–52), Petition for Bail dated 29 Dec. 1951.

58 Galipeault had been born in Maskinongé in 1880, the son of a notary. He obtained his education at the College of Joliette and Laval University (B.A. 1897, LL.L. 1900, LL.D. 1925), was called to the bar of Québec in 1900, and received a KC in 1910. He served as Bâtonnier of the Québec bar, and as Bâtonnier General of the bar of the province of Québec. He was elected to the legislative assembly from 1909–27, serving as speaker of the legislative assembly and minister of public works and labour. He married Ernestine Lamontagne in 1903, and had three sons (two of whom practised law in partnership with him) and one daughter. He was made a judge of the Court of King's Bench in 1930, and Chief Justice of the province in 1950. He is noted for having disapproved of racial segregation in Québec, in a dissenting judgment in *York Corporation v. Christie* (1938), 65 Que. B.R. 104 (Que. K.B.) at 125–39. *Who's Who in Canada, 1951–52* (Toronto: International Press, 1952) at 105–6.

59 Defence counsel Maloney argued at the appeal that the evidence of recent complaint should not have been admitted, since it was "elicited after a lengthy questioning, covering many days" and because its admissibility had "caused a serious prejudice to the accused." The appellate judges felt no need to rule on this. Judge Bernard Bissonnette and Judge George Miller Hyde both wrote concurring opinions on the point that the recent complaint could not constitute corroboration. For biographic details on Judge Bissonnette, see below note 67. Judge Hyde was born in Sewickley, Pennsylvania, in 1905, and educated at Selwyn House School, Lower Canada College, and McGill, where he received his B.A. in 1926 and his B.C.L. in 1929. He married N.E. Anne Coghlin in 1938 and had two male children. He obtained a KC in 1949, and was appointed to the Court of Queen's Bench in 1950. *The Canadian Who's Who*, vol. 7 (1955–57) (Toronto: Trans-Canada Press, 1957) at 536.

60 See, for example, *Hubin v. The King* (1927), 36 Man. R. 373 (Man. C.A.), and [1927] S.C.R. 442; Backhouse, "Doctrine of Corroboration," above note 23 at 297–338.

61 R.S.C. 1927, c.59, s.16(2); R.S.C. 1927, c.36, s.1003(2).

62 *Rex v. Baskerville*, [1916] 2 K.B. 658 dealt with the evidence of accomplices, who also required corroboration under common law. The introduction of the word "independent" seems to have been an afterthought. The focus of the decision was to insist that the evidence of an accomplice be corroborated not only "as to the circumstances of the crime, but also as to the identity of the prisoner." The court stated that *Rex v. Wilson* (1911), 6 Cr. App. R. 125 (Ct. Crim. App.), had held that "it must not be supposed that corroboration is required amounting to independent evidence implicating the accused," and then added: "If this means that the judge should not warn the jury to require independent corroboration of some part of the story which implicates or involves the accused, it goes too far." The court offered no reason for requiring "independent" corroboration.

63 *Hubin v. The King*, [1927] S.C.R. 442 (S.C.C.). The complainant, a twelve-year-old girl, had accepted a car ride from a man she had not known previously. She alleged that he forcibly raped her and left her weeping at the side of the road. She wrote his car's licence plate number down before he drove out of sight, and was able to tell the police that the car contained an unusual cushion. She subsequently identified the car and the cushion, and picked Hubin out of a police line-up. All of this identification evidence was dismissed as failing to meet the criteria for corroboration because it was not "independent." See Backhouse, "Doctrine of Corroboration," above note 23.

64 *Rex v. Ellerton*, [1927] 3 W.W.R. 564 (Sask. C.A.); *Rex v. Mudge*, [1930] 1 W.W.R. 193 (Sask. C.A.); *Rex v. Stern*, [1932] 3 W.W.R. 688 (Sask. C.A.); *Rex v. Drew* (1932), 60 C.C.C. 37 (Sask. C.A.); *Rex v. Jones*, [1935] 3 D.L.R. 237 (B.C.C.A.); *Rex v. Reeves* (1941), 77 C.C.C. 89 (B.C.C.A.); *Rex v. Reardon* (1945), 83 C.C.C. 114 (Ont. C.A.); *Rex v. O'Hara* (1946), 88 C.C.C. 74 (B.C.C.A.); *Rex v. Yott*, [1946] 1 D.L.R. 683 (Ont. C.A.); *Rex v. Stelmasczuk* (1948), 23 M.P.R. 253 (N.S.S.C.).

65 *Thomas v. The Queen* (1952), 103 C.C.C. 193 (S.C.C.) rev'ing (1951), 100 C.C.C. 112 (Ont. C.A.), was the first Canadian sexual assault decision expressly to stipulate that there was no distinction in the nature of the corroboration required between cases where corroboration was a statutory requirement and those that fell into the "rule of practice" at common law. For later cases insisting on independent corroboration, see *Regina v. Wishart* (1954), 110 C.C.C. 129 (B.C.C.A.); *Regina v. Cross, Cassell, Bryan & Foley*, [1970] 1 C.C.C. 216 (Ont. C.A.); *Regina v. Scott*, [1974] 15 CCC (2d) 234 (N.S.C.A.); *Regina v. Pelletier*, [1973] 12 C.C.C. (2d) 527 (Sask. C.A.); *Regina v. White, Dubeau & McCullough*, [1974] 16 C.C.C. (2d) 162 (Ont. C.A.); *Regina v. Mace*, [1976] 25 C.C.C. (2d) 121 (Ont. C.A.).

66 For other cases rejecting mere opportunity as corroboration, see *Rex v. Drew* (1932), 60 C.C.C. 37 (Sask. C.A.); *Rex v. Newes* (1934), 61 C.C.C. 316 (Alta. C.A.). Born in Rivière du Loup, Québec, in 1900, Pratte had obtained a B.A. and an L.Ph. from the University of Ottawa in 1920, and an LL.L. from Laval in 1923. He married Georgine, the daughter of the Hon. Adjutor Rivard in 1924, and had two male children. He was called to the bar of Québec in 1923, and made a KC in 1935. He became dean of the Faculty of Law at Laval, and was appointed to the Superior Court of Québec in 1937, and elevated to the Court of Queen's Bench (Appeal) in 1945. *The Canadian Who's Who*, vol. 7 (1955–57) (Toronto: Trans-Canada Press, 1957) at 882.

67 Bissonnette's parents were Dr. Pierre-Julien-Léonidas Bissonnette and Juliette Lamarche. He served as the law clerk for Amédée Monet, and practised law with François-Joseph Bisaillon and Louis-Joseph Béique from 1920 to 1929, and with Honoré Mercier (fils) in the law firm of Mercier, Blain, Bissonnette, and Fauteux until 1935. In 1935, he founded his own law firm with Châteauguay Perreault, Albert Lagnade, and Rock Pinard. The same year, he married Jacqueline Masson. He obtained a doctorate in law from the Université of Montréal in 1947, where he served as a professor of constitutional law, civil procedure, and civil law. He received the Canadian Bar Association medal in 1952 and an honorary doctorate of law from the University of Sherbrooke in 1955. He was a member of the Chamber of Commerce of Montréal, the Canadian Club, le Cercle universitaire, le Club de réforme de Montréal, and le

Club de la garnison de Québec. He died in 1964. "Bernard Bissonnette," *Dictionnaire des parlementaires du Québec, 1792–1992* (Sainte-Foy, QC: Presses de l'Université Laval, 1993) at 75; Jean Cournoyer, *La mémoire du Québec de 1534 à nos jours* (Montréal: Stanké, 2001) at 143; J.-A. Fortin *Biographies canadiennes-françaises*, 5th ed. (Montréal: 1948) at 508; "Monsieur l'Orateur" *Montréal La Presse* (25 avril 1940) 4; Valmore Bienvenue, "La carrière du président de l'Assemblée législative" *Le Soleil* (21 fév. 1940) 8; n.a., *Monsieur le Président: les orateurs et les présidents depuis 1792* (Sainte-Foy, QC: Publications du Québec, 1997) at 75–77; n.a., "Nos disparus: Bernard Bissonnette," above note 67; *Who's Who in Canada, 1951–52* (Toronto: International Press, 1952) at 889; *Études juridiques en hommage à monsieur le juge Bernard Bissonnette, par un groupe de professeurs et d'amis* (Montréal: Presses de l'université de Montréal, 1963); Bernard Bissonnette, *Essai sur la Constitution du Canada* (Montréal: Éditions du Jour, 1963.

68   "Obituaries, Dr. Antonio Barbeau" (August 1947) 57 *Canadian Medical Association Journal* at 177, Division des archives de l'Université de Montréal, P22/N, 92. Judge Bissonnette's wife, Jacqueline Masson, was the daughter of Docteur Médéric Masson and Yvonne (Barbeau) Masson, and the granddaughter of Henry Barbeau, a Montréal banker and economist. See n.a., "Nos disparus: Bernard Bissonnette" (1965) 25 *Revue du Barreau de la province du Québec* 157–64; *Who's Who in Canada, 1951–52* (Toronto: International Press, 1952) at 889; Antonio Barbeau, *Sous les platanes de Cos* (Canada: Bernard Valiquette, 1942) at 113–15.

69   Barbeau was the son of Jean-Baptiste Barbeau and Nathalie Desparois. His grandfather, Médéric Barbeau, had been a farmer in St-Constant, Laprairie, Québec. Dr. Barbeau's doctoral thesis was titled "Sur la fréquence des influx nerveux au cours des réflexes de flexion" (Dec. 1930). Dr. Barbeau devoted much extracurricular time to the Catholic Boy Scout movement in Québec. His wife, Rachel Jodoin, was the daughter of Moise Jodoin and Gertrude-Rose Laprès of Montréal. Initially chief of staff of the department of physiology and professeur titulaire de neurologie at Université de Montréal, he became its chair in 1939. He was also consulting neurologist at the Montréal Neurological Institute. "Deuil cruel pour la profession médicale: Le Dr Antonio Barbeau, éminent neuro-psychiatre, est décédé à Paris" *Montréal La Presse* (14 June 1947) 1; "Dr A. Barbeau Dies in Paris, Aged 46" *Montéal Gazette* (16 June 1947) 21; Répertoire informatisé du groupe BMS2000; ISQ Marriage database; ISQ Deceased database.

70   Antonio Barbeau, "Évolution de la médecine canadienne-française" in *Sous les platanes de Cos*, above note 68 at 147–54, spoke of the important historical ties of French-Canadian physicians to France. Although Barbeau welcomed some cross-fertilization with the United States, England, and Germany, particularly because of their burgeoning scientific knowledge, he expressed grave doubts about the prospect of full assimilation. Dr. Barbeau was president of the French-Canadian Association for the Advancement of Science, and worked actively with "le Comité de propagande canadienne-française" founded by Abbé Lionel Groulx. Jean-Marie Morin, "Le Dr Barbeau, ambassadeur de la médecine canadienne-française" in *Le Journal de l'Hôtel-Dieu*, no. 1–4 (juillet–déc. 1947), Division des archives de l'Université de Montréal, P22/N, 92 at 281; "Dr A. Barbeau Dies in Paris, Aged 46," above note 69.

71 A full bibliography of Dr. Barbeau's publications is contained in *Le Journal de l'Hôtel-Dieu*, no. 1–4 (juillet–déc. 1947), Division des archives de l'Université de Montréal, P22/N, 92.

72 See, for example, Antonio Barbeau, "Bilan de six ans et demi de malariathérapie à l'Hôpital de Bordeaux," *ibid.*; Antonio Barbeau & Paul Lecavalier, "Profil criminologique de la démence précoce" (1939) 68 *L'Union médicale du Canada* at 1192.

73 Barbeau, *Sous les platanes de Cos*, above note 68 at 111. The chapter is divided into three parts: the child as witness, the child as victim, and the child as juvenile delinquent. The latter is the only section that contains any empirical data. For republication of the chapter, see n.a., *L'hygiène mentale et l'éducation* (Montréal: Éditions de L'Oeuvre de presse dominicaine, 1940) at 39–64.

74 Barbeau, *Sous les platanes de Cos*, above note 68 at 113–15.

75 *Ibid.* at 114–15.

76 *Ibid.* at 115–16.

77 Herman, *Father-Daughter Incest*, above note 30 noted at 9–11 that Freud's deep discomfort with the number of female patients who reported abusive childhood sexual encounters with men they had trusted led him to repudiate his initial research documenting childhood sexual trauma, and to falsify his findings: "He concluded that his patients' numerous reports of sexual abuse were untrue. This conclusion was based not on any new evidence from patients, but rather on Freud's own growing unwillingness to believe that licentious behaviour on the part of fathers could be so widespread. . . . Freud concluded that his patients' reports of sexual abuse were fantasies, based upon their own incestuous wishes." See also Jeffrey M. Masson, *The Assault on Truth: Freud's Suppression of the Seduction Theory* (New York: Farrar, Straus & Giroux, 1984); Alice Miller, *Thou Shalt Not Be Aware: Society's Betrayal of the Child*, trans. Hildegarde Hannum & Hunter Hannum (New York: Farrar, Straus & Giroux, 1984); J. Peters, "Children Who Are Victims of Sexual Assault and the Psychology of Offenders" (1976) 30 *American Journal of Psychotherapy* 398; Lynn Sacco, "Sanitized for Your Protection: Medical Discourse and the Denial of Incest in the United States, 1890–1940" (Autumn 2002) 14 *Journal of Women's History* 80–104; Florence Rush, *The Best Kept Secret: Sexual Abuse of Children* (Englewood Cliffs, NJ: Prentice-Hall, 1980); Florence Rush, "The Freudian Cover-Up" (1977) 1 *Chrysalis* 31; Elizabeth Hanfin Pleck, *Domestic Tyranny: The Making of Social Policy against Family Violence from Colonial Times to the Present* (New York: Oxford University Press, 1987) at 150–57.

Jean Piaget, *The Moral Judgment of the Child* (London: Routledge & Kegan Paul, 1968; orig. pub. 1932), writing about the credibility of children, noted at 160: "To him a proposition has value less as a statement than as a wish, and the stories, testimony and explanations given by a child should be regarded as the expression of his feelings rather than of beliefs that may be true or false." Piaget based his conclusions on conversations with "about 20 boys ranging from 4 to 12–13," who were interviewed about rules for marble games, and an undisclosed number of girls who were interviewed about rules for hopscotch. The children were also questioned about clumsiness and lying. The author indicated that he was "more conscious than anybody of the defects as of the advantages of the method we have used" (at vii, 13, 69–71, 116–30, and 136).

78 Sherene H. Razack, *Looking White People in the Eye: Gender, Race and Culture in Courtrooms and Classrooms* (Toronto: University of Toronto Press, 1998) at 29.

79 Jeffrey J. Haugaard & N. Dickon Reppucci, "Children and the Truth" in Stephen J. Ceci, Michelle DeSimone Leichtman, & Maribeth Putnick, *Cognitive and Social Factors in Early Deception* (Hillsdale, NJ: Lawrence Erlbaum, 1992) at 44. Kay Bussey, "Children's Lying and Truthfulness: Implications for Children's Testimony" in Ceci et al., *ibid.*, noted at 97 and 106: "[S]temming largely from the legacy of Piaget . . . children are often viewed by the public and judiciary as more prone to lying than adults. There is mounting evidence, however, attesting that children are not convincing liars; they are not very skilled at masking their deception and hence their underlying affect leaks out. In conclusion . . . it is difficult to conclude that children would be any more capable than adults of intentionally and successfully leading a jury to a false understanding of a witnessed event. If anything, the inverse holds true." Carol Satterfield Tate, Amye R. Warren, & Thomas M. Hess, "Adults' Liability for Children's Lie-Ability": Can Adults Coach Children to Lie Successfully" in Ceci et al., *ibid.*, at 70–71 noted: "Whatever popular belief and common knowledge may hold, empirical consensus regarding this opinion [that children are prone to lie] heretofore has been lacking." Gail S. Goodman & Alison Clarke-Stewart, "Suggestibility in Children's Testimony: Implications for Sexual Abuse Investigations" in John Doris, ed., *The Suggestibility of Children's Recollections* (Washington, DC: American Psychological Assoc., 1991) noted at 92: "Despite strong claims by both sides, ecologically valid and scientifically sound research to determine whether, when, and to what extent children's testimony [in cases of sexual assault] is accurate or is influenced by suggestive questioning has been virtually nonexistent." The Ontario Law Reform Commission, *Report on Child Witnesses* (Toronto: OLRC, 1991) concluded at 17–18: "The behavioural science research conducted in the past twenty years has demonstrated that the traditional views about the unreliability of children's evidence has no empirical support. Children, as a class of witnesses, do not have poorer memories than adults and they do not have greater difficulty distinguishing fact from fantasy in the context of witnessed events. Moreover, studies show that adult witnesses are susceptible to distortions as a result of suggestions and post-event influences in their description of particular events. Finally, modern research has demonstrated that there is no foundation to the statement that a relationship exists between age and honesty — the testimony of a child is as trustworthy as the evidence furnished by an adult witness." See also Law Reform Commission of Canada, *Report on Evidence* (Ottawa: Information Canada, 1975). *An Act to amend the Criminal Code and the Canada Evidence Act*, S.C. 1987, c.24, abolished the corroboration requirement for the testimony of child witnesses.

80 *Rex v. Reeves* (1941), 77 C.C.C. 89 (B.C.C.A.).

81 *Regina v. Cullen*, [1976] 26 C.C.C. (2d) 79 (B.C.C.A.).

82 *Regina v. Ball* (1957), 117 C.C.C. 366 (B.C.C.A.); *Regina v. Cross, Cassel, Bryan and Foley*, [1970] 1 C.C.C. 216 (Ont. C.A.); *Regina v. Willett*, [1973] 10 C.C.C. (2d) 36 (Ont. C.A.).

83   *Regina v. Kelso* (1953), 105 C.C.C. 305 (Ont. C.A.); *Regina v. Fennell* (1957), 119 C.C.C. 344
      (B.C.C.A.).
84   *Regina v. Plantus* (1957), 118 C.C.C. 260 (Ont. C.A.).
85   *Regina v. Schmidt & Gole*, [1973] 9 C.C.C. (2d) 101 (Ont. C.A.).
86   *Rex v. Fushtor* (1946), 85 C.C.C. 283 (Sask. C.A.). See also *Rex v. Arnold*, [1947] 2 D.L.R.
      438 (Ont. C.A.), in which the judge listed potentially corroborative evidence in his
      charge to the jury, adding "that is, of course, if you believe it." The appellate court
      quashed the conviction, holding that this was insufficient instruction that the jurors
      were the decision-makers.
87   *Regina v. Ethier* (1959), 124 C.C.C. 332 (Ont. C.A.). Failure to specify which corrobora-
      tion related to which accused in cases with multiple parties also provoked reversal;
      Regina v. Lieberman, Teaney, Legault & Cosgrove, [1974] 17 C.C.C. (2d) 536 (Ont. C.A.).
88   *Regina v. Kavanagh* (1960), 128 C.C.C. 191 (Nfld. S.C.).

Chapter 8: Canada's First Capital "L" Lesbian Sexual Assault

1   I have found no prior prosecutions in the reported cases across Canada, or the ar-
      chival records I have searched in British Columbia, Saskatchewan, Ontario, Québec,
      or Nova Scotia. It is possible that a fuller search of archival records in these and oth-
      er provinces might turn up another same-sex prosecution of a woman. The charge
      would have to be something other than rape, because this was defined as a crime
      that could be committed only by "a male person," and the requirement for "sexual
      intercourse" mandated vaginal-penile penetration. *Criminal Code*, S.C. 1953-54, c.51,
      s.135. *R. v. Mercier et al.*, [1973] 12 C.C.C. (2d) 377 (Que. C.A.), appears to be the first
      reported Canadian case in which a spouse was charged as an accessory to rape. Hu-
      guette Mercier was convicted with her husband and three other males, all charged
      as parties who aided and abetted one another and other unknown male persons to
      rape a woman, but the conviction was overturned on appeal because the Crown at-
      torney had interfered in the jury deliberations. Carolyn Strange, "Patriarchy Modi-
      fied: The Criminal Prosecution of Rape in York County, Ontario, 1880–1930" in Jim
      Phillips, Tina Loo, & Susan Lewthwaite, *Essays in the History of Canadian Law: Crime
      and Criminal Justice* (Toronto: The Osgoode Society, 1994) 204 notes at 221–22 another
      (unreported) case in 1899, when police laid charges against eight young Irishmen
      and one woman. The men had allegedly gang-raped an elderly woman, while the
      woman with them yelled, "Go ahead and give it to her." All accused were acquitted;
      Toronto Telegram (9 Nov. 1899). *R. v. Halliday*, [1974] 16 C.C.C. (2d) 362 (Ont. Ct. Gen'l
      Sessions of the Peace), would later entertain a constitutional challenge regarding
      the one-sidedness of sexual assault law. A man accused of indecent assault upon
      a female brought a motion to quash the indictment on the ground that there was
      no parallel provision protecting men who were indecently assaulted by a female.
      The argument that this violated s.1(a) of the *Canadian Bill of Rights,* the guarantee to
      security of the person without discrimination on the basis of sex, was rejected, with
      the court holding that under the *Code*, both men and women could be charged with
      indecently assaulting a female. "[T]he argument . . . really goes to the protection
      which is lacking in favour of a male person who may be indecently assaulted by a

female person. Parliament has not seen fit to create such an offence." Holding that all citizens were treated equally under s.149(1), the court found that there was no discrimination.

2   On the legal harassment for cross-dressing, see the decision of New Brunswick immigration officials to detain a female second-cabin passenger on the CPR liner, *Empress of Britain*, for being attired in male costume: "A Fine Lot of New Settlers" *Regina Daily Province* (15 April 1911) 1. Mary Peterson, a young Saskatchewan woman, was arrested in Minneapolis on an unspecified charge for posing as a man: "Nokomis 'Youth' Turns Out to be Real Canadian Girl" *Regina Leader* (26 April 1912) 10; "Found Girl in Boy's Clothes" *Regina Daily Province* (26 April 1912) 9. Violet Clements was arrested for vagrancy in Regina for posing as a male: "Buddy's Giggle Betrays Her to Wideawake Police" *Regina Leader* (30 Oct. 1924) 12. Dot Bryan was convicted of vagrancy in Edmonton, based on evidence that she was "a mannish girl decked out in pseudo male attire": *Edmonton Bulletin* (24 March 1932). Virginia Innes was arrested for a similar offence: *Edmonton Bulletin* (20 Aug. 1932); David Bright, "'Go Home. Straighten Up. Live Decent Lives': Female Vagrancy and Social Respectability in Alberta, 1918–1993" (Fall 2003) 28 *Prairie Forum* 161–72.

3   Steven Maynard, "Through a Hole in the Lavatory Wall: Homosexual Subcultures, Police Surveillance, and the Dialectics of Discovery, Toronto 1890–1930" (Oct. 1994) 15 *Journal of the History of Sexuality* 207; *Criminal Code*, S.C. 1953–54, c.51, ss.147, 148, & 149.

4   *Regina v. A.B.* (1955), 113 C.C.C. 325 (Alta. C.A.). It took extended searching and the intercession of numerous judicial, territorial, and archival volunteers before A.B. was identified as Willimae Moore. The court clerks initially listed cases by the first two initials of the alphabet, as a placeholder, when they did not have full names for the parties. Why this case remained "A.B." in the law report, long after the court clerks learned the full name of the accused, remains a mystery. The Court of Appeal file was finally located in the Provincial Archives of Alberta, GR1987.095, Box 71, #4088, from which all the details and quotations that follow have been taken. The file contained appeal facta, correspondence, a transcript of the original trial, and miscellaneous printed forms. The proper reference to *R. v. Moore* later showed up in Quicklaw in 2000: [1955] A.J. No. 1 (Alta. S.C. (A.D.)), which copied the unreported judgments from the Provincial Court Libraries in Edmonton.

5   Interview with Lewis Bernstein, 6 Dec. 2004, by Constance Backhouse; Interview with Don Berkey, 15 June 2005, by Constance Backhouse; "Copy Typing Of Any Kind — Reasonable Rates — Fast, Accurate Work Guaranteed — Apply W. Moore, Phone 20," the advertisement placed by Willimae Moore in *News of the North* (17 Sept. 1954) 6.

6   Yellowknife dated from 1934, when a group of prospectors wintered there after gold was discovered by C.J. "Yellowknife Johnney" Baker and Herb Dixon. Another group arrived in the summer of 1935, and their location on the west shore of Yellowknife Bay became the first permanent settlement. During the Second World War, the predominantly young, single, male population left for war service or Southern jobs. Shacks were shuttered, storekeepers closed up shop, and the mines struggled for ex-

istence. After the war, an influx of returning veterans swelled the population again. Terry Foster & Ronnie Heming, eds., *Yellowknife Tales: Sixty Years of Stories from Yellowknife* (Yellowknife: Outcrop, 2000) at xi, 1–2, 111–12, 129–30, 137–38, 270–71, and 275; Ray Price, *Yellowknife* (Toronto: Peter Martin Associates, 1967) at 176 and 299.

7 Indian and Northern Affairs, *North of 60: Facts and Figures Northwest Territories* (Ottawa: Ministry of Indian and Northern Affairs, 1977) at 7; John David Hamilton, *Arctic Revolution: Social Change in the Northwest Territories, 1935–1994* (Toronto: Dundurn, 1994) at 27; Price, *Yellowknife*, above note 6 at 2 and 297; Max Ward, *The Max Ward Story: A Bush Pilot in the Bureaucratic Jungle* (Toronto: McClelland & Stewart, 1991) at 69; George Sian, "I Remember Yellowknife" in Foster & Heming, eds., *Yellowknife Tales*, above note 6 at 76–78.

8 In 1948, Gilbert LaBine, Charlie LaBine, and Bill Wright opened the Giant Mine, but by the mid-fifties, gold fever was subsiding in favour of a uranium boom. Prospectors, bush pilots, and hard-rock miners were being supplanted by lawyers, doctors, teachers, pharmacists, nurses, storekeepers, movie projectionists, bricklayers, mechanics, editors, printers, real estate salespeople, and insurance agents, who began to settle in Yellowknife not as "birds of passage" but "looking to the North for their future." Hamilton, *Arctic Revolution*, above note 7 at 25–29 and 83–86; "Stan Snideman: A Miner Comes to Town 1948–49" in Susan Jackson, ed., *Yellowknife N.W.T.: An Illustrated History* (Sechelt, BC: Nor'West Publishing, 1990) at 129; Price, *Yellowknife*, above note 6 at 297–98 and 300; Foster & Heming, eds., *Yellowknife Tales*, above note 6 at 112 and 274. The Dene Aboriginal population lived mostly on the land, hunting game, fish, and furs. When some of them tried to set up residence in the settlement, white anxiety and racism resulted in their removal to Rainbow Valley.

9 See "Rosemary McAnany, Stenographer, 1946–48," "Pat Bennett: Keeping the Cash Flowing, 1948–53," and "Ruth Scilley: Setting Up Housekeeping, 1949–51" in Jackson, *Yellowknife N.W.T*, above note 8 at 102–3, 131–32, and 145–46.

10 John D'Emilio, *Sexual Politics, Sexual Communities: The Making of a Homosexual Minority in the United States, 1940–1970*, 2d ed. (Chicago: University of Chicago Press, orig. pub. 1983) at 31 and 38; Paul Jackson, *One of the Boys: Homosexuality in the Military during World War II* (Montréal: McGill-Queen's University Press, 2004).

11 Previously, entry was forbidden to persons convicted of a crime of "moral turpitude": *Immigration Act, 1910*, S.C. 1910, c.27, s.3(d). The first draft of the amendment prohibited entry to "homosexuals" and "lesbians," but the word "lesbians" was dropped, leaving the prohibited class as: "homosexuals or persons living on the avails of . . . homosexualism." R.S.C. 1952, c.325, s.5(e). Philip Girard, (1987) 2 "From Subversion to Liberation: Homosexuals and the Immigration Act 1952–1977" *Canadian Journal of Law and Society* 1 notes that the new law resulted from lobbying by the RCMP and the Department of National Defence, who were responding to McCarthyist Cold War campaigns in the United States to root out subversives in national security interests.

12 The project resulted in the infamous "Fruit Machine," an instrument designed to confirm homosexuality by measuring a person's reaction to homo-erotic imagery. The RCMP focused primarily upon gay men, but also questioned lesbians about

names of friends and colleagues. Gary Kinsman, "'Character Weakness' and 'Fruit Machines': Towards an Analysis of the Anti-homosexual Security Campaign in the Canadian Civil Service" (Spring 1995) 35 *Labour/Le Travail* 133–61; Daniel J. Robinson & David Kimmel, "The Queer Career of Homosexual Security Vetting in Cold War Canada" (September 1994) 75 *Canadian Historical Review* 319–45.

13 Dr. Alfred C. Kinsey's *Sexual Behavior in the Human Male* (Philadelphia: W.B. Saunders Co., 1948) and *Sexual Behavior in the Human Female* (Philadelphia: W.B. Saunders Co., 1953), based on interviews of over 12 000 white Americans and Canadians, found 50 percent of males admitted erotic responses to other males, 37 percent admitted at least one homosexual experience, 13 percent had been involved in more homosexual than heterosexual activity for at least three consecutive years, and 4 percent reported being exclusively homosexual. Among women, 28 percent had responded erotically to other women, 13 percent had experienced orgasm with another woman, and the numbers of women involved exclusively with other women amounted to between 1/3 and 1/2 of the equivalent figure for men. On the controversy sparked in Canada, see Girard, "From Subversion to Liberation," above note 11; Mary Louise Adams, *The Trouble with Normal: Postwar Youth and the Making of Heterosexuality* (Toronto: University of Toronto Press, 1997) at 167. See also Sheila Jeffreys, *Anticlimax: A Feminist Perspective on the Sexual Revolution* (London: Women's Press, 1990) at 50–56.

14 Mary Louise Adams, "Youth, Corruptibility, and English-Canadian Postwar Campaigns against Indecency, 1948–1955" (July 1995) 6 *Journal of the History of Sexuality* 89 at 104–5.

15 *R. v. National News Company Ltd.*, AO RG 4-32, 1953, no. 830, 8 October 1952, "Reasons for Judgment" of Ottawa Judge A.G. McDougall. The novel was Tereska Torres, *Women's Barracks* (New York: Fawcett, 1950). See Adams, *The Trouble with Normal*, above note 13 at 135–65; Becki L. Ross, *The House That Jill Built: A Lesbian Nation in Formation* (Toronto: University of Toronto Press, 1995).

16 Lilyan Brock, *Queer Patterns* (New York: Eton Books, 1935) at 23, 34, 97, and back cover.

17 For these references, see Laycock, M.A., M.Ed., Ph.D., Dean of Education, Professor of Educational Psychology at the University of Saskatchewan, and the Director of the Division of Education and Mental Health of the Canadian Mental Hygiene Association, "Homosexuality — A Mental Hygiene Problem" at 245–50. There was very little research published on homosexuality in Canada before 1955. The following journals, some based in Canada and others held in Canadian medical libraries, were reviewed: *Canadian Journal of Public Health* (1940–55); *Canadian Medical Association Journal* (1921–55); *Canadian Psychiatric Association Journal* (1956–66); *International Journal of Psychoanalysis* (1920–55); *Journal of Hygiene* (1949–55); *Journal of Nervous and Mental Disease* (1932–55); *Journal of Mental Science* (1939–55); *McGill Medical Journal* (1939–56); *Ontario Medical Review* (1934–55); *Montéal Medical Journal* (1900–10); *Psychoanalytic Review* (1913–55); *Psychoanalytic Quarterly* (1932–55); *Psychiatric Quarterly* (1927–55).

The only articles that mentioned homosexuality were as follows: Laycock, "Homosexuality — A Mental Hygiene Problem," *ibid.*; Daniel Cappon, Calvin Ezrin, & Patrick Lynes, "Psychosexual Identification (Psychogender) in the Intersexed" (1959) 14 *Canadian Psychiatric Association Journal* 90; N.E. McKinnon's book review of "The Invert and His Social Adjustment" (Feb. 1950) 41 *Canadian Journal of Public Health* 99–100; B. Kanee & C.L. Hunt, "Homosexuality as a Source of Venereal Disease" (Aug. 1951) 65 *Canadian Medical Association Journal* 135–40; David Abrahamsen, "Psychodynamics in Criminal Behavior" (July–Dec. 1945) 102 *Journal of Nervous and Mental Disease* 65; W. Norwood East, "Sexual Offenders" (Jan.–June 1946) 103 *Journal of Nervous and Mental Disease* 626.

18 N.E. McKinnon, "The Invert and His Social Adjustment," reviewed a book of this title, by an anonymous author, published by Macmillan (Toronto: 1948) in (Feb. 1950) 41 *Canadian Journal of Public Health* 99–100. The Canadian experts were in agreement with sexologists and psychologists elsewhere, who had depicted lesbianism as a "congenital, mannish abnormality and/or a pathological sickness born of complex neuroses" since the late nineteenth century; Ross, *The House That Jill Built*, above note 15 at 12. Ross quoted American psychoanalyst Frank Caprio, describing lesbians as "unhappy, sexually maladjusted, and prone to extreme jealousy, sexual immaturity, and sadomasochistic tendencies" who could be "restored to normal sex outlook by sympathetic and expert treatment, usually at the hands of a psychiatrist or psychoanalyst who believes in cure." Frank Caprio, *Female Homosexuality: A Psychodynamic Study of Lesbianism* (New York: Citadel Press, 1954) at 171 and 294. But see also A.J. Kilgour, M.B., "Sex Delinquency — A Review of 100 Court Cases Referred to the Toronto Psychiatric Hospital" (Sept. 1933) *Ontario Journal of Neuro-Psychiatry* 34–50, which recommended at 50 "greater tolerance in sexual matters" and noted that "what is normal in these matters today, was not always the norm of yesterday, and may not be considered so in the future."

19 Ross, *ibid.*

20 Interview with former Yellowknife resident Ralph Moyle, 5 Feb. 2005, by Constance Backhouse; Foster & Heming, *Yellowknife Tales*, above note 6 at 113–15. On Harold and Maureen Mitchell's arrival from Hay River, see *News of the North* (27 Aug. 1954) 12.

21 Valere J. Korinek, "'The most openly gay person for at least a thousand miles': Doug Wilson and the Politicization of a Province, 1975–83" (Dec. 2003) 84 *Canadian Historical Review* 517 at 520. Others have suggested that large industrial cities populated by migrants offered greater opportunity for gays and lesbians to congregate anonymously, and perhaps this was the flip-side of the freedom offered by isolated northern towns; see Elizabeth Lapovsky Kennedy & Madeline D. Davis, *Boots of Leather, Slippers of Gold: The History of a Lesbian Community* (New York: Penguin, 1994) at 9.

22 In *Klippert v. The Queen*, [1968] 2 C.C.C. 129 (S.C.C.), a gay man who lived at Pine Point, N.W.T., was charged in Hay River with four counts of gross indecency. He told the court that he had left Calgary, to avoid bringing shame upon his family, and headed north. Interview with former Yellowknife resident, Charlotte (Suzie) Graham, 9 Dec. 2004, by Constance Backhouse, describing Yellowknife as "a close-knit

community of misfits. They were all running from somewhere. People went there to escape the scrutiny of others. Some were running from the law, some from their wives . . . our next door neighbour was a gay man and we knew it."

23 *Yellowknife News of the North* (18 March 1955) 4; Interview with Ralph Moyle; Interview with appellate defence counsel Lewis Bernstein, 6 Dec. 2004, by Constance Backhouse, in which he noted: "It really affected [Miss Gonzales's] position here, at the high school. They must have thought she would be attacking the girls next."

24 *Childs v. The Queen* (1958), 122 C.C.C. 126 (N.B.C.A.).

25 *R. v. Duguay*, [1966] 3 C.C.C. 266 (Sask. C.A.).

26 *R. v. Resener*, [1968] 64 W.W.R. 257 (B.C.C.A.).

27 R. v. Patrick Gerald Scallen, (1911) Archives nationales du Quebéc, Québec City, Cour des Sessions de la Paix, TP12, S1, SS1, SSS1, cont. 1960-01-357/600.

28 *Ibid.*

29 *R. v. Druz* (1928), 34 O.W.N. 119 (Ont. Div. Ct.).

30 *R. v. Marion* (1956), 118 C.C.C. 388 (Ont. C.A.).

31 *R. v. Backshall* (1956), 115 C.C.C. 221 (S.C.C.).

32 *R. v. Tilley* (1953), 106 C.C.C. 42 (Ont. C.A.).

33 *R. v. Marr* (1955), 114 C.C.C. 318 (N.B.C.A.).

34 The only case that came close was *R. v. Thorpe* (1973), 11 C.C.C. (2d) 502 (Ont. Co. Ct.), of a thirty-one-year-old married man who attempted to kiss a fourteen-year-old girl and then initiated a "conversation . . . of a provocative or suggestive nature." The accused met the complainant when he was out jogging and she was walking home late at night. The Crown attorney stated that this "was not a serious case," and that he was "not anxious to continue with the prosecution." After six adjournments, five at the request of the Crown, the court stayed the proceedings because the delay amounted to "unwarranted harassment." See also discussion of *R. v. Edgett* (1947), 90 C.C.C. 274 (N.B.C.A.), below note 76.

35 She had been released on bail of $100 on 7 February, and committed for trial at the preliminary hearing on 18 and 19 February.

36 The "filthy" practice that the trial judge was discussing was cunnilingus perpetrated by a man upon a woman, which had given rise to a charge of gross indecency: *R. v. St. Pierre* (1972), 7 C.C.C. (2d) 307 (Ont. C.A.) at 310.

37 The death certificate indicates the date of birth; Ron Thornber, "Woman UBC Graduate Carves Amazing Career in Europe" *Vancouver Sun* (7 Jan. 1947) 11 lists the birthplace.

38 George's marriage certificate, 26 June 1906, lists his parents as John Gonzales and Louisa Williams. Lilly Rae's parents were George Rae (from England) and Sarah Brock (from Ontario). Births, Deaths and Marriages Certificate B11373, 1906-09-052466, Vancouver Public Library, correspondence 8 and 15 Sept. 2005; Death Certificate for Lilly Wellington, B13296, 1969-09-006600, Province of British Columbia, certified 30 April 1969; Obituary for "Wellington" *Vancouver Sun* (26 April 1969).

39 Beatrice's brother was uncertain whether his mother's first marriage ended in divorce or her husband died: Interview with Dr. W.G. Wellington, Vancouver, 23 May 2005, by Constance Backhouse. George Wellington's death certificate, B13578,

1977-09-010499, Province of British Columbia, certified 18 July 1977; Obituary for "Wellington" *Vancouver Sun* (16 July 1977); B.C. *City Directories*, 1922, 1923, 1925, and 1929–32, and *Vancouver City Directories*, 1934–35.

40 William Wellington later obtained a doctorate in entomology from the University of British Columbia, taught at the University of Toronto, and then took a position as director of the Institute of Fisheries/Animal Resources Ecology at UBC between 1975 and 1980. In 1986, he became a professor emeritus of Plant Sciences at UBC; (24 Oct. 1979) 25 *UBC Reports* 3; *Vancouver Sun* (18 Oct. 1968) 26.

41 "UBC Co-ed Talked Back to Gestapo in Czecho-Slovakia" *The Ubyssey* (15 May 1941) 2; Interview with Dr. W.G. Wellington. Bollert had an M.A. from Toronto and an M.A. from Columbia University in English and Education, had been active in social welfare activities within the women's club movement, and had joined the UBC faculty as "Advisor" (later Dean) of Women in 1921. *The Ubyssey* (6 Oct. 1921) 1; Katie Pickles, "Colonial Counterparts: The First Academic Women in Anglo-Canada, New Zealand and Australia" (2001) 10 *Women's History* 273–97. With the exception of the year 1927, when Beatrice lived at 3946 W. 10th Ave., during the years she was a student, she lived with her stepfather and family at #37-709 Dunsmuir in the Tunstall Block: B.C. *City Directories*, 1925–27.

42 Later in the cross-examination, Crown attorney Parker asked: "This degree *which you say you got* from Columbia University was awarded under the name of Wellington?"[emphasis added]. The Transcript Department at Columbia University verified that Margaret Wellington attended Teachers College starting in 1931, was awarded an M.A. in 1940, and took additional courses in 1950–51.

43 Parker was born in 1911 in Brentwood, Essex, in England. He came to New York City with his father in 1920, and enrolled in St. Andrews School in Toronto in 1922. He took his B.A. at Queen's University, and attended Osgoode Hall Law School while articled to Sir Alan Aylesworth's firm in Toronto. After his call, Parker practised law in Kirkland Lake, and then served as the RCAF liaison officer with the American government, posted in Washington, D.C. Frank Wade, *Advocate for the North: Judge John Parker, His Life and Times in the Northwest Territories* (Victoria: Trafford, 2004); Jackson, *Yellowknife N.W.T.*, above note 8 at 100–1; Price, *Yellowknife*, above note 6 at 229.

44 Interview with former Yellowknife resident Charlotte (Suzie) Graham, 9 Dec. 2004, by Constance Backhouse; Interview with Ralph Moyle; Interview with Lewis Bernstein.

45 In 1929, she moved with her family to 3477 W. 29th, where she resided until 1933. In 1935 and 1936, she lived in Chilliwack. B.C. *City Directories*, 1927–32; *Vancouver City Directories*, 1933; B.C. *Provincial Directory*, 1935–36. Beatrice often sent young female students to study and board with her family in Vancouver, if she felt their educational horizons were limited in their home communities: Interview with Dr. W.G. Wellington.

46 Thornber, "Woman UBC Graduate," above note 37 at 11. Dean Mary Bollert had recommended Beatrice for the Geneva position: Interview with Dr. W.G. Wellington.

47 Letter from Clara S. Roe, World's YWCA to Pavla Molnarova, YWCA of Czechoslovakia, 31 March 1938; Report of Beatrice Wellington on the YWCA of Czechoslovakia's 1938 Summer Camp Program. World YWCA Archives.

48 J.W. Wheeler-Bennett, *Munich: Prologue to Tragedy* (London: Macmillan, 1948); Thornber, "Woman UBC Graduate," above note 37; "UBC Co-ed Talked Back," above note 41. Clara Roe, World YWCA Secretary, Travel Report 1 June 1939, described the work in Prague: "[R]ecommending women refugees for household employment in England has gone on quietly, the permission to leave the country being secured through cooperation with Miss Beatrice Wellington. Since they are now encountering increasing opposition on the part of the Gestapo in getting permission for Czech women as well as men, this probably cannot go on very much longer. . . . That they have succeeded in helping so many seems to me almost a miracle. Miss Beatrice Wellington leads this group most ably." World YWCA Archives.

49 Frank Munk, "My Century and My Many Lives," Memoirs, 1993, Postscript 1994, www.theragens.com/MunkBio/Munk_Autobiography.htm, accessed 9/7/2004, a memoir regarding the family's escape to England in May 1939.

50 "I was called to the dean's office to meet this gentleman, and he was from Czechoslovakia, and wanted by the Nazis. He told me that he wasn't alone — that there were something like 1500 people like him she had helped to evacuate to England. He said well if you have never heard what your sister was doing, I can understand, because she was risking her life." Interview with Dr. W.G. Wellington.

51 Thornber, "Woman UBC Graduate," above note 37; "UBC Co-ed Talked Back," above note 41.

52 *Ibid.*; extract from the Report of the Sub-Committee on Strategy for Mutual Service and Extension, Minutes of the World's YWCA Executive Committee, 25–30 May 1948; Correspondence from Beatrice Wellington to Lilian Espy, Foreign Division, YWCA, New York City, 28 December 1947, World YWCA Archives.

53 Thornber, "Woman UBC Graduate," above note 37.

54 Correspondence from Beatrice Wellington to Margaret Forsyth, National YWCA, New York City, 8 July 1946, and to Lilian Espy, Foreign Division, YWCA, New York City, 28 December 1947, World YWCA Archives. She also complained that the Polish YMCA had "no room for the Jewish boys as members."

55 Correspondence from Ruth F. Woodsmall, general secretary, International YWCA, to Margaret Forsyth, Foreign Division, National YWCA, New York City, 25 March 1947, World YWCA Archives. The letter also referred to "a nervous breakdown of Miss Wellington when she was working with Miss Dingman. I never knew the full details but nervous instability seemed to be the root of it. As I say, I have no documentation for this and would not want to be quoted." The reference was at odds with the bulk of the letter, which was positive about Beatrice's performance in her many European jobs.

56 Thornber, "Woman UBC Graduate," above note 37.

57 Beatrice's brother indicated that his sister had a nervous breakdown in New York, which he attributed to the pressures she had lived through in Europe. Several of Beatrice's New York friends contacted him, then in Sault Ste Marie, to explain that

she needed psychiatric treatment, that she was "losing her mind" and "talking as though she was somebody else." They arranged for Beatrice to be hospitalized. Beatrice objected to the hospitalization, and enlisted the support of a cousin who secured her release, against the advice of the treating psychiatrist, Beatrice's New York City friends, and her brother. Beatrice then returned home briefly to Vancouver, before leaving to teach in northern B.C. Interview with Dr. W.G. Wellington.

58 The name change occurred after the departure from New York City and prior to the arrival at Yellowknife. Beatrice continued to use Gonzales until her death.

59 Kilgour, M.B., "Sex Delinquency — A Review of 100 Court Cases Referred to the Toronto Psychiatric Hospital," above note 18.

60 See www.answers.com/topic/lesbian-1, accessed 26 March 2005. Similar thinking was exhibited in 1921, when the British Parliament considered a bill to provide that "any act of gross indecency between female persons shall be a misdemeanour and punishable in the same manner as any act committed by male persons." The House of Lords defeated the bill, "because it was believed that legislating against lesbianism would do 'a very great mischief' and increase it by 'creating the idea of an offence' and bringing it to the 'notice of women who have never heard of it, never thought of it, never dreamed of it.'" British Parliament, *House of Commons Debates*, series 5, vol. 145 at 1799–808; *House of Lords Debates*, series 5, vol. 46 at 567–77; Ruth Ford "'Lady-friends' and 'sexual deviationists': Lesbians and Law in Australia, 1920–1950s" in Diane Kirkby, ed., *Sex, Power and Justice: Historical Perspectives on Law in Australia* (Melbourne: Oxford University Press, 1955) at 33–49.

61 Jackson, *One of the Boys*, above note 10 at 22.

62 Rochelle G. Saidel, *The Jewish Women of Ravensbruck Concentration Camp* (Madison, WI: University of Wisconsin Press, 2004).

63 Beatrice's brother did not believe that his sister had sexual relations with women, adding that she had them as "companions — Beatrice always collected companions." He noted that she never spoke of marriage or romance, but once mentioned an Australian man she had met in Europe, with whom "it really didn't work out." He suggested that Beatrice "might have been a little bit forbidding for an awful lot of fellows because she had such an enormous breadth." Interview with Dr. W.G. Wellington. Kennedy & Davis, *Boots of Leather, Slippers of Gold*, above note 21, suggested at 2–3 that working-class lesbians in the 1940s and 1950s were able to be more open about their sexual lives than "middle-class lesbians who held teaching and other professional jobs [and] had to be secretive about their identities because their jobs and status in life depended on their reputations as morally upstanding women."

64 For further discussion of the legal doctrine of "recent complaint," see chapter 7.

65 Elsie Smith operated the ambulance service in Yellowknife, along with her husband, Wally, the undertaker. In 1956, she was elected to the local school board. Jackson, *Yellowknife N.W.T.*, above note 8 at 156; *News of the North* (23 Nov. 1956) 1. Lillian Crate and her husband, Charles, had a local radio program on CFYK: *News of the North* (15 June 1956) 3; Price, *Yellowknife*, above note 6 at 298.

66 John Gibben Fonds, 1917–1956, Yukon Archives, 82/253, MSS O/S 1; Foster & Heming, *Yellowknife Tales*, above note 6 at 15; Obituary, *Whitehorse Star* (30 Jan. 1958) 1. His first wife, Ina, died in 1950; he married Rhoda MacDonald in 1951.

67 Recollections of J. Worsell, former clerk, sent to Graham Price, 13 January 1977, as quoted in Graham Price "Lawyers on Circuit in the North in the Twentieth Century," unpublished manuscript. I am indebted to Graham Price for sharing this passage with me.

68 See, respectively, chapters 2, 4, and 6.

69 There was no statutory requirement for corroboration with the offence of indecent assault, but there was a common law duty to note that it was dangerous to convict without it. For more details on the law of corroboration, see chapter 7.

70 See chapters 2, 3, 4, and 6.

71 S.C. 1953–54, c.51, s.141: "Every one who indecently assaults a female person is guilty of an indictable offence and is liable to imprisonment for five years and to be whipped."

72 Letter from Beatrice Gonzales to the Clerk of the Court, 22 May, 5, 7, and 8 June 1955; Archival file.

73 Interview with Lewis Bernstein. Bernstein described his failed four years of practice in England: "If you wanted to be a barrister in England, you had to choose your parents with great care."

74 Sully argued that the judge had correctly dismissed the alibi evidence, in findings of credibility that could not be overruled at appeal.

75 *Beal v. Kelley*, [1951] 2 All E.R. 763. (K.B.) Bernstein also cited *Rex. v. Louie Chong* (1914), 23 C.C.C. 250 (Ont. C.A.): "It is in each case a question of fact whether the thing which was done, in the circumstances in which it was done, was done indecently. If it was, an indecent assault has been committed."

76 Bernstein did not cite *R. v. Horn* (1923), 40 C.C.C. 117 (Alta. C.A.), which might have been equally helpful. The accused had taken a four-year-old boy on a drive, and later confessed to the police: "[I] took out my penis. I tried to kiss the kid and he jerked his head away." The court concluded: "I have no hesitation in saying that this in itself is sufficient evidence of an indecent assault. Archbold, on Criminal Pleading, at p.930, says that: – 'an assault includes an attempt to commit a battery' and that a battery 'includes every touching or laying hold (however trifling) of another's person or clothes in an angry, revengeful, rude, insolent or hostile manner' citing 1 Hawk. P.C., ch.15, sec.2. . . . I think there can be no doubt of the rude and insolent manner of the attempt to touch the child's person. . . . And it was accompanied by the act of indecency." See also *R. v. Edgett* (1947), 90 C.C.C. 274 (N.B.C.A.), where a returned serviceman who had been drinking at the Legion in Fredericton accosted a woman on the street, and made a series of verbal overtures, including "Could I date youse up?" and "I will razz you." He grabbed the woman's arm, threw his coat over her head, made "dirty remarks," mumbled, cursed, and pointed to his elbow, saying "I have one of these things for you." At trial, the magistrate convicted, finding that indecency was a "fair inference" from the whole of the evidence. The conviction was

upheld on appeal, although a dissenting judge complained that there was nothing indecent about an elbow.

77 The notion of a hostile element was approved in later cases. See *R. v. Hay* (1959), 125 C.C.C. 137 (Man. C.A.), where the court concluded that "a hostile act" had been proven, along with "circumstances of indecency." *R. v. McCallum*, [1970] 2 C.C.C. 366 (P.E.I.S.C.) involved a charge for indecent assault where the accused man appeared nude before a young girl and invited her to "handle his private parts." He did not touch her, or threaten to apply force to her. Quoting *Beal v. Kelley* as well as Willimae Moore's case, the court quashed the conviction. *R. v. Baney*, [1972] 6 C.C.C. (2d) 75 (Ont. C.A.), quashed a conviction for indecent assault where an accused took his penis out in front of a four-year-old boy and told him to play with it, but desisted when the boy said no. The court held there was no "aggressive act" on the part of the accused, but "merely a request that the other person act." However, the court quoted J.C. Smith & Brian Hogan, *Criminal Law*, 2d ed. (London: Butterworths, 1969) at 302, commenting that the element of "hostility" causes difficulty: "In indecent assaults D's attitude to P will frequently not be 'hostile' in the ordinary sense, but unduly affectionate!" See also *R. v. Beamish*, [1966] 1 C.C.C. 64 (N.S.S.C.), where the court overturned an acquittal for indecent assault upon a thirteen-year-old girl. The trial judge had concluded that there was "tacit acquiescence and the total absence of any 'hostile act.'" On appeal, the court determined that the girl was below the age of consent and substituted a verdict of guilty.

Chief Justice O'Connor was born in Walkerton, Ontario, in 1883, and graduated with an LL.B. from Osgoode Hall in 1905. He was admitted to the bar in Edmonton in 1905, and practised with Griesbach, O'Connor. He was appointed to the bench in 1941, elevated to the court of appeal in 1946, and named Chief Justice in 1950. He died in 1957. Judge Johnson was born in Medonte Township, Simcoe County, Ontario, in 1899. He received his LL.B. from the University of Alberta in 1929. He practised law in Edmonton with Short and Cross until his appointment to the bench in 1954. He retired in 1973 and died in 1982. Louis Knafla & Richard Klumpenhouwer, *Lords of the Western Bench: A Biographical History of the Supreme and District Courts of Alberta, 1876–1990* (Edmonton: The Legal Archives of Alberta, 1997) at 78–79 and 139.

78 Clinton Ford was born near Corinth, Ontario, in 1882. He attended schools in Tillsonburg and Aylmer, and then taught for three years. He matriculated to Victoria College, Toronto, and graduated from the University of Toronto in 1907. He began his legal studies at Osgoode Hall, and completed them at the University of Alberta, where he received his LL.B. in 1910. He practised law in Calgary until his appointment to the bench in 1942. He would be named Chief Justice in 1957, a post he held until his death in 1961. He was extremely active in the community, serving as president of the Alberta Poultry Federation, on the council of the Calgary Board of Trade, on the board of governors of Mount Royal College, as chair of the Institute of Family and Personal Counselling, and as president of the Alberta Liberal Association. He had served as president of the local and vice-president of the national YMCA. Knafla & Klumpenhouwer, *Lords of the Western Bench*, above note 77 at 43–44.

79 *R. v. P.*, [1968] 63 W.W.R. 222 (Man. C.A.). The former *Criminal Code*, R.S.C. 1927, c.36, s.206, prohibited acts of gross indecency committed by a "male person" with another "male person." The amended S.C. 1953–54, c.53, s.149 referred to acts of gross indecency committed by "every one" with "another person."

80 I found no other lesbian sexual assault trials or prosecutions for gross indecency against lesbians in this research sample from 1900–1975; future research may locate more. On the 1954 amendment, Joseph Sedgwick QC (1955) 33 *Canadian Bar Review* 63 noted at 70: "A clause I find difficult to understand is effected by the new section 149. . . . I do not know what an act of gross indecency between a man and a woman is, but, whatever it may be, it is now an offence. Nothing in the section requires that the act take place in public and thus what two lovers — or man and wife — may do in the privacy of their own apartment may turn out to be an offence. To some narrow minds all acts of sex are grossly indecent. And what a potent weapon of blackmail is thus provided for a woman who is loved, possibly too vigorously, and later scorned!" Cases would eventually clarify that heterosexual fellatio and cunnilingus were the target of prosecution under the amended provision. Chief Justice Calvert Charleton Miller declared in *R. v. LeFrançois*, [1965] 4 C.C.C. 255 (Man. C.A.) that an act of fellatio was "a clear example of gross indecency," describing it as "repugnant to ordinary standards of morality and decency," and "unnatural and depraved." He concluded: "Counsel for the accused . . . endeavoured to justify this type of conduct as being ordinary love-making and pointed to the conduct of animals which indulge in somewhat similar actions. However, we do not think that we are, as yet, prepared to accept the actions or conduct of animals as a proper norm by which to judge human behaviour." Alfred Maurice Monnin echoed these views in *R. v. P.*, [1968] 63 W.W.R. 222 (Man. C.A.), claiming that consensual fellatio between a man and woman "outraged" public decency, was "socially harmful to the community," and could be equated with "abnormal sex practice, sex deviation, aberrant sex behaviour, perversion, [a] crime against nature, unnatural oral coitus or oral copulation." He wrote in dissent however, with Brian Dickson speaking for the majority when he held the act insufficient to warrant conviction for gross indecency. Dickson noted that the expert psychiatrists who had testified had disagreed with each other, two describing fellatio between male and female as acceptable and normal, another regarding it as normal only if infrequently practised, and a fourth regarding it as an abnormal sexual perversion. Commenting on the gender-neutral amendment of 1954, Dickson cautioned that this did not mean that "parliament suddenly decided to enter the portals of the home . . . to require the courts to sit in judgment . . . upon any heterosexual sex act . . . done in private between consenting adults." He ruled that "the act of fellatio between male and female may be grossly indecent depending on time, place and circumstances" but that it was not so here. This view was later reenforced in S.C. 1968–69, c.38, s.7, which provided an exception from criminal liability for gross indecency when an act was committed in private between any two persons, each of whom was twenty-one years or more, and both consented to the act.

A conviction for gross indecency arising out of cunnilingus perpetrated by a man upon a woman was reversed on appeal in *R. v. St. Pierre* (1972), 7 C.C.C. (2d)

307 (Ont. C.A.), rejecting the trial judge's following charge to the jury: "Well, can you think of a much more grossly indecent act? This is said, not in evidence, but by counsel to you, in our modern society you see this in plays. Well, you consider whether any of you ever saw such a filthy act as this in a play or referred to on radio or on television or otherwise. . . . [A] dirty, filthy practice such as this that is resorted to by no one but by sexual perverts, is surely an infringement of the *Criminal Code*." See also *R. v. St. Pierre*, (1974) 17 C.C.C. (2d) 489 (Ont. C.A.) where Charles Dubin held that "an act of *cunnilingus* does not *per se* constitute an act of gross indecency," adding: "Attitudes relating to sexual behaviour are constantly changing. In determining whether the conduct of the accused was a very marked departure from decent conduct, it would have been of great assistance to the jury to have been apprised by an admittedly qualified expert as to sexual practices being carried on in this country, which are not regarded by many as abnormal or perverted."

In *R. v. B. and S.* (1957), 119 C.C.C. 296 (Alta. S.C.), William Gordon Neil Egbert held that "the mere contact of the male mouth with the female genital organs" would not constitute gross indecency without "something more proven." In *R. v. J.* (1957), 118 C.C.C. 30 (Alta. C.A.), the court upheld the decision of Magistrate Walter Dupre that consensual heterosexual fellatio did not constitute gross indecency, based on evidence of psychiatrists and psychologists from the University of Alberta who cited the Kinsey Report and testified that "the conduct is common, not unusual...not abnormal." In *The Queen v. Lupien*, [1970] 2 C.C.C. 193 (S.C.C.), Emmett Hall dealt with a charge of gross indecency against a male accused who claimed he had picked up a man cross-dressed as a female at a bar, and been completely surprised by the individual's gender. Although Hall referred to homosexuality as "an acquired aberration from the normal state," and noted the importance of admitting psychiatric evidence in the courtroom, he also added these further comments: "Homosexuality is not a disease of the mind nor a mental illness nor a condition arising out of mental incapacity or deficiency. It is a sexual attraction and interest between members of the same sex. . . . No one is destined at birth to be a homosexual any more than any given individual is earmarked to be an alcoholic or a drug addict. Heredity plays no part in the development. Environment is said to be the decisive factor. The literature on the subject of homosexuality is very divergent in attributing specific causes or reasons for the condition, but all writers are agreed that whatever other causes there may be, psychological factors are of great importance."

81 Interview with Charlotte (Suzie) Graham, former student at Yellowknife High School, 9 Dec. 2004, by Constance Backhouse; Interview with Ralph Moyle, former student at Yellowknife High School, 7 Feb. 2005, by Constance Backhouse.

82 *City of Edmonton Henderson's Directories*, 1962. I have found no record of Beatrice's whereabouts between 1955 and 1962; Beatrice's brother William was not in regular touch with his sister during these years, because of the falling out they had over her New York hospitalization.

83 A letter she wrote to Anezka Lelwisova, general secretary of Prague YWCA, on 12 September 1938, reveals something of her feelings about new starts. Counselling her friend, who was thinking about abandoning her life in Czechoslovakia after "severe

strain arising from a train of events of a personal nature," Beatrice wrote about her own life: "If the suggestion is of any use to you, my personal experience has been, through a very dark problem, that in spite of real assistance rendered by friends whose aim was to provide a suitable setting for a 'comeback,' I had to do the spade work, which consisted in the main of sorting out my ideas, putting them down on paper, then standing off objectively and having a good look at them. I discovered that there were many reactions, intellectual and emotional, that I did not want to keep, these having no useful purpose in reconstruction. Since I am human, I could only put them aside temporarily, but this was done firmly, with the resolution as I put my stake down, that I would go on from this or that disappointing place, rather than back over it. This is not easy to do, but it must be done, otherwise one runs the risk of arriving in a new setting with decayed bits of past unhappy experience cling-ing like fungus to one's mental processes, and not only are *you* handicapped before you've begun, but also you present a handicap to those who want to help you. One could go on indefinitely analyzing human situations and philosophizing regard-ing how to meet them, especially if one's own experience has been very deep and some bad scars still show. But I only say all this because I do understand and really care, and you must feel free to write me as a friend whenever it will help to write to someone." Correspondence from World YWCA Archives.

84 *City of Edmonton Henderson's Directories*, 1962–67; Interview with Dr. W.G. Welling-ton.

85 Beatrice Gonzales taught at 1963/64 Senior High Temp Victoria High School (voca-tional); 1964/66 McNally Senior High; 1966/67 Harry Ainlay; 1969/70 Senior High Temp Old Scona (semester); 1970/71 Eastglen. She served as the teacher liaison of the Debating Club at McNally. Edmonton Public School Archives and Museum; *McNally Composite High School Yearbook, TREND 1965/66* at 7, 54, and 62. Curiously, her moth-er's obituary lists Beatrice as living in Manville, Alberta, in 1969, which is 110 miles east of Edmonton: *Vancouver Sun* (26 April 1969).

86 She was interred in the Ocean View Cemetery in Vancouver beside her mother: Vital Statistics, Government of Alberta, 18 Oct. 2004. Her death was caused by an accident. Beatrice had been trying to assist a driver whose automobile was stuck in the snow, and the wheel ran over her foot, which subsequently became infected. Her leg was amputated too late to save her life; Interview with Dr. W.G. Wellington. On the significance of the Stonewall Riots in Canada, see Steven Maynard, "In Search of 'Sodom North': The Writings of Lesbian and Gay History in English Canada, 1970–1990" (March–June 1994) 21 *Canadian Review of Comparative Literature* 117–32. Korinek, "'The most openly gay person,'" above note 21, noted at 522 that prior to Stonewall, there were few homophile groups in Canada, most notably the Associa-tion of Social Knowledge established in Vancouver in 1964, and that most Canadian gay organizations were established after the riots. The year 1969 also marked the Parliamentary amendment that decriminalized some aspects of male homosexuali-ty. *Criminal Law Amendment Act, 1968–69*, S.C. 1968–69, c.38, s.7 provided: (1) Sections 147 and 149 do not apply to any act committed in private between (a) a husband and his wife; or (b) any two persons, each of whom is twenty-one years or more of age,

both of whom consent to the commission of the act. (2) For the purposes of subsection (1), (a) an act shall be deemed not to have been committed in private if it is committed in a public place, or if more than two persons take part or are present; and (b) a person shall be deemed not to consent to the commission of an act (i) if the consent is extorted by force, threats or fear of bodily harm or is obtained by false and fraudulent misrepresentations as to the nature and quality of the act, or (ii) if that person is, and the other party to the commission of the act knows or has good reason to believe that that person is feeble-minded, insane, or an idiot or imbecile."

87   Correspondence from Dr. W.G. Wellington to Dean Walter H. Gage, UBC. The initial endowment of $1100, paid from Beatrice's life insurance policy, was increased by subsequent donations from Dr. Wellington and his wife, and other friends of Beatrice, to the point that it provided for an annual income of $350. Dr. Wellington added: "I got a flood of letters from ex-students, which didn't surprise me, although it was nice to know that she was still good at her teaching . . . and she was able to galvanize students . . . there were dozens of ex-students who wrote me and said they wanted to donate to the scholarship. Each made it very clear how she had affected their lives. That was what she was like all the time. She really was wonderful. She was incredible." See www.library.ubc.ca/archives/pdfs/senate/ UBC Senate Minutes 1971 10 13.pdf; Interview with Dr. W.G. Wellington.

88   *News of the North* (25 March 1955) 8 reported that she "left last week for 'outside.'"

89   Had her conviction not been reversed, Willimae Moore might have faced deportation. The press had indicated that "it is believed that deportation to the United States, Miss Moore's native country, may follow." See *News of the North* (18 March 1955) 4. The *Immigration Act*, R.S.C. 1952, c.325, s.19(2) provided that a visitor to Canada was subject to deportation if a special inquiry officer found that the person had "practise(d), assist(ed), in the practice of, or share(d) in the avails of . . . homosexualism." Section 19(1)(e)(ii) also permitted deportation for conviction under the *Criminal Code*, and s.19(1)(e)(iv) if discovered to have been a member of a prohibited class at time of admission, and s.19(1)(e)(v) if having become, since entering Canada, a member of a prohibited class. The legislation was not repealed until 1977. Girard, "From Subversion to Liberation," above note 11. A search of the *Edmonton Journal* and the *Calgary Herald*, from 10–25 March 1955 and 11–28 October 1955 revealed no further press coverage of the trial or the appeal.

90   This revelation came during an interview conducted near the end of the research for this chapter. Bernstein further explained: "Probably Miss [White] wouldn't have been so upset if she wasn't Black. The police wouldn't have pushed it if Miss Moore wasn't Black. Some people have funny ideas about Black people." Interview with Lewis Bernstein. Canadian authorities have always been reluctant to record racial identification in legal proceedings, in a tradition that I have earlier described as an "ideology of racelessness." For discussion of this, and the lengthy history of racism against Blacks in Canada, see Constance Backhouse, *Colour-Coded: A Legal History of Racism in Canada, 1900–1950* (Toronto: University of Toronto, 1999) at 12–14, chapters 6 and 7. Without the input of the individuals who actually remembered Willimae Moore, to correct the presumptions of whiteness that pervade the legal records and

our reading of them, we might never have known that racial discrimination combined with homophobia to initiate Canada's first lesbian sexual assault prosecution.

Chapter 9: "Sordid" but "Understandable under the Circumstances"

1 "Trio Arrested after Death" *Williams Lake Tribune* (12 April 1967) 1. Details of the case are drawn from the report of the appeal of the acquittals, *Regina v. Kohnke, Croft and Wilson*, [1968] 3 C.C.C. 333 (B.C.C.A.), and the unreported decisions on the appeal of the sentence, Public Archives of British Columbia, British Columbia Court of Appeal, Call No. 83-1244, Box No. 34, File No. 604/67. The archival records contain the notice and grounds of appeal, correspondence from counsel, and the judicial appellate decisions. No records of the preliminary inquiry or trial appear to have survived. These records are supplemented by Interviews with Sandra (Roper) Archie, Dog Creek Reserve, British Columbia, 16–18 Aug. 2006, and email correspondence 20, 25, and 26 Jan. 2006; Interview with Dianne (Roper) Crosina, Williams Lake, British Columbia, 17 Aug. 2006; Interview with Herbert Lee Skipp, 4 Dec. 2006, and press coverage from the *Vancouver Daily Province* (11 April 1967) 9; (12 April 1967) 28; the *Williams Lake Tribune* (12 April 1967) 1–2; (14 June 1967) 1–2; (21 June 1967) 1; (13 Sept. 1967) 1–2; (20 Sept. 1967) 1–2; (28 Feb. 1968) 1; (2 April 1968) 1. Although the papers described Rose as either nineteen or "in her early twenties," she was almost six months short of her eighteenth birthday.

2 See, for example, *Rex v. Ducharme* (1950), 97 C.C.C. 247 (B.C.C.A.); *Rex v. Sykes* (1951), 101 C.C.C. 57 (B.C.C.A.); *Regina v. Fitton* (1956), 115 C.C.C. 225 (Ont. C.A.) and 116 C.C.C. 1 (S.C.C.); *Regina v. Eaton* (1957), 117 C.C.C. 375 (B.C.C.A.); *Regina v. Truscott* (1960), 126 C.C.C. 109 (Ont. C.A.) and *Reference re Regina v. Truscott*, [1967] 2 C.C.C. 285 (S.C.C.); *Fisher v. The Queen* (1961), 130 C.C.C. 1 (S.C.C.); *Regina v. Haase*, [1965] 2 C.C.C. 56 (B.C.C.A.); *Regina v. Hage*, [1968] 65 W.W.R. 309 (Alta. C.A.); *Regina v. Ortt*, [1968] 4 C.C.C. 92 (Ont. C.A.); *Regina v. Frank*, [1970] 2 C.C.C. 102 (B.C.C.A.); *Regina v. Kully*, [1974] 15 C.C.C. (2d) 488 (Ont. H. Ct.); *Lingley v. New Brunswick Board of Review*, [1974] 13 C.C.C. (2d) 303 (Fed. Ct. T.D.). See also *Regina v. Warner* (1960), 127 C.C.C. 394 (Alta. C.A.), where a man killed another man during an assault involving gross indecency.

3 *Criminal Code*, S.C. 1953–54, c.51, s.206.

4 S.C. 1953–54, c.51, s.201.

5 S.C. 1953–54, c.51, s.201 (c).

6 S.C. 1953–54, c.51, s.202 (a).

7 S.C. 1953–54, c.51, s.205 provided that "culpable homicide that is not murder or infanticide is manslaughter." The penalty was set out in s.207.

8 Email correspondence from Sandra (Roper) Archie, 20 Jan. 2006, to the author.

9 Christine Haines was the daughter of Charlie Haines (Hance) from Toosey Reserve. Email correspondence from Sandra Archie, 11 Jan. and 14 Feb. 2007.

10 Interviews with Sandra Archie, Dog Creek Reserve, British Columbia, 16–18 Aug. 2006, and email correspondence 20, 25, and 26 Jan. 2006; Interview with Dianne (Roper) Crosina, Williams Lake, British Columbia, 17 Aug. 2006. Further references will simply be to "Interviews."

11 *Publications of the Jesup North Pacific Expedition*, vol. 2, part 7: James Alexander Teit, *The Shuswap* (New York: AMS Press, 1909); Elizabeth Furniss, *Victims of Benevolence: The Dark Legacy of the Williams Lake Residential School*, 2d ed. (Vancouver: Arsenal Pulp Press, 1995) at 37–43 and 114; Elizabeth Furniss, "Resistance, Coercion, and Revitalization: The Shuswap Encounter with Roman Catholic Missionaries, 1860–1900" (Spring 1995) 42 *Ethnohistory* 231; Edward Sleigh Hewlett, "The Chilcotin Uprising of 1864" (1973) *B.C. Studies* 50; Museum of Cariboo Chilcotin, *Williams Lake: The Heart of the Cariboo* (Williams Lake: Progressive Printers, 2003) introduction, 1–5, and 99–105; Irene Stangoe, *Looking Back at the Cariboo-Chilcotin* (Vancouver: Heritage House, 1997); Irene Stangoe, *Cariboo-Chilcotin: Pioneer People and Places* (Surrey: Heritage House, 1994); *Land Ordinance, 1870*, No. 144, as found in *The Laws of British Columbia, Revised 1871*, s.55 at 503.

12 Teit, *The Shuswap*, above note 11; Furniss, *Victims of Benevolence*, above note 11 at 37–43 and 114; Museum of Cariboo Chilcotin, *Williams Lake*, above note 11 at introduction, 1–5, and 99–105; Stangoe, *Looking Back*, above note 11; Stangoe, *Cariboo-Chilcotin*, above note 11. "The Honour of All," part 1, video of Filmwest Associates, indicates that between 1960 and 1972, almost 100 percent of the people at Alkali Lake Reserve were alcoholics. Due to the courageous leadership of a few of its members who pulled Alkali Lake back from despair, the community dried up, and by 1985, it was 95 percent sober.

13 Christine Haines, Rose's paternal grandmother, had been taken away from her family to residential school at the age of eight: email correspondence from Sandra Archie, 11 Jan. 2007.

14 Interviews with Sandra Archie and Dianne Crosina; "Rose Marie Mildred Roper" #121-1199, Baptism Register, Oblat Record 925.1, Alkali Band Office.

15 On the gentler side of her father's character, Sandra Archie noted that "people would say he was kind, and were later surprised when we told them everything he had done." Interviews with Sandra Archie.

16 Interviews with Sandra Archie and Dianne Crosina.

17 "150 Mile House," as well as "100 Mile House," "125 Mile House," and "93 Mile House," obtained its name from the number of miles that istwas distant from Lillooet, the start of the former stage route to the Cariboo gold rush trail. "Lillooet — Mile 'o' — How the Road-Houses Got Their Name" (Aug. 1971) *100 Mile House Free Press, Centennial Edition* 40D.

18 National Archives of Canada, Indian Affairs, RG 10, file 962/36-4, vol. 10323, HQ; Agreement for the Operation of Cariboo Indian Residential School, between Her Majesty the Queen in Right of Canada represented by the Minister of Citizenship and Immigration (Oblate Indian and Eskimo Commission), 25 Sept. 1962, 989/25-13, B.C. Region, vol. 1. The residential school closed in 1981.

19 *Report of the Royal Commission on Aboriginal Peoples*, vol. 1: *Looking Forward, Looking Back* at 333–44 and 365.

20 On documented complaints from 1902, 1920, 1927, 1928, 1935, 1943, 1945, 1947, and 1949, see Furniss, *Victims of Benevolence*, above note 11 at 62–88 and 92–98; National Archives of Canada, Indian Affairs, RG 10, vol. 6436, file 878-1, parts 1, 2, and 3;

vol. 6437, file 878-5, parts 1, 3, document 62003A; vol. 6438, file 878-5, parts 3 and 6; Department of Mines and Resources, Indian Affairs Branch, Inspector's Report, Cariboo Residential Indian School, 6 Nov. 1947, RG 10, vol. 85-86/476, 989/23-5, part 1, Temp. Box A-15, 11/47-6/54, Bay 2283-84, NAC — Burnaby. A 1902 inquiry into the death of eight-year-old runaway Duncan Sticks of Alkali Lake, who died from exposure by the roadside on 8 February, revealed that he had earlier complained about being whipped "with guirt" and being forced to eat bad food. His sister, Mary, age eleven, who had tried to run away earlier, stated she was "whipped with a strap." Augustin, age seven, who had run away with Duncan, claimed that they fled because they were whipped with a strap on the legs for not knowing their lessons. Louis, age twelve, and François, age ten, claimed they ran away earlier because they were whipped with a horse-whip and because they were starving. Ellen Batiste, age ten, claimed she had been hit with a strap on the head several times. Ellen Charlie, age sixteen, had run away four times, and claimed to have been whipped "with a strap on the face." She stated the food was "fit only for pigs," that the "meat was rotten and had a bad smell and taste" but that when she refused to eat it, the sisters gave it to her again "for the next meal." Christine Haines stated that the food was so bad it had made her and others sick. Refusal to eat the food meant that they got "nothing else till it was eaten." Haines also claimed that she had been beaten "with a strap, sometimes on the face, and [they] sometimes took my clothes off and beat me." Principal Rev. Henry Boening admitted that there had been incidents of children confined in dark rooms, girls confined alone in a room for a week, and whippings administered across the face, but swore that none of this had occurred while he was in charge.

In 1920, an investigation confirmed that a supervisor had flogged a student with a rod, and that the boy had run away and never been brought back. In response, nine students attempted to carry out a suicide pact. Augustine Allan from Canim Lake died, and the other eight became seriously ill from ingesting poisonous hemlock. The Indian Agent, A. O'N. Daunt, advised on 16 Aug. 1920 that "the general Indian attitude towards Mission Schools throughout Central B.C. is *not* friendly." Further correspondence, 7 Sept. 1920, stated that "the Indians are not at all satisfied with the conduct of the Missionary Schools in this part of the country."

21 Archives Deschâtelets, 175 Main, Ottawa, PC 101 .W72C 38, 235–38, Report, 23 May 1946, correspondence, 27 and 31 May 1946, 4 and 6 June 1946, 12 and 20 Aug. 1946.

22 National Archives of Canada, Indian Affairs, RG 10, vol. 8703, file 962/6-1, parts 2, 4, and 5; vol. 8760, file 901/25-1, part 2. Rose's year of admission is an estimate, based on her sister Sandra's recollection, and the fact that most students started at age six.

23 National Archives of Canada, Indian Affairs, RG 10, vol. 8703, file 962/6-1, part 6, file 962/25-13-014, vol. 1, 1965/03/01-1972/05-01, Acc. V77-F12, Box 3620, DIAND, BC Central Registry; RG 10, vol. 8704, file 962/6-1, part 11; RG 10, FA 10-379, Acc. #1999-01431-6, Box 368, 962/6-1, part 12, 1965–1966, NAC Ottawa; Department of Citizenship and Immigration, Indian Affairs Branch, Correspondence from Indian Commissioner W.S. Arneil, 4 Dec. 1956, 962/23-16, vol. 1, 05/53-05/68, (34-13), IRSRHFC; Principal's Monthly Report, Jan. 1960, 962/23-16, vol. 1, 05/53-05/68, (34-13), IRSRHFC; Interviews

with Sandra Archie. Sandra mentioned that even into adulthood, the former residential school pupils all knew each other by number.

24 Interviews with Sandra Archie.

25 "Scottish-Indian Pipers from the Cariboo" in Irene Stangoe, *Looking Back*, above note 11 at 136–40; Interviews with Sandra Archie.

26 Edward John & C.C. Barnett, *Alkali Residential School Inquiry Report*, submitted to Alkali Lake First Nation, 26 June 1997. Suzanne Fournier & Ernie Crey, *Stolen from Our Embrace* (Vancouver: Douglas & McIntyre, 1997) noted at 73 that McIntee pleaded guilty to sexual and indecent assault in 1989, and Doughty did likewise in 1991. J.R. Miller, *Shingwauk's Vision: A History of Native Residential Schools* (Toronto: University of Toronto Press, 1996) noted at 329 that McIntee was convicted of sexual assaults on thirteen boys, many of them assaulted "more than 30 times each while they slept in the group dormitory or after luring them to a shower." O'Connor was charged in 1991 with two acts of rape, three indecent assaults, and one act of gross indecency committed between 1964 and 1967 against four young Aboriginal women, all former students employed at the school; *R. v. O'Connor* (1994), 89 C.C.C. (3d) 109 (B.C.C.A.). Larry Still, "Catholic Bishop, Student Were Lovers: Lawyers Tell Judge Prelate Likely Father of Child Born in '60s" *Vancouver Sun* (17 Oct. 1992) A.1, noted four charges of rape involving two women employees of the school and two counts of indecent assault on two female students. Furniss, *Victims of Benevolence*, above note 11 notes at 115 that two other Oblates implicated in student allegations were not charged.

27 Correspondence from Rev. Fr. H. O'Connor, O.M.I., 8 March 1965, National Archives of Canada, 962/16-2 vol. 2, 1965–70, RCAP; Miller, *Shingwauk's Vision*, above note 26 at 331; Andy Ivens, "Bishop Beats Sex Charge: But Appeal Court Orders New Trial on Rape Count" *Vancouver Province* (25 March 1998) A39 and "O'Connor Appeal Dropped after Healing Circle" *Vancouver Sun* (18 June 1998) A1 and A6.

28 Miller, *Shingwauk's Vision*, above note 26 at 331; *R. v. O'Connor* (1992), 18 C.R. (4th) 98 (B.C.S.C.) quashed the charges on the ground that the Crown had failed to disclose the women's medical, counselling, and school records, despite the Crown's claim that the extensive disclosure order entailed "gender bias." *R. v. O'Connor* (1994), 89 C.C.C. (3d) 109 (B.C.C.A.) reversed the order to stay the proceedings and ordered a new trial. See also *Regina v. O'Connor (No. 2)* (1994), 90 C.C.C. (3d) 257 (B.C.C.A.). A subsequent appeal to the Supreme Court of Canada was dismissed: *O'Connor v. The Queen*, [1995] 4 S.C.R. 411. The case provoked a great deal of public debate, and resulted in revisions to the *Criminal Code* regarding the production of records to the accused, in an effort to balance the privacy rights of the complainant with concerns about due process; see S.C. 1997, c.30. The second trial in 1996 resulted in a conviction for indecent assault on one complainant, and rape on another: "Bishop Jailed 2½ Years" *Calgary Herald* (14 Sept. 1996) A3; "Sentence Hailed by Native Leaders" *Toronto Globe and Mail* (14 Sept. 1996) A1. The appeal court quashed the indecent assault conviction, and ordered a new trial on the rape charge, on the basis that the trial court had wrongly found O'Connor to be in a position of authority over the women. The matter was sent back for retrial on the proof of lack of consent. See Ivens, "Bishop Beats Sex Charge," above note 27 at A39 and "O'Connor Appeal

Dropped," above note 27 at A1 and A6. The press noted that O'Connor admitted fathering a child with one of the complainants. Thirty-eight participants took part in the private seven-hour-long healing circle in the meeting hall at Alkali Lake in June 1998.

29 On the transfer of Cariboo Indian Residential School students to these two public schools for grade 9 (commencing in fall 1961) and grade 10 (commencing in 1962), see National Archives of Canada, Indian Affairs, RG 10, vol. 1996–97/914, Box 1, File #27-8-878, 08/1961–03/1968, NAC Burnaby. On the racist incidents at the high schools, see Interviews with Sandra Archie.

30 Interviews with Sandra Archie.

31 Interviews with Sandra Archie and Dianne Crosina.

32 I have drawn the details and quotes that follow from the legal records and the press coverage: "Trio Arrested after Death" *Williams Lake Tribune* (12 April 196) 1; "Charges Hiked in Girl's Death" and "More about Hearing" *Williams Lake Tribune* (14 June 1967) 1 and 2; "Trio Ordered to Face Trial" *Williams Lake Tribune* (21 June 1967) 1 and 2; "Murder Charge Reduced" *Williams Lake Tribune* (13 Sept. 1967) 1 and 2; "One Man Acquitted, Two Fined following Manslaughter Trial" *Williams Lake Tribune* (20 Sept. 1967) 1 and 2. References will only be inserted to indicate sources other than the above.

33 Museum of Cariboo Chilcotin, *Williams Lake*, above note 11 at introduction, 1–5, and 99–105; Stangoe, *Looking Back*, above note 11; Stangoe, *Cariboo-Chilcotin*, above note 11.

34 On the long-standing practice of travelling "20 miles in 40 below weather to attend a dance," see "Of the Pioneers" (Aug. 1971) *100 Mile House Free Press, Centennial Edition* 49.

35 Rose's sister Sandra recalled that Rose used to "go out" with Alfred, but advised that this would not have meant "dates" but probably "getting together, hanging around together, drinking." Interviews with Sandra Archie.

36 Herbert Lee Skipp, Kohnke's defence counsel, advised that "it would have been very uncommon" to see a white and Aboriginal couple in an "open relationship" at the time. Interview with Herbert Lee Skipp, 4 Dec. 2006. Museum of Cariboo Chilcotin, *Williams Lake*, above note 11, notes at 17, 90, and 189 that although the First Nations were among the top competitors in the stampede arena, they were not admitted to the stampede pavilion for the dances, but were forced to hold theirs at the barbershop and pool-hall; "social events . . . were segregated, as were restaurants and other services." "Squaw Hall," an outdoor dance hall, was built on stampede grounds to accommodate "native people who were not welcome at the downtown dances." The local hospital segregated First Nations' patients until the 1950s. The uneasy race relations were occasionally set on display for "entertainment" at the Williams Lake Stampede. Stangoe, *Cariboo-Chilcotin*, above note 11, notes at 35 that in an early 1920s stampede, a "fort was built of rough lumber" and then "Indians — genuine local ones — would attack the fort and set it on fire. Then cowboys would charge from the top of the hill and drive them away, at the same time rescuing the maiden — Ollie Curtis — who had been 'captured.'" Stangoe notes at 40 that in later years, whites

began to invade the stampede dances at "Squaw Hall as it was more fun than the uptown dances," and that violence and drunkenness ensued until 1975, when the decision was taken to burn the hall to the ground. "With it went almost 30 years of memories, some good and some bad."

37 Museum of Cariboo Chilcotin, *Williams Lake*, above note 11, notes at 184 that Joan Palmantier, a rodeo competitor, trainer, and later a rodeo judge, was the "first First Nations to win in open competition" when she took the title "Stampede Queen" in 1966. She went on to win the title of "BC Indian Princess" and then "Canadian Indian Princess" in Montréal at Expo 67. (The Cariboo Indian Girls Pipe Band also performed live at Expo 67.) Palmantier (Gentles) later became the director of Indian Education for the Cariboo Chilcotin School District and was awarded the Order of British Columbia.

38 Museum of Cariboo Chilcotin, *Williams Lake*, above note 11 at 33, 39, 86, 89, and 103; Interview with Herbert Lee Skipp. Skipp described the Kohnke family as "very, very well known in Williams Lake. They had come from Vancouver and were quite a colourful family . . . but not exactly members of the first families of Williams Lake." Diana French, "French Connection" *Williams Lake Tribune* (6 June 2006) notes that the Kohnke wrestlers "raised huge amounts of money (over $50,000 in the 1950s–60s) staging wrestling bouts and donating the money to the community."

39 Interviews with Sandra Archie.

40 Two white witnesses, Joseph Lamarche and Marvin Bates, would testify to this. Beer parlours began to serve First Nations on 15 December 1951, but only to drink on the premises, and not to buy bottled stock to take off premises, or to buy hard liquor; see Museum of Cariboo Chilcotin, *Williams Lake*, above note 11 at 81.

41 "Body of Girl Found in Dump" *Vancouver Province* (11 April 1967) 9.

42 Interviews with Sandra Archie.

43 In June 1967, the charge was raised to "non-capital murder" under s.206(2), and then reduced by the time of the trial in Assize Court in September 1967. On the distinctions between capital murder and non-capital murder, see *An Act to amend the Criminal Code (Capital Murder)*, S.C. 1960–61, c.44, s.1; S.C. 1967–68, c.15, s.1.

44 On the erasure of racial identities from Canadian legal records, see Constance Backhouse, *Colour-Coded: A Legal History of Racism in Canada, 1900–1950* (Toronto: University of Toronto, 1999).

45 See, for example, the prosecution of a Chippewa from Caradox, Muncey, in Rex v. Edward Hall (1915) Middlesex County Crown Attorney and Crown Prosecutor Criminal Court Records, #1264, UWO Regional Room, Box 560. Hall was described as an "illiterate labourer" without "elementary instruction," and "a half-breed Indian . . . whose presence is a menace to every woman in the neighbourhood." *R. v. Fidler* (1921), 36 C.C.C. 239 (Man. C.A.) involved the prosecution of a "half-breed" that encompassed an intense debate about the "marked characteristics" and "racial features" of "half-breeds." Asian prosecutions include Rex v. Jack Lee (1922) Middlesex County Crown Attorney and Crown Prosecutor Criminal Court Records, #376, file 3387 (copy on file with author); Rex v. Charlie Ging (1922) Middlesex County Crown Attorney and Crown Prosecutor Criminal Court Records, #628, file 4009 (copy on file

with author); *The King v. Tom Ging* (1924), 57 N.S.R. 196 (N.S.C.A.); *Rex v. Yee Jam Hong (alias George Kee)* (1928), 23 Sask. L.R. 173 (Sask. C.A.); *Rex v. Bakshish Singh* (1943), 80 C.C.C. 79 (B.C.C.A.); *Regina v. Jumbo Singh* (1955), 112 C.C.C. 289 (B.C.C.A.). African-Canadian prosecutions include *Regina v. Olbey*, [1971] 4 C.C.C. (2d) 103 (Ont. C.A.); *Re Regina and Grant* (1973), 13 C.C.C. (2d) 495 (Ont. H. Ct.); *Regina v. Rivera*, [1975] 22 C.C.C. (2d) 105 (B.C.C.A.). Ethnic and religious discrimination that was often akin to "racism" also beset other groups. See, for example, Henry Kissel's Jewish identity in chapter 4. In *Rex v. Stelmasczuk* (1948), 23 M.P.R. 253 (N.S.S.C.), which involved a Ukrainian accused, the trial judge charged the jury: "I know you will bear in mind that these people are foreigners. Some of them, at least, have not much English. In that connection, it is for you to judge with regard to the accused. He has been in this country nineteen years and apparently has not yet learned the meaning of yes, and no, or December, or a word of English. You will draw from that whatever inference appeals to your judgment and your common sense. . . . These people are foreigners."

46 In *Rex v. Harms*, [1944] 2 D.L.R. 61 (Sask. C.A.), a sixty-three-year-old white man who called himself "Doctor Harms" purported to provide medical treatment to a twenty-year-old Aboriginal woman in Melfort, Saskatchewan. He lured her into his office by offering to treat her "for free as she was an Indian girl." Promising to cure her chest pains and irregular periods, he gave her pills to make her dizzy, inserted pills vaginally, and then had non-consensual sexual intercourse with her. Despite the argument of the defence counsel that the victim had not been deceived "as to the nature and quality of the act," Harms was convicted of inducing consent by fraud. In *Regina v. Bannerman*, [1966] 55 W.W.R. 257 (Man. C.A.) and [1966] 57 W.W.R. 736 (S.C.C.), a twenty-nine-year-old white man preyed upon two unsupervised Aboriginal children, a boy aged thirteen and a girl aged twelve. He abducted them from their home and took them to a hotel under a false name, where he showered with them and then had forcible intercourse with the girl (leaving her with a bruised lip and ruptured hymen) and fellatio with the boy. He was convicted of sexual intercourse with a female under fourteen and gross indecency with another male. The verdict was upheld, although not unanimously on appeal. The racism that could motivate assailants is clear in *Regina v. Vandervoort* (1961), 130 C.C.C. 158 (Ont. C.A.), where two white men were accused of raping a "young coloured woman of Jamaican descent" who was working as a domestic in Toronto. The complainant testified that she had been forcibly pulled into a taxi, driven far away, and raped. The version put forth by the accused men is laced with racist notions about the sexuality of African-Canadian women. They testified that they were driving by in a taxi when the coloured woman waved to them, and got into the front seat. She purportedly kissed one of them, and when he got out to urinate (he had been drinking), she "lifted her skirt and said: 'there it is boys, black and white.'" The testimony of the accused continued: "Sitting on the front seat with her legs out the door, she removed her own pants, and laid back on the seat with her legs wide open, and her skirt pulled up to her waist." After they drove her to the vicinity of the home in which she was employed, she allegedly "waved goodnight to them and seemed happy and all smiles."

The trial conviction was set aside on appeal because the court felt that due to drunkenness, the men may not have formed specific intent.

The members of the Royal Commission on the Status of Women that held hearings in Yellowknife in 1968 heard several people speak about the "exploitation of native women" and the "brutal sexual behaviour" that some white men exhibited towards Aboriginal women. Marilyn Assheton-Smith, a regional program director for the Company of Young Canadians, noted that Aboriginal women were "considered fair game for normal and respectable men" who had "learned unconsciously to differentiate between women whose social status permits them to be abused and those whose social level does not." She cited examples of two Aboriginal women she had encountered who "had probably been gang-raped by transient men working on construction or survey crews." Her observation was that "it destroyed them." See Barbara M. Freeman, *The Satellite Sex: The Media and Women's Issues in English Canada, 1966–1971* (Waterloo, ON: Wilfrid Laurier University Press, 2001) at 201. Previously in 1921, in a woefully misguided effort to prevent just such situations, the House of Commons had debated introducing an amendment to the *Criminal Code* that would have made it a crime "for any white man to have illicit connection with an Indian woman." Minister of Justice Charles Joseph Doherty, of Montréal (St. Ann's riding), justified the proposed legislation by noting that "there is a practical disregard on the part of white men of any obligation to respect these Indian women, and on the other hand the Indian women are, perhaps, not as alive as women of other races in the country to the importance of maintaining their chastity, and so forth." The legislation was opposed by Jacques Bureau, a former solicitor general and M.P. from Trois-Rivières and St. Maurice, who claimed that it provided "an inducement for blackmail," adding: "As the clause stands, there is nothing to prevent any Indian female laying a charge against a white man and having her buck Indian coming behind her for the few dollars and holding up the white man. We do not want to give the buck Indian an opportunity, by such legislation, to take money out of white people's pockets." In the face of such arguments, Doherty withdrew the amendment. *House of Commons Debates* (26 May 1921) at 3906–8; Colonel Ernest J. Chambers, *The Canadian Parliamentary Guide, 1921* (Ottawa: Mortimer Co. Ltd., 1921) at 112–13 and 128.

47 Character witnesses for Kohnke were Alfred Knull and Alfred Poelvoorde of Vancouver, and Mrs. Mae Johnson of Williams Lake. Mrs. Lillian McKay of Williams Lake and Clifford D. Gibbons of North Burnaby appeared for Croft. Frederick deMoore of Vancouver, and Mrs. Lillian Deschene and Gordon Hamilton of Williams Lake, appeared for Wilson.

48 Adjusted for inflation, $500 in 1967 is the equivalent of $2981.65 in 2006. "Inflation Calculator" at www.bankofcanada.ca/en/rates/inflation_calc.html. In 1967, Vancouver carpenters earned $4.14 an hour, newsprint machine tenders $5.05 an hour, and loggers $113.64 a week. Statistics Canada, *Historic Statistics of Canada*, 2d ed., electronic edition, F.H. Leacy, ed. (Ottawa: Statistics Canada) series E248-267 and E86-103, at 11-516-X1E. Two white men tried in Saskatchewan in 1995 for the murder of Pamela George, an Aboriginal woman described as a "prostitute," testified that they

had offered her $60 to have sex with both of them. Despite the inflationary factor of thirty years, this amount was strikingly less than what Kohnke claimed he and his friends had offered in 1967. See Sherene H. Razack, "Gendered Racial Violence and Spatialized Justice: The Murder of Pamela George" in Sherene H. Razack, ed., *Race, Space, and the Law* (Toronto: Between the Lines, 2002) at 141.

49 This information from the autopsy report is taken from the Unreported Reasons for Judgment of Judge Bull, British Columbia Court of Appeal, 27 March 1968, Public Archives of British Columbia, British Columbia Court of Appeal, Call No. 83-1244, Box No. 34, File No. 604/67.

50 Inquisition at 100 Mile House upon the death of Rosemarie Roper, 20 Nov. 1967 at 2; copy held by Sandra Archie, and on file with the author.

51 For the written report, see Inquisition at 100 Mile House upon the death of Rosemarie Roper, *ibid*. Details of Dr. Bilbey's court testimony regarding his report are drawn from the press and the Report of Judge Dohm to the Chief Justice of the British Columbia Court of Appeal, 23 Oct. 1967, and Unreported Reasons for Judgment of Judge McFarlane, British Columbia Court of Appeal, 27 March 1968, Public Archives of British Columbia, British Columbia Court of Appeal, Call No. 83-1244, Box No. 34, File No. 604/67.

52 Interview with Herbert Lee Skipp, 4 Dec. 2006. Skipp was born in 1926 in Edmonton to James Herbert Skipp and Olive (Mills). His father, a sergeant in the British Army, had immigrated to Canada after the First World War, worked in the post office and then ran a series of grocery stores. Lee Skipp worked for the Hudson's Bay Company in the Northwest Territories for a brief period after he completed grade 10, and then returned to high school. He obtained his B.A. (1948) and LL.B. (1951) from the University of British Columbia, and then moved to Williams Lake to join Jack Cade's law practice. He met and married his wife (Mary Latin) there. Skipp's busy general practice in Williams Lake encompassed criminal law and mortgage and housing work. "We did alright for a number of reasons," he recalled. "The Cariboo bar at that time was justly famous for consisting of about 80% alcoholics. We weren't, which was a distinct advantage." By the time of this trial, he was practising in partnership with Alan Vanderburgh, who had joined the firm in 1961. Skipp unsuccessfully contested the provincial election in 1966, running for the Liberals against Robert Bonner, the Socred candidate, and Hartley Dent, the NDP candidate. Bonner won. Museum of Cariboo Chilcotin, *Williams Lake*, above note 11 at 101 and 105.

53 Unless indicated otherwise, all of the references to the lawyers' submissions are drawn from the press coverage.

54 These are recollections of the jury summation from the Interview with Herbert Lee Skipp, 4 Dec. 2006.

55 Hardinge practised with the Prince George firm of Cumming, Bird, Hardinge, and Fraser.

56 Dohm was born in Edmonton in 1916, the son of Elizabeth D. and Martin Lawrence Dohm. He married Faith Cameron in 1939, and they had nine children. He received his B.A. from the University of British Columbia in 1937, and was called to the bar in British Columbia in 1940. A Roman Catholic and former vice-president of the B.C.

Liberal Association, he was elevated to the British Columbia Supreme Court in 1966, and served until 1972. He chaired the board of governors of the University of British Columbia, and served as a director of the Canadian Council of Christians and Jews, and a member of the advisory board for the Salvation Army. *Canadian Who's Who*, vol. 13 (Toronto: Who's Who Canadian Publications, 1975) at 281.

57 Skipp recalled that it was "paper inserted into her vagina," adding that "one of the judges, perhaps one of the naive ones," had asked him what the meaning of that was at the appeal. Interview with Herbert Lee Skipp.

58 Report of the Hon. Mr. Justice Dohm, made pursuant to Section 588(1) of the *Criminal Code* to the British Columbia Court of Appeal, 23 Oct. 1967, Public Archives of British Columbia, British Columbia Court of Appeal, Call No. 83-1244, Box No. 34, File No. 604/67; *Regina v. Kohnke, Croft and Wilson*, [1968] 3 C.C.C. 333 (B.C.C.A.).

59 On the racial identity of the jurors, Skipp recalled: "I believe that as was customary, the jury was all white. Jury selection then wasn't big on racial representation. It wasn't my practice ever to keep natives off, but I didn't have to really worry too much about that, because the jury pool would have been majority white, and short on native Indians." Interview with Herbert Lee Skipp.

60 Report of the Hon. Mr. Justice Dohm; "One man acquitted, two fined following manslaughter trial" *Williams Lake Tribune* (20 Sept. 1967) 1.

61 Interviews with Sandra Archie and Dianne Crosina.

62 *Criminal Code*, S.C. 1953–54, c.51, ss.191, 192, and 194.

63 Interview with Herbert Lee Skipp.

64 Murray, who was born in 1917, "built a career as one of the province's top criminal attorneys in the 1950s and 1960s." He was known to have a "stern manner," to be a voracious reader, and to have a "Falstaffian love of good food and wine." Obituary for George L. Murray, *National Post* (18 Jan. 1999) A13.

65 Notice of Appeal, Public Archives of British Columbia, British Columbia Court of Appeal, Call No. 83-1244, Box No. 34, File No. 604/67, mentions several additional grounds of appeal, all abandoned before the hearing. These included a claim that the trial judge had erred when he refused to permit Dr. Bilbey to "express his expert medical opinion on the likelihood, as opposed to the possibility, that the deceased, Rose Marie Roper, met her death by mere accident," and a claim that "in charging the jury on the law relating to common intention, the learned judge expressed himself in several different ways the effect of which must have been to cause confusion in the minds of the jurors."

66 Davey was born in 1899 in Victoria, educated there in public schools, and called to the B.C. bar in 1921. He had practised with Crease, Davey, Lawson, Davis, Gordon & Baker. MacLean was born in 1903 in Victoria, the son of Hugh Archibald, KC, and Charlotte Grace (Barrett). He graduated from Victoria College in 1922, and received a B.A. from McGill in 1924. An Anglican, he married Margaret Jean Wilson in 1931, and they had two children. He was called to the bar in 1927, and practised in Kamloops and Vancouver. He became assistant deputy attorney general in 1944, and deputy attorney general from 1954 until 1957, when he was appointed to the bench. He became a member of the court of appeal in 1965. (Alexander) Bruce Robertson

was born in Victoria in 1904, the son of the Hon. Mr. Justice Harold Bruce and Helen (Rogers). He studied at Trinity College in Port Hope, Ontario, and obtained a B.A. from the University of Toronto in 1925. An Anglican, he married Jean Keefer Campbell in 1924, and had two children. He was called to the B.C. bar in 1928, where he practised with Robertson, Douglas & Symes until 1946. He then became general solicitor for B.C. Electric Railway Co., and later served as chairman and president of B.C. Power Corp., and also with B.C. Electric Co. He served as associate counsel to Russell & DuMoulin from 1964–67, when he was appointed to the court of appeal. He was also a director of the B.C. Save the Children Fund. *Canadian Who's Who*, vol. 11 (Toronto: Who's Who Canadian Publication, 1969) at 256, 689, and 939; *Canadian Who's Who*, vol. 13 (Toronto: Who's Who Canadian Publication, 1975) at 637 and 852.

67 *Regina v. Kohnke, Croft and Wilson*, [1968] 3 C.C.C. 333 (B.C.C.A.); "No Re-Trial in Roper Case" *Williams Lake Tribune* (28 Feb. 1968) 1.

68 Meredith ("Med") McFarlane was born in Ontario in 1908, and educated at Magee High School in Vancouver and Trinity College in Port Hope, Ontario. He obtained a B.A. from the University of British Columbia in 1928. The son of a druggist, he was the first in his family to obtain a law degree. He served his first year of articles with Vancouver lawyer E.J. Bird, who had acted for the Sikhs, Muslims, and Hindus from India denied admission to Canada in the notorious Komagata Maru affair in 1914. He attended Osgoode Hall Law School and articled in Toronto for his second year, and did his third year of articles with Vancouver barrister J.A. McInnis. Called to the B.C. bar in 1931, he initially practised with McInnis's firm, but became deputy registrar of companies in 1934. Subsequently, he practised with McFarlane and White in Vancouver, served with the army during the war, and then practised with Lawrence, Shaw & McFarlane. Regarded as one of the "finest practitioners in the province," he taught company law on a part-time, voluntary basis at the University of British Columbia Faculty of Law for seventeen years, and served as a bencher and treasurer of the B.C. Law Society. In 1964, he was appointed to the bench, and elevated to the B.C. Court of Appeal in 1965. Tony Sheppard, "Interview with the Hon. Meredith Milner McFarlane" 31 May 1995, unpublished, copy on file with author; W. Wesley Pue, *Law School: The Story of Legal Education in British Columbia* (Vancouver: University of British Columbia Faculty of Law, 1995).

69 Reasons for Judgment, 27 March 1968, Public Archives of British Columbia, British Columbia Court of Appeal, Call No. 83-1244, Box No. 34, File No. 604/67.

70 Bull was born in 1907 in Vancouver, the son of Alfred Edwin and Margaret Elizabeth (McKenney). An Anglican, he studied at University School in Victoria, obtained a B.A. from the University of British Columbia, and married Margaret Jean Carder in 1934. He was called to the B.C. bar in 1931, and practised with Farris & Co. from 1931 to 1933, and with Farris, Stultz, Bull & Farris from 1933 to 1964, when he was appointed to the court of appeal. During the Second World War, he served as a major with the Seaforth Highlanders of Canada, and with the Judge Advocate's office. He was a member of the Canadian Bar Association Council, and president of the Vancouver Bar Association. He also acted as president and director of Vancou-

ver Children's Aid Society. *Canadian Who's Who*, vol. 11 (Toronto: Who's Who Canadian Publications, 1969) at 145.

71 Reasons for Judgment, above note 69.

72 Interview with Herbert Lee Skipp; "Two Jailed Year in Roper Climax" *Williams Lake Tribune* (3 April 1968) 1.

73 *Vancouver Province* (2 July 1989) 16; Interview with Herbert Lee Skipp.

74 Elena Cherney, "Judge's Stern Courtroom Manner Hid Love of Wine," Obituary for George L. Murray, above note 64.

75 Interviews with Sandra Archie.

76 Sarah Carter, *Capturing Women: The Manipulation of Cultural Imagery in Canada's Prairie West* (Montréal: McGill-Queen's University Press, 1997) at 189–90; Donald Smith, "Bloody Murder Almost Became Miscarriage of Justice" *Herald Sunday Magazine* (23 July 1989) 13; *Calgary Weekly Herald* (17 and 24 July 1889), (11 Sept. 1889), and (6 March 1889). Fisk was acquitted on the first trial, but convicted of manslaughter on the second.

77 *Regina v. Price and Hansen*, [1969] 1 C.C.C. 226 (Ont. C.A.). G. Arthur Martin, QC, counsel for the defence, argued that the complainant had cooperatively consented to enter a car with two men she had never met before, and to drive to an isolated location to have consensual sex with each of the men twice. He claimed that her bruises and two buttons torn off her coat outside the laundromat did not constitute corroboration. He offered testimony from a defence witness who said she had seen the accused and the complainant walk around the block earlier that evening as evidence that there was some preliminary activity. The trial judge asked: "Do you want me to tell the jury that that is Arctic Circle love making?" Judge Bora Laskin, ruling in dissent on the appeal, would have preferred to acquit the men. He noted that the girl's clothes were intact and the men had testified that she had asked them for $20 to pay a fine for consuming liquor under age, and they had given her cigarettes.

78 *Regina v. Warkentin, Hanson and Brown*, [1975] 20 C.C.C. (2d) 321 (B.C.C.A.). Much turned at trial and appeal on the nature of the human hair found "on her slacks," with counsel questioning whether it was "caucasian, white or in the narrow sense Indian." The dissenting judge stated that there was no lawful corroboration in the complainant's distraught condition, the presence of "pine needles in the girl's panties," or the "spermatozoa in her crotch area."

79 *Regina v. Murphy and Butt*, [1975] 2 W.W.R. 723 (B.C.C.A.). The men were convicted at trial, a verdict upheld on appeal. The dissenting judge preferred to assert that the young woman's "distraught condition" was not corroboration, because it was as consistent with "an all night harrowing experience in a strange city as it was with an act of sexual intercourse which she said occurred without her genuine consent."

80 Manitoba, *Report of the Aboriginal Justice Inquiry of Manitoba: The Deaths of Helen Betty Osborne and John Joseph Harper*, vol. 2 (Winnipeg: Queen's Printer, 1991) at 5–19, 52, and 90.

81 Interviews with Sandra Archie and Dianne Crosina.

82 The first board members were Hugh Mahon, Rev. Dick Hunt, Dr. W. Meekison, Evelyn Ignatius, Angelina Lulua, Jean Sandy, Tom Sellers, and Marvin Bates. Volunteers

included Irene and Sammie Peters, Martha Sellars, Mary Jane More, Marvin Alexander, and George and Bonnie Keener. Drug and alcohol counsellors included Brother Ed Lynch and Margaret Coldwell. George Keener served as president of what would become the Cariboo Friendship Centre for more than thirty-five years. The existence of the organization was described as a "high note" of the decade in Museum of Cariboo Chilcotin, *Williams Lake*, above note 11 at 107.

83   Interviews with Sandra Archie.
84   Email from Sandra Archie, 11 April 2007.
85   Interviews with Sandra Archie.

Chapter 10: "Imprisonment Would Be of No Assistance to the Accused"

1   Details of the case are drawn from *Regina v. A.*, [1976] 26 C.C.C. (2d) 474 (Ont. High Ct.); R. v. Angione, Archives of Ontario, RG22-1890, May–Sept. 1974, containing the Probation Order, Indictment, Indictable Informations, Undertaking, Transcript of the Preliminary Hearing, Subpoenas, Reasons for Judgment. The written files were supplemented by Interviews with Frank Montello, 7 Sept. 2005 by Megan Reid, 2 Nov. 2005 by Constance Backhouse, and 27 Dec. 2005 by Constance Backhouse and Megan Reid. Ray Houlahan advised he could not remember the case when contacted.
2   "Jury Convicts Men of Rape" *Windsor Star* (17 Sept. 1974) 5; "Pair Sentenced to Prison for Rape" *Windsor Star* (21 Sept. 1974) 5; Interviews with Frank Montello.
3   *An Act to amend the Jurors Act*, S.O. 1951, c.41, s.1. The first Canadian rape crisis centre was established in Vancouver in 1973, and by 1975 there were twenty centres across Canada. That year the first national conference of rape crisis centres was held in Ottawa. n.a., *Canadian Association of Sexual Assault Centres: Evaluation 1979–1982 to the Department of Health and Welfare* (Vancouver: n.p., 1986) at 14–15; Dianne Kinnon, *Report on Sexual Assault in Canada* (Ottawa: Canadian Advisory Council on the Status of Women, 1981) at 63.
4   Interviews with Frank Montello.
5   The federal records on the statistical outcomes of sexual assault trials for the years 1910, 1920, 1930, 1940, 1950, 1960, and 1970 do not show a pattern of increasing or decreasing rates of convictions. However, it is difficult to evaluate data that were not kept consistently over time. Conviction rates were reported separately for "crimes of indecency" and "assault on females" in 1910, but given as one unit called "rape and other crimes against decency" with no category for "assault on females" in 1920. The records only began to classify offences using terms found in the *Criminal Code* such as "rape," "attempted rape," and "seduction" in 1930. In some years, the numbers of individuals "detained for lunacy" after being tried for rape were noted, in other years not; given that the insanity verdict encompassed a finding that the act had been committed and resulted in a penalty for the accused, I have added these to the conviction rates. The data do not purport to make corrections for the many cases where convictions at trial were successfully quashed on appeal. Recognizing the inadequacies of these inconsistent statistics, it is still useful to view them over time. In 1910, since rape was not classified separately, I have calculated the convic-

tion rate of both "crimes of indecency" and "assault on females" together, resulting in a rate of 70 percent. In 1920, the conviction rate for "rape and other crimes against decency" was 56 percent. In 1930, the conviction rate for "rape" was 34 percent; in 1940 it was 50 percent; in 1950, it was 43 percent; in 1960, it was 54 percent; and in 1970, it was 33 percent. The average for these years was 49 percent. The average conviction rates for the other crimes cited during this same period are drawn from the same records. See Canada, *Appendix to the Report of the Minister of Agriculture for the Year 1910, Criminal Statistics, Sessional Paper No. 17* at viii–ix; Canada, Dominion Bureau of Statistics, *Annual Report of Criminal Statistics for the Year Ended Sept. 30, 1920* at xiv; *Annual Report of Statistics of Criminal and Other Offences for the Year Ended Sept. 30, 1930* at 10; *Annual Report of Statistics of Criminal and Other Offences for the Year Ended September 30, 1940* at 19–20; *Annual Report of Statistics of Criminal and Other Offences for the Period October 1, 1949 to December 31, 1950* at 84; *Statistics of Criminal and Other Offences, 1960* at 46; *Annual Report of Statistics of Criminal and Other Offences for the Period January 1, 1970 to December 31, 1970* at Table 11. Other researchers have also noted conviction rates averaging 49 percent for rape in a sample of twenty-five rural Ontario counties for the years 1880–1929: Karen Dubinsky & Adam Givertz, "It Was Only a Matter of Passion: Masculinity and Sexual Danger" in Kathryn McPherson et al., eds., *Gendered Pasts: Historical Essays in Femininity and Masculinity in Canada* (Don Mills, ON: Oxford University Press, 1999) at 65–66; Karen Dubinsky, *Improper Advances: Rape and Heterosexual Conflict in Ontario, 1880–1929* (Chicago: University of Chicago Press, 1993). Carolyn Strange, "Patriarchy Modified: The Criminal Prosecution of Rape in York County, Ontario, 1880–1930" in Jim Phillips, Tina Loo, & Susan Lewthwaite, eds., *Essays in the History of Canadian Law: Crime and Criminal Justice* (Toronto: The Osgoode Society, 1994) at 215 noted an average of 20 percent convicted of rape as charged, rising to 37 percent when those convicted on lesser and included offences were included. Jonathan Swainger, "Dime Novel Toughs: Legal Culture and Criminal Law in Red Deer, Alberta, 1907–1920" (1993) 14 *Criminal Justice History: An International Annual* 109–33 noted an average of 46 percent convictions on sex-related charges. Julian Roberts, *Overview: Sexual Assault Legislation in Canada, an Evaluation* (Ottawa: Dept of Justice, 1991) refers at 3 to Canadian conviction rate data for 1971, combining those convicted of rape and those charged with rape but convicted of a lesser offence, for a total of 54.7 percent, compared to an overall 86 percent rate for criminal offences generally. Audrey A. Wakeling, *Corroboration in Canadian Law* (Toronto: Carswell, 1977) at 122 cites data compiled by Statistics Canada in 1972 showing a conviction rate of 44.4 percent for rape, compared with 85.5 percent for indictable offences generally.

6   *Might's Metropolitan Windsor City Directory* (Toronto: Might Directories, 1974) at 7; Trevor Price & Larry Kulisek, *Windsor 1892–1992* (Windsor: Chamber Publications, 1992) at 89 and 94; Greater Windsor Industrial Commission, *Windsor: Essex County* (Woodland Hills, CA: Windsor Publications, 1972); "Mediation Talks Set for Thursday" *Windsor Star* (18 Sept. 1974) 5; "Lewis Visits Picket Lines" *Windsor Star* (19 Sept. 1974) 1; "Farm Labour Organizers Fight Migrant Workers' Plight" *Windsor Star* (19

Sept. 1974) 3–4; "First Law Firm Strike Launched" *Windsor Star* (19 Sept. 1974) 1; "Striking Legal Secretaries Replaced" *Windsor Star* (20 Sept. 1974) 5.

7   "Prison System Criticized" *Windsor Star* (28 Sept. 1974) 5; "Panel Calls for Law Changes" *Windsor Star* (30 Sept. 1974) 3–4; Law Reform Commission of Canada, *The Principles of Sentencing and Dispositions*, Working Paper No. 3 (March 1974). Morris Shumiatcher, who held a master's and doctoral degree in law, was the chief architect of Canada's first human rights legislation, passed in Saskatchewan; see Carmela Patrias, "Socialists, Jews, and the 1947 Saskatchewan Bill of Rights" (June 2006) 87 *Canadian Historical Review* 265.

8   Frank's father was Anthony Montello of 624 Mercer Street. Interviews with Frank Montello; Ellen van Wagenlingen, "Case Closed: Frank Montello Is Retiring" *Windsor Star* (19 June 1999) E1; Walter Temelini, "The Italians in Windsor" (1985) 7 *Polyphony* 73 at 75–80.

9   Interviews with Frank Montello. Other members of the cohort who brought respectability to criminal law were, in Montello's opinion, Charles Dubin, Joseph Sedgwick, Patrick Hartt, and David Humphrey.

10 Interviews with Montello; "Case Closed," above note 8.

11 "Key Players in the Trial" *Edmonton Journal* (1 May 1995) A3; D'Arcy Jenish, "Horror Stories: The Prosecution Sets Out the Shocking Accusations against Paul Bernardo" *Maclean's* (29 May 1995) at 14; Interviews with Frank Montello. Houlahan was named QC in 1981.

12 His parents were Charles Frederick Haines and Evelyn Eliza (Douglas). He was married to Keitha Towriss, divorced, and remarried to Vera Lorraine Jones, both of whom predeceased him. He had six children. "E.L. Haines," *Canadian Who's Who* (1952–54); "Haines, Hon. Edson Livingstone," *Canadian Who's Who* vol. 26 (Toronto: University of Toronto Press, 1991) at 419; Law Society of Upper Canada Archives, Past Member Database; Jack Batten, *Learned Friends: A Tribute to Fifty Remarkable Ontario Advocates 1950–2000* (Toronto: Irwin Law, 2005) at 24–25; Obituary *Toronto Star* (7 Dec 1996) B8; "Mr. Justice Edson Haines," Osgoode Society Oral History, part A at 18–24, 54.

13 *Canadian Who's Who* (1952–54); *Canadian Who's Who* (1991) at 419; Batten, *Learned Friends*, above note 12 at 24–25; Obituary *Toronto Star* (7 Dec. 1996) B8.

14 Alan Barnes, "Top Judge Edson Haines Was Critic of Legal System" *Toronto Star* (5 Dec. 1996) A4.

15 Ellen Anderson, *Judging Bertha Wilson* (Toronto: University of Toronto Press, 2001) at 90.

16 Interviews with Frank Montello; Barnes, "Edson Haines," above note 14.

17 Rose Weitz, *Rapunzel's Daughters: What Women's Hair Tells Us about Women's Lives* (New York: Farrar, Straus & Giroux, 2004) at 20–22, 27, 55, and 180–83; Richard Corson, *Fashions in Hair: The First Five Thousand Years* (New York: Hillary House, 1971) at 680; *Actors and Actresses, The International Dictionary of Films and Filmmakers*, vol. 3 (Chicago: St. James Press, 1986) at 61.

18 *Might's Metropolitan Windsor City Directory* (Toronto: Might Directories Ltd., 1974).

19 *Might's Metropolitan Windsor City Directory* (Toronto: Might Directories Ltd., 1970)
   shows Angione's residence as 1062 Goyeau Street, and in 1975 as 2735 Rivard. On
   Angione's birthplace and year of arrival, see "Grape Fest Spurs Memories of Old
   Country" *Windsor Star* (17 Sept. 1990) A5. The interpreter was Anthony Como. Ru-
   dolph A. Helling, *The Position of Negroes, Chinese and Italians in the Social Structure
   of Windsor, Ontario* (Toronto: Ontario Human Rights Commission, 1965) at 71–73;
   Walter Temelini, "The Italians in Windsor" (1985) 7 *Polyphony* 73 at 73–78; Ontario,
   Ministry of Citizenship and Culture, *Maps and Demographic Statistics for Selected
   Mother Tongue Groups: Windsor* (Toronto: Ministry of Citizenship and Culture, 1982),
   Population Data 10; Walter Temelini, "The Italians' Cultural Presence in Windsor,
   1920–1990" in Julius Molinaro & Maddalena Kuitunen, eds., *The Luminous Mosaic*
   (Welland: Editions Soleil, 1993) 203 at 211; Interviews with Frank Montello.
20 Interviews with Frank Montello.
21 Rex v. Frank Fraser (1934) Sask. Archives Board, Judicial District of Arcola, Ben-
   son District, 24 Jan. 1934, Police Magistrate's Court; 24 April 1934, Court of King's
   Bench; *Rex v. Jones*, [1935] 3 D.L.R. 237 (B.C.C.A.); *Rex v. Blanchard* (1941), 75 C.C.C. 279
   (B.C.C.A.).
22 *Rex v. Christakos* (1945), 85 C.C.C. 48 (Man. K.B.), aff'd. *Rex v. Christakos* (1946), 87
   C.C.C. 40 (Man. C.A.); *Regina v. Collerman*, [1964] 46 W.W.R. 300 (B.C.C.A.).
23 *Re H.C.S.* (1949), 96 C.C.C. 107 (Man. K.B.); *Regina v. Shanower*, [1972] 8 C.C.C. (2d) 527
   (Ont. C.A.). *Rex v. Probe*, [1943] 2 W.W.R. 62 (Sask. C.A.) also involved a babysitting
   component, but the employment feature was not emphasized in the case; see chapter 6.
24 On the legislative debates, see Constance Backhouse & Leah Cohen, *The Secret Oppression: Sexual Harassment of Working Women* (Toronto: Macmillan of Canada, 1979).
   Criminal Code, S.C. 1890, c.37, s.4 provided: "Every one who . . . seduces or has illicit
   connection with any woman or girl of previously chaste character and under the
   age of twenty-one years who is in his employment in a factory, mill or workshop, or
   who, being in a common employment with him, in such factory, mill or workshop,
   is, in respect of her employment or work in such factory, mill or workshop, under, or
   in any way subject to, his control or direction, is guilty of a misdemeanor and liable
   to two years' imprisonment." See also S.C. 1892, c.29, ss.183, 184.2, 551, and 684.
25 S.C. 1900, c.46, s.183. The section also noted that being in "similar" employment as
   well as "common" employment was sufficient, and expanded the provision to cover
   women who received "wages or salary directly or indirectly" from the accused. Section 183A added: "The burden of proof of previous unchastity on the part of the girl
   or woman . . . shall be upon the accused." See also R.S.C. 1906, c.146, s.213. S.C. 1920,
   c.43, s.5, reworded the earlier s.213 to create sanction for anyone "who seduces or has
   illicit connection with any girl previously chaste and under the age of twenty-one
   years who is in his employment, or who, being in a common, but not necessarily
   similar, employment with him is, in respect of her employment or work, under or in
   any way subject to his control or direction, or receives her wages or salary directly
   or indirectly from him. Proof that a girl has on previous occasions had illicit connection with the accused shall not be deemed to be evidence that she was not previ-

ously chaste." The same statute added at s.17: "On the trial of any offence against section . . . 5 . . . of this Act, the trial judge may instruct the jury that if, in their view the evidence does not show that the accused is wholly or chiefly to blame for the commission of said offence, they may find a verdict of acquittal." See also R.S.C. 1927, c.36, s.213; S.C. 1953–54, c.51, s.145. S.C. 1959, c.41, s.10 revised the last phrase to read: "the court may find the accused not guilty if it is of opinion that the evidence does not show that as between the accused and the female person, the accused is more to blame than the female person." See also R.S.C. 1970, c.C-34, s.153; R.S.C. 1985, c.C-46, s.158. The entire provision was repealed by S.C. 1987, c.24, s.3.

26 *Rex v. Jones*, [1935] 3 D.L.R. 237 (B.C.C.A.). The court noted that the provision had initially encompassed "women" and "girls," but that the word "woman" was deleted in the 1920 amendment. The defence had argued that the section was "designed to apply only to those females under 21 who had not entered the matrimonial state and therefore presumably required a special protection which was not necessary for those experienced females who had acquired sexual knowledge, and also presumably wisdom and caution from their marital experiences." The court concluded that the word "girl" must be "restricted to unmarried women." During the Parliamentary debates on the amendment, senators had claimed that "the blackmailer is the married woman. She is past the time when her sexual desire is very strong; certainly it is not so strong as her love of making money." *Senate Debates* (24 June 1920) 4th Sess., 13th Parl. at 707–8.

27 *Rex v. Blanchard* (1941), 75 C.C.C.279 (B.C.C.A.).

28 *Regina v. St. Hilaire*, [1966] 3 C.C.C. 31 (Que. C.A.).

29 Lin Farley, *Sexual Shakedown: The Sexual Harassment of Women on the Job* (New York: McGraw-Hill, 1978); Backhouse & Cohen, *The Secret Oppression*, above note 24. The third book published, Catharine A. MacKinnon, *Sexual Harassment of Working Women* (New Haven: Yale University Press, 1979) would become the most influential.

30 Several earlier criminal decisions also recognized the coercive potential of the employment setting. The King v. Bates (1921) Public Archives of Nova Scotia, RG39 "C" {Halifax} vol. 705, #B75 involved a prosecution against James Bates, the owner of Hollis Sea Grill, for attempting to rape Alice Williams, who worked at the restaurant. In *Rex v. Christakos* (1946), 87 C.C.C. 40 (Man. C.A.), a manager of the Silver Grill café was convicted of "contributing to the juvenile delinquency" of his waitresses and cashiers: "Their stories make clear that the accused used his position to compel them to submit to his sexual desires. He followed the same plan with all of them. It was his custom to drive them home at night or early morning in his motor car on an invitation to take them home after work. He took them, as a rule, one at a time, and the method of his first approach was the same. Instead of driving a new victim home he would drive into the country and attempt seduction, even using force, which was at first resisted. . . . The whole evidence goes to show that he used his authority for the purpose of debauching his employees if he could do so, or else penalized them by discharge from their employment without the means of subsistence." In *Re H.C.S.* (1949), 96 C.C.C. 107 (Man. K.B.), the accused was convicted of "contributing to juvenile delinquency" for sexually assaulting a babysitter: "Such

girls [who are enabled to supplement incomes in, perhaps, the only way available to them] must be protected. When, to the danger of going home late at night or early in the morning, is added the danger of attack or seduction by a male employer, either on the way home or actually in the employer's house, the need for protection is even greater."

31 *Law Enforcement Compensation Act, 1967,* S.O. 1967, c.45 offered compensation to persons killed or injured assisting a peace officer. S.O. 1968–69, c.59 broadened the act to cover all victims of crime. *Compensation for Victims of Crime Act,* S.O. 1971, c.51 provided compensation to victims injured or killed as a result of a "crime of violence" for medical expenses, incapacity for work, pain and suffering, "maintenance of a child born of rape," and death benefits, up to a maximum of $182 500. Amounts could be reduced where the victim's behaviour contributed to the injury. By March 1976, 3377 applications had been received, of which 105 (3 percent) related to sexual assault. In 1974, the highest sexual assault award was paid to a fourteen-year-old girl, who lost the sight of an eye after being raped with a knife. She was awarded $10 331. The previous year, a twenty-year-old woman raped by five motorcycle gang members received $1938 ($1000 of which was for pain and suffering). In 1971, the lowest sexual assault award was paid to a seventy-one-year-old woman indecently assaulted by an unknown intruder in her home. She was paid $556. Ontario *Reports of the Criminal Injuries Compensation Board* (Toronto: Criminal Injuries Compensation Board, 1970, 1971, 1972, 1973, 1974, 1975, and 1976).

32 Law Reform Commission of Canada, *The Principles of Sentencing and Dispositions,* Working Paper No. 3 (March 1974) at 2; Law Reform Commission of Canada, *Restitution and Compensation,* Working Paper No. 5 (Oct. 1974) at 7–8.

33 Canada, Canadian Committee on Corrections *Report of the Canadian Committee on Corrections* (Ottawa: Queen's Printer, 1969) at 200–1. Roger Ouimet chaired the committee, and G. Arthur Martin, Frank Montello's long-standing mentor, was the vice-chair.

34 S.C. 1921, c.25, s.19 provided that such conditions could be ordered as part of a suspended sentence, but only where the accused had no previous conviction, and it seemed expedient having regard to the "age, character, and antecedents of the offender, to the trivial nature of the offence, and to any extenuating circumstances." See also R.S.C. 1906, c.146, s.1081; R.S.C. 1927, c.36, s.1081(6); S.C. 1953–54, c.51, s.638. Section 638 was broadened in S.C. 1968–69, c.38, to allow its application to offenders with previous convictions, who were fined or imprisoned for a term not exceeding two years. See also R.S.C. 1970, s.663(2)(e). Earlier enactments also authorized compensation for damage to property, to a *bona fide* purchaser of property, and restitution of property. See R.S.C. 1986, c.174, ss.250–51; R.S.C. 1886, c.176, s.27; S.C. 1888, c.41, s.15; S.C. 1892, c.29, ss. 803, 836–38; R.S.C. 1906, c.146, ss.795, 1048–50; S.C. 1923, c.41, s.1017; R.S.C. 1927, c.36, ss.795, 1039, 1048–50; S.C. 1943–44, c.23, s.24; S.C. 1953–54, c.51, ss.628–30.

35 *Report of the Canadian Committee on Corrections,* above note 33 at 201. *Regina v. Dashner* (1973), 15 C.C.C. (2d) 139 (B.C.C.A.) struck out the $1000 order for restitution to two assault victims, because the trial judge failed to ensure that the offender was "able

to pay" and that the amount represented "actual loss or damage sustained." The court preferred that compensation come from "ordinary civil suit" or through the criminal injuries compensation scheme.

36 Interviews with Frank Montello. For rare instances in which such activities were mentioned in legal decisions, see *Rex v. Bateman* (1906) Middlesex County Crown Attorney and Crown Prosecutor Criminal Court Records, #866, UWO Regional Room, Box 558, where a Strathroy physician purporting to remove a woman's ovary was charged with attempting to rape her while she was on his examining table. Archival depositions suggest that, prior to the acquittal, the physician's lawyer had undertaken negotiations regarding payment to the girl's family. In *Viens v. Senecal* (1922), 40 C.C.C. 260 (Que. C.A.), the father of the child victim declined to give evidence against an accused charged with "abduction of a minor" because he had been reimbursed $390 in cash by the accused ($90 of which went to his attorney). The court found that this sum represented "an indemnity to which the plaintiff might lay claim civilly for travelling expenses, loss of time, detectives' fees, etc." When the accused later refused to pay an additional promissory note for $500, the father's suit to recover the sum in civil court was dismissed. With one dissent, the court held the $500 to be money promised to abandon the prosecution, making it an illegal contract, or contrary to good morals or public order. In both these cases, it appears that a family member, and not the complainant herself, stood to benefit financially.

37 On the influence of the sentencing judge's background characteristics, attitudes, and penal philosophy to the actual sentence imposed, see John Hogarth, *Sentencing as a Human Process* (Toronto: University of Toronto Press, 1971) who concluded at 382 that "only about 9 per cent of the variation in sentencing could be explained by objectively defined facts, whilst over 50 per cent of such variation could be accounted for simply by knowing certain pieces of information about the judge himself."

38 *Re Torek and the Queen* (1974), 15 C.C.C. (2d) 296 (Ont. H.C.). The offender was ordered under s.653 to pay $4377.50 to replace stolen property, after he was convicted of breaking and entering and theft. Haines equated s.653 and s.663(2)(e), noting that he saw no "meaningful distinction" between them. Responding to critique that a criminal process did not permit assessment of damages, Haines noted that the preliminary inquiry could be used to "get discovery as broad or broader than . . . in a civil action."

39 Interviews with Frank Montello.

40 *Rex v. DeYoung, Liddiard and Darling* (1927), 60 O.L.R. 155 (Ont. C.A.) noted that the death penalty was no longer imposed "in practice." S.C. 1953–54, c.51, s.136 removed the death penalty. In *Rex v. McCathern* (1927), 60 O.L.R. 334 (Ont. C.A.), the trial judge had imposed a death sentence for a "very brutal" rape. The appellate court reduced this to twenty years and twenty lashes, due to the offender's addiction to alcohol, "low mentality and baneful environment." In *Rex v. De Young, Liddiard & Darling*, the trial judge imposed fifteen years for rape, and the Crown appealed, arguing that it was "the worst case of rape which had happened in Ontario," and that the "deliberate, premeditated, concerted nature of the crime, and the horrible circumstances surrounding it made it so outrageous and terrible as to deserve the severest penalty

which the law could impose, namely, death." In the next sentence, the Crown added
he "hardly expected, however, that that sentence would be inflicted." The appellate
court held to the fifteen year sentence but added twenty lashes.

41 For rape, see *Criminal Code*, S.C. 1892, c.29, s.267; R.S.C. 1906, c.146, s.299; R.S.C. 1927,
c.36, s.299; S.C. 1953–54, c.51, s.136; R.S.C. 1970, c.C-34, s.144. For carnal knowledge of
a girl under fourteen, see S.C. 1892, c.29, s.269; R.S.C. 1906, c.146, s.301; R.S.C. 1927,
c.36, s.301; S.C. 1953–54, c.51, s.138(1); R.S.C. 1970, c.C-34, s.146(1). Buggery also carried a potential life sentence until 1954, when it was reduced to fourteen years; see
S.C. 1892, c.29, s.174; R.S.C. 1906, c.146, s.202; R.S.C. 1927, c.36, s.202; S.C. 1953–54, c.51,
s.147; R.S.C. 1970, c.C-34, s.155. For rare cases where life was imposed, see *The King
v. Spuzzum* (1906), 12 C.C.C. 287 (B.C.S.C.), where a man had broken into a house
and raped a sixteen-year-old. *Rex v. Belt* (1944), 84 C.C.C. 403 (B.C.C.A.) imposed life
upon a man for buggery; he had a long record of sexual offences involving small
boys. *Regina v. Head* (1970), 1 C.C.C. (2d) 436 (Sask. C.A.) upheld a life sentence for the
rape of a six-year-old girl who had extensive vaginal-rectal injuries; the accused had
previously been convicted of indecent assault on a young girl, and psychiatric evidence predicted that he posed a future danger. *Regina v. Leech*, [1973] 10 C.C.C. (2d)
149 (Alta. S.C.) imposed life upon a man for the forcible seizure of a woman, theft of
an automobile, rape, and buggery. His defence of insanity failed, and the court held
that he was a psychopath with irresistible impulses who was a danger to the public.
Regina v. Hill, [1974] 15 C.C.C. (2d) 145 (Ont. C.A.), aff'd [1977] 1 S.C.R. 827 (S.C.C.) increased the twelve-year sentence imposed at trial to life, for raping and wounding
a fourteen-year-old babysitter. The offender had stabbed the victim repeatedly in
the face, and she risked the loss of one eye. In *Rex v. Stonehouse and Pasquale*, [1928]
1 W.W.R. 161 (B.C.C.A.), two British Columbia teenagers were sentenced to life for
rape, but had their sentences reduced on appeal to three years, due to the "thoroughly immoral" background of the seventeen-year-old complainant. *Rex v. Willaert*
(1953), 105 C.C.C. 172 (Ont. C.A.) imposed life at trial for raping an eight-year-old
girl; this was reduced on appeal to five years, due to the offender's experiences in
war-torn Europe. The court explicitly noted that "the tendency in recent years has
been to impose more moderate sentences." *Regina v. Craig*, [1976] 28 C.C.C. (2d) 311
(Alta. C.A.) imposed life at trial for raping a fourteen-year-old girl; this was reduced
on appeal to eight years because there was insufficient "brutality" and no "record
of similar offences." A life sentence for rape was upheld in *Regina v. Haig* (1974),
26 C.R.N.S. 247 (Ont. C.A.) as this was the nineteen-year-old accused's third rape.
Carolyn Strange, "Patriarchy Modified," above note 5, refers at 233–35 to another life
sentence ordered for Michael O'Hara convicted of rape in Toronto in 1919; he was released on parole in 1927, and a year later was convicted of rape again, and sentenced
to fifteen years and twenty lashes.

42 In *Regina v. Deschenes et al.*, [1963] 2 C.C.C. 295 (Que. C.A.), the majority upheld sentences of 25, 22, 20 and 20 years with lashes for four men involved in a gang rape,
who had committed thirty-five to forty acts of forcible intercourse with a married
woman aged thirty-four, a crime described as "nauseating in . . . brutality." The dissenting judges noted that there "should be some special circumstances warranting

the imposition of sentences in excess of ten years" and added that a 1962 Queen's University sentencing seminar had concluded that "very few prisoners warranted sentences of more than five years." *Rex v. Donovan* (1947), 88 C.C.C. 86 (N.B.C.A.) appealed a sentence of fifteen years for raping a stepdaughter under the age of fourteen. The court reduced this to seven years, noting that "in recent years there has been a tendency to impose a more moderate sentence even in the case of serious offences than formerly" in recognition that "although a generation ago sentences of ten years' penal servitude were common, today they are rarely passed." For sexual assault sentences above ten years, see *Rex v. DeYoung, Liddiard and Darling* (1927), 60 O.L.R. 155 (Ont. C.A.) fifteen years and whipping for rape; *Rex v. McCathern* (1927), 60 O.L.R. 334 (Ont. C.A.) twenty years and whipping for rape; *Rex v. Carey* (1951), 102 C.C.C. 25 (Ont. C.A.) twenty years for rape; *Regina v. Gillingham* (1955), 112 C.C.C. 78 (Nfld. C.A.) two terms of seven years to be served consecutively (14 years) for two offences of carnal knowledge of girls aged 8 and 9; *Regina v. Woods* (1961), 130 C.C.C. 181 (N.B.C.A.) twenty years for sexual intercourse with a thirteen-year-old girl; *Regina v. Bell, Christiansen, Coolen and MacDonald*, [1974] 14 C.C.C. (2d) 225 (N.S.C.A.) sentences of ten, ten, ten, and twelve years for four men who gang-raped a sixteen-year-old girl. For sentences between five and ten years for rape or carnal knowledge, see *Rex v. Fox* (1925), 44 C.C.C. 262 (Ont. C.A.) seven years and whipping for rape; *Rex v. Hill* (1928), 61 O.L.R. 645 (Ont. C.A.) ten years and whipping for rape; *Rex v. Childs* (1938), 71 C.C.C. 70 (Ont. C.A.) seven years for carnal knowledge of a girl under fourteen; *Rex v. Bakshish Singh* (1943), 80 C.C.C. 79 (B.C.C.A.) ten years for rape; *Rex v. Sveinsson* (1950), 102 C.C.C. 366 (B.C.C.A.) concurrent terms of five years for rape and carnal knowledge of a girl under fourteen; *Rex v. Fenn* (1951), 100 C.C.C. 55 (Ont. C.A.) five years for rape; *Regina v. Willaert* (1953), 105 C.C.C. 172 (Ont. C.A.) five years for rape; *Regina v. Manuel* (1955), 112 C.C.C. 139 (N.S.S.C.) eight years for rape; *Regina v. Harrison* (1956), 115 C.C.C. 347 (Ont. C.A.) five years for rape; *Regina v. Nightingale* (1957), 124 C.C.C. 214 (N.B.C.A.) seven years and whipping for rape; *Regina v. Huffman, Huffman & Davignon* (1958), 120 C.C.C. 323 (Ont. C.A.) terms of eight, eight, and six years for rape; *Regina v. Wilmott*, [1967] 1 C.C.C. 171 (Ont. C.A.) eight years for rape; *Regina v Bear, Bear & Tinker*, [1974] 13 C.C.C. (2d) 570 (Sask. C.A.) three terms of five years for rape; *Regina v. Craig*, [1976] 28 C.C.C. (2d) 311 (Alta. C.A.) eight years for rape. On the lower penalties, see *Rex v. Hicks* (1925), 44 C.C.C. 13 (Sask. C.A.) three months for carnal knowledge of a girl under fourteen; *Rex v. Drew (No. 2)* (1933), 60 C.C.C. 229 (Sask. C.A.) three and a half years and twenty-one lashes for carnal knowledge of a girl under fourteen; *Rex v. Taylor* (1936), 67 C.C.C. 172 (Man. C.A.) three years for carnal knowledge of a girl under fourteen; Rex v. Stanley Peckham (1940) Middlesex County Crown Attorney and Crown Prosecutor Criminal Court Records, Judge's Notebooks for Criminal County Court, vol. 2, Sept. 1934–June 1945, UWO Regional Room, Box 169, at pp. 165–219, two years and ten lashes for carnal knowledge of a girl under fourteen; *Rex v. Harms*, [1944] 2 D.L.R. 61 (Sask. C.A.) eighteen months for rape; *Regina v. Zamal et al.*, [1964] 1 C.C.C.12 (Ont. C.A.) three terms of six, four, and two years for rape; *Regina v. Morrissette et al.*, [1970] 75 W.W.R. 644 (Sask. C.A.) three terms of five years, two years less a day, and one year; *Regina v. Messina*, [1973] 1 W.W.R. 283 (Sask.C.A.) eighteen months for attempted rape and buggery; *Regina v. Simmons, Allen & Bezzo*, [1974] 13 C.C.C. (2d) 65 (Ont. C.A.) four years for rape; *Regina v. Shonias* (1974), 21 C.C.C. (2d) 301 (Ont. C.A.) one year imprisonment and eighteen months probation for rape; *Regina v. Basken & Kohl*, [1975] 21 CCC (2d) 321 (Sask. C.A.) two terms of three years and two years less a day for rape; *Regina v. Plummer & Brown* (1975), 31 C.R.N.S. 220 (Ont. C.A.) three years for rape.

43 *Criminal Code*, S.C. 1892, c.29, s.957 authorized whipping for men (but not women) convicted of incest, gross indecency, indecent assault on a female, indecent assault on a male, and carnal knowledge of a girl under fourteen. S.C. 1900, c.46, s.957 provided that a "cat of nine tails" should be used unless some other instrument was specified in the sentence. See also R.S.C. 1906, c.146, s.1060. S.C. 1920, c.43, s.7 added attempted rape to the list of offences. S.C. 1921, c.25, s.4 added rape to the list of offences (in recognition that the death penalty was no longer being imposed.) See also R.S.C. 1927, c.36, s.1060; S.C. 1938, c.44, s.52. Gross indecency was removed from the list by S.C. 1953–54, c.51, and incest by S.C. 1972, c.13, s.10.

44 Thirty lashes were ordered for rape in *Rex v. Hill* (1928), 61 O.L.R. 645 (Ont. C.A.). See also twenty for rape in *Rex v. McCathern* (1927), 60 O.L.R. 334 (Ont. C.A.); twenty for rape in *Rex v. De Young, Liddiard and Darling* (1927), 60 O.L.R. 155 (Ont. C.A.); twenty-one for carnal knowledge of a girl under fourteen in *Rex v. Drew (No. 2)* (1933), 60 C.C.C. 229 (Sask. C.A.); seven for incest in *Rex v. Guilbault* (1939), 72 C.C.C. 254 (Que. K.B.); ten for carnal knowledge of a girl under fourteen in Rex v. Stanley Peckham (1940) Middlesex County Crown Attorney and Crown Prosecutor Criminal Court Records, Judge's Notebooks for Criminal County Court, vol. 2 (Sept. 1934–June 1945), UWO Regional Room, Box 169, at 165–219; five for gross indecency in *Rex v. Hall* (1943), 81 C.C.C. 31 (B.C.C.A.); ten for indecent assault and assault causing bodily harm in *Rex v. Robertson* (1946), 2 C.R. 222 (Ont. C.A.); an undisclosed number for indecent assault in *Regina v. Marion* (1956), 118 C.C.C. 388 (Ont. C.A.); and nine for rape in *Regina v. Nightingale* (1957), 124 C.C.C. 214 (N.B.C.A.). A Joint Committee of the Senate and the House of Commons on Capital and Corporal Punishment and Lotteries noted in 1956 that the courts rarely ordered whipping anymore, and recommended its complete abolition, but Parliament did not do so; *Senate Debates* (27 June 1956) 873. Whipping was also critiqued as "cruel and degrading" in Canada, *Report of the Royal Commission on the Status of Women in Canada* (Ottawa: Queen's Printer, 1970) at 373. Ontario Court of Appeal judge William Edward Middleton was the first to criticize whipping from the bench, describing it as degrading, uncivilized, and ineffective in deterrence, in *Rex v. Childs* (1938), 71 C.C.C. 70. Overturning an order for ten lashes for rape, Middleton noted that "modern thought revolts at the idea of torture, whipping and solitary confinement. . . . Society should, in our view, be slow to authorize a form of punishment which may degrade the brutal man still further and may deprive the less hardened man of the last remaining traces of self-respect. . . . While we are content to remain among the backward nations of the earth and have upon our *Criminal Code* provisions for punishment having their origin in the dark ages, Judges can do but little. Parliament alone can interfere. But . . . it is, I think, our duty in all but very exceptional cases to exercise as a Court of Appeal our discre-

tion by refusing to uphold sentences involving whipping." Chief Justice John Babbitt McNair of the New Brunswick Court of Appeal adopted Middleton's position in *Regina v. Woods* (1961), 130 C.C.C. 181 (N.B.C.A.), overturning an order for nine lashes for sexual intercourse with a girl under fourteen. Judge Louis McCoskery Ritchie dissented, approving the deterrent potential of the lash, and concluding that any abolition of whipping was "a matter for Parliament, not the Courts, to decide." In *Rex v. Lemire & Gosselin* (1948), 92 C.C.C. 201, where five lashes were ordered for robbery with violence, Québec Court of Appeal judge Bernard Bissonnette wrote that "in certain cases it is imposed and is inevitable. . . . For some, it is an anachronism in the evolution of our modern sociology. For others, in fact, it is the rigorous application of Mosaic legislation, of the law of retaliation." Judge Errol Malcolm William McDougall added: "There is no question of the propriety of whipping as a punishment in certain offences. . . . it is idle to speculate as to the merits or demerits of such form of punishment. It is for the Court to apply the law, not to make or modify it." In *Regina v. Dick, Penner & Finnigan*, [1965] 1 C.C.C. 171, Manitoba Court of Appeal judge Ivan Schultz upheld an order for ten strokes of the paddle for gang rape of an eighteen-year-old girl. Although he noted that orders for corporal punishment were "not common in this Province," he held them justified in certain cases, and dismissed the argument that corporal punishment ran contrary to s.2 of the *Canadian Bill of Rights*, which provided that no law of Canada should be construed to "impose or authorize the imposition of cruel and unusual treatment or punishment." Judge Samuel Freedman, dissenting, would have struck out the order for corporal punishment. See also *Regina v. Deschenes et al.*, [1963] 2 C.C.C. 295 (Que. C.A.).

45 *Criminal Code*, S.C. 1948, c.39, s.1054A. The accused first had to be convicted of indecent assault on a female, indecent assault on a male, rape, attempted rape, carnal knowledge of a girl under fourteen or between fourteen and sixteen, or attempted carnal knowledge of a girl under fourteen. Then there had to be evidence from at least two psychiatrists, one of them nominated by the minister of justice, that the accused's "course of misconduct in sexual matters" indicated "a lack of power to control his sexual impulses" and that he was "likely to attack or otherwise inflict injury, loss, pain or other evil" on others. The minister had to review the case every three years to determine if altered conditions warranted release. S.C. 1953–54, c.51, ss.659, 661–67 added buggery, bestiality, and gross indecency to the list of offences. Minor revisions were recommended in the Canada, *Report of the Royal Commission on Criminal Law Relating to Criminal Sexual Psychopaths* (Ottawa: Queen's Printer, 1961). S.C. 1960–61, c.43, ss.32–40 substituted the term "dangerous sexual offender," and expanded the definition to "a person who, by his conduct in any sexual matter, has shown a failure to control his sexual impulses, and who is likely to cause injury, pain or other evil to any person, through failure in the future to control his sexual impulses or is likely to commit a further sexual offence." It also required annual detention reviews by the minister of justice. S.C. 1968–69, c.38, ss.76–80 changed the definition of "dangerous sexual offender" to remove the phrase "or is likely to commit a further sexual offence." It also provided that the accused must be present in the court when the matter was considered, unless he "misconducts himself by inter-

rupting the proceedings so that to continue the proceedings in his presence would not be feasible." See also R.S.C. 1970, c.C-34, ss.687, 689–95.

For cases on preventive detention, see *Regina v. Tilley* (1952), 104 C.C.C. 315 (Ont. Co. Ct.), upheld in (1953), 106 C.C.C. 42 (Ont. C.A.); *Regina v. Hoyt* (1953), 107 C.C.C. 59 (Ont. C.A.); *Regina v. Ferguson* (1955), 113 C.C.C. 67 (B.C.C.A.); *Regina v. Cline* (1956), 115 C.C.C. 18 (Ont. C.A.); *Regina v. Neil* (1957), 119 C.C.C. 1 (S.C.C.); *Regina v. Pitt* (1958), 122 C.C.C. 74 (B.C.C.A.); *Regina v. Leggo* (1962), 133 C.C.C. 149 (B.C.C.A.); *Regina v. Binette*, [1965] 3 C.C.C. 216 (B.C.C.A.); *Regina v. McKenzie*, [1965] 51 W.W.R. 641 (Alta. C.A.); *Regina v. Wilband*, [1965] 51 W.W.R. 251 (B.C.C.A.) upheld in [1967] 2 C.C.C. 6 (S.C.C.); *Regina v. Johnston*, [1965] 3 C.C.C. 42 (Man. C.A.); *Regina v. Canning*, [1966] 4 C.C.C. 379 (B.C.C.A.); *Regina v. Sanders*, [1966] 2 C.C.C. 345 (B.C.S.C.), upheld in [1968] 4 C.C.C. 156 (B.C.C.A.) and [1970] 2 C.C.C. 57 (S.C.C.); *Regina v. Kanester*, [1968] 1 C.C.C. 351 (B.C.C.A.); *Klippert v. The Queen*, [1968] 2 C.C.C. 129 (S.C.C.); *Regina v. Dawson*, [1970] 71 W.W.R. 455 (B.C.C.A.); *Regina v. McAmmond*, [1970] 1 C.C.C. 175 (Man. C.A.); *Regina v. Loos*, [1970] 74 W.W.R. 467 (B.C.C.A.), rev'd [1971] 3 W.W.R. 634 (S.C.C.); *Regina v. Galbraith*, [1972] 5 C.C.C. (2d) 37 (B.C.C.A.), leave to appeal denied [1972] 2 W.W.R. 80 (S.C.C.); *Regina v. Kelman*, [1971] 4 C.C.C. (2d) 8 (B.C.S.C.); *Regina v. Roestad*, [1972] 5 C.C.C. (2d) 564 (Ont. Co. Ct.) finding the provisions did not violate ss. 1 and 2 of the *Canadian Bill of Rights; Regina v. Gordon*, [1972] 8 C.C.C. (2d) 132 (B.C.C.A.); *Regina v. Bolduc*, [1974] 16 C.C.C. (2d) 280 (Que. C.A.); *Regina v. Loysen*, [1974] 13 C.C.C. (2d) 202 (B.C.S.C.); *Re Campbell and the Queen*, [1975] 22 C.C.C. (2d) 65 (B.C.C.A.); *Regina v. Lawson*, [1974] 6 W.W.R. 625 (Alta. C.A.); *Regina v. Knight*, [1976] 27 C.C.C. (2d) 343 (Ont. H. Ct.). The Ouimet Committee reported that in 1968, there were 57 persons in Canadian penitentiaries sentenced to preventive detention as dangerous sexual offenders. It recommended the repeal of the provisions because they had been applied against sexual offenders who were "not dangerous," the basis for finding a person to be a dangerous sexual offender was "inadequate," and the dangerous sexual offender was only one class of dangerous offender, but the legislation obscured that fact. Canada, Canadian Committee on Corrections, *Report of the Canadian Committee on Corrections* (Ottawa: Queen's Printer, 1969) at 253–58. See also Elise Chenier, "The Criminal Sexual Psychopath in Canada: Sex, Psychiatry and the Law at Mid-Century" (2003) 20 *Canadian Bulletin of Medical History* 75; Elise Chenier, "Stranger in Our Midst: Male Sexual Deviance in Postwar Ontario" (Ph.D. Thesis, Queen's University, 2001); Mary Louise Adams, *The Trouble with Normal: Postwar Youth and the Making of Heterosexuality* (Toronto: University of Toronto Press, 1997).

46 Incest carried a maximum of fourteen years; S.C. 1892, c.29, s.176; R.S.C. 1906, c.146, s.204; R.S.C. 1927, c.36, s.204; S.C. 1953–54, c.51, s.142(2); R.S.C. 1970, c.C-34, s.150(2). Indecent assault on a male carried a maximum of seven years until 1906, when it was increased to ten; S.C. 1892, c.29, s.260; R.S.C. 1906, c.146, s.293; R.S.C. 1927, c.36, s.293; S.C. 1953–54, c.51, s.148; R.S.C. 1970, c.C-34, s.156. Attempted rape carried a maximum of seven years until 1954, when it was also increased to ten; S.C. 1892, c.29, s.268; R.S.C. 1906, c.146, s.300; R.S.C. 1927, c.36, s.300; S.C. 1953–54, c.51, s.137; R.S.C. 1970, c.C-34, s.146. Gross indecency carried a maximum of five years; S.C. 1892, c.29, s.178; R.S.C. 1906, c.146, s.206; R.S.C. 1927, c.36, s.206; S.C. 1953–54, c.51, s.149; R.S.C. 1970,

c.C-34, s.157. Carnal knowledge of a girl between fourteen and sixteen years (later defined as sexual intercourse with a girl between fourteen and sixteen) carried a maximum of five years; S.C. 1920, c.43, s.8; R.S.C. 1927, c.36, s.301(2); S.C. 1953–54, c.51, s.138(2); R.S.C. 1970, c.C-34, s.146(2). Carnal knowledge of an insane, deaf, or dumb woman (later defined as sexual intercourse with a feeble-minded woman) carried a maximum of four years until 1954, when it was increased to five; S.C. 1900, c.46, s.189; R.S.C. 1906, c.146, s.219; R.S.C. 1927, c.36, s.219; S.C. 1953–54, c.51, s.140; R.S.C. 1970, c.C-34, s.148. Indecent assault on a female carried a maximum of two years until 1954 when it was increased to five; S.C. 1892, c.29, s.259; R.S.C. 1906, c.146, s.292; R.S.C. 1927, c.36, s.292; S.C. 1953–54, c.51, s.141; R.S.C. 1970, c.C-34, s.149(1). Seduction of girls between sixteen and eighteen years carried a maximum of two years; S.C. 1920, c.43, s.4; R.S.C. 1927, c.36, s.211; S.C. 1953–54, c.51, s.143; R.S.C. 1970, c.C-34, s.151. Seduction of girls between fourteen and sixteen carried a maximum of two years; S.C. 1892, c.29, s.181; R.S.C. 1906, c.146, s.211. (The offence was no longer listed in R.S.C. 1927, c.36.) Seduction under promise of marriage carried a maximum of two years; S.C. 1892, c.29, s.182; R.S.C. 1906, c.146, s.212; R.S.C. 1927, c.36, s.212; S.C. 1953–54, c.51, s.144; R.S.C. 1970, c.C-34, s.152. Seduction of a ward or stepdaughter or employee carried a maximum of two years; S.C. 1892, c.29, s.183; R.S.C. 1906, c.146, s.213; R.S.C. 1927, c.36, s.213; S.C. 1953–54, c.51, s.145; R.S.C. 1970, c.C-34, s.153(1). Seduction of female passengers on vessels carried a maximum of one year until 1954, when it was increased to two; S.C. 1892, s.29, s.184; R.S.C. 1906, c.146, s.214; R.S.C. 1927, c.36, s.214; S.C. 1953–54, c.51, s.146; R.S.C. 1970, c.C-34, s.154.

47 For indecent assault on a female, see R. v. Eusèbe Bilodeau, (29 July 1914) Archives nationales center, ArchivHisto, Thémis II docs 260396 - TP12, S1, SS1, SSS1 UR 38 Cont 216, Cour des Sessions de la Paix, Québec City, one month; R. v. Evengéliste Turcotte (29 May 1916) Archives nationales center, ArchivHisto, Thémis II docs 260646 - TP12, S1, SS1, SSS1 UR 38 Cont 216, Cour des Sessions de la Paix, Québec City, twelve months; *Rex v. Warner* (1933), 61 C.C.C. 36 (N.S.S.C.) two years; *R. v. Kirkham* (1935), 64 C.C.C. 255 (B.C.C.A.) six months; *Rex v. Tolhurst* (1939), 73 C.C.C. 32 (Sask. C.A.) three months; *Rex v. O'Hara* (1946), 88 C.C.C. 74 (B.C.C.A.) two years; *Rex v. Terrell*, [1947] 3 D.L.R. 523 (B.C.C.A.) two years; *Rex v. Edgett* (1947), 90 C.C.C. 274 (N.B.C.A.) four months; *R. v. Hoyt* (1949), 93 C.C.C. 306 (N.B.C.A.) two years; *Rex v. Deschamps* (1951), 100 C.C.C. 191 (Ont. C.A.) ten months; *Descoteau v. The Queen* (1952), 104 C.C.C. 299 (Que. C.A.) six months; *The Queen v. Thorne*, [1951–52] 29 M.P.R. 144 (N.B.C.A.) two years; *R. v. Allen* (1954), 108 C.C.C. 102 (Sask. C.A.) four months; *Regina v. Marr* (1955) 114 C.C.C. 318 (N.B.C.A.) eighteen months; *R. v. Childs*, [1959] 42 M.P.R. 79 (N.B.C.A.) three months; *R. v. Mabee*, [1965] 3 C.C.C. 150 (Ont. C.A.) five years; *R. v. Diehl* (1972), 5 N.S.R. (2d) 21 (N.S.C.A.) three months; *R. v. Hurd*, [1972] 6 C.C.C. (2d) 180 (Ont. Co. Ct.) one-year probation; *R. v. Gehue*, [1975] 12 N.B.R. (2d) 564 (N.B.C.A.) one year.

For penalties for indecent assault on a male, see R. v. Higgins (1910) Archives nationales du Québec, ArchivHisto, Thémis II, TP12, S1, SS1, SSS1, Cont. 1960-01-357/600 and TP12, S1, SS1, SSS1, Cont. 1960-01-357/213, DOXS 251817 to 251819 and 251815 to 251816, and TP12, S1, SS1, SSS1, Cont. 1960-0-1-357/212, DOCS 250578 to

250580, Cour des Sessions de la Paix, Québec City, six months; R. v. Charles John Paige (3 Oct. 1916) Archives nationales center, ArchivHisto, Thémis II docs 196745 at 196748 - TP12, S1, SS1, SSS1 UR 7 Cont. 185, Cour des Sessions de la Paix, Québec City, two years with whipping; *R. v. Horn* (1923), 40 C.C.C. 117 (Alta. C.A.) three years; *Rex v. Kagna* (1942), 78 C.C.C. 342 (Alta. C.A.) three years. *R. v. Belt* (1938), 53 B.C.R. 118 (B.C.C.A.) involved two indecent assaults on two different boys; the accused voluntarily admitted to nine similar offences. He received three years on each of the two indecent assaults to be served consecutively. *Rex v. Hall* (1943), 81 C.C.C. 31 (B.C.C.A.) imposed five years and whipping for gross indecency upon a male.

For penalties for incest, see *Rex v. Adams* (1921), 17 Alta. L.R. 52 (Alta. C.A.) seven months; *Bergeron v. The King* (1930), 56 C.C.C. 62 (Que. K.B.) two and a half years; *Rex v. Guilbault* (1939), 72 C.C.C. 254 (Que. K.B.) seven years and whipping; *Rex v. Wyatt* (1944), 60 B.C.R. 255 (B.C.C.A.) five years; *Rex v. Rivet* (1944), 81 C.C.C. 377 (Alta. C.A.) three years; Rex v. Samuel McKay (1946) Public Archives of Nova Scotia, RG 39 "C" Halifax, vol. 756 #1888 three years; *Regina v. Beddoes* (1952), 103 C.C.C. 131 (Sask. C.A.) two and a half years; *Charest v. The Queen* (1957), 119 C.C.C. 197 (Que. C.A.) three terms of twelve years to run concurrently; *Regina v. DesLauriers*, [1973] 10 C.C.C. (2d) 309 (Ont. C.A.) thirty-six months and two years probation; *Regina v. Richardson* (1973), 6 N.S.R. (2d) 130 (N.S.C.A.) three years. Penalties for seduction included two years less a day in *Rex v. Armstrong* (1922), 38 C.C.C. 98 (Ont. S.C.) and suspended sentence in *Rex v. Hirsch*, [1924] 2 W.W.R. 342 (Sask. C.A.).

48 R. v. Hildevert Loupret (5 Feb. 1919) Archives nationales center, ArchivHisto, Thémis II, TP12, S1, SS1, SSS1, Cont. 1960-01-357/604 and TP12, S1, SS1, SSS1, Cont. 1960-01-357/186, docs 200204 to 200216, Cour des Sessions de la Paix, Québec City, imposed a suspended sentence upon a painter described as a long-term, satisfactory, and honest employee, from an "honourable and respectable family." The offence was attempted seduction of a woman between fourteen and sixteen years. *Rex v. McLean* (1931), 57 C.C.C. 239 (N.S.S.C.) imposed a suspended sentence for indecent assault, along with a recognizance of $500 to keep the peace for two years, based on a jury "recommendation to mercy." *Rex v. Johnston* (1948), 91 C.C.C. 59 (Ont. C.A.) imposed a fine of $3500 for carnal knowledge of a girl between fourteen and sixteen years, noting that the accused was a mason contractor whose skills were in great demand for new housing projects; the conviction was overturned on other grounds on appeal, with the court noting in *obiter* that a term of imprisonment would have been more suitable. *Rex v. Smullin* (1948), 91 C.C.C. 274 (N.B.C.A.) imposed a suspended sentence for indecent assault of a nine-year-old girl upon a twelve-year-old boy, noting that he had a "good character," was "too young to appreciate the seriousness of the offence," "helped his father in his store," and "had a good home." *Rex v. Wilson* (1950), 97 C.C.C. 350 (Ont. C.A.) imposed a suspended sentence for indecent assault upon a female; no further facts appeared. *Regina v. Allen* (1954), 108 C.C.C. 239 (B.C.C.A.) imposed probation with an order for psychiatric treatment at a clinic, noting that the accused, who had been convicted of indecent assault on a young girl, had been "over exerting himself in his real estate work," that he was "happily married in spite of his wife's domination," and that the psychiatrists had reported

he posed no future risk and would benefit from out-patient counselling. In *Regina v. Jones* (1956), 115 C.C.C. 273 (Ont. C.A.), the Crown appealed a fine of $450 imposed at trial for the indecent assault of three young girls; the court concluded that deterrence required six months, plus twelve months of an indeterminate term. The dissent preferred the fine, noting that the accused was an electrician with steady employment, of "good family background," and that his psychiatrists had testified that he was "likely to respond well to psychiatric treatment," while prison was not "a curative institution." See also *Regina v. Backshall* (1956), 115 C.C.C.221 (Ont. C.A.). *Regina v. Hurd*, [1972] 6 C.C.C. (2d) 180 (Ont. Co. Ct.) imposed a suspended sentence upon an accused convicted of indecent assault of a girl under fourteen, noting that she was less than three weeks shy of fourteen; no further details were given. In *Regina v. D.*, [1972] 5 C.C.C. (2d) 366 (Ont. C.A.), a trial judge imposed twelve months and an additional six months indeterminate term upon a schoolteacher convicted of assaulting young girls. The appellate court released him with time served, and placed him upon probation on condition that he submit to treatment with his private psychiatrist, noting that he was "of previously good character" was "regarded as a competent and dedicated school-teacher," and that treatment outside of prison was "likely to effect" a cure, while "imprisonment may not." In *Regina v. Shanower*, [1972] 8 C.C.C. (2d) 527 (Ont. C.A.), the Crown appealed a suspended sentence imposed upon "a good father, a good husband, and a good citizen in his community" who had raped the fifteen-year-old babysitter who was looking after his children. Noting the importance of deterrence, the court raised the sentence to three years. In *Regina v. McKeachnie*, [1976] 26 C.C.C. (2d) 317 (Ont. C.A.), the trial judge imposed a fine of $150 upon a "good worker as a maintenance man [who] largely supported his mother, who was in poor health" for attempted indecent assault on a young girl. The court found he should have been convicted of indecent assault and sentenced to six months, with two years probation. In *Regina v. Wood*, [1976] 26 C.C.C. (2d) 100 (Alta. C.A.), the accused pleaded guilty to gross indecency upon his nine-year-old stepdaughter. At trial he was sentenced to thirty months probation, conditional upon his receiving psychiatric care. His counsel had argued that the consulting psychiatrists did not believe he posed a continuing danger, and that he was "making a success of his own business, and to remove him from society at the present time . . . would be unfortunate." On appeal, the majority upheld the penalty because the accused had "lived up to the strict terms of his probation" for about a year, and a sentence of imprisonment after such a delay would be unfair. The dissenting judge would have imposed a prison sentence for deterrence.

49 *Regina v. Wilmott*, [1967] 1 C.C.C. 171 (Ont. C.A.); *Regina v. Deschenes et al.*, [1963] 2 C.C.C. 295 (Que. C.A.).

50 The federal government did not begin to offer "treatment programs" for "dangerous sexual offenders" until 1971. On the ineffectiveness of treatment, see Chenier, "Criminal Sexual Psychopath," above note 45 at 88 and 92; Chenier "Stranger in Our Midst," above note 45 at ch. 4; A.M. McFarthing, Sudbury psychiatrist and consultant to the Ontario Correctional Service, "A Survey of the Social, Legal, Historical

and 'Psycho-Babble' Factors Leading to Sex Offenders Legislation in the Areas of British Common Law Heritage" (1990) 9 *Medicine and the Law* at 1278.

51 *Regina v. Wilmott*, [1967] 1 C.C.C. 171 (Ont. C.A.); *Regina v. Deschenes et al.*, [1963] 2 C.C.C. 295 (Que. C.A.); *Regina v. Morrissette et al.*, [1970] 75 W.W.R. 644 (Sask. C.A.).

52 In *Regina v. Jones* (1956), 115 C.C.C. 273 (Ont. C.A.), psychiatric evidence indicated that "a prison term will be definitely detrimental" to the condition of a man convicted of indecent assault, and would have "no deterrent effect upon other . . . sex perverts." Judge Laidlaw, writing in dissent, also noted: "I am not persuaded that prison is a curative institution. I think prison life would impede treatment and probably aggravate the respondent's condition of maladjustment. The nature of prison environment renders questionable the efficacy of treatment in that institution. The prisoner is under stress; he is deprived of the comfort and encouragement of friends and of opportunities to test the progress made and is subject to conditions which are often disadvantageous in other ways. . . . There is substantial likelihood of detriment to him and increased danger to society upon his release." *Regina v. D.*, [1972] 5 C.C.C. (2d) 366 (Ont. C.A.) also noted that "pedophiles" were "not deterred by punishment to others." Hogarth, *Sentencing as a Human Process*, above note 37, surveyed the recent research and concluded at 5 that "the little evidence which exists tends to show that, as far as it can be determined, penal measures are irrelevant to the chance that offenders will commit further offences," adding the evidence for deterrence was "at best, equivocal." A.M. Kirkpatrick, "The Prison Dilemma" (1974) 16 *Canadian Journal of Criminology and Corrections* 282, noted at 289 that with some exceptions, penal institutions had "failed in the correction of the offenders who have entered their gates and all too often the offender has been returned no better or even worse than when he entered." David McLaren, "Cons, Hacks and Educated Screws: The Prison Politics of Discipline and Rehabilitation" (1973) 15 *Canadian Journal of Criminology and Corrections* 25, noted at 35 that if the objective was to rehabilitate and avoid high rates of recidivism, "perhaps the best [solution was] to avoid the prison experience altogether with its teaching problems of 'prisonalization' and its alienation and its conflicts between custody and treatment."

53 Much of the anti-rape activism of the second wave Canadian women's movement still remains undocumented, but I was one of a number of feminists who personally advocated more and lengthier prison sentences, in my public lectures to women's organizations and clubs, media interviews, and in high school, college, and university classrooms. Dianne Kinnon, *Report on Sexual Assault in Canada* (Ottawa: Canadian Advisory Council on the Status of Women, 1981), argued at 34 and 79 that "sentencing often does not reflect the seriousness of the crime" and recommended that "penalties must be brought in line." Some feminists believed that long prison terms might be a factor disinclining judges and jurors to convict, and therefore suggested a range of penalties with some less severe options. Lorenne Clark & Debra Lewis, *Rape: The Price of Coercive Sexuality* (Toronto: Women's Press, 1977), would attempt to redefine rape as a crime of violence against women, rather than sexuality, and to argue for a new tiered offence with graduated penalties. However, even they took no issue with the validity of imprisonment, or the use of long sentences in

serious cases. In 1983, when the new tiered offence of "sexual assault" was enacted, all three tiers maintained penalties of imprisonment. Several Canadian feminists deserve to be mentioned as rising above this trend. Christine Boyle critiqued feminists' failure to scrutinize the inhumanity of prisons in a public lecture "Women and Criminal Law Reform," Oct. 1987 at the University of Western Ontario. Dianne Martin wrote about the discriminatory essence of prisons in the early 1990s: see Dianne L. Martin, "Casualties of the Criminal Justice System: Women and Justice under the War on Drugs" (1993) 6 *Canadian Journal of Women and the Law* 305 and "Retribution Revisited: A Reconsideration of Feminist Criminal Law Reform Strategies" (1998) 36 *Osgoode Hall Law Journal* 151. See also Laureen Snider, "The Potential of the Criminal Justice System to Promote Feminist Concerns" (1990) 10 *Studies in Law, Policy and Society* 143; Laureen Snider, "Feminism, Punishment and the Potential for Empowerment" (1994) 9 *Canadian Journal of Law and Society* 75.

54 *Regina v. Farley*, [1976] W.W.D. 128 (Man. C.A.).

55 *Regina v. Groves* (1977), 79 D.L.R. (3d) 561 (Ont. H. Ct.) rejected Haines's conclusion that the preliminary inquiry could be used for discovery: "The purpose of the preliminary is not to provide discovery to the accused but to satisfy the Court that there is sufficient evidence to put the accused on trial. . . . Given the difficulty of assessing damages for personal injuries and the large figures which may be involved, the importance of such discovery is apparent. Inadequate discovery mechanisms and lack of procedural safeguards will not bring about the reform and rehabilitation of the accused." The case also held that the provision was *intra vires* and constitutionally valid federal criminal law. See also *Turcotte v. Gagnon*, [1974] R.P.Q. 309 (Que. C.S.); *R. v. Zelensky* (1976), 33 C.C.C. (2d) 147 (Man. C.A.); rev'd in part [1978] 2 S.C.R. 940 (S.C.C.); Kenneth L. Chasse, "Restitution in Canadian Criminal Law" (1977) 36 C.R.N.S. 201.

56 *Regina v. Wood*, [1976] 26 C.C.C. (2d) 100 (Alta. C.A.).

57 Van Wagenlingen, "Case Closed," above note 8.

58 S.C. 1900, c.46, s.550A; R.S.C. 1906, c.146, s.645; R.S.C. 1927, c.36, s.645. S.C. 1938, c.44, s.207A prohibited printing or publishing "in relation to any judicial proceeding any indecent matter or indecent medical, surgical or physiological details . . . which would be calculated to injure public morals" except for (i) the names, addresses and occupations of the parties and witnesses; (ii) a concise statement of the charges, defences and counthercharges; (iii) submissions on any point of law arising, and the decision of the court; (iv) the summing up of the judge and the finding of the jury (if any) and the judgment of the court and observations made by the judge. Judicial pleadings and published law reports were excluded. The consent of the attorney general was a precondition to prosecution. S.C. 1953–54, c.51, s.482 expanded the prohibition to provide: "The trial of an accused that is a corporation or who is or appears to be sixteen years of age or more shall be held in open court, but where the court . . . is of opinion that it is in the interest of public morals, the maintenance of order or the proper administration of justice to exclude all or any members of the public forum from the court room, he may so order." See also R.S.C. 1970, c.C-34, s.442. There is evidence that feminist organizations, such as the National Council of

Women, had criticized the "unwholesome exploitation of sex" in newspaper crime coverage as well: see Chenier, "Stranger in Our Midst," above note 45 at ch. 3, citing *Toronto Telegram* (18 May 1955).

59 In both Mary Ann Burton's (1907) and Yvonne Collin's (1917) cases, their names and the names of the assailants were published in the press; see chapters 2 and 3.

60 For Montello's views, see Rob Hornberger, "Chatham Man Found Not Guilty" *Windsor Star* (20 Aug. 1987) A5; "Proposed Law Lauded by Parents of Victim" *Windsor Star* (26 May 1993) A6.

61 Interviews with Tom McMahon, 9 and 10 March 2006, by Megan Reid and Constance Backhouse; Tom McMahon, "Victim Gets $1000 Award" *Windsor Free Press* (26 Sept. 1974) 5.

Chapter 11: Conclusion

1 *R. v. Kummerfield*, [1998] 9 W.W.R. 619; *R. v. Kummerfield and Ternowetsky*, [1998] 163 Sask. R. 257; see also the exceptional description of the case by Sherene H. Razack, "Gendered Racial Violence and Spatialized Justice: The Murder of Pamela George" in Sherene H. Razack, ed., *Race, Space, and the Law* (Toronto: Between the Lines, 2002) at 121–56.

INDEX

PUBLICATIONS OF THE
OSGOODE SOCIETY FOR CANADIAN LEGAL HISTORY

2008   Constance Backhouse, *Carnal Crimes: Sexual Assault Law in Canada, 1900–1975*
Jim Phillips, R. Roy McMurtry & John Saywell, eds., *Essays in the History of Canadian Law, Vol. X: A Tribute to Peter N. Oliver*
Gregory Taylor, *The Law of the Land: Canada's Receptions of the Torrens System*
Hamar Foster, Benjamin Berger & A.R. Buck, eds., *The Grand Experiment: Law and Legal Culture in British Settler Societies*

2007   Robert Sharpe & Patricia McMahon, *The Persons Case: The Origins and Legacy of the Fight for Legal Personhood*
Lori Chambers, *Misconceptions: Unmarried Motherhood and the Ontario Children of Unmarried Parents Act, 1921–1969*
Jonathan Swainger, ed., *The Alberta Supreme Court at 100: History & Authority*
Martin Friedland, *My Life in Crime and Other Academic Adventures*

2006   Donald Fyson, *Magistrates, Police and People: Everyday Criminal Justice in Quebec and Lower Canada, 1764-1837*
Dale Brawn, *The Court of Queen's Bench of Manitoba 1870–1950: A Biographical History*
R.C.B. Risk, *A History of Canadian Legal Thought: Collected Essays*, edited and introduced by G.Blaine Baker & Jim Phillips

2005   Philip Girard, *Bora Laskin: Bringing Law to Life*
Christopher English, ed., *Essays in the History of Canadian Law, Vol. IX: Two Islands, Newfoundland and Prince Edward Island*
Fred Kaufman, *Searching for Justice: An Autobiography*

2004   John D. Honsberger, *Osgoode Hall: An Illustrated History*
Frederick Vaughan, *Aggressive in Pursuit: The Life of Justice Emmett Hall*
Constance Backhouse & Nancy Backhouse, *The Heiress versus the Establishment: Mrs. Campbell's Campaign for Legal Justice*
Philip Girard, Jim Phillips & Barry Cahill, es., *The Supreme Court of Nova Scotia,1754–2004: From Imperial Bastion to Provincial Oracle*

2003   Robert Sharpe & Kent Roach, *Brian Dickson: A Judge's Journey*
George Finlayson, *John J. Robinette: Peerless Mentor*
Peter Oliver, *The Conventional Man: The Diaries of Ontario Chief Justice Robert A. Harrison, 1856-1878*
Jerry Bannister, *The Rule of the Admirals: Law, Custom and Naval Government in Newfoundland, 1699-1832*

2002   John T. Saywell, *The Law Makers: Judicial Power and the Shaping of Canadian Federalism*

David Murray, *Colonial Justice: Justice, Morality and Crime in the Niagara District, 1791–1849*

F. Murray Greenwood & Barry Wright, eds., *Canadian State Trials, Volume Two: Rebellion and Invasion in the Canadas, 1837–8*

Patrick Brode, *Courted and Abandoned: Seduction in Canadian Law*

2001   Ellen Anderson, *Judging Bertha Wilson: Law as Large as Life*

Judy Fudge & Eric Tucker, *Labour Before the Law: Collective Action in Canada, 1900–1948*

Laurel Sefton MacDowell, *Renegade Lawyer: The Life of J.L. Cohen*

2000   Barry Cahill, "The Thousandth Man": *A Biography of James McGregor Stewart*

A.B. McKillop, *The Spinster and the Prophet: Florence Deeks, H.G. Wells, and the Mystery of the Purloined Past*

Beverley Boissery & F. Murray Greenwood, *Uncertain Justice: Canadian Women and Capital Punishment*

Bruce Ziff, *Unforeseen Legacies: Reuben Wells Leonard and the Leonard Foundation Trust*

1999   Constance Backhouse, *Colour-Coded: A Legal History of Racism in Canada, 1900–1950*

G. Blaine Baker & Jim Phillips, eds., *Essays in the History of Canadian Law, Vol. VIII: In Honour of R.C.B. Risk*

Richard W. Pound, *Chief Justice W.R. Jackett: By the Law of the Land*

David Vanek, *Fulfilment: Memoirs of a Criminal Court Judge*

1998   Sidney Harring, *White Man's Law: Native People in Nineteenth-Century Canadian Jurisprudence*

Peter Oliver, *"Terror to Evil-Doers": Prisons and Punishments in Nineteenth-Century Ontario*

1997   James W. St.G. Walker, *"Race," Rights and the Law in the Supreme Court of Canada: Historical Case Studies*

Lori Chambers, *Married Women and Property Law in Victorian Ontario*

Patrick Brode, *Casual Slaughters and Accidental Judgments: Canadian War Crimes and Prosecutions, 1944–1948*

Ian Bushnell, *The Federal Court of Canada: A History, 1875–1992*

1996   Carol Wilton, ed., *Essays in the History of Canadian Law, Vol. VII: Inside the Law — Canadian Law Firms in Historical Perspective*

William Kaplan, *Bad Judgment: The Case of Mr. Justice Leo A. Landreville*

Murray Greenwood & Barry Wright, eds., *Canadian State Trials, Volume I: Law, Politics and Security Measures, 1608–1837*

1995   David Williams, *Just Lawyers: Seven Portraits*

Hamar Foster & John McLaren, eds., *Essays in the History of Canadian Law, Vol. VI: British Columbia and the Yukon*

W.H. Morrow, ed., *Northern Justice: The Memoirs of Mr. Justice William G. Morrow*

Beverley Boissery, *A Deep Sense of Wrong: The Treason, Trials and Transportation to New South Wales of Lower Canadian Rebels after the 1838 Rebellion*

1994   Patrick Boyer, *A Passion for Justice: The Legacy of James Chalmers McRuer*

Charles Pullen, *The Life and Times of Arthur Maloney: The Last of the Tribunes*

Jim Phillips, Tina Loo, & Susan Lewthwaite, eds., *Essays in the History of Canadian Law, Vol. V: Crime and Criminal Justice*

Brian Young, *The Politics of Codification: The Lower Canadian Civil Code of 1866*

1993 Greg Marquis, *Policing Canada's Century: A History of the Canadian Association of Chiefs of Police*

Murray Greenwood, *Legacies of Fear: Law and Politics in Quebec in the Era of the French Revolution*

1992 Brendan O'Brien, *Speedy Justice: The Tragic Last Voyage of His Majesty's Vessel Speedy*

Robert Fraser, ed., *Provincial Justice: Upper Canadian Legal Portraits from the Dictionary of Canadian Biography*

1991 Constance Backhouse, *Petticoats and Prejudice: Women and Law in Nineteenth-Century Canada*

1990 Philip Girard & Jim Phillips, eds., *Essays in the History of Canadian Law, Vol. III: Nova Scotia*

Carol Wilton, ed., *Essays in the History of Canadian Law, Vol. IV: Beyond the Law — Lawyers and Business in Canada 1830–1930*

1989 Desmond Brown, *The Genesis of the Canadian Criminal Code of 1892*

Patrick Brode, *The Odyssey of John Anderson*

1988 Robert Sharpe, *The Last Day, the Last Hour: The Currie Libel Trial*

John D. Arnup, *Middleton: The Beloved Judge*

1987 C. Ian Kyer & Jerome Bickenbach, *The Fiercest Debate: Cecil A. Wright, the Benchers and Legal Education in Ontario, 1923-1957*

1986 Paul Romney, *Mr. Attorney: The Attorney General for Ontario in Court, Cabinet and Legislature, 1791–1899*

Martin Friedland, *The Case of Valentine Shortis: A True Story of Crime and Politics in Canada*

1985 James Snell and Frederick Vaughan, *The Supreme Court of Canada: History of the Institution*

1984 Patrick Brode, *Sir John Beverley Robinson: Bone and Sinew of the Compact*

David Williams, *Duff: A Life in the Law*

1983 David H. Flaherty, ed., *Essays in the History of Canadian Law, Vol. II*

1982 Marion MacRae & Anthony Adamson, *Cornerstones of Order: Courthouses and Town Halls of Ontario, 1784–1914*

1981 David H. Flaherty, ed., *Essays in the History of Canadian Law, Vol. I*